California Corporations Code

2023 Edition

(Volume 1 of 2)

Aurum Codex Print™

Division - GENERAL PROVISIONS

Section 1 - Short title

This act shall be known as the Corporations Code.
Ca. Corp. Code § 1
Enacted by Stats. 1947, Ch. 1038.

Section 2 - Construction as restatements and continuations

The provisions of this code, insofar as they are substantially the same as existing statutory provisions relating to the same subject matter, shall be construed as restatements and continuations, and not as new enactments.
Ca. Corp. Code § 2
Enacted by Stats. 1947, Ch. 1038.

Section 3 - Offices

All persons who, at the time this code goes into effect, hold office under any of the acts repealed by this code, which offices are continued by this code, continue to hold them according to their former tenure.
Ca. Corp. Code § 3
Enacted by Stats. 1947, Ch. 1038.

Section 4 - Action or proceeding commenced before effective date; right accrued; procedures thereafter

No action or proceeding commenced before this code takes effect, and no right accrued, is affected by the provisions of this code, but all procedure thereafter taken therein shall conform to the provisions of this code so far as possible.
Ca. Corp. Code § 4
Enacted by Stats. 1947, Ch. 1038.

Section 5 - Construction of code

Unless the provision or the context otherwise requires, these general provisions, rules of construction, and definitions govern the construction of this code.
Ca. Corp. Code § 5
Enacted by Stats. 1947, Ch. 1038.

Section 6 - Effect of headings

Title, division, part, chapter, article, and section headings contained herein do not in any manner affect the scope, meaning, or intent of the provisions of this code.

Ca. Corp. Code § 6

Enacted by Stats. 1947, Ch. 1038.

Section 7 - Exercise of power or performance of duty by deputy or authorized person

Whenever, by the provisions of this code, a power is granted to, or a duty imposed upon, a public officer, the power may be exercised or the duty performed by a deputy of the officer or by a person authorized, pursuant to law, by the officer, unless this code expressly provides otherwise.

Ca. Corp. Code § 7

Enacted by Stats. 1947, Ch. 1038.

Section 8 - Writing; mailing of notice or other communications

Writing includes any form of recorded message capable of comprehension by ordinary visual means; and when used to describe communications between a corporation, partnership, or limited liability company and its shareholders, members, partners, directors, or managers, writing shall include electronic transmissions by and to a corporation (Sections 20 and 21), electronic transmissions by and to a partnership (subdivisions (4) and (5) of Section 16101), and electronic transmissions by and to a limited liability company (paragraphs (1) and (2) of subdivision (o) of Section 17001). Whenever any notice, report, statement, or record is required or authorized by this code, it shall be made in writing in the English language.

Wherever any notice or other communication is required by this code to be mailed by registered mail by or to any person or corporation, the mailing of such notice or other communication by certified mail shall be deemed to be a sufficient compliance with the requirements of law.

Ca. Corp. Code § 8

Amended by Stats 2004 ch 254 (SB 1306),s 2, eff. 1/1/2005

Section 9 - Reference to portion of code or other law

Whenever reference is made to any portion of this code or of any other law of this State, the reference applies to all amendments and additions now or hereafter made.

Ca. Corp. Code § 9

Enacted by Stats. 1947, Ch. 1038.

Section 10 - "Section" and "subdivision" defined

"Section" means a section of this code unless some other statute is specifically mentioned. "Subdivision" means a subdivision of the section in which the term appears unless some other section is expressly mentioned.

Ca. Corp. Code § 10
Enacted by Stats. 1947, Ch. 1038.

Section 11 - Tenses

The present tense includes the past and future tenses, and the future tense includes the present.
Ca. Corp. Code § 11
Enacted by Stats. 1947, Ch. 1038.

Section 12 - Gender

The masculine gender includes the feminine and neuter.
Ca. Corp. Code § 12
Enacted by Stats. 1947, Ch. 1038.

Section 12.2 - Spouse defined

"Spouse" includes "registered domestic partner," as required by Section 297.5 of the Family Code.
Ca. Corp. Code § 12.2
Added by Stats 2016 ch 50 (SB 1005),s 19, eff. 1/1/2017.

Section 13 - Numbers

The singular number includes the plural, and the plural number includes the singular.
Ca. Corp. Code § 13
Enacted by Stats. 1947, Ch. 1038.

Section 14 - "County"

"County" includes "city and county."
Ca. Corp. Code § 14
Enacted by Stats. 1947, Ch. 1038.

Section 15 - "Shall" and "may"

"Shall" is mandatory and "may" is permissive.
Ca. Corp. Code § 15
Enacted by Stats. 1947, Ch. 1038.

Section 16 - "Oath"

"Oath" includes affirmation.

Ca. Corp. Code § 16
Enacted by Stats. 1947, Ch. 1038.

Section 17 - "Signature" defined

"Signature" includes mark when the signer cannot write, such signer's name being written near the mark by a witness who writes his own name near the signer's name; but a signature by mark can be acknowledged or can serve as a signature to a sworn statement only when two witnesses so sign their own names thereto.

Ca. Corp. Code § 17
Enacted by Stats. 1947, Ch. 1038.

Section 17.1 - Signature in facsimile document

(a) In addition to the definition set forth in Section 17, the term "signature" includes a signature in a facsimile document filed pursuant to this code or pursuant to regulations adopted under this code, and presented to the Secretary of State.

(b) The terms "signed" and "executed," when used with respect to the documents filed pursuant to this code or pursuant to regulations adopted under this code, and presented to the Secretary of State, include a document bearing a signature under subdivision (a).

(c) The Secretary of State shall accept facsimile signatures on documents that are delivered by mail or by hand.

(d) A person on whose behalf a document bearing a facsimile signature is submitted for filing to the Secretary of State shall maintain the originally signed document for at least five years from the date of filing.

(e) The Secretary of State may adopt procedures permitting the direct electronic or facsimile presentation of the documents specified in subdivisions (a) and (b). However, the Secretary of State is not required to accept those direct electronic or facsimile filings until procedures are adopted.

Ca. Corp. Code § 17.1
Added by Stats 2003 ch 273 (SB 220),s 1, eff. 1/1/2004.

Section 18 - "person" defined

"Person" includes a corporation as well as a natural person.

Ca. Corp. Code § 18
Enacted by Stats. 1947, Ch. 1038.

Section 19 - Severability

If any provision of this code, or the application thereof to any person or circumstance, is held invalid, the remainder of the code, or the application of such provision to other persons or circumstances, shall not be affected thereby.

Ca. Corp. Code § 19
Enacted by Stats. 1947, Ch. 1038.

Section 20 - "Electronic transmission by the corporation" defined

"Electronic transmission by the corporation" means a communication (a) delivered by (1) facsimile telecommunication or electronic mail when directed to the facsimile number or electronic mail address, respectively, for that recipient on record with the corporation, (2) posting on an electronic message board or network which the corporation has designated for those communications, together with a separate notice to the recipient of the posting, which transmission shall be validly delivered upon the later of the posting or delivery of the separate notice thereof, or (3) other means of electronic communication, (b) to a recipient who has provided an unrevoked consent to the use of those means of transmission for communications under or pursuant to this code, and (c) that creates a record that is capable of retention, retrieval, and review, and that may thereafter be rendered into clearly legible tangible form. However, an electronic transmission under this code by a corporation to an individual shareholder or member of the corporation who is a natural person, and if an officer or director of the corporation, only if communicated to the recipient in that person's capacity as a shareholder or member, is not authorized unless, in addition to satisfying the requirements of this section, the consent to the transmission has been preceded by or includes a clear written statement to the recipient as to (a) any right of the recipient to have the record provided or made available on paper or in nonelectronic form, (b) whether the consent applies only to that transmission, to specified categories of communications, or to all communications from the corporation, and (c) the procedures the recipient must use to withdraw consent.

Ca. Corp. Code § 20
Amended by Stats 2009 ch 96 (AB 285),s 1, eff. 1/1/2010.
Added by Stats 2004 ch 254 (SB 1306),s 3, eff. 1/1/2005.

Section 21 - "Electronic transmission to the corporation" defined

"Electronic transmission to the corporation" means a communication (a) delivered by (1) facsimile telecommunication or electronic mail when directed to the facsimile number or electronic mail address, respectively, which the corporation has provided from time to time to shareholders or members and directors for sending communications to the corporation, (2) posting on an electronic message board or network which the corporation has designated for those communications, and which transmission shall be validly delivered upon the posting, or (3) other means of electronic communication, (b) as to which the corporation has placed in effect reasonable measures to verify that the sender is the shareholder or member (in person or by proxy) or director purporting to send the transmission, and (c) that creates a record that is capable of retention, retrieval, and review, and that may thereafter be rendered into clearly legible tangible form.

Ca. Corp. Code § 21
Added by Stats 2004 ch 254 (SB 1306),s 4, eff. 1/1/2005.

Title 1 - CORPORATIONS

Division 1 - GENERAL CORPORATION LAW

Chapter 1 - GENERAL PROVISIONS AND DEFINITIONS

Section 100 - Short title; amendment or repeal

(a) This division shall be known and may be cited as the General Corporation Law.
(b) This title of the Corporations Code, or any division, part, chapter, article or section thereof, may at any time be amended or repealed.
Ca. Corp. Code § 100
Repealed and added by Stats. 1975, Ch. 682.

Section 101 - Construction of division

Unless the provision or the context otherwise requires, the general provisions and definitions set forth in this chapter govern the construction of this division.
Ca. Corp. Code § 101
Repealed and added by Stats. 1975, Ch. 682.

Section 102 - Applicability of division

(a) Subject to Chapter 23 (commencing with Section 2300) (transition provisions), this division applies to corporations organized under this division and to domestic corporations that are not subject to Division 1.5 (commencing with Section 2500), and to domestic corporations that are not subject to Division 2 (commencing with Section 5000) or Part 1 (commencing with Section 12000), 2 (commencing with Section 12200), 3 (commencing with Section 13200), or 5 (commencing with Section 14000) of Division 3 on December 31, 1976, and that are not organized or existing under any statute of this state other than this code; this division applies to any other corporation only to the extent expressly included in a particular provision of this division.
(b) The existence of corporations formed or existing on the date of enactment or reenactment of this division shall not be affected by the enactment or reenactment of this division nor by any change in the requirements for the formation of corporations nor by the amendment or repeal of the laws under which they were formed or created.
(c) Neither the repeals effected by the enactment or reenactment of this division nor the enactment of this title nor the amendment thereof shall impair or take away any existing liability or cause of action against any corporation, its shareholders, directors,

or officers incurred prior to the time of the enactment, reenactment, or amendment.

    Ca. Corp. Code § 102

Amended by Stats 2011 ch 740 (SB 201),s 1, eff. 1/1/2012.

Section 103 - Agency and instrumentality of United States

Every corporation organized under the laws of this state, any other state of the United States or the District of Columbia or under an act of the Congress of the United States, all of the capital stock of which is beneficially owned by the United States, an agency or instrumentality of the United States or any corporation the whole of the capital stock of which is owned by the United States or by an agency or instrumentality of the United States, is conclusively presumed to be an agency and instrumentality of the United States and is entitled to all privileges and immunities to which the holders of all of its stock are entitled as agencies of the United States.

    Ca. Corp. Code § 103

Repealed and added by Stats. 1975, Ch. 682.

Section 104 - Reference to state or federal statute

Unless otherwise expressly provided, whenever reference is made in this division to any other state or federal statute, such reference is to that statute as it may be amended from time to time, whether before or after the enactment of this division.

    Ca. Corp. Code § 104

Repealed and added by Stats. 1975, Ch. 682.

Section 105 - Suing corporation or association

A corporation or association may be sued as provided in the Code of Civil Procedure.

    Ca. Corp. Code § 105

Repealed and added by Stats. 1975, Ch. 682.

Section 106 - Attachment of corporate property

Any corporation heretofore or hereafter formed under this division shall, as a condition of its existence as a corporation, be subject to the provisions of the Code of Civil Procedure authorizing the attachment of corporate property.

    Ca. Corp. Code § 106

Repealed and added by Stats. 1975, Ch. 682.

Section 107 - Issuance or putting in circulation money

No corporation, social purpose corporation, association, or individual shall issue or put in circulation, as money, anything but the lawful money of the United States.

    Ca. Corp. Code § 107

Amended by Stats 2014 ch 694 (SB 1301),s 1, eff. 1/1/2015.
Repealed by Stats 2014 ch 74 (AB 129),s 1, eff. 1/1/2015.
Amended by Stats 2011 ch 740 (SB 201),s 2, eff. 1/1/2012.

Section 108 - Fees for filing instruments

The fees of the Secretary of State for filing instruments by or on behalf of corporations are prescribed in Article 3 (commencing with Section 12180) of Chapter 3 of Part 2 of Division 3 of Title 2 of the Government Code.
    Ca. Corp. Code § 108
Repealed and added by Stats. 1975, Ch. 682.

Section 109 - Certificate of correction

(a) Any agreement, certificate or other instrument relating to a domestic or foreign corporation filed pursuant to this division may be corrected with respect to any misstatement of fact contained therein, any defect in the execution thereof or any other error or defect contained therein, by filing a certificate of correction entitled "Certificate of Correction of _____ (insert here the title of the agreement, certificate or other instrument to be corrected and name(s) of corporation or corporations)"; provided, however, that no such certificate of correction shall alter the wording of any resolution or written consent which was in fact adopted by the board or the shareholders or effect a corrected amendment of articles which amendment as so corrected would not in all respects have complied with the requirements of this division at the time of filing of the agreement, certificate, or other instrument being corrected.
(b) If the certificate of correction corrects original articles, the certificate of correction shall be either an officers' certificate or a certificate signed and verified by the incorporators, or a majority of them. If the certificate of correction corrects an agreement of merger or an officers' certificate accompanying an agreement of merger, the certificate of correction shall be an officers' certificate of the surviving corporation only. In all other instances, the certificate of correction shall be either an officer's certificate or a certificate signed and verified as provided in this division with respect to the agreement, certificate or other instrument being corrected.
(c) A certificate of correction shall set forth the following:

    (1) The name or names of the corporation or corporations.

    (2) The date the agreement, certificate or other instrument being corrected was filed.

    (3) The provision in the agreement, certificate or other instrument as corrected and, if the execution was defective, wherein it was defective.

(4) If applicable, that the certificate does not alter the wording of any resolution or written consent which was in fact adopted by the board or the shareholders.

(d) A provision of the articles, amended articles, restated articles, or certificate of determination being corrected by a certificate of correction shall be identified in the certificate of correction in accordance with subdivision (a) of Section 907.

(e) The filing of the certificate of correction shall not alter the effective time of the agreement, certificate or instrument being corrected, which shall remain as its original effective time, and such filing shall not affect any right or liability accrued or incurred before such filing, except that any right or liability accrued or incurred by reason of the error or defect being corrected shall be extinguished by such filing if the person having that right has not detrimentally relied on the original instrument.

Ca. Corp. Code § 109

Amended by Stats. 1988, Ch. 919, Sec. 1.

Section 109.5 - Dependence upon facts ascertainable outside articles or agreement

(a) Provisions of the articles described in paragraph (3) of subdivision (g) of Section 202 and subdivisions (a) and (b) of Section 204 may be made dependent upon facts ascertainable outside the articles, if the manner in which those facts shall operate upon those provisions is clearly and expressly set forth in the articles. Similarly, any of the terms of an agreement of merger pursuant to Section 1101 may be made dependent upon facts ascertainable outside that agreement, if the manner in which those facts shall operate upon the terms of the agreement is clearly and expressly set forth in the agreement of merger.

(b) Notwithstanding subdivision (a), when any provisions or terms of articles or an agreement of merger are made dependent upon facts ascertainable outside the filed instrument through a reference to an agreement or similar document, the corporation filing that instrument shall (1) maintain at its principal office a copy of any such agreement or document and all amendments and (2) provide to its shareholders, in the case of articles, or to shareholders of any constituent corporation, in the case of an agreement of merger, a copy of them upon written request and without charge.

(c) If the reference to an agreement or contract is a reference to an agreement or contract to which the corporation is a party (a "referenced agreement" in this section), any amendment or revision of the referenced agreement requires shareholder approval, in addition to approvals otherwise required, in the following instances and no other:

(1) If the amendment or revision of the referenced agreement would result in a material change in the rights, preferences, privileges, or restrictions of a class or series of shares, the amendment or revision of the referenced agreement is required to be approved by the outstanding shares (Section 152) of that class or series.

(2) If the amendment or revision of the referenced agreement would result in a material change in the rights or liabilities of any class or series of shares with respect to the subject matter of paragraph (1), (2), (3), (5), or (9) of subdivision (a) of Section 204, the amendment or revision of the referenced agreement is required to be approved by the outstanding shares (Section 152) of that class or series.

(3)If the amendment or revision of the referenced agreement would result in a material change in the restrictions on transfer or hypothecation of any class or series of shares, the amendment or revision of the referenced agreement is required to be approved by the outstanding shares (Section 152) of that class or series.

(4)If the amendment or revision of the referenced agreement would result in a change of any of the principal terms of an agreement of merger, the amendment or revision of the referenced agreement is required to be approved in the same manner as required by Section 1104 for a change in the principal terms of an agreement of merger.

Ca. Corp. Code § 109.5

Amended by Stats 2022 ch 617 (SB 1202),s 3, eff. 1/1/2023.

Amended by Stats 2014 ch 834 (SB 1041),s 1, eff. 1/1/2015.

Section 110 - Filing by Secretary of State; date of filing

(a)Upon receipt of any instrument by the Secretary of State for filing pursuant to this division, if it conforms to law, it shall be filed by, and in the office of, the Secretary of State and the date of filing endorsed thereon. Except for instruments filed pursuant to Section 1502, the date of filing shall be the date the instrument is received by the Secretary of State unless the instrument provides that it is to be withheld from filing until a future date, other than instruments filed pursuant to Section 119, or, unless in the judgment of the Secretary of State, the filing is intended to be coordinated with the filing of some other corporate document which cannot be filed. The Secretary of State shall file a document as of any requested future date not more than 90 days after its receipt, including a Saturday, Sunday, or legal holiday, if the document is received in the Secretary of State's office at least one business day prior to the requested date of filing. An instrument does not fail to conform to law because it is not accompanied by the full filing fee if the unpaid portion of the fee does not exceed the limits established by the policy of the Secretary of State for extending credit in these cases.

(b)If the Secretary of State determines that an instrument submitted for filing or otherwise submitted does not conform to law and returns it to the person submitting it, the instrument may be resubmitted accompanied by a written opinion of the member of the State Bar of California submitting the instrument, or representing the person submitting it, to the effect that the specific provision of the instrument objected to by the Secretary of State does conform to law and stating the points and authorities upon which the opinion is based. The Secretary of State shall rely, with respect to any disputed point of law (other than the application of Sections 119, 201, 2101, and 2106), upon that written opinion in determining whether the instrument conforms to law. The date of filing in that case shall be the date the instrument is received on resubmission.

(c) Any instrument filed with respect to a corporation, other than original articles or instruments filed pursuant to Section 119, may provide that it is to become effective not more than 90 days subsequent to its filing date. In case such a delayed effective date is specified, the instrument may be prevented from becoming effective by a certificate stating that by appropriate corporate action it has been revoked and is null and void, executed in the same manner as the original instrument and filed before the specified effective date. In the case of a merger agreement, the certificate revoking the earlier filing need only be executed on behalf of one of the constituent corporations. If no revocation certificate is filed, the instrument becomes effective on the date specified.

(d) Any instrument submitted to the Secretary of State for filing by a domestic corporation or a foreign corporation that is qualified to transact business in California under Section 2105 shall include the entity name and number as they exist on the Secretary of State's records.

Ca. Corp. Code § 110

Amended by Stats 2022 ch 217 (SB 218),s 1, eff. 1/1/2023.

Amended by Stats 2020 ch 361 (SB 522),s 1, eff. 1/1/2021.

Amended by Stats 2012 ch 494 (SB 1532),s 3, eff. 1/1/2013.

Section 110.5 - Cancellation of filing of articles of domestic corporation or filing of statement and designation by foreign corporation

The Secretary of State may cancel the filing of articles of a domestic corporation, including articles effecting a conversion, or the filing of a statement and designation by a foreign corporation if a check or other remittance accepted in payment of the filing fee or franchise tax is not paid upon presentation. Within 90 days of receiving written notification that the item presented for payment has not been honored for payment, the Secretary of State shall give written notice of the applicability of this section and the cancellation date, which shall be not less than 20 days from the date of mailing the written notice as certified by the Secretary of State, to the agent for service of process or to the person submitting the instrument. Thereafter, if the amount has not been paid by cashier's check or equivalent before the date of cancellation as stated in the written notice of cancellation, the cancellation shall thereupon be effective.

Ca. Corp. Code § 110.5

Amended by Stats 2022 ch 617 (SB 1202),s 4, eff. 1/1/2023.

Amended by Stats. 1988, Ch. 508, Sec. 1.

Section 111 - References to voting of shares

All references in this division to the voting of shares include the voting of other securities given voting rights in the articles pursuant to subdivision (a)(7) of Section

204.

Ca. Corp. Code § 111
Repealed and added by Stats. 1975, Ch. 682.

Section 112 - More or less than one vote for any share; shares disqualified from voting

If the articles provide for more or less than one vote for any share on any matter, the references in Sections 152, 153 and 602 to a majority or other proportion of shares means, as to such matter, a majority or other proportion of the votes entitled to be cast. Whenever in this division shares are disqualified from voting on any matter, they shall not be considered outstanding for the determination of a quorum at any meeting to act upon, or the required vote to approve action upon, that matter under any other provision of this division or the articles or bylaws.

Ca. Corp. Code § 112
Repealed and added by Stats. 1975, Ch. 682.

Section 113 - Reference to mailing

Any reference in this division to mailing means first-class mail, postage prepaid, unless registered or some other form of mail is specified or permitted. Registered mail includes certified mail.

Ca. Corp. Code § 113
Amended by Stats. 1978, Ch. 370.

Section 114 - References to financial statements or comparable statements or items

All references in this division to financial statements, balance sheets, income statements, and statements of cashflows, and all references to assets, liabilities, earnings, retained earnings, and similar accounting items of a corporation mean those financial statements or comparable statements or items prepared or determined in conformity with generally accepted accounting principles then applicable, fairly presenting in conformity with generally accepted accounting principles the matters that they purport to present, subject to any specific accounting treatment required by a particular section of this division. Unless otherwise expressly stated, all references in this division to financial statements mean, in the case of a corporation that has subsidiaries, consolidated statements of the corporation and each of its subsidiaries as are required to be included in the consolidated statements under generally accepted accounting principles then applicable and all references to accounting items mean the items determined on a consolidated basis in accordance with the consolidated financial statements. Financial statements other than annual statements may be condensed or otherwise presented as permitted by authoritative accounting pronouncements.

Ca. Corp. Code § 114
Amended by Stats 2006 ch 214 (AB 1959),s 1, eff. 1/1/2007.

Section 115 - Independent accountant

As used in this division, independent accountant means a certified public accountant or public accountant who is independent of the corporation as determined in accordance with generally accepted auditing standards and who is engaged to audit financial statements of the corporation or perform other accounting services.
Ca. Corp. Code § 115
Amended by Stats. 1976, Ch. 641.

Section 116 - No modification of availability of exemption

Nothing contained in this division modifies the provisions of subdivision (h) of Section 25102 or the conditions provided therein to the availability of an exemption under that subdivision.
Ca. Corp. Code § 116
Repealed and added by Stats. 1975, Ch. 682.

Section 117 - Vote of each class of outstanding shares

Any requirement in this division for a vote of each class of outstanding shares means such a vote regardless of limitations or restrictions upon the voting rights thereof, unless expressly limited to voting shares.
Ca. Corp. Code § 117
Added by Stats. 1976, Ch. 641.

Section 118 - Reference to time notice is given or sent

Any reference in this division to the time a notice is given or sent means, unless otherwise expressly provided, any of the following:
(a) The time a written notice by mail is deposited in the United States mails, postage prepaid.
(b) The time any other written notice, including facsimile, telegram, or electronic mail message, is personally delivered to the recipient or is delivered to a common carrier for transmission, or actually transmitted by the person giving the notice by electronic means, to the recipient.
(c) The time any oral notice is communicated, in person or by telephone, including a voice messaging system or other system or technology designed to record and communicate messages, or wireless, to the recipient, including the recipient's designated voice mailbox or address on the system, or to a person at the office of the recipient who the person giving the notice has reason to believe will promptly communicate it to the recipient.

Ca. Corp. Code § 118
Amended by Stats 2006 ch 538 (SB 1852),s 78, eff. 1/1/2007.

Section 119 - Ratification or validation of noncompliant corporate actions

(a)

(1) Otherwise lawful corporate actions not in compliance, or purportedly not in compliance, with this division or the articles, bylaws, or a plan or agreement to which the corporation is a party in effect at the time of the corporate action, may be ratified, or validated by the superior court, in accordance with the provisions of this section.

(2) Except as otherwise determined by the superior court pursuant to subdivision (e), a ratification or validation of a corporate action in accordance with this section is conclusive in the absence of fraud.

(3) This section does not limit the authority of the board, the shareholders, or the corporation to effect any other lawful means of ratification or validation of a corporate action or correction of a record.

(4) No corporate action may be ratified under subdivision (b) by a dissolved corporation or a foreign corporation, and no petition may be filed under subdivision (e) in respect of any corporate action or security of such a corporation.

(5) This section shall not be used to ratify or validate any corporate action in respect of any of the following:

(A) Noncompliance with subdivision (a) of Section 309.

(B) Noncompliance with subdivision (a) or (b) of Section 310.

(C) Noncompliance with Section 315.

(D) Noncompliance with subdivision (a) of Section 500.

(E) Noncompliance with Section 501.

(b)

(1)

(A)A ratification of a corporate action pursuant to this section, other than a ratification relating to the election of the initial directors pursuant to paragraph (2) of this subdivision, shall be approved by the board and, as applicable, approved by the shareholders or approved by the outstanding shares in accordance with any provision set forth in this division or the articles, bylaws, or a plan or agreement to which the corporation is a party that is applicable to the type of corporate action proposed to be ratified and in effect at the time of the ratification, unless there are no shares outstanding and entitled to vote on the ratification at the time of the ratification, in which case the ratification shall be approved solely by the board, or a higher approval standard that was or would have been applicable to the original taking or purported taking of the corporate action, in which case the ratification shall be approved in accordance with such higher approval standard. In order to approve a ratification of a corporate action pursuant to this paragraph, the board and, as applicable, the shareholders or the outstanding shares shall adopt resolutions setting forth all of the following:

(i)Each corporate action to be ratified.

(ii)The date when each such corporate action was purportedly taken, and the date any such corporate action shall be deemed to have become effective pursuant to this section if different than the date the corporate action was purportedly taken.

(iii)For a corporate action involving the purported issuance of shares, the number and type of shares purportedly issued and the date or dates upon which such shares were purported to have been issued.

(iv)The nature of the noncompliance or purported noncompliance of each such corporate action.

(v)A statement that the ratification of each such corporate action is approved.

(B)The votes of any shares issued, or purportedly issued, pursuant to any corporate action being ratified shall be disregarded for all purposes of approval of the ratification as required by this subdivision, including, but not limited to, for the purpose of determining a quorum at a meeting of shareholders or required class vote.

(2)If the corporate action to be ratified relates to the election of the initial directors pursuant to Section 210, a majority of the persons who, at the time of the ratification, are exercising the powers of directors may approve that ratification by adopting resolutions setting forth all of the following:

(A)The name of the person or persons who first took action in the name of the corporation as the initial directors of the corporation.

(B) The earlier of the date on which such persons first took such action or were purported to have been elected as the initial directors, and the date on which such person or persons shall be deemed to have become the initial directors of the corporation pursuant to this section if different than the date of such first action or purported election, as applicable.

(C) That the ratification of the election of such person or persons as the initial directors is approved.

(c) Notice of any ratification of a corporate action pursuant to this section shall be given promptly after ratification pursuant to subdivision (b) to each shareholder and holder of shares purportedly issued at the time of the ratification, regardless of whether approval of the shareholders or of the outstanding shares is required for the ratification. The notice shall be given as provided in subdivision (b) of Section 601 and shall include a copy of any resolutions adopted pursuant to subdivision (b) and a copy of this section. If a corporation that is subject to the reporting requirements of Section 13 or 15(d) of the federal Securities Exchange Act of 1934 includes the disclosures required by this section in a report, proxy statement, or information statement filed with or furnished to the Securities and Exchange Commission, notice shall be deemed given when that report or statement is filed with or furnished to the Securities and Exchange Commission.

(d)

(1) If a corporate action ratified pursuant to this section would have required the filing of an instrument with the Secretary of State pursuant to the provisions of this division, or if such ratification would cause any instrument previously filed with the Secretary of State to be inaccurate or incomplete in any material respect after giving effect to the ratification, the corporation shall file a certificate of ratification to make, amend, or correct each such instrument. The certificate of ratification shall have the effect as specified therein, and shall be filed with the Secretary of State. A certificate of ratification shall consist of an officers' certificate setting forth all of the following:

(A) The name of the corporation and the Secretary of State's file number of the corporation.

(B) The title of any such instrument whose making, amendment, or correction is being effected by the certificate of ratification.

(C) The date any such instrument was filed with the Secretary of State, or a statement that any such instrument was not previously filed with the Secretary of State and, as applicable, a statement that the ratification approved pursuant to the resolutions set forth in the certificate of ratification would cause any such instrument to be inaccurate or incomplete in any material respect after giving effect to the ratification.

(D) The date any such instrument shall be deemed to have become effective pursuant to this section, which may be prior to or after the filing date.

(E)A statement that the certificate of ratification is making, amending, or correcting any such instrument, as applicable, and a copy of any such instrument containing all of the information required to be included under this division for such instrument to be so made, amended, or corrected. An instrument attached to a certificate of ratification pursuant to this subparagraph need not be separately executed and acknowledged and need not include any statement required by any other section of this division that such instrument has been approved and adopted in accordance with the provisions of such other section.

(F)A statement that the ratification has been approved pursuant to subdivision (b), a copy of the resolutions adopted pursuant to subdivision (b) in respect of the ratification including, in the case of the ratification of any corporate action involving the purported issuance of shares, the number and type of shares purportedly issued and the date or dates upon which such shares were purported to have been issued and, if applicable, a statement of the total number of outstanding shares of each class entitled to vote with respect to the ratification.

(G)A statement that the number of shares of each class voting in favor of the ratification equaled or exceeded the vote required, specifying the percentage vote required of each class entitled to vote.

(2) The office of the Secretary of State may, in its discretion, refuse to file any certificate of ratification if the instrument would render prior filings with the Secretary of State inaccurate, ambiguous, or unintelligible. Upon refusal of the Secretary of State to file a certificate of ratification pursuant to this subdivision, the corporation shall seek validation pursuant to subdivision (e).

(e)

(1) Upon the filing of a petition by an authorized person, the superior court of the proper county shall have jurisdiction in equity to determine the validity of any corporate action (whether or not such corporate action is a ratification or has been the subject of any ratification) or security of the corporation, validate and declare effective any such corporate action or security of the corporation, and declare the date any such corporate action or security of the corporation shall be deemed to have become effective or valid, as applicable, pursuant to this section.

(2) This section does not prescribe or circumscribe the facts and circumstances the superior court may consider or which remedies the superior court may grant in exercising its jurisdiction under this section, except as described in this subdivision.

The superior court may make any order concerning the corporate action as justice and equity may require.

(3)Any petition relating to a ratification taken or proposed to be taken pursuant to this section shall be filed not later than 180 days after the notice required by subdivision (c) is given, except this paragraph shall not apply to an action asserting that a ratification was not accomplished in accordance with this section or to any person to whom notice of the ratification was required to have been given pursuant to subdivision (c), but to whom such notice was not given.

(4)For purposes of this subdivision, the proper county shall be the county where the principal office of the corporation is located or, if the principal office is not located in this state, in the county in which the corporation's agent for service of process is located.

(5)Service of the petition under paragraph (1) upon the registered agent of the corporation shall be deemed to be service upon the corporation, and no other party need be joined in order for the superior court to adjudicate the matter. The superior court may require notice of the action to be provided to other persons specified by the court and permit those other persons to intervene in the action.

(6)For purposes of this subdivision, "authorized person" means the corporation, any successor entity to the corporation, any director, any shareholder or holder of shares purportedly issued, any shareholder or holder of shares purportedly issued as of the time of a corporate action ratified pursuant to this section, or any other person, so long as the other person claims to be substantially and adversely affected by the ratification of a corporate action pursuant to this section.

(7)Any petition seeking validation of a corporate action shall identify every pending legal proceeding of which the petitioner is aware and in which (A) the validity of the corporate action is being directly challenged or (B) the validation of the corporate action would result in the dismissal of the proceeding in whole or in part. If the petitioner becomes aware of any additional such legal proceeding, the petitioner shall amend, or, to the extent required by applicable rules, move for leave to amend, the petition within 10 court days to identify each such proceeding. Identification of a proceeding shall include the venue or forum in which the proceeding was filed, any case number or other unique identifier assigned to the proceeding in that venue or forum, the names of the parties to the proceeding, and the date on which the proceeding was filed.

(f)If a corporate action validated by the superior court pursuant to this section would have required the filing of an instrument with the Secretary of State pursuant to the provisions of this division, or if such validation would cause any instrument previously filed with the Secretary of State to be inaccurate or incomplete in any material respect after giving effect to the validation, the corporation shall file a certificate of validation to make, amend, or correct each such instrument. The certificate of validation shall have the effect as specified therein, and shall be filed with the Secretary of State. A certificate of validation shall consist of an officers' certificate setting forth all of the following:

(1)The name of the corporation and the Secretary of State's file number of the corporation.

(2)The title of any such instrument whose making, amendment, or correction is being effected by the certificate of validation.

(3)The date any such instrument was filed with the Secretary of State, or a statement that any such instrument was not previously filed with the Secretary of State and, as applicable, a statement that the validation ordered pursuant to the superior court order set forth in the certificate of validation would cause any such instrument to be inaccurate or incomplete in any material respect after giving effect to the validation.

(4)The date any such instrument shall be deemed to have become effective pursuant to this section, which may be prior to or after the filing date.

(5)A statement that the certificate of validation is making, amending, or correcting any such instrument, as applicable, and a copy of any such instrument containing all of the information required to be included under this division for such instrument to be so made, amended, or corrected. An instrument attached to a certificate of validation pursuant to this paragraph need not be separately executed and acknowledged and need not include any statement required by any other section of this division that such instrument has been approved and adopted in accordance with the provisions of such other section.

(6)A statement that the validation has been ordered pursuant to subdivision (e), and a copy of the superior court order issued pursuant to subdivision (e) in respect of such validation.
(g)Unless otherwise stated in resolutions adopted pursuant to subdivision (b) or determined by the superior court pursuant to subdivision (e), a corporate action or security of the corporation ratified or validated in accordance with this section relates back to the date of the original corporate action.
(h)As used in this section:

(1)"Corporate action" means any of the following:

(A)Any action or purported action of the board.

(B)Any action or purported action of the shareholders.

(C) Any other action or transaction taken, or purportedly taken, by or on behalf of the corporation, including, but not limited to, any issuance, or purported issuance, of securities of the corporation.

(2)"Higher approval standard" means any provision set forth in this division or the articles, bylaws, or a plan or agreement to which the corporation was a party in effect at the time of the original taking or purported taking of a corporate action:

(A) Requiring action of the board or shareholders, at a meeting or by written consent, to be taken by a proportion greater than would have been required pursuant to this division or the articles, bylaws, or a plan or agreement to which the corporation is a party in effect at the time of the ratification of the corporate action pursuant to this section.

(B) Requiring a greater proportion of the directors or shareholders to constitute a quorum for the transaction of business at a meeting than would have been required pursuant to this division or the articles, bylaws, or a plan or agreement to which the corporation is a party in effect at the time of the ratification of the corporate action pursuant to this section.

(C) Requiring, prohibiting, or prescribing conditions on action of the board or shareholders at a meeting or by written consent, which would not have been required, prohibited, or prescribed pursuant to this division or the articles, bylaws, or a plan or agreement to which the corporation is a party in effect at the time of the ratification of the corporate action pursuant to this section.

(D) Requiring separate action of the holders of any class or series of the corporation's shares or of directors elected, appointed, or nominated by the holders of any class or series of the corporation's shares voting as a class or series, which would not have been required pursuant to this division or the articles, bylaws, or a plan or agreement to which the corporation is a party in effect at the time of the ratification of the corporate action pursuant to this section, unless no shares of that class or series are outstanding at the time of the ratification of the corporate action pursuant to this section.

(E) Requiring separate action of the holders of securities of the corporation other than shares, which would not have been required pursuant to this division or the articles, bylaws, or a plan or agreement to which the corporation is a party in effect at the time of the ratification of the corporate action pursuant to this section, unless those securities are not outstanding at the time of the ratification of the corporate action pursuant to this section.

(F) Requiring separate action of any specified person or persons, which would not have been required pursuant to this division or the articles, bylaws, or a plan or agreement to which the corporation is a party in effect at the time of the ratification of the corporate action pursuant to this section.

(3)"Security" means a share, option, or other security of a corporation.
(i)The corporation shall retain all records related to the ratification or validation of a corporate action under this section in accordance with Section 1500.
(j)If the corporation is a party to a pending legal proceeding in which (1) the validity of a corporate action sought to be ratified or validated pursuant to this section is at issue or (2) the ratification or validation of a corporate action pursuant to this section would result in the dismissal in whole or in part of the proceeding, the corporation shall notify the judge, arbitrator, or other person presiding over the proceeding at least 10 court days prior to adopting resolutions pursuant to subdivision (b) or filing a petition pursuant to subdivision (e) with respect to that corporate action. That person shall have power to stay the ratification or validation as justice and equity may require.

Ca. Corp. Code § 119
Added by Stats 2022 ch 217 (SB 218),s 2, eff. 1/1/2023.

Section 149 - "Acknowledged" defined

"Acknowledged" means that an instrument is either:
(a) Formally acknowledged as provided in Article 3 (commencing with Section 1180) of Chapter 4 of Title 4 of Part 4 of Division 2 of the Civil Code, or
(b) Accompanied by a declaration in writing signed by the persons executing the same that they are such persons and that the instrument is the act and deed of the person or persons executing the same. Any certificate of acknowledgment taken without this state before a notary public or a judge or clerk of a court of record having an official seal need not be further authenticated.

Ca. Corp. Code § 149
Amended by Stats. 1976, Ch. 641.

Section 150 - "Affiliate" of or "affiliated" with defined

A corporation is an "affiliate" of, or a corporation is "affiliated" with, another specified corporation if it directly, or indirectly through one or more intermediaries, controls, is controlled by or is under common control with the other specified corporation.

Ca. Corp. Code § 150
Added by Stats. 1975, Ch. 682.

Section 151 - "Approved by (or approval of) the board" defined

"Approved by (or approval of) the board" means approved or ratified by the vote of the board or by the vote of a committee authorized to exercise the powers of the board, except as to matters not within the competence of the committee under Section 311.

Ca. Corp. Code § 151
Added by Stats. 1975, Ch. 682.

Section 152 - "Approved by (or approval of) the outstanding shares" defined

"Approved by (or approval of) the outstanding shares" means approved by the affirmative vote of a majority of the outstanding shares entitled to vote. Such approval shall include the affirmative vote of a majority of the outstanding shares of each class or series entitled, by any provision of the articles or of this division, to vote as a class or series on the subject matter being voted upon and shall also include the affirmative vote of such greater proportion (including all) of the outstanding shares of any class or series if such greater proportion is required by the articles or this division.

Ca. Corp. Code § 152
Amended by Stats. 1976, Ch. 641.

Section 153 - "Approved by (or approval of) the shareholders" defined

"Approved by (or approval of) the shareholders" means approved or ratified by the affirmative vote of a majority of the shares represented and voting at a duly held meeting at which a quorum is present (which shares voting affirmatively also constitute at least a majority of the required quorum) or by the written consent of shareholders (Section 603) or by the affirmative vote or written consent of such greater proportion (including all) of the shares of any class or series as may be provided in the articles or in this division for all or any specified shareholder action.

Ca. Corp. Code § 153
Amended by Stats. 1977, Ch. 235.

Section 154 - "Articles" defined

"Articles" includes the articles of incorporation, amendments thereto, amended articles, restated articles, certificate of incorporation and certificates of determination. All references in this division to a vote required by the "articles" include, in the case of a close corporation (Section 158), any vote required by a shareholders' agreement.

Ca. Corp. Code § 154
Amended by Stats. 1976, Ch. 641.

Section 155 - "Board" defined

"Board" means the board of directors of the corporation.

Ca. Corp. Code § 155
Added by Stats. 1975, Ch. 682.

Section 156 - "Certificate of determination" defined

"Certificate of determination" means a certificate executed and filed pursuant to Section 401.

    Ca. Corp. Code § 156

Added by Stats. 1975, Ch. 682.

Section 156.1 - "Certificated security" defined

"Certificated security" means a share (Section 184), as defined in paragraph (4) of subdivision (a) of Section 8102 of, or an obligation of the issuer as described in paragraph (15) of subdivision (a) of, the Commercial Code.

    Ca. Corp. Code § 156.1

Amended by Stats. 1996, Ch. 497, Sec. 25. Effective January 1, 1997.

Section 156.5 - "Certificate of Redomestication" defined

"Certificate of Redomestication" is the document by which the appropriate official of another state approves the redomestication of a California insurer.

    Ca. Corp. Code § 156.5

Added by Stats. 1995, Ch. 702, Sec. 1. Effective January 1, 1996.

Section 156.6 - Chairperson of the board

All references in this division to "chairperson of the board" shall be deemed to refer to all permissible titles for the chairperson of the board, as permitted by Section 312.

    Ca. Corp. Code § 156.6

Added by Stats 2015 ch 98 (SB 351),s 1, eff. 1/1/2016.

Section 157 - "Chapter" defined

"Chapter" refers to a chapter of this Division 1 of Title 1 of the Corporations Code, unless otherwise expressly stated.

    Ca. Corp. Code § 157

Added by Stats. 1975, Ch. 682.

Section 158 - "Close corporation" defined

(a) "Close corporation" means a corporation, including a close social purpose corporation, whose articles contain, in addition to the provisions required by Section 202, a provision that all of the corporation's issued shares of all classes shall be held of record by not more than a specified number of persons, not exceeding 35, and a statement, "This corporation is a close corporation."

(b) The special provisions referred to in subdivision (a) may be included in the articles by amendment, but if such amendment is adopted after the issuance of shares only by the affirmative vote of all of the issued and outstanding shares of all classes.
(c) The special provisions referred to in subdivision (a) may be deleted from the articles by amendment, or the number of shareholders specified may be changed by amendment, but if such amendment is adopted after the issuance of shares, only by the affirmative vote of at least two-thirds of each class of the outstanding shares; provided, however, that the articles may provide for a lesser vote, but not less than a majority of the outstanding shares, or may deny a vote to any class, or both.
(d) In determining the number of shareholders for the purposes of the provision in the articles authorized by this section, spouses and the personal representative of either shall be counted as one regardless of how shares may be held by either or both of them, a trust or personal representative of a decedent holding shares shall be counted as one regardless of the number of trustees or beneficiaries, and a partnership or corporation or business association holding shares shall be counted as one (except that any such trust or entity the primary purpose of which was the acquisition or voting of the shares shall be counted according to the number of beneficial interests therein).
(e) A corporation shall cease to be a close corporation upon the filing of an amendment to its articles pursuant to subdivision (c) or, if it shall have more than the maximum number of holders of record of its shares specified in its articles as a result of an inter vivos transfer of shares which is not void under subdivision (d) of Section 418, the transfer of shares on distribution by will or pursuant to the laws of descent and distribution, the dissolution of a partnership or corporation or business association, or the termination of a trust which holds shares, by court decree upon dissolution of a marriage or otherwise by operation of law. Promptly upon acquiring more than the specified number of holders of record of its shares, a close corporation shall execute and file an amendment to its articles deleting the special provisions referred to in subdivision (a) and deleting any other provisions not permissible for a corporation which is not a close corporation, which amendment shall be promptly approved and filed by the board and need not be approved by the outstanding shares.
(f) Nothing contained in this section shall invalidate any agreement among the shareholders to vote for the deletion from the articles of the special provisions referred to in subdivision (a) upon the lapse of a specified period of time or upon the occurrence of a certain event or condition or otherwise.
(g) The following sections contain specific references to close corporations: Sections 186, 202, 204, 300, 418, 421, 1111, 1201, 1800, and 1904.

    Ca. Corp. Code § 158

Amended by Stats 2016 ch 50 (SB 1005),s 20, eff. 1/1/2017.
Amended by Stats 2014 ch 694 (SB 1301),s 2, eff. 1/1/2015.
Amended by Stats 2011 ch 740 (SB 201),s 3, eff. 1/1/2012.
Amended by Stats 2000 ch 485 (AB 1895), s 1, eff. 1/1/2001.

Section 159 - "Common shares" defined

"Common shares" means shares which have no preference over any other shares with respect to distribution of assets on liquidation or with respect to payment of dividends.

> *Ca. Corp. Code § 159*
Added by Stats. 1975, Ch. 682.

Section 160 - "Control" defined

(a) Except as provided in subdivision (b), "control" means the possession, direct or indirect, of the power to direct or cause the direction of the management and policies of a corporation.
(b) "Control" in Sections 181, 1001, and 1200 means the ownership directly or indirectly of shares or equity securities possessing more than 50 percent of the voting power of a domestic corporation, a foreign corporation, or an other business entity.

> *Ca. Corp. Code § 160*
Amended 9/21/1999 (Bill Number: AB 198) (Chapter 437).

Section 161 - "Constituent corporation" defined

"Constituent corporation" means a corporation which is merged with or into one or more other corporations or one or more other business entities and includes a surviving corporation.

> *Ca. Corp. Code § 161*
Amended by Stats. 1994, Ch. 1200, Sec. 9. Effective September 30, 1994.

Section 161.5 - "Constituent limited partnership" defined

"Constituent limited partnership" means a limited partnership which is merged with one or more corporations and includes the surviving limited partnership.

> *Ca. Corp. Code § 161.5*
Added by Stats. 1993, Ch. 543, Sec. 2. Effective January 1, 1994.

Section 161.7 - "Constituent other business entity" defined

"Constituent other business entity" means an other business entity that is merged with or into one or more corporations and includes the surviving other business entity.

> *Ca. Corp. Code § 161.7*
Added by Stats. 1994, Ch. 1200, Sec. 10. Effective September 30, 1994.

Section 161.9 - "Conversion" defined

"Conversion" means a conversion pursuant to Chapter 11.5 (commencing with Section 1150).

    Ca. Corp. Code § 161.9

Added by Stats 2002 ch 480 (SB 399),s 1, eff. 1/1/2003.

Section 162 - "Corporation" defined

"Corporation", unless otherwise expressly provided, refers only to a corporation organized under this division or a corporation subject to this division under the provisions of subdivision (a) of Section 102.

    Ca. Corp. Code § 162

Amended by Stats. 1976, Ch. 641.

Section 163 - "Corporation subject to the Banking Law" defined

"Corporation subject to the Banking Law" (Division 1.1 (commencing with Section 1000) of the Financial Code) means:

(a) Any corporation which, with the approval of the Commissioner of Financial Protection and Innovation, is incorporated for the purpose of engaging in, or which is authorized by the Commissioner of Financial Protection and Innovation to engage in, the commercial banking business under Division 1.1 (commencing with Section 1000) of the Financial Code.

(b) Any corporation which, with the approval of the Commissioner of Financial Protection and Innovation, is incorporated for the purpose of engaging in, or which is authorized by the Commissioner of Financial Protection and Innovation to engage in, the industrial banking business under Division 1.1 (commencing with Section 1000) of the Financial Code.

(c) Any corporation (other than a corporation described in subdivision (d)) which, with the approval of the Commissioner of Financial Protection and Innovation, is incorporated for the purpose of engaging in, or which is authorized by the Commissioner of Financial Protection and Innovation to engage in, the trust business under Division 1.1 (commencing with Section 1000) of the Financial Code.

(d) Any corporation which is authorized by the Commissioner of Financial Protection and Innovation and the Commissioner of Insurance to maintain a title insurance department to engage in title insurance business and a trust department to engage in trust business; or

(e) Any corporation which, with the approval of the Commissioner of Financial Protection and Innovation, is incorporated for the purpose of engaging in, or which is authorized by the Commissioner of Financial Protection and Innovation to engage in, business under Article 1 (commencing with Section 1850), Chapter 21, Division 1.1 of the Financial Code.

    Ca. Corp. Code § 163

Amended by Stats 2022 ch 452 (SB 1498),s 43, eff. 1/1/2023.
Amended by Stats 2014 ch 401 (AB 2763),s 16, eff. 1/1/2015.
Amended by Stats 2000 ch 1015 (SB 2148), s 1, eff. 9/29/2000.

Section 163.1 - "Cumulative dividends in arrears" defined

For purposes of subdivision (b) of Section 500 and subdivision (b) of Section 506, "cumulative dividends in arrears" means only cumulative dividends that have not been paid as required on a scheduled payment date set forth in, or determined pursuant to, the articles of incorporation, regardless of whether those dividends had been declared prior to that scheduled payment date.
   Ca. Corp. Code § 163.1
Amended by Stats 2011 ch 203 (AB 571),s 1, eff. 1/1/2012.
Added by Stats 2000 ch 485 (AB 1895), s 2, eff. 1/1/2001.

Section 164 - "Directors" defined

"Directors" means natural persons designated in the articles as such or elected by the incorporators and natural persons designated, elected or appointed by any other name or title to act as directors, and their successors.
   Ca. Corp. Code § 164
Amended by Stats. 1976, Ch. 641.

Section 165 - "Disappearing corporation" defined

"Disappearing corporation" means a constituent corporation which is not the surviving corporation.
   Ca. Corp. Code § 165
Added by Stats. 1975, Ch. 682.

Section 165.5 - "Disappearing limited partnership" defined

"Disappearing limited partnership" means a constituent limited partnership which is not the surviving limited partnership.
   Ca. Corp. Code § 165.5
Added by Stats. 1993, Ch. 543, Sec. 3. Effective January 1, 1994.

Section 166 - "Distribution to its shareholders" defined

"Distribution to its shareholders" means the transfer of cash or property by a corporation to its shareholders without consideration, whether by way of dividend or otherwise, except a dividend in shares of the corporation, or the purchase or redemption of its shares for cash or property, including the transfer, purchase, or redemption by a subsidiary of the corporation. The time of any distribution by way of dividend shall be the date of declaration thereof and the time of any distribution by purchase or redemption of shares shall be the date cash or property is transferred by the corporation, whether or not pursuant to a contract of an earlier date; provided, that where a debt obligation that is a security (as defined in Section 8102 of the Commercial Code) is issued in exchange for shares the time of the distribution is the date when the corporation acquires the shares in the exchange. In the case of a sinking fund payment, cash or property is transferred within the meaning of this section at the time that it is delivered to a trustee for the holders of preferred shares to be used for the redemption of the shares or physically segregated by the corporation in trust for that purpose. "Distribution to its shareholders" shall not include (a) satisfaction of a final judgment of a court or tribunal of appropriate jurisdiction ordering the rescission of the issuance of shares, (b) the rescission by a corporation of the issuance of it shares, if the board determines (with any director who is, or would be, a party to the transaction not being entitled to vote) that (1) it is reasonably likely that the holder or holders of the shares in question could legally enforce a claim for the rescission, (2) that the rescission is in the best interests of the corporation, and (3) the corporation is likely to be able to meet its liabilities (except those for which payment is otherwise adequately provided) as they mature, or (c) the repurchase by a corporation of its shares issued by it pursuant to Section 408, if the board determines (with any director who is, or would be, a party to the transaction not being entitled to vote) that (1) the repurchase is in the best interests of the corporation and that (2) the corporation is likely to be able to meet its liabilities (except those for which payment is otherwise adequately provided) as they mature.

 Ca. Corp. Code § 166
Amended by Stats. 1996, Ch. 497, Sec. 26. Effective January 1, 1997.

Section 167 - "Domestic corporation" defined

"Domestic corporation" means a corporation formed under the laws of this state.

 Ca. Corp. Code § 167
Added by Stats. 1975, Ch. 682.

Section 167.3 - "Domestic limited liability company" defined

"Domestic limited liability company" means a limited liability company as defined in subdivision (t) of Section 17000.

 Ca. Corp. Code § 167.3
Added by Stats. 1994, Ch. 1200, Sec. 11. Effective September 30, 1994.

Section 167.5 - "Domestic limited partnership" defined

"Domestic limited partnership" means any limited partnership formed under the laws of this state.

Ca. Corp. Code § 167.5
Amended by Stats 2006 ch 495 (AB 339),s 4, eff. 1/1/2007.

Section 167.7 - "Domestic other business entity" defined

"Domestic other business entity" means an other business entity organized under the laws of this state.
   Ca. Corp. Code § 167.7
Added by Stats. 1994, Ch. 1200, Sec. 12. Effective September 30, 1994.

Section 167.8 - "Disappearing other business entity" defined

"Disappearing other business entity" means a constituent other business entity that is not the surviving other business entity.
   Ca. Corp. Code § 167.8
Added by Stats. 1994, Ch. 1200, Sec. 13. Effective September 30, 1994.

Section 168 - "Equity security" defined

"Equity security" in Sections 181, 1001, 1113, 1200, and 1201 means any share or membership of a domestic or foreign corporation; any partnership interest, membership interest, or equivalent equity interest in an other business entity; and any security convertible with or without consideration into, or any warrant or right to subscribe to or purchase, any of the foregoing.
   Ca. Corp. Code § 168
Amended 9/21/1999 (Bill Number: AB 198) (Chapter 437).

Section 169 - "Filed" defined

"Filed", unless otherwise expressly provided, means filed in the office of the Secretary of State.
   Ca. Corp. Code § 169
Added by Stats. 1975, Ch. 682.

Section 170 - "Foreign association" defined

"Foreign association" means a business association organized as a trust under the laws of a foreign jurisdiction.
   Ca. Corp. Code § 170
Added by Stats. 1975, Ch. 682.

Section 171 - "Foreign corporation" defined

"Foreign corporation" means any corporation other than a domestic corporation and, when used in Section 191, Section 201, Section 2203, Section 2258 and Section 2259 and Chapter 21, includes a foreign association, unless otherwise stated. "Foreign corporation" as used in Chapter 21 does not include a corporation or association chartered under the laws of the United States.

Ca. Corp. Code § 171
Amended by Stats. 1977, Ch. 235.

Section 171.03 - "Foreign limited liability company" defined

"Foreign limited liability company" means a foreign limited liability company as defined in subdivision (j) of Section 17701.02.

Ca. Corp. Code § 171.03
Amended by Stats 2012 ch 419 (SB 323),s 5, eff. 1/1/2013, op. 1/1/2014.

Section 171.05 - "Foreign limited partnership" defined

"Foreign limited partnership" means any limited partnership, including a limited liability limited partnership, formed under the laws of any state other than this state or of the District of Columbia or under the laws of a foreign country.

Ca. Corp. Code § 171.05
Amended by Stats 2006 ch 495 (AB 339),s 5, eff. 1/1/2007.

Section 171.07 - "Foreign other business entity" defined

"Foreign other business entity" means an other business entity organized under the laws of any state, other than this state, or of the District of Columbia or under the laws of a foreign country.

Ca. Corp. Code § 171.07
Added by Stats. 1994, Ch. 1200, Sec. 15. Effective September 30, 1994.

Section 171.08 - "Social purpose corporation" defined

"Social purpose corporation" means any social purpose corporation formed under Division 1.5 (commencing with Section 2500).

Ca. Corp. Code § 171.08
Amended by Stats 2014 ch 694 (SB 1301),s 3, eff. 1/1/2015.
Added by Stats 2011 ch 740 (SB 201),s 4, eff. 1/1/2012.

Section 171.1 - "Initial transaction statement" defined

"Initial transaction statement" means a statement signed by or on behalf of the issuer sent to the new registered owner or registered pledgee, and "written statements," when used in connection with uncertificated securities, means the written statements that are periodically, or at the request of the registered owner or registered pledgee, sent by the issuer to the registered owner or registered pledgee describing the issue of which the uncertificated security is a part.

Ca. Corp. Code § 171.1

Amended by Stats. 1996, Ch. 497, Sec. 27. Effective January 1, 1997.

Section 171.3 - "Limited liability company" defined

"Limited liability company" means a limited liability company as defined in subdivision (k) of Section 17701.02.

Ca. Corp. Code § 171.3

Amended by Stats 2012 ch 419 (SB 323),s 6, eff. 1/1/2013, op. 1/1/2014.

Section 171.5 - "Limited partnership" defined

"Limited partnership" means a partnership formed by two or more persons and having one or more general partners and one or more limited partners, or their equivalents under any name.

Ca. Corp. Code § 171.5

Added by Stats. 1993, Ch. 543, Sec. 6. Effective January 1, 1994.

Section 172 - "Liquidation price" or "liquidation preference" defined

"Liquidation price" or "liquidation preference" means amounts payable on shares of any class upon voluntary or involuntary dissolution, winding up or distribution of the entire assets of the corporation, including any cumulative dividends accrued and unpaid, in priority to shares of another class or classes.

Ca. Corp. Code § 172

Added by Stats. 1975, Ch. 682.

Section 173 - "Officers' certificate" defined

"Officers' certificate" means a certificate signed and verified by the chairperson of the board, the president or any vice president and by the secretary, the chief financial officer, the treasurer or any assistant secretary or assistant treasurer.

Ca. Corp. Code § 173

Amended by Stats 2015 ch 98 (SB 351),s 2, eff. 1/1/2016.

Section 174 - "On the certificate" defined

"On the certificate" means that a statement appears on the face of a share certificate or on the reverse thereof with a reference thereto on the face or, in the case of an uncertificated security, that the applicable provisions of subdivision (a) of Section 8202 and Section 8204 of the Commercial Code have been complied with.

Ca. Corp. Code § 174
Amended by Stats. 1996, Ch. 497, Sec. 28. Effective January 1, 1997.

Section 174.5 - "Other business entity" defined

"Other business entity" means a domestic or foreign limited liability company, limited partnership, general partnership, business trust, real estate investment trust, unincorporated association (other than a nonprofit association), or a domestic reciprocal insurer organized after 1974 to provide medical malpractice insurance as set forth in Article 16 (commencing with Section 1550) of Chapter 3 of Part 2 of Division 1 of the Insurance Code. As used herein, "general partnership" means a "partnership" as defined in subdivision (7) of Section 16101; "business trust" means a business organization formed as a trust; "real estate investment trust" means a "real estate investment trust" as defined in subsection (a) of Section 856 of the Internal Revenue Code of 1986, as amended; and "unincorporated association" has the meaning set forth in Section 18035.
    Ca. Corp. Code § 174.5
Amended by Stats 2004 ch 178 (SB 1746),s 4, eff. 1/1/2005
Amended September 21, 1999 (Bill Number: AB 198) (Chapter 437).

Section 175 - "Parent" defined

Except as used in Sections 1001, 1101, and 1113, a "parent" of a specified corporation is an affiliate in control (Section 160(a)(a)) of that corporation directly or indirectly through one or more intermediaries. In Sections 1001, 1101, and 1113, "parent" means a person in control (Section 160(b)(b)) of a domestic corporation, a foreign corporation, or an other business entity.
    Ca. Corp. Code § 175
Amended 9/21/1999 (Bill Number: AB 198) (Chapter 437).

Section 176 - "Preferred shares" defined

"Preferred shares" means shares other than common shares.
    Ca. Corp. Code § 176
Added by Stats. 1975, Ch. 682.

Section 177 - "Proper county" defined

"Proper county" means the county where the principal office of the corporation is located or, if the principal office of the corporation is not located in this state, or the corporation has no such office, the County of Sacramento.
    Ca. Corp. Code § 177
Amended by Stats 2022 ch 617 (SB 1202),s 5, eff. 1/1/2023.
Added by Stats. 1975, Ch. 682.

Section 178 - "Proxy" defined

"Proxy" means a written authorization signed or an electronic transmission authorized by a shareholder or the shareholder's attorney in fact giving another person or persons power to vote with respect to the shares of such shareholder. "Signed" for the purpose of this section means the placing of the shareholder's name or other authorization on the proxy (whether by manual signature, typewriting, telegraphic, or electronic transmission or otherwise) by the shareholder or the shareholder's attorney in fact.

A proxy may be transmitted by an oral telephonic transmission if it is submitted with information from which it may be determined that the proxy was authorized by the shareholder, or his or her attorney in fact.

  Ca. Corp. Code § 178
Amended by Stats. 1991, Ch. 308, Sec. 1.

Section 179 - "Proxyholder" defined

"Proxyholder" means the person or persons to whom a proxy is given.

  Ca. Corp. Code § 179
Added by Stats. 1975, Ch. 682.

Section 180 - "Redemption price" defined

"Redemption price" means the amount or amounts (in cash, property or securities, or any combination thereof) payable on shares of any class or series upon the redemption of the shares. Unless otherwise expressly provided, the redemption price is payable in cash.

  Ca. Corp. Code § 180
Added by Stats. 1975, Ch. 682.

Section 180.5 - "Redomestication" defined

"Redomestication" means the transfer of an insurer's place of incorporation from another state to this state or from this state to another state.

  Ca. Corp. Code § 180.5
Added by Stats. 1995, Ch. 702, Sec. 2. Effective January 1, 1996.

Section 181 - "Reorganization" defined

"Reorganization" means either:

(a) A merger pursuant to Chapter 11 (commencing with Section 1100) other than a short-form merger (a "merger reorganization").

(b) The acquisition by one domestic corporation, foreign corporation, or other business entity in exchange, in whole or in part, for its equity securities (or the equity securities of a domestic corporation, a foreign corporation, or an other business entity which is in control of the acquiring entity) of equity securities of another domestic corporation, foreign corporation, or other business entity if, immediately after the acquisition, the acquiring entity has control of the other entity (an "exchange reorganization").

(c) The acquisition by one domestic corporation, foreign corporation, or other business entity in exchange in whole or in part for its equity securities (or the equity securities of a domestic corporation, a foreign corporation, or an other business entity which is in control of the acquiring entity) or for its debt securities (or debt securities of a domestic corporation, foreign corporation, or other business entity which is in control of the acquiring entity) which are not adequately secured and which have a maturity date in excess of five years after the consummation of the reorganization, or both, of all or substantially all of the assets of another domestic corporation, foreign corporation, or other business entity (a "sale-of-assets reorganization").

Ca. Corp. Code § 181
Amended 9/21/1999 (Bill Number: AB 198) (Chapter 437).

Section 182 - "Reverse stock split" defined

"Reverse stock split" means the pro rata combination of all the outstanding shares of a class into a smaller number of shares of the same class by an amendment to the articles stating the effect on outstanding shares.

Ca. Corp. Code § 182
Added by Stats. 1975, Ch. 682.

Section 183 - "Series" defined

"Series" of shares means those shares within a class which have the same rights, preferences, privileges and restrictions but which differ in one or more rights, preferences, privileges or restrictions from other shares within the same class. Certificated securities and uncertificated securities do not constitute different series if the only difference is certificated and uncertificated status.

Ca. Corp. Code § 183
Amended by Stats. 1986, Ch. 766, Sec. 9.

Section 183.5 - "Share exchange tender offer" defined

"Share exchange tender offer" means any acquisition by one corporation in exchange in whole or in part for its equity securities (or the equity securities of a corporation which is in control of the acquiring corporation) of shares of another corporation, other than an exchange reorganization (subdivision (b) of Section 181).

Ca. Corp. Code § 183.5
Added by Stats. 1989, Ch. 1116, Sec. 4. Effective September 30, 1989.

Section 184 - "Shares" defined

"Shares" means the units into which the proprietary interests in a corporation are divided in the articles.
Ca. Corp. Code § 184
Added by Stats. 1975, Ch. 682.

Section 185 - "Shareholder" defined

"Shareholder" means one who is a holder of record of shares.
Ca. Corp. Code § 185
Added by Stats. 1975, Ch. 682.

Section 186 - "Shareholders' agreement" defined

"Shareholders' agreement" means a written agreement among all of the shareholders of a close corporation, or if a close corporation has only one shareholder between such shareholder and the corporation, as authorized by subdivision (b) of Section 300.
Ca. Corp. Code § 186
Amended by Stats. 1976, Ch. 641.

Section 187 - "Short-form merger" defined

"Short-form merger" means a merger pursuant to Section 1110.
Ca. Corp. Code § 187
Added by Stats. 1975, Ch. 682.

Section 188 - "Stock-split" defined

"Stock split" means the pro rata division, otherwise than by a share dividend, of all the outstanding shares of a class into a greater number of shares of the same class by an amendment to the articles stating the effect on outstanding shares.
Ca. Corp. Code § 188
Added by Stats. 1975, Ch. 682.

Section 189 - "Subsidiary" defined

(a) Except as provided in subdivision (b), "subsidiary" of a specified corporation means a corporation shares of which possessing more than 50 percent of the voting power are owned directly or indirectly through one or more subsidiaries by the specified corporation.
(b) For the purpose of Section 703, "subsidiary" of a specified corporation means a corporation shares of which possessing more than 25 percent of the voting power are

owned directly or indirectly through one or more subsidiaries as defined in subdivision (a) by the specified corporation.

Ca. Corp. Code § 189

Amended by Stats. 1976, Ch. 641.

Section 190 - "Surviving corporation" defined

"Surviving corporation" means a corporation into which one or more other corporations or one or more other business entities are merged.

Ca. Corp. Code § 190

Amended by Stats. 1994, Ch. 1200, Sec. 18. Effective September 30, 1994.

Section 190.5 - "Surviving limited partnership" defined

"Surviving limited partnership" means a limited partnership into which one or more other limited partnerships or one or more corporations are merged.

Ca. Corp. Code § 190.5

Added by Stats. 1993, Ch. 543, Sec. 8. Effective January 1, 1994.

Section 190.7 - "Surviving other business entity" defined

"Surviving other business entity" means an other business entity into which one or more other business entities or one or more corporations are merged.

Ca. Corp. Code § 190.7

Added by Stats. 1994, Ch. 1200, Sec. 19. Effective September 30, 1994.

Section 191 - "Transact intrastate business" defined

(a) For the purposes of Chapter 21 (commencing with Section 2100), "transact intrastate business" means entering into repeated and successive transactions of its business in this state, other than interstate or foreign commerce.

(b) A foreign corporation shall not be considered to be transacting intrastate business merely because its subsidiary transacts intrastate business or merely because of its status as any one or more of the following:

(1) A shareholder of a domestic corporation.

(2) A shareholder of a foreign corporation transacting intrastate business.

(3) A limited partner of a domestic limited partnership.

(4) A limited partner of a foreign limited partnership transacting intrastate business.

(5) A member or manager of a domestic limited liability company.

(6) A member or manager of a foreign limited liability company transacting intrastate business.

(c) Without excluding other activities that may not constitute transacting intrastate business, a foreign corporation shall not be considered to be transacting intrastate business within the meaning of subdivision (a) solely by reason of carrying on in this state any one or more of the following activities:

(1) Maintaining or defending any action or suit or any administrative or arbitration proceeding, or effecting the settlement thereof or the settlement of claims or disputes.

(2) Holding meetings of its board or shareholders or carrying on other activities concerning its internal affairs.

(3) Maintaining bank accounts.

(4) Maintaining offices or agencies for the transfer, exchange, and registration of its securities or depositaries with relation to its securities.

(5) Effecting sales through independent contractors.

(6) Soliciting or procuring orders, whether by mail or through employees or agents or otherwise, where those orders require acceptance outside this state before becoming binding contracts.

(7) Creating evidences of debt or mortgages, liens or security interests on real or personal property.

(8) Conducting an isolated transaction completed within a period of 180 days and not in the course of a number of repeated transactions of like nature.

(d) Without excluding other activities that may not constitute transacting intrastate business, any foreign lending institution, including, but not limited to: any foreign banking corporation, any foreign corporation all of the capital stock of which is owned by one or more foreign banking corporations, any foreign savings and loan association, any foreign insurance company or any foreign corporation or association authorized by its charter to invest in loans secured by real and personal property, whether organized under the laws of the United States or of any other state, district or territory of the United States, shall not be considered to be doing, transacting, or engaging in business in this state solely by reason of engaging in any or all of the following activities either on its own behalf or as a trustee of a pension plan, employee profit sharing or retirement plan, testamentary or inter vivos trust, or in any other fiduciary capacity:

(1) The acquisition by purchase, by contract to purchase, by making of advance commitments to purchase or by assignment of loans, secured or unsecured, or any interest therein, if those activities are carried on from outside this state by the lending institution.

(2) The making by an officer or employee of physical inspections and appraisals of real or personal property securing or proposed to secure any loan, if the officer or employee making any physical inspection or appraisal is not a resident of and does not maintain a place of business for that purpose in this state.

(3) The ownership of any loans and the enforcement of any loans by trustee's sale, judicial process, or deed in lieu of foreclosure or otherwise.

(4) The modification, renewal, extension, transfer, or sale of loans or the acceptance of additional or substitute security therefor or the full or partial release of the security therefor or the acceptance of substitute or additional obligors thereon, if the activities are carried on from outside this state by the lending institution.

(5) The engaging by contractual arrangement of a corporation, firm, or association, qualified to do business in this state, that is not a subsidiary or parent of the lending institution and that is not under common management with the lending institution, to make collections and to service loans in any manner whatsoever, including the payment of ground rents, taxes, assessments, insurance, and the like and the making, on behalf of the lending institution, of physical inspections and appraisals of real or personal property securing any loans or proposed to secure any loans, and the performance of any such engagement.

(6) The acquisition of title to the real or personal property covered by any mortgage, deed of trust, or other security instrument by trustee's sale, judicial sale, foreclosure or deed in lieu of foreclosure, or for the purpose of transferring title to any federal agency or instrumentality as the insurer or guarantor of any loan, and the retention of title to any real or personal property so acquired pending the orderly sale or other disposition thereof.

(7) The engaging in activities necessary or appropriate to carry out any of the foregoing activities. Nothing contained in this subdivision shall be construed to permit any foreign banking corporation to maintain an office in this state otherwise than as provided by the laws of this state or to limit the powers conferred upon any foreign banking corporation as set forth in the laws of this state or to permit any foreign lending institution to maintain an office in this state except as otherwise permitted under the laws of this state.

Ca. Corp. Code § 191

Amended by Stats 2019 ch 143 (SB 251),s 21, eff. 1/1/2020.
Amended by Stats 2006 ch 57 (SB 1183),s 1, eff. 1/1/2007.

Section 191.1 - "Uncertificated security" defined

"Uncertificated security" means a share (Section 184), or an obligation of the issuer, described in paragraphs (15) and (18) of subdivision (a) of Section 8102 of the Commercial Code.
  Ca. Corp. Code § 191.1
Amended by Stats. 1996, Ch. 497, Sec. 29. Effective January 1, 1997.

Section 192 - "Vacancy" defined

"Vacancy" when used with respect to the board means any authorized position of director which is not then filled by a duly elected director, whether caused by death, resignation, removal, change in the authorized number of directors (by the board or the shareholders) or otherwise.
  Ca. Corp. Code § 192
Amended by Stats. 1976, Ch. 641.

Section 193 - "Verified" defined

"Verified" means that the statements contained in a certificate or other document are declared to be true of the own knowledge of the persons executing the same in either:
(a) An affidavit signed by them under oath before an officer authorized by the laws of this state or of the place where it is executed to administer oaths, or
(b) A declaration in writing executed by them "under penalty of perjury" and stating the date and place (whether within or without this state) of execution. Any affidavit sworn to without this state before a notary public or a judge or clerk of a court of record having an official seal need not be further authenticated.
  Ca. Corp. Code § 193
Added by Stats. 1975, Ch. 682.

Section 194 - "Vote" defined

"Vote" includes authorization by written consent, subject to the provisions of subdivision (b) of Section 307 and subdivision (d) of Section 603.
  Ca. Corp. Code § 194
Repealed and added by Stats. 1993, Ch. 128, Sec. 3. Effective January 1, 1994.

Section 194.5 - "Voting power" defined

"Voting power" means the power to vote for the election of directors at the time any determination of voting power is made and does not include the right to vote upon the happening of some condition or event which has not yet occurred. In any case where different classes of shares are entitled to vote as separate classes for different members of the board, the determination of percentage of voting power shall be made on the basis of the percentage of the total number of authorized directors which the shares in question (whether of one or more classes) have the power to elect in an election at which all shares then entitled to vote for the election of any directors are voted.

    Ca. Corp. Code § 194.5
Added by Stats. 1976, Ch. 641.

Section 194.7 - "Voting shift" defined

"Voting shift" means a change, pursuant to or by operation of a provision of the articles, in the relative rights of the holders of one or more classes or series of shares, voting as one or more separate classes or series, to elect one or more directors.

    Ca. Corp. Code § 194.7
Added by Stats. 1988, Ch. 495, Sec. 1.

Section 195 - "Written" or "in writing" defined

"Written" or "in writing" includes facsimile, telegraphic, and other electronic communication when authorized by this code, including an electronic transmission by a corporation that satisfies the requirements of Section 20.

    Ca. Corp. Code § 195
Amended by Stats 2004 ch 254 (SB 1306),s 5, eff. 1/1/2005

Chapter 2 - ORGANIZATION AND BYLAWS

Section 200 - Formation of corporation

(a) One or more natural persons, partnerships, associations or corporations, domestic or foreign, may form a corporation under this division by executing and filing articles of incorporation.
(b) If initial directors are named in the articles, each director named in the articles shall sign and acknowledge the articles; if initial directors are not named in the articles, the articles shall be signed by one or more persons described in subdivision (a) who thereupon are the incorporators of the corporation.
(c) The corporate existence begins upon the filing of the articles and continues perpetually, unless otherwise expressly provided by law or in the articles.

    Ca. Corp. Code § 200
Amended by Stats. 1983, Ch. 1223, Sec. 1.

Section 200.5 - Incorporation of existing business organization organized as trust

(a) An existing business association organized as a trust under the laws of this state or of a foreign jurisdiction may incorporate under this division upon approval by its board of trustees or similar governing body and approval by the affirmative vote of a majority of the outstanding voting shares of beneficial interest (or such greater proportion of the outstanding shares of beneficial interest or the vote of such other classes of shares of beneficial interest as may be specifically required by its declaration of trust or bylaws) and the filing of articles of incorporation with certificate attached pursuant to this chapter.

(b) In addition to the matters required to be set forth in the articles pursuant to Section 202, the articles in the case of an incorporation authorized by subdivision (a) shall set forth that an existing unincorporated association, stating its name, is being incorporated by the filing of the articles.

(c) The articles filed pursuant to this section shall be signed by the president, or any vice president, and the secretary, or any assistant secretary, of the existing association and shall be accompanied by a certificate signed and verified by such officers signing the articles and stating that the incorporation of the association has been approved by the trustees and by the required vote of holders of shares of beneficial interest in accordance with subdivision (a).

(d) Upon the filing of articles of incorporation pursuant to this section, the corporation shall succeed automatically to all of the rights and property of the association being incorporated and shall be subject to all of its debts and liabilities in the same manner as if the corporation had itself incurred them. The incumbent trustees of the association shall constitute the initial directors of the corporation and shall continue in office until the next annual meeting of the shareholders, unless they die, resign or are removed prior thereto. All rights of creditors and all liens upon the property of the association shall be preserved unimpaired. Any action or proceeding pending by or against the association may be prosecuted to judgment, which shall bind the corporation, or the corporation may be proceeded against or substituted in its place.

(e) The filing for record in the office of the county recorder of any county in this state in which any of the real property of the association is located of a copy of the articles of incorporation filed pursuant to this section, certified by the Secretary of State, shall evidence record ownership in the corporation of all interests of the association in and to the real property located in that county.

Ca. Corp. Code § 200.5
Added by Stats. 1978, Ch. 370.

Section 201 - Prohibited filing of articles with certain names

(a) The Secretary of State shall not file articles setting forth a name in which "bank," " trust," "trustee," or related words appear, unless the certificate of approval of the

Commissioner of Financial Protection and Innovation is attached thereto. This subdivision does not apply to the articles of any corporation subject to the Banking Law on which is endorsed the approval of the Commissioner of Financial Protection and Innovation.

(b) The name of a corporation shall not be a name that the Secretary of State determines is likely to mislead the public and shall be distinguishable in the records of the Secretary of State from all of the following:

(1) The name of any corporation.

(2) The name of any foreign corporation authorized to transact intrastate business in this state.

(3) Each name that is under reservation pursuant to this title.

(4) The name of a foreign corporation that has registered its name pursuant to Section 2101.

(5) An alternate name of a foreign corporation under subdivision (b) of Section 2106.

(6)A name that will become the record name of a domestic or foreign corporation upon a corporate instrument when there is a delayed effective or file date.

(c) Subject to Section 2106, this section applies to a foreign corporation transacting business in this state or that has applied for a certificate of qualification.

(d) The use by a corporation of a name in violation of this section may be enjoined notwithstanding the filing of its articles by the Secretary of State.

(e) Any applicant may, upon payment of the fee prescribed therefor in Article 3 (commencing with Section 12180) of Chapter 3 of Part 2 of Division 3 of Title 2 of the Government Code, obtain from the Secretary of State a certificate of reservation of any name not prohibited by subdivision (b), and upon the issuance of the certificate the name stated therein shall be reserved for a period of 60 days. The Secretary of State shall not, however, issue certificates reserving the same name for two or more consecutive 60-day periods to the same applicant or for the use or benefit of the same person; nor shall consecutive reservations be made by or for the use or benefit of the same person; of names so similar as to fall within the prohibitions of subdivision (b).

Ca. Corp. Code § 201

Amended by Stats 2022 ch 617 (SB 1202),s 6, eff. 1/1/2023.
Amended by Stats 2022 ch 452 (SB 1498),s 44, eff. 1/1/2023.
Amended by Stats 2020 ch 361 (SB 522),s 2, eff. 1/1/2021.
Amended by Stats 2015 ch 189 (AB 1471),s 1, eff. 1/1/2016.
Amended by Stats 2014 ch 401 (AB 2763),s 17, eff. 1/1/2015.
Amended by Stats 2011 ch 740 (SB 201),s 5, eff. 1/1/2012.

Section 201.3 - [Repealed]

Ca. Corp. Code § 201.3
Repealed by Stats 2000 ch 1015 (SB 2148), s 2, eff. 9/29/2000.

Section 201.5 - Prohibited filing of article in which business is insurer

The Secretary of State shall not file articles in which the business is to be an insurer unless the certificate of the Insurance Commissioner approving the corporate name is attached thereto.
Ca. Corp. Code § 201.5
Added by Stats. 1979, Ch. 737.

Section 201.6 - Redomestication of insurer

(a)

(1) When an insurer has been approved by the Insurance Commissioner pursuant to Section 709.5 of the Insurance Code to redomesticate to this state, the redomesticating insurer shall file with the Secretary of State articles of incorporation that include a provision setting forth all of the following information:

(A) The name and former jurisdiction of the redomesticating insurer.

(B) The redomesticating insurer's Secretary of State file number.

(C) A statement that the redomesticating insurer was authorized to effect the redomestication by the laws under which it formerly was organized.

(D) A statement that the redomesticating insurer has approved a plan of redomestication or other instrument as may be required to effect the redomestication to this state pursuant to the laws under which the redomesticating insurer was organized.

(E) A statement that the Insurance Commissioner has approved the redomestication of the insurer to this state.

(2) The Secretary of State shall not file articles of incorporation containing the information required by paragraph (1) unless a copy of the amended certificate of authority, evidencing the approval of the redomestication by the Insurance Commissioner, is attached thereto.
(b) If a redomesticating insurer is qualified to transact business in this state, by virtue of its filing of articles of incorporation in this state, the redomesticating insurer shall

automatically surrender its right to transact intrastate business.

(c)

(1) An insurer that has filed articles of incorporation in this state and has been approved by the Insurance Commissioner pursuant to Section 709.5 of the Insurance Code to redomesticate to another jurisdiction, shall file with the Secretary of State a statement of redomestication, on a form prescribed by the Secretary of State, containing all of the following information:

(A) The name of the redomesticating insurer.

(B) The redomesticating insurer's Secretary of State file number.

(C) The jurisdiction of the redomesticated insurer.

(D) The name and street address of the redomesticated insurer's agent for service of process.

(E) A statement that the redomesticating insurer is authorized to effect the redomestication under California law and the jurisdiction to which the insurer is redomesticating.

(F) A statement that the redomesticating insurer has complied with the requirements to redomesticate as required by California law and the jurisdiction to which the insurer is redomesticating.

(G) A statement that the Insurance Commissioner has approved the redomestication of the insurer.

(2) The Secretary of State shall not file the statement of redomestication required by paragraph (1) unless a copy of the amended certificate of authority, evidencing the approval of the redomestication by the Insurance Commissioner, is attached thereto.

Ca. Corp. Code § 201.6
Added by Stats 2017 ch 417 (AB 1696),s 2, eff. 1/1/2018.

Section 201.7 - Acceptance for filing of articles of incorporation of domestic mutual insurer or mutual holding company and stock holding company

Upon receipt of a certified copy of the commissioner's authorization issued pursuant to subdivision (a) of Section 11542 or subdivision (a) of Section 4097.11 of the Insurance Code and subject to subdivision (a) of Section 110 of the Corporations Code, the Secretary of State shall accept for filing the certificate of amendment of the articles of incorporation of the domestic mutual insurer certified by the secretary thereof.

Upon receipt of a certified copy of the commissioner's authorization to file articles of incorporation of a mutual holding company and a stock holding company authorized pursuant to conversion proceedings pursuant to subdivision (a) of Section 11542 or subdivision (a) of Section 4097.11 of the Insurance Code and subject to subdivision (a) of Section 110 of the Corporations Code, the Secretary of State shall accept for filing the articles of incorporation of the mutual holding company and stock holding company.

Ca. Corp. Code § 201.7

Amended by Stats. 1998, Ch. 421, Sec. 1. Effective January 1, 1999.

Section 202 - Articles of incorporation

The articles of incorporation shall set forth:

(a) The name of the corporation; provided, however, that in order for the corporation to be subject to the provisions of this division applicable to a close corporation (Section 158), the name of the corporation must contain the word "corporation," "incorporated," or "limited" or an abbreviation of one of such words.

(b)

(1) The applicable one of the following statements:

(A) The purpose of the corporation is to engage in any lawful act or activity for which a corporation may be organized under the General Corporation Law of California other than the banking business, the trust company business or the practice of a profession permitted to be incorporated by the California Corporations Code; or

(B) The purpose of the corporation is to engage in the profession of _____ (with the insertion of a profession permitted to be incorporated by the California Corporations Code) and any other lawful activities (other than the banking or trust company business) not prohibited to a corporation engaging in such profession by applicable laws and regulations.

(2) In case the corporation is a corporation subject to the Banking Law (Division 1.1 (commencing with Section 1000) of the Financial Code), the articles shall set forth a statement of purpose which is prescribed in the applicable provision of the Banking Law.

(3) In case the corporation is a corporation subject to the Insurance Code as an insurer, the articles shall additionally state that the business of the corporation is to be an insurer.

(4) If the corporation is intended to be a "professional corporation" within the meaning of the Moscone-Knox Professional Corporation Act (Part 4 (commencing with Section 13400) of Division 3), the articles shall additionally contain the statement required by Section 13404. The articles shall not set forth any further or additional statement with respect to the purposes or powers of the corporation, except by way of limitation or except as expressly required by any law of this state other than this division or any federal or other statute or regulation (including the Internal Revenue Code and regulations thereunder as a condition of acquiring or maintaining a particular status for tax purposes).

(c) The name and street address in this state of the corporation's initial agent for service of process in accordance with subdivision (b) of Section 1502.

(d) The initial street address of its principal office.

(e) The initial mailing address of the corporation, if different from the initial street address.

(f) If the corporation is authorized to issue only one class of shares, the total number of shares which the corporation is authorized to issue.

(g) If the corporation is authorized to issue more than one class of shares, or if any class of shares is to have two or more series:

(1) The total number of shares of each class the corporation is authorized to issue, and the total number of shares of each series which the corporation is authorized to issue or that the board is authorized to fix the number of shares of any such series;

(2) The designation of each class, and the designation of each series or that the board may determine the designation of any such series; and

(3) The rights, preferences, privileges, and restrictions granted to or imposed upon the respective classes or series of shares or the holders thereof, or that the board, within any limits and restrictions stated, may determine or alter the rights, preferences, privileges, and restrictions granted to or imposed upon any wholly unissued class of shares or any wholly unissued series of any class of shares. As to any series the number of shares of which is authorized to be fixed by the board, the articles may also authorize the board, within the limits and restrictions stated therein or stated in any resolution or resolutions of the board originally fixing the number of shares constituting any series, to increase or decrease (but not below the number of shares of such series then outstanding) the number of shares of any such series subsequent to the issue of shares of that series. In case the number of shares of any series shall be so decreased, the shares constituting such decrease shall resume the status which they had before the adoption of the resolution originally fixing the number of shares of such series.

Ca. Corp. Code § 202

Amended by Stats 2022 ch 617 (SB 1202),s 7, eff. 1/1/2023.
Amended by Stats 2014 ch 64 (AB 2742),s 3, eff. 1/1/2015.

Amended by Stats 2012 ch 494 (SB 1532),s 4, eff. 1/1/2013.
Amended by Stats 2000 ch 485 (AB 1895), s 3, eff. 1/1/2001.

Section 203 - Classes or series of shares or holders

Except as specified in the articles or in any shareholders' agreement, no distinction shall exist between classes or series of shares or the holders thereof.

Ca. Corp. Code § 203
Added by Stats. 1975, Ch. 682.

Section 203.5 - Number of shares

(a) If the articles include the designation and number of shares of one or more series within a class, the stated number of shares for all series within the class shall not exceed, and may be less than, the stated number of shares for the class.

(b) If so authorized in the articles and if the articles state the number of shares of the class, the articles may be amended by approval of the board alone to increase or decrease (but not below the number of shares of the series then outstanding) the number of shares of a series.

(c) If the articles authorize a class of shares which is stated to be issuable in series, the articles shall include either the designation and number of shares for at least one series within that class or an authorization of common shares.

Ca. Corp. Code § 203.5
Added by Stats. 1988, Ch. 919, Sec. 2.

Section 204 - Contents of articles of incorporation

The articles of incorporation may set forth:

(a) Any or all of the following provisions, which shall not be effective unless expressly provided in the articles:

(1) Granting, with or without limitations, the power to levy assessments upon the shares or any class of shares.

(2) Granting to shareholders preemptive rights to subscribe to any or all issues of shares or securities.

(3) Special qualifications of persons who may be shareholders.

(4) A provision limiting the duration of the corporation's existence to a specified date.

(5) A provision requiring, for any or all corporate actions, except as provided in Section 303, subdivision (b) of Section 402.5, subdivision (c) of Section 708, and

Section 1900, the vote of a larger proportion or of all of the shares of any class or series, or the vote or quorum for taking action of a larger proportion or of all of the directors, than is otherwise required by this division.

(6) A provision limiting or restricting the business in which the corporation may engage or the powers which the corporation may exercise or both.

(7) A provision conferring upon the holders of any evidences of indebtedness, issued or to be issued by the corporation, the right to vote in the election of directors and on any other matters on which shareholders may vote.

(8) A provision conferring upon shareholders the right to determine the consideration for which shares shall be issued.

(9) A provision requiring the approval of the shareholders (Section 153) or the approval of the outstanding shares (Section 152) for any corporate action, even though not otherwise required by this division.

(10) Provisions eliminating or limiting the personal liability of a director for monetary damages in an action brought by or in the right of the corporation for breach of a director's duties to the corporation and its shareholders, as set forth in Section 309, provided, however, that (A) such a provision may not eliminate or limit the liability of directors (i) for acts or omissions that involve intentional misconduct or a knowing and culpable violation of law, (ii) for acts or omissions that a director believes to be contrary to the best interests of the corporation or its shareholders or that involve the absence of good faith on the part of the director, (iii) for any transaction from which a director derived an improper personal benefit, (iv) for acts or omissions that show a reckless disregard for the director's duty to the corporation or its shareholders in circumstances in which the director was aware, or should have been aware, in the ordinary course of performing a director's duties, of a risk of serious injury to the corporation or its shareholders, (v) for acts or omissions that constitute an unexcused pattern of inattention that amounts to an abdication of the director's duty to the corporation or its shareholders, (vi) under Section 310, or (vii) under Section 316, (B) no such provision shall eliminate or limit the liability of a director for any act or omission occurring prior to the date when the provision becomes effective, and (C) no such provision shall eliminate or limit the liability of an officer for any act or omission as an officer, notwithstanding that the officer is also a director or that his or her actions, if negligent or improper, have been ratified by the directors.

(11) A provision authorizing, whether by bylaw, agreement, or otherwise, the indemnification of agents (as defined in Section 317) in excess of that expressly permitted by Section 317 for those agents of the corporation for breach of duty to the corporation and its stockholders, provided, however, that the provision may not

provide for indemnification of any agent for any acts or omissions or transactions from which a director may not be relieved of liability as set forth in the exception to paragraph (10) or as to circumstances in which indemnity is expressly prohibited by Section 317. Notwithstanding this subdivision, in the case of a close corporation any of the provisions referred to above may be validly included in a shareholders' agreement. Notwithstanding this subdivision, bylaws may require for all or any actions by the board the affirmative vote of a majority of the authorized number of directors. Nothing contained in this subdivision shall affect the enforceability, as between the parties thereto, of any lawful agreement not otherwise contrary to public policy.

(b) Reasonable restrictions upon the right to transfer or hypothecate shares of any class or classes or series, but no restriction shall be binding with respect to shares issued prior to the adoption of the restriction unless the holders of such shares voted in favor of the restriction.

(c) The names and addresses of the persons appointed to act as initial directors.

(d) Any other provision, not in conflict with law, for the management of the business and for the conduct of the affairs of the corporation, including any provision which is required or permitted by this division to be stated in the bylaws.

(e) This section shall become operative on January 1, 2022.

   Ca. Corp. Code § 204

Added by Stats 2018 ch 889 (SB 838),s 2, eff. 1/1/2019.

Section 204.5 - Provision regarding directors' liability

(a) If the articles of a corporation include a provision reading substantially as follows: "The liability of the directors of the corporation for monetary damages shall be eliminated to the fullest extent permissible under California law"; the corporation shall be considered to have adopted a provision as authorized by paragraph (10) of subdivision (a) of Section 204 and more specific wording shall not be required.

(b) This section shall not be construed as setting forth the exclusive method of adopting an article provision as authorized by paragraph (10) of subdivision (a) of Section 204.

(c) This section shall not change the otherwise applicable standards or duties to make full and fair disclosure to shareholders when approval of such a provision is sought.

   Ca. Corp. Code § 204.5

Added by Stats. 1987, Ch. 1203, Sec. 1.5. Effective September 27, 1987.

Section 205 - Nominal or par value of shares

Solely for the purpose of any statute or regulation imposing any tax or fee based upon the capitalization of a corporation, all authorized shares of a corporation organized under this division shall be deemed to have a nominal or par value of one dollar ($1) per share. If any federal or other statute or regulation applicable to a particular corporation requires that the shares of such corporation have a par value, such shares shall have the par value determined by the board in order to satisfy the requirements of such statute or regulation.

Ca. Corp. Code § 205
Added by Stats. 1975, Ch. 682.

Section 206 - Business activity

Subject to any limitation contained in the articles and to compliance with any other applicable laws, any corporation other than a corporation subject to the Banking Law or a professional corporation may engage in any business activity; and a corporation subject to the Banking Law or a professional corporation may engage in any business activity not prohibited by the respective statutes and regulations to which it is subject.

Ca. Corp. Code § 206
Amended by Stats. 1978, Ch. 370.

Section 207 - Powers of natural person in carrying out business activities

Subject to any limitations contained in the articles and to compliance with other provisions of this division and any other applicable laws, a corporation shall have all of the powers of a natural person in carrying out its business activities, including, without limitation, the power to:

(a) Adopt, use, and at will alter a corporate seal, but failure to affix a seal does not affect the validity of any instrument.

(b) Adopt, amend, and repeal bylaws.

(c) Qualify to do business in any other state, territory, dependency, or foreign country.

(d) Subject to the provisions of Section 510, issue, purchase, redeem, receive, take or otherwise acquire, own, hold, sell, lend, exchange, transfer or otherwise dispose of, pledge, use, and otherwise deal in and with its own shares, bonds, debentures, and other securities.

(e) Make donations, regardless of specific corporate benefit, for the public welfare or for community fund, hospital, charitable, educational, scientific, civic, or similar purposes.

(f) Pay pensions, and establish and carry out pension, profit-sharing, share bonus, share purchase, share option, savings, thrift, and other retirement, incentive, and benefit plans, trusts, and provisions for any or all of the directors, officers, and employees of the corporation or any of its subsidiary or affiliated corporations, and to indemnify and purchase and maintain insurance on behalf of any fiduciary of such plans, trusts, or provisions.

(g) Subject to the provisions of Section 315, assume obligations, enter into contracts, including contracts of guaranty or suretyship, incur liabilities, borrow and lend money, and otherwise use its credit, and secure any of its obligations, contracts, or liabilities by mortgage, pledge, or other encumbrance of all or any part of its property, franchises, and income.

(h) Participate with others in any partnership, joint venture, or other association, transaction, or arrangement of any kind, whether or not such participation involves sharing or delegation of control with or to others.

(i)

(1) In anticipation of or during an emergency, take either or both of the following actions necessary to conduct the corporation's business operations and affairs, unless emergency bylaws provide otherwise pursuant to subdivision (c) of Section 212:

(A) Modify lines of succession to accommodate the incapacity of any director, officer, employee, or agent resulting from the emergency.

(B) Relocate the principal office, designate alternative principal offices or regional offices, or authorize the officers to do so.

(2) During an emergency, take either or both of the following actions necessary to conduct the corporation's business operations and affairs, unless emergency bylaws provide otherwise pursuant to subdivision (c) of Section 212:

(A) Give notice to a director or directors in any practicable manner under the circumstances, including, but not limited to, by publication and radio, when notice of a meeting of the board cannot be given to that director or directors in the manner prescribed by the bylaws or Section 307.

(B) Deem that one or more officers of the corporation present at a board meeting is a director, in order of rank and within the same rank in order of seniority, as necessary to achieve a quorum for that meeting.

(3) In anticipation of or during an emergency, the board may take any action that it determines to be necessary or appropriate to respond to the emergency, mitigate the effects of the emergency, or comply with lawful federal and state government orders, but shall not take any action that requires the vote of the shareholders, unless the required vote of the shareholders was obtained prior to the emergency.

(4) Any actions taken in good faith in anticipation of or during an emergency under this subdivision bind the corporation and shall not be used to impose liability on a corporate director, officer, employee, or agent.

(5) For purposes of this subdivision, "emergency" means any of the following events or circumstances as a result of which, and only so long as, a quorum of the corporation's board of directors cannot be readily convened for action:

(A) A natural catastrophe, including, but not limited to, a hurricane, tornado, storm, high water, wind-driven water, tidal wave, tsunami, earthquake, volcanic eruption, landslide, mudslide, snowstorm, drought, epidemic, pandemic, or disease outbreak, or, regardless of cause, any fire, flood, or explosion.

(B) An attack on or within this state or on the public security of its residents by an enemy of this state or on the nation by an enemy of the United States of America, or upon receipt by this state of a warning from the federal government indicating that any such enemy attack is probable or imminent.

(C) An act of terrorism or other manmade disaster that results in extraordinary levels of casualties or damage or disruption severely affecting the infrastructure, environment, economy, government functions, or population, including, but not limited to, mass evacuations.

(D) A state of emergency proclaimed by the Governor of this state, including any person serving as Governor in accordance with Section 10 of Article V of the California Constitution and Section 12058 of the Government Code, or by the President of the United States of America.

Ca. Corp. Code § 207
Amended by Stats 2021 ch 523 (AB 663),s 1, eff. 1/1/2022.
Amended by Stats 2013 ch 255 (AB 491),s 1, eff. 1/1/2014.

Section 208 - Assertion of limitation as between corporation or shareholder and third person; contract or conveyance made in name of corporation

(a) No limitation upon the business, purposes or powers of the corporation or upon the powers of the shareholders, officers or directors, or the manner of exercise of such powers, contained in or implied by the articles or by Chapters 18, 19 and 20 or by any shareholders' agreement shall be asserted as between the corporation or any shareholder and any third person, except in a proceeding (1) by a shareholder or the state to enjoin the doing or continuation of unauthorized business by the corporation or its officers, or both, in cases where third parties have not acquired rights thereby, or (2) to dissolve the corporation or (3) by the corporation or by a shareholder suing in a representative suit against the officers or directors of the corporation for violation of their authority.

(b) Any contract or conveyance made in the name of a corporation which is authorized or ratified by the board, or is done within the scope of the authority, actual or apparent, conferred by the board or within the agency power of the officer executing it, except as the board's authority is limited by law other than this division, binds the corporation, and the corporation acquires rights thereunder, whether the contract is executed or wholly or in part executory.

(c) This section applies to contracts and conveyances made by foreign corporations in this state and to all conveyances by foreign corporations of real property situated in this state.

Ca. Corp. Code § 208
Added by Stats. 1975, Ch. 682.

Section 209 - Prima facie evidence of corporate existence

For all purposes other than an action in the nature of quo warranto, a copy of the articles of a corporation duly certified by the Secretary of State is conclusive evidence of the formation of the corporation and prima facie evidence of its corporate existence.

Ca. Corp. Code § 209
Added by Stats. 1975, Ch. 682.

Section 210 - Powers of incorporators

If initial directors have not been named in the articles, the incorporator or incorporators, until the directors are elected, may do whatever is necessary and proper to perfect the organization of the corporation, including the adoption and amendment of bylaws of the corporation and the election of directors and officers.

Ca. Corp. Code § 210
Added by Stats. 1975, Ch. 682.

Section 211 - Adoption, amendment, or repeal of bylaws

Bylaws may be adopted, amended or repealed either by approval of the outstanding shares (Section 152) or by the approval of the board, except as provided in Section 212. Subject to subdivision (a)(5) of Section 204, the articles or bylaws may restrict or eliminate the power of the board to adopt, amend or repeal any or all bylaws.

Ca. Corp. Code § 211
Added by Stats. 1975, Ch. 682.

Section 212 - Content of bylaws

(a) The bylaws shall set forth (unless such provision is contained in the articles, in which case it may only be changed by an amendment of the articles) the number of directors of the corporation; or that the number of directors shall be not less than a stated minimum nor more than a stated maximum (which in no case shall be greater than two times the stated minimum minus one), with the exact number of directors to be fixed, within the limits specified, by approval of the board or the shareholders (Section 153) in the manner provided in the bylaws, subject to paragraph (5) of subdivision (a) of Section 204. The number or minimum number of directors shall not be less than three; provided, however, that (1) before shares are issued, the number may be one, (2) before shares are issued, the number may be two, (3) so long as the corporation has only one shareholder, the number may be one, (4) so long as the corporation has only one shareholder, the number may be two, and (5) so long as the corporation has only two shareholders, the number may be two. After the issuance of shares, a bylaw specifying or changing a fixed number of directors or the maximum or minimum number or changing from a fixed to a variable board or vice versa may only be adopted by approval of the outstanding shares (Section 152); provided, however, that a bylaw or amendment of the articles reducing the fixed number or the minimum number of directors to a number less than five cannot be adopted if the votes cast against its adoption at a meeting or the shares not consenting in the case of action by written consent are equal to more than $16\,{}^2/_3$ percent of the outstanding shares entitled to vote.

(b) The bylaws may contain any provision, not in conflict with law or the articles for the management of the business and for the conduct of the affairs of the corporation, including, but not limited to:

(1) Any provision referred to in subdivision (b), (c), or (d) of Section 204.

(2) The time, place, and manner of calling, conducting, and giving notice of shareholders', directors', and committee meetings.

(3) The manner of execution, revocation, and use of proxies.

(4) The qualifications, duties, and compensation of directors; the time of their annual election; and the requirements of a quorum for directors' and committee meetings.

(5) The appointment and authority of committees of the board.

(6) The appointment, duties, compensation, and tenure of officers.

(7) The mode of determination of holders of record of its shares.

(8) The making of annual reports and financial statements to the shareholders.

(c)

(1) The bylaws may contain any provision, not in conflict with the articles, to manage and conduct the business affairs of the corporation effective only in an emergency as defined in Section 207, including, but not limited to, procedures for calling a board meeting, quorum requirements for a board meeting, and designation of additional or substitute directors.

(2) During an emergency, the board may take any action that it determines to be necessary or appropriate to respond to the emergency, mitigate the effects of the emergency, or comply with lawful federal and state government orders, but shall not take any action that requires the vote of the shareholders, unless the required vote of the shareholders was obtained prior to the emergency.

(3) All provisions of the regular bylaws consistent with the emergency bylaws shall remain effective during the emergency, and the emergency bylaws shall not be effective after the emergency ends.

(4) Corporate action taken in good faith in accordance with the emergency bylaws binds the corporation, and shall not be used to impose liability on a corporate director, officer, employee, or agent.

Ca. Corp. Code § 212

Amended by Stats 2021 ch 523 (AB 663),s 2, eff. 1/1/2022.

Amended by Stats 2013 ch 255 (AB 491),s 2, eff. 1/1/2014.

Section 213 - Principal office

Every corporation shall keep at its principal office in this state, or if its principal office is not in this state at its principal business office in this state, the original or a copy of its bylaws as amended to date, which shall be open to inspection by the shareholders at all reasonable times during office hours. If the principal office of the corporation is outside this state and the corporation has no principal office in this state, it shall upon the written request of any shareholder furnish to such shareholder a copy of the bylaws as amended to date.

Ca. Corp. Code § 213

Amended by Stats 2022 ch 617 (SB 1202),s 8, eff. 1/1/2023.

Added by Stats. 1975, Ch. 682.

Chapter 3 - DIRECTORS AND MANAGEMENT

Section 300 - Management of business and affairs and exercise of corporate powers

(a) Subject to the provisions of this division and any limitations in the articles relating to action required to be approved by the shareholders (Section 153) or by the outstanding shares (Section 152), or by a less than majority vote of a class or series of preferred shares (Section 402.5), the business and affairs of the corporation shall be managed and all corporate powers shall be exercised by or under the direction of the board. The board may delegate the management of the day-to-day operation of the business of the corporation to a management company or other person provided that the business and affairs of the corporation shall be managed and all corporate powers shall be exercised under the ultimate direction of the board.

(b) Notwithstanding subdivision (a) or any other provision of this division, but subject to subdivision (c), no shareholders' agreement, which relates to any phase of the affairs of a close corporation, including but not limited to management of its business, division of its profits or distribution of its assets on liquidation, shall be invalid as between the parties thereto on the ground that it so relates to the conduct of the affairs of the corporation as to interfere with the discretion of the board or that it is an attempt to treat the corporation as if it were a partnership or to arrange their relationships in a manner that would be appropriate only between partners. A transferee of shares covered by such an agreement which is filed with the secretary of the corporation for inspection by any prospective purchaser of shares, who has actual knowledge thereof or notice thereof by a notation on the certificate pursuant to Section 418, is bound by its provisions and is a party thereto for the purposes of subdivision (d). Original issuance of shares by the corporation to a new shareholder who does not become a party to the agreement terminates the agreement, except that if the agreement so provides it shall continue to the extent it is enforceable apart from this subdivision. The agreement may not be modified, extended or revoked without the consent of such a transferee, subject to any provision of the agreement permitting modification, extension or revocation by less than unanimous agreement of the parties. A transferor of shares covered by such an agreement ceases to be a party thereto upon ceasing to be a shareholder of the corporation unless the transferor is a party thereto other than as a shareholder. An agreement made pursuant to this subdivision shall terminate when the corporation ceases to be a close corporation, except that if the agreement so provides it shall continue to the extent it is enforceable apart from this subdivision. This subdivision does not apply to an agreement authorized by subdivision (a) of Section 706.

(c) No agreement entered into pursuant to subdivision (b) may alter or waive any of the provisions of Sections 158, 417, 418, 500, 501, and 1111, subdivision (e) of Section 1201, Sections 2009, 2010, and 2011, or of Chapters 15 (commencing with Section 1500), 16 (commencing with Section 1600), 18 (commencing with Section 1800), and 22 (commencing with Section 2200). All other provisions of this division may be altered or waived as between the parties thereto in a shareholders' agreement, except the required filing of any document with the Secretary of State.

(d) An agreement of the type referred to in subdivision (b) shall, to the extent and so long as the discretion or powers of the board in its management of corporate affairs is controlled by such agreement, impose upon each shareholder who is a party thereto liability for managerial acts performed or omitted by such person pursuant thereto that is otherwise imposed by this division upon directors, and the directors shall be relieved to that extent from such liability.

(e) The failure of a close corporation to observe corporate formalities relating to meetings of directors or shareholders in connection with the management of its affairs, pursuant to an agreement authorized by subdivision (b), shall not be considered a factor tending to establish that the shareholders have personal liability for corporate obligations.

Ca. Corp. Code § 300

Amended by Stats. 1983, Ch. 1223, Sec. 3.

Section 301 - Election of directors

(a) Except as provided in Section 301.5, at each annual meeting of shareholders, directors shall be elected to hold office until the next annual meeting. However, to effectuate a voting shift (Section 194.7) the articles may provide that directors hold office for a shorter term. The articles may provide for the election of one or more directors by the holders of the shares of any class or series voting as a class or series.

(b) Each director, including a director elected to fill a vacancy, shall hold office until the expiration of the term for which elected and until a successor has been elected and qualified.

Ca. Corp. Code § 301

Amended by Stats. 1989, Ch. 876, Sec. 1.

Section 301.3 - Female directors on corporate boards

(a) No later than the close of the 2019 calendar year, a publicly held domestic or foreign corporation whose principal executive offices, according to the corporation's SEC 10-K form, are located in California shall have a minimum of one female director on its board. A corporation may increase the number of directors on its board to comply with this section.

(b) No later than the close of the 2021 calendar year, a publicly held domestic or foreign corporation whose principal executive offices, according to the corporation's SEC 10-K form, are located in California shall comply with the following:

(1) If its number of directors is six or more, the corporation shall have a minimum of three female directors.

(2) If its number of directors is five, the corporation shall have a minimum of two female directors.

(3) If its number of directors is four or fewer, the corporation shall have a minimum of one female director.

(c) No later than July 1, 2019, the Secretary of State shall publish a report on its internet website documenting the number of domestic and foreign corporations whose principal executive offices, according to the corporation's SEC 10-K form, are located in California and who have at least one female director.

(d) No later than March 1, 2020, and annually thereafter, the Secretary of State shall publish a report on its internet website regarding, at a minimum, information required by subdivision (c) of Section 301.4 and all of the following:

(1) The number of corporations subject to this section that were in compliance with the requirements of this section during at least one point during the preceding calendar year.

(2) The number of publicly held corporations that moved their United States headquarters to California from another state or out of California into another state during the preceding calendar year.

(3) The number of publicly held corporations that were subject to this section during the preceding year, but are no longer publicly traded.

(e)

(1) The Secretary of State may adopt regulations to implement this section. The Secretary of State may impose fines for violations of this section as follows:

(A) For failure to timely file board member information with the Secretary of State pursuant to a regulation adopted pursuant to this paragraph, the amount of one hundred thousand dollars ($100,000).

(B) For a first violation, the amount of one hundred thousand dollars ($100,000).

(C) For a second or subsequent violation, the amount of three hundred thousand dollars ($300,000).

(2) For the purposes of this subdivision, each director seat required by this section to be held by a female, which is not held by a female during at least a portion of a calendar year, shall count as a violation.

(3) For purposes of this subdivision, a female director having held a seat for at least a portion of the year shall not be a violation.

(4) Fines collected pursuant to this section shall be available, upon appropriation by the Legislature, for use by the Secretary of State to offset the cost of administering this section.

(f) For purposes of this section, the following definitions apply:

(1) "Female" means an individual who self-identifies her gender as a woman, without regard to the individual's designated sex at birth.

(2) "Publicly held corporation" means a corporation with outstanding shares listed on a major United States stock exchange.

Ca. Corp. Code § 301.3

Amended by Stats 2020 ch 316 (AB 979),s 2, eff. 1/1/2021.
Added by Stats 2018 ch 954 (SB 826),s 2, eff. 1/1/2019.

Section 301.4 - Member of underrepresented community on corporate boards

(a) No later than the close of the 2021 calendar year, a publicly held domestic or foreign corporation whose principal executive offices, according to the corporation's

SEC 10-K form, are located in California shall have a minimum of one director from an underrepresented community on its board. A corporation may increase the number of directors on its board to comply with this section.

(b) No later than the close of the 2022 calendar year, a publicly held domestic or foreign corporation whose principal executive offices, according to the corporation's SEC 10-K form, are located in California shall comply with the following:

(1) If its number of directors is nine or more, the corporation shall have a minimum of three directors from underrepresented communities.

(2) If its number of directors is more than four but fewer than nine, the corporation shall have a minimum of two directors from underrepresented communities.

(3) If its number of directors is four or fewer, the corporation shall have a minimum of one director from an underrepresented community.

(c) No later than March 1, 2022, and annually thereafter, the Secretary of State shall include in its report required by subdivision (d) of Section 301.3, at a minimum, all of the following:

(1) The number of corporations subject to this section that were in compliance with the requirements of this section during at least one point during the preceding calendar year.

(2) The number of publicly held corporations that moved their United States headquarters to California from another state or out of California into another state during the preceding calendar year.

(3) The number of publicly held corporations that were subject to this section during the preceding year, but are no longer publicly traded.

(d)

(1) The Secretary of State may adopt regulations to implement this section. The Secretary of State may impose fines for violations of this section as follows:

(A) For failure to timely file board member information with the Secretary of State pursuant to a regulation adopted pursuant to this paragraph, the amount of one hundred thousand dollars ($100,000).

(B) For a first violation, as described in paragraph (2), the amount of one hundred thousand dollars ($100,000).

(C) For a second or subsequent violation, as described in paragraph (2), the amount of three hundred thousand dollars ($300,000).

(2) For the purposes of this subdivision, both of the following apply:

(A) Each director seat required by this section to be held by a director from an underrepresented community, which is not held by a director from an underrepresented community during at least a portion of a calendar year, shall count as a violation.

(B) A director from an underrepresented community having held a seat for at least a portion of the year shall not be a violation.

(3) Fines collected pursuant to this section shall be available, upon appropriation by the Legislature, for use by the Secretary of State to offset the cost of administering this section.

(e) For purposes of this section, the following definitions apply:

(1) "Director from an underrepresented community" means an individual who self-identifies as Black, African American, Hispanic, Latino, Asian, Pacific Islander, Native American, Native Hawaiian, or Alaska Native, or who self-identifies as gay, lesbian, bisexual, or transgender.

(2) "Publicly held corporation" means a corporation with outstanding shares listed on a major United States stock exchange.

Ca. Corp. Code § 301.4
Added by Stats 2020 ch 316 (AB 979),s 3, eff. 1/1/2021.

Section 301.5 - Division of board of directors into classes

(a)A listed corporation may, by amendment of its articles or bylaws, adopt provisions to divide the board of directors into two or three classes to serve for terms of two or three years respectively, or to eliminate cumulative voting, or both. After the issuance of shares, a corporation that is not a listed corporation may, by amendment of its articles or bylaws, adopt provisions to be effective when the corporation becomes a listed corporation to divide the board of directors into two or three classes to serve for terms of two or three years respectively, or to eliminate cumulative voting, or both. An article or bylaw amendment providing for division of the board of directors into classes, or any change in the number of classes, or the elimination of cumulative voting may only be adopted by the approval of the board and the outstanding shares (Section 152) voting as a single class, notwithstanding Section 903.

(b) If the board of directors is divided into two classes pursuant to subdivision (a), the authorized number of directors shall be no less than six and one-half of the directors or as close an approximation as possible shall be elected at each annual meeting of shareholders. If the board of directors is divided into three classes, the authorized number of directors shall be no less than nine and one-third of the directors or as close an approximation as possible shall be elected at each annual meeting of shareholders. Directors of a listed corporation may be elected by classes at a meeting of shareholders at which an amendment to the articles or bylaws described in subdivision (a) is approved, but the extended terms for directors are contingent on that approval, and in the case of an amendment to the articles, the filing of any necessary amendment to the articles pursuant to Section 905 or 910.

(c)If directors for more than one class are to be elected by the shareholders at any one meeting of shareholders and the election is by cumulative voting pursuant to Section 708, votes may be cumulated only for directors to be elected within each class.

(d)For purposes of this section, a "listed corporation" means a corporation with outstanding shares listed on the New York Stock Exchange, the NYSE American, the NASDAQ Global Market, or the NASDAQ Capital Market.

(e)Subject to subdivision (h), if a listed corporation having a board of directors divided into classes pursuant to subdivision (a) ceases to be a listed corporation for any reason, unless the articles of incorporation or bylaws of the corporation provide for the elimination of classes of directors at an earlier date or dates, the board of directors of the corporation shall cease to be divided into classes as to each class of directors on the date of the expiration of the term of the directors in that class and the term of each director serving at the time the corporation ceases to be a listed corporation (and the term of each director elected to fill a vacancy resulting from the death, resignation, or removal of any of those directors) shall continue until its expiration as if the corporation had not ceased to be a listed corporation.

(f)Subject to subdivision (h), if a listed corporation having a provision in its articles or bylaws eliminating cumulative voting pursuant to subdivision (a) or permitting noncumulative voting in the election of directors pursuant to that subdivision, or both, ceases to be a listed corporation for any reason, the shareholders shall be entitled to cumulate their votes pursuant to Section 708 at any election of directors occurring while the corporation is not a listed corporation notwithstanding that provision in its articles of incorporation or bylaws.

(g)Subject to subdivision (i), if a corporation that is not a listed corporation adopts amendments to its articles of incorporation or bylaws to divide its board of directors into classes or to eliminate cumulative voting, or both, pursuant to subdivision (a) and then becomes a listed corporation, unless the articles of incorporation or bylaws provide for those provisions to become effective at some other time and, in cases where classes of directors are provided for, identify the directors who, or the directorships that, are to be in each class or the method by which those directors or directorships are to be identified, the provisions shall become effective for the next election of directors after the corporation becomes a listed corporation at which all directors are to be elected.

(h)If a corporation ceases to be a listed corporation on or after the record date for a meeting of shareholders and before the conclusion of the meeting, including the conclusion of the meeting after an adjournment or postponement that does not require or result in the setting of a new record date, then, solely for purposes of subdivisions (e) and (f), the corporation shall not be deemed to have ceased to be a listed corporation until the conclusion of the meeting of shareholders.

(i) If a corporation becomes a listed corporation on or after the record date for a meeting of shareholders and before the conclusion of the meeting, including the conclusion of the meeting after an adjournment or postponement that does not require or result in the setting of a new record date, then, solely for purposes of subdivision (g), the corporation shall not be deemed to have become a listed corporation until the conclusion of the meeting of shareholders.

(j) If an article amendment referred to in subdivision (a) is adopted by a listed corporation, the certificate of amendment shall include a statement of the facts showing that the corporation is a listed corporation within the meaning of subdivision (d). If an article or bylaw amendment referred to in subdivision (a) is adopted by a corporation which is not a listed corporation, the provision, as adopted, shall include the following statement or the substantial equivalent: "This provision shall become effective only when the corporation becomes a listed corporation within the meaning of Section 301.5 of the Corporations Code."

Ca. Corp. Code § 301.5

Amended by Stats 2022 ch 617 (SB 1202),s 9, eff. 1/1/2023.
Amended by Stats 2009 ch 131 (AB 991),s 1, eff. 1/1/2010.
Amended by Stats 2000 ch 485 (AB 1895), s 4, eff. 1/1/2001.

Section 301.7 - Division of board of directors into classes by listed corporation engaged in recreation venture having golf and tennis facilities and ancillary dining and beverage services

(a) A listed corporation engaged in business limited to the operation and maintenance of a recreation venture having golf and tennis facilities and ancillary dining and beverage services may, by amendment of its articles or bylaws, adopt provisions allowing division of its board of directors into two classes, with one-half of the directors or as close an approximation as possible to be elected at each annual meeting of shareholders, provided that the corporation's bylaws or articles limit each holder of the securities to no more than five shares and require some of those holders to occupy dwellings immediately contiguous to the real property of the corporation. An article or bylaw amendment providing for division of the board of directors into classes may only be adopted by the approval of the board and the outstanding shares (Section 152) voting as a single class, notwithstanding Section 903. Directors of a listed corporation that meet these conditions may be elected by classes at a meeting of shareholders at which an amendment to the articles or bylaws described in this paragraph is approved, but the extended terms for directors are contingent on that approval, and in the case of an amendment to the articles, the filing of any necessary amendment to the articles pursuant to Section 905 or 910.

(b) For purposes of this section, a "listed corporation" means a corporation described in subdivision (d) of Section 301.5.

(c) If an article amendment referred to in subdivision (a) is adopted by a listed corporation, the certificate of amendment shall include a statement of the facts showing that the corporation is a listed corporation within the meaning of subdivision (b).

Ca. Corp. Code § 301.7

Amended by Stats 2009 ch 131 (AB 991),s 2, eff. 1/1/2010.

Section 301.9 - Directors of mutual water company to serve staggered terms

Notwithstanding Section 301, a mutual water company organized under this division may elect directors to serve staggered four-year terms if authorized in the corporation's articles of incorporation or bylaws. Upon the initial election of directors to staggered terms, the elected directors shall determine by lot who among them shall serve initial two-year terms and who among them shall serve four-year terms. Prior to any election in which the terms of elected directors shall be determined by lot, the mutual water company shall notify its shareholders that the terms of the directors elected shall be determined among those directors by lot.

Ca. Corp. Code § 301.9

Added by Stats 2011 ch 89 (SB 918),s 1, eff. 1/1/2012.

Section 302 - Vacancy if director declared of unsound mind or convicted of felony

The board may declare vacant the office of a director who has been declared of unsound mind by an order of court or convicted of a felony.

Ca. Corp. Code § 302

Repealed and added by Stats. 1975, Ch. 682.

Section 303 - Removal of directors

(a) Any or all of the directors may be removed without cause if the removal is approved by the outstanding shares (Section 152), subject to the following:

(1) Except for a corporation to which paragraph (3) is applicable, no director may be removed (unless the entire board is removed) when the votes cast against removal, or not consenting in writing to the removal, would be sufficient to elect the director if voted cumulatively at an election at which the same total number of votes were cast (or, if the action is taken by written consent, all shares entitled to vote were voted) and the entire number of directors authorized at the time of the director's most recent election were then being elected.

(2) When by the provisions of the articles the holders of the shares of any class or series, voting as a class or series, are entitled to elect one or more directors, any director so elected may be removed only by the applicable vote of the holders of the shares of that class or series.

(3) A director of a corporation whose board of directors is classified pursuant to Section 301.5 may not be removed if the votes cast against removal of the director, or not consenting in writing to the removal, would be sufficient to elect the director if voted cumulatively (without regard to whether shares may otherwise be voted cumulatively) at an election at which the same total number of votes were cast (or, if the action is taken by written consent, all shares entitled to vote were voted) and either the number of directors elected at the most recent annual meeting of shareholders, or if greater, the number of directors for whom removal is being sought, were then being elected.

(b) Any reduction of the authorized number of directors or amendment reducing the number of classes of directors does not remove any director prior to the expiration of the director's term of office.

(c) Except as provided in this section and Sections 302 and 304, a director may not be removed prior to the expiration of the director's term of office.

Ca. Corp. Code § 303

Amended by Stats. 1989, Ch. 876, Sec. 3.

Section 304 - Removal in case of fraudulent or dishonest acts or gross abuse of authority or discretion

The superior court of the proper county may, at the suit of shareholders holding at least 10 percent of the number of outstanding shares of any class, remove from office any director in case of fraudulent or dishonest acts or gross abuse of authority or discretion with reference to the corporation and may bar from reelection any director so removed for a period prescribed by the court. The corporation shall be made a party to such action.

Ca. Corp. Code § 304

Repealed and added by Stats. 1975, Ch. 682.

Section 305 - Filling of vacancies

(a) Unless otherwise provided in the articles or bylaws and except for a vacancy created by the removal of a director, vacancies on the board may be filled by approval of the board (Section 151) or, if the number of directors then in office is less than a quorum, by (1) the unanimous written consent of the directors then in office, (2) the affirmative vote of a majority of the directors then in office at a meeting held pursuant to notice or waivers of notice complying with Section 307 or (3) a sole remaining director. Unless the articles or a bylaw adopted by the shareholders provide that the board may fill vacancies occurring in the board by reason of the removal of directors, such vacancies may be filled only by approval of the shareholders (Section 153).

(b) The shareholders may elect a director at any time to fill any vacancy not filled by the directors. Any such election by written consent other than to fill a vacancy created by removal, which requires the unanimous consent of all shares entitled to vote for the election of directors, requires the consent of a majority of the outstanding shares entitled to vote.

(c) If, after the filling of any vacancy by the directors, the directors then in office who have been elected by the shareholders shall constitute less than a majority of the directors then in office, then both of the following shall be applicable:

(1) Any holder or holders of an aggregate of 5 percent or more of the total number of shares at the time outstanding having the right to vote for those directors may call a special meeting of shareholders, or

(2) The superior court of the proper county shall, upon application of such shareholder or shareholders, summarily order a special meeting of shareholders, to be held to elect the entire board. The term of office of any director shall terminate upon that election of a successor. The hearing on any application filed pursuant to this subdivision shall be held on not less than 10 business days notice to the corporation. If the corporation intends to oppose the application, it shall file with the court a notice of opposition not later than five business days prior to the date set for the hearing. The application and any notice of opposition shall be supported by appropriate affidavits and the court's determination shall be made on the basis of the papers in the record; but, for good cause shown, the court may receive and consider at the hearing additional evidence, oral or documentary, and additional points and authorities. The hearing shall take precedence over all other matters not of a similar nature pending on the date set for the hearing.

(d) Any director may resign effective upon giving written notice to the chairperson of the board, the president, the secretary or the board of directors of the corporation, unless the notice specifies a later time for the effectiveness of such resignation. If the resignation is effective at a future time, a successor may be elected to take office when the resignation becomes effective.

Ca. Corp. Code § 305

Amended by Stats 2015 ch 98 (SB 351),s 3, eff. 1/1/2016.
Amended by Stats 2000 ch 485 (AB 1895), s 5, eff. 1/1/2001.

Section 306 - Appointment of directors by superior court

If (a) a corporation has not issued shares and all the directors resign, die, or become incompetent, or (b) a corporation's initial directors have not been named in the articles, and all the incorporators resign, die, or become incompetent prior to the election of the initial directors, the superior court of any county may appoint directors of the corporation upon application by any party in interest.

Ca. Corp. Code § 306

Amended by Stats 2000 ch 485 (AB 1895), s 6, eff. 1/1/2001.

Section 307 - Meetings of board

(a) Unless otherwise provided in the articles or, subject to paragraph (5) of subdivision (a) of Section 204, in the bylaws, all of the following apply:

(1) Meetings of the board may be called by the chairperson of the board or the president or any vice president or the secretary or any two directors.

(2) Regular meetings of the board may be held without notice if the time and place of the meetings are fixed by the bylaws or the board. Special meetings of the board shall be held upon four days' notice by mail or 48 hours' notice delivered personally or by telephone, including a voice messaging system or by electronic transmission by the corporation (Section 20). The articles or bylaws may not dispense with notice of a special meeting. A notice, or waiver of notice, need not specify the purpose of any regular or special meeting of the board.

(3) Notice of a meeting need not be given to a director who provides a waiver of notice or a consent to holding the meeting or an approval of the minutes thereof in writing, whether before or after the meeting, or who attends the meeting without protesting, prior thereto or at its commencement, the lack of notice to that director. These waivers, consents and approvals shall be filed with the corporate records or made a part of the minutes of the meeting.

(4) A majority of the directors present, whether or not a quorum is present, may adjourn any meeting to another time and place. If the meeting is adjourned for more than 24 hours, notice of an adjournment to another time or place shall be given prior to the time of the adjourned meeting to the directors who were not present at the time of the adjournment.

(5) Meetings of the board may be held at a place within or without the state that has been designated in the notice of the meeting or, if not stated in the notice or there is no notice, designated in the bylaws or by resolution of the board.

(6) Members of the board may participate in a meeting through use of conference telephone, electronic video screen communication, or electronic transmission by and to the corporation (Sections 20 and 21). Participation in a meeting through use of conference telephone or electronic video screen communication pursuant to this subdivision constitutes presence in person at that meeting as long as all members participating in the meeting are able to hear one another. Participation in a meeting through electronic transmission by and to the corporation (other than conference telephone and electronic video screen communication), pursuant to this subdivision constitutes presence in person at that meeting if both of the following apply:

(A) Each member participating in the meeting can communicate with all of the other members concurrently.

(B) Each member is provided the means of participating in all matters before the board, including, without limitation, the capacity to propose, or to interpose an objection to, a specific action to be taken by the corporation.

(7) A majority of the authorized number of directors constitutes a quorum of the board for the transaction of business. The articles or bylaws may not provide that a quorum shall be less than one-third the authorized number of directors or less than two, whichever is larger, unless the authorized number of directors is one, in which case one director constitutes a quorum.

(8) An act or decision done or made by a majority of the directors present at a meeting duly held at which a quorum is present is the act of the board, subject to the provisions of Section 310 and subdivision (e) of Section 317. The articles or bylaws may not provide that a lesser vote than a majority of the directors present at a meeting is the act of the board. A meeting at which a quorum is initially present may continue to transact business notwithstanding the withdrawal of directors, if any action taken is approved by at least a majority of the required quorum for that meeting.

(b) An action required or permitted to be taken by the board may be taken without a meeting, if all members of the board shall individually or collectively consent in writing to that action and if the number of members of the board serving at the time constitutes a quorum. The written consent or consents shall be filed with the minutes of the proceedings of the board. For purposes of this subdivision only, "all members of the board" shall include an "interested director" as described in subdivision (a) of Section 310 or a "common director" as described in subdivision (b) of Section 310 who abstains in writing from providing consent, where the disclosures required by Section 310 have been made to the noninterested or noncommon directors, as applicable, prior to their execution of the written consent or consents, the specified disclosures are conspicuously included in the written consent or consents executed by the noninterested or noncommon directors, and the noninterested or noncommon directors, as applicable, approve the action by a vote that is sufficient without counting the votes of the interested or common directors. If written consent is provided by the directors in accordance with the immediately preceding sentence and the disclosures made regarding the action that is the subject of the consent do not comply with the requirements of Section 310, the action that is the subject of the consent shall be deemed approved, but in any suit brought to challenge the action, the party asserting the validity of the action shall have the burden of proof in establishing that the action was just and reasonable to the corporation at the time it was approved.

(c) This section applies also to committees of the board and incorporators and action by those committees and incorporators, mutatis mutandis.

Ca. Corp. Code § 307

Amended by Stats 2015 ch 98 (SB 351),s 4, eff. 1/1/2016.

Amended by Stats 2010 ch 91 (AB 2158),s 1, eff. 1/1/2011.
Amended by Stats 2010 ch 91 (AB 2158),s 2, eff. 1/1/2011.
Amended by Stats 2005 ch 102 (SB 119),s 1, eff. 1/1/2006
Amended by Stats 2004 ch 254 (SB 1306),s 6, eff. 1/1/2005
Amended by Stats 2003 ch 168 (SB 735),s 1, eff. 1/1/2004.
Amended by Stats 2002 ch 1008 (AB 3028),s 7, eff. 1/1/2003.

Section 308 - Appointment of provisional director

(a) If a corporation has an even number of directors who are equally divided and cannot agree as to the management of its affairs, so that its business can no longer be conducted to advantage or so that there is danger that its property and business will be impaired or lost, the superior court of the proper county may, notwithstanding any provisions of the articles or bylaws and whether or not an action is pending for an involuntary winding up or dissolution of the corporation, appoint a provisional director pursuant to this section. Action for such appointment may be brought by any director or by the holders of not less than 33 $^1/_3$ percent of the voting power.
(b) If the shareholders of a corporation are deadlocked so that they cannot elect the directors to be elected at an annual meeting of shareholders, the superior court of the proper county may, notwithstanding any provisions of the articles or bylaws, upon petition of a shareholder or shareholders holding 50 percent of the voting power, appoint a provisional director or directors pursuant to this section or order such other equitable relief as the court deems appropriate.
(c) A provisional director shall be an impartial person, who is neither a shareholder nor a creditor of the corporation, nor related by consanguinity or affinity within the third degree according to the common law to any of the other directors of the corporation or to any judge of the court by which such provisional director is appointed. A provisional director shall have all the rights and powers of a director until the deadlock in the board or among shareholders is broken or until such provisional director is removed by order of the court or by approval of the outstanding shares (Section 152). Such person shall be entitled to such compensation as shall be fixed by the court unless otherwise agreed with the corporation.
(d) This section does not apply to corporations subject to the Public Utilities Act (Part 1 (commencing with Section 201) of Division 1 of the Public Utilities Code).
Ca. Corp. Code § 308
Amended by Stats. 1995, Ch. 154, Sec. 3. Effective January 1, 1996.

Section 309 - Performance of duties of director

(a) A director shall perform the duties of a director, including duties as a member of any committee of the board upon which the director may serve, in good faith, in a manner such director believes to be in the best interests of the corporation and its shareholders and with such care, including reasonable inquiry, as an ordinarily prudent person in a like position would use under similar circumstances.

(b) In performing the duties of a director, a director shall be entitled to rely on information, opinions, reports or statements, including financial statements and other financial data, in each case prepared or presented by any of the following:

(1) One or more officers or employees of the corporation whom the director believes to be reliable and competent in the matters presented.

(2) Counsel, independent accountants or other persons as to matters which the director believes to be within such person's professional or expert competence.

(3) A committee of the board upon which the director does not serve, as to matters within its designated authority, which committee the director believes to merit confidence, so long as, in any such case, the director acts in good faith, after reasonable inquiry when the need therefor is indicated by the circumstances and without knowledge that would cause such reliance to be unwarranted.

(c) A person who performs the duties of a director in accordance with subdivisions (a) and (b) shall have no liability based upon any alleged failure to discharge the person's obligations as a director. In addition, the liability of a director for monetary damages may be eliminated or limited in a corporation's articles to the extent provided in paragraph (10) of subdivision (a) of Section 204.

Ca. Corp. Code § 309
Amended by Stats. 1987, Ch. 1203, Sec. 2. Effective September 27, 1987.

Section 310 - Material financial interest of director in contract or other transaction

(a) No contract or other transaction between a corporation and one or more of its directors, or between a corporation and any corporation, firm or association in which one or more of its directors has a material financial interest, is either void or voidable because such director or directors or such other corporation, firm or association are parties or because such director or directors are present at the meeting of the board or a committee thereof which authorizes, approves or ratifies the contract or transaction, if

(1) The material facts as to the transaction and as to such director's interest are fully disclosed or known to the shareholders and such contract or transaction is approved by the shareholders (Section 153) in good faith, with the shares owned by the interested director or directors not being entitled to vote thereon, or

(2) The material facts as to the transaction and as to such director's interest are fully disclosed or known to the board or committee, and the board or committee authorizes, approves or ratifies the contract or transaction in good faith by a vote sufficient without counting the vote of the interested director or directors and the contract or transaction is just and reasonable as to the corporation at the time it is authorized, approved or ratified, or

(3) As to contracts or transactions not approved as provided in paragraph (1) or (2) of this subdivision, the person asserting the validity of the contract or transaction sustains the burden of proving that the contract or transaction was just and reasonable as to the corporation at the time it was authorized, approved or ratified. A mere common directorship does not constitute a material financial interest within the meaning of this subdivision. A director is not interested within the meaning of this subdivision in a resolution fixing the compensation of another director as a director, officer or employee of the corporation, notwithstanding the fact that the first director is also receiving compensation from the corporation.

(b) No contract or other transaction between a corporation and any corporation or association of which one or more of its directors are directors is either void or voidable because such director or directors are present at the meeting of the board or a committee thereof which authorizes, approves or ratifies the contract or transaction, if

(1) The material facts as to the transaction and as to such director's other directorship are fully disclosed or known to the board or committee, and the board or committee authorizes, approves or ratifies the contract or transaction in good faith by a vote sufficient without counting the vote of the common director or directors or the contract or transaction is approved by the shareholders (Section 153) in good faith, or

(2) As to contracts or transactions not approved as provided in paragraph (1) of this subdivision, the contract or transaction is just and reasonable as to the corporation at the time it is authorized, approved or ratified. This subdivision does not apply to contracts or transactions covered by subdivision (a).

(c) Interested or common directors may be counted in determining the presence of a quorum at a meeting of the board or a committee thereof which authorizes, approves or ratifies a contract or transaction.

Ca. Corp. Code § 310
Amended by Stats. 1976, Ch. 641.

Section 311 - Committees

The board may, by resolution adopted by a majority of the authorized number of directors, designate one or more committees, each consisting of two or more directors, to serve at the pleasure of the board. The board may designate one or more directors as alternate members of any committee, who may replace any absent member at any meeting of the committee. The appointment of members or alternate members of a committee requires the vote of a majority of the authorized number of directors. Any such committee, to the extent provided in the resolution of the board or in the bylaws, shall have all the authority of the board, except with respect to:

(a) The approval of any action for which this division also requires shareholders' approval (Section 153) or approval of the outstanding shares (Section 152).

(b) The filling of vacancies on the board or in any committee.

(c) The fixing of compensation of the directors for serving on the board or on any committee.

(d) The amendment or repeal of bylaws or the adoption of new bylaws.

(e) The amendment or repeal of any resolution of the board which by its express terms is not so amendable or repealable.

(f) A distribution (Section 166), except at a rate, in a periodic amount or within a price range set forth in the articles or determined by the board.

(g) The appointment of other committees of the board or the members thereof.

Ca. Corp. Code § 311

Amended by Stats. 1983, Ch. 1223, Sec. 4.

Section 312 - Officers

(a)A corporation shall have (1) a chairperson of the board, who may be given the title of chair of the board, chairperson of the board, chairperson, or a president or both, (2) a secretary, (3) a chief financial officer, and (4) such other officers with such titles and duties as shall be stated in the bylaws or determined by the board and as may be necessary to enable it to sign instruments and share certificates. The president, or if there is no president the chairperson of the board, is the general manager and chief executive officer of the corporation, unless otherwise provided in the articles or bylaws. Any number of offices may be held by the same person unless the articles or bylaws provide otherwise.

(b) Except as otherwise provided by the articles or bylaws, officers shall be chosen by the board and serve at the pleasure of the board, subject to the rights, if any, of an officer under any contract of employment. Any officer may resign at any time upon written notice to the corporation without prejudice to the rights, if any, of the corporation under any contract to which the officer is a party.

Ca. Corp. Code § 312

Amended by Stats 2022 ch 617 (SB 1202),s 10, eff. 1/1/2023.

Amended by Stats 2015 ch 98 (SB 351),s 5, eff. 1/1/2016.

Section 313 - Authority of signing officers

Subject to the provisions of subdivision (a) of Section 208, any note, mortgage, evidence of indebtedness, contract, share certificate, initial transaction statement or written statement, conveyance, or other instrument in writing, and any assignment or endorsement thereof, executed or entered into between any corporation and any other person, when signed by the chairperson of the board, the president or any vice president and the secretary, any assistant secretary, the chief financial officer or any assistant treasurer of such corporation, is not invalidated as to the corporation by any lack of authority of the signing officers in the absence of actual knowledge on the part of the other person that the signing officers had no authority to execute the same.

Ca. Corp. Code § 313
Amended by Stats 2015 ch 98 (SB 351),s 6, eff. 1/1/2016.

Section 314 - Prima facie evidence of adoption of bylaws, resolution, or holding

The original or a copy in writing or in any other form capable of being converted into clearly legible tangible form of the bylaws or of the minutes of any incorporators', shareholders', directors', committee or other meeting or of any resolution adopted by the board or a committee thereof, or shareholders, certified to be a true copy by a person purporting to be the secretary or an assistant secretary of the corporation, is prima facie evidence of the adoption of such bylaws or resolution or of the due holding of such meeting and of the matters stated therein.
Ca. Corp. Code § 314
Amended by Stats 2004 ch 254 (SB 1306),s 7, eff. 1/1/2005

Section 315 - Loans or guaranties

(a) A corporation shall not make any loan of money or property to, or guarantee the obligation of, any director or officer of the corporation or of its parent, unless the transaction, or an employee benefit plan authorizing the loans or guaranties after disclosure of the right under such a plan to include officers or directors, is approved by a majority of the shareholders entitled to act thereon.
(b) Notwithstanding subdivision (a), if the corporation has outstanding shares held of record by 100 or more persons (determined as provided in Section 605) on the date of approval by the board, and has a bylaw approved by the outstanding shares (Section 152) authorizing the board alone to approve such a loan or guaranty to an officer, whether or not a director, or an employee benefit plan authorizing such a loan or guaranty to an officer, such a loan or guaranty or employee benefit plan may be approved by the board alone by a vote sufficient without counting the vote of any interested director or directors if the board determines that such a loan or guaranty or plan may reasonably be expected to benefit the corporation.
(c) A corporation shall not make any loan of money or property to, or guarantee the obligation of, any person upon the security of shares of the corporation or of its parent if the corporation's recourse in the event of default is limited to the security for the loan or guaranty, unless the loan or guaranty is adequately secured without considering these shares, or the loan or guaranty is approved by a majority of the shareholders entitled to act thereon.
(d) Notwithstanding subdivision (a), a corporation may advance money to a director or officer of the corporation or of its parent for any expenses reasonably anticipated to be incurred in the performance of the duties of the director or officer, provided that in the absence of the advance the director or officer would be entitled to be reimbursed for the expenses by the corporation, its parent, or any subsidiary.
(e) The provisions of subdivision (a) do not apply to the payment of premiums in

whole or in part by a corporation on a life insurance policy on the life of a director or officer so long as repayment to the corporation of the amount paid by it is secured by the proceeds of the policy and its cash surrender value.

(f) This section does not apply to any of the following:

(1) Any transaction, plan, or agreement permitted under Section 408.

(2) Any depository institution, as defined in Section 202 of the Depository Institutions Management Interlocks Act (12 U.S.C. Sec. 3201) .

(3) Any loan or guaranty made by a corporation that makes loans or guaranties in the ordinary course of its business if statutes or regulations pertaining to the corporation expressly regulate the making by the corporation of loans to its officers or directors or the undertaking of guaranties of the obligations of its officers or directors.

(g) For the purposes of subdivisions (a) and (c), "approval by a majority of the shareholders entitled to act" means either (1) written consent of a majority of the outstanding shares without counting as outstanding or as consenting any shares owned by any officer or director eligible to participate in the plan or transaction that is subject to this approval, (2) the affirmative vote of a majority of the shares present and voting at a duly held meeting at which a quorum is otherwise present, without counting for purposes of the vote as either present or voting any shares owned by any officer or director eligible to participate in the plan or transaction that is subject to the approval, or (3) the unanimous vote or written consent of the shareholders. In the case of a corporation which has more than one class or series of shares outstanding, the "shareholders entitled to act" within the meaning of this section includes only holders of those classes or series entitled under the articles to vote on all matters before the shareholders or to vote on the subject matter of this section, and includes a requirement for separate class or series voting, or for more or less than one vote per share, only to the extent required by the articles.

Ca. Corp. Code § 315
Amended by Stats. 1984, Ch. 812, Sec. 1.

Section 316 - Joint and several liability regarding distributions

(a) Subject to the provisions of Section 309, directors of a corporation who approve any of the following corporate actions shall be jointly and severally liable to the corporation for the benefit of all of the creditors or shareholders entitled to institute an action under subdivision (c):

(1) The making of any distribution to its shareholders to the extent that it is contrary to the provisions of Sections 500 to 503, inclusive.

(2) The distribution of assets to shareholders after institution of dissolution proceedings of the corporation, without paying or adequately providing for all known

liabilities of the corporation, excluding any claims not filed by creditors within the time limit set by the court in a notice given to creditors under Chapters 18 (commencing with Section 1800), 19 (commencing with Section 1900) and 20 (commencing with Section 2000).

(3) The making of any loan or guaranty contrary to Section 315.

(b) A director who is present at a meeting of the board, or any committee thereof, at which action specified in subdivision (a) is taken and who abstains from voting shall be considered to have approved the action.

(c) Suit may be brought in the name of the corporation to enforce the liability (1) under paragraph (1) of subdivision (a) against any or all directors liable by the persons entitled to sue under subdivision (b) of Section 506, (2) under paragraph (2) or (3) of subdivision (a) against any or all directors liable by any one or more creditors of the corporation whose debts or claims arose prior to the time of any of the corporate actions specified in paragraph (2) or (3) of subdivision (a) and who have not consented to the corporate action, whether or not they have reduced their claims to judgment, or (3) under paragraph (3) of subdivision (a) against any or all directors liable by any one or more holders of shares outstanding at the time of any corporate action specified in paragraph (3) of subdivision (a) who have not consented to the corporate action, without regard to the provisions of Section 800.

(d) The damages recoverable from a director under this section shall be the amount of the illegal distribution (or if the illegal distribution consists of property, the fair market value of that property at the time of the illegal distribution) plus interest thereon from the date of the distribution at the legal rate on judgments until paid, together with all reasonably incurred costs of appraisal or other valuation, if any, of that property or loss suffered by the corporation as a result of the illegal loan or guaranty, as the case may be, but not exceeding the liabilities of the corporation owed to nonconsenting creditors at the time of the violation and the injury suffered by nonconsenting shareholders, as the case may be.

(e) Any director sued under this section may implead all other directors liable and may compel contribution, either in that action or in an independent action against directors not joined in that action.

(f) Directors liable under this section shall also be entitled to be subrogated to the rights of the corporation:

(1) With respect to paragraph (1) of subdivision (a), against shareholders who received the distribution.

(2) With respect to paragraph (2) of subdivision (a), against shareholders who received the distribution of assets.

(3) With respect to paragraph (3) of subdivision (a), against the person who received the loan or guaranty. Any director sued under this section may file a cross-complaint against the person or persons who are liable to the director as a result of

the subrogation provided for in this subdivision or may proceed against them in an independent action.

Ca. Corp. Code § 316

Amended by Stats. 1994, Ch. 1064, Sec. 1. Effective January 1, 1995.

Section 317 - Indemnification

(a) For the purposes of this section, "agent" means any person who is or was a director, officer, employee or other agent of the corporation, or is or was serving at the request of the corporation as a director, officer, employee or agent of another foreign or domestic corporation, partnership, joint venture, trust or other enterprise, or was a director, officer, employee or agent of a foreign or domestic corporation which was a predecessor corporation of the corporation or of another enterprise at the request of the predecessor corporation; "proceeding" means any threatened, pending or completed action or proceeding, whether civil, criminal, administrative or investigative; and "expenses" includes without limitation attorneys' fees and any expenses of establishing a right to indemnification under subdivision (d) or paragraph (4) of subdivision (e).

(b) A corporation shall have power to indemnify any person who was or is a party or is threatened to be made a party to any proceeding (other than an action by or in the right of the corporation to procure a judgment in its favor) by reason of the fact that the person is or was an agent of the corporation, against expenses, judgments, fines, settlements, and other amounts actually and reasonably incurred in connection with the proceeding if that person acted in good faith and in a manner the person reasonably believed to be in the best interests of the corporation and, in the case of a criminal proceeding, had no reasonable cause to believe the conduct of the person was unlawful. The termination of any proceeding by judgment, order, settlement, conviction, or upon a plea of nolo contendere or its equivalent shall not, of itself, create a presumption that the person did not act in good faith and in a manner which the person reasonably believed to be in the best interests of the corporation or that the person had reasonable cause to believe that the person's conduct was unlawful.

(c) A corporation shall have power to indemnify any person who was or is a party or is threatened to be made a party to any threatened, pending, or completed action by or in the right of the corporation to procure a judgment in its favor by reason of the fact that the person is or was an agent of the corporation, against expenses actually and reasonably incurred by that person in connection with the defense or settlement of the action if the person acted in good faith, in a manner the person believed to be in the best interests of the corporation and its shareholders. No indemnification shall be made under this subdivision for any of the following:

(1) In respect of any claim, issue or matter as to which the person shall have been adjudged to be liable to the corporation in the performance of that person's duty to the corporation and its shareholders, unless and only to the extent that the court in which the proceeding is or was pending shall determine upon application that, in view of all the circumstances of the case, the person is fairly and reasonably entitled to indemnity for expenses and then only to the extent that the court shall determine.

(2) Of amounts paid in settling or otherwise disposing of a pending action without court approval.

(3) Of expenses incurred in defending a pending action which is settled or otherwise disposed of without court approval.

(d) To the extent that an agent of a corporation has been successful on the merits in defense of any proceeding referred to in subdivision (b) or (c) or in defense of any claim, issue, or matter therein, the agent shall be indemnified against expenses actually and reasonably incurred by the agent in connection therewith.

(e) Except as provided in subdivision (d), any indemnification under this section shall be made by the corporation only if authorized in the specific case, upon a determination that indemnification of the agent is proper in the circumstances because the agent has met the applicable standard of conduct set forth in subdivision (b) or (c), by any of the following:

(1) A majority vote of a quorum consisting of directors who are not parties to such proceeding.

(2) If such a quorum of directors is not obtainable, by independent legal counsel in a written opinion.

(3) Approval of the shareholders (Section 153), with the shares owned by the person to be indemnified not being entitled to vote thereon.

(4) The court in which the proceeding is or was pending upon application made by the corporation or the agent or the attorney or other person rendering services in connection with the defense, whether or not the application by the agent, attorney or other person is opposed by the corporation.

(f) Expenses incurred in defending any proceeding may be advanced by the corporation prior to the final disposition of the proceeding upon receipt of an undertaking by or on behalf of the agent to repay that amount if it shall be determined ultimately that the agent is not entitled to be indemnified as authorized in this section. The provisions of subdivision (a) of Section 315 do not apply to advances made pursuant to this subdivision.

(g) The indemnification authorized by this section shall not be deemed exclusive of any additional rights to indemnification for breach of duty to the corporation and its shareholders while acting in the capacity of a director or officer of the corporation to the extent the additional rights to indemnification are authorized in an article provision adopted pursuant to paragraph (11) of subdivision (a) of Section 204. The indemnification provided by this section for acts, omissions, or transactions while acting in the capacity of, or while serving as, a director or officer of the corporation but not involving breach of duty to the corporation and its shareholders shall not be deemed exclusive of any other rights to which those seeking indemnification may be entitled under any bylaw, agreement, vote of shareholders or disinterested directors, or otherwise, to the extent the additional rights to indemnification are authorized in the articles of the corporation. An article provision authorizing indemnification "in excess of that otherwise permitted by Section 317" or "to the fullest extent permissible under California law" or the substantial equivalent thereof shall be construed to be both a provision for additional indemnification for breach of duty to the corporation and its shareholders as referred to in, and with the limitations required by, paragraph (11) of subdivision (a) of Section 204 and a provision for additional indemnification as referred to in the second sentence of this subdivision. The rights to indemnity hereunder shall continue as to a person who has ceased to be a director, officer, employee, or agent and shall inure to the benefit of the heirs, executors, and administrators of the person. Nothing contained in this section shall affect any right to indemnification to which persons other than the directors and officers may be entitled by contract or otherwise.

(h) No indemnification or advance shall be made under this section, except as provided in subdivision (d) or paragraph (4) of subdivision (e), in any circumstance where it appears:

(1) That it would be inconsistent with a provision of the articles, bylaws, a resolution of the shareholders, or an agreement in effect at the time of the accrual of the alleged cause of action asserted in the proceeding in which the expenses were incurred or other amounts were paid, which prohibits or otherwise limits indemnification.

(2) That it would be inconsistent with any condition expressly imposed by a court in approving a settlement.

(i) A corporation shall have power to purchase and maintain insurance on behalf of any agent of the corporation against any liability asserted against or incurred by the agent in that capacity or arising out of the agent's status as such whether or not the corporation would have the power to indemnify the agent against that liability under this section. The fact that a corporation owns all or a portion of the shares of the company issuing a policy of insurance shall not render this subdivision inapplicable if either of the following conditions are satisfied:

(1) if the articles authorize indemnification in excess of that authorized in this section and the insurance provided by this subdivision is limited as indemnification is required to be limited by paragraph (11) of subdivision (a) of Section 204; or

(2) (A) the company issuing the insurance policy is organized, licensed, and operated in a manner that complies with the insurance laws and regulations applicable to its jurisdiction of organization, (B) the company issuing the policy provides procedures for processing claims that do not permit that company to be subject to the direct control of the corporation that purchased that policy, and (C) the policy issued provides for some manner of risk sharing between the issuer and purchaser of the policy, on one hand, and some unaffiliated person or persons, on the other, such as by providing for more than one unaffiliated owner of the company issuing the policy or by providing that a portion of the coverage furnished will be obtained from some unaffiliated insurer or reinsurer.

(j) This section does not apply to any proceeding against any trustee, investment manager, or other fiduciary of an employee benefit plan in that person's capacity as such, even though the person may also be an agent as defined in subdivision (a) of the employer corporation. A corporation shall have power to indemnify such a trustee, investment manager, or other fiduciary to the extent permitted by subdivision (f) of Section 207.

Ca. Corp. Code § 317
Amended by Stats. 1995, Ch. 154, Sec. 4. Effective January 1, 1996.

Section 318 - Registry of distinguished women and minorities available to serve on corporate boards of directors

(a) The Secretary of State shall develop and maintain a registry of distinguished women and minorities who are available to serve on corporate boards of directors. As used in this section, "minority" means an ethnic person of color including American Indians, Asians (including, but not limited to, Chinese, Japanese, Koreans, Pacific Islanders, Samoans, and Southeast Asians), Blacks, Filipinos, and Hispanics.

(b) For each woman or minority who participates in the registry, the Secretary of State shall maintain information on his or her educational, professional, community service, and corporate governance background. That information may include, but is not limited to:

(1) Paid or volunteer employment.

(2) Service in elected public office or on public boards or commissions.

(3) Directorships, officerships, and trusteeships of business and nonprofit entities, including committee experience.

(4) Professional, academic, or community awards or honors.

(5) Publications.

(6) Government relations experience.

(7) Experience with corporate constituents.

(8) Any other areas of special expertise.

(c) In addition to the information subdivision (b) requires, each woman or minority who participates in the registry may disclose any number of personal attributes that may contribute to board diversity. Those attributes may include, but are not limited to, gender, physical disability, race, or ethnic origin.

(d) In addition to the information subdivision (b) requires, each woman or minority who participates in the registry may indicate characteristics of corporations for which he or she would consider, or is especially interested in, serving as a director. These characteristics may include, but are not limited to, company size, industry, geographic location, board meeting frequency, director time commitments, director compensation, director insurance or indemnification, or social policy concerns.

(e) Any woman or minority may nominate himself or herself to the registry by filing with the Secretary of State the information required by subdivision (b) on a form the secretary prescribes. Any registrant may attach a copy of his or her resume and up to two letters of recommendation to his or her registration form. Each registrant's registration form, together with any attached resume or letters of recommendation, shall constitute his or her registry transcript.

(f) The Secretary of State shall make appropriate rules requiring registrants to renew or update their filings with the registry, as necessary to ensure continued accuracy of registry information.

(g) The Secretary of State shall assign each registrant a file number, then enter the information described in subdivisions (b), (c), and (d) into a data base, using the registrant's file number to identify him or her. The registry data base shall not disclose any registrant's name or street address, but may list the city, county, or ZIP Code of his or her business or residence address. The secretary shall make data base information available to those persons described in subdivisions (i) and (j). The secretary may provide that access either by permitting direct data base searches or by performing data base searches on written request.

(h) The Secretary of State may also make information contained in the registry data base available to any person or entity qualified to transact business in California that regularly engages in the business of providing data base access or search services; provided, that data base access will not be construed to entitle the user to access to any registrant's transcript.

(i) The Secretary of State shall make information contained in a reasonable number of registrants' transcripts available to any corporation or its representative. A "representative," for purposes of this subdivision, may be an attorney, an accountant, or a retained executive recruiter. A "retained executive recruiter," for purposes of this subdivision, is an individual or business entity engaged in the executive search business that is regularly retained to locate qualified candidates for appointment or election as corporate directors or executive officers.

(j) The Secretary of State may also grant access to a reasonable number of registrants' transcripts to any other person who demonstrates to the secretary's satisfaction that the person does both of the following:

(1) Seeks access to the registry in connection with an actual search for a corporate director.

(2) Intends to use any information obtained from the registry only for the purpose of finding qualified candidates for an open position on a corporate board of directors.

(k) The Secretary of State may employ reasonable means to verify that any party seeking access to registry transcript information is one of those specified in subdivision (i) or (j). To that end, the secretary may require a representative to identify its principal, but may not disclose that principal's identity to any other person.

(l) Upon written request specifying the registrant's file number, the Secretary of State shall provide any party entitled to access to registry transcripts with a copy of any registrant's transcript. The secretary may by rule or regulation specify other reasonable means by which persons entitled thereto may order copies of registrants' transcripts.

(m) Notwithstanding any other law, a person shall not be entitled to access to information the registry contains, except as this section specifically provides.

(n) The Secretary of State shall charge fees for registering with the registry, obtaining access to the registry data base, and obtaining copies of registrants' transcripts. The Secretary of State, in consultation with the Senate Commission on Corporate Governance, Shareholder Rights, and Securities Transactions, shall fix those fees by regulation. Fees shall be fixed so that the aggregate amount of all fees collected shall be sufficient to cover the total cost of administering the registry program. Registration fees shall be fixed so as to encourage qualified women and minorities to participate. Fees shall be deposited into the Secretary of State's Business Fee Fund.

(o) The Secretary of State may make any rule, regulation, guideline, or agreement the secretary deems necessary to carry out the purposes and provisions of this section.

(p) The Secretary of State may cooperate with the Commission on the Status of Women and Girls, the California Council to Promote Business Ownership by Women, the Senate Commission on Corporate Governance, Shareholder Rights, and Securities Transactions, women's organizations, minority organizations, business and professional organizations, and any other individual or entity the secretary deems appropriate, for any of the following purposes:

(1) Promoting corporate use of the registry.

(2) Locating qualified women and minorities and encouraging them to participate in the registry.

(3) Educating interested parties on the purpose and most effective use of the registry. The secretary may also prepare and distribute publications designed to promote informed use of the registry.

(q) The Secretary of State may seek registrants' consent to be listed in a published directory of women and minorities eligible to serve as corporate directors, which will contain a summary of each listed registrant's qualifications. The secretary may periodically publish, or cause to be published, such a directory. Only those registrants who so consent in writing may be included in the directory. The printed directory shall be provided to any person upon payment of a fee, which the Secretary of State will determine by regulation, in consultation with the Senate Commission on Corporate Governance, Shareholder Rights, and Securities Transactions.

(r) The Secretary of State shall implement this section no later than January 1, 1995.

(s) At least once in each three-year period during which the registry is available for corporate use, the Secretary of State, in consultation with the Senate Commission on Corporate Governance, Shareholder Rights, and Securities Transactions, shall report to the Legislature on the extent to which the registry has helped women and minorities progress toward achieving parity in corporate board appointments or elections.

(t) The Secretary of State shall notify each University of California campus and each California State University campus of the opportunity to maintain the registry created pursuant to this section. If more than one campus of the university or state university expresses interest in maintaining the registry, the Secretary of State shall select a campus based on a competitive selection process. If a campus is selected, the Secretary of State shall transfer the information contained in the registry, free of cost, to that campus. Any University of California or California State University campus selected to maintain the registry shall do so in a manner consistent with this section. Funds deposited in the Secretary of State's Business Fees Fund pursuant to this section shall be transferred to the university selected to maintain the registry, and shall be used to administer the registry program. The Secretary of State shall maintain the registry until a University of California or California State University campus agrees to do so.

Ca. Corp. Code § 318

Amended by Stats 2012 ch 46 (SB 1038),s 2, eff. 6/27/2012.

Chapter 4 - SHARES AND SHARE CERTIFICATES

Section 400 - Issuance of classes or series of shares

(a) A corporation may issue one or more classes or series of shares or both, with full, limited or no voting rights and with such other rights, preferences, privileges and restrictions as are stated or authorized in its articles. No denial or limitation of voting rights shall be effective unless at the time one or more classes or series of outstanding shares or debt securities, singly or in the aggregate, are entitled to full voting rights; and no denial or limitation of dividend or liquidation rights shall be effective unless at the time one or more classes or series of outstanding shares, singly or in the aggregate, are entitled to unlimited dividend and liquidation rights.

(b) All shares of any one class shall have the same voting, conversion and redemption rights and other rights, preferences, privileges and restrictions, unless the class is divided into series. If a class is divided into series, all the shares of any one series shall have the same voting, conversion and redemption rights and other rights, preferences, privileges and restrictions.

Ca. Corp. Code § 400

Amended by Stats. 1976, Ch. 641.

Section 401 - Certificate of determination

(a) Before any corporation issues any shares of any class or series of which the rights, preferences, privileges, and restrictions, or any of them, or the number of shares constituting any series or the designation of the series, are not set forth in its articles but are fixed in a resolution adopted by the board pursuant to authority given by its articles, an officers' certificate shall be executed and filed, setting forth:

(1) a copy of the resolution;

(2) the number of shares of the class or series; and (3) that none of the shares of the class or series has been issued.

(b) After any certificate of determination has been filed, but before the corporation issues any shares of the class or series covered thereby, the board may alter or revoke any right, preference, privilege, or restriction fixed or determined by the resolution set forth therein by the adoption of another resolution appropriate for that purpose and the execution and filing of an officers' certificate setting forth a copy of the resolution, and stating that none of the shares of the class or the series affected has been issued.

(c) After any certificate of determination has been filed, the board may, if authorized in the articles pursuant to subdivision (e) of Section 202, increase or decrease the number of shares constituting any series, by the adoption of another resolution appropriate for that purpose and the execution and filing of an officers' certificate setting forth a copy of the resolution, the number of shares of the series then outstanding and the increase or decrease in the number of shares constituting the series. If any certificate of determination has been incorporated in restated articles filed pursuant to Section 910, the action authorized by this subdivision may, notwithstanding Section 902, be accomplished by an amendment of the articles approved by the board alone.

(d) After shares of a class or series have been issued, the provisions of the resolution set forth in a certificate of determination may be amended only by the adoption and approval of an amendment in accordance with Section 902, 903, or 904 and the filing of a certificate of amendment in accordance with Sections 905 and 908. Notwithstanding the preceding sentence, a certificate to increase or decrease the number of shares of a series also may be filed as permitted by subdivision (c).

(e) A provision in a certificate of determination being amended pursuant to subdivision (b), (c), or (d) shall be identified in the amendment in accordance with subdivision (a) of Section 907.

(f) If a certificate is filed pursuant to subdivision (c) to decrease the number of shares of a series to zero, the certificate of determination whereby the series was established is thereupon no longer in force and the series is no longer an authorized series of the corporation.

(g) If the rights, preferences, privileges, and restrictions of the class or series contain a supermajority vote provision, as defined in subdivision (b) of Section 710, subject to Section 710, the officers' certificate shall also state that the provision has been approved by the shareholders in accordance with subdivision (c) of Section 710.

Ca. Corp. Code § 401

Amended by Stats. 1993, Ch. 128, Sec. 4. Effective January 1, 1994.

Section 402 - Redemption

(a) A corporation may provide in its articles for one or more classes or series of shares which are redeemable, in whole or in part, (1) at the option of the corporation or (2) to the extent and upon the happening of one or more specified events, and not otherwise except as herein provided. A corporation may provide in its articles for one or more classes or series of preferred shares which are redeemable, in whole or in part, (1) as specified above, (2) at the option of the holder, or (3) upon the vote of at least a majority of the outstanding shares of the class or series to be redeemed. An open-end investment company registered under the United States Investment Company Act of 1940 may, if its articles so provide, issue shares which are redeemable at the option of the holder at a price approximately equal to the shares' proportionate interest in the net assets of the corporation and a shareholder may compel redemption of such shares in accordance with their terms.

(b) Any such redemption shall be effected at such price or prices, within such time and upon such terms and conditions as are stated in the articles. When the articles permit partial redemption of a class or series of shares, the articles shall prescribe the method of selecting the shares to be redeemed, which may be pro rata, by lot, at the discretion of, or in a manner approved by, the board or upon such other terms as are specified in the articles.

(c) No redeemable common shares, other than (1) shares issued by an open-end investment company registered under the United States Investment Company Act of 1940, (2) shares of a corporation which has a license or franchise from a governmental agency to conduct its business or is a member corporation of a national securities exchange registered under the United States Securities Exchange Act of 1934, which license, franchise or membership is conditioned upon some or all of the holders of its stock possessing prescribed qualifications, to the extent necessary to prevent the loss of such license, franchise or membership or to reinstate it, or (3) shares of a professional corporation, as defined in Part 4 (commencing with Section 13400) of Division 3 of Title 1, shall be issued or redeemed unless the corporation at the time has outstanding a class of common shares that is not subject to redemption.

(d) Any redemption by a corporation of its shares shall be subject to the provisions of Chapter 5 (commencing with Section 500). Nothing in this section shall prevent a corporation from creating a sinking fund or similar provision for, or entering into an agreement for, the redemption or purchase of its shares to the extent permitted by

Chapter 5, but unless such purchase or redemption is permitted under Chapter 5, the holder of shares to be so purchased or redeemed shall not become a creditor of the corporation.

Ca. Corp. Code § 402

Amended by Stats 2022 ch 617 (SB 1202),s 11, eff. 1/1/2023.

Amended by Stats. 1983, Ch. 1223, Sec. 5.

Section 402.5 - Preferred shares

The rights, preferences, privileges, and restrictions granted to or imposed upon a class or series of preferred shares (Section 176), the designation of which includes either the word "preferred" or the word "preference," may:

(a) Notwithstanding paragraph (9) of subdivision (a) of Section 204, include a provision requiring a vote of a specified percentage or proportion of the outstanding shares of the class or series that is less than a majority of the class or series to approve any corporate action, except where the vote of a majority or greater proportion of the class or series is required by this division, regardless of restrictions or limitations on the voting rights thereof.

(b) Notwithstanding paragraph (5) of subdivision (a) of Section 204, provide that in addition to the requirement of subdivision (a) of Section 1900 the corporation may voluntarily wind up and dissolve only upon the vote of a specified percentage (which shall not exceed $66^2/_3$ percent) of such class or series.

(c) Notwithstanding subdivision (a) of Section 500, provide that a distribution may be made without regard to the preferential dividends arrears amount, or any preferential rights amount, or both, as described in paragraphs (1) and (2) of subdivision (a) of Section 500.

Ca. Corp. Code § 402.5

Amended by Stats 2014 ch 71 (SB 1304),s 22, eff. 1/1/2015.

Amended by Stats 2013 ch 38 (AB 434),s 1, eff. 1/1/2014.

Section 403 - Convertible shares

(a) When so provided in the articles, a corporation may issue shares convertible within the time or upon the happening of one or more specified events and upon the terms and conditions that are stated in the articles if any of the following conditions apply:

(1) At the option of the holder or automatically upon either the vote of at least a majority of the outstanding shares of the class or series to be converted or upon the happening of one or more specified events, into shares of any class or series.

(2) If it is a corporation which has a license or franchise from a governmental agency to conduct its business or a member corporation of a national securities exchange registered under the United States Securities Exchange Act of 1934, the license, franchise or membership of which is conditioned upon some or all of the holders of its stock possessing prescribed qualifications, to the extent necessary to prevent the loss of such license, franchise or membership or to reinstate it, at the option of the corporation, into shares of any class or series or into any other security of the corporation.

(3) If the corporation is a "listed corporation" as defined in subdivision (d) of Section 301.5, both at the time of the original issuance of the convertible shares and at the time of the conversion, at the option of the corporation into shares of any class or series or into any other security of the corporation, provided that any such securities received upon conversion are listed or qualified for trading on a stock exchange or market system defined in subdivision (d) of Section 301.5.

(b) Unless otherwise provided in the articles, a corporation may issue its debt securities convertible into other debt securities or into shares of the corporation within such time or upon the happening of one or more specified events and upon such terms and conditions as are fixed by the board.

Ca. Corp. Code § 403

Amended by Stats. 1996, Ch. 477, Sec. 1. Effective January 1, 1997.

Section 404 - Option rights

Either in connection with the issue, subscription or sale of any of its shares, bonds, debentures, notes or other securities or independently thereof, a corporation may grant options to purchase or subscribe for shares of any class or series upon such terms and conditions as may be deemed expedient. Option rights may be transferable or nontransferable and separable or inseparable from other securities of the corporation.

Ca. Corp. Code § 404

Added by Stats. 1975, Ch. 682.

Section 405 - Amendment of articles relating to option or conversion rights

(a) If at the time of granting option or conversion rights or at any later time the corporation is not authorized by its articles to issue all the shares required for the satisfaction of the rights, if and when exercised, the additional number of shares required to be issued upon the exercise of such option or conversion rights shall be authorized by an amendment to the articles.

(b) If a corporation has obtained approval of the outstanding shares (Section 152) for the issue of options to purchase shares or of securities convertible into shares of the corporation, the board may, without further approval of the outstanding shares (Section 152), amend the articles to increase the authorized shares of any class or series to such number as will be sufficient from time to time, when added to the previously authorized but unissued shares of such class or series, to satisfy any such option or conversion rights.

Ca. Corp. Code § 405

Added by Stats. 1975, Ch. 682.

Section 406 - Issuance of shares options or securities having conversion or option rights without offering to shareholders

Unless the articles provide otherwise, the board may issue shares, options or securities having conversion or option rights without first offering them to shareholders of any class.

Ca. Corp. Code § 406

Added by Stats. 1975, Ch. 682.

Section 407 - Fractions of share

A corporation may, but is not required to, issue fractions of a share originally or upon transfer. If it does not issue fractions of a share, it shall in connection with any original issuance of shares (a) arrange for the disposition of fractional interests by those entitled thereto, (b) pay in cash the fair value of fractions of a share as of the time when those entitled to receive those fractions are determined or (c) issue scrip or warrants in registered form, as certificated securities or uncertificated securities, or bearer form as certificated securities, which shall entitle the holder to receive a certificate for a full share upon the surrender of the scrip or warrants aggregating a full share; provided, however, that if the fraction of a share that any person would otherwise be entitled to receive in a merger, conversion, or reorganization is less than one-half of 1 percent of the total shares that person is entitled to receive, a merger, conversion, or reorganization agreement may provide that fractions of a share will be disregarded or that shares issuable in the merger or conversion will be rounded off to the nearest whole share; and provided, further, that a corporation may not pay cash for fractional shares if that action would result in the cancellation of more than 10 percent of the outstanding shares of any class. A determination by the board of the fair value of fractions of a share shall be conclusive in the absence of fraud. A certificate for a fractional share shall, but scrip or warrants shall not unless otherwise provided therein, entitle the holder to exercise voting rights, to receive dividends thereon and to participate in any of the assets of the corporation in the event of liquidation. The board may cause scrip or warrants to be issued subject to the condition that they shall become void if not exchanged for full shares before a specified date or that the shares for which scrip or warrants are exchangeable may be sold by the corporation and the proceeds thereof distributed to the holder of the scrip or warrants or any other condition that the board may impose.

Ca. Corp. Code § 407

Amended by Stats 2002 ch 480 (SB 399),s 2, eff. 1/1/2003.

Section 408 - Stock purchase plan or agreement or stock option plan or

agreement

(a) A corporation may adopt and carry out a stock purchase plan or agreement or stock option plan or agreement providing for the issue and sale for such consideration as may be fixed of its unissued shares, or of issued shares acquired or to be acquired, to one or more of the employees or directors of the corporation or of a subsidiary or parent thereof or to a trustee on their behalf and for the payment for such shares in installments or at one time, and may provide for aiding any such persons in paying for such shares by compensation for services rendered, promissory notes or otherwise.

(b) A stock purchase plan or agreement or stock option plan or agreement may include, among other features, the fixing of eligibility for participation therein, the class and price of shares to be issued or sold under the plan or agreement, the number of shares which may be subscribed for, the method of payment therefor, the reservation of title until full payment therefor, the effect of the termination of employment, an option or obligation on the part of the corporation to repurchase the shares upon termination of employment, subject to the provisions of Chapter 5, restrictions upon transfer of the shares and the time limits of and termination of the plan.

(c) Sections 406 and 407 of the Labor Code shall not apply to shares issued by any foreign or domestic corporation to the following persons:

(1) Any employee of the corporation or of any parent or subsidiary thereof, pursuant to a stock purchase plan or agreement or stock option plan or agreement provided for in subdivision (a).

(2) In any transaction in connection with securing employment, to a person who is or is about to become an officer of the corporation or of any parent or subsidiary thereof.

Ca. Corp. Code § 408
Amended by Stats. 1982, Ch. 266, Sec. 1.

Section 409 - Issuance of shares

(a) Shares may be issued:

(1) For such consideration as is determined from time to time by the board, or by the shareholders if the articles so provide, consisting of any or all of the following: money paid; labor done; services actually rendered to the corporation or for its benefit or in its formation or reorganization; debts or securities canceled; and tangible or intangible property actually received either by the issuing corporation or by a wholly owned subsidiary; but neither promissory notes of the purchaser (unless adequately secured by collateral other than the shares acquired or unless permitted by Section 408) nor future services shall constitute payment or part payment for shares of the corporation; or

(2) As a share dividend or upon a stock split, reverse stock split, reclassification of outstanding shares into shares of another class, conversion of outstanding shares into shares of another class, exchange of outstanding shares for shares of another class or other change affecting outstanding shares.

(b) Except as provided in subdivision (d), shares issued as provided in this section or Section 408 shall be declared and taken to be fully paid stock and not liable to any further call nor shall the holder thereof be liable for any further payments under the provisions of this division. In the absence of fraud in the transaction, the judgment of the directors as to the value of the consideration for shares shall be conclusive.

(c) If the articles reserve to the shareholders the right to determine the consideration for the issue of any shares, such determination shall be made by approval of the outstanding shares (Section 152).

(d) A corporation may issue the whole or any part of its shares as partly paid and subject to call for the remainder of the consideration to be paid therefor. On the certificate issued to represent any such partly paid shares or, for uncertificated securities, on the initial transaction statement for such partly paid shares, the total amount of the consideration to be paid therefor and the amount paid thereon shall be stated. Upon the declaration of any dividend on fully paid shares, the corporation shall declare a dividend upon partly paid shares of the same class, but only upon the basis of the percentage of the consideration actually paid thereon.

(e) The board shall state by resolution its determination of the fair value to the corporation in monetary terms of any consideration other than money for which shares are issued. This subdivision does not affect the accounting treatment of any transaction, which shall be in conformity with generally accepted accounting principles.

Ca. Corp. Code § 409
Amended by Stats. 1986, Ch. 766, Sec. 13.

Section 410 - Liability for consideration for shares

(a) Every subscriber to shares and every person to whom shares are originally issued is liable to the corporation for the full consideration agreed to be paid for the shares.

(b) The full agreed consideration for shares shall be paid prior to or concurrently with the issuance thereof, unless the shares are issued as partly paid pursuant to subdivision (d) of Section 409, in which case the consideration shall be paid in accordance with the agreement of subscription or purchase.

Ca. Corp. Code § 410
Added by Stats. 1975, Ch. 682.

Section 411 - Liability of transferee of shares for unpaid consideration

A transferee of shares for which the full agreed consideration has not been paid to the issuing corporation, who acquired them in good faith, without knowledge that they were not paid in full or to the extent stated on the certificate representing them or, in the case of uncertificated securities, on the applicable initial transaction statement, is liable only for the amount shown by the certificate or statement to be unpaid on the shares represented thereby, until the transferee transfers the shares to one who becomes liable therefor; provided that the transferor shall remain personally liable if so provided on the certificate or statement or agreed upon in writing. The liability of any holder of such shares who derives title through such a transferee and who is not a party to any fraud affecting the issue of the shares is the same as that of the transferee through whom title is derived.

Ca. Corp. Code § 411
Amended by Stats. 1986, Ch. 766, Sec. 14.

Section 412 - Holder in good faith

Every transferee of partly paid shares who acquired them under a certificate or initial transaction statement showing the fact of part payment, and every transferee of such shares (other than a transferee who derives title through a holder in good faith without knowledge and who is not a party to any fraud affecting the issue of such shares) who acquired them with actual knowledge that the full agreed consideration had not been paid to the extent stated on the certificate or initial transaction statement, is personally liable to the corporation for installments of the amount unpaid becoming due until the shares are transferred to one who becomes liable therefor; provided that the transferor shall remain personally liable if so provided on the certificate, initial transaction statement, or written statement, or agreed upon in writing.

Ca. Corp. Code § 412
Amended by Stats. 1986, Ch. 766, Sec. 15.

Section 413 - Liability of person holding shares in representative or fiduciary capacity

A person holding shares as pledgee, executor, administrator, guardian, conservator, trustee, receiver or in any representative or fiduciary capacity is not personally liable for any unpaid balance of the subscription price of the shares because the shares are so held but the estate and funds in the hands of such fiduciary or representative are liable and the shares are subject to sale therefor.

Ca. Corp. Code § 413
Amended by Stats. 1979, Ch. 730.

Section 414 - Action by creditor

(a) No action shall be brought by or on behalf of any creditor to reach and apply the liability, if any, of a shareholder to the corporation to pay the amount due on such shareholder's shares unless final judgment has been rendered in favor of the creditor against the corporation and execution has been returned unsatisfied in whole or in part or unless such proceedings would be useless.

(b) All creditors of the corporation, with or without reducing their claims to judgment, may intervene in any such creditor's action to reach and apply unpaid subscriptions and any or all shareholders who hold partly paid shares may be joined in such action. Several judgments may be rendered for and against the parties to the action or in favor of a receiver for the benefit of the respective parties thereto.

(c) All amounts paid by any shareholder in any such action shall be credited on the unpaid balance due the corporation upon such shareholder's shares.

Ca. Corp. Code § 414
Added by Stats. 1975, Ch. 682.

Section 415 - No derogation of rights or remedies of creditor or shareholder

Nothing in this division shall be construed as a derogation of any rights or remedies which any creditor or shareholder may have against any promoter, shareholder, director, officer or the corporation because of participation in any fraud or illegality practiced upon such creditor or shareholder by any such person or by the corporation in connection with the issue or sale of shares or other securities or in derogation of any rights which the corporation may have by rescission, cancellation or otherwise because of any fraud or illegality practiced on it by any such person in connection with the issue or sale of shares or other securities.

Ca. Corp. Code § 415
Added by Stats. 1975, Ch. 682.

Section 416 - Certificates; system of issuance, recordation, and transfer of shares by electronic means

(a) Every holder of shares in a corporation shall be entitled to have a certificate signed in the name of the corporation by the chairperson or vice chairperson of the board or the president or a vice president and by the chief financial officer or an assistant treasurer or the secretary or any assistant secretary, certifying the number of shares and the class or series of shares owned by the shareholder. Any or all of the signatures on the certificate may be facsimile. In case any officer, transfer agent or registrar who has signed or whose facsimile signature has been placed upon a certificate has ceased to be such officer, transfer agent or registrar before such certificate is issued, it may be issued by the corporation with the same effect as if such person were an officer, transfer agent or registrar at the date of issue.

(b) Notwithstanding subdivision (a), a corporation may adopt a system of issuance, recordation and transfer of its shares by electronic or other means not involving any issuance of certificates, including provisions for notice to purchasers in substitution for the required statements on certificates under Sections 417, 418, and 1302, and as may be required by the commissioner in administering the Corporate Securities Law of 1968, which system (1) has been approved by the United States Securities and Exchange Commission, (2) is authorized in any statute of the United States, or (3) is in accordance with Division 8 (commencing with Section 8101) of the Commercial Code. Any system so adopted shall not become effective as to issued and outstanding certificated securities until the certificates therefor have been surrendered to the corporation.

Ca. Corp. Code § 416
Amended by Stats 2015 ch 98 (SB 351),s 7, eff. 1/1/2016.

Section 417 - Certificates for classified shares

If the shares of the corporation are classified or if any class of shares has two or more series, there shall appear on the certificate or, in the case of uncertificated securities, the initial transaction statement and written statements, one of the following:

(a) A statement of the rights, preferences, privileges and restrictions granted to or imposed upon each class or series of shares authorized to be issued and upon the holders thereof.

(b) A summary of such rights, preferences, privileges and restrictions with reference to the provisions of the articles and any certificates of determination establishing the same.

(c) A statement setting forth the office or agency of the corporation from which shareholders may obtain, upon request and without charge, a copy of the statement referred to in subdivision (a).

Ca. Corp. Code § 417
Amended by Stats. 1986, Ch. 766, Sec. 17.

Section 418 - Required statements on certificate

(a) There shall also appear on the certificate, the initial transaction statement, and written statements (unless stated or summarized under subdivision (a) or (b) of Section 417) the statements required by all of the following clauses to the extent applicable:

(1) The fact that the shares are subject to restrictions upon transfer.

(2) If the shares are assessable or are not fully paid, a statement that they are assessable or the statements required by subdivision (d) of Section 409 if they are not fully paid.

(3) The fact that the shares are subject to a voting agreement under subdivision (a) of Section 706 or an irrevocable proxy under subdivision (e) of Section 705 or restrictions upon voting rights contractually imposed by the corporation.

(4) The fact that the shares are redeemable.

(5) The fact that the shares are convertible and the period for conversion. Any such statement or reference thereto (Section 174) on the face of the certificate, the initial transaction statement, and written statements required by paragraph (1) or (2) shall be conspicuous.

(b) Unless stated on the certificate, the initial transaction statement, and written statements as required by subdivision (a), no restriction upon transfer, no right of redemption and no voting agreement under subdivision (a) of Section 706, no irrevocable proxy under subdivision (e) of Section 705, and no voting restriction imposed by the corporation shall be enforceable against a transferee of the shares without actual knowledge of such restriction, right, agreement or proxy. With regard only to liability to assessment or for the unpaid portion of the subscription price, unless stated on the certificate as required by subdivision (a), that liability shall not be enforceable against a transferee of the shares. For the purpose of this subdivision, "transferee" includes a purchaser from the corporation.

(c) All certificates representing shares of a close corporation shall contain in addition to any other statements required by this section, the following conspicuous legend on the face thereof: "This corporation is a close corporation. The number of holders of record of its shares of all classes cannot exceed _____ [a number not in excess of 35]. Any attempted voluntary inter vivos transfer which would violate this requirement is void. Refer to the articles, bylaws and any agreements on file with the secretary of the corporation for further restrictions."

(d) Any attempted voluntary inter vivos transfer of the shares of a close corporation which would result in the number of holders of record of its shares exceeding the maximum number specified in its articles is void if the certificate contains the legend required by subdivision (c).

Ca. Corp. Code § 418
Amended by Stats. 1986, Ch. 766, Sec. 18.

Section 419 - Issuance of new certificate for lost, stolen, or destroyed certificate

(a) A domestic or foreign corporation may issue a new share certificate or a new certificate for any other security in the place of any certificate theretofore issued by it, alleged to have been lost, stolen or destroyed, and the corporation may require the owner of the lost, stolen or destroyed certificate or the owner's legal representative to give the corporation a bond (or other adequate security) sufficient to indemnify it against any claim that may be made against it (including any expense or liability) on account of the alleged loss, theft or destruction of any such certificate or the issuance of such new certificate.

(b) If a corporation refuses to issue a new share certificate or other certificate in place of one theretofore issued by it, or by any corporation of which it is the lawful successor, alleged to have been lost, stolen or destroyed, the owner of the lost, stolen or destroyed certificate or the owner's legal representative may bring an action in the superior court of the proper county for an order requiring the corporation to issue a new certificate in place of the one lost, stolen or destroyed.

(c) If the court is satisfied that the plaintiff is the lawful owner of the number of shares or other securities, or any part thereof, described in the complaint and that the certificate therefor has been lost, stolen or destroyed, and no sufficient cause has been shown why a new certificate should not be issued in place thereof, it shall make an order requiring the corporation to issue and deliver to the plaintiff a new certificate for such shares or other securities. In its order the court shall direct that, prior to the issuance and delivery to the plaintiff of such new certificate, the plaintiff give the corporation a bond (or other adequate security) as to the court appears sufficient to indemnify the corporation against any claim that may be made against it (including any expense or liability) on account of the alleged loss, theft or destruction of any such certificate or the issuance of such new certificate.

Ca. Corp. Code § 419
Added by Stats. 1975, Ch. 682.

Section 420 - Liability of transfer agent or registrar

Neither a domestic nor foreign corporation nor its transfer agent or registrar is liable:
(a) For transferring or causing to be transferred on the books of the corporation to the surviving joint tenant or tenants any share or shares or other securities issued to two or more persons in joint tenancy, whether or not the transfer is made with actual or constructive knowledge of the existence of any understanding, agreement, condition or evidence that the shares or securities were held other than in joint tenancy or of a breach of trust by any joint tenant.

(b) To a minor or incompetent person in whose name shares or other securities are of record on its books or to any transferee of or transferor to either for transferring the shares or other securities on its books at the instance of or to the minor or incompetent or for the recognition of or dealing with the minor or incompetent as a shareholder or security holder, whether or not the corporation, transfer agent or registrar had notice, actual or constructive, of the nonage or incompetency, unless a guardian or conservator of the property of the minor or incompetent has been appointed and the corporation, transfer agent or registrar has received written notice thereof.

(c) To any married person or to any transferee of such person for transferring shares or other securities on its books at the instance of the person in whose name they are registered, without the signature of such person's spouse and regardless of whether the registration indicates that the shares or other securities are community property, in the same manner as if such person were unmarried.

(d) For transferring or causing to be transferred on the books of the corporation shares or other securities pursuant to a judgment or order of a court which has been set aside, modified or reversed unless, prior to the registration of the transfer on the books of the corporation, written notice is served upon the corporation or its transfer agent in the manner provided by law for the service of a summons in a civil action, stating that an appeal or other further court proceeding has been or is to be taken from or with regard to such judgment or order. After the service of such notice neither the corporation nor its transfer agent has any duty to register the requested transfer until the corporation or its transfer agent has received a certificate of the clerk of the court in which the judgment or order was entered or made, showing that the judgment or order has become final.

(e) The Commercial Code shall not affect the limitations of liability set forth in this section. Section 1100 of the Family Code shall be subject to the provisions of this section and shall not be construed to prevent transfers, or result in liability to the corporation, transfer agent or registrar permitting or effecting transfers, which comply with this section.

Ca. Corp. Code § 420

Amended by Stats 2002 ch 784 (SB 1316),s 89, eff. 1/1/2003.

Section 421 - Effect of acceptance of certificates with legend regarding close corporation

Each holder of shares of a close corporation, whether original or subsequent, by accepting the certificates for the shares which contain the legend required by subdivision (c) of Section 418 agrees and consents that such holder cannot make any transfer of shares which would violate the provisions of subdivision (d) of Section 418 and waives any right which such holder might otherwise have under any other law to sell such shares to a greater number of purchasers or to demand any registration thereof under the Securities Act of 1933, as now or hereafter amended, or as provided in any statute adopted in substitution therefor, or otherwise, so long as the corporation is a close corporation.

Ca. Corp. Code § 421

Added by Stats. 1975, Ch. 682.

Section 422 - Surrender and exchange of certificates for new certificates

(a) When the articles are amended in any way affecting the statements contained in the certificates for outstanding shares, or it becomes desirable for any reason, in the discretion of the board, to cancel any outstanding certificate for shares and issue a new certificate therefor conforming to the rights of the holder, the board may order any holders of outstanding certificates for shares to surrender and exchange them for new certificates within a reasonable time to be fixed by the board.

(b) The order may provide that a holder of any certificates so ordered to be surrendered is not entitled to vote or to receive dividends or exercise any of the other rights of shareholders until the holder has complied with the order, but such order operates to suspend such rights only after notice and until compliance. The duty of surrender of any outstanding certificates may also be enforced by civil action.

(c) When the articles are amended in any way affecting the statements contained in the initial transaction statement or other written statements for outstanding uncertificated securities, or it becomes desirable for any reason, in the discretion of the board, to amend, revise, or supersede outstanding initial transaction statements or written statements, the board may order the issuance and delivery to holders of record of amended, revised, or superseding initial transaction statements or written statements.

Ca. Corp. Code § 422

Amended by Stats. 1986, Ch. 766, Sec. 19.

Section 423 - Assessment

(a) Shares are not assessable except as provided in this section or as otherwise provided by a statute other than this division. If the articles expressly confer such authority upon the corporation or the board, and subject to any limitations therein contained, the board may in its discretion levy and collect assessments upon all shares of any or all classes made subject to assessment by the articles. This authority is in addition to the right of the corporation to recover the unpaid subscription price of shares or the remainder of the consideration to be paid therefor.

(b) Every levy of an assessment shall: specify the amount thereof and to whom and where it is payable; fix, or if proceedings or filings with any governmental or other agency for any qualification, permit, registration or exemption therefrom are required as a condition precedent to the levy or payment of an assessment provide for the establishment of, a date on which the assessment is payable; fix a date, not less than 30 nor more than 60 days from the date on which the assessment is payable, on which such assessment becomes delinquent if not paid; and fix a date, not less than 15 nor more than 60 days from the date on which the unpaid assessment becomes delinquent, for the sale of delinquent shares. The levy also shall fix the hour and place of sale, which place shall be in the county where the corporation is required to keep a copy of its bylaws pursuant to Section 213, or if there is no such county, in Sacramento.

(c) On or before the date an assessment is payable, the secretary of the corporation shall give notice thereof in substantially the following form: (Name of corporation in full. Location of principal office.)

Notice is hereby given that the board of directors on (date) has levied an assessment of (amount) per share upon the (name or designation of class or series of shares) of the corporation payable (to whom and where). Any shares upon which this assessment remains unpaid on (date fixed) will be delinquent. Unless payment is made before delinquency, the said shares, or as many of them as may be necessary, will be sold at (particular place) on (date) at (hour) of such date, to pay the delinquent assessment, together with a penalty of 5 percent of the amount of the assessment on such shares, or be forfeited to the corporation. (Name of secretary with location of office.)

(d) The notice shall be served personally upon each holder of record of shares assessed; provided, however, that in lieu of personal service the notice may be mailed to each such shareholder addressed to the last address of the shareholder appearing on the books of the corporation or given by the shareholder to the corporation for the purpose of notice, or if no such address appears or is given, at the place where the principal office of the corporation is located, and published once in some newspaper of general circulation in the county in which the principal office of the corporation is located. If there is no such newspaper in such county, the publication shall be made in some newspaper of general circulation in an adjoining county.

(e) The assessment is a lien upon the shares assessed from the time of personal service or the publication of the notice of assessment, unless the articles provide for such lien from the time of the levy. Unless otherwise provided by law, a transfer of the shares on the books of the corporation after the lien of an assessment has attached is a waiver of the lien unless a conspicuous legend is placed on the face of any certificate issued upon such transfer or, in the case of uncertificated securities, on the initial transaction statement, setting forth the information contained in the notice required by subdivision (c). Such legend shall be removed if the assessment on the shares evidenced by the certificate is paid or if the shares are sold to pay the assessment or forfeited for nonpayment.

(f) The date of sale of delinquent shares fixed in any levy of an assessment may be extended from time to time for not more than 30 days at a time by order of the board entered on the records of the corporation, or when the sale is restrained by order of a court. Notice of such extension shall be given by announcement by the secretary, or other person authorized to conduct the sale, made at the time and place of sale last theretofore fixed. If a date of sale of delinquent shares is extended for more than five days the corporation shall cause a notice to be mailed to the shareholder or shareholders whose shares are to be the subject of such sale setting forth the date and time to which the date of sale has been extended.

(g) If payment is made after delinquency and before the sale, the shareholder shall pay a penalty of 5 percent of the amount of the assessment on the shares in addition to the assessment.

(h) At the place and time appointed in the notice of levy any officer or an agent of the corporation, shall, unless otherwise ordered by the board, sell or cause to be sold to the highest bidder for cash as many shares of each delinquent holder of the assessed shares as may be necessary to pay the assessment and charges thereon according to the notice. The person offering at the sale to pay the assessment and penalty for the smallest number of shares is the highest bidder. The shares purchased shall be transferred to the highest bidder on the share register of the corporation on the payment of the assessment and penalty and a new certificate or initial transaction statement therefor issued to such highest bidder.

A corporation is not required to accept an offer for a fraction of a share.

(i) If no bidder offers to pay the amount due on the shares, together with the penalty of 5 percent thereof, the shares shall be forfeited to the corporation in satisfaction of the assessment and penalty thereon.

(j) After a sale or forfeiture of shares for nonpayment of an assessment, the holder or owner of delinquent shares shall, if they are certificated securities, surrender the certificate for such shares to the corporation for cancellation or, if they are uncertificated securities, have no further rights with respect to such shares. This duty may be enforced by order or decree of court and such holder or owner shall be liable for damages to the corporation for failure to surrender the certificate for cancellation upon demand without good cause or excuse. Any certificate not so surrendered forthwith becomes null and void and ceases to be evidence of the right or title of the holder or any transferee to the shares purporting to be represented thereby, and neither the corporation nor the purchaser of such shares incurs any liability thereon to any such transferee.

The purchaser of any shares, at a sale for delinquent assessments thereon, whenever made, is entitled to the issue of a new certificate representing the shares so purchased.

(k) The certificate of the secretary or assistant secretary of the corporation is prima facie evidence of the time and place of sale and any postponement thereof, of the quantity and particular description of the shares sold, to whom, for what price, and of the fact of payment of the purchase money. The certificate shall be filed in the office of the corporation, and copies of the certificate, certified by the secretary or an assistant secretary of the corporation, are prima facie evidence of the facts therein stated.

(l) An assessment is not invalidated by a failure to publish the notice of assessment, nor by the nonperformance of any act required in order to enforce the payment of the assessment; but in case of any substantial error or omission in the course of proceedings for collection of an assessment on any shares, all previous proceedings, except the levy of the assessment, are void as to such shares, and shall be taken anew.

(m) No action shall be maintained to recover shares sold for delinquent assessments, upon the ground of irregularity in the assessment, irregularity or defect of the notice of sale, or defect or irregularity in the sale, unless the party seeking to maintain the action first pays or tenders to the corporation, or the party holding the shares sold, the sum for which the shares were sold, together with all subsequent assessments which may have been paid thereon and interest on such sums from the time they were paid. No such action shall be maintained unless it is commenced by the filing of a complaint and the issuing of a summons thereon within six months after the sale was made.

(n) The only remedy for the collection of an assessment on fully paid shares is sale or forfeiture of the shares unless (1) remedy by action is expressly authorized in the original articles or by an amendment of the articles adopted before August 21, 1933, or by an amendment adopted on or after August 21, 1933, by unanimous consent of the shareholders, and (2) unless a statement of such remedy appears on the face of any share certificate issued on or after August 21, 1933.

Ca. Corp. Code § 423

Amended by Stats 2022 ch 617 (SB 1202),s 12, eff. 1/1/2023.
Amended by Stats. 1986, Ch. 766, Sec. 20.

Chapter 5 - DIVIDENDS AND REACQUISITIONS OF SHARES

Section 500 - Distribution

(a) Neither a corporation nor any of its subsidiaries shall make any distribution to the corporation's shareholders (Section 166) unless the board of directors has determined in good faith either of the following:

(1)The amount of retained earnings of the corporation immediately prior to the distribution equals or exceeds the sum of (A) the amount of the proposed distribution plus (B) the preferential dividends arrears amount.

(2)Immediately after the distribution, the value of the corporation's assets would equal or exceed the sum of its total liabilities plus the preferential rights amount.
(b)For the purpose of applying paragraph (1) of subdivision (a) to a distribution by a corporation, "preferential dividends arrears amount" means the amount, if any, of cumulative dividends in arrears on all shares having a preference with respect to payment of dividends over the class or series to which the applicable distribution is being made, provided that if the articles of incorporation provide that a distribution can be made without regard to preferential dividends arrears amount, then the preferential dividends arrears amount shall be zero. For the purpose of applying paragraph (2) of subdivision (a) to a distribution by a corporation, "preferential rights amount" means the amount that would be needed if the corporation were to be dissolved at the time of the distribution to satisfy the preferential rights, including accrued but unpaid dividends, of other shareholders upon dissolution that are superior to the rights of the shareholders receiving the distribution, provided that if the articles of incorporation provide that a distribution can be made without regard to any preferential rights, then the preferential rights amount shall be zero. In the case of a distribution of cash or property in payment by the corporation in connection with the purchase of its shares, (1) there shall be added to retained earnings all amounts that had been previously deducted therefrom with respect to obligations incurred in connection with the corporation's repurchase of its shares and reflected on the corporation's balance sheet, but not in excess of the principal of the obligations that remain unpaid immediately prior to the distribution and (2) there shall be deducted from liabilities all amounts that had been previously added thereto with respect to the obligations incurred in connection with the corporation's repurchase of its shares and reflected on the corporation's balance sheet, but not in excess of the principal of the obligations that will remain unpaid after the distribution, provided that no addition to retained earnings or deduction from liabilities under this subdivision shall occur on account of any obligation that is a distribution to the corporation's shareholders (Section 166) at the time the obligation is incurred.
(c)The board of directors may base a determination that a distribution is not prohibited under subdivision (a) or under Section 501 on any of the following:

(1)Financial statements prepared on the basis of accounting practices and principles that are reasonable under the circumstances.

(2)A fair valuation.

(3) Any other method that is reasonable under the circumstances.

(d) The effect of a distribution under paragraph (1) or (2) of subdivision (a) is measured as of the date the distribution is authorized if the payment occurs within 120 days after the date of authorization.

(e)

(1) If terms of indebtedness provide that payment of principal and interest is to be made only if, and to the extent that, payment of a distribution to shareholders could then be made under this section, indebtedness of a corporation, including indebtedness issued as a distribution, is not a liability for purposes of determinations made under paragraph (2) of subdivision (a).

(2) If indebtedness is issued as a distribution, each payment of principal or interest on the indebtedness shall be treated as a distribution, the effect of which is measured on the date the payment of the indebtedness is actually made.

(f) This section does not apply to a corporation licensed as a broker-dealer under Chapter 2 (commencing with Section 25210) of Part 3 of Division 1 of Title 4, if immediately after giving effect to any distribution the corporation is in compliance with the net capital rules of the Commissioner of Financial Protection and Innovation and the Securities and Exchange Commission.

Ca. Corp. Code § 500
Amended by Stats 2022 ch 452 (SB 1498),s 45, eff. 1/1/2023.
Amended by Stats 2019 ch 143 (SB 251),s 22, eff. 1/1/2020.
Amended by Stats 2012 ch 162 (SB 1171),s 18, eff. 1/1/2013.
Amended by Stats 2011 ch 203 (AB 571),s 2, eff. 1/1/2012.

Section 501 - Prohibited distribution

Neither a corporation nor any of its subsidiaries shall make any distribution to the corporation's shareholders (Section 166) if the corporation or the subsidiary making the distribution is, or as a result thereof would be, likely to be unable to meet its liabilities (except those whose payment is otherwise adequately provided for) as they mature.

Ca. Corp. Code § 501
Repealed and added by Stats. 1975, Ch. 682.

Section 502 - [Repealed]

Ca. Corp. Code § 502
Repealed by Stats 2011 ch 203 (AB 571),s 3, eff. 1/1/2012.

Section 503 - Inapplicability to purchase or redemption of shares of deceased or disabled shareholder

(a) The provisions of Sections 500 and 501 shall not apply to a purchase or redemption of shares of a deceased shareholder from the proceeds of insurance on the life of that shareholder in excess of the total amount of all premiums paid by the corporation for that insurance, in order to carry out the provisions of an agreement between the corporation and that shareholder to purchase or redeem those shares upon the death of the shareholder.

(b) The provisions of Sections 500 and 501 shall not apply to the purchase or redemption of shares of a disabled shareholder from the proceeds of disability insurance applicable to the disabled shareholder in excess of the total amount of all premiums paid by the corporation for the insurance, in order to carry out the provisions of an agreement between the corporation and the shareholder to purchase or redeem shares upon the disability of the shareholder as defined within that policy. For the purposes of this subdivision, "disability insurance" means an agreement of indemnification against the insured's loss of the ability to work due to accident or illness.

Ca. Corp. Code § 503
Added by Stats 2011 ch 203 (AB 571),s 5, eff. 1/1/2012.

Section 503.1 - [Repealed]

Ca. Corp. Code § 503.1
Repealed by Stats 2011 ch 203 (AB 571),s 6, eff. 1/1/2012.

Section 503.2 - [Repealed]

Ca. Corp. Code § 503.2
Repealed by Stats 2011 ch 203 (AB 571),s 7, eff. 1/1/2012.

Section 504 - Applicability to regulated investment company, real estate investment company, or registered open-end investment company

(a) The provisions of Section 500 do not apply to a dividend declared by either of the following:

(1) A regulated investment company, as defined in the federal Internal Revenue Code, as amended, to the extent that the dividend is necessary to maintain the status of the corporation as a regulated investment company under the provisions of that code.

(2) A real estate investment trust, as defined in Part II of Subchapter M of Chapter 1 of Subtitle A of the federal Internal Revenue Code, as amended, to the extent that the dividend is necessary to maintain the status of the corporation as a real estate investment trust under the provisions of that code.

(b) The provisions of this chapter do not apply to any purchase or redemption of shares redeemable at the option of the holder by a registered open-end investment company under the United States Investment Company Act of 1940, so long as the right of redemption remains unsuspended under the provisions of that statute and the articles and bylaws of the corporation.

Ca. Corp. Code § 504

Amended by Stats 2000 ch 112 (SB 1517), s 1, eff. 1/1/2001.

Section 505 - Additional restrictions not prohibited

Nothing in this chapter prohibits additional restrictions upon the declaration of dividends or the purchase or redemption of a corporation's own shares by provision in the articles or bylaws or in any indenture or other agreement entered into by the corporation.

Ca. Corp. Code § 505

Added by Stats. 1975, Ch. 682.

Section 506 - Liability of shareholder receiving prohibited distribution

(a) Any shareholder who receives any distribution prohibited by this chapter with knowledge of facts indicating the impropriety thereof is liable to the corporation for the benefit of all of the creditors or shareholders entitled to institute an action under subdivision (b) for the amount so received by the shareholder with interest thereon at the legal rate on judgments until paid, but not exceeding the liabilities of the corporation owed to nonconsenting creditors at the time of the violation and the injury suffered by nonconsenting shareholders, as the case may be. For purposes of determining the value of any noncash property received in a distribution described in the preceding sentence, the shareholder receiving that illegal distribution shall be liable to the corporation for an amount equal to the fair market value of the property at the time of the illegal distribution plus interest thereon from the date of the distribution at the legal rate on judgments until paid, together with all reasonably incurred costs of appraisal or other valuation, if any, of that property, but not exceeding the liabilities of the corporation owed to nonconsenting creditors at the time of the violation and the injury suffered by nonconsenting shareholders, as the case may be.

(b) Suit may be brought in the name of the corporation to enforce the liability (1) to creditors arising under subdivision (a) for a violation of Section 500 or 501 against any or all shareholders liable by any one or more creditors of the corporation whose debts or claims arose prior to the time of the distribution to shareholders and who have not consented thereto, whether or not they have reduced their claims to judgment, or (2) to shareholders arising under subdivision (a) for a violation of Section 500 against any or all shareholders liable by one or more holders of shares having preferential rights with respect to cumulative dividends in arrears, in the case of a violation of paragraph (1) of subdivision (a) of Section 500, or upon dissolution, in the case of a violation of paragraph (2) of subdivision (a) of Section 500, in each case who have not consented to the applicable distribution, without regard to the provisions in Section 800, and in each case to the extent the applicable shares with preferential rights were outstanding at the time of the distribution; provided that holders of shares of preferential rights shall not have the right to bring suit in the name of the corporation under this subdivision unless the preferential dividends arrears amount, in the case of a violation of paragraph (1) of subdivision (a) of Section 500, or the preferential rights amount, in the case of a violation of paragraph (2) of subdivision (a) of Section 500, was greater than zero. A cause of action with respect to an obligation to return a distribution pursuant to this section shall be extinguished unless the action is brought within four years after the date the distribution is made.

(c) Any shareholder sued under this section may implead all other shareholders liable under this section and may compel contribution, either in that action or in an independent action against shareholders not joined in that action.

(d) Nothing contained in this section affects any liability which any shareholder may have under Chapter 1 (commencing with Section 3439) of Title 2 of Part 2 of Division 4 of the Civil Code.

Ca. Corp. Code § 506
Amended by Stats 2011 ch 203 (AB 571),s 8, eff. 1/1/2012.

Section 507 - [Repealed]

Ca. Corp. Code § 507
Repealed by Stats 2011 ch 203 (AB 571),s 9, eff. 1/1/2012.

Section 508 - Inapplicability of chapter

This chapter does not apply in connection with any proceeding for winding up and dissolution under Chapter 18 or 19.

Ca. Corp. Code § 508
Added by Stats. 1975, Ch. 682.

Section 509 - Redemption of shares

(a)A corporation may redeem any or all shares which are redeemable at its option by (1) giving notice of redemption as provided in subdivisions (b) and (c) or as otherwise provided in its articles of incorporation, and (2) payment or deposit of the redemption price of the shares as provided in its articles or deposit of the redemption price pursuant to subdivision (d).

(b) Subject to any provisions in the articles with respect to the notice required for redemption of shares, the corporation may give notice of the redemption of any or all shares subject to redemption by causing a notice of redemption to be published in a newspaper of general circulation in the county in which the principal office of the corporation is located at least once a week for two successive weeks, in each instance on any day of the week, commencing not earlier than 60 nor later than 20 days before the date fixed for redemption. The notice of redemption shall set forth all of the following:

(1)The class or series of shares or part of any class or series of shares to be redeemed.

(2)The date fixed for redemption.

(3)The redemption price.

(4)If the shares are certificated securities, the place at which the shareholders may obtain payment of the redemption price upon surrender of their share certificates.
(c)If the corporation gives notice of redemption pursuant to subdivision (b), it shall also mail a copy of the notice of redemption to each holder of record of shares to be redeemed as of the date of mailing or record date fixed in accordance with Section 701, addressed to the holder at the address of such holder appearing on the books of the corporation or given by the holder to the corporation for the purpose of notice, or if no such address appears or is given at the place where the principal office of the corporation is located, not earlier than 60 nor later than 20 days before the date fixed for redemption. Failure to comply with this subdivision does not invalidate the redemption of the shares.
(d)If, on or before any date fixed for redemption of redeemable shares, the corporation deposits with any bank or trust company in this state as a trust fund, (1) a sum sufficient to redeem, on the date fixed for redemption thereof, the shares called for redemption, (2) in the case of the redemption of any uncertificated securities, an officer's certificate setting forth the holders thereof registered on the books of the corporation and the number of shares held by each, and (3) irrevocable instructions and authority to the bank or trust company to publish the notice of redemption thereof (or to complete publication if theretofore commenced) and to pay, on and after the date fixed for redemption or prior thereto, the redemption price of the shares to their respective holders upon the surrender of their share certificates, in the case of certificated securities, or the delivery of the officer's certificate in the case of uncertificated securities, then from and after the date of the deposit (although before the date fixed for redemption) the shares called shall be redeemed and the dividends on those shares shall cease to accrue after the date fixed for redemption. The deposit shall constitute full payment of the shares to their holders and from and after the date of the deposit the shares shall no longer be outstanding and the holders thereof shall cease to be shareholders with respect to the shares and shall have no rights with respect thereto except the right to receive from the bank or trust company payment of the redemption price of the shares without interest, upon surrender of their certificates therefor, in the case of certificated securities, and any right to convert the shares which may exist and then continue for any period fixed by its terms. In determining the holders of uncertificated securities, the bank or trust company shall

be entitled to rely on any officer's certificate deposited with it in accordance with this subdivision.

Ca. Corp. Code § 509

Amended by Stats 2022 ch 617 (SB 1202),s 13, eff. 1/1/2023.

Amended by Stats 2011 ch 203 (AB 571),s 10, eff. 1/1/2012.

Section 510 - Reacquisition of shares

(a) When a corporation reacquires its own shares, those shares are restored to the status of authorized but unissued shares, unless the articles prohibit the reissuance thereof.

(b) When a corporation reacquires authorized shares of a class or series and the articles prohibit the reissuance of those shares:

(1) If all of the authorized shares of that class or series, as the case may be, are reacquired, then (A) that class or series is automatically eliminated, (B) in the case of reacquisition of all of the authorized shares of a series, the authorized number of shares of the class to which the shares belonged is reduced by the number of shares so reacquired, and (C) the articles shall be amended to eliminate any statement of rights, preferences, privileges, and restrictions relating solely to that class or series.

(2) If less than all of the authorized shares but all of the issued and outstanding shares of that class or series, as the case may be, are reacquired, the authorized number of shares of the class or series is automatically reduced by the number of shares so reacquired, and the board shall determine either (A) to eliminate that class or series, whereupon the articles shall be amended to eliminate any statement of rights, preferences, privileges, and restrictions relating solely to that class or series, or (B) not to eliminate that class or series, whereupon the articles shall be amended to reflect that reduction of the number of authorized shares of that class or series by the shares so reacquired.

(3) If less than all of the authorized shares and less than all of the issued and outstanding shares of a class or series, as the case may be, are reacquired, the authorized number of shares of that class or series shall be automatically reduced by the number of shares reacquired, and the articles shall be amended to reflect that reduction.

(c) When a corporation reacquires authorized shares of a series of shares and the articles only prohibit the reissuance of those shares as shares of the same series:

(1) If all of the authorized shares of that series are reacquired, then that series is automatically eliminated, the articles shall be amended to eliminate any statement of rights, preferences, privileges, and restrictions relating solely to that series, and the board shall determine either (A) to return those shares to the status of authorized but undesignated shares of the class to which they belong or (B) to eliminate those shares entirely, whereupon the articles in either case shall be amended to reflect the reduction in the authorized shares of that series and the effect, if any, on the class to which that series belongs.

(2) If all of the issued and outstanding shares of that series (but less than all of the authorized shares of that series) are reacquired, the board shall determine either (A) to eliminate that series, whereupon the articles shall be amended to eliminate any statement of rights, preferences, privileges, and restrictions relating solely to that series, or (B) not to eliminate that series, whereupon the articles shall be amended to reflect the return of the reacquired shares to the status of authorized but undesignated shares of the class to which they belong.

(3) If less than all of the issued and outstanding shares of that series are reacquired, the authorized number of shares of that series shall be automatically reduced by the number of shares reacquired, and the board shall determine either (A) to return those shares to the status of authorized but undesignated shares of the class to which they belong, or (B) to eliminate those shares entirely, whereupon the articles in either case shall be amended to reflect the reduction in the authorized shares of that series and the effect, if any, on the class to which that series belongs.

(d) "Reacquires" as used in this section means that a corporation purchases, redeems, acquires by way of conversion to another class or series, or otherwise acquires its own shares or that issued and outstanding shares cease to be outstanding.

(e) The provisions of this section are subject to any contrary or inconsistent provision in the articles.

(f) A certificate of amendment shall be filed in accordance with the requirements of Chapter 9 (commencing with Section 900) reflecting any elimination or reduction of authorized shares set forth in subdivisions (b) and (c), and any related elimination from the articles of the designation and the rights, preferences, privileges, and restrictions of any series or class of stock that is eliminated, except that approval by the outstanding shares (Section 152) shall not be required to adopt any such amendment. Nothing contained in this section is intended to alter or otherwise affect the powers of the board to amend the articles as contemplated in Sections 202 and 401.

Ca. Corp. Code § 510

Amended by Stats. 1995, Ch. 154, Sec. 5. Effective January 1, 1996.

Section 511 - Enforceability of negotiable instrument issued by corporation for purchase or redemption of shares

Notwithstanding the provisions of this chapter, a negotiable instrument issued by a corporation for the purchase or redemption of shares shall be enforceable by a holder in due course (Section 3302 of the Commercial Code) without notice that it was issued for that purpose or by a person who acquired the instrument through such a holder.

Ca. Corp. Code § 511
Added by Stats. 1978, Ch. 370.

Chapter 6 - SHAREHOLDERS' MEETINGS AND CONSENTS

Section 600 - Meetings of shareholders

(a) Meetings of shareholders may be held at any place within or without this state as may be stated in or fixed in accordance with the bylaws. If no other place is stated or so fixed, shareholder meetings shall be held at the principal office of the corporation. Subject to any limitations in the articles or bylaws of the corporation, if authorized by the board of directors in its sole discretion, and subject to those guidelines and procedures as the board of directors may adopt, shareholders not physically present in person or by proxy at a meeting of shareholders may, by electronic transmission by and to the corporation (Sections 20 and 21), electronic video screen communication, conference telephone, or other means of remote communication, participate in a meeting of shareholders, be deemed present in person or by proxy, and vote at a meeting of shareholders, subject to subdivision (e).

(b) An annual meeting of shareholders shall be held for the election of directors on a date and at a time stated in or fixed in accordance with the bylaws. However, if the corporation is a regulated management company, a meeting of shareholders shall be held as required by the Federal Investment Company Act of 1940 (15 U.S.C. Sec. 80a-1, et seq.). Any other proper business may be transacted at the annual meeting. For purposes of this subdivision, "regulated management company" means a regulated investment company as defined in Section 851 of the federal Internal Revenue Code.

(c) If there is a failure to hold the annual meeting for a period of 60 days after the date designated therefor or, if no date has been designated, for a period of 15 months after the organization of the corporation or after its last annual meeting, the superior court of the proper county may summarily order a meeting to be held upon the application of any shareholder after notice to the corporation giving it an opportunity to be heard. The shares represented at the meeting, either in person or by proxy, and entitled to vote thereat shall constitute a quorum for the purpose of the meeting, notwithstanding any provision of the articles or bylaws or in this division to the contrary. The court may issue any orders as may be appropriate, including, without limitation, orders designating the time and place of the meeting, the record date for determination of shareholders entitled to vote, and the form of notice of the meeting.

(d) Special meetings of the shareholders may be called by the board, the chairperson of the board, the president, the holders of shares entitled to cast not less than 10 percent of the votes at the meeting, or any additional persons as may be provided in the articles or bylaws.

(e) A meeting of the shareholders may be conducted, in whole or in part, by electronic transmission by and to the corporation, electronic video screen communication, conference telephone, or other means of remote communication if the corporation implements reasonable measures:

(1) to provide shareholders and proxyholders a reasonable opportunity to participate in the meeting and to vote on matters submitted to the shareholders, including an opportunity to read or hear the proceedings of the meeting concurrently with those proceedings,

(2) if any shareholder or proxyholder votes or takes other action at the meeting by means of electronic transmission to the corporation, electronic video screen communication, conference telephone, or other means of remote communication, to maintain a record of that vote or action in its books and records, and

(3) to verify that each person who has voted remotely is a shareholder or proxyholder. A corporation shall not conduct a meeting of shareholders solely by electronic transmission by and to the corporation, electronic video screen communication, conference telephone, or other means of remote communication unless one or more of the following conditions apply:

(A) all of the shareholders consent;

(B) the board determines it is necessary or appropriate because of an emergency, as defined in paragraph (5) of subdivision (i) of Section 207; or

(C) notwithstanding the absence of consent from all shareholders pursuant to (A) or subdivision (b) of Section 20, the meeting is conducted on or before December 31, 2025, and includes a live audiovisual feed for the duration of the meeting. A de minimis disruption of an audio, visual, or audiovisual feed does not require a corporation to end a shareholder meeting under, or render the corporation out of compliance with, this subdivision.

Ca. Corp. Code § 600
Amended by Stats 2022 ch 951 (AB 1780),s 1.5, eff. 1/1/2023.
Amended by Stats 2022 ch 617 (SB 1202),s 14, eff. 1/1/2023.
Amended by Stats 2022 ch 12 (AB 769),s 1, eff. 3/25/2022.
Amended by Stats 2021 ch 523 (AB 663),s 3, eff. 1/1/2022.
Amended by Stats 2006 ch 214 (AB 1959),s 2, eff. 1/1/2007.
Amended by Stats 2004 ch 254 (SB 1306),s 8, eff. 1/1/2005

Section 601 - Notice of shareholders' meeting or report

(a) Whenever shareholders are required or permitted to take any action at a meeting a written notice of the meeting shall be given not less than 10 (or, if sent by third-class mail, 30) nor more than 60 days before the date of the meeting to each shareholder entitled to vote thereat. That notice shall state the place, date and hour of the meeting, the means of electronic transmission by and to the corporation (Sections 20 and 21), electronic video screen communication, conference telephone, or other means of remote communication, if any, by which shareholders may participate in that meeting, and (1) in the case of a special meeting, the general nature of the business to be transacted, and no other business may be transacted, or (2) in the case of the annual meeting, those matters that the board, at the time of the mailing of the notice, intends to present for action by the shareholders, but subject to the provisions of subdivision (f) any proper matter may be presented at the meeting for that action. The notice of any meeting at which directors are to be elected shall include the names of nominees intended at the time of the notice to be presented by the board for election.

(b)

(1)Notice of a shareholders' meeting or any report shall be given personally, by electronic transmission by the corporation, or by first-class mail, or, in the case of a corporation with outstanding shares held of record by 500 or more persons (determined as provided in Section 605) on the record date for the shareholders' meeting, notice may also be sent third-class mail, or other means of written communication, addressed to the shareholder at the address of that shareholder appearing on the books of the corporation or given by the shareholder to the corporation for the purpose of notice, or if no address appears or is given, at the place where the principal office of the corporation is located or by publication at least once in a newspaper of general circulation in the county in which the principal office is located. The notice or report shall be deemed to have been given at the time when delivered personally, sent by electronic transmission by the corporation, deposited in the mail, or sent by other means of written communication. Notwithstanding the foregoing, the notice of a shareholder's meeting or any report may be sent by electronic communication or other means of remote communication if the board determines it is necessary or appropriate because of an emergency, as defined in paragraph (5) of subdivision (i) of Section 207. An affidavit of mailing or electronic transmission by the corporation, or electronic communication or other means of remote communication as permitted because of an emergency, of any notice or report in accordance with the provisions of this division, executed by the secretary, assistant secretary, or any transfer agent, shall be prima facie evidence of the giving of the notice or report.

(2)If any notice or report addressed to the shareholder at the address of that shareholder appearing on the books of the corporation is returned to the corporation by the United States Postal Service marked to indicate that the United States Postal Service is unable to deliver the notice or report to the shareholder at that address, all future notices or reports shall be deemed to have been duly given without further mailing if the same shall be available for the shareholder upon written demand of the shareholder at the principal office of the corporation for a period of one year from the date of the giving of the notice or report to all other shareholders.

(3)

(A) Notice given by electronic transmission by the corporation under this subdivision shall be valid only if it complies with Section 20. Notwithstanding the foregoing, notice shall not be given by electronic transmission by the corporation under this subdivision after either of the following:

(i) The corporation is unable to deliver two consecutive notices to the shareholder by that means.

(ii) The inability to so deliver the notices to the shareholder becomes known to the secretary, any assistant secretary, the transfer agent, or other person responsible for the giving of the notice.

(B) This paragraph shall not apply if notices are provided by electronic communication or other means of remote communication as permitted because of an emergency.

(c) Upon request in writing to the corporation addressed to the attention of the chairperson of the board, president, vice president or secretary by any person (other than the board) entitled to call a special meeting of shareholders, the officer forthwith shall cause notice to be given to the shareholders entitled to vote that a meeting will be held at a time requested by the person or persons calling the meeting, not less than 35 nor more than 60 days after the receipt of the request. If the notice is not given within 20 days after receipt of the request, the persons entitled to call the meeting may give the notice or the superior court of the proper county shall summarily order the giving of the notice, after notice to the corporation giving it an opportunity to be heard. The procedure provided in subdivision (c) of Section 305 shall apply to that application. The court may issue orders as may be appropriate, including, without limitation, orders designating the time and place of the meeting, the record date for determination of shareholders entitled to vote, and the form of notice.

(d) When a shareholders' meeting is adjourned to another time or place, unless the bylaws otherwise require and except as provided in this subdivision, notice need not be given of the adjourned meeting if the time and place thereof (or the means of electronic transmission by and to the corporation or, electronic video screen communication, conference telephone, or other means of remote communication, if any, by which the shareholders may participate) are announced at the meeting at which the adjournment is taken. At the adjourned meeting the corporation may transact any business that might have been transacted at the original meeting. If the adjournment is for more than 45 days or if after the adjournment a new record date is fixed for the adjourned meeting, a notice of the adjourned meeting shall be given to each shareholder of record entitled to vote at the meeting.

(e) The transactions of any meeting of shareholders, however called and noticed, and wherever held, are as valid as though had at a meeting duly held after regular call and notice, if a quorum is present either in person or by proxy, and if, either before or after the meeting, each of the persons entitled to vote, not present in person or by proxy, provides a waiver of notice or consent to the holding of the meeting or an approval of the minutes thereof in writing. All those waivers, consents, and approvals shall be filed with the corporate records or made a part of the minutes of the meeting. Attendance of a person at a meeting shall constitute a waiver of notice of and presence at the meeting, except when the person objects, at the beginning of the meeting, to the transaction of any business because the meeting is not lawfully called or convened and except that attendance at a meeting is not a waiver of any right to object to the consideration of matters required by this division to be included in the notice but not so included, if the objection is expressly made at the meeting. Neither the business to be transacted at nor the purpose of any regular or special meeting of shareholders need be specified in any written waiver of notice, consent to the holding of the meeting or approval of the minutes thereof, unless otherwise provided in the articles or bylaws, except as provided in subdivision (f).

(f) Any shareholder approval at a meeting, other than unanimous approval by those entitled to vote, pursuant to Section 310, 902, 1152, 1201, 1900, or 2007 shall be valid only if the general nature of the proposal so approved was stated in the notice of meeting or in any written waiver of notice.

Ca. Corp. Code § 601

Amended by Stats 2022 ch 617 (SB 1202),s 15, eff. 1/1/2023.
Amended by Stats 2021 ch 523 (AB 663),s 4, eff. 1/1/2022.
Amended by Stats 2004 ch 254 (SB 1306),s 9, eff. 1/1/2005
Amended by Stats 2002 ch 480 (SB 399),s 3, eff. 1/1/2003.

Section 602 - Quorum

(a) Unless otherwise provided in the articles, a majority of the shares entitled to vote, represented in person or by proxy, shall constitute a quorum at a meeting of the shareholders, but in no event shall a quorum consist of less than one-third (or, in the case of a mutual water company, 20 percent) of the shares entitled to vote at the meeting or, except in the case of a close corporation, of more than a majority of the shares entitled to vote at the meeting. Except as provided in subdivision (b), the affirmative vote of a majority of the shares represented and voting at a duly held meeting at which a quorum is present (which shares voting affirmatively also constitute at least a majority of the required quorum) shall be the act of the shareholders, unless the vote of a greater number or voting by classes is required by this division or the articles.

(b) The shareholders present at a duly called or held meeting at which a quorum is present may continue to transact business until adjournment notwithstanding the withdrawal of enough shareholders to leave less than a quorum, if any action taken (other than adjournment) is approved by at least a majority of the shares required to constitute a quorum or, if required by this division or the articles, the vote of a greater number or voting by classes.

(c) In the absence of a quorum, any meeting of shareholders may be adjourned from time to time by the vote of a majority of the shares represented either in person or by proxy, but no other business may be transacted, except as provided in subdivision (b).

Ca. Corp. Code § 602

Amended by Stats 2000 ch 485 (AB 1895), s 8, eff. 1/1/2001.

Section 603 - Action taken without meeting and prior notice

(a) Unless otherwise provided in the articles, any action that may be taken at any annual or special meeting of shareholders may be taken without a meeting and without prior notice, if a consent in writing, as specified in Section 195, setting forth the action so taken, shall be provided by the holders of outstanding shares having not less than the minimum number of votes that would be necessary to authorize or take that action at a meeting at which all shares entitled to vote thereon were present and voted.

(b) Unless the consents of all shareholders entitled to vote have been solicited in writing, both of the following shall apply:

(1) Notice of any shareholder approval pursuant to Section 310, 317, 1152, 1201 (except for a reorganization as to which shareholders have the right, pursuant to Chapter 13 (commencing with Section 1300) to demand payment of cash for their shares), or 2007 without a meeting by less than unanimous written consent shall be given at least 10 days before the consummation of the action authorized by that approval. Notice shall be given as provided in subdivision (b) of Section 601.

(2) Prompt notice shall be given of the taking of any other corporate action approved by shareholders without a meeting by less than unanimous written consent, to those shareholders entitled to vote who have not consented in writing. Notice shall be given as provided in subdivision (b) of Section 601.

(c) Any shareholder giving a written consent, or the shareholder's proxyholders, or a transferee of the shares or a personal representative of the shareholder or their respective proxyholders, may revoke the consent personally or by proxy by a writing received by the corporation prior to the time that written consents of the number of shares required to authorize the proposed action have been filed with the secretary of the corporation, but may not do so thereafter. The revocation is effective upon its receipt by the secretary of the corporation.

(d) Notwithstanding subdivision (a), directors may not be elected by written consent except by unanimous written consent of all shares entitled to vote for the election of directors; provided that the shareholders may elect a director to fill a vacancy, other than a vacancy created by removal, by the written consent of a majority of the outstanding shares entitled to vote.

Ca. Corp. Code § 603

Amended by Stats 2013 ch 109 (AB 457),s 1, eff. 1/1/2014.

Amended by Stats 2006 ch 214 (AB 1959),s 3, eff. 1/1/2007.

Amended by Stats 2004 ch 254 (SB 1306),s 10, eff. 1/1/2005

Amended by Stats 2002 ch 480 (SB 399),s 4, eff. 1/1/2003.
Amended by Stats 2000 ch 485 (AB 1895), s 9, eff. 1/1/2001.

Section 604 - Proxy or written consent

(a) Any form of proxy or written consent distributed to 10 or more shareholders of a corporation with outstanding shares held of record by 100 or more persons shall afford an opportunity on the proxy or form of written consent to specify a choice between approval and disapproval of each matter or group of related matters intended to be acted upon at the meeting for which the proxy is solicited or by such written consent, other than elections to office, and shall provide, subject to reasonable specified conditions, that where the person solicited specifies a choice with respect to any such matter the shares will be voted in accordance therewith.
(b) In any election of directors, any form of proxy in which the directors to be voted upon are named therein as candidates and which is marked by a shareholder "withhold" or otherwise marked in a manner indicating that the authority to vote for the election of directors is withheld shall not be voted for the election of a director.
(c) Failure to comply with this section shall not invalidate any corporate action taken, but may be the basis for challenging any proxy at a meeting and the superior court may compel compliance therewith at the suit of any shareholder.
(d) This section does not apply to any corporation with an outstanding class of securities registered under Section 12 of the Securities Exchange Act of 1934 or whose securities are exempted from such registration by Section 12(g)(2)(g)(2) of that act.
   Ca. Corp. Code § 604
Amended by Stats. 1980, Ch. 501.

Section 605 - Determination of whether corporation has outstanding shares held of record by 100 or more persons

(a) For the purpose of determining whether a corporation has outstanding shares held of record by 100 or more persons, shares shall be deemed to be "held of record" by each person who is identified as the owner of such shares on the record of shareholders maintained by or on behalf of the corporation, subject to the following:

   (1) In any case where the record of shareholders has not been maintained in accordance with accepted practice, any additional person who would be identified as such an owner on such record if it had been maintained in accordance with accepted practice shall be included as a holder of record.

   (2) Shares identified as held of record by a corporation, a partnership, a limited liability company, a trust, whether or not the trustees are named, or other organization shall be included as so held by one person.

   (3) Shares identified as held of record by one or more persons as trustees, executors, guardians, conservators, custodians or in other fiduciary capacities with respect to a single trust, estate or account shall be included as held of record by one person.

(4) Shares held by two or more persons as coowners shall be included as held by one person.

(5) Shares registered in substantially similar names, where the corporation (or other person soliciting proxies) has reason to believe because of the address or other indications that such names represent the same person, may be included as held of record by one person.

(b) Notwithstanding subdivision (a):

(1) Shares held, to the knowledge of the corporation (or other person soliciting proxies), subject to a voting trust, deposit agreement or similar arrangement shall be included as held of record by the recordholders of the voting trust certificates, certificates of deposit, receipts or similar evidences of interest in such securities; provided, however, that the corporation (or other person soliciting proxies) may rely in good faith on such information as is received in response to its request from a nonaffiliated issuer of the certificates or evidences of interest.

(2) If the corporation (or other person soliciting proxies) knows or has reason to know that the form of holding shares of record is used primarily to circumvent the provisions of this section, the beneficial owners of such shares shall be deemed to be the record owners thereof.

Ca. Corp. Code § 605
Amended by Stats. 1994, Ch. 1010, Sec. 65. Effective January 1, 1995.

Chapter 7 - VOTING OF SHARES

Section 700 - One vote per outstanding share; voting by holder of shares

(a) Except as provided in Section 708 and except as may be otherwise provided in the articles, each outstanding share, regardless of class, shall be entitled to one vote on each matter submitted to a vote of shareholders.

(b) Any holder of shares entitled to vote on any matter may vote part of the shares in favor of the proposal and refrain from voting the remaining shares or vote them against the proposal, other than elections to office, but, if the shareholder fails to specify the number of shares such shareholder is voting affirmatively, it will be conclusively presumed that the shareholder's approving vote is with respect to all shares such shareholder is entitled to vote.

Ca. Corp. Code § 700
Added by Stats. 1975, Ch. 682.

Section 701 - Record date

(a) In order that the corporation may determine the shareholders entitled to notice of any meeting or to vote or entitled to receive payment of any dividend or other distribution or allotment of any rights or entitled to exercise any rights in respect of any other lawful action, the board may fix, in advance, a record date, which shall not be more than 60 nor less than 10 days prior to the date of such meeting nor more than 60 days prior to any other action.

(b) If no record date is fixed:

(1) The record date for determining shareholders entitled to notice of or to vote at a meeting of shareholders shall be at the close of business on the business day next preceding the day on which notice is given or, if notice is waived, at the close of business on the business day next preceding the day on which the meeting is held.

(2) The record date for determining shareholders entitled to give consent to corporate action in writing without a meeting, when no prior action by the board has been taken, shall be the day on which the first written consent is given.

(3) The record date for determining shareholders for any other purpose shall be at the close of business on the day on which the board adopts the resolution relating thereto, or the 60th day prior to the date of such other action, whichever is later.

(c) A determination of shareholders of record entitled to notice of or to vote at a meeting of shareholders shall apply to any adjournment of the meeting unless the board fixes a new record date for the adjourned meeting, but the board shall fix a new record date if the meeting is adjourned for more than 45 days from the date set for the original meeting.

(d) Shareholders at the close of business on the record date are entitled to notice and to vote or to receive the dividend, distribution or allotment of rights or to exercise the rights, as the case may be, notwithstanding any transfer of any shares on the books of the corporation after the record date, except as otherwise provided in the articles or by agreement or in this division.

Ca. Corp. Code § 701
Amended by Stats. 1977, Ch. 235.

Section 702 - Voting of shares held by representative or fiduciary

(a) Subject to subdivision (c) of Section 703, shares held by an administrator, executor, guardian, conservator or custodian may be voted by such holder either in person or by proxy, without a transfer of such shares into the holder's name; and shares standing in the name of a trustee may be voted by the trustee, either in person or by proxy, but no trustee shall be entitled to vote shares held by such trustee without a transfer of such shares into the trustee's name.

(b) Shares standing in the name of a receiver may be voted by such receiver; and shares held by or under the control of a receiver may be voted by such receiver without the transfer thereof into the receiver's name if authority to do so is contained in the order of the court by which such receiver was appointed.

(c) Subject to the provisions of Section 705 and except where otherwise agreed in writing between the parties, a shareholder whose shares are pledged shall be entitled to vote such shares until the shares have been transferred into the name of the pledgee, and thereafter the pledgee shall be entitled to vote the shares so transferred.

(d) Shares standing in the name of a minor may be voted and the corporation may treat all rights incident thereto as exercisable by the minor, in person or by proxy, whether or not the corporation has notice, actual or constructive, of the nonage, unless a guardian of the minor's property has been appointed and written notice of such appointment given to the corporation.

(e) If authorized to vote the shares by the power of attorney by which the attorney in fact was appointed, shares held by or under the control of an attorney in fact may be voted and the corporation may treat all rights incident thereto as exercisable by the attorney in fact, in person or by proxy, without the transfer of the shares into the name of the attorney in fact.

Ca. Corp. Code § 702
Amended by Stats. 1985, Ch. 403, Sec. 13.

Section 703 - Voting of shares held by corporation

(a) Shares standing in the name of another corporation, domestic or foreign, may be voted by an officer, agent, or proxyholder as the bylaws of the other corporation may prescribe or, in the absence of such provision, as the board of the other corporation may determine or, in the absence of that determination, by the chairperson of the board, president or any vice president of the other corporation, or by any other person authorized to do so by the chairperson of the board, president, or any vice president of the other corporation. Shares which are purported to be voted or any proxy purported to be executed in the name of a corporation (whether or not any title of the person signing is indicated) shall be presumed to be voted or the proxy executed in accordance with the provisions of this subdivision, unless the contrary is shown.

(b) Shares of a corporation owned by its subsidiary shall not be entitled to vote on any matter.

(c) Shares held by the issuing corporation in a fiduciary capacity, and shares of an issuing corporation held in a fiduciary capacity by its subsidiary, shall not be entitled to vote on any matter, except as follows:

(1) To the extent that the settlor or beneficial owner possesses and exercises a right to vote or to give the corporation binding instructions as to how to vote such shares.

(2) Where there are one or more cotrustees who are not affected by the prohibition of this subdivision, in which case the shares may be voted by the cotrustees as if it or they are the sole trustee.

    Ca. Corp. Code § 703

Amended by Stats 2015 ch 98 (SB 351),s 8, eff. 1/1/2016.

Section 704 - Voting of shares in names of two or more persons

(a) If shares stand of record in the names of two or more persons, whether fiduciaries, members of a partnership, joint tenants, tenants in common, spouses as community property, tenants by the entirety, voting trustees, persons entitled to vote under a shareholder voting agreement or otherwise, or if two or more persons (including proxyholders) have the same fiduciary relationship respecting the same shares, unless the secretary of the corporation is given written notice to the contrary and is furnished with a copy of the instrument or order appointing them or creating the relationship wherein it is so provided, their acts with respect to voting shall have the following effect:

    (1) If only one votes, such act binds all.

    (2) If more than one vote, the act of the majority so voting binds all.

    (3) If more than one vote, but the vote is evenly split on any particular matter, each faction may vote the securities in question proportionately.

(b) If the instrument so filed or the registration of the shares shows that any such tenancy is held in unequal interests, a majority or even split for the purpose of this section shall be a majority or even split in interest.

    Ca. Corp. Code § 704

Amended by Stats 2016 ch 50 (SB 1005),s 21, eff. 1/1/2017.

Section 705 - Proxy

(a) Every person entitled to vote shares may authorize another person or persons to act by proxy with respect to such shares. Any proxy purporting to be executed in accordance with the provisions of this division shall be presumptively valid.

(b) No proxy shall be valid after the expiration of 11 months from the date thereof unless otherwise provided in the proxy. Every proxy continues in full force and effect until revoked by the person executing it prior to the vote pursuant thereto, except as otherwise provided in this section. Such revocation may be effected by a writing delivered to the corporation stating that the proxy is revoked or by a subsequent proxy executed by the person executing the prior proxy and presented to the meeting, or as to any meeting by attendance at such meeting and voting in person by the person executing the proxy. The dates contained on the forms of proxy presumptively determine the order of execution, regardless of the postmark dates on the envelopes in which they are mailed.

(c) A proxy is not revoked by the death or incapacity of the maker unless, before the vote is counted, written notice of such death or incapacity is received by the corporation.

(d) Except when other provision shall have been made by written agreement between the parties, the recordholder of shares which such person holds as pledgee or otherwise as security or which belong to another shall issue to the pledgor or to the owner of such shares, upon demand therefor and payment of necessary expenses thereof, a proxy to vote or take other action thereon.

(e) A proxy which states that it is irrevocable is irrevocable for the period specified therein (notwithstanding subdivision (c)) when it is held by any of the following or a nominee of any of the following:

   (1) A pledgee.

   (2) A person who has purchased or agreed to purchase or holds an option to purchase the shares or a person who has sold a portion of such person's shares in the corporation to the maker of the proxy.

   (3) A creditor or creditors of the corporation or the shareholder who extended or continued credit to the corporation or the shareholder in consideration of the proxy if the proxy states that it was given in consideration of such extension or continuation of credit and the name of the person extending or continuing credit.

   (4) A person who has contracted to perform services as an employee of the corporation, if a proxy is required by the contract of employment and if the proxy states that it was given in consideration of such contract of employment, the name of the employee and the period of employment contracted for.

   (5) A person designated by or under an agreement under Section 706.

   (6) A beneficiary of a trust with respect to shares held by the trust. Notwithstanding the period of irrevocability specified, the proxy becomes revocable when the pledge is redeemed, the option or agreement to purchase is terminated or the seller no longer owns any shares of the corporation or dies, the debt of the corporation or the shareholder is paid, the period of employment provided for in the contract of employment has terminated, the agreement under Section 706 has terminated, or the person ceases to be a beneficiary of the trust. In addition to the foregoing clauses (1) through (5), a proxy may be made irrevocable (notwithstanding subdivision (c)) if it is given to secure the performance of a duty or to protect a title, either legal or equitable, until the happening of events which, by its terms, discharge the obligations secured by it.

(f) A proxy may be revoked, notwithstanding a provision making it irrevocable, by a transferee of shares without knowledge of the existence of the provision unless the existence of the proxy and its irrevocability appears, in the case of certificated securities, on the certificate representing such shares, or in the case of uncertificated securities, on the initial transaction statement and written statements.

Ca. Corp. Code § 705

Amended by Stats. 1986, Ch. 766, Sec. 22.

Section 706 - Voting agreement

(a) Notwithstanding any other provision of this division, an agreement between two or more shareholders of a corporation, if in writing and signed by the parties thereto, may provide that in exercising any voting rights the shares held by them shall be voted as provided by the agreement, or as the parties may agree or as determined in accordance with a procedure agreed upon by them, and the parties may but need not transfer the shares covered by such an agreement to a third party or parties with authority to vote them in accordance with the terms of the agreement. Such an agreement shall not be denied specific performance by a court on the ground that the remedy at law is adequate or on other grounds relating to the jurisdiction of a court of equity.

(b) Shares in any corporation may be transferred by written agreement to trustees in order to confer upon them the right to vote and otherwise represent the shares for such period of time, not exceeding 10 years, as may be specified in the agreement. The validity of a voting trust agreement, otherwise lawful, shall not be affected during a period of 10 years from the date when it was created or last extended as hereinafter provided by the fact that under its terms it will or may last beyond such 10-year period. At any time within two years prior to the time of expiration of any voting trust agreement as originally fixed or as last extended as provided in this subdivision, one or more beneficiaries under the voting trust agreement may, by written agreement and with the written consent of the voting trustee or trustees, extend the duration of the voting trust agreement with respect to their shares for an additional period not exceeding 10 years from the expiration date of the trust as originally fixed or as last extended as provided in this subdivision. A duplicate of the voting trust agreement and any extension thereof shall be filed with the secretary of the corporation and shall be open to inspection by a shareholder, a holder of a voting trust certificate or the agent of either, upon the same terms as the record of shareholders of the corporation is open to inspection.

(c) No agreement made pursuant to subdivision (a) shall be held to be invalid or unenforceable on the ground that it is a voting trust that does not comply with subdivision (b) or that it is a proxy that does not comply with Section 705.

(d) This section shall not invalidate any voting or other agreement among shareholders or any irrevocable proxy complying with subdivision (e) of Section 705, which agreement or proxy is not otherwise illegal.

Ca. Corp. Code § 706

Amended by Stats. 1997, Ch. 136, Sec. 3. Effective January 1, 1998.

Section 707 - Inspectors of election

(a) In advance of any meeting of shareholders the board may appoint inspectors of election to act at the meeting and any adjournment thereof. If inspectors of election are not so appointed, or if any persons so appointed fail to appear or refuse to act, the chairperson of any meeting of shareholders may, and on the request of any shareholder or a shareholder's proxy shall, appoint inspectors of election (or persons to replace those who so fail or refuse) at the meeting. The number of inspectors shall be either one or three. If appointed at a meeting on the request of one or more shareholders or proxies, the majority of shares represented in person or by proxy shall determine whether one or three inspectors are to be appointed.

(b) The inspectors of election shall determine the number of shares outstanding and the voting power of each, the shares represented at the meeting, the existence of a quorum and the authenticity, validity and effect of proxies, receive votes, ballots or consents, hear and determine all challenges and questions in any way arising in connection with the right to vote, count and tabulate all votes or consents, determine when the polls shall close, determine the result and do such acts as may be proper to conduct the election or vote with fairness to all shareholders.

(c) The inspectors of election shall perform their duties impartially, in good faith, to the best of their ability and as expeditiously as is practical. If there are three inspectors of election, the decision, act or certificate of a majority is effective in all respects as the decision, act or certificate of all. Any report or certificate made by the inspectors of election is prima facie evidence of the facts stated therein.

Ca. Corp. Code § 707

Amended by Stats 2022 ch 617 (SB 1202),s 16, eff. 1/1/2023.

Added by Stats. 1975, Ch. 682.

Section 708 - Cumulative voting

(a) Except as provided in Sections 301.5 and 708.5, every shareholder complying with subdivision (b) and entitled to vote at any election of directors may cumulate such shareholder's votes and give one candidate a number of votes equal to the number of directors to be elected multiplied by the number of votes to which the shareholder's shares are normally entitled, or distribute the shareholder's votes on the same principle among as many candidates as the shareholder thinks fit.

(b) No shareholder shall be entitled to cumulate votes (i.e., cast for any candidate a number of votes greater than the number of votes that the shareholder normally is entitled to cast) unless the candidate or candidates' names have been placed in nomination prior to the voting and the shareholder has given notice at the meeting prior to the voting of the shareholder's intention to cumulate the shareholder's votes. If any one shareholder has given that notice, all shareholders may cumulate their votes for candidates in nomination.

(c) Except as provided in Section 708.5, in any election of directors, the candidates receiving the highest number of affirmative votes of the shares entitled to be voted for them up to the number of directors to be elected by those shares are elected; votes against the director and votes withheld shall have no legal effect.

(d) Subdivision (a) applies to the shareholders of any mutual water company organized or existing for the purpose of delivering water to its shareholders at cost on lands located within the boundaries of one or more reclamation districts now or hereafter legally existing in this state and created by or formed under the provisions of any statute of this state, but does not otherwise apply to the shareholders of mutual water companies unless their articles or bylaws so provide.

(e) Elections for directors need not be by ballot unless a shareholder demands election by ballot at the meeting and before the voting begins or unless the bylaws so require.

Ca. Corp. Code § 708

Amended by Stats 2006 ch 871 (SB 1207),s 1, eff. 1/1/2007.

Section 708.5 - Uncontested election of listed corporation

(a) For purposes of this section,the following definitions shall apply:

(1) "Uncontested election" means an election of directors in which, at the expiration of the time fixed under the articles of incorporation or bylaws requiring advance notification of director candidates or, absent such a provision in the articles of incorporation or bylaws, at a time fixed by the board of directors that is not more than 14 days before notice is given of the meeting at which the election is to occur, the number of candidates for election does not exceed the number of directors to be elected by the shareholders at that election.

(2) "Listed corporation" means a domestic corporation that qualifies as a listed corporation under subdivision (d) of Section 301.5.

(b) Notwithstanding paragraph (5) of subdivision (a) of Section 204, a listed corporation that has eliminated cumulative voting pursuant to subdivision (a) of Section 301.5 may amend its articles of incorporation or bylaws to provide that, in an uncontested election, approval of the shareholders, as specified in Section 153, shall be required to elect a director.

(c) Notwithstanding subdivision (b) of Section 301, if an incumbent director fails to be elected by approval of the shareholders (Section 153) in an uncontested election of a listed corporation that has amended its articles of incorporation or bylaws pursuant to subdivision (b), then, unless the incumbent director has earlier resigned, the term of the incumbent director shall end on the date that is the earlier of 90 days after the date on which the voting results are determined pursuant to Section 707 or the date on which the board of directors selects a person to fill the office held by that director pursuant to subdivision (d).

(d) Any vacancy on the board of directors resulting from any failure of a candidate to be elected by approval of the shareholders (Section 153) in an uncontested election of a listed corporation that has amended its articles of incorporation or bylaws pursuant to subdivision (b) shall be filled in accordance with the procedures set forth in Section

305.

Ca. Corp. Code § 708.5
Added by Stats 2006 ch 871 (SB 1207),s 2, eff. 1/1/2007.

Section 709 - Action by shareholder or person claiming denial of right to vote

(a) Upon the filing of an action therefor by any shareholder or by any person who claims to have been denied the right to vote, the superior court of the proper county shall try and determine the validity of any election or appointment of any director of any domestic corporation, or of any foreign corporation if the election was held or the appointment was made in this state. In the case of a foreign corporation the action may be brought at the option of the plaintiff in the county in which the corporation has its principal office in California or in the county in which the election was held or the appointment was made.

(b) Upon the filing of the complaint, and before any further proceedings are had, the court shall enter an order fixing a date for the hearing, which shall be within five days unless for good cause shown a later date is fixed, and requiring notice of the date for the hearing and a copy of the complaint to be served upon the corporation and upon the person whose purported election or appointment is questioned and upon any person (other than the plaintiff) whom the plaintiff alleges to have been elected or appointed, in the manner in which a summons is required to be served, or, if the court so directs, by registered mail; and the court may make such further requirements as to notice as appear to be proper under the circumstances.

(c) The court may determine the person entitled to the office of director or may order a new election to be held or appointment to be made, may determine the validity, effectiveness and construction of voting agreements and voting trusts, the validity of the issuance of shares and the right of persons to vote and may direct such other relief as may be just and proper.

Ca. Corp. Code § 709
Amended by Stats 2022 ch 617 (SB 1202),s 17, eff. 1/1/2023.
Added by Stats. 1975, Ch. 682.

Section 710 - Supermajority vote requirement

(a) This section applies to a corporation with outstanding shares held of record by 100 or more persons (determined as provided in Section 605) that files an amendment of articles or certificate of determination containing a "supermajority vote" provision on or after January 1, 1989. This section shall not apply to a corporation that files an amendment of articles or certificate of determination on or after January 1, 1994, if, at the time of filing, the corporation has (1) outstanding shares of more than one class or series of stock, (2) no class of equity securities registered under Section 12(b)(b) or 12(g)(g) of the Securities Exchange Act of 1934, and (3) outstanding shares held of record by fewer than 300 persons determined as provided by Section 605.

(b) A "supermajority vote" is a requirement set forth in the articles or in a certificate of determination authorized under any provision of this division that specified corporate action or actions be approved by a larger proportion of the outstanding shares than a majority, or by a larger proportion of the outstanding shares of a class or series than a majority, but no supermajority vote that is subject to this section shall require a vote in excess of 66 $^2/_3$ percent of the outstanding shares or 66 $^2/_3$ percent of the outstanding shares of any class or series of those shares.

(c) An amendment of the articles or a certificate of determination that includes a supermajority vote requirement shall be approved by at least as large a proportion of the outstanding shares (Section 152) as is required pursuant to that amendment or certificate of determination for the approval of the specified corporate action or actions.

(d) The amendments made to this section by the act amending this section in the 2001-02 Regular Session shall not affect the rights of minority shareholders existing under law.

Ca. Corp. Code § 710

Amended by Stats 2006 ch 57 (SB 1183),s 2, eff. 1/1/2007.
Amended by Stats 2002 ch 173 (SB 1472),s 1, eff. 1/1/2003.

Section 711 - Person on whose behalf shares are voted

(a) The Legislature finds and declares that: Many of the residents of this state are the legal and beneficial owners or otherwise the ultimate beneficiaries of shares of stock of domestic and foreign corporations, title to which may be held by a variety of intermediate owners as defined in subdivision (b). The informed and active involvement of such beneficial owners and beneficiaries in holding legal owners and, through them, management, accountable in their exercise of corporate power is essential to the interest of those beneficiaries and beneficial owners and to the economy and well-being of this state.

The purpose of this section is to serve the public interest by ensuring that voting records are maintained and disclosed as provided in this section. In the event that by statute or regulation pursuant to the federal Employee Retirement Income Security Act of 1974 (29 U.S.C. Sec. 1001 et seq.), there are imposed upon investment managers as defined in Sec. 2(38) thereof, duties substantially the same as those set forth in this section, compliance with those statutory or regulatory requirements by persons subject to this section shall be deemed to fulfill the obligations contained in this section.

This section shall be construed liberally to achieve that purpose.

(b) For purposes of this section, a person on whose behalf shares are voted includes, but is not limited to:

(1) A participant or beneficiary of an employee benefit plan with regard to shares held for the benefit of the participant or beneficiary.

(2) A shareholder, beneficiary, or contract owner of any entity (or of any portfolio of any entity) as defined in Section 3(a) of the federal Investment Company Act of 1940 (15 U.S.C. Sec. 80a-1 et seq.), as amended, to the extent the entity (or portfolio) holds the shares for which the record is requested.

(c) For the purposes of this section, a person on whose behalf shares are voted does not include:

(1) A person who possesses the right to terminate or withdraw from the shareholder, contract owner, participant, or beneficiary relationship with any entity (or any portfolio of any entity) defined in subdivision (b). This exclusion does not apply in the event the right of termination or withdrawal cannot be exercised without automatic imposition of a tax penalty. The right to substitute a relationship with an entity or portfolio, the shares of which are voted by or subject to the direction of the investment adviser (as defined in Section 2 of the federal Investment Company Act of 1940 (15 U.S.C. Sec. 80a-1 et seq.), as amended), of the prior entity or portfolio, or an affiliate of the investment adviser, shall not be deemed to be a right of termination or withdrawal within the meaning of this subdivision.

(2) A person entitled to receive information about a trust pursuant to Section 16061 of the Probate Code.

(3) A beneficiary, participant, contract owner, or shareholder whose interest is funded through the general assets of a life insurance company authorized to conduct business in this state.

(d) Every person possessing the power to vote shares of stock on behalf of another shall maintain a record of the manner in which the shares were voted. The record shall be maintained for a period of 12 consecutive months from the effective date of the vote.

(e) Upon a reasonable written request, the person possessing the power to vote shares of stock on behalf of another, or a designated agent, shall disclose the voting record with respect to any matter involving a specific security or securities in accordance with the following procedures:

(1) Except as set forth in paragraph (2), disclosure shall be made to the person making the request. The person making the disclosure may require identification sufficient to identify the person making the request as a person on whose behalf the shares were voted. A request for identification, if made, shall be reasonable, shall be made promptly, and may include a request for the person's social security number.

(2) If the person possessing the power to vote shares on behalf of another holds that power pursuant to an agreement entered into with a party other than the person making the request for disclosure, the person maintaining and disclosing the record pursuant to this section may, instead, make the requested disclosure to that party.

Disclosure to that party shall be deemed compliance with the disclosure requirement of this section. If disclosure is made to that party and not to the person making the request, subdivision (i) shall not apply. However, nothing herein shall prohibit that party and the person possessing the power to vote on shares from entering into an agreement between themselves for the payment or assessment of a reasonable charge to defray expenses of disclosing the record.

(f) Where the entity subject to the requirements of this section is organized as a unit investment trust as defined in Section 4(2) of the federal Investment Company Act of 1940 (15 U.S.C. Sec. 80a-1 et seq.), the open-ended investment companies underlying the unit investment trust shall promptly make available their proxy voting records to the unit investment trust upon evidence of a bona fide request for voting record information pursuant to subdivision (e).

(g) Signing a proxy on another's behalf and forwarding it for disposition or receiving voting instructions does not constitute the power to vote. A person forwarding proxies or receiving voting instructions shall disclose the identity of the person having the power to vote shares upon reasonable written request by a person entitled to request a voting record under subdivision (c).

(h) For purposes of this section, if one or more persons has the power to vote shares on behalf of another, unless a governing instrument provides otherwise, the person or persons may designate an agent who shall maintain and disclose the record in accordance with subdivisions (b) and (c).

(i) Except as provided in paragraph (2) of subdivision (e), or as otherwise provided by law or a governing instrument, a person maintaining and disclosing a record pursuant to this section may assess a reasonable charge to the requesting person in order to defray expenses of disclosing the record in accordance with subdivision (e). Disclosure shall be made within a reasonable period after payment is received.

(j) Upon the petition of any person who successfully brings an action pursuant to or to enforce this section, the court may award costs and reasonable attorney's fees if the court finds that the defendant willfully violated this section.

(k) The obligation to maintain and disclose a voting record in accordance with subdivisions (b) and (c) shall commence January 1, 1990.

    Ca. Corp. Code § 711

Added by Stats. 1988, Ch. 1360, Sec. 1.

Chapter 8 - SHAREHOLDER DERIVATIVE ACTIONS

Section 800 - Shareholder derivative actions

(a) As used in this section, "corporation" includes an unincorporated association; "board" includes the managing body of an unincorporated association; "shareholder" includes a member of an unincorporated association; and "shares" includes memberships in an unincorporated association.

(b) No action may be instituted or maintained in right of any domestic or foreign corporation by any holder of shares or of voting trust certificates of the corporation unless both of the following conditions exist:

(1) The plaintiff alleges in the complaint that plaintiff was a shareholder, of record or beneficially, or the holder of voting trust certificates at the time of the transaction or any part thereof of which plaintiff complains or that plaintiff's shares or voting trust certificates thereafter devolved upon plaintiff by operation of law from a holder who was a holder at the time of the transaction or any part thereof complained of; provided, that any shareholder who does not meet these requirements may nevertheless be allowed in the discretion of the court to maintain the action on a preliminary showing to and determination by the court, by motion and after a hearing, at which the court shall consider such evidence, by affidavit or testimony, as it deems material, that (i) there is a strong prima facie case in favor of the claim asserted on behalf of the corporation, (ii) no other similar action has been or is likely to be instituted, (iii) the plaintiff acquired the shares before there was disclosure to the public or to the plaintiff of the wrongdoing of which plaintiff complains, (iv) unless the action can be maintained the defendant may retain a gain derived from defendant's willful breach of a fiduciary duty, and (v) the requested relief will not result in unjust enrichment of the corporation or any shareholder of the corporation; and

(2) The plaintiff alleges in the complaint with particularity plaintiff's efforts to secure from the board such action as plaintiff desires, or the reasons for not making such effort, and alleges further that plaintiff has either informed the corporation or the board in writing of the ultimate facts of each cause of action against each defendant or delivered to the corporation or the board a true copy of the complaint which plaintiff proposes to file.

(c) In any action referred to in subdivision (b), at any time within 30 days after service of summons upon the corporation or upon any defendant who is an officer or director of the corporation, or held such office at the time of the acts complained of, the corporation or the defendant may move the court for an order, upon notice and hearing, requiring the plaintiff to furnish a bond as hereinafter provided. The motion shall be based upon one or both of the following grounds:

(1) That there is no reasonable possibility that the prosecution of the cause of action alleged in the complaint against the moving party will benefit the corporation or its shareholders.

(2) That the moving party, if other than the corporation, did not participate in the transaction complained of in any capacity. The court on application of the corporation or any defendant may, for good cause shown, extend the 30-day period for an additional period or periods not exceeding 60 days.

(d) At the hearing upon any motion pursuant to subdivision (c), the court shall consider such evidence, written or oral, by witnesses or affidavit, as may be material (1) to the ground or grounds upon which the motion is based, or (2) to a determination of the probable reasonable expenses, including attorneys' fees, of the corporation and the moving party which will be incurred in the defense of the action. If the court determines, after hearing the evidence adduced by the parties, that the moving party has established a probability in support of any of the grounds upon which the motion is based, the court shall fix the amount of the bond, not to exceed fifty thousand dollars ($50,000), to be furnished by the plaintiff for reasonable expenses, including attorneys' fees, which may be incurred by the moving party and the corporation in connection with the action, including expenses for which the corporation may become liable pursuant to Section 317. A ruling by the court on the motion shall not be a determination of any issue in the action or of the merits thereof. If the court, upon the motion, makes a determination that a bond shall be furnished by the plaintiff as to any one or more defendants, the action shall be dismissed as to the defendant or defendants, unless the bond required by the court has been furnished within such reasonable time as may be fixed by the court.

(e) If the plaintiff shall, either before or after a motion is made pursuant to subdivision (c), or any order or determination pursuant to the motion, furnish a bond in the aggregate amount of fifty thousand dollars ($50,000) to secure the reasonable expenses of the parties entitled to make the motion, the plaintiff has complied with the requirements of this section and with any order for a bond theretofore made, and any such motion then pending shall be dismissed and no further or additional bond shall be required.

(f) If a motion is filed pursuant to subdivision (c), no pleadings need be filed by the corporation or any other defendant and the prosecution of the action shall be stayed until 10 days after the motion has been disposed of.

Ca. Corp. Code § 800
Amended by Stats. 1982, Ch. 517, Sec. 186.

Chapter 9 - AMENDMENT OF ARTICLES

Section 900 - Amendment of articles

(a) By complying with the provisions of this chapter, a corporation may amend its articles from time to time, in any and as many respects as may be desired, so long as its articles as amended contain only such provisions as it would be lawful to insert in original articles filed at the time of the filing of the amendment and, if a change in shares or the rights of shareholders or an exchange, reclassification or cancellation of shares or rights of shareholders is to be made, such provisions as may be necessary to effect such change, exchange, reclassification or cancellation. It is the intent of the Legislature in adopting this section to exercise to the fullest extent the reserve power of the state over corporations and to authorize any amendment of the articles covered by the preceding sentence regardless of whether any provision contained in the amendment was permissible at the time of the original incorporation of the corporation.

(b) A corporation shall not amend its articles to add any statement or to alter any statement that may appear in the original articles of the initial street address and initial mailing address of the corporation, the names and addresses of the first directors, or the name and address of the initial agent, except to correct an error in the statement or to delete the information after the corporation has filed a statement under Section 1502.

Ca. Corp. Code § 900

Amended by Stats 2012 ch 494 (SB 1532),s 5, eff. 1/1/2013.

Section 901 - Amendment of articles before shares issued

Before any shares have been issued, any amendment of the articles may be adopted by a writing signed by a majority of the incorporators, if directors were not named in the original articles and have not been elected, or, if directors were named in the original articles or have been elected, by a majority of the directors.

Ca. Corp. Code § 901

Added by Stats. 1975, Ch. 682.

Section 902 - Amendment of articles after shares issued

(a) After any shares have been issued, amendments may be adopted if approved by the board and approved by the outstanding shares (Section 152), either before or after the approval by the board.

(b) Notwithstanding subdivision (a), an amendment extending the corporate existence or making the corporate existence perpetual may be adopted by a corporation organized prior to August 14, 1929, with approval by the board alone.

(c) Notwithstanding subdivision (a), unless the corporation has more than one class of shares outstanding, an amendment effecting only a stock split (including an increase in the authorized number of shares in proportion thereto) may be adopted with approval by the board alone.

(d) Notwithstanding subdivision (a), an amendment deleting the initial street address and initial mailing address of the corporation, the names and addresses of the first directors, or the name and address of the initial agent may be adopted with approval by the board alone.

(e) Whenever the articles require for corporate action the vote of a larger proportion or of all of the shares of any class or series, or of a larger proportion or of all of the directors, than is otherwise required by this division, the provision in the articles requiring such greater vote shall not be altered, amended or repealed except by such greater vote unless otherwise provided in the articles.

(f) Notwithstanding subdivision (a), any amendment reducing the vote required for an amendment pursuant to subdivision (c) of Section 158 may not be adopted unless approved by the affirmative vote of at least two-thirds of each class of outstanding shares or such other vote as may then be specified by the articles of the corporation.

Ca. Corp. Code § 902

Amended by Stats 2012 ch 494 (SB 1532),s 6, eff. 1/1/2013.

Section 903 - Approval of proposed amendment

(a) A proposed amendment must be approved by the outstanding shares (Section 152) of a class, whether or not such class is entitled to vote thereon by the provisions of the articles, if the amendment would:

(1) Increase or decrease the aggregate number of authorized shares of such class, other than an increase as provided in either subdivision (b) of Section 405 or subdivision (c) of Section 902.

(2) Effect an exchange, reclassification, or cancellation of all or part of the shares of such class, including a reverse stock split but excluding a stock split.

(3) Effect an exchange, or create a right of exchange, of all or part of the shares of another class into the shares of such class.

(4) Change the rights, preferences, privileges or restrictions of the shares of such class.

(5) Create a new class of shares having rights, preferences or privileges prior to the shares of such class, or increase the rights, preferences or privileges or the number of authorized shares of any class having rights, preferences or privileges prior to the shares of such class.

(6) In the case of preferred shares, divide the shares of any class into series having different rights, preferences, privileges or restrictions or authorize the board to do so.

(7) Cancel or otherwise affect dividends on the shares of such class which have accrued but have not been paid.

(b) Different series of the same class shall not constitute different classes for the purpose of voting by classes except when a series is adversely affected by an amendment in a different manner than other shares of the same class.

(c) In addition to approval by a class as provided in subdivision (a), a proposed amendment must also be approved by the outstanding voting shares (Section 152).

Ca. Corp. Code § 903

Amended by Stats. 1997, Ch. 136, Sec. 4. Effective January 1, 1998.

Section 904 - Approval of amendment making shares assessable or authorizing remedy by action for collection of assessment

(a) Except as provided in subdivision (b), if any amendment of the articles would make shares assessable or would authorize remedy by action for the collection of an assessment on fully paid shares, it shall be approved by all of the outstanding shares affected regardless of limitations or restrictions on the voting rights thereof.

(b) If a corporation is a mutual water company within the meaning of Section 2705 of the Public Utilities Code, an amendment of the articles to make the shares assessable or to amend prior article provisions authorizing assessment of shares shall be approved by the holders of at least two-thirds of the outstanding shares of any class affected by the amendment regardless of limitations or restrictions on the voting rights thereof. However, if the amendment would authorize remedy by action for the collection of an assessment on fully paid shares, the amendment shall be approved pursuant to subdivision (a).

Ca. Corp. Code § 904

Amended by Stats. 1990, Ch. 677, Sec. 1.

Section 905 - Certificate of amendment if amendment adopted after issuance of shares

In the case of amendments adopted after the corporation has issued any shares, the corporation shall file a certificate of amendment, which shall consist of an officers' certificate stating:

(a) The wording of the amendment or amended articles in accordance with Section 907;

(b) That the amendment has been approved by the board;

(c) If the amendment is one for which the approval of the outstanding shares (Section 152) is required, that the amendment was approved by the required vote of shareholders in accordance with Section 902, 903 or 904; the total number of outstanding shares of each class entitled to vote with respect to the amendment; and that the number of shares of each class voting in favor of the amendment equaled or exceeded the vote required, specifying the percentage vote required of each class entitled to vote; and

(d) If the amendment is one which may be adopted with approval by the board alone, a statement of the facts entitling the board alone to adopt the amendment. In the event of an amendment of the articles pursuant to a merger, the filing of the officers' certificate and agreement pursuant to Section 1103 or a certificate of ownership pursuant to subdivision (d) of Section 1110 shall be in lieu of any filing required under this chapter.

Ca. Corp. Code § 905

Amended by Stats. 1976, Ch. 641.

Section 906 - Certificate of amendment if amendment adopted by incorporators or board

In the case of amendments adopted by the incorporators or the board under Section 901, the corporation shall file a certificate of amendment signed and verified by a majority of the incorporators or of the board, as the case may be, which shall state that the signers thereof constitute at least a majority of the incorporators or of the board, that the corporation has issued no shares and that they adopt the amendment or amendments therein set forth. In the case of amendments adopted by the incorporators, the certificate shall also state that directors were not named in the original articles and have not been elected.

In the case of amendments adopted by the board under Section 901, the corporation may file a certificate of amendment pursuant to Section 905 in lieu of a certificate of amendment pursuant to this section.

Ca. Corp. Code § 906
Amended by Stats. 1978, Ch. 370.

Section 907 - Content of certificate of amendment

(a) The certificate of amendment shall establish the wording of the amendment or amended articles by one or more of the following means:

(1) By stating that the articles shall be amended to read as therein set forth in full.

(2) By stating that any provision of the articles, which shall be identified by the numerical or other designation given it in the articles or by stating the wording thereof, shall be stricken from the articles or shall be amended to read as set forth in the certificate.

(3) By stating that the provisions set forth therein shall be added to the articles.

(b) If the purpose of the amendment is to effect a stock split or reverse stock split or to reclassify, cancel, exchange, or otherwise change outstanding shares, the amended articles shall state the effect thereof on outstanding shares.

(c) In the event of an amendment to change the statement of authorized shares from a single class of shares to two classes, the shares outstanding immediately prior to the amendment are automatically considered to be the same number of shares of the common stock class. If the designation of only one of the two classes includes "common," that class is the common stock class. If the designation of both classes or of neither class includes "common" but one of the two classes has limited or no voting rights, the class whose voting rights are not limited is the common stock class for the purpose of this subdivision. This subdivision has no application if the amendment of articles includes a statement of the effect of the amendment on outstanding shares pursuant to subdivision (b).

(d) An amendment which adds or eliminates a stated par value or changes the stated par value and which does not also state the effect of the amendment on outstanding shares is not thereby subject to subdivision (b).

Ca. Corp. Code § 907
Amended by Stats. 1985, Ch. 764, Sec. 1.

Section 908 - Effect of filing of certificate of amendment

Upon the filing of the certificate of amendment, the articles shall be amended in accordance with the certificate and any stock split, reverse stock split, reclassification, cancellation, exchange or other change in shares shall be effected, and a copy of the certificate, certified by the Secretary of State, is prima facie evidence of the performance of the conditions necessary to the adoption of the amendment.

Ca. Corp. Code § 908

Amended by Stats. 1979, Ch. 711.

Section 909 - Extension of term of existence by amendment

A corporation formed for a limited period may at any time subsequent to the expiration of the term of its corporate existence, if it has continuously acted as a corporation and done business as such, extend the term of its existence by an amendment to its articles removing any provision limiting the term of its existence and providing for perpetual existence. If the filing of the certificate of amendment providing for perpetual existence would be prohibited if it were original articles by the provisions of Section 201, the Secretary of State shall not file such certificate unless by the same or a concurrently filed certificate of amendment the articles of such corporation are amended to adopt a new available name. For the purpose of the adoption of any such amendment, persons who have been functioning as directors of such corporation shall be considered to have been validly elected even though their election may have occurred after the expiration of the original term of the corporate existence. The certificate of amendment shall set forth that the corporation continuously acted as a corporation and did business as such from the expiration of its term of corporate existence to the date of the amendment.

Ca. Corp. Code § 909

Added by Stats. 1975, Ch. 682.

Section 910 - Restatement of articles

(a)A corporation may restate in a single certificate the entire text of its articles as amended by filing an officers' certificate or, in circumstances where incorporators or the board may amend a corporation's articles pursuant to Sections 901 and 906, a certificate signed and verified by a majority of the incorporators or the board, as applicable, entitled Restated Articles of Incorporation, which shall set forth the articles as amended to the date of the filing of the certificate, except that the signatures and acknowledgments of the articles by the incorporators and any statements regarding the effect of any prior amendment upon outstanding shares and any provisions of agreements of merger (other than amendments to the articles of the surviving corporation) and the initial street address and initial mailing address of the corporation and the names and addresses of the first directors and of the initial agent for service of process shall be omitted (except that the initial street address and initial mailing address of the corporation, the names and addresses of the initial agent for service of process and, if previously set forth in the articles, the initial directors, shall not be omitted before the time that the corporation has filed a statement under Section 1502). Such omissions are not alterations or amendments of the articles. The certificate may also itself alter or amend the articles in any respect, in which case the certificate must comply with Section 905 or 906, as the case may be, and Section 907.

(b) If the certificate does not itself alter or amend the articles in any respect, it shall be approved by the board or, before the issuance of any shares and the naming and election of directors, by a majority of the incorporators, and shall be subject to the provisions of this chapter relating to an amendment of the articles not requiring any approval of the outstanding shares (Section 152). If the certificate does itself alter or amend the articles, it shall be subject to the provisions of this chapter relating to the amendment or amendments so made and, except for certificates approved by a majority of the incorporators, the certificate shall also state that the board has approved the restated articles.

(c) Certificates of determination are a part of the articles within the meaning of this section. The provisions of such a certificate shall be given an article designation in the restated articles.

(d) Restated articles of incorporation filed pursuant to this section shall supersede for all purposes the original articles and all amendments and certificates of determination filed prior thereto.

   Ca. Corp. Code § 910

Amended by Stats 2022 ch 617 (SB 1202),s 18, eff. 1/1/2023.
Amended by Stats 2012 ch 494 (SB 1532),s 7, eff. 1/1/2013.

Section 911 - Amendment of articles to convert to nonprofit corporation

(a) A corporation may, by amendment of its articles pursuant to this section, change its status to that of a social purpose corporation, nonprofit public benefit corporation, nonprofit mutual benefit corporation, nonprofit religious corporation, or cooperative corporation.

(b) The amendment of the articles to change status to a nonprofit corporation shall revise the statement of purpose, delete the authorization for shares and any other provisions relating to authorized or issued shares, make such other changes as may be necessary or desired, and, if any shares have been issued, provide either for the cancellation of those shares or for the conversion of those shares to memberships of the nonprofit corporation. The amendment of the articles to change status to a cooperative corporation shall revise the statement of purpose, make such other changes as may be necessary or desired, and, if any shares have been issued, provide for the cancellation of those shares or for the conversion of those shares to memberships of the cooperative corporation, if necessary.

(c) If shares have been issued, an amendment to change status to a nonprofit corporation shall be approved by all of the outstanding shares of all classes regardless of limitations or restrictions on the voting rights thereof and an amendment to change status to a cooperative corporation shall be approved by the outstanding shares (Section 152) of each class regardless of limitations or restrictions on the voting rights thereof.

(d) In the case of a change of status to a social purpose corporation:

(1) The corporation shall modify the name of the corporation, revise the statement of purpose, include the statement required by subparagraph (B) of paragraph (3) of subdivision (b) of Section 2602, and make such other conforming changes as may be necessary or desired.

(2) The amendment shall be approved by the affirmative vote of at least two-thirds of each class, or a greater vote if required in the articles, of outstanding shares (Section 152) of that changing corporation.

(e) If an amendment pursuant to this section is included in a merger agreement, the provisions of this section apply, except that any provision for cancellation or conversion of shares shall be in the merger agreement rather than in the amendment of the articles.

(f) Notwithstanding subdivision (c), if a corporation is a mutual water company within the meaning of Section 2705 of the Public Utilities Code and under the terms of the status change each outstanding share is converted to a membership of a nonprofit mutual benefit corporation, an amendment to change status to a nonprofit mutual benefit corporation shall be approved by the outstanding shares (Section 152) of each class regardless of limitations or restrictions on the voting rights thereof.

Ca. Corp. Code § 911
Amended by Stats 2014 ch 694 (SB 1301),s 4, eff. 1/1/2015.

Chapter 10 - SALES OF ASSETS

Section 1000 - Mortgage, deed of trust, pledge, or other hypothecation of corporation's property

Any mortgage, deed of trust, pledge or other hypothecation of all or any part of the corporation's property, real or personal, for the purpose of securing the payment or performance of any contract or obligation may be approved by the board. Unless the articles otherwise provide, no approval of shareholders (Section 153) or of the outstanding shares (Section 152) shall be necessary for such action.

Ca. Corp. Code § 1000
Added by Stats. 1975, Ch. 682.

Section 1001 - Sale, lease, conveyance, exchange, transfer or other disposition of assets

(a) A corporation may sell, lease, convey, exchange, transfer, or otherwise dispose of all or substantially all of its assets when the principal terms are approved by the board, and, unless the transaction is in the usual and regular course of its business, approved by the outstanding shares (Section 152), either before or after approval by the board and before or after the transaction. A transaction constituting a reorganization (Section 181) is subject to the provisions of Chapter 12 (commencing with Section 1200) and not this section (other than subdivision (d)). A transaction constituting a conversion (Section 161.9) is subject to the provisions of Chapter 11.5 (commencing with Section 1150) and not this section.

(b) Notwithstanding approval of the outstanding shares (Section 152), the board may abandon the proposed transaction without further action by the shareholders, subject to the contractual rights, if any, of third parties.

(c) The sale, lease, conveyance, exchange, transfer, or other disposition may be made upon those terms and conditions and for that consideration as the board may deem in the best interests of the corporation. The consideration may be money, securities, or other property.

(d) If the acquiring party in a transaction pursuant to subdivision (a) of this section or subdivision (g) of Section 2001 is in control of or under common control with the disposing corporation, the principal terms of the sale must be approved by at least 90 percent of the voting power of the disposing corporation unless the disposition is to a domestic or foreign corporation or other business entity in consideration of the nonredeemable common shares or nonredeemable equity securities of the acquiring party or its parent.

(e) Subdivision (d) does not apply to any transaction if the Commissioner of Financial Protection and Innovation, the Insurance Commissioner, or the Public Utilities Commission has approved the terms and conditions of the transaction and the fairness of those terms and conditions pursuant to Section 25142 of this code, or Section 1209, 5750, or 5802 of the Financial Code, Section 838.5 of the Insurance Code, or Section 822 of the Public Utilities Code.

Ca. Corp. Code § 1001

Amended by Stats 2022 ch 617 (SB 1202),s 19, eff. 1/1/2023.
Amended by Stats 2022 ch 452 (SB 1498),s 46, eff. 1/1/2023.
Amended by Stats 2019 ch 143 (SB 251),s 23, eff. 1/1/2020.
Amended by Stats 2002 ch 480 (SB 399),s 5, eff. 1/1/2003.
Previously Amended September 21, 1999 (Bill Number: AB 198) (Chapter 437).

Section 1002 - Certificate annexed to deed or instrument transferring assets

Any deed or instrument conveying or otherwise transferring any assets of a corporation may have annexed to it the certificate of the secretary or an assistant secretary of the corporation, setting forth that the transaction has been validly approved by the board and (a) stating that the property described in said deed or instrument is less than substantially all of the assets of the corporation or that the transfer is in the usual and regular course of the business of the corporation, if such be the case, or (b) if such property constitutes all or substantially all of the assets of the corporation and the transfer is not in the usual and regular course of the business of the corporation, stating the fact of approval thereof by the outstanding shares

(Section 152) pursuant to this chapter or Chapter 12, as the case may be, or that such approval is not required by Chapter 12. Such certificate is prima facie evidence of the existence of the facts authorizing such conveyance or other transfer of the assets and conclusive evidence in favor of any innocent purchaser or encumbrancer for value.

Ca. Corp. Code § 1002
Added by Stats. 1975, Ch. 682.

Chapter 11 - MERGER

Section 1100 - Merger of corporations

Any two or more corporations may be merged into one of those corporations. A corporation may merge with one or more domestic corporations (Section 167), social purpose corporations (Section 171.08), foreign corporations (Section 171), or other business entities (Section 174.5) pursuant to this chapter. Mergers in which a foreign corporation but no other business entity is a constituent party are governed by Section 1108, mergers in which a social purpose corporation but no other business entity is a constituent party are governed by Section 1112.5, and mergers in which an other business entity is a constituent party are governed by Section 1113.

Ca. Corp. Code § 1100
Amended by Stats 2014 ch 694 (SB 1301),s 5, eff. 1/1/2015.
Amended by Stats 2011 ch 740 (SB 201),s 6, eff. 1/1/2012.
Amended September 21, 1999 (Bill Number: AB 198) (Chapter 437).

Section 1101 - Agreement of merger

(a) The board of each corporation that desires to merge shall approve an agreement of merger. The constituent corporations shall be parties to the agreement of merger and other persons, including a parent party (Section 1200), may be parties to the agreement of merger. The agreement shall state all of the following:

(1) The terms and conditions of the merger.

(2) The amendments, subject to Sections 900 and 907, to the articles of the surviving corporation to be effected by the merger, if any. If any amendment changes the name of the surviving corporation the new name may be the same as or similar to the name of a disappearing domestic or foreign corporation, subject to subdivision (b) of Section 201.

(3) The name and place of incorporation of each constituent corporation and which of the constituent corporations is the surviving corporation.

(4) The manner of converting the shares of each of the constituent corporations into shares or other securities of the surviving corporation and, if any shares of any of the constituent corporations are not to be converted solely into shares or other securities of the surviving corporation, the cash, rights, securities, or other property which the holders of those shares are to receive in exchange for the shares, which cash, rights, securities, or other property may be in addition to or in lieu of shares or other securities of the surviving corporation, or that the shares are canceled without consideration.

(5)Other details or provisions as are desired, if any, including, without limitation, a provision for the payment of cash in lieu of fractional shares or for any other arrangement with respect thereto consistent with the provisions of Section 407. (b)Each share of the same class or series of any constituent corporation (other than the cancellation of shares held by a constituent corporation or its parent or a wholly owned subsidiary of either in another constituent corporation) shall, unless all shareholders of the class or series consent and except as provided in Section 407, be treated equally with respect to any distribution of cash, rights, securities, or other property. Notwithstanding paragraph (4) of subdivision (a), except in a short-form merger, and in the merger of a corporation into its subsidiary in which it owns at least 90 percent of the outstanding shares of each class, the nonredeemable common shares or nonredeemable equity securities of a constituent corporation may be converted only into nonredeemable common shares of the surviving party or a parent party if a constituent corporation or its parent owns, directly or indirectly, before the merger shares of another constituent corporation representing more than 50 percent of the voting power of the other constituent corporation before the merger, unless all of the shareholders of the class consent and except as provided in Section 407.

Ca. Corp. Code § 1101

Amended by Stats 2022 ch 617 (SB 1202),s 20, eff. 1/1/2023.

Amended 9/21/1999 (Bill Number: AB 198) (Chapter 437).

Section 1101.1 - Approval by Commissioner of Financial Protection and Innovation, the Insurance Commissioner, or Public Utilities Commission

Subdivision (c) of Section 1113 and subdivision (b) of Section 1101 do not apply to any transaction if the Commissioner of Financial Protection and Innovation, the Insurance Commissioner, or the Public Utilities Commission has approved the terms and conditions of the transaction and the fairness of those terms and conditions pursuant to Section 25142 or Section 1209, 5750, or 5802 of the Financial Code, Section 838.5 of the Insurance Code, or Section 822 of the Public Utilities Code.

Ca. Corp. Code § 1101.1

Amended by Stats 2022 ch 617 (SB 1202),s 21, eff. 1/1/2023.

Amended by Stats 2015 ch 190 (AB 1517),s 7, eff. 1/1/2016.

Amended September 21, 1999 (Bill Number: AB 198) (Chapter 437).

Section 1102 - Signing agreement

Each corporation shall sign the agreement by its chairperson of the board, president or a vice president and secretary or an assistant secretary acting on behalf of their respective corporations.

Ca. Corp. Code § 1102
Amended by Stats 2015 ch 98 (SB 351),s 9, eff. 1/1/2016.

Section 1103 - Filing of agreement of merger

After approval of a merger by the board and any approval of the outstanding shares (Section 152) required by Chapter 12 (commencing with Section 1200), the surviving corporation shall file a copy of the agreement of merger with an officers' certificate of each constituent corporation attached stating the total number of outstanding shares of each class entitled to vote on the merger, that the principal terms of the agreement in the form attached were approved by that corporation by a vote of a number of shares of each class which equaled or exceeded the vote required, specifying each class entitled to vote and the percentage vote required of each class, or that the merger agreement was entitled to be and was approved by the board alone under the provisions of Section 1201. If equity securities of a parent of a constituent corporation are to be issued in the merger, the officers' certificate of that constituent corporation shall state either that no vote of the shareholders of the parent was required or that the required vote was obtained. The merger and any amendment of the articles of the surviving corporation contained in the merger agreement shall thereupon be effective (subject to subdivision (c) of Section 110 and subject to the provisions of Section 1108) and the several parties thereto shall be one corporation. The Secretary of State may certify a copy of the merger agreement separate from the officers' certificates attached thereto.

Ca. Corp. Code § 1103
Amended by Stats 2006 ch 773 (AB 2341),s 1, eff. 9/29/2006.

Section 1104 - Amendment to agreement

Any amendment to the agreement may be adopted and the agreement so amended may be approved by the board and, if it changes any of the principal terms of the agreement, by the outstanding shares (Section 152) (if required by Chapter 12) of any constituent corporation in the same manner as the original agreement. If the agreement so amended is approved by the board and the outstanding shares (if required) of each of the corporations, the agreement so amended shall then constitute the agreement of merger.

Ca. Corp. Code § 1104
Amended by Stats. 1979, Ch. 711.

Section 1105 - Abandonment of merger

The board may, in its discretion, abandon a merger, subject to the contractual rights, if any, of third parties, including other constituent corporations, without further approval by the outstanding shares (Section 152), at any time before the merger is effective.

Ca. Corp. Code § 1105

Repealed and added by Stats. 1975, Ch. 682.

Section 1106 - Effect of certified copy of agreement of merger

A copy of an agreement of merger certified on or after the effective date by an official having custody thereof has the same force in evidence as the original and, except as against the state, is conclusive evidence of the performance of all conditions precedent to the merger, the existence on the effective date of the surviving corporation and the performance of the conditions necessary to the adoption of any amendment to the articles contained in the agreement of merger.

Ca. Corp. Code § 1106

Amended by Stats. 1976, Ch. 641.

Section 1107 - Disappearing corporation; surviving corporation

(a) Upon merger pursuant to this chapter the separate existence of the disappearing corporations ceases and the surviving corporation shall succeed, without other transfer, to all the rights and property of each of the disappearing corporations and shall be subject to all the debts and liabilities of each in the same manner as if the surviving corporation had itself incurred them.

(b) For purposes of subdivision (a), a surviving corporation may succeed without the payment of any local agency transfer fee to all licenses, permits, registrations, and other privileges granted by any local agency provided the merger does not result in a change of ownership. Examples of mergers that do not result in a change of ownership are mergers between any of the following:

(1) a corporation and its wholly owned subsidiary;

(2) a corporation and the wholly owned subsidiary of that corporation's wholly owned subsidiary; or

(3) two wholly owned subsidiaries of the same parent corporation. The surviving corporation shall be subject to the same duties and obligations in connection with the license, permit, registration, or other privileges acquired from the disappearing corporations.

(c) All rights of creditors and all liens upon the property of each of the constituent corporations shall be preserved unimpaired, provided that any liens upon property of a disappearing corporation shall be limited to the property affected thereby immediately prior to the time the merger is effective.

(d) Any action or proceeding pending by or against any disappearing corporation may be prosecuted to judgment, which shall bind the surviving corporation, or the surviving corporation may be proceeded against or substituted in its place.

(e) Nothing in subdivision (b) shall limit or restrict a tax assessor from reassessing real property upon transfer of title. Privileges granted by any local agency do not include property tax assessments.

(f) Nothing in subdivision (b) shall limit or restrict a local agency from reevaluating privileges received by a successor corporation from disappearing corporations if the local agency determines in its sole discretion that the reevaluation is necessary for public health, safety, or welfare purposes.

(g) For purposes of this section, "local agency" means a county, city, city and county, political subdivision, district, or municipal corporation.

Ca. Corp. Code § 1107

Amended by Stats. 1998, Ch. 381, Sec. 1. Effective January 1, 1999.

Section 1107.5 - Assumption of liability by surviving corporation or other business entity

(a) Upon merger pursuant to this chapter, a surviving domestic or foreign corporation or other business entity shall be deemed to have assumed the liability of each disappearing domestic or foreign corporation or other business entity that is taxed under Part 10 (commencing with Section 17001) of, or under Part 11 (commencing with Section 23001) of, Division 2 of the Revenue and Taxation Code for the following:

    (1) To prepare and file, or to cause to be prepared and filed, tax and information returns otherwise required of that disappearing entity as specified in Chapter 2 (commencing with Section 18501) of Part 10.2 of Division 2 of the Revenue and Taxation Code.

    (2) To pay any tax liability determined to be due.

(b) If the surviving entity is a domestic limited liability company, domestic corporation, or registered limited liability partnership or a foreign limited liability company, foreign limited liability partnership, or foreign corporation that is registered or qualified to do business in California, the Secretary of State shall notify the Franchise Tax Board of the merger.

Ca. Corp. Code § 1107.5

Amended by Stats 2006 ch 495 (AB 339),s 6, eff. 1/1/2007.
Amended by Stats 2006 ch 773 (AB 2341),s 2, eff. 9/29/2006.
Amended by Stats 2005 ch 286 (AB 241),s 1, eff. 1/1/2006
Amended by Stats 2001 ch 50 (SB 324), s 1, eff. 1/1/2002.
Added October 10, 1999 (Bill Number: SB 284) (Chapter 1000).

Section 1108 - Merger of domestic corporations with foreign corporations

(a) The merger of any number of domestic corporations with any number of foreign corporations may be effected if the foreign corporations are authorized by the laws under which they are formed to effect the merger. The surviving corporation may be any one of the constituent corporations and shall continue to exist under the laws of the state or place of its incorporation.

(b) If the surviving corporation is a domestic corporation, the merger proceedings with respect to that corporation and any domestic disappearing corporation shall conform to the provisions of this chapter governing the merger of domestic corporations, but if the surviving corporation is a foreign corporation, then, subject to the requirements of subdivision (d) and of Section 407 and Chapters 12 (commencing with Section 1200) and 13 (commencing with Section 1300) (with respect to any domestic constituent corporations), the merger proceedings may be in accordance with the laws of the state or place of incorporation of the surviving corporation.

(c) If the surviving corporation is a domestic corporation, the agreement and the officers' certificate of each domestic or foreign constituent corporation shall be filed as provided in Section 1103, or the certificate of ownership shall be filed as provided in Section 1110, and thereupon, subject to subdivision (c) of Section 110, the merger shall be effective as to each domestic constituent corporation; and each foreign disappearing corporation that is qualified for the transaction of intrastate business shall by virtue of the filing, subject to subdivision (c) of Section 110, automatically surrender its right to transact intrastate business.

(d) If the surviving corporation is a foreign corporation, the merger shall become effective in accordance with the law of the jurisdiction in which it is organized, but, except as provided in subdivision (e), the merger shall be effective as to any domestic disappearing corporation as of the time of effectiveness in the foreign jurisdiction upon the filing in this state as required by this subdivision. There shall be filed as to the domestic disappearing corporation or corporations the documents described in any one of the following paragraphs:

(1) A copy of the agreement, certificate or other document filed by the surviving foreign corporation in the state or place of its incorporation for the purpose of effecting the merger, which copy shall be certified by the public officer having official custody of the original.

(2) An executed counterpart of the agreement, certificate or other document filed by the surviving foreign corporation in the state or place of its incorporation for the purpose of effecting the merger.

(3) A copy of the agreement of merger with an officers' certificate of the surviving foreign corporation and of each constituent domestic corporation attached, which officers' certificates shall conform to the requirements of Section 1103.

(4) A certificate of ownership pursuant to Section 1110.

(e) If the date of the filing in this state pursuant to subdivision (d) is more than six months after the time of the effectiveness in the foreign jurisdiction, or if the powers of the domestic corporation are suspended at the time of effectiveness in the foreign jurisdiction, the merger shall be effective as to the domestic disappearing corporation or corporations as of the date of filing in this state. Each foreign disappearing corporation that is qualified for the transaction of intrastate business shall, by virtue of the filing pursuant to subdivision (d), automatically surrender its right to transact intrastate business as of the date of filing in this state regardless of the time of effectiveness as to a domestic disappearing corporation.

(f) The provisions of the last two sentences of Section 1101 and Chapter 12 (commencing with Section 1200) and Chapter 13 (commencing with Section 1300) apply to the rights of the shareholders of any of the constituent corporations that are domestic corporations and of any domestic corporation that is a parent party of any foreign constituent corporation.

   Ca. Corp. Code § 1108

Amended by Stats 2006 ch 773 (AB 2341),s 3, eff. 9/29/2006.
Amended by Stats 2000 ch 201 (AB 1894), s 1, eff. 1/1/2001.

Section 1109 - Evidence of record ownership in surviving or consolidated party to merger

Whenever a domestic or foreign corporation or domestic or foreign other business entity having any real property in this state merges or consolidates with another domestic or foreign corporation or other business entity pursuant to the laws of this state or of the state or place in which any constituent party to the merger was incorporated or organized, and the laws of the state or place of incorporation or organization (including this state) of any disappearing party to the merger provide substantially that the making and filing of the agreement of merger or consolidation or certificate of ownership or certificate of merger vests in the surviving or consolidated party to the merger all the real property of any disappearing party to the merger, the filing for record in the office of the county recorder of any county in this state in which any of the real property of that disappearing party to the merger is located of a copy of the agreement of merger or consolidation or certificate of ownership or certificate of merger, certified by the Secretary of State or an authorized public official of the state or place pursuant to the laws of which the merger or consolidation is effected, shall evidence record ownership in the surviving or consolidated party to the merger, of all interest of the disappearing party to the merger in and to the real property located in that county.

   Ca. Corp. Code § 1109

Amended 9/21/1999 (Bill Number: AB 198) (Chapter 437).

Section 1110 - Merger of parent corporation and subsidiary

(a) If a domestic corporation owns all the outstanding shares, or owns less than all the outstanding shares but at least 90 percent of the outstanding shares of each class, of a corporation or corporations, domestic or foreign, the merger of the subsidiary corporation or corporations into the parent corporation or the merger into the subsidiary corporation of the parent corporation and any other subsidiary corporation or corporations, may be effected by a resolution or plan of merger adopted and approved by the board of the parent corporation and the filing of a certificate of ownership as provided in subdivision (e). The resolution or plan of merger shall provide for the merger and shall provide that the surviving corporation assumes all the liabilities of each disappearing corporation and shall include any other provisions required by this section.

(b) If the parent corporation owns less than all the outstanding shares but at least 90 percent of the outstanding shares of each class of the subsidiary corporation that is a party to the merger, the resolution or plan of merger also shall set forth the securities, cash, property, or rights to be issued, paid, delivered, or granted upon surrender of each outstanding share of the subsidiary corporation not owned by the parent corporation and the entire resolution or plan of merger as well as the consideration to be received for each share of the subsidiary corporation not owned by the parent corporation, shall be approved by the board of that subsidiary corporation.

(c) If the parent corporation is to be merged into one of its subsidiary corporations, the resolution or plan of merger also shall provide for the pro rata conversion of the outstanding shares of the parent corporation into shares of the surviving subsidiary corporation. In this case, the entire resolution or plan of merger shall be approved by the board of the surviving subsidiary corporation and, if the merger, but for the operation of this section, would be a merger reorganization (Section 181) the principal terms of which would be required to be approved by the outstanding shares (Section 152) of any class of the parent corporation pursuant to subdivision (d) of Section 1201, the principal terms of the resolution or plan of merger shall be approved by the outstanding shares (Section 152) of that same class of the parent corporation.

(d) In any merger pursuant to this section, the resolution or plan of merger may provide for the amendment of the articles of the surviving corporation to change its name, subject to Section 201, regardless of whether the name so adopted is the same as or similar to that of one of the disappearing corporations. The provision shall establish the wording of the amendment pursuant to paragraph (2) of subdivision (a) of Section 907 and the resolution or plan of merger shall not provide for the amendment of the articles of the surviving corporation other than to change its name.

(e) After the required approval or approvals of the resolution or plan of merger, a certificate of ownership consisting of an officers' certificate of the parent corporation shall be filed, and a copy thereof for each domestic subsidiary corporation and qualified foreign disappearing subsidiary corporation which is a party to the merger shall also be filed. The certificate of ownership shall:

(1) Identify the parent and subsidiary corporation or corporations.

(2) Set forth the share ownership by the parent corporation of each subsidiary corporation as 100 percent of the outstanding shares or as at least 90 percent of the

outstanding shares of each class, as the case may be.

(3) Set forth the resolution or plan of merger.

(4) Set forth approval of the resolution or plan of merger by the board of the parent corporation.

(5) Set forth other approvals of the resolution or plan of merger as required under subdivision (b) or (c), if applicable.

(f) Upon the filing of the certificate of ownership, the merger shall be effective and any amendment of the articles of the surviving corporation set forth in the certificate shall be effective.

(g) A merger pursuant to this section may be effected if the parent corporation is a foreign corporation and if at least one subsidiary corporation is a domestic corporation but in such a case the certificate of ownership prepared as in subdivision (e) or the document required by subdivision (d) of Section 1108 shall be filed as to each domestic and qualified foreign subsidiary corporation, but no filing shall be made as to the foreign parent corporation. No merger into or with a foreign corporation may be effected as provided by this section unless the laws of the state or place of its incorporation permit that action.

(h) In the event all of the outstanding shares of a subsidiary domestic corporation party to a merger effected under this section are not owned by the parent corporation immediately prior to the merger, the parent corporation shall, at least 20 days before the effective date of the merger, give notice to each shareholder of such subsidiary corporation that the merger will become effective on or after a specified date. The notice shall contain a copy of the resolution or plan of merger and the information required by subdivision (a) of Section 1301. The notice shall be sent by mail addressed to the shareholder at the address of the shareholder as it appears on the records of the corporation. The shareholder shall have the right to demand payment of cash for the shares of the shareholder pursuant to Chapter 13 (commencing with Section 1300).

(i) If an agreement of merger is entered into between a parent corporation and one or more of its subsidiary corporations and the share ownership requirements of subdivision (a) are met, the agreement of merger may be filed as a plan of merger with a certificate of ownership in accordance with the requirements of this section, in which case Sections 1101, 1102, 1103, 1200, 1201, and 1202 shall not apply; or the agreement of merger may be filed pursuant to Section 1103, in which case this section shall not apply.

Ca. Corp. Code § 1110

Amended by Stats 2006 ch 773 (AB 2341),s 4, eff. 9/29/2006.

Section 1111 - Disappearing corporation close corporation and surviving corporation not close corporation

If any disappearing corporation in a merger is a close corporation and the surviving corporation is not a close corporation, the merger shall be approved by the affirmative vote of at least two-thirds of each class of the outstanding shares of such disappearing corporation; provided, however, that the articles may provide for a lesser vote, but not less than a majority of the outstanding shares of each class.

Ca. Corp. Code § 1111

Amended by Stats. 1976, Ch. 641.

Section 1112 - Surviving corporation nonprofit corporation

If a disappearing corporation in a merger is a corporation governed by this division and the surviving corporation is a nonprofit public benefit corporation, a nonprofit mutual benefit corporation, or a nonprofit religious corporation, the merger shall be approved by all of the outstanding shares of all classes of the disappearing corporation, regardless of limitations or restrictions on the voting rights thereof, notwithstanding any provision of Chapter 12 (commencing with Section 1200).

Ca. Corp. Code § 1112

Added by Stats. 1979, Ch. 711.

Section 1112.5 - Surviving corporation social purpose corporation

If a disappearing corporation in a merger is a corporation governed by this division and the surviving corporation is a social purpose corporation, both of the following shall apply:

(a) The merger shall be approved by the affirmative vote of at least two-thirds of each class, or a greater vote if required in the articles, of the outstanding shares (Section 152) of the disappearing corporation, notwithstanding any provision of Chapter 12 (commencing with Section 1200).

(b) The shareholders of the disappearing corporation shall have all of the rights under Chapter 13 (commencing with Section 1300) of the shareholders of a corporation involved in a reorganization requiring the approval of its outstanding shares (Section 152), and the disappearing corporation shall have all of the obligations under Chapter 13 (commencing with Section 1300) of a corporation involved in the reorganization.

Ca. Corp. Code § 1112.5

Amended by Stats 2014 ch 694 (SB 1301),s 6, eff. 1/1/2015.

Added by Stats 2011 ch 740 (SB 201),s 7, eff. 1/1/2012.

Section 1113 - Merger of corporation with business entity

(a) Any one or more corporations may merge with one or more other business entities (Section 174.5). One or more domestic corporations (Section 167) not organized under this division and one or more foreign corporations (Section 171) may be parties to the merger. Notwithstanding the provisions of this section, the merger of any number of corporations with any number of other business entities may be effected only if:

(1) In a merger in which a domestic corporation not organized under this division or a domestic other business entity is a party, it is authorized by the laws under which it is organized to effect the merger.

(2) In a merger in which a foreign corporation is a party, it is authorized by the laws under which it is organized to effect the merger.

(3) In a merger in which a foreign other business entity is a party, it is authorized by the laws under which it is organized to effect the merger.
(b) Each corporation and each other party that desires to merge shall approve, and shall be a party to, an agreement of merger. Other persons, including a parent party (Section 1200), may be parties to the agreement of merger. The board of each corporation that desires to merge and, if required, the shareholders shall approve the agreement of merger. The agreement of merger shall be approved on behalf of each party by those persons required to approve the merger by the laws under which it is organized. The agreement of merger shall state:

(1) The terms and conditions of the merger.

(2) The name and place of incorporation or organization of each party to the merger and the identity of the surviving party.

(3) The amendments, if any, subject to Sections 900 and 907, to the articles of the surviving corporation, if applicable, to be effected by the merger. If any amendment changes the name of the surviving corporation, if applicable, the new name may be, subject to subdivision (b) of Section 201, the same as or similar to the name of a disappearing party to the merger.

(4) The manner of converting the shares of each constituent corporation into shares, interests, or other securities of the surviving party. If any shares of any constituent corporation are not to be converted solely into shares, interests, or other securities of the surviving party, the agreement of merger shall state (A) the cash, rights, securities, or other property which the holders of those shares are to receive in exchange for the shares, which cash, rights, securities, or other property may be in addition to or in lieu of shares, interests, or other securities of the surviving party, or (B) that the shares are canceled without consideration.

(5) Any other details or provisions required by the laws under which any party to the merger is organized, including, if a public benefit corporation or a religious corporation is a party to the merger, Section 6019.1, or, if a mutual benefit corporation is a party to the merger, Section 8019.1, or, if a consumer cooperative corporation is a party to the merger, Section 12540.1, or if an unincorporated association is a party to the merger, Section 18370, or, if a domestic limited partnership is a party to the merger, Section 15911.12, or, if a domestic partnership is a party to the merger, Section 16911, or, if a domestic limited liability company is a party to the merger, Section 17710.12.

(6) Any other details or provisions as are desired, including, without limitation, a provision for the payment of cash in lieu of fractional shares or for any other arrangement with respect thereto consistent with the provisions of Section 407.

(c) Each share of the same class or series of any constituent corporation (other than the cancellation of shares held by a party to the merger or its parent, or a wholly owned subsidiary of either, in another constituent corporation) shall, unless all shareholders of the class or series consent and except as provided in Section 407, be treated equally with respect to any distribution of cash, rights, securities, or other property. Notwithstanding paragraph (4) of subdivision (b), the unredeemable common shares of a constituent corporation may be converted only into unredeemable common shares of a surviving corporation or a parent party (Section 1200) or unredeemable equity securities of a surviving party other than a corporation if another party to the merger or its parent owns, directly or indirectly, prior to the merger shares of that corporation representing more than 50 percent of the voting power of that corporation, unless all of the shareholders of the class consent and except as provided in Section 407.

(d) Notwithstanding its prior approval, an agreement of merger may be amended prior to the filing of the agreement of merger or the certificate of merger, as is applicable, if the amendment is approved by the board of each constituent corporation and, if the amendment changes any of the principal terms of the agreement, by the outstanding shares (Section 152), if required by Chapter 12 (commencing with Section 1200), in the same manner as the original agreement of merger. If the agreement of merger as so amended and approved is also approved by each of the other parties to the agreement of merger, the agreement of merger as so amended shall then constitute the agreement of merger.

(e) The board of a constituent corporation may, in its discretion, abandon a merger, subject to the contractual rights, if any, of third parties, including other parties to the agreement of merger, without further approval by the outstanding shares (Section 152), at any time before the merger is effective.

(f) Each constituent corporation shall sign the agreement of merger by its chairperson of the board, president or a vice president, and also by its secretary or an assistant secretary acting on behalf of their respective corporations.

(g)

(1) If the surviving party is a corporation or a foreign corporation, or if a social purpose corporation (Section 171.08), a public benefit corporation (Section 5060), a mutual benefit corporation (Section 5059), a religious corporation (Section 5061), or a corporation organized under the Consumer Cooperative Corporation Law (Section 12200) is a party to the merger, after required approvals of the merger by each constituent corporation through approval of the board (Section 151) and any approval of the outstanding shares (Section 152) required by Chapter 12 (commencing with Section 1200) and by the other parties to the merger, the surviving party shall file a copy of the agreement of merger with an officers' certificate of each constituent domestic and foreign corporation attached stating the total number of outstanding shares or membership interests of each class entitled to vote on the merger (and identifying any other person or persons whose approval is required), that the agreement of merger in the form attached or its principal terms, as required, were approved by that corporation by a vote of a number of shares or membership interests of each class that equaled or exceeded the vote required, specifying each class entitled to vote and the percentage vote required of each class and, if applicable, by that other person or persons whose approval is required, or that the merger agreement was entitled to be and was approved by the board alone (as provided in Section 1201, in the case of corporations subject to that section). If equity securities of a parent party (Section 1200) are to be issued in the merger, the officers' certificate of that controlled party shall state either that no vote of the shareholders of the parent party was required or that the required vote was obtained. In lieu of an officers' certificate, a certificate of merger, on a form prescribed by the Secretary of State, shall be filed for each constituent other business entity. The certificate of merger shall be executed and acknowledged by each domestic constituent limited liability company by all managers of the limited liability company (unless a lesser number is specified in its articles of organization or operating agreement) and by each domestic constituent limited partnership by all general partners (unless a lesser number is provided in its certificate of limited partnership or partnership agreement) and by each domestic constituent general partnership by two partners (unless a lesser number is provided in its partnership agreement) and by each foreign constituent limited liability company by one or more managers and by each foreign constituent general partnership or foreign constituent limited partnership by one or more general partners, and by each constituent reciprocal insurer by the chairperson of the board, president, or vice president, and by the secretary or assistant secretary, or, if a constituent reciprocal insurer has not appointed those officers, by the chairperson of the board, president, or vice president, and by the secretary or assistant secretary of the constituent reciprocal insurer's attorney-in-fact, and by each other party to the merger by those persons required or authorized to execute the certificate of merger by the laws under which that party is organized, specifying for that party the provision of law or other basis for the authority of the signing persons. The certificate of merger shall set forth, if a vote of the shareholders, members, partners, or other holders of interests of the constituent other business entity was required, a statement setting forth the total number of outstanding interests of each class entitled to vote on the merger and that the agreement of merger in the form attached or its principal terms, as required, were approved by a vote of the number of interests of each class that equaled or exceeded the vote required, specifying each class entitled to vote and the percentage vote required of each class, and any other information required to be set forth under the laws under which the constituent other business entity is organized, including, if a domestic limited partnership is a party to the merger, subdivision (a) of

Section 15911.14, if a domestic partnership is a party to the merger, subdivision (b) of Section 16915, and, if a domestic limited liability company is a party to the merger, subdivision (a) of Section 17710.04. The certificate of merger for each constituent foreign other business entity, if any, shall also set forth the statutory or other basis under which that foreign other business entity is authorized by the laws under which it is organized to effect the merger. The merger and any amendment of the articles of the surviving corporation, if applicable, contained in the agreement of merger shall be effective upon filing of the agreement of merger with an officer's certificate of each constituent domestic and foreign corporation and a certificate of merger for each constituent other business entity, subject to subdivision (c) of Section 110 and subject to the provisions of subdivision (j), and the several parties thereto shall be one entity. If a domestic reciprocal insurer organized after 1974 to provide medical malpractice insurance is a party to the merger, the agreement of merger or certificate of merger shall not be filed until there has been filed the certificate issued by the Insurance Commissioner approving the merger pursuant to Section 1555 of the Insurance Code. The Secretary of State may certify a copy of the agreement of merger separate from the officers' certificates and certificates of merger attached thereto.

(2) If the surviving entity is an other business entity, and no public benefit corporation (Section 5060), mutual benefit corporation (Section 5059), religious corporation (Section 5061), or corporation organized under the Consumer Cooperative Corporation Law (Section 12200) is a party to the merger, after required approvals of the merger by each constituent corporation through approval of the board (Section 151) and any approval of the outstanding shares (Section 152) required by Chapter 12 (commencing with Section 1200) and by the other parties to the merger, the parties to the merger shall file a certificate of merger in the office of, and on a form prescribed by, the Secretary of State. The certificate of merger shall be executed and acknowledged by each constituent domestic and foreign corporation by its chairperson of the board, president or a vice president, and also by its secretary or an assistant secretary and by each domestic constituent limited liability company by all managers of the limited liability company (unless a lesser number is specified in its articles of organization or operating agreement) and by each domestic constituent limited partnership by all general partners (unless a lesser number is provided in its certificate of limited partnership or partnership agreement) and by each domestic constituent general partnership by two partners (unless a lesser number is provided in its partnership agreement) and by each foreign constituent limited liability company by one or more managers and by each foreign constituent general partnership or foreign constituent limited partnership by one or more general partners, and by each constituent reciprocal insurer by the chairperson of the board, president, or vice president, and by the secretary or assistant secretary, or, if a constituent reciprocal insurer has not appointed those officers, by the chairperson of the board, president, or vice president, and by the secretary or assistant secretary of the constituent reciprocal insurer's attorney-in-fact. The certificate of merger shall be signed by each other party to the merger by those persons required or authorized to

execute the certificate of merger by the laws under which that party is organized, specifying for that party the provision of law or other basis for the authority of the signing persons. The certificate of merger shall set forth all of the following:

(A) The name, place of incorporation or organization, and the Secretary of State's file number, if any, of each party to the merger, separately identifying the disappearing parties and the surviving party.

(B) If the approval of the outstanding shares of a constituent corporation was required by Chapter 12 (commencing with Section 1200), a statement setting forth the total number of outstanding shares of each class entitled to vote on the merger and that the principal terms of the agreement of merger were approved by a vote of the number of shares of each class entitled to vote and the percentage vote required of each class.

(C) The future effective date or time, not more than 90 days subsequent to the date of filing of the merger, if the merger is not to be effective upon the filing of the certificate of merger with the office of the Secretary of State.

(D) A statement, by each party to the merger which is a domestic corporation not organized under this division, a foreign corporation, or an other business entity, of the statutory or other basis under which that party is authorized by the laws under which it is organized to effect the merger.

(E) Any other information required to be stated in the certificate of merger by the laws under which each party to the merger is organized, including, if a domestic limited liability company is a party to the merger, subdivision (a) of Section 17710.14, if a domestic partnership is a party to the merger, subdivision (b) of Section 16915, and, if a domestic limited partnership is a party to the merger, subdivision (a) of Section 15911.14.

(F) Any other details or provisions that may be desired. Unless a future effective date or time is provided in a certificate of merger, in which event the merger shall be effective at that future effective date or time, a merger shall be effective upon the filing of the certificate of merger in the office of the Secretary of State and the several parties thereto shall be one entity. The surviving other business entity shall keep a copy of the agreement of merger at its principal place of business which, for purposes of this subdivision, shall be the office referred to in Section 17710.13 if a domestic limited liability company, at the business address specified in paragraph (5) of subdivision (a) of Section 17710.14 if a foreign limited liability company, at the office referred to in subdivision (a) of Section 16403 if a domestic general partnership, at the business address specified in subdivision (f) of Section 16911 if a foreign partnership, at the office referred to in subdivision (a) of Section 15901.14 if a domestic limited partnership, or at the business address specified in paragraph (3) of subdivision (a) of Section 15909.02 if a foreign limited partnership. Upon the request of a holder of equity securities of a party to the merger, a person with authority to do so on behalf of the surviving other business entity shall promptly deliver to that holder, a copy of the agreement of merger. A waiver by that holder of the rights provided in the foregoing sentence shall be unenforceable. If a domestic reciprocal insurer organized after 1974 to provide medical malpractice insurance is a party to the merger the agreement of merger or certificate of merger shall not be filed until there has been filed the certificate issued by the Insurance Commissioner approving the merger in accordance with Section 1555 of the Insurance Code.

(h)

(1) A copy of an agreement of merger certified on or after the effective date by an official having custody thereof has the same force in evidence as the original and, except as against the state, is conclusive evidence of the performance of all conditions precedent to the merger, the existence on the effective date of the surviving party to the merger, and the performance of the conditions necessary to the adoption of any amendment to the articles, if applicable, contained in the agreement of merger.

(2) For all purposes for a merger in which the surviving entity is a domestic other business entity and the filing of a certificate of merger is required by paragraph (2) of subdivision (g), a copy of the certificate of merger duly certified by the Secretary of State is conclusive evidence of the merger of the constituent corporations, either by themselves or together with the other parties to the merger, into the surviving other business entity.

(i)

(1) Upon a merger pursuant to this section, the separate existences of the disappearing parties to the merger cease and the surviving party to the merger shall succeed, without other transfer, to all the rights and property of each of the disappearing parties to the merger and shall be subject to all the debts and liabilities of each in the same manner as if the surviving party to the merger had itself incurred them.

(2) All rights of creditors and all liens upon the property of each of the constituent corporations and other parties to the merger shall be preserved unimpaired, provided that those liens upon property of a disappearing party shall be limited to the property affected thereby immediately prior to the time the merger is effective.

(3) Any action or proceeding pending by or against any disappearing corporation or disappearing party to the merger may be prosecuted to judgment, which shall bind the surviving party, or the surviving party may be proceeded against or substituted in its place.

(4) If a limited partnership or a general partnership is a party to the merger, nothing in this section is intended to affect the liability a general partner of a disappearing limited partnership or general partnership may have in connection with the debts and liabilities of the disappearing limited partnership or general partnership existing prior to the time the merger is effective.

(j)

(1) The merger of domestic corporations with foreign corporations or foreign other business entities in a merger in which one or more other business entities is a party shall comply with subdivision (a) and this subdivision.

(2) If the surviving party is a domestic corporation or domestic other business entity, the merger proceedings with respect to that party and any domestic disappearing corporation shall conform to the provisions of this section. If the surviving party is a foreign corporation or foreign other business entity, then, subject to the requirements of subdivision (c), and of Section 407 and Chapter 12 (commencing with Section 1200) and Chapter 13 (commencing with Section 1300), and, if applicable, corresponding provisions of the Nonprofit Corporation Law or the Consumer Cooperative Corporation Law, with respect to any domestic constituent corporations, Article 11 (commencing with Section 17711.01) of Title 2.6 with respect to any domestic constituent limited liability companies, Article 6 (commencing with Section 16601) of Chapter 5 of Title 2 with respect to any domestic constituent general partnerships, and Article 11.5 (commencing with Section 15911.20) of Chapter 5.5 of Title 2 with respect to any domestic constituent limited partnerships, the merger proceedings may be in accordance with the laws of the state or place of incorporation or organization of the surviving party.

(3) If the surviving party is a domestic corporation or domestic other business entity, the certificate of merger or the agreement of merger with attachments shall be filed as provided in subdivision (g) and thereupon, subject to subdivision (c) of Section 110 or paragraph (2) of subdivision (g), as is applicable, the merger shall be effective as to each domestic constituent corporation and domestic constituent other business entity.

(4) If the surviving party is a foreign corporation or foreign other business entity, the merger shall become effective in accordance with the law of the jurisdiction in which the surviving party is organized, but, except as provided in paragraph (5), the merger shall be effective as to any domestic disappearing corporation as of the time of effectiveness in the foreign jurisdiction upon the filing in this state of a copy of the agreement of merger with an officers' certificate of each constituent foreign and domestic corporation and a certificate of merger of each constituent other business entity attached, which officers' certificates and certificates of merger shall conform to the requirements of paragraph (1) of subdivision (g). If one or more domestic other business entities is a disappearing party in a merger pursuant to this subdivision in which a foreign other business entity is the surviving entity, a certificate of merger required by the laws under which that domestic other business entity is organized, including subdivision (a) of Section 15911.14, subdivision (b) of Section 16915, or subdivision (a) of Section 17710.14, as is applicable, shall also be filed at the same time as the filing of the agreement of merger.

(5) If the date of the filing in this state pursuant to this subdivision is more than six months after the time of the effectiveness in the foreign jurisdiction, or if the powers of a domestic disappearing corporation are suspended at the time of effectiveness in the foreign jurisdiction, the merger shall be effective as to the domestic disappearing corporation as of the date of filing in this state.

(6) In a merger described in paragraph (3) or (4), each foreign disappearing corporation that is qualified for the transaction of intrastate business shall by virtue of the filing pursuant to this subdivision, subject to subdivision (c) of Section 110, automatically surrender its right to transact intrastate business in this state. The filing of the agreement of merger or certificate of merger, as is applicable, pursuant to this subdivision, by a disappearing foreign other business entity registered for the transaction of intrastate business in this state shall, by virtue of that filing, subject to subdivision (c) of Section 110, automatically cancels the registration for that foreign other business entity, without the necessity of the filing of a certificate of cancellation.

Ca. Corp. Code § 1113

Amended by Stats 2014 ch 694 (SB 1301),s 7, eff. 1/1/2015.
Amended by Stats 2012 ch 419 (SB 323),s 7, eff. 1/1/2013, op. 1/1/2014.
Amended by Stats 2011 ch 740 (SB 201),s 8.5, eff. 1/1/2012.
Amended by Stats 2011 ch 442 (AB 1211),s 1, eff. 1/1/2012.
Amended by Stats 2006 ch 773 (AB 2341),s 5.5, eff. 9/29/2006.
Amended by Stats 2006 ch 495 (AB 339),s 7, eff. 1/1/2007.
Amended by Stats 2000 ch 201 (AB 1894), s 2, eff. 1/1/2001.
Previously Amended September 21, 1999 (Bill Number: AB 198) (Chapter 437).

Chapter 11.5 - CONVERSIONS

Section 1150 - Definitions

For purposes of this chapter, the following definitions shall apply:
(a)"Converted corporation" means a corporation that results from a conversion of a domestic other business entity, foreign other business entity, or foreign corporation pursuant to Section 1157.
(b)"Converted entity" means a domestic other business entity, foreign other business entity, or foreign corporation that results from a conversion of a corporation under this chapter.
(c)"Converting corporation" means a corporation that converts into a domestic other business entity, foreign other business entity, or foreign corporation pursuant to this chapter.

(d)"Converting entity" means a domestic other business entity, foreign other business entity, or foreign corporation that converts into a corporation pursuant to Section 1157.

(e)"Domestic other business entity" has the meaning provided in Section 167.7.

(f)"Foreign corporation" has the meaning provided in Section 171.

(g)"Foreign other business entity" has the meaning provided in Section 171.07.

(h)"Other business entity" has the meaning provided in Section 174.5.

Ca. Corp. Code § 1150

Amended by Stats 2022 ch 237 (SB 49),s 1, eff. 1/1/2023.

Added by Stats 2002 ch 480 (SB 399),s 6, eff. 1/1/2003.

Section 1151 - Conversion of corporation into domestic other business entity

(a)A corporation may be converted into a domestic other business entity, foreign other business entity, or foreign corporation pursuant to this chapter if, pursuant to the proposed conversion, (1) each share of the same class or series of the converting corporation shall, unless all the shareholders of the class or series consent, be treated equally with respect to any cash, rights, securities, or other property to be received by, or any obligations or restrictions to be imposed on, the holder of that share, and (2) nonredeemable common shares of the converting corporation shall be converted only into nonredeemable equity securities of the converted entity unless all of the shareholders of the class consent; provided, however, that clause (1) shall not restrict the ability of the shareholders of a converting corporation to appoint one or more managers, if the converted entity is a limited liability company, or one or more general partners, if the converted entity is a limited partnership, in the plan of conversion or in the converted entity's governing documents.

(b) Notwithstanding this section, the conversion of a corporation into a domestic other business entity foreign other business entity, or foreign corporation may be effected only if both of the following conditions are met:

(1) The law under which the converted entity will exist expressly permits the formation of that entity pursuant to a conversion.

(2) The corporation complies with any and all other requirements of any other law that applies to conversion to the converted entity.

Ca. Corp. Code § 1151

Amended by Stats 2022 ch 237 (SB 49),s 2, eff. 1/1/2023.

Amended by Stats 2014 ch 694 (SB 1301),s 8, eff. 1/1/2015.

Added by Stats 2002 ch 480 (SB 399),s 6, eff. 1/1/2003.

Section 1152 - Plan of conversion

(a)A corporation that desires to convert to a domestic other business entity, foreign other business entity, or foreign corporation shall approve a plan of conversion. The plan of conversion shall state all of the following:

(1)The terms and conditions of the conversion.

(2)The name, form, and jurisdiction of organization of the converted entity after conversion.

(3)The manner of converting the shares of each of the shareholders of the converting corporation into securities of, or interests in, the converted entity.

(4)The provisions of the governing documents for the converted entity, including the partnership agreement if the converted entity is a partnership, the articles of organization or certificate of formation and operating agreement if the converted entity is a limited liability company, or the articles or certificate of incorporation if the converted entity is a corporation, to which the holders of interests in the converted entity are to be bound.

(5)Any other details or provisions that are required by the laws under which the converted entity is organized, or that are desired by the converting corporation.
(b)The plan of conversion shall be approved by the board of the converting corporation (Section 151), and the principal terms of the plan of the conversion shall be approved by the outstanding shares (Section 152) of each class of the converting corporation. The approval of the outstanding shares may be given before or after approval by the board. Notwithstanding the foregoing, if a converting corporation is a close corporation, the conversion shall be approved by the affirmative vote of at least two-thirds of each class, or a greater vote if required in the articles, of outstanding shares (Section 152) of that converting corporation; provided, however, that the articles may provide for a lesser vote, but not less than a majority of the outstanding shares of each class.
(c)If the corporation is converting into a general or limited partnership or a foreign general or limited partnership or into a limited liability company or a foreign limited liability company, then in addition to the approval of the shareholders set forth in subdivision (b), the plan of conversion shall be approved by each shareholder who will become a general partner or manager, as applicable, of the converted entity pursuant to the plan of conversion unless the shareholders have dissenters' rights pursuant to Section 1159 and Chapter 13 (commencing with Section 1300).
(d)Upon the effectiveness of the conversion, all shareholders of the converting corporation, except those that exercise dissenters' rights as provided in Section 1159 and Chapter 13 (commencing with Section 1300), shall be deemed parties to any agreement or agreements constituting the governing documents for the converted entity adopted as part of the plan of conversion, irrespective of whether a shareholder has executed the plan of conversion or those governing documents for the converted entity. Any adoption of governing documents made pursuant thereto shall be effective

at the effective time or date of the conversion.

(e) Notwithstanding its prior approval by the board and the outstanding shares or either of them, a plan of conversion may be amended before the conversion takes effect if the amendment is approved by the board and, if it changes any of the principal terms of the plan of conversion, by the shareholders of the converting corporation in the same manner and to the same extent as was required for approval of the original plan of conversion.

(f)A plan of conversion may be abandoned by the board of a converting corporation, or by the shareholders of a converting corporation if the abandonment is approved by the outstanding shares, in each case in the same manner as required for approval of the plan of conversion, subject to the contractual rights of third parties, at any time before the conversion is effective.

(g) The converted entity shall keep the plan of conversion at (1) the principal place of business of the converted entity if the converted entity is a domestic partnership, (2) the office at which records are to be kept under Section 15901.11 if the converted entity is a domestic limited partnership, (3) the office at which records are to be kept under Section 17701.13 if the converted entity is a domestic limited liability company, or (4) the office at which records are to be kept under the laws of the jurisdiction applicable to the converted entity if the converted entity is a foreign other business entity or foreign corporation. Upon the request of a shareholder of a converting corporation, the authorized person on behalf of the converted entity shall promptly deliver to the shareholder, at the expense of the converted entity, a copy of the plan of conversion. A waiver by a shareholder of the rights provided in this subdivision shall be unenforceable.

Ca. Corp. Code § 1152

Amended by Stats 2022 ch 237 (SB 49),s 3, eff. 1/1/2023.
Amended by Stats 2014 ch 694 (SB 1301),s 9, eff. 1/1/2015.
Amended by Stats 2012 ch 419 (SB 323),s 8, eff. 1/1/2013, op. 1/1/2014.
Amended by Stats 2011 ch 740 (SB 201),s 9, eff. 1/1/2012.
Amended by Stats 2006 ch 495 (AB 339),s 8, eff. 1/1/2007.
Added by Stats 2002 ch 480 (SB 399),s 6, eff. 1/1/2003.

Section 1153 - Filing of documents

(a) After the approval, as provided in Section 1152, of a plan of conversion by the board and the outstanding shares of a corporation, the converting corporation shall cause the filing of all documents required by law, including, in the case of a corporation converting into a foreign corporation or foreign other business entity, the laws of the state or place of organization of the foreign corporation or foreign other business entity, to effect the conversion and create the converted entity, which documents shall include a certificate of conversion or a statement of conversion as required by Section 1155, and the conversion shall thereupon be effective, or, in the case of a corporation converting into a foreign corporation or foreign other business entity, shall be effective in accordance with the laws of the state or place of organization of the foreign corporation or foreign other business entity.

(b)A copy of the statement of partnership authority, certificate of limited partnership, or articles of organization, or certificate of conversion complying with Section 1155, duly certified by the Secretary of State on or after the effective date, is conclusive evidence of the conversion of the corporation.

Ca. Corp. Code § 1153

Amended by Stats 2022 ch 237 (SB 49),s 4, eff. 1/1/2023.
Added by Stats 2002 ch 480 (SB 399),s 6, eff. 1/1/2003.

Section 1154 - Secretary of State as agent for service of process in proceedings against foreign entities

(a) To enforce an obligation of a corporation that has converted to a foreign corporation or foreign other business entity, the Secretary of State shall only be the agent for service of process in an action or proceeding against that converted foreign entity, if the agent designated for the service of process for that entity is a natural person and cannot be found with due diligence or if the agent is a corporation and no person, to whom delivery may be made, may be located with due diligence, or if no agent has been designated and if none of the officers, members, managers, or agents of that entity may be located after diligent search, and it is shown by affidavit to the satisfaction of the court. The court then may make an order that service be made by personal delivery to the Secretary of State or to an assistant or Deputy Secretary of State of two copies of the process together with two copies of the order, and the order shall set forth an address to which the process shall be sent by the Secretary of State. Service in this manner is deemed complete on the 10th day after delivery of the process to the Secretary of State.

(b) Upon receipt of the process and order and the fee set forth in Section 12197 of the Government Code, the Secretary of State shall provide notice to that entity of the service of the process by forwarding by certified mail, return receipt requested, a copy of the process and order to the address specified in the order.

(c) The Secretary of State shall keep a record of all process served upon the Secretary of State and shall record the time of service and the Secretary of State's action with respect to the process served. The certificate of the Secretary of State, under the Secretary of State's official seal, certifying to the receipt of process, the providing of notice of process to that entity, and the forwarding of the process shall be competent and prima facie evidence of the matters stated therein.

Ca. Corp. Code § 1154

Added by Stats 2022 ch 237 (SB 49),s 5, eff. 1/1/2023.

Section 1155 - Conversion of corporation

(a) To convert a corporation:

(1)If the corporation is converting into a domestic limited partnership, a statement of conversion shall be completed on the certificate of limited partnership for the converted entity.

(2)If the corporation is converting into a domestic partnership, a statement of conversion shall be completed on the statement of partnership authority for the converted entity, or if no statement of partnership authority is filed then a certificate of conversion shall be filed separately.

(3)If the corporation is converting into a domestic limited liability company, a statement of conversion shall be completed on the articles of organization for the converted entity.

(4)If the corporation is converting into a foreign other business entity or a foreign corporation, a certificate of conversion shall be filed with the Secretary of State. (b)Any statement or certificate of conversion of a converting corporation shall be executed and acknowledged by those officers of the converting corporation as would be required to sign an officers' certificate (Section 173), and shall set forth all of the following:

(1)The name of the converting corporation and the Secretary of State's file number of the converting corporation.

(2)A statement of the total number of outstanding shares of each class entitled to vote on the conversion, that the principal terms of the plan of conversion were approved by a vote of the number of shares of each class which equaled or exceeded the vote required under Section 1152, specifying each class entitled to vote and the percentage vote required of each class.

(3)The name, form, and jurisdiction of organization of the converted entity.

(4)The name, mailing address, and street address of the converted entity's agent for service of process. If a corporation qualified under Section 1505 is designated as the agent, no address for it shall be set forth.
(c)For the purposes of this chapter, the certificate of conversion shall be on a form prescribed by the Secretary of State.
(d)The filing with the Secretary of State of a statement of conversion on an organizational document or a certificate of conversion as set forth in subdivision (a) shall have the effect of the filing of a certificate of dissolution by the converting corporation and no converting corporation that has made the filing is required to file a certificate of election under Section 1901 or a certificate of dissolution under Section 1905 as a result of that conversion.
(e)Upon the effectiveness of a conversion pursuant to this chapter, a converted entity shall be deemed to have assumed the liability of the converting corporation (1) to prepare and file or cause to be prepared and filed all tax and information returns

otherwise required of the converting corporation under the Corporation Tax Law (Part 11 (commencing with Section 23001) of Division 2 of the Revenue and Taxation Code) and (2) to pay any tax liability determined to be due pursuant to that law.

Ca. Corp. Code § 1155

Amended by Stats 2022 ch 237 (SB 49),s 6, eff. 1/1/2023.
Amended by Stats 2015 ch 189 (AB 1471),s 2, eff. 1/1/2016.
Amended by Stats 2014 ch 834 (SB 1041),s 2.5, eff. 1/1/2015.
Amended by Stats 2014 ch 694 (SB 1301),s 10, eff. 1/1/2015.
Amended by Stats 2011 ch 740 (SB 201),s 10, eff. 1/1/2012.
Amended by Stats 2006 ch 773 (AB 2341),s 6, eff. 9/29/2006.
Added by Stats 2002 ch 480 (SB 399),s 6, eff. 1/1/2003.

Section 1156 - Record ownership of real property; effect of recording

(a) Whenever a corporation or other business entity having any real property in this state converts into a corporation or an other business entity pursuant to the laws of this state or of the state or place in which the corporation or other business entity was organized, and the laws of the state or place of organization, including this state, of the converting corporation or other converting entity provide substantially that the conversion vests in the converted corporation or other converted entity all the real property of the converting corporation or other converting entity, the filing for record in the office of the county recorder of any county in this state in which any of the real property of the converting corporation or other converting entity is located of either (1) a certificate of conversion or a statement of partnership authority, certificate of limited partnership or articles of organization containing a statement of conversion complying with Section 1155 and certified on or after the effective date of the conversion by the Secretary of State or (2) a copy of a certificate of conversion or a statement of partnership authority, certificate of limited partnership, articles of organization, articles of incorporation, or other comparable organizing document evidencing the creation of a foreign other business entity or foreign corporation, containing a statement of conversion, meeting the requirements of subdivision (b) and certified on or after the effective date of the conversion by the Secretary of State or any other authorized public official of the state or place pursuant to the laws of which the converted entity is organized, shall evidence record ownership in the converted corporation or other converted entity of all interest of the converting corporation or other converting entity in and to the real property located in that county.

(b) A filed and, if appropriate, recorded certificate of conversion or a statement of partnership authority, certificate of limited partnership, articles of organization, articles of incorporation, or other comparable organizing document evidencing the formation of a foreign other business entity or a foreign corporation referred to in clause (2) of subdivision (a) above which contains a statement of conversion, stating the name of the converting corporation or other converting entity in whose name property was held before the conversion and the name of the converted entity or converted corporation, but not containing all of the other information required by Section 1155, operates with respect to the converted entity named to the extent provided in subdivision (a).

(c) Recording of a certificate of conversion or a statement of partnership authority, certificate of limited partnership, articles of organization, articles of incorporation, or other comparable organizing document evidencing the creation of an other business entity or a corporation, containing a statement of conversion, in accordance with subdivision (a), shall create, in favor of bona fide purchasers or encumbrances for value, a conclusive presumption that the conversion was validly completed.

Ca. Corp. Code § 1156

Added by Stats 2002 ch 480 (SB 399),s 6, eff. 1/1/2003.

Section 1157 - Conversion of other business entity or foreign other business entity or foreign corporation into corporation

(a)A domestic other business entity, foreign other business entity, or foreign corporation may be converted into a corporation pursuant to this chapter only if the converting entity is authorized by the laws under which it is organized to effect the conversion.

(b)A domestic other business entity, foreign other business entity, or foreign corporation that desires to convert into a corporation shall approve a plan of conversion or other instrument as is required to be approved to effect the conversion pursuant to the laws under which that entity is organized.

(c) The conversion of a domestic other business entity, foreign other business entity, or foreign corporation shall be approved by the number or percentage of the partners, members, shareholders, or other holders of interest of the converting entity that is required by the laws under which that entity is organized, or a greater or lesser percentage as may be set forth in the converting entity's partnership agreement, articles of organization, operating agreement, articles of incorporation, or other governing document in accordance with applicable laws.

(d) The conversion by a domestic other business entity, foreign other business entity, or foreign corporation shall be effective under this chapter upon the filing with the Secretary of State of the articles of incorporation of the converted corporation, containing a statement of conversion that complies with subdivision (e).

(e)A statement of conversion of an entity converting into a corporation pursuant to this chapter shall set forth all of the following:

(1) The name, form, and jurisdiction of organization of the converting entity.

(2) The Secretary of State's file number, if any, of the converting entity.

(3) If the converting entity is a foreign other business entity or a foreign corporation, the statement of conversion shall contain the following:

(A) A statement that the converting entity is authorized to effect the conversion by the laws under which it is organized.

(B) A statement that the converting entity has approved a plan of conversion or other instrument as is required to be approved to effect the conversion pursuant to the laws under which the converting entity is organized.

(C) A statement that the conversion has been approved by the number or percentage of the partners, members, shareholders, or other holders of interest of the converting entity that is required by the laws under which that entity is organized, or a greater or lesser percentage as may be set forth in the converting entity's partnership agreement, articles of organization, operating agreement, articles of incorporation, or other governing document in accordance with applicable laws.

(f) The filing with the Secretary of State of articles of incorporation containing a statement pursuant to subdivision (e) shall have the effect of the filing of a certificate of cancellation by a converting foreign limited liability company or foreign limited partnership, and no converting foreign limited liability company or foreign limited partnership that has made the filing is required to file a certificate of cancellation under Section 15909.07 or 17708.06 as a result of that conversion. If a converting entity is a foreign corporation qualified to transact business in this state, the foreign corporation shall, by virtue of the filing, automatically surrender its right to transact intrastate business.

Ca. Corp. Code § 1157

Amended by Stats 2022 ch 237 (SB 49),s 7, eff. 1/1/2023.
Amended by Stats 2012 ch 419 (SB 323),s 9, eff. 1/1/2013, op. 1/1/2014.
Amended by Stats 2007 ch 130 (AB 299),s 39, eff. 1/1/2008.
Amended by Stats 2006 ch 495 (AB 339),s 9, eff. 1/1/2007.
Added by Stats 2002 ch 480 (SB 399),s 6, eff. 1/1/2003.

Section 1158 - Effect of conversion

(a) An entity that converts into another entity pursuant to this chapter is for all purposes other than for the purposes of Part 10 (commencing with Section 17001) of, Part 10.20 (commencing with Section 18401) of, and Part 11 (commencing with Section 23001) of, Division 2 of the Revenue and Taxation Code, the same entity that existed before the conversion.

(b) Upon a conversion taking effect, all of the following apply:

(1) All the rights and property, whether real, personal, or mixed, of the converting entity or converting corporation are vested in the converted entity or converted corporation.

(2) All debts, liabilities, and obligations of the converting entity or converting corporation continue as debts, liabilities, and obligations of the converted entity or converted corporation.

(3) All rights of creditors and liens upon the property of the converting entity or converting corporation shall be preserved unimpaired and remain enforceable against the converted entity or converted corporation to the same extent as against the converting entity or converting corporation as if the conversion had not occurred.

(4) Any action or proceeding pending by or against the converting entity or converting corporation may be continued against the converted entity or converted corporation as if the conversion had not occurred.

(c) A shareholder of a converting corporation is liable for:

(1) All obligations of the converting corporation for which the shareholder was personally liable before the conversion, but only to the extent that the shareholder was personally liable for the obligations of the converting corporation before the conversion.

(2) All obligations of the converted entity incurred after the conversion takes effect if (A) the shareholder becomes a general partner of a converted entity that is a general or limited partnership and, as a general partner, has liability under the laws under which the converted entity is organized or under the converted entity's governing documents or (B) the shareholder becomes a holder of other interests in the converted entity and, as a holder, has liability under the laws under which the converted entity is organized or under the converted entity's governing documents.

(d) A shareholder of a converted corporation remains liable for any and all obligations of the converting entity for which the shareholder was personally liable before the conversion, but only to the extent that the shareholder was personally liable for the obligations of the converting entity prior to the conversion.

(e) If a party to a transaction with a converted corporation that converted from a partnership reasonably believes when entering into the transaction that a shareholder of the converted corporation continues to be a general partner of the converting entity after the conversion is effective, and the shareholder was a general partner of the partnership that converted into the converted corporation, the shareholder is liable for an obligation incurred by the converted corporation within 90 days after the conversion takes effect. The shareholder's liability for all other obligations of the converted corporation incurred after the conversion takes effect is that of a shareholder of a corporation.

(f) The converted entity shall cause written notice of the conversion to be given by mail within 90 days after the effective date of the conversion to all known creditors and claimants whose addresses appear on the records of the converting entity. Failure to comply with this subdivision shall not affect the validity of the conversion, extend the 90-day period set forth in subdivision (e), or otherwise affect the rights of a creditor or claimant under this section.

Ca. Corp. Code § 1158
Added by Stats 2002 ch 480 (SB 399),s 6, eff. 1/1/2003.

Section 1159 - Rights of shareholders of converting corporation

The shareholders of a converting corporation shall have all of the rights under
Chapter 13 (commencing with Section 1300) of the shareholders of a corporation
involved in a reorganization requiring the approval of its outstanding shares (Section
152), and the converting corporation shall have all of the obligations under Chapter 13
(commencing with Section 1300) of a corporation involved in the reorganization.
Solely for purposes of applying the provisions of Chapter 13 (and not for purposes of
Chapter 12), a conversion pursuant to Section 1151 or 1157 shall be deemed to
constitute a reorganization.
   Ca. Corp. Code § 1159
Added by Stats 2002 ch 480 (SB 399),s 6, eff. 1/1/2003.

Section 1160 - [Repealed]

   Ca. Corp. Code § 1160
Repealed by Stats 2022 ch 237 (SB 49),s 8, eff. 1/1/2023.
Added by Stats 2002 ch 480 (SB 399),ss 6, 6 eff. 1/1/2003.

Chapter 12 - REORGANIZATIONS

Section 1200 - Approval of reorganization or share exchange tender offer by boards

A reorganization (Section 181) or a share exchange tender offer (Section 183.5) shall
be approved by the board of:
(a) Each constituent corporation in a merger reorganization;
(b) The acquiring corporation in an exchange reorganization;
(c) The acquiring corporation and the corporation whose property and assets are
acquired in a sale-of-assets reorganization;
(d) The acquiring corporation in a share exchange tender offer (Section 183.5); and
(e) The corporation in control of any constituent or acquiring domestic or foreign
corporation or other business entity under subdivision (a), (b) or (c) and whose equity
securities are issued, transferred, or exchanged in the reorganization (a "parent
party").
   Ca. Corp. Code § 1200
Amended 9/21/1999 (Bill Number: AB 198) (Chapter 437).

Section 1201 - Approval of principal terms of reorganization

(a) The principal terms of a reorganization shall be approved by the outstanding shares (Section 152) of each class of each corporation the approval of whose board is required under Section 1200, except as provided in subdivision (b) and except that (unless otherwise provided in the articles) no approval of any class of outstanding preferred shares of the surviving or acquiring corporation or parent party shall be required if the rights, preferences, privileges, and restrictions granted to or imposed upon that class of shares remain unchanged (subject to the provisions of subdivision (c)). For the purpose of this subdivision, two classes of common shares differing only as to voting rights shall be considered as a single class of shares.

(b) No approval of the outstanding shares (Section 152) is required by subdivision (a) in the case of any corporation if that corporation, or its shareholders immediately before the reorganization, or both, shall own (immediately after the reorganization) equity securities, other than any warrant or right to subscribe to or purchase those equity securities, of the surviving or acquiring corporation or a parent party (subdivision (e) of Section 1200) possessing more than five-sixths of the voting power of the surviving or acquiring corporation or parent party. In making the determination of ownership by the shareholders of a corporation, immediately after the reorganization, of equity securities pursuant to the preceding sentence, equity securities which they owned immediately before the reorganization as shareholders of another party to the transaction shall be disregarded. For the purpose of this section only, the voting power of a corporation shall be calculated by assuming the conversion of all equity securities convertible (immediately or at some future time) into shares entitled to vote but not assuming the exercise of any warrant or right to subscribe to or purchase those shares.

(c) Notwithstanding subdivision (b), the principal terms of a reorganization shall be approved by the outstanding shares (Section 152) of the surviving corporation in a merger reorganization if any amendment is made to its articles that would otherwise require that approval.

(d) Notwithstanding subdivision (b), the principal terms of a reorganization shall be approved by the outstanding shares (Section 152) of any class of a corporation that is a party to a merger or sale-of-assets reorganization if holders of shares of that class receive shares of the surviving or acquiring corporation or parent party having different rights, preferences, privileges, or restrictions than those surrendered. Shares in a foreign corporation received in exchange for shares in a domestic corporation have different rights, preferences, privileges, and restrictions within the meaning of the preceding sentence.

(e) Notwithstanding subdivisions (a) and (b), the principal terms of a reorganization shall be approved by the affirmative vote of at least two-thirds of each class, or a greater vote if required in the articles, of the outstanding shares (Section 152) of any close corporation if the reorganization would result in their receiving shares of a corporation that is not a close corporation. However, the articles may provide for a lesser vote, but not less than a majority of the outstanding shares of each class.

(f) Notwithstanding subdivisions (a) and (b), the principal terms of a reorganization shall be approved by at least two-thirds of each class, or a greater vote if required in the articles, of the outstanding shares (Section 152) of a corporation that is a party to a merger reorganization if holders of shares receive shares of a surviving social purpose corporation in the merger.

(g) Notwithstanding subdivisions (a) and (b), the principal terms of a reorganization shall be approved by the outstanding shares (Section 152) of any class of a corporation that is a party to a merger reorganization if holders of shares of that class receive interests of a surviving other business entity in the merger.

(h) Notwithstanding subdivisions (a) and (b), the principal terms of a reorganization shall be approved by all shareholders of any class or series if, as a result of the reorganization, the holders of that class or series become personally liable for any obligations of a party to the reorganization, unless all holders of that class or series have the dissenters' rights provided in Chapter 13 (commencing with Section 1300).

(i) Any approval required by this section may be given before or after the approval by the board. Notwithstanding approval required by this section, the board may abandon the proposed reorganization without further action by the shareholders, subject to the contractual rights, if any, of third parties.

Ca. Corp. Code § 1201

Amended by Stats 2022 ch 617 (SB 1202),s 22, eff. 1/1/2023.

Amended by Stats 2014 ch 694 (SB 1301),s 11, eff. 1/1/2015.

Amended by Stats 2011 ch 740 (SB 201),s 11, eff. 1/1/2012.

Amended September 21, 1999 (Bill Number: AB 198) (Chapter 437).

Section 1201.5 - Approval of principal terms of share exchange tender offer

(a) The principal terms of a share exchange tender offer (Section 183. 5) shall be approved by the outstanding shares (Section 152) of each class of the corporation making the tender offer or whose shares are to be used in the tender offer, except as provided in subdivision (b) and except that (unless otherwise provided in the articles) no approval of any class of outstanding preferred shares of either corporation shall be required, if the rights, preferences, privileges, and restrictions granted to or imposed upon that class of shares remain unchanged. For the purpose of this subdivision, two classes of common shares differing only as to voting rights shall be considered as a single class of shares.

(b) No approval of the outstanding shares (Section 152) is required by subdivision (a) in the case of any corporation if the corporation, or its shareholders immediately before the tender offer, or both, shall own (immediately after the completion of the share exchange proposed in the tender offer) equity securities, (other than any warrant or right to subscribe to or purchase the equity securities), of the corporation making the tender offer or of the corporation whose shares were used in the tender offer, possessing more than five-sixths of the voting power of either corporation. In making the determination of ownership by the shareholders of a corporation, immediately after the tender offer, of equity securities pursuant to the preceding sentence, equity securities which they owned immediately before the tender offer as shareholders of another party to the transaction shall be disregarded. For the purpose of this section only, the voting power of a corporation shall be calculated by assuming the conversion of all equity securities convertible (immediately or at some future time) into shares entitled to vote but not assuming the exercise of any warrant or right to subscribe to, or purchase, shares.

Ca. Corp. Code § 1201.5
Amended by Stats. 1990, Ch. 616, Sec. 2.

Section 1202 - Approval of principal terms of merger reorganization or sale-of-assets reorganization

(a) In addition to the requirements of Section 1201, the principal terms of a merger reorganization shall be approved by all the outstanding shares of a corporation if the agreement of merger provides that all the outstanding shares of that corporation are canceled without consideration in the merger.

(b) In addition to the requirements of Section 1201, if the terms of a merger reorganization or sale-of-assets reorganization provide that a class or series of preferred shares is to have distributed to it a lesser amount than would be required by applicable article provisions, the principal terms of the reorganization shall be approved by the same percentage of outstanding shares of that class or series which would be required to approve an amendment of the article provisions to provide for the distribution of that lesser amount.

(c) If a parent party within the meaning of Section 1200 is a foreign corporation (other than a foreign corporation to which subdivision (a) of Section 2115 is applicable), any requirement or lack of a requirement for approval by the outstanding shares of the foreign corporation shall be based, not on the application of Sections 1200 and 1201, but on the application of the laws of the state or place of incorporation of the foreign corporation.

Ca. Corp. Code § 1202
Added by Stats. 1988, Ch. 919, Sec. 7.

Section 1203 - Delivery of affirmative opinion as to fairness of consideration to shareholders if tender offer is made by interested party proposal

(a) If a tender offer, including a share exchange tender offer (Section 183.5), or a written proposal for approval of a reorganization subject to Section 1200 or for a sale of assets subject to subdivision (a) of Section 1001 is made to some or all of a corporation's shareholders by an interested party (herein referred to as an "Interested Party Proposal"), an affirmative opinion in writing as to the fairness of the consideration to the shareholders of that corporation shall be delivered as follows:

(1) If no shareholder approval or acceptance is required for the consummation of the transaction, the opinion shall be delivered to the corporation's board of directors not later than the time that consummation of the transaction is authorized and approved by the board of directors.

(2) If a tender offer is made to the corporation's shareholders, the opinion shall be delivered to the shareholders at the time that the tender offer is first made in writing to the shareholders. However, if the tender offer is commenced by publication and tender offer materials are subsequently mailed or otherwise distributed to the shareholders, the opinion may be omitted in that publication if the opinion is included in the materials distributed to the shareholders.

(3) If a shareholders' meeting is to be held to vote on approval of the transaction, the opinion shall be delivered to the shareholders with the notice of the meeting (Section 601).

(4) If consents of all shareholders entitled to vote are solicited in writing (Section 603), the opinion shall be delivered at the same time as that solicitation.

(5) If the consents of all shareholders are not solicited in writing, the opinion shall be delivered to each shareholder whose consent is solicited prior to that shareholder's consent being given, and to all other shareholders at the time they are given the notice required by subdivision (b) of Section 603. For purposes of this section, the term "interested party" means a person who is a party to the transaction and (A) directly or indirectly controls the corporation that is the subject of the tender offer or proposal, (B) is, or is directly or indirectly controlled by, an officer or director of the subject corporation, or (C) is an entity in which a material financial interest (subdivision (a) of Section 310) is held by any director or executive officer of the subject corporation. For purposes of the preceding sentence, "any executive officer" means the president, any vice president in charge of a principal business unit, division, or function such as sales, administration, research, development, or finance, and any other officer or other person who performs a policymaking function or has the same duties as those of a president or vice president. The opinion required by this subdivision shall be provided by a person who is not affiliated with the offeror and who, for compensation, engages in the business of advising others as to the value of properties, businesses, or securities. The fact that the opining person previously has provided services to the offeror or a related entity or is simultaneously engaged in providing advice or assistance with respect to the proposed transaction in a manner which makes its compensation contingent on the success of the proposed transaction shall not, for those reasons, be deemed to affiliate the opining person with the offeror. Nothing in this subdivision shall limit the applicability of the standards of review of the transaction in the event of a challenge thereto under Section 310 or subdivision (c) of Section 1312.

This subdivision shall not apply to an Interested Party Proposal if the corporation that is the subject thereof does not have shares held of record by 100 or more persons (determined as provided in Section 605), or if the transaction has been qualified under Section 25113 or 25121 and no order under Section 25140 or subdivision (a) of

Section 25143 is in effect with respect to that qualification.

(b) If a tender of shares or a vote or written consent is being sought pursuant to an Interested Party Proposal and a later tender offer or written proposal for a reorganization subject to Section 1200 or sale of assets subject to subdivision (a) of Section 1001 that would require a vote or written consent of shareholders is made to the corporation or its shareholders (herein referred to as a "Later Proposal") by any other person at least 10 days prior to the date for acceptance of the tendered shares or the vote or notice of shareholder approval on the Interested Party Proposal, then each of the following shall apply:

(1) The shareholders shall be informed of the Later Proposal and any written material provided for this purpose by the later offeror shall be forwarded to the shareholders at that offeror's expense.

(2) The shareholders shall be afforded a reasonable opportunity to withdraw any vote, consent, or proxy previously given before the vote or written consent on the Interested Party Proposal becomes effective, or a reasonable time to withdraw any tendered shares before the purchase of the shares pursuant to the Interested Party Proposal. For purposes of this subdivision, a delay of 10 days from the notice or publication of the Later Proposal shall be deemed to provide a reasonable opportunity or time to effect that withdrawal.

Ca. Corp. Code § 1203
Amended by Stats. 1990, Ch. 216, Sec. 9.

Chapter 13 - DISSENTERS' RIGHTS

Section 1300 - Purchase of dissenting shares

(a) If the approval of the outstanding shares (Section 152) of a corporation is required for a reorganization under subdivisions (a) and (b) or subdivision (e) or (f) of Section 1201, each shareholder of the corporation entitled to vote on the transaction and each shareholder of a subsidiary corporation in a short-form merger may, by complying with this chapter, require the corporation in which the shareholder holds shares to purchase for cash at their fair market value the shares owned by the shareholder which are dissenting shares as defined in subdivision (b). The fair market value shall be determined as of the day of, and immediately prior to, the first announcement of the terms of the proposed reorganization or short-form merger, excluding any appreciation or depreciation in consequence of the proposed reorganization or short-form merger, as adjusted for any stock split, reverse stock split, or share dividend that becomes effective thereafter.

(b) As used in this chapter, "dissenting shares" means shares to which all of the following apply:

(1) That were not, immediately prior to the reorganization or short-form merger, listed on any national securities exchange certified by the Commissioner of Financial Protection and Innovation under subdivision (o) of Section 25100, and the notice of meeting of shareholders to act upon the reorganization summarizes this section and Sections 1301, 1302, 1303, and 1304; provided, however, that this provision does not apply to any shares with respect to which there exists any restriction on transfer imposed by the corporation or by any law or regulation; and provided, further, that this provision does not apply to any shares where the holder of those shares is required, by the terms of the reorganization or short-form merger, to accept for the shares anything except:

(A) shares of any other corporation, which shares, at the time the reorganization or short-form merger is effective, are listed on any national securities exchange certified by the Commissioner of Financial Protection and Innovation under subdivision (o) of Section 25100;

(B) cash in lieu of fractional shares described in the foregoing subparagraph (A); or (C) any combination of the shares and cash in lieu of fractional shares described in the foregoing subparagraphs (A) and (B).

(2)That were outstanding on the date for the determination of shareholders entitled to vote on the reorganization and (A) were not voted in favor of the reorganization or, (B) if described in paragraph (1), were voted against the reorganization, or were held of record on the effective date of a short-form merger; provided, however, that subparagraph (A) rather than subparagraph (B) of this paragraph applies in any case where the approval required by Section 1201 is sought by written consent rather than at a meeting.

(3)That the dissenting shareholder has demanded that the corporation purchase at their fair market value, in accordance with Section 1301.

(4)That the dissenting shareholder has submitted for endorsement, in accordance with Section 1302.
(c)As used in this chapter, "dissenting shareholder" means the recordholder of dissenting shares and includes a transferee of record.
  Ca. Corp. Code § 1300
Amended by Stats 2022 ch 452 (SB 1498),s 48, eff. 1/1/2023.
Amended by Stats 2019 ch 143 (SB 251),s 24, eff. 1/1/2020.
Amended by Stats 2012 ch 473 (AB 1680),s 1, eff. 1/1/2013.
Amended by Stats 2009 ch 131 (AB 991),s 3, eff. 1/1/2010.
Amended September 23, 1999 (Bill Number: AB 1688) (Chapter 470).

Section 1301 - Notice of approval of reorganization, statement of price, and procedure; shareholder's demand

(a) If, in the case of a reorganization, any shareholders of a corporation have a right under Section 1300, subject to compliance with paragraphs (3) and (4) of subdivision (b) thereof, to require the corporation to purchase their shares for cash, that corporation shall mail to each of those shareholders a notice of the approval of the reorganization by its outstanding shares (Section 152) within 10 days after the date of that approval, accompanied by a copy of Sections 1300, 1302, 1303, and 1304 and this section, a statement of the price determined by the corporation to represent the fair market value of the dissenting shares, and a brief description of the procedure to be followed if the shareholder desires to exercise the shareholder's right under those sections. The statement of price constitutes an offer by the corporation to purchase at the price stated any dissenting shares as defined in subdivision (b) of Section 1300, unless they lose their status as dissenting shares under Section 1309.

(b) Any shareholder who has a right to require the corporation to purchase the shareholder's shares for cash under Section 1300, subject to compliance with paragraphs (3) and (4) of subdivision (b) thereof, and who desires the corporation to purchase shares shall make written demand upon the corporation for the purchase of those shares and payment to the shareholder in cash of their fair market value. The demand is not effective for any purpose unless it is received by the corporation or any transfer agent thereof (1) in the case of shares described in subdivision (b) of Section 1300, not later than the date of the shareholders' meeting to vote upon the reorganization, or (2) in any other case, within 30 days after the date on which the notice of the approval by the outstanding shares pursuant to subdivision (a) or the notice pursuant to subdivision (h) of Section 1110 was mailed to the shareholder.

(c) The demand shall state the number and class of the shares held of record by the shareholder which the shareholder demands that the corporation purchase and shall contain a statement of what the shareholder claims to be the fair market value of those shares as determined pursuant to subdivision (a) of Section 1300. The statement of fair market value constitutes an offer by the shareholder to sell the shares at that price.

Ca. Corp. Code § 1301

Amended by Stats 2012 ch 473 (AB 1680),s 2, eff. 1/1/2013.
Amended by Stats 2009 ch 131 (AB 991),s 4, eff. 1/1/2010.
Amended by Stats 2006 ch 214 (AB 1959),s 4, eff. 1/1/2007.

Section 1302 - Submission of shares or written notice of shares which shareholder demands that corporation purchase

Within 30 days after the date on which notice of the approval by the outstanding shares or the notice pursuant to subdivision (h) of Section 1110 was mailed to the shareholder, the shareholder shall submit to the corporation at its principal office or at the office of any transfer agent thereof, (a) if the shares are certificated securities, the shareholder's certificates representing any shares which the shareholder demands that the corporation purchase, to be stamped or endorsed with a statement that the shares are dissenting shares or to be exchanged for certificates of appropriate denomination so stamped or endorsed or (b) if the shares are uncertificated securities, written notice of the number of shares which the shareholder demands that the corporation purchase. Upon subsequent transfers of the dissenting shares on the books of the corporation, the new certificates, initial transaction statement, and other written statements issued therefor shall bear a like statement, together with the name of the original dissenting holder of the shares.

Ca. Corp. Code § 1302

Amended by Stats 2012 ch 473 (AB 1680),s 3, eff. 1/1/2013.

Section 1303 - Agreement that shares are dissenting shares and fixing price of shares

(a) If the corporation and the shareholder agree that the shares are dissenting shares and agree upon the price of the shares, the dissenting shareholder is entitled to the agreed price with interest thereon at the legal rate on judgments from the date of the agreement. Any agreements fixing the fair market value of any dissenting shares as between the corporation and the holders thereof shall be filed with the secretary of the corporation.

(b) Subject to the provisions of Section 1306, payment of the fair market value of dissenting shares shall be made within 30 days after the amount thereof has been agreed or within 30 days after any statutory or contractual conditions to the reorganization are satisfied, whichever is later, and in the case of certificated securities, subject to surrender of the certificates therefor, unless provided otherwise by agreement.

Ca. Corp. Code § 1303

Amended by Stats. 1986, Ch. 766, Sec. 24.

Section 1304 - Action to determine whether shares are dissenting shares and/or fair market value of dissenting shares

(a) If the corporation denies that the shares are dissenting shares, or the corporation and the shareholder fail to agree upon the fair market value of the shares, then the shareholder demanding purchase of such shares as dissenting shares or any interested corporation, within six months after the date on which notice of the approval by the outstanding shares (Section 152) or notice pursuant to subdivision (h) of Section 1110 was mailed to the shareholder, but not thereafter, may file a complaint in the superior court of the proper county praying the court to determine whether the shares are dissenting shares or the fair market value of the dissenting shares or both or may intervene in any action pending on such a complaint.

(b) Two or more dissenting shareholders may join as plaintiffs or be joined as defendants in any such action and two or more such actions may be consolidated.

(c) On the trial of the action, the court shall determine the issues. If the status of the shares as dissenting shares is in issue, the court shall first determine that issue. If the fair market value of the dissenting shares is in issue, the court shall determine, or shall appoint one or more impartial appraisers to determine, the fair market value of the shares.

Ca. Corp. Code § 1304

Amended by Stats 2012 ch 473 (AB 1680),s 4, eff. 1/1/2013.

Section 1305 - Appraisers

(a) If the court appoints an appraiser or appraisers, they shall proceed forthwith to determine the fair market value per share. Within the time fixed by the court, the appraisers, or a majority of them, shall make and file a report in the office of the clerk of the court. Thereupon, on the motion of any party, the report shall be submitted to the court and considered on such evidence as the court considers relevant. If the court finds the report reasonable, the court may confirm it.

(b) If a majority of the appraisers appointed fail to make and file a report within 10 days from the date of their appointment or within such further time as may be allowed by the court or the report is not confirmed by the court, the court shall determine the fair market value of the dissenting shares.

(c) Subject to the provisions of Section 1306, judgment shall be rendered against the corporation for payment of an amount equal to the fair market value of each dissenting share multiplied by the number of dissenting shares which any dissenting shareholder who is a party, or who has intervened, is entitled to require the corporation to purchase, with interest thereon at the legal rate from the date on which judgment was entered.

(d) Any such judgment shall be payable forthwith with respect to uncertificated securities and, with respect to certificated securities, only upon the endorsement and delivery to the corporation of the certificates for the shares described in the judgment. Any party may appeal from the judgment.

(e) The costs of the action, including reasonable compensation to the appraisers to be fixed by the court, shall be assessed or apportioned as the court considers equitable, but, if the appraisal exceeds the price offered by the corporation, the corporation shall pay the costs (including in the discretion of the court attorneys' fees, fees of expert witnesses and interest at the legal rate on judgments from the date of compliance with Sections 1300, 1301 and 1302 if the value awarded by the court for the shares is more than 125 percent of the price offered by the corporation under subdivision (a) of Section 1301).

Ca. Corp. Code § 1305

Amended by Stats. 1986, Ch. 766, Sec. 25.

Section 1306 - Creditors of corporation

To the extent that the provisions of Chapter 5 prevent the payment to any holders of dissenting shares of their fair market value, they shall become creditors of the corporation for the amount thereof together with interest at the legal rate on judgments until the date of payment, but subordinate to all other creditors in any liquidation proceeding, such debt to be payable when permissible under the provisions of Chapter 5.

Ca. Corp. Code § 1306

Repealed and added by Stats. 1975, Ch. 682.

Section 1307 - Cash dividends

Cash dividends declared and paid by the corporation upon the dissenting shares after the date of approval of the reorganization by the outstanding shares (Section 152) and prior to payment for the shares by the corporation shall be credited against the total amount to be paid by the corporation therefor.

Ca. Corp. Code § 1307

Repealed and added by Stats. 1975, Ch. 682.

Section 1308 - Rights and privileges of holders of dissenting shares

Except as expressly limited in this chapter, holders of dissenting shares continue to have all the rights and privileges incident to their shares, until the fair market value of their shares is agreed upon or determined. A dissenting shareholder may not withdraw a demand for payment unless the corporation consents thereto.

Ca. Corp. Code § 1308

Repealed and added by Stats. 1975, Ch. 682.

Section 1309 - Loss of status as dissenting shares

Dissenting shares lose their status as dissenting shares and the holders thereof cease to be dissenting shareholders and cease to be entitled to require the corporation to purchase their shares upon the happening of any of the following:

(a) The corporation abandons the reorganization. Upon abandonment of the reorganization, the corporation shall pay on demand to any dissenting shareholder who has initiated proceedings in good faith under this chapter all necessary expenses incurred in such proceedings and reasonable attorneys' fees.

(b) The shares are transferred prior to their submission for endorsement in accordance with Section 1302 or are surrendered for conversion into shares of another class in accordance with the articles.

(c) The dissenting shareholder and the corporation do not agree upon the status of the shares as dissenting shares or upon the purchase price of the shares, and neither files a complaint or intervenes in a pending action as provided in Section 1304, within six months after the date on which notice of the approval by the outstanding shares or notice pursuant to subdivision (h) of Section 1110 was mailed to the shareholder.

(d) The dissenting shareholder, with the consent of the corporation, withdraws the shareholder's demand for purchase of the dissenting shares.

Ca. Corp. Code § 1309

Amended by Stats 2012 ch 473 (AB 1680),s 5, eff. 1/1/2013.

Section 1310 - Effect of litigation testing sufficiency or regularity of votes in authorizing reorganization

If litigation is instituted to test the sufficiency or regularity of the votes of the shareholders in authorizing a reorganization, any proceedings under Sections 1304 and 1305 shall be suspended until final determination of such litigation.

Ca. Corp. Code § 1310
Repealed and added by Stats. 1975, Ch. 682.

Section 1311 - Inapplicability of chapter

This chapter, except Section 1312, does not apply to classes of shares whose terms and provisions specifically set forth the amount to be paid in respect to such shares in the event of a reorganization or merger.

Ca. Corp. Code § 1311
Amended by Stats. 1988, Ch. 919, Sec. 8.

Section 1312 - Right to attack validity of reorganization or short-form merger

(a) No shareholder of a corporation who has a right under this chapter to demand payment of cash for the shares held by the shareholder shall have any right at law or in equity to attack the validity of the reorganization or short-form merger, or to have the reorganization or short-form merger set aside or rescinded, except in an action to test whether the number of shares required to authorize or approve the reorganization have been legally voted in favor thereof; but any holder of shares of a class whose terms and provisions specifically set forth the amount to be paid in respect to them in the event of a reorganization or short-form merger is entitled to payment in accordance with those terms and provisions or, if the principal terms of the reorganization are approved pursuant to subdivision (b) of Section 1202, is entitled to payment in accordance with the terms and provisions of the approved reorganization.
(b) If one of the parties to a reorganization or short-form merger is directly or indirectly controlled by, or under common control with, another party to the reorganization or short-form merger, subdivision (a) shall not apply to any shareholder of such party who has not demanded payment of cash for such shareholder's shares pursuant to this chapter; but if the shareholder institutes any action to attack the validity of the reorganization or short-form merger or to have the reorganization or short-form merger set aside or rescinded, the shareholder shall not thereafter have any right to demand payment of cash for the shareholder's shares pursuant to this chapter. The court in any action attacking the validity of the reorganization or short-form merger or to have the reorganization or short-form merger set aside or rescinded shall not restrain or enjoin the consummation of the transaction except upon 10 days' prior notice to the corporation and upon a

determination by the court that clearly no other remedy will adequately protect the complaining shareholder or the class of shareholders of which such shareholder is a member.

(c) If one of the parties to a reorganization or short-form merger is directly or indirectly controlled by, or under common control with, another party to the reorganization or short-form merger, in any action to attack the validity of the reorganization or short-form merger or to have the reorganization or short-form merger set aside or rescinded, (1) a party to a reorganization or short-form merger which controls another party to the reorganization or short-form merger shall have the burden of proving that the transaction is just and reasonable as to the shareholders of the controlled party, and (2) a person who controls two or more parties to a reorganization shall have the burden of proving that the transaction is just and reasonable as to the shareholders of any party so controlled.

   Ca. Corp. Code § 1312
Amended by Stats. 1988, Ch. 919, Sec. 9.

Section 1313 - Conversion deemed reorganization

A conversion pursuant to Chapter 11.5 (commencing with Section 1150) shall be deemed to constitute a reorganization for purposes of applying the provisions of this chapter, in accordance with and to the extent provided in Section 1159.

   Ca. Corp. Code § 1313
Added by Stats 2002 ch 480 (SB 399),s 7, eff. 1/1/2003.

Chapter 14 - BANKRUPTCY REORGANIZATIONS AND ARRANGEMENTS

Section 1400 - Power and authority to carry out plan of reorganization and court orders

(a) Any domestic corporation with respect to which a proceeding has been initiated under any applicable statute of the United States, as now existing or hereafter enacted, relating to reorganizations of corporations, has full power and authority to put into effect and carry out any plan of reorganization and the orders of the court or judge entered in such proceeding and may take any proceeding and do any act provided in the plan or directed by such orders, without further action by its board or shareholders. Such power and authority may be exercised and such proceedings and acts may be taken, as may be directed by such orders, by the trustee or trustees of such corporation appointed in the reorganization proceeding (or a majority thereof), or if none is appointed and acting, by officers of the corporation designated or a master or other representative appointed by the court or judge, with like effect as if exercised and taken by unanimous action of the board and shareholders of the corporation.

(b) Such corporation may, in the manner provided in subdivision (a), but without limiting the generality or effect of subdivision (a), alter, amend or repeal its bylaws;

constitute or reconstitute its board and name, constitute or appoint directors and officers in place of or in addition to all or some of the directors or officers then in office; amend its articles; make any change in its capital stock; make any other amendment, change, alteration or provision authorized by this division; be dissolved, transfer all or part of its assets or merge as permitted by this division, in which case, however, no shareholder shall have any statutory dissenter's rights; change the location of its principal office or remove or appoint an agent to receive service of process; authorize and fix the terms, manner and conditions of the issuance of bonds, debentures or other obligations, whether or not convertible into shares of any class or bearing warrants or rights to purchase or subscribe to shares of any class; or lease its property and franchises to any corporation, if permitted by law.

Ca. Corp. Code § 1400
Amended by Stats 2022 ch 617 (SB 1202),s 23, eff. 1/1/2023.
Amended by Stats 2009 ch 500 (AB 1059),s 15, eff. 1/1/2010.

Section 1401 - Certificate of amendment, change or alteration or of dissolution or agreement of merger

(a) A certificate of any amendment, change or alteration or of dissolution or any agreement of merger made by a corporation pursuant to Section 1400 and executed as provided in subdivision (b), shall be filed and shall thereupon become effective in accordance with its terms and the provisions of this chapter.

(b) The certificate, agreement of merger, or other instrument shall be signed and verified, as may be directed by the orders of the court or judge, by the trustee or trustees appointed in the reorganization proceeding (or a majority thereof) or, if none is appointed and acting, by officers of the corporation designated or by a master or other representative appointed by the court or judge, and shall state that provision for the making of that certificate, agreement of merger, or instrument is contained in an order, identifying the same, of a court or judge having jurisdiction of a proceeding under a statute of the United States for the reorganization of that corporation.

(c) Notwithstanding subdivision (b), a trustee, liquidating agent, responsible officer, or other representative appointed by the court for a corporation, with respect to which a proceeding has been initiated under any applicable statute of the United States as described in subdivision (a) of Section 1401.5 may execute and file a certificate of dissolution as provided in subdivision (b) of Section 1401.5.

Ca. Corp. Code § 1401
Amended by Stats 2017 ch 267 (SB 340),s 1, eff. 1/1/2018.
Amended by Stats 2009 ch 500 (AB 1059),s 16, eff. 1/1/2010.

Section 1401.5 - Certificate of dissolution

(a) A trustee, liquidating agent, responsible officer, or other representative appointed by the court for a corporation subject to an order for relief entered in a case under Chapter 11 (commencing with Section 1101) of Title 11 of the United States Code may sign and verify a certificate of dissolution when the corporation has been completely wound up.

(b) The certificate of dissolution shall state the following:

(1) The name of the corporation.

(2) That an order for relief was entered in a case under Chapter 11 (commencing with Section 1101) of Title 11 of the United States Code with respect to the corporation.

(3) The identification of the court in which the order for relief was entered and the court's file number for the matter.

(4) That an order confirming a reorganization plan has been entered in that case.

(5) That the undersigned has been appointed by the court as a trustee, liquidating agent, responsible officer, or other representative of the corporation.

(6) That the shares of the corporation have been canceled pursuant to the terms of that plan.

(7) That the assets of the corporation have been distributed pursuant to the terms of that plan.

(8) That the corporation is dissolved.

Ca. Corp. Code § 1401.5
Amended by Stats 2018 ch 92 (SB 1289),s 47, eff. 1/1/2019.
Added by Stats 2017 ch 267 (SB 340),s 2, eff. 1/1/2018.

Section 1402 - Effect of entry of final decree in reorganization proceeding

The provisions of this chapter shall cease to apply to a corporation upon the entry of a final decree in the reorganization proceeding closing the case and discharging the trustee or trustees, if any, whether or not jurisdiction may be retained thereafter by the court for limited purposes which do not relate to the consummation of the plan.

Ca. Corp. Code § 1402
Amended by Stats 2009 ch 500 (AB 1059),s 17, eff. 1/1/2010.

Section 1403 - Fees

For filing any certificate, agreement or other paper pursuant to this chapter there shall be paid to the Secretary of State the same fees as are payable by corporations not in reorganization proceedings upon the filing of like certificates, agreements or other papers.

Ca. Corp. Code § 1403
Amended by Stats 2009 ch 500 (AB 1059),s 18, eff. 1/1/2010.

Chapter 15 - RECORDS AND REPORTS

Section 1500 - Books and records of accounts; minutes

Each corporation shall keep adequate and correct books and records of account and shall keep minutes of the proceedings of its shareholders, board and committees of the board and shall keep at its principal office, or at the office of its transfer agent or registrar, a record of its shareholders, giving the names and addresses of all shareholders and the number and class of shares held by each. Those minutes and other books and records shall be kept either in written form or in another form capable of being converted into clearly legible tangible form or in any combination of the foregoing. When minutes and other books and records are kept in a form capable of being converted into clearly legible paper form, the clearly legible paper form into which those minutes and other books and records are converted shall be admissible in evidence, and accepted for all other purposes, to the same extent as an original paper record of the same information would have been, provided that the paper form accurately portrays the record.

Ca. Corp. Code § 1500
Amended by Stats 2022 ch 617 (SB 1202),s 24, eff. 1/1/2023.
Amended by Stats 2004 ch 254 (SB 1306),s 11, eff. 1/1/2005

Section 1501 - Annual shareholders report

(a)

(1) The board shall cause an annual report to be sent to the shareholders not later than 120 days after the close of the fiscal year, unless in the case of a corporation with less than 100 holders of record of its shares (determined as provided in Section 605) this requirement is expressly waived in the bylaws. Unless otherwise provided by the articles or bylaws and if approved by the board of directors, that report and any accompanying material sent pursuant to this section may be sent by electronic transmission by the corporation (Section 20). This report shall contain a balance sheet as of the end of that fiscal year and an income statement and a statement of cashflows for that fiscal year, accompanied by any report thereon of independent accountants or, if there is no report, the certificate of an authorized officer of the corporation that the statements were prepared without audit from the books and records of the corporation.

(2) Unless so waived, the report specified in paragraph (1) shall be sent to the shareholders at least 15 (or, if sent by third-class mail, 35) days before the annual meeting of shareholders to be held during the next fiscal year, but this requirement shall not limit the requirement for holding an annual meeting as required by Section 600.

(3) Notwithstanding Section 114, the financial statements of any corporation with fewer than 100 holders of record of its shares (determined as provided in Section 605) required to be furnished by this subdivision and subdivision (c) are not required to be prepared in conformity with generally accepted accounting principles if they reasonably set forth the assets and liabilities and the income and expense of the corporation and disclose the accounting basis used in their preparation.

(4) The requirements described in paragraphs (1) and (2) shall be satisfied if a corporation with an outstanding class of securities registered under Section 12 of the Securities Exchange Act of 1934 complies with Section 240.14a-16 of Title 17 of the Code of Federal Regulations, as it may be amended from time to time, with respect to the obligation of a corporation to furnish an annual report to shareholders pursuant to Section 240.14a-3(b) of Title 17 of the Code of Federal Regulations.
(b) In addition to the financial statements required by subdivision (a), the annual report of any corporation having 100 or more holders of record of its shares (determined as provided in Section 605) either not subject to the reporting requirements of Section 13 of the Securities Exchange Act of 1934, or exempted from those reporting requirements by Section 12(g)(2) of that act, shall also describe briefly both of the following:

(1) Any transaction (excluding compensation of officers and directors) during the previous fiscal year involving an amount in excess of forty thousand dollars ($40,000) (other than contracts let at competitive bid or services rendered at prices regulated by law) to which the corporation or its parent or subsidiary was a party and in which any director or officer of the corporation or of a subsidiary or (if known to the corporation or its parent or subsidiary) any holder of more than 10 percent of the outstanding voting shares of the corporation had a direct or indirect material interest, naming the person and stating the person's relationship to the corporation, the nature of the person's interest in the transaction and, where practicable, the amount of the interest; provided that in the case of a transaction with a partnership of which the person is a partner, only the interest of the partnership need be stated; and provided further that no report need be made in the case of any transaction approved by the shareholders (Section 153).

(2) The amount and circumstances of any indemnification or advances aggregating more than ten thousand dollars ($10,000) paid during the fiscal year to any officer or director of the corporation pursuant to Section 317; provided that no report need be made in the case of indemnification approved by the shareholders (Section 153) under paragraph (2) of subdivision (e) of Section 317.
(c) If no annual report for the last fiscal year has been sent to shareholders, the

corporation shall, upon the written request of any shareholder made more than 120 days after the close of that fiscal year, deliver or mail to the person making the request within 30 days thereafter the financial statements required by subdivision (a) for that year. A shareholder or shareholders holding at least 5 percent of the outstanding shares of any class of a corporation may make a written request to the corporation for an income statement of the corporation for the three-month, six-month, or nine-month period of the current fiscal year ended more than 30 days before the date of the request and a balance sheet of the corporation as of the end of the period and, in addition, if no annual report for the last fiscal year has been sent to shareholders, the statements referred to in subdivision (a) for the last fiscal year. The statements shall be delivered or mailed to the person making the request within 30 days thereafter. A copy of the statements shall be kept on file in the principal office of the corporation for 12 months and it shall be exhibited at all reasonable times to any shareholder demanding an examination of the statements or a copy shall be mailed to the shareholder.

(d) The quarterly income statements and balance sheets referred to in this section shall be accompanied by the report thereon, if any, of any independent accountants engaged by the corporation or the certificate of an authorized officer of the corporation that the financial statements were prepared without audit from the books and records of the corporation.

(e) In addition to the penalties provided for in Section 2200, the superior court of the proper county shall enforce the duty of making and mailing or delivering the information and financial statements required by this section and, for good cause shown, may extend the time therefor.

(f) In any action or proceeding under this section, if the court finds the failure of the corporation to comply with the requirements of this section to have been without justification, the court may award an amount sufficient to reimburse the shareholder for the reasonable expenses incurred by the shareholder, including attorney's fees, in connection with the action or proceeding.

(g) This section applies to any domestic corporation and also to a foreign corporation having its principal office in California or customarily holding meetings of its board in this state.

Ca. Corp. Code § 1501

Amended by Stats 2022 ch 617 (SB 1202),s 25, eff. 1/1/2023.
Amended by Stats 2008 ch 177 (SB 1409),s 1, eff. 7/22/2008.
Amended by Stats 2006 ch 214 (AB 1959),s 5, eff. 1/1/2007.
Amended by Stats 2004 ch 254 (SB 1306),s 12, eff. 1/1/2005

Section 1502 - Filing of statement

(a) Every corporation shall file, within 90 days after the filing of its original articles and annually thereafter during the applicable filing period, on a form prescribed by the Secretary of State, a statement containing all of the following:

(1) The name of the corporation and the Secretary of State's file number.

(2) The names and complete business or residence addresses of its incumbent directors.

(3) The number of vacancies on the board, if any.

(4) The names and complete business or residence addresses of its chief executive officer, secretary, and chief financial officer.

(5) The street address of its principal executive office.

(6) The mailing address of the corporation, if different from the street address of its principal executive office.

(7) If the address of its principal executive office is not in this state, the street address of its principal business office in this state, if any.

(8) If the corporation chooses to receive renewal notices and any other notifications from the Secretary of State by electronic mail instead of by United States mail, the corporation shall include a valid electronic mail address for the corporation or for the corporation's designee to receive those notices.

(9) A statement of the general type of business that constitutes the principal business activity of the corporation, such as, for example, manufacturer of aircraft, wholesale liquor distributor, or retail department store.

(10) A statement indicating whether any officer or any director has an outstanding final judgment issued by the Division of Labor Standards Enforcement or a court of law, for which no appeal therefrom is pending, for the violation of any wage order or provision of the Labor Code.
(b) The statement required by subdivision (a) shall also designate, as the agent of the corporation for the purpose of service of process, a natural person residing in this state or a corporation that has complied with Section 1505 and whose capacity to act as an agent has not terminated. If a natural person is designated, the statement shall set forth that person's complete business or residence street address. If a corporate agent is designated, no address for it shall be set forth.
(c) If there has been no change in the information in the last filed statement of the corporation on file in the Secretary of State's office, the corporation may, in lieu of filing the statement required by subdivisions (a) and (b), advise the Secretary of State, on a form prescribed by the Secretary of State, that no changes in the required information have occurred during the applicable filing period.
(d) For the purposes of this section, the applicable filing period for a corporation shall be the calendar month during which its original articles were filed and the

immediately preceding five calendar months. The Secretary of State shall provide a notice to each corporation to comply with this section approximately three months prior to the close of the applicable filing period. The notice shall state the due date for compliance and shall be sent to the last address of the corporation according to the records of the Secretary of State or to the last electronic mail address according to the records of the Secretary of State if the corporation has elected to receive notices from the Secretary of State by electronic mail. The failure of the corporation to receive the notice is not an excuse for failure to comply with this section.

(e) Whenever any of the information required by subdivision (a) is changed, the corporation may file a current statement containing all the information required by subdivisions (a) and (b). In order to change its agent for service of process or the address of the agent, the corporation must file a current statement containing all the information required by subdivisions (a) and (b). Whenever any statement is filed pursuant to this section, it supersedes any previously filed statement and the statement in the articles as to the agent for service of process and the address of the agent.

(f) The Secretary of State may destroy or otherwise dispose of any statement filed pursuant to this section after it has been superseded by the filing of a new statement.

(g) This section shall not be construed to place any person dealing with the corporation on notice of, or under any duty to inquire about, the existence or content of a statement filed pursuant to this section.

(h) The statement required by subdivision (a) shall be available and open to the public for inspection. The Secretary of State shall provide access to all information contained in this statement by means of an online database.

(i) In addition to any other fees required, a corporation shall pay a five-dollar ($5) disclosure fee when filing the statement required by subdivision (a). One-half of the fee shall, notwithstanding Section 12176 of the Government Code, be deposited into the Business Programs Modernization Fund established in subdivision (k), and one-half shall be deposited into the Victims of Corporate Fraud Compensation Fund established in Section 2280.

(j) A corporation shall certify that the information it provides pursuant to subdivisions (a) and (b) is true and correct. No claim may be made against the state for inaccurate information contained in the statements.

(k) There is hereby established the Business Programs Modernization Fund in the State Treasury. Moneys deposited into the fund shall, upon appropriation by the Legislature, be available to the Secretary of State to further the purposes of this section, including the development and maintenance of the online database required by subdivision (h), and by subdivision (c) of Section 2117.

(l)

    (1) This section shall become operative on January 1, 2022, or upon certification by the Secretary of State that California Business Connect is implemented, whichever date is earlier.

(2) If the Secretary of State certifies California Business Connect is implemented prior to January 1, 2022, the Secretary of State shall post notice of the certification on the homepage of its internet website and send notice of the certification to the Legislative Counsel.

Ca. Corp. Code § 1502
Added by Stats 2020 ch 357 (AB 3075),s 2, eff. 1/1/2021.

Section 1502.1 - Additional filing of statement

(a) In addition to the statement required pursuant to Section 1502, every publicly traded corporation shall file annually, within 150 days after the end of its fiscal year, a statement, on a form prescribed by the Secretary of State, that includes all of the following information:

(1) The name of the independent auditor that prepared the most recent auditor's report on the corporation's annual financial statements.

(2) A description of other services, if any, performed for the corporation during its two most recent fiscal years and the period between the end of its most recent fiscal year and the date of the statement by the foregoing independent auditor, by its parent corporation, or by a subsidiary or corporate affiliate of the independent auditor or its parent corporation.

(3) The name of the independent auditor employed by the corporation on the date of the statement, if different from the independent auditor listed pursuant to paragraph (1).

(4) The compensation for the most recent fiscal year of the corporation paid to each member of the board of directors and paid to each of the five most highly compensated executive officers of the corporation who are not members of the board of directors, including the number of any shares issued, options for shares granted, and similar equity-based compensation granted to each of those persons. If the chief executive officer is not among the five most highly compensated executive officers of the corporation, the compensation paid to the chief executive officer shall also be included.

(5) A description of any loan, including the amount and terms of the loan, made to any member of the board of directors by the corporation during the corporation's two most recent fiscal years at an interest rate lower than the interest rate available from unaffiliated commercial lenders generally to a similarly-situated borrower.

(6) A statement indicating whether an order for relief has been entered in a bankruptcy case with respect to the corporation, its executive officers, or members of the board of directors of the corporation during the 10 years preceding the date of the statement.

(7) A statement indicating whether any member of the board of directors or executive officer of the corporation was convicted of fraud during the 10 years preceding the date of the statement, if the conviction has not been overturned or expunged.

(8) A description of any material pending legal proceedings, other than ordinary routine litigation incidental to the business, to which the corporation or any of its subsidiaries is a party or of which any of their property is the subject, as specified by Item 103 of Regulation S-K of the Securities and Exchange Commission (Section 229.103 of Title 12 of the Code of Federal Regulations). A description of any material legal proceeding during which the corporation was found legally liable by entry of a final judgment or final order that was not overturned on appeal during the five years preceding the date of the statement.

(b) For purposes of this section, the following definitions apply:

(1) "Publicly traded corporation" means a corporation, as defined in Section 162, that is an issuer as defined in Section 3 of the Securities Exchange Act of 1934, as amended (15 U.S.C. Sec. 78c) , and has at least one class of securities listed or admitted for trading on a national securities exchange, on the OTC Bulletin Board, or on the electronic service operated by OTC Markets Group Inc.

(2) "Executive officer" means the chief executive officer, president, any vice president in charge of a principal business unit, division, or function, any other officer of the corporation who performs a policymaking function, or any other person who performs similar policymaking functions for the corporation.

(3) "Compensation" as used in paragraph (4) of subdivision (a) means all plan and nonplan compensation awarded to, earned by, or paid to the person for all services rendered in all capacities to the corporation and to its subsidiaries, as the compensation is specified by Item 402 of Regulation S-K of the Securities and Exchange Commission (Section 229.402 of Title 17 of the Code of Federal Regulations).

(4) "Loan" as used in paragraph (5) of subdivision (a) excludes an advance for expenses permitted under subdivision (d) of Section 315, the corporation's payment of life insurance premiums permitted under subdivision (e) of Section 315, and an advance of expenses permitted under Section 317.

(c) This statement shall be available and open to the public for inspection. The Secretary of State shall provide access to all information contained in this statement by means of an online database.

(d) A corporation shall certify that the information it provides pursuant to this section is true and correct. No claim may be made against the state for inaccurate information contained in statements filed under this section with the Secretary of State.

Ca. Corp. Code § 1502.1
Amended by Stats 2019 ch 143 (SB 251),s 25, eff. 1/1/2020.
Amended by Stats 2009 ch 131 (AB 991),s 5, eff. 1/1/2010.
Added by Stats 2004 ch 819 (AB 1000),s 3, eff. 9/27/2004.

Section 1502.5 - [Repealed]

Ca. Corp. Code § 1502.5
Repealed by Stats 2012 ch 564 (SB 1058),s 2, eff. 1/1/2013.
Amended by Stats 2004 ch 227 (SB 1102),s 14, eff. 8/16/2004.
Added by Stats 2002 ch 1015 (AB 55),s 3, eff. 1/1/2003.

Section 1503 - Resignation of agent designated for service of process

(a) An agent designated for service of process pursuant to Section 202, 1502, 2105, or 2117 may deliver to the Secretary of State, on a form prescribed by the Secretary of State for filing, a signed and acknowledged written statement of resignation as an agent for service of process. The form shall contain the name of the corporation, the Secretary of State's file number of the corporation, the name of the resigning agent for service of process, and a statement that the agent is resigning. Thereupon the authority of the agent to act in such capacity shall cease and the Secretary of State forthwith shall mail or otherwise provide written notice of the filing of the statement of resignation to the corporation at its principal office.
(b) The resignation of an agent may be effective if, on a form prescribed by the Secretary of State containing the name of the corporation, the Secretary of State's file number for the corporation, and the name of the resigning agent for service of process, the agent disclaims having been properly appointed as the agent. Similarly, a person named as an officer or director may indicate that the person was never properly appointed as the officer or director.
(c) The Secretary of State may destroy or otherwise dispose of any resignation filed pursuant to this section after a new form is filed pursuant to Section 1502 or 2117 replacing the agent for service of process that has resigned.

Ca. Corp. Code § 1503
Amended by Stats 2022 ch 617 (SB 1202),s 26, eff. 1/1/2023.
Amended by Stats 2014 ch 834 (SB 1041),s 3, eff. 1/1/2015.

Section 1504 - Designation of new agent required

If a natural person who has been designated agent for service of process pursuant to Section 202, 1502, 2105, or 2117 dies or resigns or no longer resides in the state or if the corporate agent for such purpose resigns, dissolves, withdraws from the state, forfeits its right to transact intrastate business, has its corporate rights, powers and privileges suspended or ceases to exist, the corporation shall forthwith file a designation of a new agent conforming to the requirements of Section 1502 or 2117.

Ca. Corp. Code § 1504

Amended by Stats. 1985, Ch. 764, Sec. 2. Operative July 1, 1986, by Sec. 11 of Ch. 764.

Section 1505 - Filing of certificate prior to designation of agent for purpose of service of process

(a) Any domestic or foreign corporation, before it may be designated as the agent for the purpose of service of process of any entity pursuant to any law which refers to this section, shall file a certificate executed in the name of the corporation by an officer thereof stating all of the following:

(1) The complete street address of its office or offices in this state, wherein any entity designating it as such agent may be served with process.

(2) The name of each person employed by it at each such office to whom it authorizes the delivery of a copy of any such process.

(3) Its consent that delivery thereof to any such person at the office where the person is employed shall constitute delivery of any such copy to it, as such agent.

(b) Any corporation which has filed the certificate provided for in subdivision (a) may file any number of supplemental certificates containing all the statements provided for in subdivision (a), which, upon the filing thereof, shall supersede the statements contained in the original or in any supplemental certificate previously filed.

(c) No domestic or foreign corporation may file a certificate pursuant to this section unless it is currently authorized to engage in business in this state and is in good standing on the records of the Secretary of State.

Ca. Corp. Code § 1505

Amended by Stats 2012 ch 494 (SB 1532),s 8, eff. 1/1/2013.

Section 1506 - Request of assessor for business records relevant to property

Upon request of an assessor, a domestic or foreign corporation owning, claiming, possessing or controlling property in this state subject to local assessment shall make available at the corporation's principal office in California or at a place mutually acceptable to the assessor and the corporation a true copy of business records relevant to the amount, cost and value of all property that it owns, claims, possesses or controls within the county.

Ca. Corp. Code § 1506

Repealed and added by Stats. 1975, Ch. 682.

Section 1507 - Joint and several liability for damages relating to false

documents

Any officers, directors, employees or agents of a corporation who do any of the following are liable jointly and severally for all the damages resulting therefrom to the corporation or any person injured thereby who relied thereon or to both:

(a) Make, issue, deliver or publish any prospectus, report, circular, certificate, financial statement, balance sheet, public notice or document respecting the corporation or its shares, assets, liabilities, capital, dividends, business, earnings or accounts which is false in any material respect, knowing it to be false, or participate in the making, issuance, delivery or publication thereof with knowledge that the same is false in a material respect.

(b) Make or cause to be made in the books, minutes, records or accounts of a corporation any entry which is false in any material particular knowing such entry is false.

(c) Remove, erase, alter or cancel any entry in any books or records of the corporation, with intent to deceive.

   Ca. Corp. Code § 1507
Repealed and added by Stats. 1975, Ch. 682.

Section 1508 - Actions of attorney general upon complaint

The Attorney General, upon complaint that a foreign or domestic corporation is failing to comply with the provisions of this chapter or Chapter 6 (commencing with Section 600), 7 (commencing with Section 700), or 16 (commencing with Section 1600), may in the name of the people of the State of California send to the principal office of such corporation notice of the complaint. If the answer is not satisfactory, the Attorney General may institute, maintain or intervene in such suits, actions or proceedings of any type in any court or tribunal of competent jurisdiction or before any administrative agency for such relief by way of injunction, the dissolution of entities, the appointment of receivers or any other temporary, preliminary, provisional or final remedies as may be appropriate to protect the rights of shareholders or to undo the consequences of failure to comply with such requirements. In any such action, suit or proceeding there may be joined as parties all persons and entities responsible for or affected by such activity.

   Ca. Corp. Code § 1508
Amended by Stats 2022 ch 617 (SB 1202),s 27, eff. 1/1/2023.
Amended by Stats. 1976, Ch. 641.

Section 1509 - Report following shareholders meeting

For a period of 60 days following the conclusion of an annual, regular, or special meeting of shareholders, a corporation shall, upon written request from a shareholder, forthwith inform the shareholder of the result of any particular vote of shareholders taken at the meeting, including the number of shares voting for, the number of shares voting against, and the number of shares abstaining or withheld from voting. If the matter voted on was the election of directors, the corporation shall report the number of shares (or votes if voted cumulatively) cast for each nominee for director. If more than one class or series of shares voted, the report shall state the appropriate numbers by class and series of shares.

Ca. Corp. Code § 1509
Added by Stats. 1987, Ch. 408, Sec. 1.

Section 1510 - Report following shareholders meeting by foreign corporation qualified to transact intrastate business

(a) Any foreign corporation qualified to transact intrastate business in this state shall provide the information specified in Section 1509, at the request of a shareholder resident in this state.

(b) Any of the following shall be considered to be a shareholder resident in this state:

(1) A natural person residing in this state.

(2) A bank organized under Division 1 (commencing with Section 99) of the Financial Code, whether acting for itself, acting as a sole fiduciary, or acting with one or more other persons as a fiduciary.

(3) A national bank having its head office in this state whether acting for itself, acting as a sole fiduciary, or acting with one or more other persons as a fiduciary.

(4) Any retirement fund for public employees established or authorized by any law of this state.

Ca. Corp. Code § 1510
Added by Stats. 1987, Ch. 408, Sec. 2.

Section 1511 - Report following shareholders meeting by foreign corporation not qualified to transact intrastate business

Any foreign corporation which is not qualified to transact intrastate business in this state but has one or more subsidiaries which are domestic corporations or foreign corporations qualified to transact intrastate business in this state shall provide the information specified in Section 1509, at the request of a shareholder resident in this state, as defined by subdivision (b) of Section 1510.

Ca. Corp. Code § 1511
Added by Stats. 1987, Ch. 408, Sec. 3.

Section 1512 - Shareholder for purposes of report following shareholders meeting

(a) For the purposes of Sections 1509, 1510, and 1511, a shareholder includes (1) any person named in a share certificate as a shareholder or (2) any person named as a shareholder on the records of a central depository, bank, or broker-dealer with respect to shares which are subject to the control of the central depository, bank, or broker-dealer.

(b) A beneficiary of a trust, a beneficiary of the estate of a decedent, or an employee with respect to a pension, retirement, or health care trust or fund is not a shareholder of any shares standing in the name of the trust, the fund, the decedent, or the estate of the decedent.

(c) A person who is a shareholder by reason of paragraph (2) of subdivision (a) shall provide the corporation with a photocopy of a receipt of a statement from the central depository, bank, or broker-dealer showing the person to be a shareholder and the corporation shall accept the photocopy as sufficient evidence thereof.

   Ca. Corp. Code § 1512
Added by Stats. 1987, Ch. 408, Sec. 4.

Chapter 16 - RIGHTS OF INSPECTION

Section 1600 - Shareholder's right to inspect and copy record of shareholders' names and addresses and shareholdings or to obtain list

(a) A shareholder or shareholders holding at least 5 percent in the aggregate of the outstanding voting shares of a corporation or who hold at least 1 percent of those voting shares and have filed a Schedule 14A with the United States Securities and Exchange Commission shall have an absolute right to do either or both of the following:

   (1) inspect and copy the record of shareholders' names and addresses and shareholdings during usual business hours upon five business days' prior written demand upon the corporation, or

   (2) obtain from the transfer agent for the corporation, upon written demand and upon the tender of its usual charges for such a list (the amount of which charges shall be stated to the shareholder by the transfer agent upon request), a list of the shareholders' names and addresses, who are entitled to vote for the election of directors, and their shareholdings, as of the most recent record date for which it has been compiled or as of a date specified by the shareholder subsequent to the date of demand. The list shall be made available on or before the later of five business days after the demand is received or the date specified therein as the date as of which the list is to be compiled. A corporation shall have the responsibility to cause its transfer agent to comply with this subdivision.

(b) Any delay by the corporation or the transfer agent in complying with a demand under subdivision (a) beyond the time limits specified therein shall give the shareholder or shareholders properly making the demand a right to obtain from the superior court, upon the filing of a verified complaint in the proper county and after a hearing, notice of which shall be given to such persons and in such manner as the court may direct, an order postponing any shareholders' meeting previously noticed for a period equal to the period of such delay. Such right shall be in addition to any other legal or equitable remedies to which the shareholder may be entitled.

(c) The record of shareholders shall also be open to inspection and copying by any shareholder or holder of a voting trust certificate at any time during usual business hours upon written demand on the corporation, for a purpose reasonably related to such holder's interests as a shareholder or holder of a voting trust certificate.

(d) Any inspection and copying under this section may be made in person or by agent or attorney. The rights provided in this section may not be limited by the articles or bylaws. This section applies to any domestic corporation and to any foreign corporation having its principal office in California or customarily holding meetings of its board in this state.

Ca. Corp. Code § 1600

Amended by Stats 2022 ch 617 (SB 1202),s 28, eff. 1/1/2023.

Amended by Stats. 1995, Ch. 154, Sec. 8. Effective January 1, 1996.

Section 1601 - Shareholder's right to inspect books and records and minutes

(a)

(1) The accounting books, records, and minutes of proceedings of the shareholders and the board and committees of the board of any domestic corporation, and of any foreign corporation keeping any records in this state or having its principal office in California, or a true and accurate copy thereof if the original has been lost, destroyed, or is not normally physically located within this state shall be open to inspection at the corporation's principal office in California, or if none, at the physical location for the corporation's registered agent for service of process in this state, upon the written demand on the corporation of any shareholder or holder of a voting trust certificate at any reasonable time during usual business hours, for a purpose reasonably related to the holder's interests as a shareholder or as the holder of a voting trust certificate.

(2) As an alternative to the procedure in subdivision (a), the shareholder or holder of a voting trust certificate may elect to request that the corporation produce the books, records, and minutes by mail or electronically, if the shareholder or holder of a voting trust certificate pays for the reasonable costs for copying or converting the requested documents to electronic format.

(3) The right of inspection created by this subdivision shall extend to the records of each subsidiary of a corporation subject to this subdivision.

(b) The inspection by a shareholder or holder of a voting trust certificate may be made in person or by agent or attorney, and the right of inspection includes the right to copy and make extracts. The right of the shareholders to inspect the corporate records may not be limited by the articles or bylaws.

    Ca. Corp. Code § 1601

Amended by Stats 2022 ch 617 (SB 1202),s 29, eff. 1/1/2023.

Amended by Stats 2018 ch 76 (AB 2237),s 1, eff. 1/1/2019.

Section 1602 - Director's right to inspect and copy

Every director shall have the absolute right at any reasonable time to inspect and copy all books, records and documents of every kind and to inspect the physical properties of the corporation of which such person is a director and also of its subsidiary corporations, domestic or foreign. Such inspection by a director may be made in person or by agent or attorney and the right of inspection includes the right to copy and make extracts. This section applies to a director of any foreign corporation having its principal office in California or customarily holding meetings of its board in California.

    Ca. Corp. Code § 1602

Amended by Stats 2022 ch 617 (SB 1202),s 30, eff. 1/1/2023.

Amended by Stats. 1976, Ch. 641.

Section 1603 - Enforcement of right of inspection

(a) Upon refusal of a lawful demand for inspection, the superior court of the proper county, may enforce the right of inspection with just and proper conditions or may, for good cause shown, appoint one or more competent inspectors or accountants to audit the books and records kept in this state and investigate the property, funds and affairs of any domestic corporation or any foreign corporation keeping records in this state and of any subsidiary corporation thereof, domestic or foreign, keeping records in this state and to report thereon in such manner as the court may direct.

(b) All officers and agents of the corporation shall produce to the inspectors or accountants so appointed all books and documents in their custody or power, under penalty of punishment for contempt of court.

(c) All expenses of the investigation or audit shall be defrayed by the applicant unless the court orders them to be paid or shared by the corporation.

    Ca. Corp. Code § 1603

Amended by Stats. 1976, Ch. 641.

Section 1604 - Award of reasonable expenses, including attorneys' fees

In any action or proceeding under Section 1600 or Section 1601, if the court finds the failure of the corporation to comply with a proper demand thereunder was without justification, the court may award an amount sufficient to reimburse the shareholder or holder of a voting trust certificate for the reasonable expenses incurred by such holder, including attorneys' fees, in connection with such action or proceeding.

Ca. Corp. Code § 1604

Added by Stats. 1975, Ch. 682.

Section 1605 - Record available in written form

If any record subject to inspection pursuant to this chapter is not maintained in written form, a request for inspection is not complied with unless and until the corporation at its expense makes such record available in written form.

Ca. Corp. Code § 1605

Added by Stats. 1975, Ch. 682.

Chapter 17 - SERVICE OF PROCESS

Section 1700 - Service of process upon domestic corporations

In addition to the provisions of Chapter 4 (commencing with Section 413. 10) of Title 5 of Part 2 of the Code of Civil Procedure, process may be served upon domestic corporations as provided in this chapter.

Ca. Corp. Code § 1700

Repealed and added by Stats. 1975, Ch. 682.

Section 1701 - Delivery by hand to agent

Delivery by hand of a copy of any process against the corporation (a) to any natural person designated by it as agent or (b), if a corporate agent has been designated, to any person named in the latest certificate of the corporate agent filed pursuant to Section 1505 at the office of such corporate agent shall constitute valid service on the corporation.

Ca. Corp. Code § 1701

Repealed and added by Stats. 1975, Ch. 682.

Section 1702 - Delivery by hand to Secretary of State

(a)If an agent for the purpose of service of process has resigned and has not been replaced or if the agent designated cannot with reasonable diligence be found at the address designated for personally delivering the process, or if no agent has been designated, and it is shown by affidavit to the satisfaction of the court that process against a domestic corporation cannot be served with reasonable diligence upon the designated agent by hand in the manner provided in Section 415.10, subdivision (a) of Section 415.20 or subdivision (a) of Section 415.30 of the Code of Civil Procedure or upon the corporation in the manner provided in subdivision (a), (b), or (c) of Section 416.10 or subdivision (a) of Section 416.20 of the Code of Civil Procedure, the court may make an order that the service be made upon the corporation by delivering by hand to the Secretary of State, or to any person employed in the Secretary of State's office in the capacity of assistant or deputy, one copy of the process for each defendant to be served, together with a copy of the order authorizing such service. Service in this manner is deemed complete on the 10th day after delivery of the process to the Secretary of State.

(b) Upon the receipt of any such copy of process and the fee therefor, the Secretary of State shall give notice of the service of the process to the corporation at its principal office, by forwarding to such office, by registered mail with request for return receipt, the copy of the process or, if the records of the Secretary of State do not disclose an address for its principal office, by forwarding such copy in the same manner to the last designated agent for service of process who has not resigned. If the agent for service of process has resigned and has not been replaced and the records of the Secretary of State do not disclose an address for its principal office, no action need be taken by the Secretary of State.

(c) The Secretary of State shall keep a record of all process served upon the Secretary of State under this chapter and shall record therein the time of service and the Secretary of State's action with reference thereto. The certificate of the Secretary of State, under the Secretary of State's official seal, certifying to the receipt of process, the giving of notice thereof to the corporation and the forwarding of such process pursuant to this section, shall be competent and prima facie evidence of the matters stated therein.

(d) The court order pursuant to subdivision (a) that service of process be made upon the corporation by delivery to the Secretary of State may be a court order of a court of another state, or of any federal court if the suit, action, or proceeding has been filed in that court.

Ca. Corp. Code § 1702

Amended by Stats 2022 ch 617 (SB 1202),s 31, eff. 1/1/2023.
Amended by Stats. 1989, Ch. 438, Sec. 1.

Chapter 18 - INVOLUNTARY DISSOLUTION

Section 1800 - Involuntary dissolution

(a) A verified complaint for involuntary dissolution of a corporation on any one or more of the grounds specified in subdivision (b) may be filed in the superior court of the proper county by any of the following persons:

(1) One-half or more of the directors in office.

(2) A shareholder or shareholders who hold shares representing not less than 33 $1/3$ percent of (i) the total number of outstanding shares (assuming conversion of any preferred shares convertible into common shares) or (ii) the outstanding common shares or (iii) the equity of the corporation, exclusive in each case of shares owned by persons who have personally participated in any of the transactions enumerated in

paragraph (4) of subdivision (b), or any shareholder or shareholders of a close corporation.

(3) Any shareholder if the ground for dissolution is that the period for which the corporation was formed has terminated without extension thereof.

(4) Any other person expressly authorized to do so in the articles.
(b) The grounds for involuntary dissolution are that:

(1) The corporation has abandoned its business for more than one year.

(2) The corporation has an even number of directors who are equally divided and cannot agree as to the management of its affairs, so that its business can no longer be conducted to advantage or so that there is danger that its property and business will be impaired or lost, and the holders of the voting shares of the corporation are so divided into factions that they cannot elect a board consisting of an uneven number.

(3) There is internal dissension and two or more factions of shareholders in the corporation are so deadlocked that its business can no longer be conducted with advantage to its shareholders or the shareholders have failed at two consecutive annual meetings at which all voting power was exercised, to elect successors to directors whose terms have expired or would have expired upon election of their successors.

(4) Those in control of the corporation have been guilty of or have knowingly countenanced persistent and pervasive fraud, mismanagement or abuse of authority or persistent unfairness toward any shareholders or its property is being misapplied or wasted by its directors or officers.

(5) In the case of any corporation with 35 or fewer shareholders (determined as provided in Section 605), liquidation is reasonably necessary for the protection of the rights or interests of the complaining shareholder or shareholders.

(6) The period for which the corporation was formed has terminated without extension of such period.
(c) At any time prior to the trial of the action any shareholder or creditor may intervene therein.
(d) This section does not apply to any corporation subject to the Banking Law (Division 1.1 (commencing with Section 1000) of the Financial Code), the Public Utilities Act (Part 1 (commencing with 201) of Division 1 of the Public Utilities Code), the Savings Association Law (Division 2 (commencing with Section 5000) of the Financial Code) or Article 14 (commencing with Section 1010) of Chapter 1 of Part 2 of Division 1 of the Insurance Code.
(e) For the purposes of this section, "shareholder" includes a beneficial owner of

shares who has entered into an agreement under Section 300 or 706.

Ca. Corp. Code § 1800

Amended by Stats 2014 ch 64 (AB 2742),s 4, eff. 1/1/2015.

Section 1801 - Action by attorney general

(a) The Attorney General may bring an action against any domestic corporation or purported domestic corporation in the name of the people of this state, upon the Attorney General's own information or upon complaint of a private party, to procure a judgment dissolving the corporation and annulling, vacating or forfeiting its corporate existence upon any of the following grounds:

(1) The corporation has seriously offended against any provision of the statutes regulating corporations.

(2) The corporation has fraudulently abused or usurped corporate privileges or powers.

(3) The corporation has violated any provision of law by any act or default which under the law is a ground for forfeiture of corporate existence.

(4) The corporation has failed to pay to the Franchise Tax Board for a period of five years any tax imposed upon it by the Bank and Corporation Tax Law.

(b) If the ground of the action is a matter or act which the corporation has done or omitted to do that can be corrected by amendment of its articles or by other corporate action, such suit shall not be maintained unless (1) the Attorney General, at least 30 days prior to the institution of suit, has given the corporation written notice of the matter or act done or omitted to be done and (2) the corporation has failed to institute proceedings to correct it within the 30-day period or thereafter fails to prosecute such proceedings.

(c) In any such action the court may order dissolution or such other or partial relief as it deems just and expedient. The court also may appoint a receiver for winding up the affairs of the corporation or may order that the corporation be wound up by its board subject to the supervision of the court.

(d) Service of process on the corporation may be made pursuant to Chapter 17 or by written notice to the president or secretary of the corporation at the address indicated in the corporation's last tax return filed pursuant to the Bank and Corporation Tax Law. The Attorney General shall also publish one time in a newspaper of general circulation in the proper county a notice to the shareholders of the corporation.

Ca. Corp. Code § 1801

Added by Stats. 1975, Ch. 682.

Section 1802 - Appointment of provisional director

If the ground for the complaint for involuntary dissolution of the corporation is a deadlock in the board as set forth in subdivision (b)(2) of Section 1800, the court may appoint a provisional director. The provisions of subdivision (c) of Section 308 apply to any such provisional director so appointed.

Ca. Corp. Code § 1802
Amended by Stats. 1977, Ch. 235.

Section 1803 - Appointment of receiver

If, at the time of the filing of a complaint for involuntary dissolution or at any time thereafter, the court has reasonable grounds to believe that unless a receiver of the corporation is appointed the interests of the corporation and its shareholders will suffer pending the hearing and determination of the complaint, upon the application of the plaintiff, and after a hearing upon such notice to the corporation as the court may direct and upon the giving of security pursuant to Sections 566 and 567 of the Code of Civil Procedure, the court may appoint a receiver to take over and manage the business and affairs of the corporation and to preserve its property pending the hearing and determination of the complaint for dissolution.

Ca. Corp. Code § 1803
Added by Stats. 1975, Ch. 682.

Section 1804 - Winding up and dissolution or other orders and decrees and injunctions

After hearing the court may decree a winding up and dissolution of the corporation if cause therefor is shown or, with or without winding up and dissolution, may make such orders and decrees and issue such injunctions in the case as justice and equity require.

Ca. Corp. Code § 1804
Added by Stats. 1975, Ch. 682.

Section 1805 - Involuntary proceeding for winding up

(a) Involuntary proceedings for winding up a corporation commence when the order for winding up is entered under Section 1804.
(b) When an involuntary proceeding for winding up has commenced, the board shall conduct the winding up of the affairs of the corporation, subject to the supervision of the court, unless other persons are appointed by the court, on good cause shown, to conduct the winding up. The directors or such other persons may, subject to any restrictions imposed by the court, exercise all their powers through the executive officers without any order of court.
(c) When an involuntary proceeding for winding up has commenced, the corporation shall cease to carry on business except to the extent necessary for the beneficial winding up thereof and except during such period as the board may deem necessary

to preserve the corporation's goodwill or going-concern value pending a sale of its business or assets, or both, in whole or in part. The directors shall cause written notice of the commencement of the proceeding for involuntary winding up to be given by mail to all shareholders and to all known creditors and claimants whose addresses appear on the records of the corporation, unless the order for winding up has been stayed by appeal therefrom or otherwise or the proceeding or the execution of the order has been enjoined.

Ca. Corp. Code § 1805
Added by Stats. 1975, Ch. 682.

Section 1806 - Jurisdiction of court

When an involuntary proceeding for winding up has been commenced, the jurisdiction of the court includes:

(a) The requirement of the proof of all claims and demands against the corporation, whether due or not yet due, contingent, unliquidated or sounding only in damages, and the barring from participation of creditors and claimants failing to make and present claims and proof as required by any order.

(b) The determination or compromise of all claims of every nature against the corporation or any of its property, and the determination of the amount of money or assets required to be retained to pay or provide for the payment of claims.

(c) The determination of the rights of shareholders and of all classes of shareholders in and to the assets of the corporation.

(d) The presentation and filing of intermediate and final accounts of the directors or other persons appointed to conduct the winding up and hearing thereon, the allowance, disallowance or settlement thereof and the discharge of the directors or such other persons from their duties and liabilities.

(e) The appointment of a commissioner to hear and determine any or all matters, with such power or authority as the court may deem proper.

(f) The filling of any vacancies on the board which the directors or shareholders are unable to fill.

(g) The removal of any director if it appears that the director has been guilty of dishonesty, misconduct, neglect or abuse of trust in conducting the winding up or if the director is unable to act. The court may order an election to fill the vacancy so caused, and may enjoin, for such time as it considers proper, the reelection of the director so removed; or the court, in lieu of ordering an election, may appoint a director to fill the vacancy caused by such removal. Any director so appointed by the court shall serve until the next annual meeting of shareholders or until a successor is elected or appointed.

(h) Staying the prosecution of any suit, proceeding or action against the corporation and requiring the parties to present and prove their claims in the manner required of other creditors.

(i) The determination of whether adequate provision has been made for payment or satisfaction of all debts and liabilities not actually paid.

(j) The making of orders for the withdrawal or termination of proceedings to wind up and dissolve, subject to conditions for the protection of shareholders and creditors.

(k) The making of an order, upon the allowance or settlement of the final accounts of the directors or such other persons, that the corporation has been duly wound up and is dissolved. Upon the making of such order, the corporate existence shall cease except for purposes of further winding up if needed.

(l) The making of orders for the bringing in of new parties as the court deems proper for the determination of all questions and matters.

   Ca. Corp. Code § 1806

Added by Stats. 1975, Ch. 682.

Section 1807 - Creditors and claimants

(a) All creditors and claimants may be barred from participation in any distribution of the general assets if they fail to make and present claims and proofs within such time as the court may direct, which shall not be less than four nor more than six months after the first publication of notice to creditors unless it appears by affidavit that there are no claims, in which case the time limit may be three months. If it is shown that a claimant did not receive notice because of absence from the state or other cause, the court may allow a claim to be filed or presented at any time before distribution is completed.

(b) Such notice to creditors shall be published not less than once a week for three consecutive weeks in a newspaper of general circulation published in the county in which the proceeding is pending or, if there is no such newspaper published in that county, in such newspaper as may be designated by the court, directing creditors and claimants to make and present claims and proofs to the person, at the place and within the time specified in the notice. A copy of the notice shall be mailed to each person shown as a creditor or claimant on the books of the corporation, at such person's last known address.

(c) Holders of secured claims may prove for the whole debt in order to realize any deficiency. If such creditors fail to present their claims they shall be barred only as to any right to claim against the general assets for any deficiency in the amount realized on their security.

(d) Before any distribution is made the amount of any unmatured, contingent or disputed claim against the corporation which has been presented and has not been disallowed, or such part of any such claim as the holder would be entitled to if the claim were due, established or absolute, shall be paid into court and there remain to be paid over to the party when the party becomes entitled thereto or, if the party fails to establish a claim, to be paid over or distributed with the other assets of the corporation to those entitled thereto; or such other provision for the full payment of such claim, if and when established, shall be made as the court may deem adequate. A creditor whose claim has been allowed but is not yet due shall be entitled to its present value upon distribution.

(e) Suits against the corporation on claims which have been rejected shall be commenced within 30 days after written notice of rejection thereof is given to the claimant.

Ca. Corp. Code § 1807
Added by Stats. 1975, Ch. 682.

Section 1808 - Order declaring corporation duly wound up and dissolved

(a) Upon the final settlement of the accounts of the directors or other persons appointed pursuant to Section 1805 and the determination that the corporation's affairs are in condition for it to be dissolved, the court may make an order declaring the corporation duly wound up and dissolved. The order shall declare:

(1) That the corporation has been duly wound up, that a final franchise tax return, as described by Section 23332 of the Revenue and Taxation Code, has been filed with the Franchise Tax Board as required under Part 10.2 (commencing with Section 18401) of Division 2 of the Revenue and Taxation Code, and that its known debts and liabilities have been paid or adequately provided for, or that those debts and liabilities have been paid as far as its assets permitted, as the case may be. If there are known debts or liabilities for payment of which adequate provision has been made, the order shall state what provision has been made, setting forth the name and address of the corporation, person or governmental agency that has assumed or guaranteed the payment, or the name and address of the depositary with which deposit has been made or such other information as may be necessary to enable the creditor or other person to whom payment is to be made to appear and claim payment of the debt or liability.

(2) That its known assets have been distributed to the persons entitled thereto or that it acquired no known assets, as the case may be.

(3) That the accounts of directors or such other persons have been settled and that they are discharged from their duties and liabilities to creditors and shareholders.

(4) That the corporation is dissolved. The court may make such additional orders and grant such further relief as it deems proper upon the evidence submitted.
(b) Upon the making of the order declaring the corporation dissolved, corporate existence shall cease except for the purposes of further winding up if needed; and the directors or such other persons shall be discharged from their duties and liabilities, except in respect to completion of the winding up.

Ca. Corp. Code § 1808
Amended by Stats 2006 ch 773 (AB 2341),s 7, eff. 9/29/2006.

Section 1809 - Filing of order, decree, or judgment with Secretary of State

Whenever a corporation is dissolved or its existence forfeited by order, decree or judgment of a court, a copy of the order, decree or judgment, certified by the clerk of court, shall forthwith be filed in the office of the Secretary of State. The Secretary of State shall notify the Franchise Tax Board of the dissolution.

Ca. Corp. Code § 1809

Amended by Stats 2006 ch 773 (AB 2341),s 8, eff. 9/29/2006.

Chapter 19 - VOLUNTARY DISSOLUTION

Section 1900 - Voluntary election to wind up and dissolve

(a) Any corporation may elect voluntarily to wind up and dissolve by the vote of shareholders holding shares representing 50 percent or more of the voting power.

(b) Any corporation which comes within one of the following descriptions may elect by approval by the board to wind up and dissolve:

(1) A corporation as to which an order for relief has been entered under Chapter 7 of the federal bankruptcy law.

(2) A corporation which has disposed of all of its assets and has not conducted any business for a period of five years immediately preceding the adoption of the resolution electing to dissolve the corporation.

(3) A corporation which has issued no shares.

Ca. Corp. Code § 1900

Amended by Stats. 1980, Ch. 501.

Section 1900.5 - Certificate of dissolution if corporation has not issued shares

(a) Notwithstanding any other provision of this division, when a corporation has not issued shares, a majority of the directors, or, if no directors have been named in the articles or been elected, the incorporator or a majority of the incorporators may sign and verify a certificate of dissolution stating the following:

(1) That the certificate of dissolution is being filed within 12 months from the date the articles of incorporation were filed.

(2) That the corporation does not have any debts or other liabilities, except as provided in paragraph (3).

(3) That the tax liability will be satisfied on a taxes paid basis or that a person or corporation or other business entity assumes the tax liability, if any, of the dissolving corporation and is responsible for additional corporate taxes, if any, that are assessed and that become due after the date of the assumption of the tax liability.

(4) That a final franchise tax return, as described by Section 23332 of the Revenue and Taxation Code, has been or will be filed with the Franchise Tax Board as required under Part 10.2 (commencing with Section 18401) of Division 2 of the Revenue and Taxation Code.

(5) That the corporation has not conducted any business from the time of the filing of the articles of incorporation.

(6) That the known assets of the corporation remaining after payment of, or adequately providing for, known debts and liabilities have been distributed to the persons entitled thereto or that the corporation acquired no known assets, as the case may be.

(7) That a majority of the directors, or, if no directors have been named in the articles or been elected, the incorporator or a majority of the incorporators authorized the dissolution and elected to dissolve the corporation.

(8) That the corporation has not issued any shares, and if the corporation has received payments for shares from investors, those payments have been returned to those investors.

(9) That the corporation is dissolved.
(b) A certificate of dissolution signed and verified pursuant to subdivision (a) shall be filed with the Secretary of State. The Secretary of State shall notify the Franchise Tax Board of the dissolution.
(c) Upon filing a certificate of dissolution pursuant to subdivision (b), a corporation shall be dissolved and its powers, rights, and privileges shall cease.
  Ca. Corp. Code § 1900.5
Amended by Stats 2006 ch 773 (AB 2341),s 9, eff. 9/29/2006.
Added by Stats 2002 ch 390 (AB 1875),s 1, eff. 1/1/2003.

Section 1901 - Certificate evidencing election to wind up and dissolve

(a) Whenever a corporation has elected to wind up and dissolve a certificate evidencing such election shall forthwith be filed.
(b) The certificate shall be an officers' certificate or shall be signed and verified by at least a majority of the directors then in office or by one or more shareholders authorized to do so by shareholders holding shares representing 50 percent or more of the voting power and shall set forth:

(1) That the corporation has elected to wind up and dissolve.

(2) If the election was made by the vote of shareholders, the number of shares voting for the election and that the election was made by shareholders representing at least 50 percent of the voting power.

(3) If the certificate is executed by a shareholder or shareholders, that the subscribing shareholder or shareholders were authorized to execute the certificate by shareholders holding shares representing at least 50 percent of the voting power.

(4) If the election was made by the board pursuant to subdivision (b) of Section 1900, the certificate shall also set forth the circumstances showing the corporation to be within one of the categories described in said subdivision.

(c) If an election to dissolve made pursuant to subdivision (a) of Section 1900 is made by the vote of all the outstanding shares and a statement to that effect is added to the certificate of dissolution pursuant to Section 1905, the separate filing of the certificate of election pursuant to this section is not required.

Ca. Corp. Code § 1901
Amended by Stats. 1991, Ch. 280, Sec. 1.

Section 1902 - Revocation of voluntary election to wind up and dissolve

(a) A voluntary election to wind up and dissolve may be revoked prior to distribution of any assets by the vote of shareholders holding shares representing a majority of the voting power, or by approval by the board if the election was by the board pursuant to subdivision (b) of Section 1900. Thereupon a certificate evidencing the revocation shall be signed, verified and filed in the manner prescribed by Section 1901.

(b) The certificate shall set forth:

(1) That the corporation has revoked its election to wind up and dissolve.

(2) That no assets have been distributed pursuant to the election.

(3) If the revocation was made by the vote of shareholders, the number of shares voting for the revocation and the total number of outstanding shares the holders of which were entitled to vote on the revocation.

(4) If the election and revocation was by the board, that shall be stated.

Ca. Corp. Code § 1902
Amended by Stats. 1976, Ch. 641.

Section 1903 - Commencement of voluntary proceedings for winding up

(a) Voluntary proceedings for winding up the corporation commence upon the adoption of the resolution of shareholders or directors of the corporation electing to wind up and dissolve, or upon the filing with the corporation of a written consent of shareholders thereto.

(b) When a voluntary proceeding for winding up has commenced, the board shall continue to act as a board and shall have full powers to wind up and settle its affairs, both before and after the filing of the certificate of dissolution.

(c) When a voluntary proceeding for winding up has commenced, the corporation shall cease to carry on business except to the extent necessary for the beneficial winding up thereof and except during such period as the board may deem necessary to preserve the corporation's goodwill or going-concern value pending a sale of its business or assets, or both, in whole or in part. The board shall cause written notice of the commencement of the proceeding for voluntary winding up to be given by mail to all shareholders (except no notice need be given to the shareholders who voted in favor of winding up and dissolving the corporation) and to all known creditors and claimants whose addresses appear on the records of the corporation.

Ca. Corp. Code § 1903
Repealed and added by Stats. 1975, Ch. 682.

Section 1904 - Assumption of jurisdiction by superior court

If a corporation is in the process of voluntary winding up, the superior court of the proper county, upon the petition of (a) the corporation, or (b) a shareholder or shareholders who hold shares representing 5 percent or more of the total number of any class of outstanding shares, or (c) any shareholder or shareholders of a close corporation, or (d) three or more creditors, and upon such notice to the corporation and to other persons interested in the corporation as shareholders and creditors as the court may order, may take jurisdiction over such voluntary winding up proceeding if that appears necessary for the protection of any parties in interest. The court, if it assumes jurisdiction, may make such orders as to any and all matters concerning the winding up of the affairs of the corporation and for the protection of its shareholders and creditors as justice and equity may require. The provisions of Chapter 18 (commencing with Section 1800) (except Sections 1800 and 1801) shall apply to such court proceedings.

Ca. Corp. Code § 1904
Amended by Stats. 1976, Ch. 641.

Section 1905 - Certificate of dissolution when corporation completely wound up without court proceedings

(a) When a corporation has been completely wound up without court proceedings therefor, a majority of the directors then in office shall sign and verify a certificate of dissolution stating:

(1) That the corporation has been completely wound up.

(2) That its known debts and liabilities have been actually paid, or adequately provided for, or paid or adequately provided for as far as its assets permitted, or that

it has incurred no known debts or liabilities, as the case may be. If there are known debts or liabilities for payment of which adequate provision has been made, the certificate shall state what provision has been made, setting forth the name and address of the corporation, person or governmental agency that has assumed or guaranteed the payment, or the name and address of the depositary with which deposit has been made or any other information that may be necessary to enable the creditor or other person to whom payment is to be made to appear and claim payment of the debt or liability.

(3) That its known assets have been distributed to the persons entitled thereto or that it acquired no known assets, as the case may be.

(4) That the corporation is dissolved.

(5) If no certificate of election is to be filed pursuant to subdivision (c) of Section 1901, that the election to dissolve was made by the vote of all the outstanding shares.

(6) That a final franchise tax return, as described by Section 23332 of the Revenue and Taxation Code, has been or will be filed with the Franchise Tax Board, as required under Part 10.2 (commencing with Section 18401) of Division 2 of the Revenue and Taxation Code.
(b) The certificate of dissolution shall be filed with the Secretary of State and thereupon the corporate powers, rights, and privileges of the corporation shall cease. The Secretary of State shall notify the Franchise Tax Board of the dissolution.

Ca. Corp. Code § 1905
Amended by Stats 2006 ch 773 (AB 2341),s 10, eff. 9/29/2006.
Amended October 10, 1999 (Bill Number: SB 284) (Chapter 1000).

Section 1905.1 - Date of dissolution

If a corporation has filed a certificate of dissolution with the Secretary of State on or after January 1, 1992, and before the effective date of the act adding this section, pursuant to Section 1905, prior to its amendment by the act adding this section, and the Franchise Tax Board has not, as of that effective date, made the determination required by subdivision (c) of Section 1905, prior to its amendment by the act adding this section, then the corporation shall be dissolved as of the date of filing the certificate of dissolution and thereupon its corporate existence shall cease.

Ca. Corp. Code § 1905.1
Added by Stats 2006 ch 773 (AB 2341),s 11, eff. 9/29/2006.

Section 1906 - Expiration of term of existence without renewal or extension

Except as otherwise provided by law, if the term of existence for which any corporation was organized expires without renewal or extension thereof, the board shall terminate its business and wind up its affairs; and when the business and affairs of the corporation have been wound up a majority of the directors shall execute and file a certificate conforming to the requirements of Section 1905.

Ca. Corp. Code § 1906

Repealed and added by Stats. 1975, Ch. 682.

Section 1907 - Petition for order declaring corporation duly wound up and dissolved

(a) The board, in lieu of filing the certificate of dissolution, may petition the superior court of the proper county for an order declaring the corporation duly wound up and dissolved. Such petition shall be filed in the name of the corporation.

(b) Upon the filing of the petition, the court shall make an order requiring all persons interested to show cause why an order should not be made declaring the corporation duly wound up and dissolved and shall direct that the order be served by notice to all creditors, claimants and shareholders in the same manner as the notice given under subdivision (b) of Section 1807.

(c) Any person claiming to be interested as shareholder, creditor or otherwise may appear in the proceeding at any time before the expiration of 30 days from the completion of publication of the order to show cause and contest the petition, and upon failure to appear such person's claim shall be barred.

(d) Thereafter an order shall be entered and filed and have the effect as prescribed in Sections 1808 and 1809.

Ca. Corp. Code § 1907

Repealed and added by Stats. 1975, Ch. 682.

Chapter 20 - GENERAL PROVISIONS RELATING TO DISSOLUTION

Section 2000 - Avoidance of dissolution and appointment of receiver

(a) Subject to any contrary provision in the articles, which may include a reference to a separate written agreement between two or more shareholders pertaining to the purchase of shares: In any suit for involuntary dissolution, or in any proceeding for voluntary dissolution initiated by the vote of shareholders representing only 50 percent of the voting power, the corporation or, if it does not elect to purchase, the holders of 50 percent or more of the voting power of the corporation (the "purchasing parties") may avoid the dissolution of the corporation and the appointment of any receiver by purchasing for cash the shares owned by the plaintiffs or by the shareholders so initiating the proceeding (the "moving parties") at their fair value. The fair value shall be determined on the basis of the liquidation value as of the valuation date but taking into account the possibility, if any, of sale of the entire business as a going concern in a liquidation. In fixing the value, the amount of any damages resulting if the initiation of the dissolution is a breach by any moving party or parties of an agreement with the purchasing party or parties may be deducted from the amount payable to the moving party or parties, unless the ground for dissolution is that specified in paragraph (4) of subdivision (b) of Section 1800. The election of the corporation to purchase may be made by the approval of the outstanding shares (Section 152) excluding shares held by the moving parties.

(b) If the purchasing parties (1) elect to purchase the shares owned by the moving parties, and (2) are unable to agree with the moving parties upon the fair value of those shares, and (3) give bond with sufficient security to pay the estimated reasonable expenses (including attorneys' fees) of the moving parties if those expenses are recoverable under subdivision (c), the court upon application of the purchasing parties, either in the pending action or in a proceeding initiated in the superior court of the proper county by the purchasing parties in the case of a voluntary election to wind up and dissolve, shall stay the winding up and dissolution proceeding and shall proceed to ascertain and fix the fair value of the shares owned by the moving parties.

(c) The court shall appoint three disinterested appraisers to appraise the fair value of the shares owned by the moving parties, and shall make an order referring the matter to the appraisers so appointed for the purpose of ascertaining the value. The order shall prescribe the time and manner of producing evidence, if evidence is required. The award of the appraisers or of a majority of them, when confirmed by the court, shall be final and conclusive upon all parties. The court shall enter a decree, which shall provide in the alternative for winding up and dissolution of the corporation unless payment is made for the shares within the time specified by the decree. If the purchasing parties do not make payment for the shares within the time specified, judgment shall be entered against them and the surety or sureties on the bond for the amount of the expenses (including attorneys' fees) of the moving parties. Any shareholder aggrieved by the action of the court may appeal the court's decision.

(d) If the purchasing parties desire to prevent the winding up and dissolution, they shall pay to the moving parties the value of their shares ascertained and decreed within the time specified pursuant to this section, or, in case of an appeal, as fixed on appeal. On receiving payment or the tender thereof, the moving parties shall transfer their shares to the purchasing parties.

(e) For the purposes of this section, "shareholder" includes a beneficial owner of shares who has entered into an agreement under Section 300 or 706.

(f) For the purposes of this section, the valuation date shall be (1) in the case of a suit for involuntary dissolution under Section 1800, the date upon which that action was commenced, or (2) in the case of a proceeding for voluntary dissolution initiated by the vote of shareholders representing only 50 percent of the voting power, the date upon which that proceeding was initiated. However, in either case the court may, upon the hearing of a motion by any party, and for good cause shown, designate some other date as the valuation date.

Ca. Corp. Code § 2000

Amended by Stats 2017 ch 721 (AB 1535),s 1, eff. 1/1/2018.

Section 2001 - Powers of directors and officers after commencement of dissolution proceeding

The powers and duties of the directors (or other persons appointed by the court pursuant to Section 1805) and officers after commencement of a dissolution proceeding include, but are not limited to, the following acts in the name and on behalf of the corporation:

(a) To elect officers and to employ agents and attorneys to liquidate or wind up its affairs.

(b) To continue the conduct of the business insofar as necessary for the disposal or winding up thereof.

(c) To carry out contracts and collect, pay, compromise and settle debts and claims for or against the corporation.

(d) To defend suits brought against the corporation.

(e) To sue, in the name of the corporation, for all sums due or owing to the corporation or to recover any of its property.

(f) To collect any amounts remaining unpaid on subscriptions to shares or to recover unlawful distributions.

(g) To sell at public or private sale, exchange, convey or otherwise dispose of all or any part of the assets of the corporation for cash in an amount deemed reasonable by the board without compliance with the provisions of Section 1001 (except subdivision (d) thereof), or (subject to compliance with the provisions of Sections 1001, 1200 and 1201, but Chapter 13 (commencing with Section 1300) shall not be applicable thereto) upon such other terms and conditions and for such other considerations as the board deems reasonable or expedient; and to execute bills of sale and deeds of conveyance in the name of the corporation.

(h) In general, to make contracts and to do any and all things in the name of the corporation which may be proper or convenient for the purposes of winding up, settling and liquidating the affairs of the corporation.

Ca. Corp. Code § 2001
Amended by Stats. 1976, Ch. 641.

Section 2002 - Vacancy on board

A vacancy on the board may be filled during a winding up proceeding in the manner provided in Section 305.

Ca. Corp. Code § 2002
Added by Stats. 1975, Ch. 682.

Section 2003 - Identity of directors or right to hold office in doubt

When the identity of the directors or their right to hold office is in doubt, or if they are dead or unable to act, or they fail or refuse to act or their whereabouts cannot be ascertained, any interested person may petition the superior court of the proper county to determine the identity of the directors or, if there are no directors, to appoint directors to wind up the affairs of the corporation, after hearing upon such notice to such persons as the court may direct.

Ca. Corp. Code § 2003
Added by Stats. 1975, Ch. 682.

Section 2004 - Distribution of remaining corporate assets among shareholders

After determining that all the known debts and liabilities of a corporation in the process of winding up have been paid or adequately provided for, the board shall distribute all the remaining corporate assets among the shareholders according to their respective rights and preferences or, if there are no shareholders, to the persons entitled thereto. If the winding up is by court proceeding or subject to court supervision, the distribution shall not be made until after the expiration of any period for the presentation of claims which has been prescribed by order of the court.

Ca. Corp. Code § 2004
Amended by Stats. 1976, Ch. 641.

Section 2005 - Payment of debt or liability

The payment of a debt or liability, whether the whereabouts of the creditor is known or unknown, has been adequately provided for if the payment has been provided for by either of the following means:

(a) Payment thereof has been assumed or guaranteed in good faith by one or more financially responsible corporations or other persons or by the United States government or any agency thereof, and the provision (including the financial responsibility of such corporations or other persons) was determined in good faith and with reasonable care by the board to be adequate at the time of any distribution of the assets by the board pursuant to this chapter.

(b) The amount of the debt or liability has been deposited as provided in Section 2008. This section does not prescribe the exclusive means of making adequate provision for debts and liabilities.

Ca. Corp. Code § 2005
Added by Stats. 1975, Ch. 682.

Section 2006 - Distribution

Distribution may be made either in money or in property or securities and either in installments from time to time or as a whole, if this can be done fairly and ratably and in conformity with the provisions of the articles and the rights of the shareholders, and shall be made as soon as reasonably consistent with the beneficial liquidation of the corporate assets.

Ca. Corp. Code § 2006
Added by Stats. 1975, Ch. 682.

Section 2007 - Plan of distribution if corporation has both preferred and common shares

(a) If the corporation in process of winding up has both preferred and common shares outstanding, a plan of distribution of the shares, obligations or securities of any other corporation, domestic or foreign, or assets other than money which is not in accordance with the liquidation rights of the preferred shares as specified in the articles may nevertheless be adopted if approved by (1) the board and (2) by approval of the outstanding shares (Section 152) of each class. The plan may provide that such distribution is in complete or partial satisfaction of the rights of any of such shareholders upon distribution and liquidation of the assets.

(b) A plan of distribution so approved shall be binding upon all the shareholders except as provided in subdivision (c). The board shall cause notice of the adoption of the plan to be given by mail within 20 days after its adoption to all holders of shares having a liquidation preference.

(c) Shareholders having a liquidation preference who dissent from the plan of distribution are entitled to be paid the amount of their liquidation preference in cash if they file written demand for payment with the corporation within 30 days after the date of mailing of the notice of the adoption of the plan of distribution, unless the plan of distribution is abandoned. The demand shall state the number and class of the shares held of record by the shareholder in respect of which the shareholder claims payment.

(d) If any such demand for cash payment is filed, the board in its discretion may abandon the plan without further approval by the outstanding shares (Section 152), and all shareholders shall then be entitled to distribution according to their rights and liquidation preferences in the process of winding up.

(e) This section shall not apply to a distribution in accordance with a reorganization the principal terms of which have been approved pursuant to subdivision (b) of Section 1202.

Ca. Corp. Code § 2007
Amended by Stats. 1988, Ch. 919, Sec. 10.

Section 2008 - Deposit with Controller in trust

(a) If any shareholders or creditors are unknown or fail or refuse to accept their payment, dividend, or distribution in cash or property or their whereabouts cannot be ascertained after diligent inquiry, or the existence or amount of a claim of a creditor or shareholder is contingent, contested, or not determined, or if the ownership of any shares of stock is in dispute, the corporation may deposit any such payment, dividend, distribution, or the maximum amount of the claim with the Controller in trust for the benefit of those lawfully entitled to the payment, dividend, distribution, or the amount of the claim. The payment, dividend, or distribution shall be paid over by the depositary to the lawful owners, their representatives or assigns, upon satisfactory proof of title.

(b) For the purpose of providing for the transmittal, receipt, accounting for, claiming, management, and investment of all money or other property deposited with the Controller under subdivision (a), the money or other property shall be deemed to be paid or delivered for deposit with the Controller under Chapter 7 (commencing with Section 1500) of Title 10 of Part 3 of the Code of Civil Procedure, and may be recovered in the manner prescribed in that chapter.

Ca. Corp. Code § 2008

Amended by Stats. 1996, Ch. 860, Sec. 1. Effective January 1, 1997.

Section 2009 - Recovery of improper distribution to shareholder

(a) Whenever in the process of winding up a corporation any distribution of assets has been made, otherwise than under an order of court, without prior payment or adequate provision for payment of any of the debts and liabilities of the corporation, any amount so improperly distributed to any shareholder may be recovered by the corporation. Any of such shareholders may be joined as defendants in the same action or brought in on the motion of any other defendant.

(b) Suit may be brought in the name of the corporation to enforce the liability under subdivision (a) against any or all shareholders receiving the distribution by any one or more creditors of the corporation, whether or not they have reduced their claims to judgment.

(c) Shareholders who satisfy any liability under this section shall have the right of ratable contribution from other distributees similarly liable. Any shareholder who has been compelled to return to the corporation more than the shareholder's ratable share of the amount needed to pay the debts and liabilities of the corporation may require that the corporation recover from any or all of the other distributees such proportion of the amounts received by them upon the improper distribution as to give contribution to those held liable under this section and make the distribution of the assets fair and ratable, according to the respective rights and preferences of the shares, after payment or adequate provision for payment of all the debts and liabilities of the corporation.

(d) As used in this section, "process of winding up" includes proceedings under Chapters 18 and 19 and also any other distribution of assets to shareholders made in contemplation of termination or abandonment of the corporate business.

Ca. Corp. Code § 2009

Added by Stats. 1975, Ch. 682.

Section 2010 - Continued existence of dissolved corporation for purpose of winding up

(a) A corporation which is dissolved nevertheless continues to exist for the purpose of winding up its affairs, prosecuting and defending actions by or against it and enabling it to collect and discharge obligations, dispose of and convey its property and collect and divide its assets, but not for the purpose of continuing business except so far as necessary for the winding up thereof.

(b) No action or proceeding to which a corporation is a party abates by the dissolution of the corporation or by reason of proceedings for winding up and dissolution thereof.

(c) Any assets inadvertently or otherwise omitted from the winding up continue in the dissolved corporation for the benefit of the persons entitled thereto upon dissolution of the corporation and on realization shall be distributed accordingly.

Ca. Corp. Code § 2010

Amended by Stats 2006 ch 773 (AB 2341),s 12, eff. 9/29/2006.

Section 2011 - Causes of action against dissolved corporation or shareholders of dissolved corporation

(a)

(1) Causes of action against a dissolved corporation, whether arising before or after the dissolution of the corporation, may be enforced against any of the following:

(A) Against the dissolved corporation, to the extent of its undistributed assets, including, without limitation, any insurance assets held by the corporation that may be available to satisfy claims.

(B) If any of the assets of the dissolved corporation have been distributed to shareholders, against shareholders of the dissolved corporation to the extent of their pro rata share of the claim or to the extent of the corporate assets distributed to them upon dissolution of the corporation, whichever is less. A shareholder's total liability under this section may not exceed the total amount of assets of the dissolved corporation distributed to the shareholder upon dissolution of the corporation.

(2) Except as set forth in subdivision (c), all causes of action against a shareholder of a dissolved corporation arising under this section are extinguished unless the claimant commences a proceeding to enforce the cause of action against that shareholder of a dissolved corporation prior to the earlier of the following:

(A) The expiration of the statute of limitations applicable to the cause of action.

(B) Four years after the effective date of the dissolution of the corporation.

(3) As a matter of procedure only, and not for purposes of determining liability, shareholders of the dissolved corporation may be sued in the corporate name of the corporation upon any cause of action against the corporation. This section does not affect the rights of the corporation or its creditors under Section 2009, or the rights, if any, of creditors under the Uniform Voidable Transactions Act, which may arise against the shareholders of a corporation.

(4) This subdivision applies to corporations dissolved on and after January 1, 1992. Corporations dissolved prior to that date are subject to the law in effect prior to that date.

(b) Summons or other process against such a corporation may be served by delivering a copy thereof to an officer, director, or person having charge of its assets or, if no such person can be found, to any agent upon whom process might be served at the time of dissolution. If none of those persons can be found with due diligence and it is so shown by affidavit to the satisfaction of the court, then the court may make an order that summons or other process be served upon the dissolved corporation by personally delivering a copy thereof, together with a copy of the order, to the Secretary of State or an assistant or deputy secretary of state. Service in this manner is deemed complete on the 10th day after delivery of the process to the Secretary of State.

(c) Every such corporation shall survive and continue to exist indefinitely for the purpose of being sued in any quiet title action. Any judgment rendered in any such action shall bind each and all of its shareholders or other persons having any equity or other interest in that corporation, to the extent of their interest therein, and that action shall have the same force and effect as an action brought under the provisions of Sections 410.50 and 410.60 of the Code of Civil Procedure. Service of summons or other process in any such action may be made as provided in Chapter 4 (commencing with Section 413.10) of Title 5 of Part 2 of the Code of Civil Procedure or as provided in subdivision (b).

(d) Upon receipt of that process and the fee therefor, the Secretary of State forthwith shall give notice to the corporation as provided in Section 1702.

(e) For purposes of Article 4 (commencing with Section 19071) of Chapter 4 of Part 10.2 of Division 2 of the Revenue and Taxation Code, the liability described in this section shall be considered a liability at law with respect to a dissolved corporation.

Ca. Corp. Code § 2011

Amended by Stats 2019 ch 143 (SB 251),s 26, eff. 1/1/2020.
Amended by Stats 2006 ch 773 (AB 2341),s 13, eff. 9/29/2006.

Chapter 21 - FOREIGN CORPORATIONS

Section 2100 - Applicability

This chapter applies only to foreign corporations transacting intrastate business, except as otherwise expressly provided.

Ca. Corp. Code § 2100

Added by Stats. 1975, Ch. 682.

Section 2101 - Registration of corporate name

(a) Any foreign corporation (other than a foreign association) not transacting intrastate business may register its corporate name with the Secretary of State, provided its corporate name would be available pursuant to Section 201 to a new corporation organized under this division at the time of such registration.

(b) Such registration may be made by filing (1) an application for registration signed by a corporate officer stating the name of the corporation, the state or place under the laws of which it is incorporated, and that it desires to register its name under this section; and (2) a certificate of an authorized public official of the state or place in which it is organized issued within the past six months from the submission of the application for registration in California stating that such corporation is in good standing under those laws. Such registration shall be effective until the close of the calendar year in which the application for registration is filed.

(c) A corporation that has in effect a registration of its corporate name may renew such registration from year to year by annually filing an application for renewal setting forth the facts required to be set forth in an original application for registration and a certificate of good standing as required for the original registration between the first day of October and the 31st day of December in each year. Such renewal application shall extend the registration for the following calendar year.

(d) A corporation that has in effect a registration of its corporate name may cancel the registration by delivering to the Secretary of State, on a form prescribed by the Secretary of State for filing, a certificate of cancellation of foreign name registration signed by a corporate officer containing the name of the corporation and the Secretary of State's file number of the corporation.

Ca. Corp. Code § 2101

Amended by Stats 2022 ch 617 (SB 1202),s 32, eff. 1/1/2023.
Amended by Stats 2014 ch 834 (SB 1041),s 4, eff. 1/1/2015.

Section 2102 - Designation of agent for service of process

A foreign corporation which has filed a designation of an agent for the service of process, pursuant to the requirements of any law relating to the qualification of foreign corporations in force at the time of the filing, need not file the statement provided for in Section 2105, but shall file an amended statement and designation when required by Section 2107.

Ca. Corp. Code § 2102

Added by Stats. 1975, Ch. 682.

Section 2103 - Effect of chapter

Nothing in this chapter repeals, alters or amends the provisions of Sections 1600 to 1605, inclusive, of the Insurance Code or prevents any foreign insurance company from carrying out contracts made before the surrender of its right to engage in intrastate business or contracts made with citizens of other states who subsequently become citizens of or residents in this state.

Ca. Corp. Code § 2103

Amended by Stats 2022 ch 617 (SB 1202),s 33, eff. 1/1/2023.

Added by Stats. 1975, Ch. 682.

Section 2104 - Secretary of State as agent for service of process for foreign lending institution

Any foreign lending institution which has not qualified to do business in this state and which engages in any of the activities set forth in subdivision (d) of Section 191 shall be considered by such activities to have appointed the Secretary of State as its agent for service of process for any action arising out of any such activities, and, on or before June 30th of each year, shall file a statement showing the address to which any notice or process may be sent in the manner and with the effect provided in Section 2111. No foreign lending institution solely by reason of engaging in any one or more of the activities set forth in subdivision (d) of Section 191 shall be required to qualify to do business in this state nor be subject to (a) any of the provisions of the Bank and Corporation Tax Law (commencing with Section 23001) of the Revenue and Taxation Code or (b) any of the provisions of this code or the Financial Code or Insurance Code relating to qualifications for doing or transacting business in this state or to requirements pertaining thereto or to the effects or results of failure to qualify to do business in this state.

Ca. Corp. Code § 2104

Amended by Stats. 1976, Ch. 641.

Section 2105 - Certificate of qualification

(a)A foreign corporation shall not transact intrastate business without having first obtained from the Secretary of State a certificate of qualification. To obtain that certificate it shall file, on a form prescribed by the Secretary of State, a statement and designation signed by a corporate officer or, in the case of a foreign association that has no officers, signed by a trustee stating:

(1) The name of the corporation, and, if the name does not comply with Section 201, an alternate name adopted pursuant to subdivision (b) of Section 2106.

(2) The state or place of its incorporation or organization and a statement that the foreign corporation is authorized to exercise its powers and privileges in that state or place of its incorporation or organization.

(3) The street address of its principal office.

(4) The street address of its principal office in California, if any.

(5) The mailing address of its principal office, if different from the addresses specified pursuant to paragraphs (3) and (4).

(6) The name of an agent upon whom process directed to the corporation may be served within this state. The designation shall comply with subdivision (b) of Section 1502.

(7)

(A) Its irrevocable consent to service of process directed to it upon the agent designated and to service of process on the Secretary of State if the agent designated or the agent's successor is no longer authorized to act or cannot be found at the address given.

(B) Consent under this paragraph extends to service of process directed to the foreign corporation's agent in this state for a search warrant issued pursuant to Section 1524.2 of the Penal Code, or for any other validly issued and properly served search warrant, for records or documents that are in the possession of the foreign corporation and are located inside or outside of this state. This subparagraph shall apply to a foreign corporation that is a party or a nonparty to the matter for which the search warrant is sought. For purposes of this subparagraph, "properly served" means delivered by hand, or in a manner reasonably allowing for proof of delivery if delivered by United States mail, overnight delivery service, or facsimile to a person or entity listed in Section 2110, or any other means specified by the foreign corporation, including, but not limited to, email or submission via an internet web portal that the foreign corporation has designated for the purpose of service of process.

(8) If it is a corporation that will be subject to the Insurance Code as an insurer, it shall state that fact.
(b) Annexed to the statement and designation shall be a certificate by an authorized public official of the state or place of incorporation of the corporation to the effect that the corporation is an existing corporation in good standing in that state or place or, in the case of an association, an officers' certificate stating that it is a validly organized and existing business association under the laws of a specified foreign jurisdiction.
(c) Before it may be designated by a foreign corporation as its agent for service of process, a corporate agent must comply with Section 1505.
Ca. Corp. Code § 2105
Amended by Stats 2022 ch 617 (SB 1202),s 34, eff. 1/1/2023.
Amended by Stats 2016 ch 86 (SB 1171),s 47, eff. 1/1/2017.
Amended by Stats 2015 ch 57 (AB 844),s 1, eff. 1/1/2016.
Amended by Stats 2014 ch 834 (SB 1041),s 5, eff. 1/1/2015.

Amended by Stats 2012 ch 494 (SB 1532),s 9, eff. 1/1/2013.
Amended by Stats 2004 ch 629 (AB 1776),s 1, eff. 1/1/2005
Amended October 10, 1999 (Bill Number: SB 662) (Chapter 896).

Section 2106 - Issuance of certificate of qualification; assumed name

(a) Subject to the provisions of subdivision (b), upon payment of the fees required by law the Secretary of State shall file the statement and designation prescribed in Section 2105 and shall issue to the corporation a certificate of qualification stating the date of filing of said statement and designation and that the corporation is qualified to transact intrastate business, subject, however, to any licensing requirements otherwise imposed by the laws of this state.

(b) No foreign corporation having a name which would not be available pursuant to subdivision (b) of Section 201 to a new corporation organized under this division shall transact intrastate business in this state or qualify to do so under this chapter or file an amended statement and designation containing such name unless either:

(1) it obtains and files an order from a court of competent jurisdiction permanently enjoining the other corporation having a conflicting name from doing business in this state under that name; or

(2) the Secretary of State finds, upon proof by affidavit or otherwise as the Secretary of State may determine, that the business to be conducted in this state by the foreign corporation is not the same as or similar to the business being conducted by the corporation (or to be conducted by the proposed corporation) with whose name it may conflict and that the public is not likely to be deceived, and the foreign corporation agrees that it will transact business in this state under an alternate name disclosed to the Secretary of State and that it will use the alternate name in all of its dealings with the Secretary of State and in the conduct of its affairs in this state. The alternate name may be its name with the addition of some distinguishing word or words acceptable to the Secretary of State or a name available for the name of a domestic corporation pursuant to subdivision (b) of Section 201. A corporation which has made such an agreement with the Secretary of State shall not do business in this state except under the name agreed upon, so long as the agreement remains in effect. This subdivision shall not apply to any corporation that is subject to the Insurance Code as an insurer unless the insurer has first obtained from the Insurance Commissioner a certificate approving the alternate name.

Ca. Corp. Code § 2106

Amended by Stats 2022 ch 617 (SB 1202),s 35, eff. 1/1/2023.
Amended by Stats. 1979, Ch. 737.

Section 2106.5 - Certificate of insurance commissioner approving corporate name

215

The Secretary of State shall not file any statement and designation pursuant to Section 2106 or any amended statement and designation pursuant to Section 2107, where it appears that the business is that of an insurer subject to the Insurance Code unless a certificate of the Insurance Commissioner approving the corporate name is attached thereto.

Ca. Corp. Code § 2106.5
Added by Stats. 1979, Ch. 737.

Section 2107 - Change of name

(a) If any foreign corporation (but not a foreign association) qualified to transact intrastate business shall change its name or make a change affecting an alternate name under Section 2106, it shall file, on a form prescribed by the Secretary of State, an amended statement signed by a corporate officer setting forth the change made. The amended statement shall set forth the name relinquished as well as the new name alternate and there shall be annexed to the amended statement a certificate of an authorized public official of its state or place of incorporation issued within the past six months from the submission of the amended statement for filing in California that the change of name was made in accordance with the laws of that state or place of incorporation. Upon the filing of the amended statement, the Secretary of State shall issue a new certificate of qualification.

(b) If any foreign association qualified to transact intrastate business shall change its name, the address of its principal office in California, the address of its principal office or its agent for the service of process, or if the stated address of any natural person designated as agent is changed, it shall file, on a form prescribed by the Secretary of State, an amended statement and designation signed by an officer or, in the case of a foreign association that has no officers, signed by a trustee setting forth the change or changes made. In the case of a change of name, the amended statement and designation shall set forth the name relinquished as well as the new name alternate and there shall be annexed to the amended statement and designation an officer's certificate, or trustee's certificate, if applicable, stating that such change of name was made in accordance with its declaration of trust. If the change includes a change of name, or a change affecting an alternate name pursuant to Section 2106, upon the filing of the amended statement, the Secretary of State shall issue a new certificate of qualification.

(c) If the change includes a change of name of an insurer subject to the Insurance Code, the form shall include a statement that the corporation is such an insurer if it does not already so appear.

(d) If a foreign corporation qualified to transact business in this state shall change the address of its principal office in California, the address of its principal office, or its agent for the service of process, or if the stated address of any natural person designated as agent is changed, the filing of a statement pursuant to Section 2117 shall supersede the statement and designation with respect thereto.

Ca. Corp. Code § 2107

Amended by Stats 2022 ch 617 (SB 1202),s 36, eff. 1/1/2023.
Amended by Stats 2014 ch 834 (SB 1041),s 6, eff. 1/1/2015.

Section 2110 - Delivery by hand of copy of process

Delivery by hand of a copy of any process against a foreign corporation (a) to any officer of the corporation or its general manager in this state, or if the corporation is a bank to a cashier or an assistant cashier, (b) to any natural person designated by it as agent for the service of process, or (c), if the corporation has designated a corporate agent, to any person named in the latest certificate of the corporate agent filed pursuant to Section 1505 shall constitute valid service on the corporation. A copy of the statement and designation, or a copy of the latest statement filed pursuant to Section 2117, certified by the Secretary of State, is sufficient evidence of the appointment of an agent for the service of process.

  Ca. Corp. Code § 2110
Amended by Stats. 1989, Ch. 438, Sec. 2.

Section 2110.1 - Serving of process upon foreign corporation

In addition to the provisions of Chapter 4 (commencing with Section 413.10) of Title 5 of Part 2 of the Code of Civil Procedure, process may be served upon a foreign corporation as provided in this chapter.

  Ca. Corp. Code § 2110.1
Added by Stats. 1977, Ch. 235.

Section 2111 - Personal delivery to Secretary of State

(a) If the agent designated for the service of process is a natural person and cannot be found with due diligence at the address stated in the designation or if the agent is a corporation and no person can be found with due diligence to whom the delivery authorized by Section 2110 may be made for the purpose of delivery to the corporate agent, or if the agent designated is no longer authorized to act, or if no agent has been designated and if no one of the officers or agents of the corporation specified in Section 2110 can be found after diligent search and it is so shown by affidavit to the satisfaction of the court, then the court may make an order that service be made by personal delivery to the Secretary of State or to an assistant or deputy secretary of state of two copies of the process together with two copies of the order, except that if the corporation to be served has not filed the statement required to be filed by Section 2105 then only one copy of the process and order need be delivered but the order shall include and set forth an address to which the process shall be sent by the Secretary of State. Service in this manner is deemed complete on the 10th day after delivery of the process to the Secretary of State.

(b) Upon receipt of the process and order and the fee therefor the Secretary of State forthwith shall give notice to the corporation of the service of the process by forwarding by registered or certified mail, with request for return receipt, a copy of the process and order to the address specified in the order if the corporation has not filed the statement required by Section 2105 or to the two stated addresses of the corporation set forth in the latest statement filed pursuant to Section 2105 or 2117, or if only one address is set forth in the latest statement, to the sole stated address of the corporation.

(c) The Secretary of State shall keep a record of all process served upon the Secretary of State and shall record therein the time of service and the Secretary of State's action with respect thereto. The certificate of the Secretary of State, under the Secretary of State's official seal, certifying to the receipt of process, the giving of notice thereof to the corporation, and the forwarding of the process pursuant to this section, shall be competent and prima facie evidence of the matters stated therein.

Ca. Corp. Code § 2111
Amended by Stats. 1989, Ch. 438, Sec. 3.

Section 2112 - Certificate of surrender

(a) Subject to Section 2113, a foreign corporation which has qualified to transact intrastate business may surrender its right to engage in that business within this state by filing a certificate of surrender signed by a corporate officer or, in the case of a foreign association that has no officers, signed by a trustee stating:

(1) The name of the corporation as shown on the records of the Secretary of State, and the state or place of incorporation or organization.

(2) That it revokes its designation of agent for service of process.

(3) That it surrenders its authority to transact intrastate business.

(4) That it consents that process against it in any action upon any liability or obligation incurred within this state before the filing of the certificate of surrender may be served upon the Secretary of State.

(5)A post office address to which the Secretary of State may mail a copy of any process against the corporation that is served upon the Secretary of State, which address or the name to which the process should be sent may be changed from time to time by filing a statement signed by a corporate officer or, in the case of a foreign association that has no officers, signed by a trustee stating the new address or name or both.

(6) Except in the case of a foreign association, that a final franchise tax return, as described by Section 23332 of the Revenue and Taxation Code, has been or will be filed with the Franchise Tax Board, as required under Part 10.2 (commencing with Section 18401) of Division 2 of the Revenue and Taxation Code.

(b) The Secretary of State shall notify the Franchise Tax Board of the surrender.

Ca. Corp. Code § 2112

Amended by Stats 2022 ch 617 (SB 1202),s 37, eff. 1/1/2023.

Amended by Stats 2014 ch 834 (SB 1041),s 7, eff. 1/1/2015.

Amended by Stats 2006 ch 773 (AB 2341),s 14, eff. 9/29/2006.

Section 2113 - Filing of agreement of merger as surrender of right to engage in intrastate business

(a) The filing of an agreement of merger of a foreign disappearing corporation qualified to transact intrastate business in this state pursuant to Section 1103, or the filing pursuant to subdivision (d) of Section 1108 of an agreement, certificate, or other document as to a merger that includes a disappearing foreign corporation qualified to transact intrastate business, or the filing of a certificate of ownership as to a foreign subsidiary corporation qualified to transact intrastate business in this state pursuant to Section 1110, or the filing by a foreign corporation qualified to transact intrastate business in this state of an organizational document containing a statement of conversion pursuant to Section 15911.08, 16908, or 17710.08, constitutes the surrender by the foreign corporation of its right to engage in intrastate business within this state.

(b) With respect to corporations for which documents have not been filed as provided in subdivision (a), a certificate of surrender as prescribed by Section 2112 shall be filed by a foreign corporation qualified to transact intrastate business upon its merger into another foreign corporation.

(c) In lieu of a signature as prescribed by Section 2112, a certificate of surrender pursuant to subdivision (b) for a merged foreign corporation may be signed in the name of the surviving corporation by an officer thereof. In that case, the certificate of surrender shall be accompanied by a certificate of an authorized public official of the state or place of incorporation of the merged foreign corporation stating that the corporation has been merged into another foreign corporation and setting forth the name and state or place of incorporation of the surviving foreign corporation.

Ca. Corp. Code § 2113

Amended by Stats 2012 ch 419 (SB 323),s 10, eff. 1/1/2013, op. 1/1/2014.

Amended by Stats 2006 ch 495 (AB 339),s 10, eff. 1/1/2007.

Amended by Stats 2000 ch 201 (AB 1894), s 3, eff. 1/1/2001.

Section 2114 - Service of process upon withdrawal from business in state, surrender of right to transact intrastate business, or forfeiture of right to transact intrastate business

(a) A foreign corporation that has transacted intrastate business and has thereafter withdrawn from business in this state may be served with process in the manner provided in this chapter in any action brought in this state arising out of that business, whether or not it has ever complied with the requirements of this chapter.

(b) A foreign corporation that has surrendered its right to transact intrastate business pursuant to Section 2112 or 2113 may be served with process in any action upon a liability or obligation incurred within this state prior to that surrender by delivery of the process to the Secretary of State, or an assistant or a deputy to the Secretary of State pursuant to this chapter and no court order authorizing this service shall be required. The process shall be mailed in the manner prescribed in this chapter except that it shall be sent to the address to which process is authorized to be sent in the certificate of surrender or to the address of the surviving domestic corporation in the case of a surrender under Section 2113.

(c) If a foreign corporation that is qualified to transact intrastate business has its right to transact such business forfeited by the Franchise Tax Board pursuant to the Bank and Corporation Tax Law (Part 11 (commencing with Section 23001) of Division 2 of the Revenue and Taxation Code), service of process on that corporation may be effected in the manner set forth in Sections 2110 and 2111, as if the right to transact intrastate business had not been forfeited.

(d) The fact that a corporation ceases to transact intrastate business without filing a certificate of surrender does not revoke the appointment of any agent for the service of process.

Ca. Corp. Code § 2114

Amended by Stats. 1997, Ch. 187, Sec. 5. Effective January 1, 1998.

Section 2115 - Laws applicable to foreign corporation

(a) A foreign corporation (other than a foreign association or foreign nonprofit corporation but including a foreign parent corporation even though it does not itself transact intrastate business) is subject to the requirements of subdivision (b) commencing on the date specified in subdivision (d) and continuing until the date specified in subdivision (e) if:

(1) The average of the property factor, the payroll factor, and the sales factor (as defined in Sections 25129, 25132, and 25134 of the Revenue and Taxation Code) with respect to it is more than 50 percent during its latest full income year and

(2) more than one-half of its outstanding voting securities are held of record by persons having addresses in this state appearing on the books of the corporation on the record date for the latest meeting of shareholders held during its latest full income year or, if no meeting was held during that year, on the last day of the latest full income year. The property factor, payroll factor, and sales factor shall be those used in computing the portion of its income allocable to this state in its franchise tax return or, with respect to corporations the allocation of whose income is governed by special formulas or that are not required to file separate or any tax returns, which would have been so used if they were governed by this three-factor formula. The determination of these factors with respect to any parent corporation shall be made on a consolidated basis, including in a unitary computation (after elimination of intercompany transactions) the property, payroll, and sales of the parent and all of its subsidiaries in which it owns directly or indirectly more than 50 percent of the outstanding shares entitled to vote for the election of directors, but deducting a percentage of the property, payroll, and sales of any subsidiary equal to the percentage minority ownership, if any, in the subsidiary. For the purpose of this subdivision, any securities held to the knowledge of the issuer in the names of broker-dealers, nominees for broker-dealers (including clearing corporations), or banks, associations, or other entities holding securities in a nominee name or otherwise on behalf of a beneficial owner (collectively "nominee holders"), shall not be considered outstanding. However, if the foreign corporation requests all nominee holders to certify, with respect to all beneficial owners for whom securities are held, the number of shares held for those beneficial owners having addresses (as shown on the records of the nominee holder) in this state and outside of this state, then all shares so certified shall be considered outstanding and held of record by persons having addresses either in this state or outside of this state as so certified, provided that the certification so provided shall be retained with the record of shareholders and made available for inspection and copying in the same manner as is provided in Section 1600 with respect to that record. A current list of beneficial owners of a foreign corporation's securities provided to the corporation by one or more nominee holders or their agent pursuant to the requirements of Rule 14b-1(b)(3) or 14b-2(b)(3) as adopted on January 6, 1992, promulgated under the Securities Exchange Act of 1934, shall constitute an acceptable certification with respect to beneficial owners for the purposes of this subdivision.

(b) Except as provided in subdivision (c), the following chapters and sections of this division shall apply to a foreign corporation as defined in subdivision (a) (to the exclusion of the law of the jurisdiction in which it is incorporated): Chapter 1 (general provisions and definitions), to the extent applicable to the following provisions;

Section 301 (annual election of directors);

Section 303 (removal of directors without cause);

Section 304 (removal of directors by court proceedings);

Section 305, subdivision (c) (filling of director vacancies where less than a majority in office elected by shareholders);

Section 309 (directors' standard of care);

Section 316 (excluding paragraph (3) of subdivision (a) and paragraph (3) of subdivision (f)) (liability of directors for unlawful distributions);

Section 317 (indemnification of directors, officers, and others);

Sections 500 to 505, inclusive (limitations on corporate distributions in cash or property);

Section 506 (liability of shareholder who receives unlawful distribution);

Section 600, subdivisions (b) and (c) (requirement for annual shareholders' meeting and remedy if same not timely held);

Section 708, subdivisions (a), (b), and (c) (shareholder's right to cumulate votes at any election of directors);

Section 710 (supermajority vote requirement);

Section 1001, subdivision (d) (limitations on sale of assets);

Section 1101, subdivision (b) (limitations on mergers);

Section 1151 (first sentence only) (limitations on conversions);

Section 1152 (requirements of conversions);

Chapter 12 (commencing with Section 1200) (reorganizations);

Chapter 13 (commencing with Section 1300) (dissenters' rights);

Sections 1500 and 1501 (records and reports);

Section 1508 (action by Attorney General);

Chapter 16 (commencing with Section 1600) (rights of inspection).

(c) This section does not apply to any corporation (1) with outstanding securities listed on the New York Stock Exchange, the NYSE American, the NASDAQ Global Market, or the NASDAQ Capital Market, or (2) if all of its voting shares (other than directors' qualifying shares) are owned directly or indirectly by a corporation or corporations not subject to this section.

(d) For purposes of subdivision (a), the requirements of subdivision (b) shall become applicable to a foreign corporation only upon the first day of the first income year of the corporation (1) commencing on or after the 135th day of the income year immediately following the latest income year with respect to which the tests referred to in subdivision (a) have been met or (2) commencing on or after the entry of a final order by a court of competent jurisdiction declaring that those tests have been met.

(e) For purposes of subdivision (a), the requirements of subdivision (b) shall cease to be applicable to a foreign corporation (1) at the end of the first income year of the corporation immediately following the latest income year with respect to which at least one of the tests referred to in subdivision (a) is not met or (2) at the end of the income year of the corporation during which a final order has been entered by a court of competent jurisdiction declaring that one of those tests is not met, provided that a contrary order has not been entered before the end of the income year.

(f) Any foreign corporation that is subject to the requirements of subdivision (b) shall advise any shareholder of record, any officer, director, employee, or other agent (within the meaning of Section 317) and any creditor of the corporation in writing, within 30 days of receipt of written request for that information, whether or not it is subject to subdivision (b) at the time the request is received. Any party who obtains a final determination by a court of competent jurisdiction that the corporation failed to provide to the party information required to be provided by this subdivision or provided the party information of the kind required to be provided by this subdivision that was incorrect, then the court, in its discretion, shall have the power to include in its judgment recovery by the party from the corporation of all court costs and reasonable attorneys' fees incurred in that legal proceeding to the extent they relate to obtaining that final determination.

Ca. Corp. Code § 2115

Amended by Stats 2022 ch 617 (SB 1202),s 38, eff. 1/1/2023.

Amended by Stats 2009 ch 131 (AB 991),s 6, eff. 1/1/2010.

Amended by Stats 2002 ch 480 (SB 399),s 8, eff. 1/1/2003.

Amended by Stats 2000 ch 206 (SB 1488), s 1, eff. 1/1/2001.

Section 2115.5 - Female directors on corporate boards

(a) Section 301.3 shall apply to a foreign corporation that is a publicly held corporation to the exclusion of the law of the jurisdiction in which the foreign corporation is incorporated.

(b) For purposes of this section, a "publicly held corporation" means a foreign corporation with outstanding shares listed on a major United States stock exchange.

Ca. Corp. Code § 2115.5

Added by Stats 2018 ch 954 (SB 826),s 3, eff. 1/1/2019.

Section 2115.6 - Underrepresented community on foreign corporation boards; applicability of section 301.4

(a) Section 301.4 shall apply to a foreign corporation that is a publicly held corporation to the exclusion of the law of the jurisdiction in which the foreign corporation is incorporated.

(b) For purposes of this section, a "publicly held corporation" means a foreign corporation with outstanding shares listed on a major United States stock exchange.

Ca. Corp. Code § 2115.6

Added by Stats 2020 ch 316 (AB 979),s 4, eff. 1/1/2021.

Section 2116 - Liability of directors

The directors of a foreign corporation transacting intrastate business are liable to the corporation, its shareholders, creditors, receiver, liquidator or trustee in bankruptcy for the making of unauthorized dividends, purchase of shares or distribution of assets or false certificates, reports or public notices or other violation of official duty according to any applicable laws of the state or place of incorporation or organization, whether committed or done in this state or elsewhere. Such liability may be enforced in the courts of this state.

Ca. Corp. Code § 2116

Added by Stats. 1975, Ch. 682.

Section 2117 - Filing of statement

(a) Every foreign corporation (other than a foreign association) qualified to transact intrastate business shall file, within 90 days after the filing of its original statement and designation of foreign corporation and annually thereafter during the applicable filing period, on a form prescribed by the Secretary of State, a statement containing all of the following:

(1) The name of the corporation as registered in California and the California Secretary of State's file number.

(2) The names and complete business or residence addresses of its chief executive officer, secretary, and chief financial officer.

(3) The street address of its principal executive office.

(4) The mailing address of the corporation, if different from the street address of its principal executive office.

(5) The street address of its principal business office in this state, if any.

(6) If the corporation chooses to receive renewal notices and any other notifications from the Secretary of State by electronic mail instead of by United States mail, the corporation shall include a valid electronic mail address for the corporation or for the corporation's designee to receive those notices.

(7) A statement of the general type of business that constitutes the principal business activity of the corporation, such as, for example, manufacturer of aircraft, wholesale liquor distributor, or retail department store.

(8) A statement indicating whether any officer or any director has an outstanding final judgment issued by the Division of Labor Standards Enforcement or a court of law, for which no appeal therefrom is pending, for the violation of any wage order or provision of the Labor Code.

(b) The statement required by subdivision (a) shall also designate, as the agent of the corporation for the purpose of service of process, a natural person residing in this state or a corporation that has complied with Section 1505 and whose capacity to act as the agent has not terminated. If a natural person is designated, the statement shall set forth the person's complete business or residence street address. If a corporate agent is designated, no address for it shall be set forth.

(c) The statement required by subdivision (a) shall be available and open to the public for inspection. The Secretary of State shall provide access to all information contained in the statement by means of an online database.

(d) In addition to any other fees required, a foreign corporation shall pay a five-dollar ($5) disclosure fee upon filing the statement required by subdivision (a). One-half of the fee shall, notwithstanding Section 12176 of the Government Code, be deposited into the Business Programs Modernization Fund established in subdivision (k) of Section 1502, and one-half shall be deposited into the Victims of Corporate Fraud Compensation Fund established in Section 2280.

(e) Whenever any of the information required by subdivision (a) is changed, the corporation may file a current statement containing all the information required by subdivisions (a) and (b). In order to change its agent for service of process or the address of the agent, the corporation shall file a current statement containing all the information required by subdivisions (a) and (b). Whenever any statement is filed pursuant to this section, it supersedes any previously filed statement and the statement in the filing pursuant to Section 2105.

(f) Subdivisions (c), (d), (f), and (g) of Section 1502 apply to statements filed pursuant to this section, except that "articles" shall mean the filing pursuant to Section 2105, and "corporation" shall mean a foreign corporation.

(g)

(1) This section shall become operative on January 1, 2022, or upon certification by the Secretary of State that California Business Connect is implemented, whichever date is earlier.

(2) If the Secretary of State certifies California Business Connect is implemented prior to January 1, 2022, the Secretary of State shall post notice of the certification on the homepage of its internet website and send notice of the certification to the Legislative Counsel.

Ca. Corp. Code § 2117

Added by Stats 2020 ch 357 (AB 3075),s 4, eff. 1/1/2021.

Section 2117.1 - Additional filing of statement

(a) In addition to the statement required pursuant to Section 2117, every publicly traded foreign corporation shall file annually, within 150 days after the end of its fiscal year, on a form prescribed by the Secretary of State, a statement that includes all of the following information:

(1) The name of the independent auditor that prepared the most recent auditor's report on the publicly traded foreign corporation's annual financial statements.

(2) A description of other services, if any, performed for the publicly traded foreign corporation during its two most recent fiscal years and the period between the end of its most recent fiscal year and the date of the statement by the foregoing independent auditor, by its parent corporation, or by a subsidiary or corporate affiliate of the independent auditor or its parent corporation.

(3) The name of the independent auditor employed by the foreign corporation on the date of the statement, if different from the independent auditor listed pursuant to paragraph (1).

(4) The compensation for the most recent fiscal year of the publicly traded foreign corporation paid to each member of the board of directors and paid to each of the five most highly compensated executive officers of the foreign corporation who are not members of the board of directors, including the number of any shares issued, options for shares granted, and similar equity-based compensation granted to each of those persons. If the chief executive officer is not among the five most highly compensated

executive officers of the corporation, the compensation paid to the chief executive officer shall also be included.

(5) A description of any loan, including the amount and terms of the loans, made to any member of the board of directors by the publicly traded foreign corporation during the foreign corporation's two most recent fiscal years at an interest rate lower than the interest rate available from unaffiliated commercial lenders generally to a similarly situated borrower.

(6) A statement indicating whether an order for relief has been entered in a bankruptcy case with respect to the foreign corporation, its executive officers, or members of the board of directors of the foreign corporation during the 10 years preceding the date of the statement.

(7) A statement indicating whether any member of the board of directors or executive officer of the publicly traded foreign corporation was convicted of fraud during the 10 years preceding the date of the statement, which conviction has not been overturned or expunged.

(8) A description of any material pending legal proceedings, other than ordinary routine litigation incidental to the business, to which the corporation or any of its subsidiaries is a party or of which any of their property is the subject, as specified by Item 103 of Regulation S-K of the Securities and Exchange Commission (Section 229.103 of Title 12 of the Code of Federal Regulations). A description of any material legal proceeding during which the corporation was found legally liable by entry of a final judgment or final order that was not overturned on appeal during the five years preceding the date of the statement.

(b) For purposes of this section, the following definitions apply:

(1) "Publicly traded foreign corporation" means a foreign corporation, as defined in Section 171, that is an issuer as defined in Section 3 of the Securities Exchange Act of 1934, as amended (15 U.S.C. Sec. 78c) , and has at least one class of securities listed or admitted for trading on a national securities exchange, on the OTC Bulletin Board, or on the electronic service operated by OTC Markets Group Inc.

(2) "Executive officer" means the chief executive officer, president, any vice president in charge of a principal business unit, division, or function, any other officer of the corporation who performs a policymaking function, or any other person who performs similar policymaking functions for the corporation.

(3) "Compensation" as used in paragraph (4) of subdivision (a) means all plan and nonplan compensation awarded to, earned by, or paid to the person for all services rendered in all capacities to the corporation and to its subsidiaries, as the compensation is specified by Item 402 of Regulation S-K of the Securities and

Exchange Commission (Section 229.402 of Title 17 of the Code of Federal Regulations).

(4) "Loan" as used in paragraph (5) of subdivision (a) excludes an advance for expenses, the foreign corporation's payment of life insurance premiums, and an advance of litigation expenses, in each instance as permitted according to the applicable law of the state or place of incorporation or organization of the foreign corporation.

(c) This statement shall be available and open to the public for inspection. The Secretary of State shall provide access to all information contained in this statement by means of an online database.

(d) A foreign corporation shall certify that the information it provides pursuant to this section is true and correct. No claim may be made against the state for inaccurate information contained in statements filed under this section with the Secretary of State.

Ca. Corp. Code § 2117.1

Amended by Stats 2019 ch 143 (SB 251),s 27, eff. 1/1/2020.

Amended by Stats 2009 ch 131 (AB 991),s 7, eff. 1/1/2010.

Added by Stats 2004 ch 819 (AB 1000),s 5, eff. 9/27/2004.

Chapter 22 - CRIMES AND PENALTIES

Section 2200 - Neglect, failure, or refusal to keep records of shareholders or books of account, prepare or submit financial statements, or give shareholder required advice

Every corporation that neglects, fails, or refuses:

(a) to keep or cause to be kept or maintained the record of shareholders or books of account required by this division to be kept or maintained,

(b) to prepare or cause to be prepared or submitted the financial statements required by this division to be prepared or submitted, or

(c) to give any shareholder of record the advice required by subdivision (f) of Section 2115, is subject to penalty as provided in this section. The penalty shall be twenty-five dollars ($25) for each day that the failure or refusal continues, up to a maximum of one thousand five hundred dollars ($1,500), beginning 30 days after receipt of the written request that the duty be performed from one entitled to make the request, except that, in the case of a failure to give advice required by subdivision (f) of Section 2115, the 30-day period shall run from the date of receipt of the request made pursuant to subdivision (f) of Section 2115, and no additional request is required by this section.

The penalty shall be paid to the shareholder or shareholders jointly making the request for performance of the duty, and damaged by the neglect, failure, or refusal, if suit therefor is commenced within 90 days after the written request is made, including any request made pursuant to subdivision (f) of Section 2115; but the maximum daily penalty because of failure to comply with any number of separate requests made on any one day or for the same act shall be two hundred fifty dollars ($250).

    Ca. Corp. Code § 2200

Amended by Stats 2000 ch 206 (SB 1488), s 2, eff. 1/1/2001.

Amended by Stats 2001 ch 159 (SB 662), s 44, eff. 1/1/2002.

Section 2201 - Neglect, failure, or refusal to enter transfer of shares upon books and issue share certificate or initial transaction statement

Any officer of a corporation charged with the duty of entering a transfer of shares upon the books of the corporation and issuing a share certificate or, with respect to uncertificated securities, an initial transaction statement or written statements, who unreasonably neglects, fails or refuses to perform such duty after written request by any person entitled thereto is subject to a penalty of one hundred dollars ($100) and the further penalty of ten dollars ($10) for each day that such default continues, beginning five days after receipt of the request, up to a maximum of five hundred dollars ($500). The penalty shall be paid to each person aggrieved. It may be enforced by action and shall be in addition to all other remedies.

Every director or other officer unreasonably causing such neglect, failure or refusal to make such entries upon the books of the corporation or to issue a certificate or, with respect to uncertificated securities, an initial transaction statement or written statements, for shares to a person entitled thereto is subject to a like penalty.

    Ca. Corp. Code § 2201

Amended by Stats. 1986, Ch. 766, Sec. 27.

Section 2202 - Penalty

Any penalty prescribed by Section 2200 or Section 2201 shall be in addition to any remedy by injunction or action for damages or by writ of mandate for the nonperformance of acts and duties enjoined by law upon the corporation or its directors or officers.

The court in which an action for any such penalty is brought may reduce, remit or suspend the penalty on such terms and conditions as it may deem reasonable when it is made to appear that the neglect, failure or refusal was inadvertent or excusable.

    Ca. Corp. Code § 2202

Repealed and added by Stats. 1975, Ch. 682.

Section 2203 - Foreign corporation which transacts intrastate business without valid certificate

(a) Any foreign corporation which transacts intrastate business and which does not hold a valid certificate from the Secretary of State may be subject to a penalty of twenty dollars ($20) for each day that unauthorized intrastate business is transacted;

and the foreign corporation, by transacting unauthorized intrastate business, shall be deemed to consent to the jurisdiction of the courts of California in any civil action arising in this state in which the corporation is named a party defendant.

(b) The penalty established by subdivision (a) of this section shall be assessed according to the number of days it is found that the corporation has been willfully doing unauthorized intrastate business. Prosecution under this section may be brought, and the money penalty recovered thereby shall be paid, in the manner provided by Section 2258 for a prosecution brought under that section. The amount of the penalty assessed shall be determined by the court based upon the circumstances, including the size of the corporation and the willfulness of the violation.

(c) A foreign corporation subject to the provisions of Chapter 21 (commencing with Section 2100) which transacts intrastate business without complying with Section 2105 shall not maintain any action or proceeding upon any intrastate business so transacted in any court of this state, commenced prior to compliance with Section 2105, until it has complied with the provisions thereof and has paid to the Secretary of State a penalty of two hundred fifty dollars ($250) in addition to the fees due for filing the statement and designation required by Section 2105 and has filed with the clerk of the court in which the action is pending receipts showing the payment of the fees and penalty and all franchise taxes and any other taxes on business or property in this state that should have been paid for the period during which it transacted intrastate business.

Ca. Corp. Code § 2203
Amended by Stats. 1990, Ch. 926, Sec. 1.

Section 2204 - Failure to file statement; certification of name of corporation to Franchise Tax Board; penalty

(a) Upon the failure of a corporation to file the statement required by Section 1502, the Secretary of State shall provide a notice of that delinquency to the corporation. The notice shall also contain information concerning the application of this section, advise the corporation of the penalty imposed by Section 19141 of the Revenue and Taxation Code for failure to timely file the required statement after notice of the delinquency has been provided by the Secretary of State, and shall advise the corporation of its right to request relief from the Secretary of State because of reasonable cause or unusual circumstances that justify the failure to file. If, within 60 days of providing notice of the delinquency, a statement pursuant to Section 1502 has not been filed by the corporation, the Secretary of State shall certify the name of the corporation to the Franchise Tax Board.

(b) Upon certification pursuant to subdivision (a), the Franchise Tax Board shall assess against the corporation the penalty provided in Section 19141 of the Revenue and Taxation Code.

(c) The penalty herein provided shall not apply to a corporation that on or prior to the date of certification pursuant to subdivision (a) has dissolved, has converted to another type of business entity, or has been merged into another corporation or other business entity.

(d) The penalty herein provided shall not apply and the Secretary of State need not provide a notice of the delinquency to a corporation if the corporate powers, rights, and privileges have been suspended by the Franchise Tax Board pursuant to Section 23301, 23301.5, or 23775 of the Revenue and Taxation Code on or prior to, and remain suspended on, the last day of the filing period pursuant to Section 1502. The Secretary of State need not provide notice of the filing requirement pursuant to Section 1502 to a corporation if the corporate powers, rights, and privileges have been so suspended by the Franchise Tax Board on or prior to, and remain suspended on, the day the Secretary of State prepares the notice for sending.

(e) If, after certification pursuant to subdivision (a), the Secretary of State finds (1) the required statement was filed before the expiration of the 60-day period after providing notice of the delinquency, or (2) the failure to provide notice of delinquency was due to an error of the Secretary of State, the Secretary of State shall promptly decertify the name of the corporation to the Franchise Tax Board. The Franchise Tax Board shall then promptly abate any penalty assessed against the corporation pursuant to Section 19141 of the Revenue and Taxation Code.

(f) If the Secretary of State determines that the failure of a corporation to file the statement required by Section 1502 is excusable because of reasonable cause or unusual circumstances that justify the failure, the Secretary of State may waive the penalty imposed by this section and by Section 19141 of the Revenue and Taxation Code, in which case the Secretary of State shall not certify the name of the corporation to the Franchise Tax Board, or if already certified, the Secretary of State shall promptly decertify the name of the corporation.

Ca. Corp. Code § 2204

Amended by Stats 2014 ch 834 (SB 1041),s 8, eff. 1/1/2015.

Amended by Stats 2011 ch 204 (AB 657),s 5, eff. 1/1/2012.

Section 2205 - Suspension for failure to file statement

(a) A corporation that (1) fails to file a statement pursuant to Section 1502 for an applicable filing period, (2) has not filed a statement pursuant to Section 1502 during the preceding 24 months, and (3) was certified for penalty pursuant to Section 2204 for the same filing period, is subject to suspension pursuant to this section rather than to penalty pursuant to Section 2204.

(b) When subdivision (a) is applicable, the Secretary of State shall provide a notice to the corporation informing the corporation that its corporate powers, rights, and privileges will be suspended after 60 days if it fails to file a statement pursuant to Section 1502.

(c) After the expiration of the 60-day period without any statement filed pursuant to Section 1502, the Secretary of State shall notify the Franchise Tax Board of the suspension and provide a notice of the suspension to the corporation, and thereupon, the corporate powers, rights, and privileges of the corporation are suspended, except for the purpose of filing an application for exempt status or amending the articles of incorporation as necessary either to perfect that application or to set forth a new name.

(d) A statement pursuant to Section 1502 may be filed notwithstanding suspension of the corporate powers, rights, and privileges pursuant to this section or Section 23301, 23301.5, or 23775 of the Revenue and Taxation Code. Upon the filing of a statement pursuant to Section 1502 by a corporation that has suffered suspension pursuant to this section, the Secretary of State shall certify that fact to the Franchise Tax Board and the corporation may thereupon be relieved from suspension unless the corporation is held in suspension by the Franchise Tax Board by reason of Section 23301, 23301.5, or 23775 of the Revenue and Taxation Code.

Ca. Corp. Code § 2205

Amended by Stats 2011 ch 204 (AB 657),s 6, eff. 1/1/2012.
Amended by Stats 2003 ch 633 (SB 1061),s 1, eff. 9/30/2003.
Amended October 10, 1999 (Bill Number: SB 284) (Chapter 1000).

Section 2205.5 - Administrative dissolution for suspension by Franchise Tax Board

(a) A domestic corporation, as defined in Section 167, may be subject to administrative dissolution pursuant to this section if, as of January 1, 2019, or at any time thereafter, the corporation's corporate powers, rights, and privileges are, and have been, suspended by the Franchise Tax Board pursuant to Article 7 (commencing with Section 23301) of Chapter 2 of Part 11 of Division 2 of the Revenue and Taxation Code for a period of not less than 60 continuous months.

(b) Prior to administrative dissolution of the corporation, the corporation shall be notified of the pending administrative dissolution as follows:

(1) The Franchise Tax Board shall mail written notice to the last known address of the corporation.

(2) If the corporation does not have a valid address in the records of the Franchise Tax Board, the notice provided in subdivision (d) shall be deemed sufficient notice prior to administrative dissolution.

(c) The Franchise Tax Board shall transmit to the Secretary of State the names and Secretary of State file numbers of the corporations subject to administrative dissolution pursuant to this section.

(d) The Secretary of State shall provide 60 days' notice of the pending administrative dissolution on its Internet Web site by listing the corporation's name and the Secretary of State's file number. The Secretary of State shall also, in conjunction with the information above, provide instructions for a corporation to submit a written objection of the pending administrative dissolution to the Franchise Tax Board, before the expiration of the 60 day's notice.

(e)

(1) A corporation may provide the Franchise Tax Board with a written objection to the administrative dissolution.

(2) The Franchise Tax Board shall notify the Secretary of State if a written objection has been received.

(f) If a written objection to the administrative dissolution is not received by the Franchise Tax Board during the 60-day period described in subdivision (d), the corporation shall be administratively dissolved pursuant to this section. The certificate of dissolution of the Secretary of State shall be prima facie evidence of the administrative dissolution.

(g)

(1) If the written objection of a corporation to the administrative dissolution has been received by the Franchise Tax Board before the expiration of the 60-day period described in subdivision (d), that corporation shall have an additional 90 days from the date the written objection is received by the Franchise Tax Board to file returns, pay or otherwise satisfy all accrued taxes, penalties, and interest, file a current Statement of Information with the Secretary of State, fulfill any other requirements to be eligible, and apply for revivor.

(2)

(A) If the conditions in paragraph (1) are satisfied, the administrative dissolution shall be canceled.

(B) If the conditions in paragraph (1) are not satisfied, the corporation shall be administratively dissolved pursuant to this section as of the later of the date that is 90 days after the receipt of the written objection or after the period in paragraph (3), if so extended.

(3) The Franchise Tax Board may extend the 90-day period in paragraph (1), but for no more than one period of 90 days.

(h) Upon administrative dissolution pursuant to this section, the corporation's liabilities for qualified taxes, interest, and penalties, as defined in paragraph (2) of subdivision (b) of Section 23310 of the Revenue and Taxation Code, if any, shall be abated. Any actions taken by the Franchise Tax Board to collect the abated liability shall be released, withdrawn, or otherwise terminated by the Franchise Tax Board and no subsequent administrative or civil action shall be taken or brought to collect all or part of that amount.

(i) If the corporation is administratively dissolved pursuant to this section, the liability to creditors, if any, is not discharged. The liability of the directors, shareholders, transferees, or other persons related to the administratively dissolved corporation is not discharged.

(j) The administrative dissolution of a corporation pursuant to this section shall not diminish or adversely affect the ability of the Attorney General to enforce liabilities as otherwise provided by law.

(k) No administrative appeal, writ, or other judicial action may be taken based on the Franchise Tax Board's or the Secretary of State's actions pursuant to this section, except pursuant to subdivision (h) if related to repayment of amounts erroneously received after administrative dissolution has occurred.

(l) Upon administrative dissolution, the corporate rights, powers, and privileges of the corporation shall cease.

Ca. Corp. Code § 2205.5
Added by Stats 2018 ch 679 (AB 2503),s 1, eff. 1/1/2019.

Section 2206 - Forfeiture of exercise of corporate powers rights and privileges for failure to file statements

(a) Sections 2204 and 2205 apply to foreign corporations with respect to the statements required to be filed by Section 2117. For this purpose, the suspension of the corporate powers, rights, and privileges of a domestic corporation shall mean the forfeiture of the exercise of the corporate powers, rights, and privileges of a foreign corporation in this state.

(b) A foreign nonprofit corporation which has suffered the forfeiture of the exercise of the corporate powers, rights, and privileges in this state may nevertheless file an application for exempt status as specified in Section 23301 of the Revenue and Taxation Code.

(c) The forfeiture of the exercise of the corporate powers, rights, and privileges of a foreign corporation in this state as used in subdivision (a) does not prohibit the transaction of business in this state by a foreign corporation if the business transacted subsequent to the forfeiture would not, considered as an entirety, require the foreign corporation to obtain a certificate of qualification pursuant to Sections 191 and 2105.

Ca. Corp. Code § 2206
Added by Stats. 1985, Ch. 764, Sec. 8. Operative July 1, 1986, by Sec. 11 of Ch. 764.

Section 2207 - Liability for civil penalty for certain acts of officer, director, manager, or agent

(a) A corporation is liable for a civil penalty in an amount not exceeding one million dollars ($1,000,000) if the corporation does both of the following:

(1) Has actual knowledge that an officer, director, manager, or agent of the corporation does any of the following:

(A) Makes, publishes, or posts, or has made, published, or posted, either generally or privately to the shareholders or other persons, either of the following:

(i) An oral, written, or electronically transmitted report, exhibit, notice, or

233

statement of its affairs or pecuniary condition that includes a material statement or omission that is false and intended to give the shares of stock in the corporation a materially greater or a materially less apparent market value than they really possess.

(ii)An oral, written, or electronically transmitted report, prospectus, account, or statement of operations, values, business, profits, or expenditures, that includes a material false statement or omission intended to give the shares of stock in the corporation a materially greater or a materially less apparent market value than they really possess.

(B)Refuses, or has refused to make, any book entry or post any notice required by law in the manner required by law.

(C)Misstates or conceals, or has misstated or concealed, from a regulatory body a material fact in order to deceive a regulatory body to avoid a statutory or regulatory duty, or to avoid a statutory or regulatory limit or prohibition.

(2)Within 30 days after actual knowledge is acquired of the actions described in paragraph (1), the corporation knowingly fails to do both of the following:

(A)Notify the Attorney General or appropriate government agency in writing, unless the corporation has actual knowledge that the Attorney General or appropriate government agency has been notified.

(B)Notify its shareholders in writing, unless the corporation has actual knowledge that the shareholders have been notified.
(b)The requirement for notification under this section does not apply if the action taken or about to be taken by the corporation, or by an officer, director, manager, or agent of the corporation under paragraph (1) of subdivision (a), is abated within the time prescribed for reporting, unless the appropriate government agency requires disclosure by regulation.
(c)If the action reported to the Attorney General pursuant to this section implicates the government authority of an agency other than the Attorney General, the Attorney General shall promptly forward the written notice to that agency.
(d)If the Attorney General was not notified pursuant to subparagraph (A) of paragraph (2) of subdivision (a), but the corporation reasonably and in good faith believed that it had complied with the notification requirements of this section by notifying a government agency listed in paragraph (5) of subdivision (e), no penalties shall apply.
(e)For purposes of this section:

(1)"Manager" means a person having both of the following:

(A)Management authority over a business entity.

(B) Significant responsibility for an aspect of a business that includes actual authority for the financial operations or financial transactions of the business.

(2) "Agent" means a person or entity authorized by the corporation to make representations to the public about the corporation's financial condition and who is acting within the scope of the agency when the representations are made.

(3) "Shareholder" means a person or entity that is a shareholder of the corporation at the time the disclosure is required pursuant to subparagraph (B) of paragraph (2) of subdivision (a).

(4) "Notify its shareholders" means to give sufficient description of an action taken or about to be taken that would constitute acts or omissions as described in paragraph (1) of subdivision (a). A notice or report filed by a corporation with the United States Securities and Exchange Commission that relates to the facts and circumstances giving rise to an obligation under paragraph (1) of subdivision (a) shall satisfy all notice requirements arising under paragraph (2) of subdivision (a), but is not the exclusive means of satisfying the notice requirements, if the Attorney General or appropriate agency is informed in writing that the filing has been made together with a copy of the filing or an electronic link where it is available online without charge.

(5) "Appropriate government agency" means an agency on the following list that has regulatory authority with respect to the financial operations of a corporation:

(A) Department of Financial Protection and Innovation.

(B) Department of Insurance.

(C) Department of Managed Health Care.

(D) United States Securities and Exchange Commission.

(6) "Actual knowledge of the corporation" means the knowledge an officer or director of a corporation actually possesses or does not consciously avoid possessing, based on an evaluation of information provided pursuant to the corporation's disclosure controls and procedures.

(7) "Refuse to make a book entry" means the intentional decision not to record an accounting transaction when all of the following conditions are satisfied:

(A) The independent auditors required recordation of an accounting transaction during the course of an audit.

(B) The corporation's audit committee has not approved the independent auditor's recommendation.

(C) The decision is made for the primary purpose of rendering the financial statements materially false or misleading.

(8)"Refuse to post any notice required by law" means an intentional decision not to post a notice required by law when all of the following conditions exist:

(A) The decision not to post the notice has not been approved by the corporation's audit committee.

(B) The decision is intended to give the shares of stock in the corporation a materially greater or a materially less apparent market value than they really possess.

(9)"Misstate or conceal material facts from a regulatory body" means an intentional decision not to disclose material facts when all of the following conditions exist:

(A) The decision not to disclose material facts has not been approved by the corporation's audit committee.

(B) The decision is intended to give the shares of stock in the corporation a materially greater or a materially less apparent market value than they really possess.

(10)"Material false statement or omission" means an untrue statement of material fact or an omission to state a material fact necessary in order to make the statements made under the circumstances under which they were made not misleading.

(11)"Officer" means any person as set forth in Rule 16a-1 promulgated under the Securities Exchange Act of 1934 or any successor regulation thereto, except an officer of a subsidiary corporation who is not also an officer of the parent corporation.
(f) This section only applies to corporations that are issuers, as defined in Section 2 of the Sarbanes-Oxley Act of 2002 (15 U.S.C. Sec. 7201 et seq.).
(g) An action to enforce this section may only be brought by the Attorney General or a district attorney or city attorney in the name of the people of the state.
Ca. Corp. Code § 2207
Amended by Stats 2022 ch 452 (SB 1498),s 49, eff. 1/1/2023.
Amended by Stats 2016 ch 86 (SB 1171),s 48, eff. 1/1/2017.
Amended by Stats 2015 ch 190 (AB 1517),s 8, eff. 1/1/2016.
Added by Stats 2004 ch 183 (AB 3082),s 49, eff. 1/1/2005.
Added by Stats 2003 ch 477 (SB 523),s 2, eff. 1/1/2004.

Section 2251 - Unlawful issuance of certificates or initial transaction

statements with intent to defraud

Any promoter, director or officer of a corporation who knowingly and willfully issues or consents to the issuance of certificates for certificated securities, or initial transaction statements or written statements for uncertificated securities, in violation of this division with intent to defraud present or future shareholders, subscribers, purchasers of shares or creditors is guilty of a misdemeanor punishable by a fine of not more than one thousand dollars ($1,000) or imprisonment for not more than one year or both.

Ca. Corp. Code § 2251
Amended by Stats. 1986, Ch. 766, Sec. 28.

Section 2252 - Unlawful signature on subscription for or agreement to take stock

Every person (a) who signs the name of a fictitious person to any subscription for or agreement to take stock in any domestic or foreign corporation, existing or proposed, or (b) who signs to any subscription or agreement the name of any person, knowing that the person has no means or does not intend in good faith to comply with all the terms thereof or that there is any understanding or agreement that the terms of the subscription or agreement are not to be complied with or enforced, is guilty of a misdemeanor.

Ca. Corp. Code § 2252
Added by Stats. 1975, Ch. 682.

Section 2253 - Unlawful concurrence in vote or act of directors to make dividend or distribution of assets

Any director of a stock corporation, domestic or foreign, who concurs in any vote or act of the directors of the corporation or any of them, knowingly and with dishonest or fraudulent purpose, to make any dividend or distribution of assets except in the cases and in the manner allowed by law, either with the design of defrauding creditors or shareholders or of giving a false appearance to the value of the stock and thereby defrauding subscribers or purchasers, is guilty of a misdemeanor, punishable by a fine of not more than one thousand dollars ($1,000) or imprisonment for not more than one year or both.

Ca. Corp. Code § 2253
Added by Stats. 1975, Ch. 682.

Section 2254 - Unlawful concurrence in false report or refusal to make book entry or post notice

Every director, officer or agent of any corporation, domestic or foreign, is guilty of a felony (a) who knowingly concurs in making, publishing or posting either generally or privately to the shareholders or other persons (1) any written report, exhibit, statement of its affairs or pecuniary condition or notice containing any material statement which is false, or (2) any untrue or willfully or fraudulently exaggerated report, prospectus, account, statement of operations, values, business, profits, expenditures or prospects, or (3) any other paper or document intended to produce or give, or having a tendency to produce or give, the shares of stock in such corporation a greater value or a less apparent or market value than they really possess, or (b) who refuses to make any book entry or post any notice required by law in the manner required by law.

Ca. Corp. Code § 2254
Added by Stats. 1975, Ch. 682.

Section 2255 - Unlawful receipt or possession of corporate property; unlawful alteration, mutilation, or falsification of books, papers, writings, or securities or making or concurring in omitting to make entry in book of accounts or other record or document

(a) Every director, officer or agent of any corporation, domestic or foreign, who knowingly receives or acquires possession of any property of the corporation, otherwise than in payment of a just demand, and, with intent to defraud, omits to make, or to cause or direct to be made, a full and true entry thereof in the books or accounts of the corporation is guilty of a public offense.

(b) Every director, officer, agent or shareholder of any corporation, domestic or foreign, who, with intent to defraud, destroys, alters, mutilates or falsifies any of the books, papers, writings or securities belonging to the corporation or makes or concurs in omitting to make any material entry in any book of accounts or other record or document kept by the corporation is guilty of a public offense.

(c) Each public offense specified in this section is punishable by imprisonment pursuant to subdivision (h) of Section 1170 of the Penal Code, or by imprisonment in a county jail not exceeding one year, or a fine not exceeding one thousand dollars ($1,000), or by both that fine and imprisonment.

Ca. Corp. Code § 2255
Amended by Stats 2011 ch 39 (AB 117),s 68, eff. 6/30/2011.
Amended by Stats 2011 ch 15 (AB 109),s 38, eff. 4/4/2011, but operative no earlier than October 1, 2011, and only upon creation of a community corrections grant program to assist in implementing this act and upon an appropriation to fund the grant program.

Section 2256 - Unlawful exhibition of false, forged or altered book, paper, voucher, security or other instrument of evidence to public officer or board with intent to deceive

Every officer, agent or clerk of any corporation, domestic or foreign, or any person proposing to organize such a corporation or to increase the capital stock of any such corporation, who knowingly exhibits any false, forged or altered book, paper, voucher, security or other instrument of evidence to any public officer or board authorized by law to examine the organization of such corporation or to investigate its affairs or to allow an increase of its capital, with intent to deceive such officer or board in respect thereto, is punishable by imprisonment pursuant to subdivision (h) of Section 1170 of the Penal Code, or by imprisonment in a county jail for not exceeding one year.

   Ca. Corp. Code § 2256

Amended by Stats 2011 ch 39 (AB 117),s 68, eff. 6/30/2011.

Amended by Stats 2011 ch 15 (AB 109),s 39, eff. 4/4/2011, but operative no earlier than October 1, 2011, and only upon creation of a community corrections grant program to assist in implementing this act and upon an appropriation to fund the grant program.

Section 2257 - Unlawful subscribing name of another or insertion of name of another in prospectus, circular, or other advertisement or announcement

Every person who, without being authorized so to do, subscribes the name of another to or inserts the name of another in any prospectus, circular or other advertisement or announcement of any corporation, domestic or foreign, whether existing or intended to be formed, with intent to permit the document to be published and thereby to lead persons to believe that the person whose name is so subscribed is an officer, agent, shareholder or promoter of such corporation, when in fact no such relationship exists to the knowledge of such person, is guilty of a misdemeanor.

   Ca. Corp. Code § 2257

Added by Stats. 1975, Ch. 682.

Section 2258 - Unlawful transaction of intrastate business by foreign corporation

Any foreign corporation subject to the provisions of Chapter 21 which transacts intrastate business without complying therewith is guilty of a misdemeanor, punishable by fine of not less than five hundred dollars ($500) nor more than one thousand dollars ($1,000), to be recovered in any court of competent jurisdiction. Prosecution under this section may be brought by the Attorney General or by any district attorney. If brought by the latter, one-half of the fine collected shall be paid to the treasurer of the county in which the conviction was had and one-half to the State Treasurer. If brought by the Attorney General the entire amount of fine collected shall be paid to the State Treasurer to the credit of the General Fund of the state.

   Ca. Corp. Code § 2258

Added by Stats. 1975, Ch. 682.

Section 2259 - Unlawful transaction of intrastate business on behalf of foreign corporation not authorized to transact such business

Any person who transacts intrastate business on behalf of a foreign corporation which is not authorized to transact such business in this state, knowing that it is not so authorized, is guilty of a misdemeanor punishable by fine of not less than fifty dollars ($50) nor more than six hundred dollars ($600).

Ca. Corp. Code § 2259

Amended by Stats. 1983, Ch. 1092, Sec. 75. Effective September 27, 1983. Operative January 1, 1984, by Sec. 427 of Ch. 1092.

Section 2260 - Finding that corporation was foreign corporation

In a prosecution for a violation of Section 2252, 2253, 2254, 2255, 2256 or 2257, the fact that the corporation was a foreign corporation is not a defense, if it was carrying on business or keeping an office therefor within this state.

Ca. Corp. Code § 2260

Amended by Stats. 1976, Ch. 641.

Chapter 22.5 - VICTIMS OF CORPORATE FRAUD COMPENSATION FUND

Section 2280 - Victims of Corporate Fraud Compensation Fund

The Victims of Corporate Fraud Compensation Fund is hereby established in the State Treasury. The fund shall be administered by the Secretary of State for the sole purpose of providing restitution to the victims of a corporate fraud. The Secretary of State shall adopt regulations in furtherance of the administration of this chapter. Notwithstanding Section 13340 of the Government Code, the money in the fund is continuously appropriated to the Secretary of State for the purposes authorized by this chapter.

Ca. Corp. Code § 2280

Added by Stats 2012 ch 564 (SB 1058),s 4, eff. 1/1/2013.

Section 2281 - Definitions

As used in this chapter:

(a) "Agent" means a person who was an officer or director of a corporation, as defined in subdivision (e), at the time the fraudulent acts occurred, was named in a final criminal restitution order in connection with the fraudulent acts, and was acting in the person's capacity as the corporation's officer or director when committing the fraudulent acts.

(b) "Application" means a request for payment from the fund submitted to the Secretary of State pursuant to this chapter.

(c) "Claimant" means an aggrieved person who resides in the state at the time of the fraud and who submits an application pursuant to this chapter.

(d) "Complaint," for the purpose of an application based on a criminal restitution order, means the facts of the underlying transaction or transactions upon which the criminal restitution order is based.

(e) "Corporation" means a domestic corporation as defined by Section 162 or 2509 or a foreign corporation that is qualified to transact business in California pursuant to Section 2105.

(f) "Court of competent jurisdiction" means a state or federal court situated in California.

(g) "Final judgment" means a judgment, arbitration award, or criminal restitution order for which appeals have been exhausted or for which the period for appeal has expired, enforcement of which is not barred by the order of any court or by any statutory provision, which has not been nullified or rendered void by any court order or statutory provision, and for which the claimant has not otherwise been fully reimbursed. The following are examples of final judgments:

(1) A civil judgment that has been entered against a corporation for fraud, misrepresentation, or deceit, with the intent to defraud, and includes findings of facts and conclusions of law.

(2) If the matter was submitted to arbitration, a copy of the arbitration decision and any other documentation supporting the arbitration award. An arbitration award against a corporation for conduct constituting fraud, misrepresentation, or deceit, with the intent to defraud, that includes findings of fact and conclusions of law rendered in accordance with the rules established by the American Arbitration Association or another recognized arbitration body, and in accordance with Sections 1280 to 1294.2, inclusive, of the Code of Civil Procedure where applicable, and where the arbitration award has been confirmed and reduced to judgment pursuant to Section 1287.4 of the Code of Civil Procedure.

(3) A criminal restitution order issued by a court of competent jurisdiction against a corporation, or an agent of the corporation, for fraud, misrepresentation, or deceit, with the intent to defraud, pursuant to subdivision (f) of Section 1202.4 of the Penal Code or Section 3663 of Title 18 of the United States Code. An application for payment from the fund that is based on a criminal restitution order shall comply with all of the requirements of this chapter.

(h) "Fund" means the Victims of Corporate Fraud Compensation Fund created by Section 2280.

(i) "Judgment debtor" means a corporation or agent against which a judgment, arbitration award, or criminal restitution order has been entered for conduct constituting intentional fraud.

Ca. Corp. Code § 2281

Amended by Stats 2016 ch 390 (AB 2759),s 1, eff. 1/1/2017.

Added by Stats 2012 ch 564 (SB 1058),s 4, eff. 1/1/2013.

Section 2282 - Application for payment from fund

(a) When an aggrieved person obtains a final judgment in a court of competent jurisdiction against a corporation based upon the corporation's fraud, misrepresentation, or deceit, made with intent to defraud, or obtains a criminal restitution order against an agent based upon the agent's fraud, misrepresentation, or deceit, made with intent to defraud while acting in the agent's capacity as the corporation's officer or director, the aggrieved person may, upon the judgment becoming final and after diligent collection efforts are made, file an application with the Secretary of State for payment from the fund, within the limitations specified in Section 2289, for the amount unpaid on the judgment that represents the awarded actual and direct loss, any awarded compensatory damages, and awarded costs to the claimant in the final judgment, excluding punitive damages.

(b) The application shall be delivered in person or by certified mail to the Secretary of State not later than 18 months after the judgment has become final.

(c) The application shall be made on a form prescribed by the Secretary of State and shall include each of the following:

(1) The name and address of the claimant.

(2) If the claimant is represented by an attorney for the application, the name, business address, and telephone number of the attorney. If the claimant is not represented by an attorney for the application, a telephone number where the claimant can be reached during regular business hours shall be included.

(3) The name and address of the corporation and the agent, if any.

(4) The identification of the final judgment, the amount of the claim that remains unreimbursed from any source, and an explanation of the claim's computation.

(5) A copy of a final judgment and a copy of the civil complaint and any amendments thereto upon which the judgment finding fraud, misrepresentation, or deceit, made with the intent to defraud, was made shall be deemed to satisfy compliance with the requirements prescribed in this paragraph. The claimant may also provide any additional documentation that he or she believes may help the Secretary of State in evaluating the application, including, but not limited to, evidence submitted to the court in the underlying judgment or a detailed narrative statement of facts in explanation of the allegations of the complaint upon which the underlying judgment is based.

(6) If the final judgment is a criminal restitution order, the claimant shall provide the charging document and the restitution order, and if the defendant is an agent, documentation showing the defendant named in the restitution order is an agent as defined in this chapter.

(7) A description of searches and inquiries conducted by or on behalf of the claimant with respect to the judgment debtor's assets liable to be sold or applied to satisfaction of the judgment. A court's determination or finding of the judgment debtor's insolvency or lack of assets to pay the claimant shall be deemed to satisfy the requirements prescribed in this paragraph.

(8) Each of the following representations by the claimant:

(A) That the claimant is not a spouse, registered domestic partner, or an immediate family member of an employee, officer, director, managing agent, or other principal of the corporation nor a personal representative of the spouse, registered domestic partner, or an immediate family member of an employee, officer, director, managing agent, or other principal of the corporation.

(B) That the claimant has complied with all of the requirements of this section.

(C) That the judgment underlying the claim meets the requirements of subdivisions (a) and (b), including all of the following:

(i) That the judgment was for fraud, misrepresentation, or deceit by the corporation or the agent of the corporation, with the intent to defraud.

(ii) That the judgment is unpaid in part or in whole.

(iii) That the underlying judgment and debt have not been discharged in bankruptcy, or the underlying judgment is statutorily nondischargeable, or, in the case of a bankruptcy proceeding that is open at or after the time of the filing of the application, that the judgment and debt have been declared to be nondischargeable by the judge or stipulated as nondischargeable by the parties in the proceeding and that the claimant has been granted permission by the bankruptcy court to proceed with collection or otherwise proceed with the claimant's claims against the judgment debtor or debtors.

(D) That the claimant does not have a pending claim and has not collected on the final judgment from any other restitution fund. If the claimant has a pending claim or has collected from another fund, a description of the nature of the pending claim and the recovery amounts from any restitution fund.
(d)

(1) Except as provided in paragraphs (2), (3), and (4) the Secretary of State shall not condition an award of payment from the fund upon a claimant providing any additional information or documents other than those prescribed in subdivision (c).

(2) If the final judgment in favor of the claimant was by default, stipulated, a consent judgment, or pursuant to Section 594 of the Code of Civil Procedure or if the action against the corporation or its agent was defended by a trustee in bankruptcy, the Secretary of State may request additional documents and information from the claimant to determine whether the claim is valid.

(3) If the final judgment does not expressly set forth the amount of damages that were awarded for actual loss and compensatory damages that are payable from the fund pursuant to Section 2289, the Secretary of State may ask the claimant to provide copies of documentation pertaining to the amount of the actual and direct loss and the awarded compensatory damages or both of those findings. For purposes of this section, "sufficient proof of money damages" may include any of the following: copies of bank account statements showing or confirming particular transactions, copies of the front and back of checks made payable to the corporation that have been negotiated, credit card statements showing or confirming particular transactions, or similar documentation demonstrating financial loss directly resulting from the fraudulent acts by the corporation or its agent and the amount of compensatory damages awarded by the court.

(4) If there is no court determination or finding of the insolvency of the judgment debtor or lack of assets to pay the claimant, the Secretary of State may request additional information and documentation from the claimant to determine what assets, if any, are available to satisfy the final judgment.

(e) The Secretary of State shall include with the application form a notice to the claimant of his or her obligation to protect the underlying judgment from discharge in bankruptcy, to be appended to the application.

(f) If a claimant is a spouse, registered domestic partner, or an immediate family member of an employee, officer, director, managing agent, or other principal of the corporation, or is a personal representative of the spouse, registered domestic partner, or an immediate family member of an employee, officer, director, managing agent, or other principal of the corporation, the claimant shall not be precluded for that reason alone from receiving an award where the claimant can otherwise meet the requirements of this section.

Ca. Corp. Code § 2282

Amended by Stats 2017 ch 561 (AB 1516),s 25, eff. 1/1/2018.
Amended by Stats 2016 ch 390 (AB 2759),s 2, eff. 1/1/2017.
Added by Stats 2012 ch 564 (SB 1058),s 4, eff. 1/1/2013.

Section 2282.1 - Notice to corporation; contesting payment of application

(a) The Secretary of State shall provide notice to the corporation and all agents named in the application that a claimant has submitted an application for payment from the fund and shall also provide within that notice, as prescribed by the Secretary of State, the method to contest the payment from the fund.

(b) The notice to the corporation shall be provided by certified mail addressed to the corporation's last designated agent for service of process of record with the Secretary of State and notice shall be deemed complete five calendar days after the notice is mailed.

(c) If the corporation or its agent wishes to contest payment of an application by the Secretary of State, the corporation or agent shall mail or deliver a written response addressed to the Secretary of State within 30 calendar days of the notice of the application, and shall mail or deliver a copy of the response to the claimant. The written response of the corporation or agent shall not be directed to issues and facts conclusively established by the underlying judgment. If the corporation fails to mail or deliver a timely response, the corporation shall have waived the corporation's right to present objections to payment of the application, and shall not thereafter be entitled to notice of any action taken or proposed to be taken by the Secretary of State with respect to the application.

Ca. Corp. Code § 2282.1

Amended by Stats 2016 ch 390 (AB 2759),s 3, eff. 1/1/2017.

Added by Stats 2012 ch 564 (SB 1058),s 4, eff. 1/1/2013.

Section 2282.2 - Response by corporation

(a) The response by the corporation shall be by an officer or director and shall contain proof of service showing that a copy of the response was sent to the claimant, or if the claimant is represented by an attorney for purposes of the application, to the claimant's attorney, at the address specified in the application for the claimant or the claimant's attorney, respectively.

(b) If the corporation is not represented by an attorney in objecting to payment of the application, the response shall contain the name, title, and address of the officer, director, managing agent, or other responsible person authorized to represent the corporation and the address at which the corporation wishes to receive correspondence and notices relating to the application, and a telephone number at which the corporation's representative can be reached during regular business hours. If the corporation is represented by an attorney in objecting to the application, the response shall contain the name, business address, and telephone number of the attorney.

Ca. Corp. Code § 2282.2

Added by Stats 2012 ch 564 (SB 1058),s 4, eff. 1/1/2013.

Section 2283 - List of deficiencies

(a) If the Secretary of State determines that the application, as submitted by the claimant, fails to comply with the requirements of Section 2282, the Secretary of State shall, within 21 calendar days after receipt of the application by a single claimant or within 40 calendar days after receipt of the application by multiple claimants, mail an itemized list of deficiencies to the claimant.

(b) The time within which the Secretary of State is required to act under Section 2284 shall be measured from the date of receipt by the Secretary of State of a completed application. In the event of an irreconcilable dispute between the claimant and the Secretary of State on the question of whether the application is complete, the claimant may immediately file the claim with the court pursuant to Section 2287.

(c) If the Secretary of State has mailed one or more itemized lists of deficiencies to a claimant, and, if after 30 calendar days the Secretary of State has not received a response to the latest list of deficiencies, the Secretary of State shall notify the claimant that, unless the claimant responds to the deficiencies within a specified period of time of not less than 15 calendar days, the application will be denied.

Ca. Corp. Code § 2283

Added by Stats 2012 ch 564 (SB 1058),s 4, eff. 1/1/2013.

Section 2284 - Final written decision on application

(a) The Secretary of State shall render a final written decision on the application within 90 calendar days after a completed application has been received unless the claimant agrees in writing to extend the time within which the Secretary of State may render a decision.

(b) The Secretary of State may deny or grant the application or may enter into a compromise with the claimant to pay less in settlement than the full amount of the claim. If the claimant refuses to accept a settlement of the claim offered by the Secretary of State, the written decision of the Secretary of State shall be to deny the claim. Evidence of settlement offers and discussions between the Secretary of State and the claimant shall not be competent evidence in judicial proceedings undertaken by the claimant pursuant to Section 2287.

(c) Upon issuance of a proposed decision to award payment or an offer to compromise, the claimant shall have 60 calendar days from the date of service of the proposed award or offer to compromise to accept the proposed award or offer to compromise. If the claimant fails to accept the proposed award or offer to compromise within the specified time, the application shall be deemed denied.

Ca. Corp. Code § 2284

Added by Stats 2012 ch 564 (SB 1058),s 4, eff. 1/1/2013.

Section 2285 - Notice of decision to claimant

The Secretary of State shall give written notice, as prescribed by the Secretary of State, of a decision rendered with respect to the application to the claimant.

Ca. Corp. Code § 2285

Added by Stats 2012 ch 564 (SB 1058),s 4, eff. 1/1/2013.

Section 2286 - Notice to corporation of decision to award funds

The Secretary of State shall give notice, as prescribed by the Secretary of State, to the corporation and all agents named in the application that the Secretary of State has made a decision to award funds to the claimant and shall provide a copy of the decision to the corporation and all agents named in the application.

Ca. Corp. Code § 2286

Amended by Stats 2016 ch 390 (AB 2759),s 4, eff. 1/1/2017.

Added by Stats 2012 ch 564 (SB 1058),s 4, eff. 1/1/2013.

Section 2287 - Petition for order directing payment

(a) A claimant against whom the Secretary of State has rendered a decision denying an application may, within six months after the mailing of the notice of the denial, file a verified petition in superior court for an Order Directing Payment Out of the Victims of Corporate Fraud Compensation Fund based upon the grounds set forth in the application to the Secretary of State. If the underlying judgment is a California state court judgment, the petition shall be filed in the court in which the underlying judgment was entered. If the underlying judgment is not a California state court judgment or is a federal court judgment, the petition shall be filed in the superior court of any county within California that would have been a proper venue if the underlying lawsuit had been filed in a California state court, or in the Superior Court of the County of Sacramento.

(b) A copy of the petition shall be served upon the Secretary of State by the claimant. A certificate or affidavit of service shall be filed by the claimant with the court. Service on the Secretary of State may be made by mail addressed to the Secretary of State's office.

(c) The Secretary of State shall have 30 calendar days after being served with the petition in which to file a written response. The court shall thereafter set the matter for hearing upon the request of the claimant. The court shall grant a request of the Secretary of State for one continuance of as much as 30 calendar days and may, upon a showing of good cause by any party, continue the hearing as the court deems appropriate.

(d) The claimant shall have the burden of proving compliance with the requirements of Section 2282 by competent evidence at an evidentiary hearing. The claimant shall be entitled to a de novo review of the merits of the application as contained in the administrative record.

(e) At any time during the court proceedings, the petition may be compromised or settled by the Secretary of State and the court shall, upon joint petition of the claimant and the Secretary of State, issue an order directing payment out of the fund.

Ca. Corp. Code § 2287

Added by Stats 2012 ch 564 (SB 1058),s 4, eff. 1/1/2013.

Section 2288 - Order of payment; defense of action

(a) Whenever the court proceeds upon a petition under Section 2287, it shall order payment out of the fund only upon a determination that the aggrieved party has a valid cause of action within the purview of Section 2282, and has complied with

Section 2287.

(b)

(1) The Secretary of State may defend any action on behalf of the fund and shall have recourse to all appropriate means of defense and review, including examination of witnesses and the right to relitigate any issues that are material and relevant in the proceeding against the fund. The claimant's judgment shall create a rebuttable presumption of the fraud, misrepresentation, or deceit by the corporation, which presumption shall affect the burden of producing evidence.

(2) If the civil judgment, arbitration award, or criminal restitution order in the underlying action on which the final judgment in favor of the petitioner was by default, stipulation, consent, or pursuant to Section 594 of the Code of Civil Procedure, or if the action against the corporation or its agent was defended by a trustee in bankruptcy, the petitioner shall have the burden of proving that the cause of action against the corporation or its agent was for fraud, misrepresentation, or deceit. **(c)** If the final judgment is a criminal restitution order against an agent, the petitioner shall have the burden of proving that the defendant named in the criminal restitution order qualifies as an agent as defined in this chapter. An active corporation, that has submitted a response to the application pursuant to Section 2282.2, may be permitted by the court to appear in the action regarding the sole issue of whether the defendant named in the criminal restitution order qualifies as its agent as defined in this chapter.
(d) The Secretary of State may move the court at any time to dismiss the petition when it appears there are no triable issues and the petition is without merit. The motion may be supported by affidavit of any person or persons having knowledge of the facts, and may be made on the basis that the petition, and the judgment referred to therein, does not form the basis for a meritorious recovery claim within the purview of Section 2282; provided, however, the Secretary of State shall give written notice at least 10 calendar days before hearing on the motion to the claimant.
  Ca. Corp. Code § 2288
Amended by Stats 2016 ch 390 (AB 2759),s 5, eff. 1/1/2017.
Added by Stats 2012 ch 564 (SB 1058),s 4, eff. 1/1/2013.

Section 2289 - Limited liability of fund

(a) Notwithstanding any other provision of this chapter and regardless of the number of persons aggrieved in an instance of corporate fraud, or misrepresentation or deceit resulting in a judgment meeting the requirements of Section 2282, or the number of judgments against a corporation or its agent, the liability of the fund shall not exceed fifty thousand dollars ($50,000) for any one claimant per single judgment finding fraud, misrepresentation, or deceit, made with the intent to defraud.
(b) When multiple corporations or their agents are involved in the same event or series of events that are the basis of the claimant's final judgment and the conduct of

two or more of the corporations or their agents results in a judgment meeting the requirements of Section 2282, the claimant may seek recovery from the fund based on the judgment against any one of the corporations or their agents, subject to the limitations of subdivision (a).

(c) When multiple claimants are involved in a corporate fraud, or in misrepresentation or deceit by a corporation or its agents, resulting in a judgment meeting the requirements of Section 2282, each claimant may seek recovery from the fund individually, subject to the limitations of subdivision (a).

(d) Claimants who are spouses, registered domestic partners, or persons other than natural persons, that have obtained an eligible final judgment shall be considered one claimant.

    Ca. Corp. Code § 2289

Amended by Stats 2016 ch 390 (AB 2759),s 6, eff. 1/1/2017.

Added by Stats 2012 ch 564 (SB 1058),s 4, eff. 1/1/2013.

Section 2290 - Satisfaction of unpaid awards or offers of settlement

If, at any time, the money deposited in the fund is insufficient to satisfy any duly authorized award or offer of settlement, the Secretary of State shall, when sufficient money has been deposited in the fund, satisfy the unpaid awards or offer of settlement, in the order that the awards or offers of settlement were originally filed.

    Ca. Corp. Code § 2290

Amended by Stats 2016 ch 390 (AB 2759),s 7, eff. 1/1/2017.

Added by Stats 2012 ch 564 (SB 1058),s 4, eff. 1/1/2013.

Section 2291 - Sums received from Secretary of State

Any sums received by the Secretary of State pursuant to any provisions of this chapter shall be deposited in the State Treasury and credited to the fund.

    Ca. Corp. Code § 2291

Added by Stats 2012 ch 564 (SB 1058),s 4, eff. 1/1/2013.

Section 2292 - Unlawful filing of notice, statement, or document

It shall be unlawful for any person or the agent of any person to file with the Secretary of State any notice, statement, or other document required under the provisions of this chapter that is false or untrue or contains any willful, material misstatement of fact. That conduct shall constitute a public offense punishable by imprisonment in a county jail for a period of not more than one year or a fine of not more than one thousand dollars ($1,000), or both.

    Ca. Corp. Code § 2292

Added by Stats 2012 ch 564 (SB 1058),s 4, eff. 1/1/2013.

Section 2293 - Subrogation and assignment of rights, title, and interest in

judgment

When the Secretary of State has paid from the fund any sum to the claimant, the Secretary of State shall be subrogated to all of the rights of the claimant and the claimant shall assign all of his or her right, title, and interest in the judgment to the Secretary of State and any amount and interest so recovered by the Secretary of State on the judgment shall be deposited in the fund.

   Ca. Corp. Code § 2293
Added by Stats 2012 ch 564 (SB 1058),s 4, eff. 1/1/2013.

Section 2293.1 - Payment by corporation to fund after Secretary of State pays amount in settlement of claim or toward satisfaction of final judgment

If the Secretary of State pays from the fund any amount in settlement of a claim or toward satisfaction of a final judgment against a corporation or its agent, the corporation or its agent shall be required to pay to the fund the amount paid plus interest at the prevailing legal rate applicable to a judgment rendered in any court of this state, within 30 calendar days of the date that the Secretary of State provided notice of the payment of the award or compromise. If the corporation or its agent fails to make the required payment to the fund within the required time, the corporation shall be suspended until the payment is made. A discharge in bankruptcy shall not relieve a corporation or its agent from the penalties and disabilities provided in this chapter.

   Ca. Corp. Code § 2293.1
Amended by Stats 2016 ch 390 (AB 2759),s 8, eff. 1/1/2017.
Added by Stats 2012 ch 564 (SB 1058),s 4, eff. 1/1/2013.

Section 2294 - No award if claimant has received payment

The Secretary of State shall not make any award to a claimant from the fund if the claimant has received payment from any other restitution funds or for the portions of the judgment that the claimant has collected from the corporation or its agent or any other defendant in the underlying judgment.

   Ca. Corp. Code § 2294
Amended by Stats 2016 ch 390 (AB 2759),s 9, eff. 1/1/2017.
Added by Stats 2012 ch 564 (SB 1058),s 4, eff. 1/1/2013.

Section 2295 - Waiver of rights

The failure of an aggrieved person to comply with all of the provisions of this chapter shall constitute a waiver of any rights hereunder.

   Ca. Corp. Code § 2295
Added by Stats 2012 ch 564 (SB 1058),s 4, eff. 1/1/2013.

Section 2296 - Applicability

This chapter shall apply to applications submitted to the Secretary of State on or after January 1, 2013.

Ca. Corp. Code § 2296

Added by Stats 2012 ch 564 (SB 1058),s 4, eff. 1/1/2013.

Chapter 23 - TRANSITION PROVISIONS

Section 2300 - "New law" and "prior law" defined

As used in this chapter, the term "new law" means this division of the Corporations Code as amended by act of the California Legislature, 1975-76 Regular Session, effective January 1, 1977, and as in effect on that date; the term "prior law" means the applicable law as in effect prior to January 1, 1977; and the term "effective date" means January 1, 1977.

Ca. Corp. Code § 2300

Added by Stats. 1975, Ch. 682.

Section 2301 - Application of new law

(a) Except as otherwise expressly provided in this chapter, the provisions of the new law apply on and after the effective date to all corporations referred to in Section 162 existing on the effective date and to all actions taken by the directors or shareholders of such corporations on and after the effective date.

(b) Except as otherwise expressly provided in this chapter, all of the sections of the new law governing acts, contracts or other transactions by a corporation or its directors or shareholders apply only to such acts, contracts or transactions occurring on or after the effective date and the prior law governs such acts, contracts or transactions occurring prior thereto.

(c) Except as otherwise expressly provided in this chapter, any vote or consent by the directors or shareholders of a corporation prior to the effective date in accordance with the prior law shall be effective in accordance with the prior law and if any certificate or document is required to be filed in any public office of this state relating to such action, it may be filed after the effective date in accordance with the prior law.

Ca. Corp. Code § 2301

Added by Stats. 1975, Ch. 682.

Section 2302 - Application of new law relating to contents of articles

The provisions of Sections 202, 204 (other than subdivision (a) thereof) and 205 of the new law relating to the contents of articles do not apply to corporations existing on the effective date unless and until an amendment of the articles is filed stating that the corporation elects to be governed by all of the provisions of the new law not otherwise applicable to it under this chapter. Such amendment may be adopted by approval of the board alone, except that, if any such amendment makes any change in the articles other than conforming the statement of purposes and powers to subdivision (b) of Section 202 and the deletion of any references to par value and location of principal office and deleting any statement regarding the number of directors or conforming any such statement to Section 212 (subject to Section 2304), it shall also be approved by the outstanding shares (Section 152) if such approval is otherwise required for the changes made. The amendment shall not name the corporation's initial agent for service of process if a report required by Section 1502 has been filed.

Ca. Corp. Code § 2302

Amended by Stats. 1977, Ch. 235.

Section 2302.1 - Application of section requiring inclusion of certain provisions in articles to bylaws

The provisions of subdivision (a) of Section 204, insofar as they require the inclusion of certain provisions in the articles, do not apply to the provisions of bylaws in effect on the effective date and valid under the prior law, unless and until an amendment is filed pursuant to Section 2302.

Ca. Corp. Code § 2302.1

Added by Stats. 1977, Ch. 235.

Section 2302.5 - Absence of reference to par value in articles of corporation

The absence of any reference to par value in the articles of a corporation which is subject to the prior law relating to the contents of articles as specified in Section 2302 is equivalent to a statement that the shares of stock are to be without par value.

Ca. Corp. Code § 2302.5

Added by Stats. 1985, Ch. 764, Sec. 8.5.

Section 2303 - Applicability of Sections 206 and 207

Sections 206 and 207 of the new law apply to corporations existing on the effective date, but any statement in the articles of such corporation, prior to an amendment thereof pursuant to Section 2302, relating to the purposes or powers of the corporation shall not be construed as a limitation unless it is expressly stated as such.

Ca. Corp. Code § 2303

Added by Stats. 1975, Ch. 682.

Section 2304 - Effect of difference between articles and bylaws in statement of number of directors

The effect of a difference between the articles and bylaws in the statement of the number of directors shall not be governed by subdivision (a) of Section 212 of the new law for a corporation existing on the effective date, which shall continue to be governed by the prior law, unless and until an amendment of its articles is filed pursuant to Section 2302. If such amendment makes any change in the number of directors or the maximum or minimum number of directors or makes a change from a fixed to a variable board or vice versa, it shall also be approved by the outstanding shares (Section 152).

Ca. Corp. Code § 2304
Amended by Stats. 1988, Ch. 919, Sec. 11.

Section 2305 - Applicability of subdivision (a) of Section 312

Subdivision (a) of Section 312 of the new law applies to a corporation existing on the effective date, but the "treasurer" of such corporation shall be deemed to be the "chief financial officer."

Ca. Corp. Code § 2305
Amended by Stats. 1976, Ch. 641.

Section 2306 - Application of new law governing proposed indemnification

Section 317 of the new law governs any proposed indemnification by a corporation after the effective date, whether the events upon which the indemnification is based occurred before or after the effective date. Any statement relating to indemnification contained in the articles or bylaws of a corporation on the effective date shall not be construed as limiting the indemnification permitted by Section 317 unless it is expressly stated as so intended.

Ca. Corp. Code § 2306
Added by Stats. 1975, Ch. 682.

Section 2307 - Application of new law relating to requirement statements on certificates representing shares

Sections 417 and 418 of the new law relating to required statements on certificates representing shares apply to certificates representing shares of corporations existing on the effective date only if the shares are originally issued after the effective date, and the prior law shall continue to govern the certificates representing shares originally issued prior to the effective date, unless and until an amendment of the articles is filed pursuant to Section 2302, and the certificate is presented for transfer.

Ca. Corp. Code § 2307
Amended by Stats. 1977, Ch. 235.

Section 2308 - Application of new law applying to distribution to shareholders

Chapter 5 of the new law applies to any distribution to its shareholders made after the effective date by a corporation existing on the effective date, except that any such distribution effected pursuant to a contract for the purchase or redemption of shares entered into by the corporation prior to the effective date may be made if permissible under Chapter 5 or under the prior law in effect at the time the contract was entered into.

Ca. Corp. Code § 2308
Added by Stats. 1975, Ch. 682.

Section 2309 - Application of new law to shares

Subdivision (a) of Section 510 of the new law applies only to shares acquired after the effective date.

Ca. Corp. Code § 2309
Added by Stats. 1975, Ch. 682.

Section 2310 - Application of new law applying to shareholder meetings

The provisions of Chapter 6 (commencing with Section 600) and Chapter 7 (commencing with Section 700) (other than Section 706) of the new law apply to any meeting of shareholders held after the effective date and to any action by shareholders pursuant to written consent which becomes effective after the effective date and to any vote cast at such a meeting or consent given for such action (whether or not a proxy or consent was executed by the shareholder prior to the effective date); provided, however, that the prior law shall apply to any such meeting of shareholders and to any vote cast at such a meeting if such meeting was initially called for a date prior to the effective date and notice thereof was given to shareholders entitled to vote thereat.

Ca. Corp. Code § 2310
Amended by Stats. 1976, Ch. 641.

Section 2311 - Application of new law to agreements and voting trusts

Section 706 of the new law applies to agreements and voting trusts entered into after the effective date and prior law governs such agreements or trusts entered into prior thereto unless the agreement or trust is amended or extended thereafter, in which event the new law applies.

Ca. Corp. Code § 2311
Added by Stats. 1975, Ch. 682.

Section 2312 - Application of new law to actions

Section 800 of the new law applies to actions commenced after the effective date and prior law governs actions pending on the effective date.

Ca. Corp. Code § 2312
Added by Stats. 1975, Ch. 682.

Section 2313 - Application of new law to transactions

Chapters 10 (commencing with Section 1000), 11 (commencing with Section 1100), 12 (commencing with Section 1200) and 13 (commencing with Section 1300) of the new law apply to transactions consummated after the effective date, unless a required approval of the outstanding shares (Section 152) has been given prior to the effective date or has been given after the effective date but at a meeting of shareholders initially called for a date prior to the effective date, in which case the transaction shall be governed by the prior law.

Ca. Corp. Code § 2313
Amended by Stats. 1976, Ch. 641.

Section 2314 - Application of new law applying to actions for involuntary dissolution

Chapters 18 (commencing with Section 1800) and 20 (commencing with Section 2000) of the new law apply to actions for involuntary dissolution commenced after the effective date, but the prior law governs any such action pending on the effective date.

Ca. Corp. Code § 2314
Amended by Stats. 1976, Ch. 641.

Section 2315 - Application of new law applying to voluntary dissolution proceedings initiated by filing of election

Chapters 19 (commencing with Section 1900) and 20 (commencing with Section 2000) of the new law apply to any voluntary dissolution proceeding initiated by the filing of an election after the effective date, but the prior law governs any such proceeding so initiated prior to the effective date.

Ca. Corp. Code § 2315
Amended by Stats. 1976, Ch. 641.

Section 2316 - No penalty for failure to obtain certificate of qualification if it is obtained no later than four months after effective date

A foreign association which has transacted intrastate business in this state prior to the effective date and which is required by Section 2105 of the new law to obtain a certificate of qualification from the Secretary of State shall not be subject to any direct or indirect penalty as a result of failure to obtain such certificate of qualification if the certificate of qualification is obtained no later than four months after the effective date.

Ca. Corp. Code § 2316
Added by Stats. 1975, Ch. 682.

Section 2317 - Service on agent

When any corporate agent for service of process has been designated prior to the effective date and such designation of agent included a name of a city, town or village wherein the corporate agent maintained an office, service on such agent may be effected at any office of the agent set forth in the certificate of the corporate agent filed pursuant to Section 1505 of the new law or filed pursuant to Section 3301.5, 3301.6, 6403.5 or 6403.6 of the prior law, whether or not such office is in said city, town or village.

Ca. Corp. Code § 2317
Amended by Stats. 1976, Ch. 641.

Section 2318 - Election to continue existence

Any corporation existing on the first day of January, 1873, formed under the laws of this state, and still existing, which has not already elected to continue its existence under the prior law, may, at any time, elect to continue its existence under the provisions of this code applicable thereto by the unanimous vote of all its directors, or such election may be made at any annual meeting of the shareholders, or at any meeting called by the directors especially for considering the subject, if voted by shareholders representing a majority of the voting power, or may be made by the directors upon the written consent of that number of the shareholders.

A certificate of the action of the directors, signed by them and their secretary, when the election is made by their unanimous vote, or upon the written consent of the shareholders, or a certificate of the proceedings of the meeting of the shareholders, when the election is made at any such meeting, signed by the chairperson and secretary of the meeting and a majority of the directors, shall be filed in the office of the Secretary of State, and thereafter the corporation continues its existence under the provisions of this code which are applicable thereto, and possesses all the rights, and powers, and is subject to all the obligations, restrictions, and limitations prescribed thereby.

Ca. Corp. Code § 2318
Amended by Stats 2022 ch 617 (SB 1202),s 39, eff. 1/1/2023.
Added by Stats. 1975, Ch. 682.

Section 2319 - Continued suspension

If the corporate rights, privileges and powers of a corporation have been suspended and are still suspended immediately prior to the effective date pursuant to Sections 5700 through 5908 of the old law and provisions of law there referred to, said sections and provisions continue to apply to such a corporation until restoration by the Controller pursuant to said sections.

Ca. Corp. Code § 2319
Added by Stats. 1975, Ch. 682.

Division 1.5 - SOCIAL PURPOSE CORPORATIONS ACT

Chapter 1 - GENERAL PROVISIONS AND DEFINITIONS

Section 2500 - Short title

This division shall be known and may be cited as the Social Purpose Corporations Act.

Ca. Corp. Code § 2500
Amended by Stats 2014 ch 694 (SB 1301),s 13, eff. 1/1/2015.
Division heading amended by Stats 2014 ch 694 (SB 1301),s 12, eff. 1/1/2015.
Added by Stats 2011 ch 740 (SB 201),s 12, eff. 1/1/2012.

Section 2501 - Applicable provisions

Except as otherwise expressly stated, the provisions of Division 1 (commencing with Section 100) shall apply to corporations organized under this division, and references in that division to the terms "close corporation," "constituent corporation," "corporation," "disappearing corporation," "domestic corporation," "foreign corporation," "surviving corporation," and similar terms shall be read to apply, in the same manner, to include the similar "social purpose corporation."

Ca. Corp. Code § 2501
Amended by Stats 2014 ch 694 (SB 1301),s 14, eff. 1/1/2015.
Added by Stats 2011 ch 740 (SB 201),s 12, eff. 1/1/2012.

Section 2502 - Division applicable only to social purpose corporations

This division applies only to social purpose corporations organized expressly under this division whether organized or existing under this division or amended, merged or converted into a social purpose corporation in accordance with Chapter 9 (commencing with Section 900) of Division 1, Chapter 11 (commencing with Section 1100) of Division 1 or Chapter 11.5 (commencing with Section 1150) of Division 1, including all flexible purpose corporations formed under this division prior to January 1, 2015, and now existing except as provided in paragraph (2) of subdivision (b) of Section 2601 and paragraph (3) of subdivision (b) of Section 2602.

Ca. Corp. Code § 2502

Amended by Stats 2014 ch 694 (SB 1301),s 15, eff. 1/1/2015.
Added by Stats 2011 ch 740 (SB 201),s 12, eff. 1/1/2012.

Section 2502.01 - Agency or instrumentality of United States

Every social purpose corporation organized under the laws of this state or similar foreign social purpose corporation, all of the capital stock of which is beneficially owned by the United States, an agency or instrumentality of the United States or any social purpose corporation or similar foreign social purpose corporation the whole of the capital stock of which is owned by the United States or by an agency or instrumentality of the United States, is conclusively presumed to be an agency and instrumentality of the United States and is entitled to all privileges and immunities to which the holders of all of its stock are entitled as agencies of the United States.

    Ca. Corp. Code § 2502.01

Amended by Stats 2014 ch 694 (SB 1301),s 16, eff. 1/1/2015.
Added by Stats 2011 ch 740 (SB 201),s 12, eff. 1/1/2012.

Section 2502.02 - Reference to state or federal statute

Unless otherwise expressly provided, whenever reference is made in this division to any other state or federal statute, that reference is to that statute as it may be amended from time to time, whether before or after the enactment of this division.

    Ca. Corp. Code § 2502.02

Added by Stats 2011 ch 740 (SB 201),s 12, eff. 1/1/2012.

Section 2502.03 - Suing social purpose corporation

A social purpose corporation may be sued in the same manner as a corporation as provided in the Code of Civil Procedure.

    Ca. Corp. Code § 2502.03

Amended by Stats 2014 ch 694 (SB 1301),s 17, eff. 1/1/2015.
Added by Stats 2011 ch 740 (SB 201),s 12, eff. 1/1/2012.

Section 2502.04 - Attachment of corporate property

A social purpose corporation formed under this division shall, in respect of its property, as a condition of its existence as a social purpose corporation, be subject, in the same manner as a corporation, to the provisions of the Code of Civil Procedure authorizing the attachment of corporate property.

    Ca. Corp. Code § 2502.04

Amended by Stats 2014 ch 694 (SB 1301),s 18, eff. 1/1/2015.
Added by Stats 2011 ch 740 (SB 201),s 12, eff. 1/1/2012.

Section 2502.05 - Fees for filing instruments

The fees of the Secretary of State for filing instruments by or on behalf of social purpose corporations shall be the same fees prescribed for corporations in Article 3 (commencing with Section 12180) of Chapter 3 of Part 2 of Division 3 of Title 2 of the Government Code.

Ca. Corp. Code § 2502.05
Amended by Stats 2014 ch 694 (SB 1301),s 19, eff. 1/1/2015.
Added by Stats 2011 ch 740 (SB 201),s 12, eff. 1/1/2012.

Section 2502.06 - Dependence upon facts ascertainable outside of articles or agreement of merger

(a) Provisions of the articles described in paragraph (3) of subdivision (e) of Section 2602 and subdivisions (a) and (b) of Section 2603 may be made dependent upon facts ascertainable outside of the articles, if the manner in which those facts shall operate upon those provisions is clearly and expressly set forth in the articles. Similarly, any of the terms of an agreement of merger pursuant to Section 1101 may be made dependent upon facts ascertainable outside of that agreement, if the manner in which those facts shall operate upon the terms of the agreement is clearly and expressly set forth in the agreement of merger.

(b) Notwithstanding subdivision (a), when any provisions or terms of articles or an agreement of merger are made dependent upon facts ascertainable outside of the filed instrument through a reference to an agreement or similar document, the social purpose corporation filing that instrument shall maintain at its principal office a copy of that referenced agreement or document and all amendments, and shall provide to its shareholders, in the case of articles, or to shareholders of any constituent corporation or other business entity, in the case of an agreement of merger, a copy of them upon written request and without charge.

(c) For the purposes of this section, "referenced agreement" means an agreement or contract to which the social purpose corporation is a party. An amendment or revision of a referenced agreement shall require shareholder approval, in addition to any other required approvals, upon any of the following circumstances:

(1) If the amendment or revision of the referenced agreement would result in a material change in the rights, preferences, privileges, or restrictions of a class or series of shares, the amendment or revision shall be approved by the outstanding shares, as defined in Section 152, of that class or series.

(2) If the amendment or revision of the referenced agreement would result in a material change in the rights or liabilities of any class or series of shares with respect to the subject matter of paragraph (1), (2), (3), (5), or (9) of subdivision (a) of Section 2603, the amendment or revision shall be approved by the outstanding shares, as defined in Section 152, of that class or series.

(3) If the amendment or revision of the referenced agreement would result in a material change in the restrictions on transfer or hypothecation of any class or series of shares, the amendment or revision shall be approved by the outstanding shares, as defined in Section 152, of that class or series.

(4) If the amendment or revision of the referenced agreement would result in a change of any of the principal terms of an agreement of merger, the amendment or revision shall be approved in the same manner as required by Section 3504 for a change in the principal terms of an agreement of merger.

Ca. Corp. Code § 2502.06

Amended by Stats 2022 ch 617 (SB 1202),s 40, eff. 1/1/2023.

Amended by Stats 2014 ch 694 (SB 1301),s 20, eff. 1/1/2015.

Added by Stats 2011 ch 740 (SB 201),s 12, eff. 1/1/2012.

Section 2502.07 - Availability of exemption

Nothing contained in this division shall be construed to modify the provisions of subdivision (h) of Section 25102, or the conditions provided therein to the availability of an exemption under that subdivision.

Ca. Corp. Code § 2502.07

Added by Stats 2011 ch 740 (SB 201),s 12, eff. 1/1/2012.

Section 2503 - "Annual report" defined

"Annual report" means the report required by subdivision (a) of Section 3500, including the information specified in subdivision (b) of Section 3500.

Ca. Corp. Code § 2503

Added by Stats 2011 ch 740 (SB 201),s 12, eff. 1/1/2012.

Section 2503.1 - "Close social purpose corporation" defined

"Close social purpose corporation" means a social purpose corporation that is also a close corporation.

Ca. Corp. Code § 2503.1

Amended by Stats 2014 ch 694 (SB 1301),s 21, eff. 1/1/2015.

Added by Stats 2011 ch 740 (SB 201),s 12, eff. 1/1/2012.

Section 2504 - "Constituent social purpose corporation" defined

"Constituent social purpose corporation" means a social purpose corporation that is merged with or into one or more corporations or one or more other business entities and includes a surviving social purpose corporation.

Ca. Corp. Code § 2504

Amended by Stats 2014 ch 694 (SB 1301),s 22, eff. 1/1/2015.

Added by Stats 2011 ch 740 (SB 201),s 12, eff. 1/1/2012.

Section 2505 - "Conversion" defined

"Conversion" means a conversion pursuant to Chapter 11.5 (commencing with Section 1150) of Division 1 and Chapter 9 (commencing with Section 3300) of this division.

Ca. Corp. Code § 2505

Added by Stats 2011 ch 740 (SB 201),s 12, eff. 1/1/2012.

Section 2506 - "Disappearing social purpose corporation" defined

"Disappearing social purpose corporation" means a constituent social purpose corporation that is not the surviving entity.

Ca. Corp. Code § 2506

Amended by Stats 2014 ch 694 (SB 1301),s 23, eff. 1/1/2015.

Added by Stats 2011 ch 740 (SB 201),s 12, eff. 1/1/2012.

Section 2507 - "Domestic social purpose corporation" defined

"Domestic social purpose corporation" means a corporation organized under this division.

Ca. Corp. Code § 2507

Amended by Stats 2014 ch 694 (SB 1301),s 24, eff. 1/1/2015.

Added by Stats 2011 ch 740 (SB 201),s 12, eff. 1/1/2012.

Section 2509 - "Social purpose corporation" defined

"Social purpose corporation," unless otherwise expressly provided, refers only to a corporation organized under this division.

Ca. Corp. Code § 2509

Amended by Stats 2014 ch 694 (SB 1301),s 25, eff. 1/1/2015.

Added by Stats 2011 ch 740 (SB 201),s 12, eff. 1/1/2012.

Section 2510 - "Social purpose corporation subject to the Banking Law" defined

"Social purpose corporation subject to the Banking Law" means any of the following:
(a)A social purpose corporation that, with the approval of the Commissioner of Financial Protection and Innovation, is incorporated for the purpose of engaging in, or that is authorized by the Commissioner of Financial Protection and Innovation to engage in, the commercial banking business under the Banking Law (Division 1.1 (commencing with Section 1000) of the Financial Code).
(b) Any social purpose corporation that, with the approval of the Commissioner of

Financial Protection and Innovation, is incorporated for the purpose of engaging in, or that is authorized by the Commissioner of Financial Protection and Innovation to engage in, the industrial banking business under the Banking Law (Division 1.1 (commencing with Section 1000) of the Financial Code).

(c)Any social purpose corporation, other than a social purpose corporation described in subdivision (d), that, with the approval of the Commissioner of Financial Protection and Innovation, is incorporated for the purpose of engaging in, or that is authorized by the Commissioner of Financial Protection and Innovation to engage in, the trust business under the Banking Law (Division 1.1 (commencing with Section 1000) of the Financial Code).

(d)Any social purpose corporation that is authorized by the Commissioner of Financial Protection and Innovation and the Commissioner of Insurance to maintain a title insurance department to engage in title insurance business and a trust department to engage in trust business.

(e)Any social purpose corporation that, with the approval of the Commissioner of Financial Protection and Innovation, is incorporated for the purpose of engaging in, or that is authorized by the Commissioner of Financial Protection and Innovation to engage in, business under Article 1 (commencing with Section 1850) of Chapter 21 of Division 1.1 of the Financial Code.

Ca. Corp. Code § 2510

Amended by Stats 2022 ch 452 (SB 1498),s 50, eff. 1/1/2023.
Amended by Stats 2016 ch 277 (AB 2907),s 4, eff. 1/1/2017.
Amended by Stats 2015 ch 190 (AB 1517),s 9, eff. 1/1/2016.
Amended by Stats 2014 ch 694 (SB 1301),s 26, eff. 1/1/2015.
Amended by Stats 2014 ch 401 (AB 2763),s 18, eff. 1/1/2015.
Added by Stats 2011 ch 740 (SB 201),s 12, eff. 1/1/2012.

Section 2510.1 - "Social purpose corporation subject to the Insurance Code as an insurer" defined

"Social purpose corporation subject to the Insurance Code as an insurer" means a social purpose corporation that has met the requirements of Sections 201.5, 201.6, and 201.7.

Ca. Corp. Code § 2510.1

Amended by Stats 2014 ch 694 (SB 1301),s 27, eff. 1/1/2015.
Added by Stats 2011 ch 740 (SB 201),s 12, eff. 1/1/2012.

Section 2511 - "Reorganization" defined

"Reorganization" means a merger reorganization, an exchange reorganization, or a sale of assets reorganization.

(a) "Merger reorganization" means a merger pursuant to Chapter 11 (commencing with Section 1100) of Division 1 and Chapter 8 (commencing with Section 3200), of this division, other than a short-form merger.

(b) "Exchange reorganization" means the acquisition by one domestic social purpose corporation, foreign social purpose corporation, or other business entity in exchange, in whole or in part, for its equity securities, or the equity securities of a domestic social purpose corporation, a foreign social purpose corporation, or an other business entity that is in control of the acquiring entity, of equity securities of another domestic social purpose corporation, foreign social purpose corporation, or other business entity if, immediately after the acquisition, the acquiring entity has control of the other entity.

(c) "Sale-of-assets reorganization" means the acquisition by one domestic social purpose corporation, foreign social purpose corporation, or other business entity in exchange in whole or in part for its equity securities, or the equity securities of a domestic social purpose corporation, a foreign social purpose corporation, or an other business entity that is in control of the acquiring entity, or for its debt securities, or debt securities of a domestic social purpose corporation, foreign social purpose corporation, or other business entity that is in control of the acquiring entity, that are not adequately secured and that have a maturity date in excess of five years after the consummation of the reorganization, or both, of all or substantially all of the assets of another domestic social purpose corporation, foreign social purpose corporation, or other business entity.

Ca. Corp. Code § 2511
Amended by Stats 2014 ch 694 (SB 1301),s 28, eff. 1/1/2015.
Added by Stats 2011 ch 740 (SB 201),s 12, eff. 1/1/2012.

Section 2512 - "Share exchange tender offer" defined

"Share exchange tender offer" means any acquisition by one social purpose corporation in exchange in whole or in part for its equity securities, or the equity securities of a corporation or a social purpose corporation that is in control of the acquiring social purpose corporation, of shares of another corporation or social purpose corporation, other than an exchange reorganization (subdivision (b) of Section 2511).

Ca. Corp. Code § 2512
Amended by Stats 2014 ch 694 (SB 1301),s 29, eff. 1/1/2015.
Added by Stats 2011 ch 740 (SB 201),s 12, eff. 1/1/2012.

Section 2513 - "Special purpose" defined

"Special purpose" means the special purpose set forth in a social purpose corporation's articles pursuant to subdivision (b) of Section 2602.

Ca. Corp. Code § 2513
Amended by Stats 2014 ch 694 (SB 1301),s 30, eff. 1/1/2015.
Added by Stats 2011 ch 740 (SB 201),s 12, eff. 1/1/2012.

Section 2514 - "Special purpose current report" defined

"Special purpose current report" means the report required of a social purpose corporation pursuant to Section 3501.

    Ca. Corp. Code § 2514

Amended by Stats 2014 ch 694 (SB 1301),s 31, eff. 1/1/2015.

Added by Stats 2011 ch 740 (SB 201),s 12, eff. 1/1/2012.

Section 2515 - "Special purpose MD&A" defined

"Special purpose MD&A" means the management discussion and analysis required of a social purpose corporation pursuant to subdivision (b) of Section 3500.

    Ca. Corp. Code § 2515

Amended by Stats 2014 ch 694 (SB 1301),s 32, eff. 1/1/2015.

Added by Stats 2011 ch 740 (SB 201),s 12, eff. 1/1/2012.

Section 2516 - "Special purpose objectives" defined

"Special purpose objectives" means those objectives set forth by management and the directors of a social purpose corporation for purposes of measuring the impact of the social purpose corporation's efforts relating to its special purpose in accordance with Section 3500.

    Ca. Corp. Code § 2516

Amended by Stats 2014 ch 694 (SB 1301),s 33, eff. 1/1/2015.

Added by Stats 2011 ch 740 (SB 201),s 12, eff. 1/1/2012.

Section 2517 - "Surviving social purpose corporation" defined

"Surviving social purpose corporation" means a social purpose corporation into which one or more other corporations or one or more other business entities is merged.

    Ca. Corp. Code § 2517

Amended by Stats 2014 ch 694 (SB 1301),s 34, eff. 1/1/2015.

Added by Stats 2011 ch 740 (SB 201),s 12, eff. 1/1/2012.

Chapter 2 - ORGANIZATION AND BYLAWS

Section 2600 - Formation of social purpose corporation

(a) One or more natural persons, partnerships, associations, social purpose corporations, or corporations, domestic or foreign, may form a social purpose corporation under this division by executing and filing articles of incorporation.
(b) If initial directors are named in the articles, each director named in the articles shall sign and acknowledge the articles. If initial directors are not named in the articles, the articles shall be signed by one or more incorporators who shall be persons described in subdivision (a).

(c) The corporate existence begins upon the filing of the articles and continues perpetually, unless otherwise expressly provided by law or in the articles.

Ca. Corp. Code § 2600

Amended by Stats 2014 ch 694 (SB 1301),s 35, eff. 1/1/2015.

Added by Stats 2011 ch 740 (SB 201),s 12, eff. 1/1/2012.

Section 2600.5 - Incorporation of existing business association organized as trust

(a) An existing business association organized as a trust under the laws of this state or of a foreign jurisdiction may incorporate under this division upon approval by its board of trustees or similar governing body and approval by the affirmative vote of two-thirds of the outstanding voting shares of beneficial interest, or a greater proportion of the outstanding shares of beneficial interest or the vote of those other classes of shares of beneficial interest as may be specifically required by its declaration of trust or bylaws, and the filing of articles with a certificate attached pursuant to this chapter.

(b) In addition to the matters required to be set forth in the articles pursuant to Section 2602, the articles filed pursuant to this section shall state that an existing unincorporated association, stating its name, is being incorporated by the filing of the articles.

(c) The articles filed pursuant to this section shall be signed by the president, or any vice president, and the secretary, or any assistant secretary, of the existing association and shall be accompanied by a certificate signed and verified by those officers signing the articles and stating that the incorporation of the association has been approved by the trustees and by the required vote of holders of shares of beneficial interest in accordance with subdivision (a).

(d) Upon the filing of articles pursuant to this section, the social purpose corporation shall succeed automatically to all of the rights and property of the association being incorporated and shall be subject to all of its debts and liabilities in the same manner as if the social purpose corporation had itself incurred them. The incumbent trustees of the association shall constitute the initial directors of the social purpose corporation and shall continue in office until the next annual meeting of the shareholders or their earlier death, resignation, or removal. All rights of creditors and all liens upon the property of the association shall be preserved unimpaired. Any action or proceeding pending by or against the association may be prosecuted to judgment, which shall bind the social purpose corporation, or the social purpose corporation may be proceeded against or substituted in its place.

(e) The filing for record in the office of the county recorder of any county in this state in which any of the real property of the association is located of a copy of the articles filed pursuant to this section, certified by the Secretary of State, shall evidence record ownership in the social purpose corporation of all interests of the association in and to the real property located in that county.

Ca. Corp. Code § 2600.5

Amended by Stats 2014 ch 694 (SB 1301),s 36, eff. 1/1/2015.
Added by Stats 2011 ch 740 (SB 201),s 12, eff. 1/1/2012.

Section 2601 - Name of social purpose corporation

(a) The Secretary of State shall not file articles setting forth a name in which "bank," "trust," "trustee," or related words appear, unless the certificate of approval of the Commissioner of Financial Protection and Innovation is attached to the articles. This subdivision does not apply to the articles of any social purpose corporation subject to the Banking Law on which is endorsed the approval of the Commissioner of Financial Protection and Innovation.

(b)

(1) The name of a social purpose corporation shall not be a name that the Secretary of State determines is likely to mislead the public and shall be distinguishable in the records of the Secretary of State from all of the following:

(A) The name of any corporation.

(B) The name of any foreign corporation authorized to transact intrastate business in this state.

(C) Each name that is under reservation pursuant to this title.

(D) The name of a foreign corporation that has registered its name pursuant to Section 2101.

(E) An alternate name of a foreign corporation under subdivision (b) of Section 2106.

(F)A name that will become the record name of a domestic or foreign corporation upon a corporate instrument when there is a delayed effective or file date.

(2) The use by a social purpose corporation of a name in violation of this section may be enjoined notwithstanding the filing of its articles by the Secretary of State.

(3)A corporation formed pursuant to this division before January 1, 2015, may elect to change its status from a flexible purpose corporation to a social purpose corporation by amending its articles of incorporation to change its name to replace "flexible purpose corporation" with "social purpose corporation" and to replace the term "flexible purpose corporation" with "social purpose corporation" as applicable in any statements contained in the articles. For any flexible purpose corporation formed before January 1, 2015, that has not amended its articles of incorporation to change its status to a social purpose corporation, any reference in this division to social purpose corporation shall be deemed a reference to "flexible purpose corporation."

(c) Any applicant may, upon payment of the fee prescribed in Article 3 (commencing with Section 12180) of Chapter 3 of Part 2 of Division 3 of Title 2 of the Government Code, obtain from the Secretary of State a certificate of reservation of any name not prohibited by subdivision (b), and upon the issuance of the certificate the name stated in the certificate shall be reserved for a period of 60 days. The Secretary of State shall not, however, issue certificates reserving the same name for two or more consecutive 60-day periods to the same applicant or for the use or benefit of the same person. No consecutive reservations shall be made by or for the use or benefit of the same person of names so similar as to fall within the prohibitions of subdivision (b).

Ca. Corp. Code § 2601

Amended by Stats 2022 ch 617 (SB 1202),s 41, eff. 1/1/2023.

Amended by Stats 2022 ch 452 (SB 1498),s 51, eff. 1/1/2023.

Amended by Stats 2020 ch 361 (SB 522),s 3, eff. 1/1/2021.

Amended by Stats 2016 ch 277 (AB 2907),s 5, eff. 1/1/2017.

Amended by Stats 2015 ch 189 (AB 1471),s 3, eff. 1/1/2016.

Amended by Stats 2014 ch 694 (SB 1301),s 37, eff. 1/1/2015.

Amended by Stats 2014 ch 401 (AB 2763),s 19, eff. 1/1/2015.

Added by Stats 2011 ch 740 (SB 201),s 12, eff. 1/1/2012.

Section 2602 - Mandatory content of articles of incorporation

The articles of incorporation shall set forth:

(a) The name of the social purpose corporation that shall contain the words "social purpose corporation" or an abbreviation of those words.

(b)

(1) Either of the following statements, as applicable:

(A) "The purpose of this social purpose corporation is to engage in any lawful act or activity for which a social purpose corporation may be organized under Division 1.5 of the California Corporations Code, other than the banking business, the trust company business or the practice of a profession permitted to be incorporated by the California Corporations Code, for the benefit of the overall interests of the social purpose corporation and its shareholders and in furtherance of the following enumerated purposes _____."

(B) "The purpose of this social purpose corporation is to engage in the profession of _____ (with the insertion of a profession permitted to be incorporated by the California Corporations Code) and any other lawful activities, other than the banking or trust company business, not prohibited to a social purpose corporation engaging in that profession by applicable laws and regulations, for the benefit of the overall interests of the social purpose corporation and its shareholders and in furtherance of the following enumerated purposes _____."

(2) A statement that a purpose of the social purpose corporation, in addition to the purpose stated pursuant to paragraph (1), is to engage in one or more of the following enumerated purposes, as also specified in the statement set forth pursuant to paragraph (1):

(A) One or more charitable or public purpose activities that a nonprofit public benefit corporation is authorized to carry out.

(B) The purpose of promoting positive effects of, or minimizing adverse effects of, the social purpose corporation's activities upon any of the following, provided that the corporation consider the purpose in addition to or together with the financial interests of the shareholders and compliance with legal obligations, and take action consistent with that purpose:

(i) The social purpose corporation's employees, suppliers, customers, and creditors.

(ii) The community and society.

(iii) The environment.

(3)

(A) For any corporation organized under this division before January 1, 2015, that has not elected to change its status to a social purpose corporation, a statement that the corporation is organized as a flexible purpose corporation under the Corporate Flexibility Act of 2011. Such a corporation is not required to revise the statements required in paragraphs (1) and (2) to conform to the changes made by the act adding this subparagraph.

(B) For any corporation organized under this division on and after January 1, 2015, or that has elected to change its status to a social purpose corporation pursuant to paragraph (2) of subdivision (b) of Section 2601, a statement that the corporation is organized as a social purpose corporation under the Social Purpose Corporations Act.

(4) If the social purpose corporation is a social purpose corporation subject to the Banking Law (Division 1.1 (commencing with Section 1000) of the Financial Code), the articles shall set forth a statement of purpose that is prescribed by the applicable provision of the Banking Law (Division 1.1 (commencing with Section 1000) of the Financial Code).

(5) If the social purpose corporation is a social purpose corporation subject to the

Insurance Code as an insurer, the articles shall additionally state that the business of the social purpose corporation is to be an insurer.

(6) If the social purpose corporation is intended to be a professional corporation within the meaning of the Moscone-Knox Professional Corporation Act (Part 4 (commencing with Section 13400) of Division 3), the articles shall additionally contain the statement required by Section 13404. The articles shall not set forth any further or additional statement with respect to the purposes or powers of the social purpose corporation, except by way of limitation or except as expressly required by any law of this state, other than this division, or any federal or other statute or regulation, including the Internal Revenue Code and regulations thereunder as a condition of acquiring or maintaining a particular status for tax purposes.

(7) If the social purpose corporation is a close social purpose corporation, a statement as required by subdivision (a) of Section 158.

(c) The name and street address in this state of the social purpose corporation's initial agent for service of process in accordance with subdivision (b) of Section 1502.

(d) The initial street address of the corporation.

(e) The initial mailing address of the corporation, if different from the initial street address.

(f) If the social purpose corporation is authorized to issue only one class of shares, the total number of shares that the social purpose corporation is authorized to issue.

(g) If the social purpose corporation is authorized to issue more than one class of shares, or if any class of shares is to have two or more series, the articles shall state:

(1) The total number of shares of each class that the social purpose corporation is authorized to issue and the total number of shares of each series that the social purpose corporation is authorized to issue or that the board is authorized to fix the number of shares of any such series.

(2) The designation of each class and the designation of each series or that the board may determine the designation of any such series.

(3) The rights, preferences, privileges, and restrictions granted to or imposed upon the respective classes or series of shares or the holders thereof, or that the board, within any limits and restrictions stated, may determine or alter the rights, preferences, privileges, and restrictions granted to or imposed upon any wholly unissued class of shares or any wholly unissued series of any class of shares. As to any series the number of shares of which is authorized to be fixed by the board, the articles may also authorize the board, within the limits and restrictions stated in the article or in any resolution or resolutions of the board originally fixing the number of shares constituting any series, to increase or decrease, but not below the number of shares of such series then outstanding, the number of shares of any series subsequent to the issue of shares of that series. If the number of shares of any series shall be so decreased, the shares constituting that decrease shall resume the status which they had prior to the adoption of the resolution originally fixing the number of shares of that series.

Ca. Corp. Code § 2602
Amended by Stats 2014 ch 694 (SB 1301),s 38, eff. 1/1/2015.
Amended by Stats 2014 ch 64 (AB 2742),s 5, eff. 1/1/2015.
Amended by Stats 2012 ch 494 (SB 1532),s 10, eff. 1/1/2013.
Added by Stats 2011 ch 740 (SB 201),s 12, eff. 1/1/2012.

Section 2603 - Content of articles of incorporation

The articles of incorporation may set forth:
(a) Any or all of the following provisions, which shall not be effective unless expressly provided in the articles:

(1) Granting, with or without limitations, the power to levy assessments upon the shares or any class of shares.

(2) Granting to shareholders preemptive rights to subscribe to any or all issues of shares or securities.

(3) Special qualifications of persons who may be shareholders.

(4) A provision limiting the duration of the social purpose corporation's existence to a specified date.

(5) A provision requiring, for any or all corporate actions, except as provided in Section 303, subdivision (b) of Section 402.5, subdivision (c) of Section 708, and Section 1900, the vote of a larger proportion or of all of the shares of any class or series, or the vote or quorum for taking action of a larger proportion or of all of the directors, than is otherwise required by Division 1 (commencing with Section 100) or this division.

(6) So long as consistent with the purpose of the social purpose corporation as set forth in the articles in accordance with subdivision (b) of Section 2602, a provision limiting or restricting the business in which the social purpose corporation may engage or the powers which the social purpose corporation may exercise, or both.

(7) A provision conferring upon the holders of any evidences of indebtedness, issued or to be issued by the social purpose corporation, the right to vote in the election of the directors and on any other matters on which shareholders may vote.

(8) A provision conferring upon shareholders the right to determine the consideration for which shares shall be issued.

(9) A provision requiring the approval of the shareholders (Section 153) or the approval of the outstanding shares (Section 152) for any corporate action, even though not otherwise required by Division 1 (commencing with Section 100) or this division.

(10) Provisions eliminating or limiting the personal liability of a director for monetary damages in an action brought by or in the right of the social purpose corporation for breach of a director's duties to the social purpose corporation and its shareholders, as set forth in Section 2700, subject to the following:

(A) The provision may not eliminate or limit the liability of directors (i) for acts or omissions that involve intentional misconduct or a knowing and culpable violation of law, (ii) for acts or omissions that a director believes to be contrary to the best interests of the social purpose corporation or its shareholders and its corporate purposes as expressed in its articles, or that involve the absence of good faith on the part of the director, (iii) for any transaction from which a director derived an improper personal benefit, (iv) for acts or omissions that show a reckless disregard for the director's duty to the social purpose corporation or its shareholders in circumstances in which the director was aware, or should have been aware, in the ordinary course of performing a director's duties, of a risk of serious injury to the social purpose corporation, its shareholders, or its corporate purposes as expressed in its articles, (v) for acts or omissions that constitute an unexcused pattern of inattention that amounts to an abdication of the director's duty to the social purpose corporation, its shareholders, or its corporate purposes as expressed in its articles pursuant to Section 2602, or (vi) under Section 310 or 2701.

(B) The provision shall not eliminate or limit the liability of a director for any act or omission occurring prior to the date on which the provision becomes effective.

(C) The provision shall not eliminate or limit the liability of an officer for any act or omission as an officer, notwithstanding that the officer is also a director or that his or her actions, if negligent or improper, have been ratified by the directors.

(11) A provision authorizing, whether by bylaw, agreement, or otherwise, the indemnification of agents of the social purpose corporation for breach of duty to the social purpose corporation and its shareholders, provided, however, that the provision may not provide for indemnification of any agent for any acts or omissions or transactions from which a director may not be relieved of liability as described in subparagraphs (A), (B), and (C) of paragraph (10). Notwithstanding this subdivision, bylaws may require, for all or any actions by the board, the affirmative vote of a majority of the authorized number of directors. Nothing contained in this subdivision shall affect the enforceability, as between the parties thereto, of any lawful agreement not otherwise contrary to public policy.

(b) Reasonable restrictions upon the right to transfer or hypothecate shares of any class or classes or series, except that no restriction shall be binding with respect to shares issued prior to the adoption of the restriction unless the holders of those shares voted in favor of the restriction.

(c) The names and addresses of the persons appointed to act as initial directors.

(d) Any other provision, not in conflict with law, for the management of the business and for the conduct of the affairs of the social purpose corporation, including any provision that is required or permitted by this division to be stated in the bylaws.

(e) This section shall become operative on January 1, 2022.

Ca. Corp. Code § 2603

Added by Stats 2018 ch 889 (SB 838),s 4, eff. 1/1/2019.

Section 2604 - Business activity

Subject to any limitation contained in the articles, to compliance with any other applicable laws, and to consistency with the special purpose of the social purpose corporation, any social purpose corporation other than a social purpose corporation subject to the Banking Law or a professional social purpose corporation may engage in any business activity. A social purpose corporation subject to the Banking Law or a professional social purpose corporation may engage in any business activity not prohibited by the respective statutes and regulations to which it is subject.

Ca. Corp. Code § 2604

Amended by Stats 2014 ch 694 (SB 1301),s 40, eff. 1/1/2015.

Added by Stats 2011 ch 740 (SB 201),s 12, eff. 1/1/2012.

Section 2605 - Powers in carrying out business activities

Subject to any limitations contained in the articles, to compliance with other provisions of this division and any other applicable laws, and to consistency with the special purpose of the social purpose corporation, a social purpose corporation shall have all the powers of a natural person in carrying out its business activities, including, without limitation, the power to:

(a) Adopt, use, and at will alter a corporate seal. Failure to affix a seal does not affect the validity of any instrument.

(b) Adopt, amend, and repeal bylaws.

(c) Qualify to do business in any other state, territory, dependency, or foreign country.

(d) Subject to the provisions of Section 510, issue, purchase, redeem, receive, take or otherwise acquire, own, hold, sell, lend, exchange, transfer or otherwise dispose of, pledge, use, and otherwise deal in and with its own shares, bonds, debentures, and other securities.

(e) Make donations, regardless of specific corporate benefit, for the public welfare or for a community fund, hospital, charitable, educational, scientific, civic, or similar purposes.

(f) Pay pensions, and establish and carry out pension, profit-sharing, share bonus, share purchase, share option, savings, thrift, and other retirement, incentive, and benefit plans, trusts, and provisions for any or all of the directors, officers, and employees of the social purpose corporation or any of its subsidiaries or affiliates, and to indemnify and purchase and maintain insurance on behalf of any fiduciary of these plans, trusts, or provisions.

(g) Subject to the provisions of Section 315, assume obligations, enter into contracts, including contracts of guaranty or suretyship, incur liabilities, borrow and lend money and otherwise use its credit, and secure any of its obligations, contracts, or liabilities by mortgage, pledge, or other encumbrance of all or any part of its property, franchises, and income.

(h) Participate with others in any partnership, joint venture, or other association, transaction, or arrangement of any kind, whether or not that participation involves sharing or delegation of control with or to others.

Ca. Corp. Code § 2605

Amended by Stats 2014 ch 694 (SB 1301),s 41, eff. 1/1/2015.

Added by Stats 2011 ch 740 (SB 201),s 12, eff. 1/1/2012.

Chapter 3 - DIRECTORS AND MANAGEMENT

Section 2700 - Duties of director

(a) A director shall perform the duties of a director, including duties as a member of any committee of the board upon which the director may serve, in good faith, in a manner the director believes to be in the best interests of the social purpose corporation and its shareholders, and with that care, including reasonable inquiry, as an ordinarily prudent person in a like position would use under similar circumstances.

(b) In performing the duties of a director, a director shall be entitled to rely upon information, opinions, reports, or statements, including financial statements and other financial data, in each case prepared or presented by any of the following:

(1) An officer or employee of the social purpose corporation whom the director believes to be reliable and competent in the matters presented.

(2) Counsel, independent accountants, or other persons as to matters which the director believes to be within that person's professional or expert competence.

(3) A committee of the board upon which the director does not serve, as to matters within its designated authority, which committee the director believes to merit confidence, so long as the director acts in good faith, after reasonable inquiry when the need therefor is indicated by the circumstances and without knowledge that would cause that reliance to be unwarranted.

(c) In discharging his or her duties, a director shall consider those factors, and give weight to those factors, as the director deems relevant, including the overall prospects of the social purpose corporation, the best interests of the social purpose corporation and its shareholders, and the purposes of the social purpose corporation as set forth in its articles.

(d) A person who performs the duties of a director in accordance with subdivisions (a), (b), and (c) shall have no liability based upon any alleged failure to discharge the person's obligations as a director. The liability of a director for monetary damages may be eliminated or limited by a social purpose corporation's articles to the extent provided in paragraph (10) of subdivision (a) of Section 2603.

(e) Notwithstanding any of the purposes set forth in its articles, a social purpose corporation shall not be deemed to hold any of its assets for the benefit of any party other than its shareholders. However, nothing in this division shall be construed as negating existing charitable trust principles or the Attorney General's authority to enforce any charitable trust created.

(f) Nothing in this section, express or implied, is intended to create or grant or shall create or grant any right in or for any person or any cause of action by or for any person, and a director shall not be responsible to any party other than the social purpose corporation and its shareholders.

Ca. Corp. Code § 2700

Amended by Stats 2014 ch 694 (SB 1301),s 42, eff. 1/1/2015.
Added by Stats 2011 ch 740 (SB 201),s 12, eff. 1/1/2012.

Section 2701 - Directors' joint and several liability to social purpose corporation for benefit of creditors or shareholders

(a) Subject to Section 2700, directors of a social purpose corporation who approve any of the following corporate actions shall be jointly and severally liable to the social purpose corporation for the benefit of all of the creditors or shareholders entitled to institute an action under subdivision (c):

(1) The making of any distribution to its shareholders to the extent that it is contrary to the provisions of Sections 500 to 503, inclusive.

(2) The distribution of assets to shareholders after institution of dissolution proceedings of the social purpose corporation, without paying or adequately providing for all known liabilities of the social purpose corporation, excluding any claims not filed by creditors within the time limit set by the court in a notice given to creditors under Chapter 18 (commencing with Section 1800) of Division 1, Chapter 20 (commencing with Section 1900) of Division 1, and Chapter 20 (commencing with Section 2000).

(3) The making of any loan or guaranty contrary to Section 2715.
(b) A director who is present at a meeting of the board, or any committee of the board, at which an action specified in subdivision (a) is taken and who abstains from

voting, shall be deemed to have approved the action.

(c) Suit may be brought in the name of the social purpose corporation to enforce the liability as follows:

(1) Under paragraph (1) of subdivision (a) against any or all directors liable, by the persons entitled to sue under subdivision (b) of Section 506.

(2) Under paragraph (2) or (3) of subdivision (a) against any or all directors liable, by any one or more creditors of the social purpose corporation whose debts or claims arose prior to the time of any of the corporate actions specified in paragraph (2) or (3) of subdivision (a) and who have not consented to the corporate action, regardless of whether they have reduced their claims to judgment.

(3) Under paragraph (3) of subdivision (a) against any or all directors liable, by any one or more holders of shares outstanding at the time of any corporate action specified in paragraph (3) of subdivision (a) who have not consented to the corporate action, without regard to the provisions of Section 2900.

(d) The damages recoverable from a director under this section shall be the amount of the illegal distribution, or if the illegal distribution consists of property, the fair market value of that property at the time of the illegal distribution, plus interest thereon from the date of the distribution at the legal rate on judgments until paid, together with all reasonably incurred costs of appraisal or other valuation, if any, of that property or loss suffered by the social purpose corporation as a result of the illegal loan or guaranty, respectively, but not exceeding the liabilities of the social purpose corporation owed to nonconsenting creditors at the time of the violation and the injury suffered by nonconsenting shareholders.

(e) Any director sued under this section may implead all other directors liable and may compel contribution, either in that action or in an independent action against directors not joined in that action.

(f) Directors liable under this section shall also be entitled to be subrogated to the rights of the social purpose corporation:

(1) With respect to paragraph (1) of subdivision (a), against shareholders who received the distribution.

(2) With respect to paragraph (2) of subdivision (a), against shareholders who received the distribution of assets.

(3) With respect to paragraph (3) of subdivision (a), against the person who received the loan or guaranty. Any director sued under this section may file a cross-complaint against the person or persons who are liable to the director as a result of the subrogation provided for in this subdivision or may proceed against them in an independent action.

Ca. Corp. Code § 2701

Amended by Stats 2014 ch 694 (SB 1301),s 43, eff. 1/1/2015.
Added by Stats 2011 ch 740 (SB 201),s 12, eff. 1/1/2012.

Section 2702 - Indemnification

(a) For the purposes of this section:

(1) "Agent" means any person who is or was a director, officer, employee, or other agent of the social purpose corporation, or is or was serving at the request of the social purpose corporation as a director, officer, employee, or agent of another foreign or domestic corporation, partnership, joint venture, trust, or other enterprise, or was a director, officer, employee, or agent of a foreign or domestic corporation which was a predecessor corporation of the social purpose corporation or of another enterprise at the request of the predecessor corporation.

(2) "Proceeding" means any threatened, pending, or completed action or proceeding, whether civil, criminal, administrative, or investigative.

(3) "Expenses" includes without limitation attorneys' fees and any expenses of establishing a right to indemnification under subdivision (b).

(b) Subject to the standards and restrictions, if any, set forth in its articles or bylaws, and subject to the limitations required by paragraph (11) of subdivision (a) of Section 2603, a social purpose corporation may indemnify and hold harmless any agent or any other person from and against any and all claims and demands whatsoever.

(c) Expenses incurred in defending any proceeding may be advanced by the social purpose corporation prior to the final disposition of the proceeding. The provisions of subdivision (a) of Section 315 do not apply to advances made pursuant to this subdivision.

(d) A social purpose corporation may purchase and maintain insurance on behalf of any of its agents against any liability asserted against or incurred by the agent in that capacity or arising out of the agent's status as an agent regardless of whether the social purpose corporation would have the power to indemnify the agent against that liability under this section. The fact that a social purpose corporation owns all or a portion of the shares of the company issuing a policy of insurance shall not render this subdivision inapplicable if either of the following conditions are satisfied:

(1) The insurance provided by this subdivision is limited as indemnification is required to be limited by paragraph (11) of subdivision (a) of Section 2603.

(2)

(A) The company issuing the insurance policy is organized, licensed, and operated in a manner that complies with the insurance laws and regulations applicable to its jurisdiction of organization.

(B) The company issuing the policy provides procedures for processing claims that do not permit that company to be subject to the direct control of the social purpose corporation that purchased that policy.

(C) The policy issued provides for some manner of risk sharing between the issuer and purchaser of the policy, on one hand, and some unaffiliated person or persons, on the other, such as by providing for more than one unaffiliated owner of the company issuing the policy or by providing that a portion of the coverage furnished will be obtained from some unaffiliated insurer or reinsurer.

(e) This section does not apply to any proceeding against any trustee, investment manager, or other fiduciary of an employee benefit plan in that person's capacity as such, even though the person may also be an agent as defined in subdivision (a) of the employer social purpose corporation. A social purpose corporation shall have power to indemnify a trustee, investment manager, or other fiduciary to the extent permitted by subdivision (f) of Section 2605.

Ca. Corp. Code § 2702

Amended by Stats 2014 ch 694 (SB 1301),s 44, eff. 1/1/2015.
Added by Stats 2011 ch 740 (SB 201),s 12, eff. 1/1/2012.

Chapter 4 - SHARES AND SHARE CERTIFICATES

Section 2800 - Certificates representing shares

(a) All certificates representing shares of a social purpose corporation shall contain, in addition to any other statements required by this section, the following conspicuous language on the face of the certificate. "This entity is a social purpose corporation organized under Division 1.5 of the California Corporations Code. The articles of this corporation state one or more purposes required by law. Refer to the articles on file with the Secretary of State, and the bylaws and any agreements on file with the secretary of the corporation, for further information."

(b) There shall also appear on the certificate, the initial transaction statement, and written statements, unless stated or summarized under subdivision (a) or (b) of Section 417, the statements required by all of the following, to the extent applicable:

(1) The fact that the shares are subject to restrictions upon transfer.

(2) If the shares are assessable or are not fully paid, a statement that they are assessable or the statements required by subdivision (d) of Section 409 if they are not fully paid.

(3) The fact that the shares are subject to a voting agreement under subdivision (a) of Section 706 or an irrevocable proxy under subdivision (e) of Section 705 or restrictions upon voting rights contractually imposed by the social purpose corporation.

(4) The fact that the shares are redeemable.

(5) The fact that the shares are convertible and the period for conversion. Statements or references to statements on the face of the certificate, the initial transaction statement, and written statements required by paragraph (1) or (2) shall be conspicuous.

(c) Unless stated on the certificate, the initial transaction statement, and written statements as required by subdivision (a), no restriction upon transfer, no right of redemption and no voting agreement under subdivision (a) of Section 706, no irrevocable proxy under subdivision (e) of Section 705, and no voting restriction imposed by the social purpose corporation shall be enforceable against a transferee of the shares without actual knowledge of the restriction, right, agreement, or proxy. With regard only to liability to assessment or for the unpaid portion of the subscription price, unless stated on the certificate as required by subdivision (a), that liability shall not be enforceable against a transferee of the shares. For the purpose of this subdivision, "transferee" includes a purchaser from the social purpose corporation.

(d) All certificates representing shares of a close social purpose corporation shall contain, in addition to any other statements required by this section, the following conspicuous legend on the face thereof: "This social purpose corporation is a close social purpose corporation. The number of holders of record of its shares of all classes cannot exceed _____ (a number not in excess of 35). Any attempted voluntary inter vivos transfer which would violate this requirement is void. Refer to the articles, bylaws, and any agreements on file with the secretary of the social purpose corporation for further restrictions."

(e) Any attempted voluntary inter vivos transfer of the shares of a close social purpose corporation that would result in the number of holders of record of its shares exceeding the maximum number specified in its articles is void if the certificate contains the legend required by subdivision (c).

(f) Notwithstanding any other subdivision, the certificates representing shares of a corporation formed pursuant to this division as a "flexible purpose corporation" before January 1, 2015, shall continue to be valid even if the certificates reference a "flexible purpose corporation." A corporation formed pursuant to this division before January 1, 2015, may, but is not required to, reissue certificates to replace "flexible purpose corporation" with "social purpose corporation" as applicable. Any reference to a "flexible purpose corporation" or any abbreviation of that term in certificates representing shares of a corporation formed pursuant to this division before January 1, 2015, shall also be a reference to "social purpose corporation."

Ca. Corp. Code § 2800

Amended by Stats 2014 ch 694 (SB 1301),s 45, eff. 1/1/2015.
Added by Stats 2011 ch 740 (SB 201),s 12, eff. 1/1/2012.

Chapter 5 - SHAREHOLDER DERIVATIVE ACTIONS

Section 2900 - Shareholder derivative actions

(a) As used in this section:

(1) "Social purpose corporation" includes an unincorporated association.

(2) "Board" includes the managing body of an unincorporated association.

(3) "Shareholder" includes a member of an unincorporated association.

(4) "Shares" includes memberships in an unincorporated association.

(b) Shareholders of a social purpose corporation may maintain a derivative lawsuit to enforce the requirements set forth in subdivision (c) of Section 2700.

(c) No action may be instituted or maintained in right of any domestic or foreign social purpose corporation under this section by any party other than a shareholder of the social purpose corporation.

(d) No action may be instituted or maintained in right of any domestic or foreign social purpose corporation by any holder of shares or of voting trust certificates of the social purpose corporation unless both of the following conditions exist:

(1) The plaintiff alleges in the complaint that plaintiff was a shareholder, of record or beneficially, or the holder of voting trust certificates at the time of the transaction or any part thereof of which plaintiff complains or that plaintiff's shares or voting trust certificates thereafter devolved upon plaintiff by operation of law from a holder who was a holder at the time of the transaction or any part thereof complained of. Any shareholder who does not meet these requirements may nevertheless be allowed, in the discretion of the court, to maintain the action on a preliminary showing to and determination by the court, by motion and after a hearing, at which the court shall consider the evidence by affidavit or testimony, as it deems material, of all of the following:

(A) There is a strong prima facie case in favor of the claim asserted on behalf of the social purpose corporation.

(B) No other similar action has been or is likely to be instituted.

(C) The plaintiff acquired the shares before there was disclosure to the public or to the plaintiff of the wrongdoing of which plaintiff complains.

(D) Unless the action can be maintained the defendant may retain a gain derived from defendant's willful breach of a fiduciary duty.

(E) The requested relief will not result in unjust enrichment of the social purpose corporation or any shareholder of the social purpose corporation.

(2) The plaintiff alleges in the complaint with particularity plaintiff's efforts to secure from the board the action as plaintiff desires, or the reasons for not making that effort, and alleges further that plaintiff has either informed the social purpose corporation or the board in writing of the ultimate facts of each cause of action against each defendant or delivered to the social purpose corporation or the board a true copy of the complaint which plaintiff proposes to file.

(e) In any action referred to in subdivision (c), at any time within 30 days after service of summons upon the social purpose corporation or upon any defendant who is an officer or director of the social purpose corporation, or held that office at the time of the acts complained of, the social purpose corporation or the defendant may move the court for an order, upon notice and hearing, requiring the plaintiff to furnish a bond as hereinafter provided. The motion shall be based upon one or both of the following grounds:

(1) There is no reasonable possibility that the prosecution of the cause of action alleged in the complaint against the moving party will benefit the social purpose corporation or its shareholders.

(2) The moving party, if other than the social purpose corporation, did not participate in the transaction complained of in any capacity. The court on application of the social purpose corporation or any defendant may, for good cause shown, extend the 30-day period for an additional period or periods not exceeding 60 days.

(f) At the hearing upon any motion pursuant to subdivision (d), the court shall consider the evidence, written or oral, by witnesses or affidavit, as may be material to the ground or grounds upon which the motion is based, or to a determination of the probable reasonable expenses, including attorney's fees, of the social purpose corporation and the moving party that will be incurred in the defense of the action. If the court determines, after hearing the evidence adduced by the parties, that the moving party has established a probability in support of any of the grounds upon which the motion is based, the court shall fix the amount of the bond, not to exceed fifty thousand dollars ($50,000), to be furnished by the plaintiff for reasonable expenses, including attorney's fees, which may be incurred by the moving party and the social purpose corporation in connection with the action, including expenses for which the social purpose corporation may become liable pursuant to Section 2702. A ruling by the court on the motion shall not be a determination of any issue in the action or of the merits thereof. If the court, upon the motion, makes a determination that a bond shall be furnished by the plaintiff as to any one or more defendants, the action shall be dismissed as to the defendant or defendants, unless the bond required by the court has been furnished within such reasonable time as may be fixed by the court.

(g) If the plaintiff, either before or after a motion is made pursuant to subdivision (d), or any order or determination pursuant to the motion, furnishes a bond in the aggregate amount of fifty thousand dollars ($50,000) to secure the reasonable expenses of the parties entitled to make the motion, the plaintiff shall be deemed to have complied with the requirements of this section and with any order for a bond theretofore made, and any motion then pending shall be dismissed and no further or additional bond shall be required.

(h) If a motion is filed pursuant to subdivision (d), no pleadings need be filed by the social purpose corporation or any other defendant and the prosecution of the action shall be stayed until 10 days after the motion has been disposed of.

Ca. Corp. Code § 2900

Amended by Stats 2014 ch 694 (SB 1301),s 46, eff. 1/1/2015.

Amended by Stats 2012 ch 162 (SB 1171),s 19, eff. 1/1/2013.

Added by Stats 2011 ch 740 (SB 201),s 12, eff. 1/1/2012.

Chapter 6 - AMENDMENT OF ARTICLES

Section 3000 - Amendment to articles of social purpose corporation

(a) A proposed amendment to the articles of a social purpose corporation shall be approved by the outstanding shares of a class, regardless of whether that class is entitled to vote thereon by the provisions of the articles, if the amendment would:

(1) Increase or decrease the aggregate number of authorized shares of that class, other than an increase as provided in either subdivision (b) of Section 405 or subdivision (b) of Section 902.

(2) Effect an exchange, reclassification, or cancellation of all or part of the shares of that class, including a reverse stock split but excluding a stock split.

(3) Effect an exchange, or create a right of exchange, of all or part of the shares of another class into the shares of that class.

(4) Change the rights, preferences, privileges, or restrictions of the shares of that class.

(5) Create a new class of shares having rights, preferences, or privileges prior to the shares of that class, or increase the rights, preferences, or privileges or the number of authorized shares of any class having rights, preferences, or privileges prior to the shares of that class.

(6) In the case of preferred shares, divide the shares of any class into series having different rights, preferences, privileges, or restrictions or authorize the board to do so.

(7) Cancel or otherwise affect dividends on the shares of that class that have accrued but have not been paid.

(b) A proposed amendment shall be approved by an affirmative vote of at least two-thirds of the outstanding shares of each class, or a greater vote if required in the articles, regardless of whether that class is entitled to vote thereon by the provisions of the articles, if the amendment would materially alter any special purpose of the social purpose corporation stated in the articles pursuant to paragraph (2) of subdivision (b) of Section 2602, regardless of whether that purpose, as amended, would comply with the provisions of that paragraph.

(c) Different series of the same class shall not constitute different classes for the purpose of voting by classes except when a series is adversely affected by an amendment in a different manner than other shares of the same class.

(d) In addition to approval by a class as provided in subdivisions (a) and (b), a proposed amendment shall also be approved by the outstanding voting shares (Section 152).

   Ca. Corp. Code § 3000

Amended by Stats 2014 ch 694 (SB 1301),s 47, eff. 1/1/2015.
Added by Stats 2011 ch 740 (SB 201),s 12, eff. 1/1/2012.

Section 3001 - Conversion to nonprofit corporation

(a) A social purpose corporation may, by amendment of its articles pursuant to this section, change its status to that of a nonprofit public benefit corporation, nonprofit mutual benefit corporation, nonprofit religious corporation, or cooperative corporation.

(b) The amendment of the articles to change its status to a nonprofit corporation shall revise the statement of purpose, delete the authorization for shares and any other provisions relating to authorized or issued shares, make other changes as may be necessary or desired, and, if any shares have been issued, provide either for the cancellation of those shares or for the conversion of those shares to memberships of the nonprofit corporation. The amendment of the articles to change status to a cooperative corporation shall revise the statement of purpose, make other changes as may be necessary or desired, and, if any shares have been issued, provide for the cancellation of those shares or for the change of those shares to memberships of the cooperative corporation, if necessary.

(c) If shares have been issued, an amendment to change status to a nonprofit corporation shall be approved by all of the outstanding shares of all classes regardless of limitations or restrictions on their voting rights and an amendment to change status to a cooperative corporation shall be approved by the outstanding shares of each class regardless of limitations or restrictions on their voting rights.

(d) If an amendment pursuant to this section is included in a merger agreement, the provisions of this section shall apply, except that any provision for cancellation or conversion of shares shall be in the merger agreement rather than in the amendment of the articles.

(e) Notwithstanding subdivision (c), if a social purpose corporation is a mutual water company within the meaning of Section 2705 of the Public Utilities Code and under the terms of the status change each outstanding share is converted to a membership of a nonprofit mutual benefit corporation, an amendment to change status to a nonprofit mutual benefit corporation shall be approved by the outstanding shares of each class regardless of limitations or restrictions on their voting rights.

Ca. Corp. Code § 3001

Amended by Stats 2014 ch 694 (SB 1301),s 48, eff. 1/1/2015.

Added by Stats 2011 ch 740 (SB 201),s 12, eff. 1/1/2012.

Section 3002 - Conversion to domestic corporation

(a) A social purpose corporation may, by amendment of its articles pursuant to this section, change its status to that of a business corporation.

(b) The amendment of the articles to change status to a business corporation shall revise the statement of purpose to delete any provisions in the articles that are permitted by Section 2602, but that are not permitted to be in the articles of a domestic corporation.

(c) If shares have been issued, an amendment to change status to a business corporation shall be approved by an affirmative vote of at least two-thirds of the outstanding shares of each class, or a greater vote if required in the articles, regardless of whether that class is entitled to vote thereon by the provisions of the articles. If the status change is approved, shareholders with dissenting shares, as defined in subdivision (b) of Section 1300, may exercise dissenters' rights pursuant to Section 3305 and Chapter 13 (commencing with Section 1300) of Division 1.

(d) If an amendment pursuant to this section is included in a merger agreement, the provisions of this section shall apply, except that any provision for cancellation or conversion of shares shall be in the merger agreement rather than in the amendment of the articles.

Ca. Corp. Code § 3002

Amended by Stats 2014 ch 694 (SB 1301),s 49, eff. 1/1/2015.

Added by Stats 2011 ch 740 (SB 201),s 12, eff. 1/1/2012.

Chapter 7 - SALES OF ASSETS

Section 3100 - Sale or other disposal of assets

(a) A social purpose corporation may sell, lease, convey, exchange, transfer, or otherwise dispose of all or substantially all of its assets when the principal terms of the transaction are approved by the board and are approved by an affirmative vote of at least two-thirds of the outstanding shares of each class, or a greater vote if required in the articles, regardless of whether that class is entitled to vote thereon by the provisions of the articles, either before or after approval by the board and before the transaction. A transaction constituting a reorganization shall be subject to Chapter 12 (commencing with Section 1200) of Division 1 and Chapter 10 (commencing with

Section 3400) of this division and shall not be subject to this section, other than subdivision (d). A transaction constituting a conversion shall be subject to Chapter 11.5 (commencing with Section 1150) of Division 1 and Chapter 9 (commencing with Section 3300) of this division and shall not be subject to this section.

(b) Notwithstanding approval of two-thirds of the outstanding shares, the board may abandon the proposed transaction without further action by the shareholders, subject to the contractual rights, if any, of third parties.

(c) The sale, lease, conveyance, exchange, transfer, or other disposition may be made upon those terms and conditions and for that consideration as the board may deem in the best interests of the social purpose corporation. The consideration may be money, securities, or other property.

(d) If the acquiring party in a transaction pursuant to subdivision (a) or subdivision (g) of Section 2001 is in control of or under common control with the disposing social purpose corporation, the principal terms of the sale shall be approved by at least 90 percent of the voting power of the disposing social purpose corporation unless the disposition is to a domestic or foreign other business entity or social purpose corporation, the articles of incorporation of which specify materially the same purposes, in consideration of the nonredeemable common shares or nonredeemable equity securities of the acquiring party or its parent.

(e) Subdivision (d) shall not apply to a transaction if the Commissioner of Financial Protection and Innovation, the Insurance Commissioner, or the Public Utilities Commission has approved the terms and conditions of the transaction and the fairness of those terms and conditions pursuant to Section 25142, Section 1209 of the Financial Code, Section 838.5 of the Insurance Code, or Section 822 of the Public Utilities Code.

Ca. Corp. Code § 3100
Amended by Stats 2022 ch 452 (SB 1498),s 52, eff. 1/1/2023.
Amended by Stats 2015 ch 190 (AB 1517),s 10, eff. 1/1/2016.
Amended by Stats 2014 ch 694 (SB 1301),s 50, eff. 1/1/2015.
Added by Stats 2011 ch 740 (SB 201),s 12, eff. 1/1/2012.

Chapter 8 - MERGER

Section 3200 - Disappearing social purpose corporation close social purpose corporation and surviving social purpose corporation not close social purpose corporation

If any disappearing social purpose corporation in a merger is a close social purpose corporation and the surviving social purpose corporation is not a close social purpose corporation, the merger shall be approved by an affirmative vote of at least two-thirds of the outstanding shares of each class, or a greater vote if required in the articles, regardless of whether that class is entitled to vote thereon by the provisions of the articles, of the disappearing social purpose corporation. The articles may provide for a lesser vote, but not less than a majority of the outstanding shares of each class.

Ca. Corp. Code § 3200
Amended by Stats 2014 ch 694 (SB 1301),s 51, eff. 1/1/2015.
Added by Stats 2011 ch 740 (SB 201),s 12, eff. 1/1/2012.

Section 3201 - Disappearing corporation social purpose corporation and surviving entity not social purpose corporation or social purpose corporation articles of incorporation of which set forth materially different purposes

If any disappearing corporation in a merger is a social purpose corporation and the surviving entity is not a social purpose corporation, or is a social purpose corporation the articles of incorporation of which set forth materially different purposes, the merger shall be approved by an affirmative vote of at least two-thirds of the outstanding shares of each class, or a greater vote if required in the articles, regardless of whether that class is entitled to vote thereon by the provisions of the articles, of the disappearing social purpose corporation. If the merger is approved, shareholders with dissenting shares, as defined in subdivision (b) of Section 1300, may exercise dissenters' rights pursuant to Section 3305 and Chapter 13 (commencing with Section 1300) of Division 1.

Ca. Corp. Code § 3201
Amended by Stats 2014 ch 694 (SB 1301),s 52, eff. 1/1/2015.
Added by Stats 2011 ch 740 (SB 201),s 12, eff. 1/1/2012.

Section 3202 - Disappearing social purpose corporation social purpose corporation and surviving corporation nonprofit corporation

If a disappearing social purpose corporation in a merger is a social purpose corporation governed by this division and the surviving corporation is a nonprofit public benefit corporation, a nonprofit mutual benefit corporation, or a nonprofit religious corporation, the merger shall be approved by all of the outstanding shares of all classes of the disappearing social purpose corporation, regardless of limitations or restrictions on their voting rights, notwithstanding any provision of Chapter 10 (commencing with Section 3400).

Ca. Corp. Code § 3202
Amended by Stats 2014 ch 694 (SB 1301),s 53, eff. 1/1/2015.
Added by Stats 2011 ch 740 (SB 201),s 12, eff. 1/1/2012.

Section 3203 - Merger of social purpose corporation with other business entity

(a) Any one or more social purpose corporations may merge with one or more other business entities. One or more domestic social purpose corporations not organized under this division and one or more foreign corporations may be parties to the merger. Notwithstanding this section, the merger of any number of social purpose corporations with any number of other business entities may be effected only if:

(1) In a merger in which a domestic social purpose corporation not organized under this division or a domestic other business entity is a party, it is authorized by the laws under which it is organized to effect the merger.

(2) In a merger in which a foreign corporation is a party, it is authorized by the laws under which it is organized to effect the merger.

(3) In a merger in which a foreign other business entity is a party, it is authorized by the laws under which it is organized to effect the merger.
(b) Each social purpose corporation and each other party that desires to merge shall approve, and shall be a party to, an agreement of merger. Other persons, including a parent party, may be parties to the agreement of merger. The board of each social purpose corporation that desires to merge, and, if required, the shareholders, shall approve the agreement of merger. The agreement of merger shall be approved on behalf of each party by those persons required to approve the merger by the laws under which it is organized. The agreement of merger shall state:

(1) The terms and conditions of the merger.

(2) The name and place of incorporation or organization of each party to the merger and the identity of the surviving party.

(3) The amendments, if any, subject to Sections 900, 902, 907, and 3002 to the articles of the surviving social purpose corporation, if applicable, to be effected by the merger. If any amendment changes the name of the surviving social purpose corporation, if applicable, the new name may be, subject to subdivision (b) of Section 2601, the same as or similar to the name of a disappearing party to the merger.

(4) The manner of converting the shares of each constituent social purpose corporation into shares, interests, or other securities of the surviving party. If any shares of any constituent social purpose corporation are not to be converted solely into shares, interests, or other securities of the surviving party, the agreement of merger shall state (A) the cash, rights, securities, or other property that the holders of those shares are to receive in exchange for the shares, which cash, rights, securities, or other property may be in addition to or in lieu of shares, interests, or other securities of the surviving party, or (B) that the shares are canceled without consideration.

(5) Any other details or provisions required by the laws under which any party to the merger is organized, including, if a domestic corporation is a party to the merger, Section 3203, if a public benefit corporation or a religious corporation is a party to the merger, Section 6019.1, if a mutual benefit corporation is a party to the merger, Section 8019.1, if a consumer cooperative corporation is a party to the merger, Section

12540.1, if a domestic limited partnership is a party to the merger, Section 15911.12, if a domestic partnership is a party to the merger, Section 16911, and if a domestic limited liability company is a party to the merger, Section 17551.

(6) Any other details or provisions as are desired, including, without limitation, a provision for the payment of cash in lieu of fractional shares or for any other arrangement with respect thereto consistent with the provisions of Section 407.

(c) Each share of the same class or series of any constituent social purpose corporation, other than the cancellation of shares held by a party to the merger or its parent, or a wholly owned subsidiary of either, in another constituent social purpose corporation, shall, unless all shareholders of the class or series consent and except as provided in Section 407, be treated equally with respect to any distribution of cash, rights, securities, or other property. Notwithstanding paragraph (4) of subdivision (b), the nonredeemable common shares of a constituent social purpose corporation may be converted only into nonredeemable common shares of a surviving social purpose corporation or a parent party or nonredeemable equity securities of a surviving party other than a social purpose corporation if another party to the merger or its parent owns, directly or indirectly, prior to the merger shares of that corporation representing more than 50 percent of the voting power of that social purpose corporation, unless all of the shareholders of the class consent and except as provided in Section 407.

(d) Notwithstanding its prior approval, an agreement of merger may be amended prior to the filing of the agreement of merger or the certificate of merger, as is applicable, if the amendment is approved by the board of each constituent social purpose corporation and, if the amendment changes any of the principal terms of the agreement, by the outstanding shares, if required by Chapter 10 (commencing with Section 3400), in the same manner as the original agreement of merger. If the agreement of merger as so amended and approved is also approved by each of the other parties to the agreement of merger, the agreement of merger as so amended shall then constitute the agreement of merger.

(e) The board of a constituent social purpose corporation may, in its discretion, abandon a merger, subject to the contractual rights, if any, of third parties, including other parties to the agreement of merger, without further approval by the outstanding shares, at any time before the merger is effective.

(f) Each constituent social purpose corporation shall sign the agreement of merger by its chairperson of the board, president, or a vice president and also by its secretary or an assistant secretary acting on behalf of their respective corporations.

(g)

(1) If the surviving party is a domestic social purpose corporation, or if a domestic corporation or a foreign corporation, a public benefit corporation, a mutual benefit corporation, a religious corporation, or a corporation organized under the Consumer Cooperative Corporation Law (Part 2 (commencing with Section 12200) of Division 3) is a party to the merger, after required approvals of the merger by each constituent social purpose corporation through approval of the board and any approval of the outstanding shares required by Chapter 10 (commencing with Section 3400) and by the other parties to the merger, the surviving party shall file a copy of the agreement of merger with an officers' certificate of each constituent domestic social purpose corporation and foreign social purpose corporation attached stating the total number of outstanding shares of each class entitled to vote on the merger, and identifying any other person or persons whose approval is required, that the agreement of merger in the form attached or its principal terms, as required, were approved by that social purpose corporation by a vote of a number of shares of each class that equaled or exceeded the vote required, specifying each class entitled to vote and the percentage vote required of each class and, if applicable, by that other person or persons whose approval is required, or that the merger agreement was entitled to be and was approved by the board alone, as provided in Section 3401, in the case of a social purpose corporation subject to that section. If equity securities of a parent party are to be issued in the merger, the officers' certificate of that controlled party shall state either that no vote of the shareholders of the parent party was required or that the required vote was obtained. In lieu of an officers' certificate, a certificate of merger, on a form prescribed by the Secretary of State, shall be filed for each constituent other business entity. The certificate of merger shall be executed and acknowledged by each domestic constituent limited liability company by all managers of the limited liability company, unless a lesser number is specified in its articles or organization or operating agreement, and by each domestic constituent limited partnership by all general partners, unless a lesser number is provided in its certificate of limited partnership or partnership agreement, and by each domestic constituent general partnership by two partners, unless a lesser number is provided in its partnership agreement, and by each foreign constituent limited liability company by one or more managers and by each foreign constituent general partnership or foreign constituent limited partnership by one or more general partners, and by each constituent reciprocal insurer by the chairperson of the board, president, or vice president, and by the secretary or assistant secretary, or, if a constituent reciprocal insurer has not appointed those officers, by the chairperson of the board, president, or vice president, and by the secretary or assistant secretary of the constituent reciprocal insurer's attorney-in-fact, and by each other party to the merger by those persons required or authorized to execute the certificate of merger by the laws under which that party is organized, specifying for that party the provision of law or other basis for the authority of the signing persons. The certificate of merger shall set forth, if a vote of the shareholders, members, partners, or other holders of interests of the constituent other business entity was required, a statement setting forth the total number of outstanding interests of each class entitled to vote on the merger and that the agreement of merger in the form attached or its principal terms, as required, were approved by a vote of the number of interests of each class that equaled or exceeded the vote required, specifying each class entitled to vote and the percentage vote required of each class, and any other information required to be set forth under the laws under which the constituent other business entity is organized, including, if a domestic limited partnership is a party to the merger, subdivision (a) of Section 15911.14, if a domestic partnership is a party to the merger, subdivision (b) of Section 16915, and, if a domestic limited liability company is a party to the merger, subdivision (a) of Section 17552. The certificate of merger for each constituent foreign other business entity, if any, shall also set forth the statutory or other basis under which that foreign other business entity is authorized by the laws under which it is organized to effect the merger. The merger and any amendment of the articles of the surviving social purpose corporation, if applicable, contained in the agreement of merger shall be effective upon filing of the agreement of merger with an officer's certificate of each constituent domestic corporation and foreign corporation and a certificate of merger for each constituent other business entity, subject to subdivision (c) of Section 110 and subject to the provisions of subdivision (j), and the several parties thereto shall be one entity. If a domestic reciprocal insurer organized after 1974 to provide medical malpractice insurance is a party to the merger, the agreement of merger or certificate of merger shall not be filed until there has been filed the certificate issued by the Insurance Commissioner approving the merger pursuant to Section 1555 of the Insurance Code. The Secretary of State may certify a copy of the agreement of merger separate from the officers' certificates and certificates of merger attached thereto.

(2) If the surviving entity is an other business entity, and no public benefit corporation, mutual benefit corporation, religious corporation, or corporation organized under the Consumer Cooperative Corporation Law (Part 2 (commencing with Section 12200) of Division 3) is a party to the merger, after required approvals of the merger by each constituent social purpose corporation through approval of the board and any approval of the outstanding shares required by Chapter 10 (commencing with Section 3400) and by the other parties to the merger, the parties to the merger shall file a certificate of merger in the office of, and on a form prescribed by, the Secretary of State. The certificate of merger shall be executed and acknowledged by each constituent domestic and foreign social purpose corporation by its chairperson of the board, president, or a vice president and also by its secretary or an assistant secretary and by each domestic constituent limited liability company by all managers of the limited liability company, unless a lesser number is specified in its articles of organization or operating agreement, and by each domestic constituent limited partnership by all general partners, unless a lesser number is provided in its certificate of limited partnership or partnership agreement, and by each domestic constituent general partnership by two partners, unless a lesser number is provided in its partnership agreement, and by each foreign constituent limited liability company by one or more managers and by each foreign constituent general partnership or foreign constituent limited partnership by one or more general partners, and by each constituent reciprocal insurer by the chairperson of the board, president, or vice president, and by the secretary or assistant secretary, or, if a constituent reciprocal insurer has not appointed those officers, by the chairperson of the board, president, or vice president, and by the secretary or assistant secretary of the constituent reciprocal insurer's attorney-in-fact. The certificate of merger shall be signed by each other party to the merger by those persons required or authorized to execute the certificate of merger by the laws under which that party is organized, specifying for that party the provision of law or other basis for the authority of the signing persons. The certificate of merger shall set forth all of the following:

(A) The name, place of incorporation or organization, and the Secretary of State's file number, if any, of each party to the merger, separately identifying the disappearing parties and the surviving party.

(B) If the approval of the outstanding shares of a constituent social purpose corporation was required by Chapter 10 (commencing with Section 3400), a statement setting forth the total number of outstanding shares of each class entitled to vote on the merger and that the principal terms of the agreement of merger were approved by a vote of the number of shares of each class entitled to vote and the percentage vote required of each class.

(C) The future effective date or time, not more than 90 days subsequent to the date of filing of the merger, if the merger is not to be effective upon the filing of the certificate of merger with the Secretary of State.

(D) A statement, by each party to the merger that is a domestic corporation not organized under this division, a foreign corporation or foreign other business entity, or an other business entity, of the statutory or other basis under which that party is authorized by the laws under which it is organized to effect the merger.

(E) Any other information required to be stated in the certificate of merger by the laws under which each respective party to the merger is organized, including, if a domestic limited liability company is a party to the merger, subdivision (a) of Section 17552, if a domestic partnership is a party to the merger, subdivision (b) of Section 16915, and, if a domestic limited partnership is a party to the merger, subdivision (a) of Section 15911.14.

(F) Any other details or provisions that may be desired. Unless a future effective date or time is provided in a certificate of merger, in which event the merger shall be effective at that future effective date or time, a merger shall be effective upon the filing of the certificate of merger with the Secretary of State and the several parties thereto shall be one entity. The surviving other business entity shall keep a copy of the agreement of merger at its principal place of business which, for purposes of this subdivision, shall be the office referred to in Section 17057 if a domestic limited liability company, at the business address specified in paragraph (5) of subdivision (a) of Section 17552 if a foreign limited liability company, at the office referred to in subdivision (a) of Section 16403 if a domestic general partnership, at the business address specified in subdivision (f) of Section 16911 if a foreign partnership, at the office referred to in subdivision (a) of Section 15901.14 if a domestic limited partnership, or at the business address specified in paragraph (5) of subdivision (a) of Section 15911.14 if a foreign limited partnership. Upon the request of a holder of equity securities of a party to the merger, a person with authority to do so on behalf of the surviving other business entity shall promptly deliver to that holder, a copy of the agreement of merger. A waiver by that holder of the rights provided in the foregoing sentence shall be unenforceable. If a domestic reciprocal insurer organized after 1974 to provide medical malpractice insurance is a party to the merger the agreement of merger or certificate of merger shall not be filed until there has been filed the certificate issued by the Insurance Commissioner approving the merger in accordance with Section 1555 of the Insurance Code.

(h)

(**1**) A copy of an agreement of merger certified on or after the effective date by an official having custody thereof has the same force in evidence as the original and, except as against the state, is conclusive evidence of the performance of all conditions precedent to the merger, the existence on the effective date of the surviving party to the merger, and the performance of the conditions necessary to the adoption of any amendment to the articles, if applicable, contained in the agreement of merger.

(**2**) For all purposes for a merger in which the surviving entity is a domestic other business entity and the filing of a certificate of merger is required by paragraph (2) of subdivision (g), a copy of the certificate of merger duly certified by the Secretary of State is conclusive evidence of the merger of the constituent corporations, either by themselves or together with the other parties to the merger, into the surviving other business entity.

(i)

(**1**) Upon a merger pursuant to this section, the separate existences of the disappearing parties to the merger cease and the surviving party to the merger shall succeed, without other transfer, to all the rights and property of each of the disappearing parties to the merger and shall be subject to all the debts and liabilities of each in the same manner as if the surviving party to the merger had itself incurred them.

(**2**) All rights of creditors and all liens upon the property of each of the constituent social purpose corporations and other parties to the merger shall be preserved unimpaired, provided that those liens upon property of a disappearing party shall be limited to the property affected thereby immediately prior to the time the merger is effective.

(**3**) Any action or proceeding pending by or against any disappearing social purpose corporation or disappearing party to the merger may be prosecuted to judgment, which shall bind the surviving party, or the surviving party may be proceeded against or substituted in its place.

(4) Nothing in this section shall be construed to affect the liability a general partner of a disappearing limited partnership or general partnership may have in connection with the debts and liabilities of the disappearing limited partnership or general partnership existing prior to the time the merger is effective.

(j)

(1) The merger of domestic social purpose corporations with foreign corporations or foreign other business entities in a merger in which one or more other business entities is a party shall comply with subdivision (a) and this subdivision.

(2) If the surviving party is a domestic social purpose corporation or domestic other business entity, the merger proceedings with respect to that party and any domestic disappearing social purpose corporation shall conform to the provisions of this section. If the surviving party is a foreign corporation or foreign other business entity, then, subject to the requirements of subdivision (c), Section 407, Chapter 10 (commencing with Section 3400), and Chapter 13 (commencing with Section 1300) of Division 1, and, if applicable, corresponding provisions of the Nonprofit Corporation Law (Division 2 (commencing with Section 5002)) or the Consumer Cooperative Corporation Law (Part 2 (commencing with Section 12200) of Division 3), with respect to any domestic constituent corporations, Chapter 13 (commencing with Section 17600) of Title 2.5 with respect to any domestic constituent limited liability companies, Article 6 (commencing with Section 16601) of Chapter 5 of Title 2 with respect to any domestic constituent general partnerships, and Article 11.5 (commencing with Section 15911.20) of Chapter 5.5 of Title 2 with respect to any domestic constituent limited partnerships, the merger proceedings may be in accordance with the laws of the state or place of incorporation or organization of the surviving party.

(3) If the surviving party is a domestic social purpose corporation or domestic other business entity, the certificate of merger or the agreement of merger with attachments shall be filed as provided in subdivision (g) and thereupon, subject to subdivision (c) of Section 110 or paragraph (2) of subdivision (g), as applicable, the merger shall be effective as to each domestic constituent social purpose corporation and domestic constituent other business entity.

(4) If the surviving party is a foreign corporation or foreign other business entity, the merger shall become effective in accordance with the law of the jurisdiction in which the surviving party is organized, but, except as provided in paragraph (5), the merger shall be effective as to any domestic disappearing social purpose corporation as of the time of effectiveness in the foreign jurisdiction upon the filing in this state of a copy of the agreement of merger with an officers' certificate of each constituent foreign and domestic social purpose corporation and a certificate of merger of each constituent other business entity attached, which officers' certificates and certificates of merger shall conform to the requirements of paragraph (1) of subdivision (g). If one or more domestic other business entities is a disappearing party in a merger pursuant to this subdivision in which a foreign other business entity is the surviving entity, a certificate of merger required by the laws under which that domestic other business entity is organized, including subdivision (a) of Section 15911.14, subdivision (b) of Section 16915, or subdivision (a) of Section 17552, as is applicable, shall also be filed at the same time as the filing of the agreement of merger.

(5) If the date of the filing in this state pursuant to this subdivision is more than six months after the time of the effectiveness in the foreign jurisdiction, or if the powers of a domestic disappearing social purpose corporation are suspended at the time of effectiveness in the foreign jurisdiction, the merger shall be effective as to the domestic disappearing social purpose corporation as of the date of filing in this state.

(6) In a merger described in paragraph (3) or (4), each foreign disappearing social purpose corporation that is qualified for the transaction of intrastate business shall by virtue of the filing pursuant to this subdivision, subject to subdivision (c) of Section 110, automatically surrender its right to transact intrastate business in this state. The filing of the agreement of merger or certificate of merger, as is applicable, pursuant to this subdivision, by a disappearing foreign other business entity registered for the transaction of intrastate business in this state shall, by virtue of that filing, subject to subdivision (c) of Section 110, automatically cancel the registration for that foreign other business entity, without the necessity of the filing of a certificate of cancellation.

Ca. Corp. Code § 3203
Amended by Stats 2014 ch 694 (SB 1301),s 54, eff. 1/1/2015.
Added by Stats 2011 ch 740 (SB 201),s 12, eff. 1/1/2012.

Chapter 9 - CONVERSIONS

Section 3300 - Definitions

For purposes of this chapter, the following definitions shall apply:
(a) "Converted social purpose corporation" means a social purpose corporation that results from a conversion of an other business entity or a foreign other business entity or a foreign corporation pursuant to Section 3307.
(b) "Converted entity" means a domestic other business entity that results from a conversion of a social purpose corporation under this chapter.
(c) "Converting social purpose corporation" means a social purpose corporation that converts into a domestic other business entity pursuant to this chapter.
(d) "Converting entity" means an other business entity or a foreign other business entity or foreign corporation that converts into a social purpose corporation pursuant to Section 3307.
(e) "Domestic other business entity" has the meaning provided in Section 167.7.

(f) "Foreign other business entity" has the meaning provided in Section 171.07.

(g) "Other business entity" has the meaning provided in Section 174.5.

  Ca. Corp. Code § 3300

Amended by Stats 2014 ch 694 (SB 1301),s 55, eff. 1/1/2015.

Added by Stats 2011 ch 740 (SB 201),s 12, eff. 1/1/2012.

Section 3301 - Conversion into domestic other business entity

(a) A social purpose corporation may be converted into a domestic other business entity pursuant to this chapter if, pursuant to the proposed conversion, each of the following conditions is met:

  (1) Each share of the same class or series of the converting social purpose corporation shall, unless all the shareholders of the class or series consent, be treated equally with respect to any cash, rights, securities, or other property to be received by, or any obligations or restrictions to be imposed on, the holder of that share.

  (2) The conversion is approved by an affirmative vote of at least two-thirds of the outstanding shares of each class, or a greater vote if required in the articles, regardless of whether that class is entitled to vote thereon by the provisions of the articles.

  (3) Nonredeemable common shares of the converting social purpose corporation shall be converted only into nonredeemable equity securities of the converted entity unless all of the shareholders of the class consent.

  (4) Paragraph (1) shall not restrict the ability of the shareholders of a converting social purpose corporation to appoint one or more managers, if the converted entity is a limited liability company, or one or more general partners, if the converted entity is a limited partnership, in the plan of conversion or in the converted entity's governing documents.

(b) Notwithstanding subdivision (a), the conversion of a social purpose corporation into a domestic other business entity may be effected only if both of the following conditions are met:

  (1) The law under which the converted entity will exist expressly permits the formation of that entity pursuant to a conversion.

  (2) The social purpose corporation complies with any and all other requirements of any other law that applies to conversion to the converted entity.

  Ca. Corp. Code § 3301

Amended by Stats 2014 ch 694 (SB 1301),s 56, eff. 1/1/2015.

Added by Stats 2011 ch 740 (SB 201),s 12, eff. 1/1/2012.

Section 3302 - Plan of conversion

(a) A social purpose corporation that desires to convert to a domestic other business entity shall approve a plan of conversion. The plan of conversion shall state all of the following:

(1) The terms and conditions of the conversion.

(2) The jurisdiction of the organization of the converted entity and of the converting social purpose corporation and the name of the converted entity after conversion.

(3) The manner of converting the shares of each of the shareholders of the converting social purpose corporation into securities of, or interests in, the converted entity.

(4) The provisions of the governing documents for the converted entity, including the articles and bylaws, partnership agreement or limited liability company articles of organization and operating agreement, to which the holders of interests in the converted entity are to be bound.

(5) Any other details or provisions that are required by the laws under which the converted entity is organized, or that are desired by the converting social purpose corporation.

(b) The plan of conversion shall be approved by the board of the converting social purpose corporation, and the principal terms of the plan of the conversion shall be approved by at least two-thirds of the outstanding shares of each class, or a greater vote if required in the articles, regardless of whether that class is entitled to vote thereon by the provisions of the articles of the converting social purpose corporation. The approval of at least two-thirds of the outstanding shares may be given before or after approval by the board. If the plan is approved, shareholders with dissenting shares, as defined in subdivision (b) of Section 1300, may exercise dissenters' rights pursuant to Section 3305 and Chapter 13 (commencing with Section 1300) of Division 1.

(c) If the social purpose corporation is converting into a general or limited partnership or into a limited liability company, then in addition to the approval of the shareholders set forth in subdivision (b), the plan of conversion shall be approved by each shareholder who will become a general partner or manager, as applicable, of the converted entity pursuant to the plan of conversion unless the shareholders have dissenters' rights pursuant to Section 3305 and Chapter 13 (commencing with Section 1300) of Division 1.

(d) Upon the effectiveness of the conversion, all shareholders of the converting social purpose corporation, except those that exercise dissenters' rights as provided in Section 3305 and Chapter 13 (commencing with Section 1300) of Division 1, shall be deemed parties to any agreement or agreements constituting the governing documents for the converted entity adopted as part of the plan of conversion, regardless of whether a shareholder has executed the plan of conversion or those governing documents for the converted entity. Any adoption of governing documents made pursuant thereto shall be effective at the effective time or date of the conversion.

(e) Notwithstanding its prior approval by the board and the outstanding shares, or either of them, a plan of conversion may be amended before the conversion takes effect if the amendment is approved by the board and, if it changes any of the principal terms of the plan of conversion, by the shareholders of the converting social purpose corporation in the same manner and to the same extent as was required for approval of the original plan of conversion.

(f) A plan of conversion may be abandoned by the board of a converting social purpose corporation, or by the shareholders of a converting social purpose corporation if the abandonment is approved by the outstanding shares, in each case in the same manner as required for approval of the plan of conversion, subject to the contractual rights of third parties, at any time before the conversion is effective.

(g) The converted entity shall keep the plan of conversion at the principal place of business of the converted entity if the converted entity is a domestic partnership, or at the office at which records are to be kept under Section 15901.14 if the converted entity is a domestic limited partnership, or at the office at which records are to be kept under Section 17701.13 if the converted entity is a domestic limited liability company. Upon the request of a shareholder of a converting social purpose corporation, the authorized person on behalf of the converted entity shall promptly deliver to the shareholder, at the expense of the converted entity, a copy of the plan of conversion. A waiver by a shareholder of the rights provided in this subdivision shall be unenforceable.

Ca. Corp. Code § 3302

Amended by Stats 2014 ch 694 (SB 1301),s 57, eff. 1/1/2015.
Added by Stats 2011 ch 740 (SB 201),s 12, eff. 1/1/2012.

Section 3303 - Filing of documents

(a) After the approval, as provided in Section 3302, of a plan of conversion by the board and the outstanding shares of a social purpose corporation converting into a domestic other business entity, the converting social purpose corporation shall cause the filing of all documents required by law to effect the conversion and create the converted entity, which documents shall include a certificate of conversion or a statement of conversion as required by Section 3304, and the conversion shall thereupon be effective.

(b) A copy of the statement of partnership authority, certificate of limited partnership, or articles of organization complying with Section 3304, duly certified by the Secretary of State on or after the effective date, shall be conclusive evidence of the conversion of the social purpose corporation.

Ca. Corp. Code § 3303

Amended by Stats 2014 ch 694 (SB 1301),s 58, eff. 1/1/2015.

Added by Stats 2011 ch 740 (SB 201),s 12, eff. 1/1/2012.

Section 3304 - Statement of conversion; certificate of conversion

(a) To convert a social purpose corporation:

(1) If the social purpose corporation is converting into a domestic limited partnership, a statement of conversion shall be completed on the certificate of limited partnership for the converted entity.

(2) If the social purpose corporation is converting into a domestic partnership, a statement of conversion shall be completed on the statement of partnership authority for the converted entity, or if no statement of partnership authority is filed, then a certificate of conversion shall be filed separately.

(3) If the social purpose corporation is converting into a domestic limited liability company, a statement of conversion shall be completed on the articles of organization for the converted entity.

(b) Any statement or certificate of conversion of a converting social purpose corporation shall be executed and acknowledged by those officers of the converting social purpose corporation as would be required to sign an officers' certificate, and shall set forth all of the following:

(1) The name and the Secretary of State's file number of the converting social purpose corporation.

(2) A statement of the total number of outstanding shares of each class entitled to vote on the conversion, that the principal terms of the plan of conversion were approved by a vote of the number of shares of each class which equaled or exceeded the vote required under Section 3302, specifying each class entitled to vote and the percentage vote required of each class.

(3) The name, form, and jurisdiction of organization of the converted entity.

(4) The name and street address of the converted entity's agent for service of process. If a corporation qualified under Section 1505 is designated as the agent, no address for it shall be set forth.

(c) The certificate of conversion shall be on a form prescribed by the Secretary of State.

(d) The filing with the Secretary of State of a statement of conversion on an organizational document or a certificate of conversion as set forth in subdivision (a) shall have the effect of the filing of a certificate of dissolution by the converting social purpose corporation and no converting social purpose corporation that has made the filing is required to file a certificate of election under Section 1901 or a certificate of dissolution under Section 1905 as a result of that conversion.

(e) Upon the effectiveness of a conversion pursuant to this chapter, a converted entity that is a domestic partnership, domestic limited partnership, or domestic limited liability company shall be deemed to have assumed the liability of the converting social purpose corporation to prepare and file or cause to be prepared and filed all tax and information returns otherwise required of the converting social purpose corporation under the Corporation Tax Law (Part 11 (commencing with Section 23001) of Division 2 of the Revenue and Taxation Code) and to pay any tax liability determined to be due pursuant to that law.

Ca. Corp. Code § 3304
Amended by Stats 2014 ch 834 (SB 1041),s 9.5, eff. 1/1/2015.
Amended by Stats 2014 ch 694 (SB 1301),s 59, eff. 1/1/2015.
Added by Stats 2011 ch 740 (SB 201),s 12, eff. 1/1/2012.

Section 3305 - Rights of shareholders of converting social purpose corporation

The shareholders with dissenting rights, as defined in subdivision (b) of Section 1300, of a converting social purpose corporation shall have all of the rights under Chapter 13 (commencing with Section 1300) of Division 1 of the shareholders of a corporation involved in a reorganization requiring the approval of its outstanding shares, and the converting social purpose corporation shall have all of the obligations under Chapter 13 (commencing with Section 1300) of Division 1 of a corporation involved in the reorganization. Solely for purposes of applying the provisions of Chapter 13 (commencing with Section 1300) of Division 1, and not for purposes of this chapter, a conversion pursuant to Section 3301 or 3307 shall be deemed to constitute a reorganization.

Ca. Corp. Code § 3305
Amended by Stats 2014 ch 694 (SB 1301),s 60, eff. 1/1/2015.
Added by Stats 2011 ch 740 (SB 201),s 12, eff. 1/1/2012.

Section 3306 - Fee

Notwithstanding any other provision of law, the Secretary of State shall charge an entity a fee not to exceed one hundred fifty dollars ($150) for its conversion made under this chapter.

Ca. Corp. Code § 3306
Added by Stats 2011 ch 740 (SB 201),s 12, eff. 1/1/2012.

Section 3307 - Conversion to social purpose corporation

(a) An other business entity or a foreign other business entity or a foreign corporation may be converted into a social purpose corporation pursuant to this chapter only if the converting entity is authorized by the laws under which it is organized to effect the conversion.

(b) An other business entity or a foreign other business entity or a foreign corporation that desires to convert into a social purpose corporation shall approve a plan of conversion or other instrument as is required to be approved to effect the conversion pursuant to the laws under which that entity is organized.

(c) The conversion of an other business entity or a foreign other business entity or a foreign corporation shall be approved by the number or percentage of the partners, members, shareholders, or other holders of interest of the converting entity that is required by the laws under which that entity is organized, or a greater or lesser percentage as may be set forth in the converting entity's partnership agreement, articles of organization, operating agreement, articles of incorporation, or other governing document in accordance with applicable laws.

(d) The conversion by an other business entity or a foreign other business entity or a foreign corporation shall be effective under this chapter upon the filing with the Secretary of State of the articles of incorporation of the converted corporation, containing a statement of conversion that complies with subdivision (e).

(e) A statement of conversion of an entity converting into a social purpose corporation pursuant to this chapter shall set forth all of the following:

(1) The name, form, and jurisdiction of organization of the converting entity.

(2) The Secretary of State's file number, if any, of the converting entity.

(3) If the converting entity is a foreign other business entity or a foreign corporation, the statement of conversion shall contain the following:

(A) A statement that the converting entity is authorized to effect the conversion by the laws under which it is organized.

(B) A statement that the converting entity has approved a plan of conversion or other instrument as is required to be approved to effect the conversion pursuant to the laws under which the converting entity is organized.

(C) A statement that the conversion has been approved by the number or percentage of the partners, members, shareholders, or other holders of interest of the converting entity that is required by the laws under which that entity is organized, or a greater or lesser percentage as may be set forth in the converting entity's partnership agreement, articles of organization, operating agreement, articles of incorporation, or other governing document in accordance with applicable laws.

(f) The filing with the Secretary of State of articles of incorporation containing a statement pursuant to subdivision (e) shall have the effect of the filing of a certificate of cancellation by a converting foreign limited liability company or foreign limited partnership, and no converting foreign limited liability company or foreign limited partnership that has made the filing is required to file a certificate of cancellation under Section 17708.06 or 15909.07 as a result of that conversion. If a converting entity is a foreign corporation qualified to transact business in this state, the foreign corporation shall, by virtue of the filing, automatically surrender its right to transact intrastate business.

Ca. Corp. Code § 3307

Added by Stats 2014 ch 694 (SB 1301),s 61, eff. 1/1/2015.

Chapter 10 - REORGANIZATIONS

Section 3400 - Approval of reorganization or share exchange tender offer

A reorganization or a share exchange tender offer shall be approved by the board of all of the following:

(a) Each constituent social purpose corporation in a merger reorganization.

(b) The acquiring social purpose corporation in an exchange reorganization.

(c) The acquiring social purpose corporation and the social purpose corporation whose property and assets are acquired in a sale-of-assets reorganization.

(d) The acquiring social purpose corporation in a share exchange tender offer.

(e) The social purpose corporation in control of any constituent or acquiring domestic or foreign social purpose corporation or other business entity under subdivision (a), (b), or (c) and whose equity securities are issued, transferred, or exchanged in the reorganization, hereafter a "parent party."

Ca. Corp. Code § 3400

Amended by Stats 2014 ch 694 (SB 1301),s 62, eff. 1/1/2015.
Added by Stats 2011 ch 740 (SB 201),s 12, eff. 1/1/2012.

Section 3401 - Approval of principal terms of reorganization

(a) The principal terms of a reorganization shall be approved by the outstanding shares of each class of each social purpose corporation the approval of whose board is required under Section 3400, except as provided in subdivision (b) and except that, unless otherwise provided in the articles, no approval of any class of outstanding preferred shares of the surviving or acquiring social purpose corporation or parent party shall be required if the rights, preferences, privileges, and restrictions granted to or imposed upon that class of shares remain unchanged, subject to the provisions of subdivision (c). For the purpose of this subdivision, two classes of common shares differing only as to voting rights shall be considered as a single class of shares.

(b) No approval of the outstanding shares is required by subdivision (a) if the social purpose corporation, or its shareholders immediately before the reorganization, or both, shall own, immediately after the reorganization, equity securities, other than any warrant or right to subscribe to or purchase those equity securities, of the surviving or acquiring social purpose corporation or a parent party possessing more than five-sixths of the voting power of the surviving or acquiring social purpose corporation or parent party. In making the determination of ownership by the shareholders of a social purpose corporation, immediately after the reorganization, of equity securities pursuant to the preceding sentence, equity securities that they owned immediately before the reorganization as shareholders of another party to the transaction shall be disregarded. For the purpose of this section, the voting power of a social purpose corporation shall be calculated by assuming the conversion of all equity securities convertible, immediately or at some future time, into shares entitled to vote but not assuming the exercise of any warrant or right to subscribe to or purchase those shares.

(c) Notwithstanding subdivisions (a) and (b), the principal terms of a reorganization shall be approved by the outstanding shares of the surviving social purpose corporation in a merger reorganization, as otherwise required by Chapter 10 (commencing with Section 3400), if any amendment is made to its articles that would otherwise require that approval.

(d) Notwithstanding subdivisions (a) and (b), the principal terms of a reorganization shall be approved by the affirmative vote of at least two-thirds of each class, or a greater vote if required in the articles, of the outstanding shares of any class of a social purpose corporation that is a party to a merger or sale-of-assets reorganization if holders of shares of that class receive shares of the surviving or acquiring social purpose corporation or parent party having different rights, preferences, privileges, or restrictions than those surrendered. Shares in a foreign corporation received in exchange for shares in a domestic social purpose corporation shall be deemed to have different rights, preferences, privileges, and restrictions within the meaning of the preceding sentence.

(e) Notwithstanding subdivisions (a) and (b), the principal terms of a reorganization shall be approved by the affirmative vote of at least two-thirds of each class, or a greater vote if required in the articles, of the outstanding shares of any social purpose corporation that is a close social purpose corporation if the reorganization would result in the holders receiving shares or other interests of a corporation or other business entity that is not a close social purpose corporation. The articles may provide for a lesser vote, but not less than a majority of the outstanding shares of each class.

(f) Notwithstanding subdivisions (a) and (b), the principal terms of a reorganization shall be approved by a vote of at least two-thirds of the outstanding shares of each class, or a greater vote if required in the articles, of a social purpose corporation that is a party to a merger reorganization, regardless of whether that class is entitled to vote thereon by the provisions of the articles, if holders of shares of that class receive interests of a surviving other business entity in the merger that is not a social purpose corporation, or receive interests of a surviving social purpose corporation the articles of incorporation of which specify a materially different purpose as part of the reorganization.

(g) Notwithstanding subdivisions (a) and (b), the principal terms of a reorganization shall be approved by all shareholders of any class or series if, as a result of the reorganization, the holders of that class or series become personally liable for any obligations of a party to the reorganization, unless all holders of that class or series have the dissenters' rights provided in Chapter 13 (commencing with Section 1300) of Division 1.

(h) Any approval required by this section may be given before or after the approval by the board. Notwithstanding approval required by this section, the board may abandon the proposed reorganization without further action by the shareholders, subject to the contractual rights, if any, of third parties.

Ca. Corp. Code § 3401

Amended by Stats 2014 ch 694 (SB 1301),s 63, eff. 1/1/2015.

Added by Stats 2011 ch 740 (SB 201),s 12, eff. 1/1/2012.

Chapter 11 - RECORDS AND REPORTS

Section 3500 - Annual shareholders report

(a) The board of a social purpose corporation shall cause an annual report to be sent to the shareholders not later than 120 days after the close of the fiscal year. The annual report shall contain (1) a balance sheet as of the end of that fiscal year and an income statement and a statement of cashflows for that fiscal year, accompanied by any report thereon of independent accountants or, if there is no report, the certificate of an authorized officer of the social purpose corporation that the statements were prepared without audit from the books and records of the corporation, and (2) the information required by subdivision (b).

(b) The board shall cause to be provided with the annual report, a management discussion and analysis (special purpose MD&A) concerning the social purpose corporation's stated purpose or purposes as set forth in its articles pursuant to paragraph (2) of subdivision (b) of Section 2602, and, to the extent consistent with reasonable confidentiality requirements, shall cause the special purpose MD&A to be made publicly available by posting it on the social purpose corporation's Internet Web site or providing it through similar electronic means. The special purpose MD&A shall include the information specified in this subdivision and any other information that the social purpose corporation's officers and directors believe to be reasonably necessary or appropriate to an understanding of the social purpose corporation's efforts in connection with its special purpose or purposes. The special purpose MD&A shall also include the following information:

(1) Identification and discussion of the overall objectives of the social purpose corporation relating to its special purpose or purposes, and an identification and explanation of any changes made in those special purpose objectives during the fiscal year.

(2) Identification and discussion of the material actions taken by the social purpose corporation during the fiscal year to achieve its special purpose objectives, the impact of those actions, including the causal relationships between the actions and the reported outcomes, and the extent to which those actions achieved the special purpose objectives for the fiscal year.

(3) Identification and discussion of material actions, including the intended impact of those actions, that the social purpose corporation expects to take in the short term and long term with respect to achievement of its special purpose objectives.

(4) A description of the process for selecting, and an identification and description of, the financial, operating, and other measures used by the social purpose corporation during the fiscal year for evaluating its performance in achieving its special purpose objectives, including an explanation of why the social purpose corporation selected those measures and identification and discussion of the nature and rationale for any material changes in those measures made during the fiscal year.

(5) Identification and discussion of any material operating and capital expenditures incurred by the social purpose corporation during the fiscal year in furtherance of achieving the special purpose objectives, a good faith estimate of any additional material operating or capital expenditures the social purpose corporation expects to incur over the next three fiscal years in order to achieve its special purpose objectives, and other material expenditures of resources incurred by the social purpose corporation during the fiscal year, including employee time, in furtherance of achieving the special purpose objectives, including a discussion of the extent to which that capital or use of other resources serves purposes other than and in addition to furthering the achievement of the special purpose objectives.

(c) Except as may otherwise be excused pursuant to subdivision (h) of Section 1501.5, the reports specified in subdivisions (a) and (b) shall be sent to the shareholders at least 15 days, or, if sent by bulk mail, 35 days, prior to the annual meeting of shareholders to be held during the next fiscal year. This requirement shall not limit the requirement for holding an annual meeting as required by Section 600.

(d) If no annual report for the last fiscal year has been sent to shareholders, the social purpose corporation shall, upon the written request of any shareholder made more than 120 days after the end of that fiscal year, deliver or mail to the person making the request within 30 days following the request, the statements required by subdivisions (a) and (b) for that fiscal year.

(e) A shareholder or shareholders holding at least 5 percent of the outstanding shares of any class of a social purpose corporation may make a written request to the social purpose corporation for an income statement of the social purpose corporation for the three-month, six-month, or nine-month period of the current fiscal year ended more than 30 days prior to the date of the request and a balance sheet of the social purpose corporation as at the end of that period and, in addition, if no annual report for the most recent fiscal year has been sent to the shareholders, the statements referred to in subdivisions (a) and (b) relating to that fiscal year. The statements shall be delivered or mailed to the person making the request within 30 days following the request. A copy of the statements shall be kept on file in the principal office of the social purpose corporation for 12 months and shall be exhibited at all reasonable times to any shareholder demanding an examination of the statements or a copy shall be mailed to the shareholder. The quarterly income statements and balance sheets referred to in this subdivision shall be accompanied by the report thereon, if any, of any independent accountants engaged by the social purpose corporation or the certificate of an authorized officer of the social purpose corporation that the financial statements were prepared without audit from the books and records of the social purpose corporation.

Ca. Corp. Code § 3500

Amended by Stats 2014 ch 694 (SB 1301),s 64, eff. 1/1/2015.

Added by Stats 2011 ch 740 (SB 201),s 12, eff. 1/1/2012.

Section 3501 - Special purpose current report

(a) The board shall cause a special purpose current report to be sent to the shareholders not later than 45 days following the occurrence of any one or more of the events specified in subdivision (b) or (c), and, to the extent consistent with reasonable confidentiality requirements, shall cause the special purpose current report to be made publicly available by posting it on the social purpose corporation's Internet Web site or providing it through similar electronic means.

(b) Unless previously reported in the most recent annual report, the special purpose current report shall identify and discuss, in reasonable detail, any expenditure or group of related or planned expenditures, excluding compensation of officers and directors, made in furtherance of the special purpose objectives, whether an operating expenditure, a capital expenditure, or some other expenditure of corporate resources, including, but not limited to, employee time, whether the expenditure was direct or indirect, and whether the expenditure was categorized as overhead or otherwise where the expenditure has or is likely to have a material adverse impact on the social purpose corporation's results of operations or financial condition for a quarterly or annual fiscal period.

(c) Unless previously reported in the most recent annual report, the special purpose current report shall identify and discuss, in reasonable detail, any decision by the board or action by management to do either of the following:

(1) Withhold expenditures or a group of related or planned expenditures, whether temporarily or permanently, that were to have been made in furtherance of the special purpose as contemplated in the most recent annual report, whether those planned expenditures were an operating expenditure, a capital expenditure, or some other expenditure of corporate resources, including, but not limited to, employee time, whether the planned expenditure was direct or indirect, and whether the planned expenditure to be made would have been categorized as overhead or otherwise, in any case, where the planned expenditure was likely to have had a material positive impact on the social purpose corporation's impact in furtherance of its special purpose objectives, as contemplated in the most recent annual report.

(2) Determine that the special purpose has been satisfied or should no longer be pursued, whether temporarily or permanently.

Ca. Corp. Code § 3501

Amended by Stats 2014 ch 694 (SB 1301),s 65, eff. 1/1/2015.

Added by Stats 2011 ch 740 (SB 201),s 12, eff. 1/1/2012.

Section 3502 - Detailing or itemization of every expenditure or action not required; liability of officers and directors

(a) Nothing contained in subdivision (b) of Section 3500 or Section 3501 shall require a detailing or itemization of every relevant expenditure incurred, or planned or action taken or planned, by the corporation. Management and the board shall use their discretion in providing that information, including the reasonable detail that a reasonable investor would consider important in understanding the corporation's objectives, actions, impacts, measures, rationale, and results of operations as they relate to the nature and achievement of the special purpose objectives.

(b) Where best practices emerge for providing the information required by subdivision (b) of Section 3500 or Section 3501, use of those best practices shall create a presumption that the social purpose corporation caused all the information required by those provisions to be provided. This presumption can only be rebutted by showing that the reporting contained either a misstatement of a material fact or omission of a material fact.

(c) Notwithstanding subdivision (b) of Section 3500 and Section 3501, under no circumstances shall the social purpose corporation be required to provide information that would result in a violation of state or federal securities laws or other applicable laws.

(d) The social purpose corporation and its officers and directors are expressly excluded from liability for any and all forward looking statements supplied in the report required by subdivision (b) of Section 3500 and Section 3501, so long as those statements are supplied in good faith. Statements are deemed to be forward looking as that term is defined in the federal securities laws.

(e) The special purpose MD&A and any special purpose current report shall be written in plain English and shall be provided in an efficient and understandable manner, avoiding repetition and disclosure of immaterial information.

(f) Unless otherwise provided by the articles or bylaws, and if approved by the board of directors, the reports specified in Sections 3500 and 3501 and any accompanying material sent pursuant to this section may be sent by electronic transmission by the corporation.

(g) The financial statements of any social purpose corporation with fewer than 100 holders of record of its shares, determined as provided in Section 605, required to be furnished by Sections 3500 and 3501 are not required to be prepared in conformity with generally accepted accounting principles if they reasonably set forth the assets and liabilities and the income and expense of the social purpose corporation and disclose the accounting basis used in their preparation.

(h) The requirements described in Section 3500 shall be satisfied if a corporation with an outstanding class of securities registered under Section 12 of the Securities Exchange Act of 1934 both complies with Section 240.14a-16 of Title 17 of the Code of Federal Regulations, as amended from time to time, with respect to the obligation of a corporation to furnish an annual report to shareholders pursuant to Section 240.14a-3(b) of Title 17 of the Code of Federal Regulations, and includes the information required by subdivision (b) of Section 3500 in the annual report.

(i) The requirements described in Section 3501 shall be satisfied if a corporation with an outstanding class of securities registered under Section 12 of the Securities Exchange Act of 1934 both complies with Section 240.13a-13 of Title 17 of the Code of Federal Regulations, as amended from time to time, with respect to the obligation of a corporation to furnish a quarterly report to shareholders, and includes the information required by subdivision (b) of Section 3501 in the quarterly report.

(j) In addition to the penalties provided for in this division, the superior court of the proper county shall enforce the duty of making and mailing or delivering the information and financial statements required by Sections 3500 and 3501 and, for good cause shown, may extend the time therefor.

(k) In any action or proceeding with respect to Section 3500 or 3501, if the court finds the failure of the social purpose corporation to comply with the requirements of those sections to have been without justification, the court may award an amount sufficient to reimburse the shareholder for the reasonable expenses incurred by the shareholder, including attorney's fees, in connection with the action or proceeding.

(l) Section 3500 and Section 3501 apply to any domestic social purpose corporation and also to a foreign social purpose corporation having its principal office in California or customarily holding meetings of its board in this state.

(m) All reports and notices required by Section 3500 and Section 3501 shall be maintained by the social purpose corporation, in an electronic form for a period of not less than 10 years.

Ca. Corp. Code § 3502

Amended by Stats 2022 ch 617 (SB 1202),s 42, eff. 1/1/2023.

Amended by Stats 2014 ch 694 (SB 1301),s 66, eff. 1/1/2015.

Added by Stats 2011 ch 740 (SB 201),s 12, eff. 1/1/2012.

Section 3503 - Joint and several liability

Any officers, directors, employees, or agents of a social purpose corporation who do any of the following shall be liable jointly and severally for all the damages resulting therefrom to the social purpose corporation or any person injured by those actions who relied on those actions or to both:

(a) Make, issue, deliver, or publish any prospectus, report, including the reports required pursuant to Sections 3500 and 3501, circular, certificate, financial statement, balance sheet, public notice, or document respecting the social purpose corporation or its shares, assets, liabilities, capital, dividends, business, earnings, or accounts which is false in any material respect, knowing it to be false, or participate in the making, issuance, delivery, or publication thereof with knowledge that the same is false in a material respect.

(b) Make or cause to be made in the books, minutes, records, or accounts of a social purpose corporation any entry that is false in any material particular knowing it to be false.

(c) Remove, erase, alter, or cancel any entry in any books or records of the social purpose corporation, with intent to deceive.

(d) With respect to the reports required pursuant to subdivision (b) of Section 3500 and Section 3501, omit to state any material fact necessary in order to make the statements contained therein, in light of the circumstances under which those statements were made, not misleading in a material respect, knowing the omission to be misleading.

Ca. Corp. Code § 3503
Amended by Stats 2014 ch 694 (SB 1301),s 67, eff. 1/1/2015.
Added by Stats 2011 ch 740 (SB 201),s 12, eff. 1/1/2012.

Division 2 - NONPROFIT CORPORATION LAW

Section 5000 - Short title

This division shall be known and may be cited as the Nonprofit Corporation Law.

Ca. Corp. Code § 5000
Added by Stats. 1978, Ch. 567.

Section 5001 - Amendment or repeal

This division of the Nonprofit Corporation Law, or any part, chapter, article or section thereof, may at any time be amended or repealed.

Ca. Corp. Code § 5001
Added by Stats. 1978, Ch. 567.

Part 1 - GENERAL PROVISIONS AND DEFINITIONS GOVERNING PARTS 1 THROUGH 5

Section 5002 - Construction

Unless the provisions or the context otherwise requires, the general provisions and definitions set forth in this part govern the construction of this part and of Part 2 (commencing with Section 5110), Part 3 (commencing with Section 7110), Part 4 (commencing with Section 9110), and Part 5 (commencing with Section 9910) of this division.

Ca. Corp. Code § 5002
Added by Stats. 1978, Ch. 567.

Section 5003 - Applicability

(a) The provisions of this part apply to:

(1) Corporations organized under Part 2, Part 3, and Part 4 of this division;

(2) Corporations expressly subject to Part 2, Part 3 or Part 4 of this division pursuant to a particular provision of this division or Division 3 (commencing with Section 12000) or other specific statutory provision;

(3) Corporations which pursuant to the express provisions of Part 1, Division 2 (commencing with Section 9000) in effect immediately prior to January 1, 1980, are subject to the provisions of Part 1 of Division 2 and which, on or after January 1, 1980, are subject to the Nonprofit Public Benefit Corporation Law, the Nonprofit Mutual Benefit Corporation Law or the Nonprofit Religious Corporation Law, pursuant to Section 9912.

(4) Corporations expressly subject to Part 1, Division 2 (commencing with Section 9000) in effect immediately prior to January 1, 1980, pursuant to a particular provision of this division or Division 3 (commencing with Section 12000) or other specific statutory provision in effect immediately prior to January 1, 1980, and which, on or after January 1, 1980, are subject to the Nonprofit Public Benefit Corporation Law, the Nonprofit Mutual Benefit Corporation Law, or the Nonprofit Religious Corporation Law, pursuant to Section 9912; and

(5) Corporations incorporated as permitted by subdivision (d) of Section 9911.
(b) The existence of corporations formed or existing on the date of enactment or reenactment of this part, Part 2, Part 3, Part 4 or Part 5 shall not be affected by the enactment or reenactment of such parts or by any change in the requirements for the formation of corporations or by the amendment or repeal of the laws under which they were formed or created.
(c) Neither the repeals effected by the enactment or reenactment of this part or of Part 2, Part 3, Part 4 or Part 5, nor the amendment thereof shall impair or take away any existing liability or cause of action against any corporation, its members, directors or officers incurred prior to the time of such enactment, reenactment or amendment.
Ca. Corp. Code § 5003
Amended by Stats. 1979, Ch. 724.

Section 5004 - Suing corporation

A corporation may be sued as provided in the Code of Civil Procedure.
Ca. Corp. Code § 5004
Added by Stats. 1978, Ch. 567.

Section 5005 - Attachment of corporate property

Any corporation shall, as a condition of its existence as a corporation, be subject to the provisions of the Code of Civil Procedure authorizing the attachment of corporate property.

Ca. Corp. Code § 5005
Added by Stats. 1978, Ch. 567.

Section 5005.1 - Insurance

(a) Except for a liability that may be insured against pursuant to Division 4 (commencing with Section 3200) of the Labor Code, an authorized corporation may do any of the following:

(1) Insure itself against all or any part of any tort liability.

(2) Insure any employee of the corporation against all or any part of his or her liability for injury resulting from an act or omission in the scope of employment.

(3) Insure any board member, officer, or volunteer of the corporation against any liability that may arise from any act or omission in the scope of participation with the corporation.

(4) Insure itself against any loss arising from physical damage to motor vehicles owned or operated by the corporation.

(5) Insure itself against the loss or damage to property of every kind, including, but not limited to, losses and expenses related to the loss of property.

(b)

(1) The arrangement authorized pursuant to this section shall only be available to an authorized corporation where that corporation has joined with two or more other authorized corporations to provide for the pooling of self-insured claims or losses. The pooling arrangement shall be organized as a nonprofit public benefit corporation pursuant to Part 2 (commencing with Section 5110) and shall not be considered insurance nor be subject to regulation under the Insurance Code.

(2) A pooling arrangement shall include in every application form for membership and every risk pooling contract issued or renewed on or after January 1, 2016, and in boldface 10-point type on the front page, the following notice: "Notice: This risk pooling contract is issued by a pooling arrangement authorized by California Corporations Code Section 5005.1. The pooling arrangement is not subject to all of the insurance laws of the State of California and is not subject to regulation by the

Insurance Commissioner. Insurance guaranty funds are not available to pay claims in the event the risk pool becomes insolvent."

(c) This section does not authorize a corporation organized pursuant to this division to pay for, or to insure, contract, or provide for payment for, any part of a claim or judgment against an employee of the corporation for punitive or exemplary damages.

(d)

(1) Any insurance pool established pursuant to this section shall have initial pooled resources of not less than two hundred fifty thousand dollars ($250,000).

(2) Any insurance pool providing the coverage described in paragraph (5) of subdivision (a) shall do all of the following:

(A) Be organized for the purpose of providing the coverage described in paragraph (1) of subdivision (a) for a period of no less than five years.

(B) Have accumulated net assets of not less than five million dollars ($5,000,000).

(e) All participating corporations in any pool established pursuant to this section are required to agree to pay premiums or make other mandatory financial contributions or commitments necessary to ensure a financially sound risk pool.

(f) For the purpose of this section, an authorized "corporation" means any corporation that meets all of the following criteria:

(1) Is organized chiefly to provide or fund health or human services, but does not include a hospital.

(2) Is exempt from federal income taxation as an organization described in Section 501(c)(3)(c)(3) of the United States Internal Revenue Code.

Ca. Corp. Code § 5005.1
Amended by Stats 2014 ch 556 (SB 1011),s 1, eff. 1/1/2015.

Section 5006 - Fees for filing instruments

The fees of the Secretary of State for filing instruments by or on behalf of corporations are prescribed in Article 3 (commencing with Section 12180) of Chapter 3 of Part 2 of Division 3 of Title 2 of the Government Code.

Ca. Corp. Code § 5006
Added by Stats. 1978, Ch. 567.

Section 5007 - Certificate of correction

Any agreement, certificate or other instrument relating to a domestic corporation, a foreign corporation, or a foreign business corporation filed pursuant to the provisions of this part, Part 2, Part 3, Part 4 or Part 5 may be corrected with respect to any misstatement of fact contained therein, any defect in the execution thereof or any other error or defect contained therein, by filing a certificate of correction entitled "Certificate of Correction of _____ (insert here the title of the agreement, certificate or other instrument to be corrected and name(s) of the corporation or corporations)"; provided, however, that no such certificate of correction shall alter the wording of any resolution which was in fact adopted by the board or the members or delegates or effect a corrected amendment of articles which amendment as so corrected would not in all respects have complied with the requirements of this part, Part 2, Part 3, Part 4 or Part 5 at the time of filing of the agreement, certificate or other instrument being corrected. Such certificate of correction shall be signed and verified or acknowledged as provided in this part with respect to the agreement, certificate or other instrument being corrected. It shall set forth the following:

(a) The name or names of the corporation or corporations.

(b) The date the agreement, certificate or other instrument being corrected was filed.

(c) The provision in the agreement, certificate or other instrument as corrected and, if the execution was defective, wherein it was defective. The filing of the certificate of correction shall not alter the effective time of the agreement, certificate or instrument being corrected, which shall remain as its original effective time, and such filing shall not affect any right or liability accrued or incurred before such filing, except that any right or liability accrued or incurred by reason of the error or defect being corrected shall be extinguished by such filing if the person having such right has not detrimentally relied on the original instrument.

Ca. Corp. Code § 5007

Amended by Stats. 1979, Ch. 724.

Section 5008 - Date of filing

(a) Upon receipt of any instrument by the Secretary of State for filing pursuant to this part, Part 2, Part 3, Part 4 or Part 5, if it conforms to law, it shall be filed by, and in the office of the Secretary of State and the date of filing endorsed thereon. Except for instruments filed pursuant to Section 6210, 8210, or 9660 the date of filing shall be the date the instrument is received by the Secretary of State unless the instrument provides that it is to be withheld from filing until a future date or unless in the judgment of the Secretary of State the filing is intended to be coordinated with the filing of some other corporate document which cannot be filed. The Secretary of State shall file a document as of any requested future date not more than 90 days after its receipt, including a Saturday, Sunday or legal holiday, if the document is received in the Secretary of State's office at least one business day prior to the requested date of filing. An instrument does not fail to conform to law because it is not accompanied by the full filing fee if the unpaid portion of such fee does not exceed the limits established by the policy of the Secretary of State for extending credit in such cases.

(b) If the Secretary of State determines that an instrument submitted for filing or otherwise submitted does not conform to law and returns it to the person submitting it, the instrument may be resubmitted accompanied by a written opinion of a member of the State Bar of California submitting the instrument, or representing the person submitting it, to the effect that the specific provision of the instrument objected to by the Secretary of State does conform to law and stating the points and authorities upon which the opinion is based. The Secretary of State shall rely, with respect to any disputed point of law (other than the application of Section 5122, 7122, or 9122), upon such written opinion in determining whether the instrument conforms to law. The date of filing in such case shall be the date the instrument is received on resubmission.

(c) Any instrument filed with respect to a corporation (other than original articles) may provide that it is to become effective not more than 90 days subsequent to its filing date. In case such a delayed effective date is specified, the instrument may be prevented from becoming effective by a certificate stating that by appropriate corporate action it has been revoked and is null and void, executed in the same manner as the original instrument and filed before the specified effective date. In the case of a merger agreement, such certificate revoking the earlier filing need only be executed on behalf of one of the constituent corporations. If no such revocation certificate is filed, the instrument becomes effective on the date specified.

(d) Any instrument submitted to the Secretary of State for filing pursuant to this part, Part 2, Part 3, Part 4, or Part 5 by a domestic corporation or foreign corporation that is qualified to transact business in California under Section 2105 shall include the entity name and number as they exist on the Secretary of State's records.

Ca. Corp. Code § 5008

Amended by Stats 2020 ch 361 (SB 522),s 4, eff. 1/1/2021.
Amended by Stats 2012 ch 494 (SB 1532),s 11, eff. 1/1/2013.

Section 5008.5 - Cancellation of filing of articles

The Secretary of State may cancel the filing of articles if a check or other remittance accepted in payment of the filing fee or franchise tax is not paid upon presentation. Within 90 days of receiving written notification that the item presented for payment has not been honored for payment, the Secretary of State shall give written notice of the applicability of this section and the cancellation date, which shall be not less than 20 days from the date of mailing the written notice as certified by the Secretary of State, to the agent for service of process or to the person submitting the instrument. Thereafter, if the amount has not been paid by cashier's check or equivalent before the date of cancellation as stated in the written notice of cancellation, the cancellation shall thereupon be effective.

Ca. Corp. Code § 5008.5

Amended by Stats 2022 ch 617 (SB 1202),s 43, eff. 1/1/2023.
Amended by Stats. 1988, Ch. 508, Sec. 2.

Section 5008.6 - Suspension

(a) A corporation that (1) fails to file a statement pursuant to Section 6210, 8210, or 9660 for an applicable filing period, (2) has not filed a statement pursuant to Section 6210, 8210, or 9660 during the preceding 24 months, and (3) was certified for penalty pursuant to Section 6810, 8810, or 9690 for the same filing period, shall be subject to suspension pursuant to this section rather than to penalty under Section 6810 or 8810.

(b) When subdivision (a) is applicable, the Secretary of State shall provide a notice to the corporation informing the corporation that its corporate powers, rights, and privileges will be suspended 60 days from the date of the notice if the corporation does not file the statement required by Section 6210, 8210, or 9660.

(c) If the 60-day period expires without the delinquent corporation filing the required statement, the Secretary of State shall notify the Franchise Tax Board of the suspension, and provide a notice of the suspension to the corporation. Thereupon, except for the purpose of filing an application for exempt status or amending the articles of incorporation as necessary either to perfect that application or to set forth a new name, the corporate powers, rights, and privileges of the corporation are suspended.

(d) A statement required by Section 6210, 8210, or 9660 may be filed, notwithstanding suspension of the corporate powers, rights, and privileges under this section or under provisions of the Revenue and Taxation Code. Upon the filing of a statement under Section 6210, 8210, or 9660, by a corporation that has suffered suspension under this section, the Secretary of State shall certify that fact to the Franchise Tax Board and the corporation may thereupon be relieved from suspension, unless the corporation is held in suspension by the Franchise Tax Board because of Section 23301, 23301.5, or 23775 of the Revenue and Taxation Code.

Ca. Corp. Code § 5008.6

Amended by Stats 2012 ch 494 (SB 1532),s 12, eff. 1/1/2013.
Amended by Stats 2003 ch 633 (SB 1061), eff. 9/30/2003.
Amended by Stats 2003 ch 633 (SB 1061),ss 2 eff. 9/30/2003.
Previously Amended October 10, 1999 (Bill Number: SB 284) (Chapter 1000).

Section 5008.9 - Suspension or forfeiture of nonprofit corporate powers; administrative dissolution or administrative surrender

(a) A nonprofit corporation described in Section 5059, 5060, or 5061, or a foreign nonprofit corporation, as defined in Section 5053, that has qualified to transact intrastate business, shall be subject to administrative dissolution or administrative surrender in accordance with this section if, as of January 1, 2016, or later, the nonprofit corporation's or foreign corporation's corporate powers are, and have been, suspended or forfeited by the Franchise Tax Board for a period of not less than 48 continuous months.

(b) Prior to the administrative dissolution or administrative surrender of the nonprofit corporation or foreign corporation, the corporation shall be notified of the pending administrative dissolution or administrative surrender as follows:

(1) The Franchise Tax Board shall mail written notice to the last known address of a nonprofit corporation or foreign corporation meeting the requirement described in subdivision (a).

(2) If the nonprofit corporation or foreign corporation does not have a valid address in the records of the Franchise Tax Board, the notice provided in subdivision (d) shall be deemed sufficient notice prior to administrative dissolution or administrative surrender.

(c) The Franchise Tax Board shall transmit to the Secretary of State and the Attorney General's Registry of Charitable Trusts the names and Secretary of State file numbers of nonprofit corporations and foreign corporations subject to the administrative dissolution or administrative surrender provisions of this section.

(d) The Secretary of State shall provide 60 calendar days' notice of the pending administrative dissolution or administrative surrender on its Internet Web site by listing the corporation name and the Secretary of State's file number for the nonprofit corporation or foreign corporation. The Secretary of State shall also, in conjunction with the information above, provide instructions for a nonprofit corporation or foreign corporation to submit a written objection of the pending administrative dissolution or administrative surrender to the Franchise Tax Board.

(e)

(1) A nonprofit corporation or foreign corporation may provide the Franchise Tax Board with a written objection to the administrative dissolution or administrative surrender.

(2) The Franchise Tax Board shall notify the Secretary of State if a written objection has been received.

(f) If no written objection to the administrative dissolution or administrative surrender is received by the Franchise Tax Board during the 60-day period described in subdivision (d), the nonprofit corporation or foreign corporation shall be administratively dissolved or administratively surrendered in accordance with this section. The certificate of the Secretary of State shall be prima facie evidence of the administrative dissolution or administrative surrender.

(g)

(1) If the written objection of a nonprofit corporation or foreign corporation to the administrative dissolution or administrative surrender has been received by the Franchise Tax Board before the expiration of the 60-day period described in subdivision (d), that nonprofit corporation or foreign corporation shall have an additional 90 days from the date the written objection is received by the Franchise Tax Board to pay or otherwise satisfy all accrued taxes, penalties, and interest and to file a current Statement of Information with the Secretary of State.

(2)

(A) If the conditions in paragraph (1) are satisfied, the administrative dissolution or administrative surrender shall be canceled.

(B) If the conditions in paragraph (1) are not satisfied, the nonprofit corporation or foreign corporation shall be administratively dissolved or administratively surrendered in accordance with this section as of the date that is 90 days after the receipt of the written objection.

(3) The Franchise Tax Board may extend the 90-day period in paragraph (1), but for no more than one period of 90 days.

(h) Upon administrative dissolution or administrative surrender in accordance with this section, the nonprofit corporation's or the foreign corporation's liabilities for qualified taxes, interest, and penalties as defined in Section 23156 of the Revenue and Taxation Code, if any, shall be abated. Any actions taken by the Franchise Tax Board to collect that abated liability shall be released, withdrawn, or otherwise terminated by the Franchise Tax Board, and no subsequent administrative or civil action shall be taken or brought to collect all or part of that amount. Any amounts erroneously received by the Franchise Tax Board in contravention of this section may be credited and refunded in accordance with Article 1 (commencing with Section 19301) of Chapter 6 of Part 10.2 of Division 2 of the Revenue and Taxation Code.

(i) If the nonprofit corporation or foreign corporation is administratively dissolved or administratively surrendered under this section, the liability to creditors, if any, is not discharged. The liability of the directors of, or other persons related to, the administratively dissolved or administratively surrendered nonprofit corporation or foreign corporation is not discharged. The administrative dissolution or administrative surrender of a nonprofit corporation or foreign corporation pursuant to this section shall not diminish or adversely affect the ability of the Attorney General to enforce liabilities as otherwise provided by law.

Ca. Corp. Code § 5008.9
Added by Stats 2015 ch 363 (AB 557),s 2, eff. 1/1/2016.

Section 5009 - Reference to mailing

Except as otherwise required, any reference in this part, Part 2, Part 3, Part 4 or Part 5 to mailing means first-, second-, or third-class mail, postage prepaid, unless registered mail is specified. Registered mail includes certified mail.

Ca. Corp. Code § 5009
Added by Stats. 1978, Ch. 567.

Section 5010 - Reference to majority or other proportion of memberships

If the articles or bylaws provide for more or less than one vote for any membership on any matter, the references in Sections 5033 and 5034 to a majority or other proportion of memberships mean, as to those matters, a majority or other proportion of the votes entitled to be cast. Whenever in Part 2 (commencing with Section 5110) or Part 3 (commencing with Section 7110) members are disqualified from voting on any matter, their memberships shall not be counted for the determination of a quorum at any meeting to act upon, or the required vote to approve action upon, that matter under any other provision of Part 2 (commencing with Section 5110) or Part 3 (commencing with Section 7110) or the articles or bylaws.

Ca. Corp. Code § 5010
Amended by Stats. 1983, Ch. 101, Sec. 9.

Section 5011 - References to voting of memberships

All references in Part 3 (commencing with Section 7110) to the voting of memberships include the voting of securities given voting rights in the articles pursuant to paragraph (3) of subdivision (a) of Section 7132.

Ca. Corp. Code § 5011
Amended by Stats. 1983, Ch. 101, Sec. 10.

Section 5012 - References to financial statements

All references in this part, Part 2 (commencing with Section 5110), Part 3 (commencing with Section 7110), or Part 4 (commencing with Section 9110) to financial statements of a corporation mean statements prepared in conformity with generally accepted accounting principles or some other basis of accounting which reasonably sets forth the assets and liabilities and the income and expenses of the corporation and discloses the accounting basis used in their preparation.

Ca. Corp. Code § 5012
Amended by Stats. 1983, Ch. 101, Sec. 11.

Section 5013 - "Independent accountant" defined

As used in this part, Part 2 (commencing with Section 5110), Part 3 (commencing with Section 7110), or Part 4 (commencing with Section 9110), "independent accountant" means a certified public accountant or public accountant who is independent of the corporation, as determined in accordance with generally accepted auditing standards, and who is engaged to audit financial statements of the corporation or perform other accounting services.

Ca. Corp. Code § 5013
Amended by Stats. 1983, Ch. 101, Sec. 12.

Section 5014 - Requirement for vote of each class of members

Any requirement in Part 3 (commencing with Section 7110) for a vote of each class of members means such a vote regardless of limitations or restrictions upon the voting rights thereof, unless expressly limited to voting memberships.

Ca. Corp. Code § 5014

Amended by Stats. 1983, Ch. 101, Sec. 13.

Section 5015 - Reference to time notice is given or sent

Any reference in this part, Part 2 (commencing with Section 5110), Part 3 (commencing with Section 7110), Part 4 (commencing with Section 9110), or Part 5 (commencing with Section 9910) to the time a notice is given or sent means, unless otherwise expressly provided, (a) the time a written notice by mail is deposited in the United States mails, postage prepaid; or (b) the time any other written notice, including facsimile, telegram, or other electronic mail message, is personally delivered to the recipient or is delivered to a common carrier for transmission, or actually transmitted by the person giving the notice by electronic means, to the recipient; or (c) the time any oral notice is communicated, in person or by telephone, including a voice messaging system or other system or technology designed to record and communicate messages, or wireless, to the recipient, including the recipient's designated voice mailbox or address on such a system, or to a person at the office of the recipient who the person giving the notice has reason to believe will promptly communicate it to the recipient.

Ca. Corp. Code § 5015

Amended by Stats. 1995, Ch. 154, Sec. 10. Effective January 1, 1996.

Section 5016 - Notice or report mailed or delivered as party of newsletter, magazine, or other organ regularly sent to members

A notice or report mailed or delivered as part of a newsletter, magazine or other organ regularly sent to members shall constitute written notice or report pursuant to this division when addressed and mailed or delivered to the member, or in the case of members who are residents of the same household and who have the same address on the books of the corporation, when addressed and mailed or delivered to one of such members, at the address appearing on the books of the corporation.

Ca. Corp. Code § 5016

Amended by Stats. 1979, Ch. 724.

Section 5030 - "Acknowledged" defined

"Acknowledged" means that an instrument is either:

(a) Formally acknowledged as provided in Article 3 (commencing with Section 1180) of Chapter 4 of Title 4 of Part 4 of Division 2 of the Civil Code; or

(b) Accompanied by a declaration in writing signed by the persons executing the same that they are such persons and that the instrument is the act and deed of the person or persons executing the same. Any certificate of acknowledgment taken without this state before a notary public or a judge or clerk of a court of record having an official seal need not be further authenticated.

Ca. Corp. Code § 5030
Added by Stats. 1978, Ch. 567.

Section 5031 - "Affiliate" and "affiliated" defined

A corporation is an "affiliate" of, or a corporation is "affiliated" with, another specified corporation if it directly, or indirectly through one or more intermediaries, controls, is controlled by or is under common control with the other specified corporation.

Ca. Corp. Code § 5031
Added by Stats. 1978, Ch. 567.

Section 5032 - "Approved by (or approval of) the board" defined

"Approved by (or approval of) the board" means approved or ratified by the vote of the board or by the vote of a committee authorized to exercise the powers of the board, except as to matters not within the competence of the committee under Section 5212, Section 7212, or Section 9212.

Ca. Corp. Code § 5032
Added by Stats. 1978, Ch. 567.

Section 5033 - "Approval by (or approval of) a majority of all members" defined

"Approval by (or approval of) a majority of all members" means approval by an affirmative vote (or written ballot in conformity with Section 5513, Section 7513, or Section 9413) of a majority of the votes entitled to be cast. Such approval shall include the affirmative vote of a majority of the outstanding memberships of each class, unit, or grouping of members entitled, by any provision of the articles or bylaws or of Part 2, Part 3, Part 4 or Part 5 to vote as a class, unit, or grouping of members on the subject matter being voted upon and shall also include the affirmative vote of such greater proportion, including all, of the votes of the memberships of any class, unit, or grouping of members if such greater proportion is required by the bylaws (subdivision (e) of Section 5151, subdivision (e) of Section 7151, or subdivision (e) of Section 9151) or Part 2, Part 3, Part 4 or Part 5.

Ca. Corp. Code § 5033
Amended by Stats. 1979, Ch. 724.

Section 5034 - "Approval by (or approval of) the members" defined

"Approval by (or approval of) the members" means approved or ratified by the affirmative vote of a majority of the votes represented and voting at a duly held meeting at which a quorum is present (which affirmative votes also constitute a majority of the required quorum) or written ballot in conformity with Section 5513, 7513, or 9413 or by the affirmative vote or written ballot of such greater proportion, including all of the votes of the memberships of any class, unit, or grouping of members as may be provided in the bylaws (subdivision (e) of Section 5151, subdivision (e) of Section 7151, or subdivision (e) of Section 9151) or in Part 2, Part 3, Part 4 or Part 5 for all or any specified member action.

Ca. Corp. Code § 5034

Amended by Stats. 1979, Ch. 724.

Section 5035 - "Articles" defined

"Articles" includes the articles of incorporation, amendments thereto, amended articles, restated articles, and certificates of incorporation.

Ca. Corp. Code § 5035

Added by Stats. 1978, Ch. 567.

Section 5036 - "Authorized number" defined

(a) Except as provided in subdivision (b) or (c), "authorized number" means 5 percent of the voting power.

(b) Where (disregarding any provision for cumulative voting which would otherwise apply) the total number of votes entitled to be cast for a director is 1,000 or more, but less than 5,000 the authorized number shall be $2 \frac{1}{2}$ percent of the voting power, but not less than 50.

(c) Where (disregarding any provision for cumulative voting which would otherwise apply) the total number of votes entitled to be cast for a director is 5,000 or more, the authorized number shall be one-twentieth of 1 percent of the voting power, but not less than 125.

(d) Any right under Part 2, Part 3, or Part 4 which may be exercised by the authorized number, or some multiple thereof, may be exercised by a member with written authorizations obtained within any 11-month period from members who, in the aggregate, hold the equivalent voting power. Any such authorization shall specify the right to be exercised thereunder and the duration thereof (which shall not exceed three years).

(e) Where any provision of Part 2, Part 3, or Part 4 specifies twice the authorized number, that means two times the number calculated according to subdivision (a), (b) or (c).

Ca. Corp. Code § 5036

Amended by Stats. 1979, Ch. 724.

Section 5037 - "Bylaws" defined

"Bylaws" includes amendments thereto and amended bylaws.

Ca. Corp. Code § 5037
Added by Stats. 1978, Ch. 567.

Section 5038 - "Board" defined

"Board" means the board of directors of the corporation.
  Ca. Corp. Code § 5038
Added by Stats. 1978, Ch. 567.

Section 5039 - "Business corporation" defined

"Business corporation" means a corporation as defined in Section 162 of the General Corporation Law.
  Ca. Corp. Code § 5039
Added by Stats. 1978, Ch. 567.

Section 5039.5 - "chairperson of the board" defined

All references in this division to "chairperson of the board," other than in Sections 5213, 7213, and 9213, shall be deemed to refer to all permissible titles for a chair of the board, as permitted by Sections 5213, 7213, and 9213.
  Ca. Corp. Code § 5039.5
Amended by Stats 2022 ch 617 (SB 1202),s 44, eff. 1/1/2023.
Amended by Stats 2015 ch 98 (SB 351),s 10, eff. 1/1/2016.
Added by Stats 2009 ch 631 (AB 1233),s 1, eff. 1/1/2010.

Section 5040 - "Chapter" defined

"Chapter" refers to a chapter of Part 2 (commencing with Section 5110), Part 3 (commencing with Section 7110), or Part 4 (commencing with Section 9110) unless otherwise expressly stated.
  Ca. Corp. Code § 5040
Amended by Stats. 1983, Ch. 101, Sec. 15.

Section 5041 - "Class" defined

"Class" refers to those memberships which:
(a) are identified in the articles or bylaws as being a different type of membership; or
(b) have the same rights with respect to voting, dissolution, redemption and transfer.
For the purpose of this section, rights shall be considered the same if they are determined by a formula applied uniformly.
  Ca. Corp. Code § 5041
Repealed and added by Stats. 1979, Ch. 724.

Section 5043 - "Common shares" defined

"Common shares," as used in Part 3 (commencing with Section 7110), means shares which have no preference over any other shares with respect to distribution of assets on liquidation or with respect to payment of dividends.

Ca. Corp. Code § 5043

Amended by Stats. 1983, Ch. 101, Sec. 17.

Section 5044 - "Constituent corporation" defined

"Constituent corporation" means a corporation which is merged with one or more other corporations and includes the surviving corporation.

Ca. Corp. Code § 5044

Added by Stats. 1978, Ch. 567.

Section 5045 - "Control" defined

"Control" means the possession, direct or indirect, of the power to direct or cause the direction of the management and policies of a corporation.

Ca. Corp. Code § 5045

Added by Stats. 1978, Ch. 567.

Section 5046 - "Corporation" defined

(a) "Corporation" as used in this part and Part 5 (commencing with Section 9910), refers to corporations defined in subdivisions (b), (c), and (d).
(b) "Corporation," as used in Part 2 (commencing with Section 5110), means a nonprofit public benefit corporation as defined in Section 5060.
(c) "Corporation," as used in Part 3 (commencing with Section 7110) means a nonprofit mutual benefit corporation as defined in Section 5059.
(d) "Corporation," as used in Part 4 (commencing with Section 9110), including those provisions of Part 2 (commencing with Section 5110) made applicable pursuant to Chapter 6 (commencing with Section 9610) of Part 4, means a nonprofit religious corporation as defined in Section 5061.

Ca. Corp. Code § 5046

Amended by Stats. 1983, Ch. 101, Sec. 18.

Section 5047 - "Directors" defined

Except as otherwise expressly provided, "directors" means natural persons, designated in the articles or bylaws or elected by the incorporators, and their successors and natural persons designated, elected, or appointed by any other name or title to act as members of the governing body of the corporation. If the articles or bylaws designate that a natural person is a director or a member of the governing body of the corporation by reason of occupying a specified position within the corporation or outside the corporation, without limiting that person's right to vote as a member of the governing body, that person shall be a director for all purposes and shall have the same rights and obligations, including voting rights, as the other directors. A person who does not have authority to vote as a member of the governing body of the corporation, is not a director as that term is used in this division regardless of title.

Ca. Corp. Code § 5047

Amended by Stats 2015 ch 303 (AB 731),s 45, eff. 1/1/2016.

Amended by Stats 2014 ch 914 (AB 2755),s 1, eff. 1/1/2015.

Amended by Stats 2009 ch 631 (AB 1233),s 2, eff. 1/1/2010.

Section 5047.5 - Liability of director or officer

(a) The Legislature finds and declares that the services of directors and officers of nonprofit corporations who serve without compensation are critical to the efficient conduct and management of the public service and charitable affairs of the people of California. The willingness of volunteers to offer their services has been deterred by a perception that their personal assets are at risk for these activities. The unavailability and unaffordability of appropriate liability insurance makes it difficult for these corporations to protect the personal assets of their volunteer decisionmakers with adequate insurance. It is the public policy of this state to provide incentive and protection to the individuals who perform these important functions.

(b) Except as provided in this section, no cause of action for monetary damages shall arise against any person serving without compensation as a director or officer of a nonprofit corporation subject to Part 2 (commencing with Section 5110), Part 3 (commencing with Section 7110), or Part 4 (commencing with Section 9110) of this division on account of any negligent act or omission occurring (1) within the scope of that person's duties as a director acting as a board member, or within the scope of that person's duties as an officer acting in an official capacity; (2) in good faith; (3) in a manner that the person believes to be in the best interest of the corporation; and (4) is in the exercise of his or her policymaking judgment.

(c) This section shall not limit the liability of a director or officer for any of the following:

(1) Self-dealing transactions, as described in Sections 5233 and 9243.

(2) Conflicts of interest, as described in Section 7233.

(3) Actions described in Sections 5237, 7236, and 9245.

(4) In the case of a charitable trust, an action or proceeding against a trustee brought by a beneficiary of that trust.

(5) Any action or proceeding brought by the Attorney General.

(6) Intentional, wanton, or reckless acts, gross negligence, or an action based on fraud, oppression, or malice.

(7) Any action brought under Chapter 2 (commencing with Section 16700) of Part 2 of Division 7 of the Business and Professions Code.

(d) This section only applies to nonprofit corporations organized to provide religious, charitable, literary, educational, scientific, social, or other forms of public service that are exempt from federal income taxation under Section 501(c)(3)(c)(3) or 501(c)(6)(c)(6) of the Internal Revenue Code.

(e) This section applies only if the nonprofit corporation maintains a liability insurance policy with an amount of coverage of at least the following amounts:

(1) If the corporation's annual budget is less than fifty thousand dollars ($50,000), the minimum required amount is five hundred thousand dollars ($500,000).

(2) If the corporation's annual budget equals or exceeds fifty thousand dollars ($50,000), the minimum required amount is one million dollars ($1,000,000). This section applies only if the claim against the director or officer can also be made directly against the corporation and a liability insurance policy is applicable to the claim. If that policy is found to cover the damages caused by the director or officer, no cause of action as provided in this section shall be maintained against the director or officer.

(f) For the purposes of this section, the payment of actual expenses incurred in attending meetings or otherwise in the execution of the duties of a director or officer shall not constitute compensation.

(g) Nothing in this section shall be construed to limit the liability of a nonprofit corporation for any negligent act or omission of a director, officer, employee, agent, or servant occurring within the scope of his or her duties.

(h) This section does not apply to any corporation that unlawfully restricts membership, services, or benefits conferred on the basis of political affiliation, age, or any characteristic listed or defined in subdivision (b) or (e) of Section 51 of the Civil Code.

(i) This section does not apply to any volunteer director or officer who receives compensation from the corporation in any other capacity, including, but not limited to, as an employee.

Ca. Corp. Code § 5047.5

Amended by Stats 2009 ch 631 (AB 1233),s 3, eff. 1/1/2010.
Amended by Stats 2007 ch 568 (AB 14),s 17, eff. 1/1/2008.

Section 5048 - "Disappearing corporation" defined

323

"Disappearing corporation" means a constituent corporation which is not the surviving corporation.

Ca. Corp. Code § 5048
Added by Stats. 1978, Ch. 567.

Section 5049 - "Distribution" defined

"Distribution" means the distribution of any gains, profits or dividends to any member as such. As used in this section, "member" means any person who is a member as defined in Section 5056 and any person who is referred to as a member as authorized by subdivision (a) of Sections 5332, 7333 and 9332.

Ca. Corp. Code § 5049
Amended by Stats. 1979, Ch. 724.

Section 5050 - "Domestic corporation" defined

"Domestic corporation" means a corporation formed under the laws of this state.

Ca. Corp. Code § 5050
Added by Stats. 1978, Ch. 567.

Section 5051 - "Filed" defined

"Filed," unless otherwise expressly provided, means filed in the office of the Secretary of State.

Ca. Corp. Code § 5051
Added by Stats. 1978, Ch. 567.

Section 5052 - "Foreign business corporation" defined

"Foreign business corporation," as used in Part 3 (commencing with Section 7110), means a foreign corporation as defined in Section 171 except that it does not include a foreign corporation as defined in Section 5053.

Ca. Corp. Code § 5052
Amended by Stats. 1983, Ch. 101, Sec. 19.

Section 5053 - "Foreign corporation" defined

"Foreign corporation" means any corporation incorporated in a jurisdiction other than California pursuant to that jurisdiction's law for the incorporation of nonprofit corporations; except that as used in subdivision (b) of Section 5122, in subdivision (c) of Section 7122, and in subdivision (b) of Section 9122, "foreign corporation" means a corporation described in Section 171.

Ca. Corp. Code § 5053
Amended by Stats. 1979, Ch. 724.

Section 5054 - "Incentive and benefit plans" defined

"Incentive and benefit plans," as used in Section 5140, in Section 7140, and in Section 9140 includes, but is not limited to, any plan or agreement under which the compensation of officers or employees is fixed, in full or in part, by reference to the financial performance of the corporation.

Ca. Corp. Code § 5054
Added by Stats. 1978, Ch. 567.

Section 5055 - "Liquidating price" or "liquidation preference" defined

"Liquidating price" or "liquidation preference," as used in Part 3 (commencing with Section 7110), means amounts payable on memberships of any class, upon voluntary or involuntary dissolution, winding up or distribution of the entire assets of the corporation, in priority to amounts payable to members of another class or classes.

Ca. Corp. Code § 5055
Amended by Stats. 1983, Ch. 101, Sec. 20.

Section 5056 - "Member" defined; rights of member

(a) "Member" means any person who, pursuant to a specific provision of a corporation's articles or bylaws, has the right to vote for the election of a director or directors or on a disposition of all or substantially all of the assets of a corporation or on a merger or on a dissolution unless the provision granting such right to vote is only effective as a result of paragraph (2) of subdivision (a) of Section 7132. "Member" also means any person who is designated in the articles or bylaws as a member and, pursuant to a specific provision of a corporation's articles or bylaws, has the right to vote on changes to the articles or bylaws.

(b) The articles or bylaws may confer some or all of the rights of a member, set forth in this part and in Parts 2 through 5 of this division, upon any person or persons who do not have any of the voting rights referred to in subdivision (a).

(c) Where a member of a corporation is not a natural person, such member may authorize in writing one or more natural persons to vote on its behalf on any or all matters which may require a vote of the members.

(d) A person is not a member by virtue of any of the following:

(1) Any rights such person has as a delegate.

(2) Any rights such person has to designate or select a director or directors.

(3) Any rights such person has as a director.

Ca. Corp. Code § 5056
Amended by Stats. 1982, Ch. 36, Sec. 5. Effective February 17, 1982.

Section 5057 - "Membership" defined

A "membership" refers to the rights a member has pursuant to a corporation's articles, bylaws and this division.
  Ca. Corp. Code § 5057
Amended by Stats. 1979, Ch. 724.

Section 5058 - "Membership certificate" defined

"Membership certificate," as used in Part 3 (commencing with Section 7110), means a document evidencing a transferable property interest in a corporation.
  Ca. Corp. Code § 5058
Amended by Stats. 1983, Ch. 101, Sec. 21.

Section 5059 - "Nonprofit mutual benefit corporation" or "mutual benefit corporation" defined

"Nonprofit mutual benefit corporation" or "mutual benefit corporation" means a corporation which is organized under Part 3 (commencing with Section 7110), or subject to Part 3 under the provisions of subdivision (a) of Section 5003.
  Ca. Corp. Code § 5059
Amended by Stats. 1979, Ch. 724.

Section 5060 - "Nonprofit public benefit corporation" or "public benefit corporation" defined

"Nonprofit public benefit corporation" or "public benefit corporation" means a corporation which is organized under Part 2 (commencing with Section 5110) or subject to Part 2 under the provisions of subdivision (a) of Section 5003.
  Ca. Corp. Code § 5060
Amended by Stats. 1979, Ch. 724.

Section 5061 - "Nonprofit religious corporation" or "religious corporation" defined

"Nonprofit religious corporation" or "religious corporation" means a corporation which is organized under Part 4 (commencing with Section 9110) or subject to Part 4 pursuant to subdivision (a) of Section 5003.
  Ca. Corp. Code § 5061
Amended by Stats. 1979, Ch. 724.

Section 5062 - "Officer's certificate" defined

"Officer's certificate" means a certificate signed and verified by the chair of the board, the president or any vice president and by the secretary, the chief financial officer, the treasurer or any assistant secretary or assistant treasurer.

Ca. Corp. Code § 5062
Amended by Stats 2009 ch 631 (AB 1233),s 4, eff. 1/1/2010.

Section 5063 - "On the certificate" defined

"On the certificate," as used in Part 3 (commencing with Section 7110), means that a statement appears on the face of a certificate or on the reverse thereof with a reference thereto on the face.

Ca. Corp. Code § 5063
Amended by Stats. 1983, Ch. 101, Sec. 22.

Section 5063.5 - "Other business entity" defined

"Other business entity" means a domestic or foreign limited liability company, limited partnership, general partnership, business trust, real estate investment trust, unincorporated association, or a domestic reciprocal insurer organized after 1974 to provide medical malpractice insurance as set forth in Article 16 (commencing with Section 1550) of Chapter 3 of Part 2 of Division 1 of the Insurance Code. As used herein, "general partnership" means a "partnership" as defined in subdivision (9) of Section 16101; "business trust" means a business organization formed as a trust; "real estate investment trust" means a "real estate investment trust" as defined in subsection (a) of Section 856 of the Internal Revenue Code of 1986, as amended; and "unincorporated association" has the meaning set forth in Section 18035.

Ca. Corp. Code § 5063.5
Amended by Stats 2009 ch 631 (AB 1233),s 5, eff. 1/1/2010.
Amended by Stats 2004 ch 178 (SB 1746),s 5, eff. 1/1/2005
Added September 21, 1999 (Bill Number: AB 198) (Chapter 437).

Section 5064 - "Parent" defined

A "parent" of a specified corporation is an affiliate controlling such corporation directly or indirectly through one or more intermediaries.

Ca. Corp. Code § 5064
Added by Stats. 1978, Ch. 567.

Section 5064.5 - "Parent party" defined

"Parent party" means the corporation in control of any constituent domestic or foreign corporation or other business entity and whose equity securities are issued, transferred, or exchanged in a merger pursuant to Section 6019.1 or 8019.1.

Ca. Corp. Code § 5064.5
Added 9/21/1999 (Bill Number: AB 198) (Chapter 437).

Section 5065 - "Person" defined

"Person," in addition to those entities specified in Section 18 and unless otherwise expressly provided, includes any association, business corporation, company, corporation, corporation sole, domestic corporation, estate, foreign corporation, foreign business corporation, individual, joint stock company, joint venture, mutual benefit corporation, public benefit corporation, religious corporation, partnership, government or political subdivision, agency or instrumentality of a government.

Ca. Corp. Code § 5065
Added by Stats. 1978, Ch. 567.

Section 5067 - "Preferred shares" defined

"Preferred shares," as used in Part 3 (commencing with Section 7110), means shares other than common shares.

Ca. Corp. Code § 5067
Amended by Stats. 1983, Ch. 101, Sec. 24.

Section 5068 - "Proper county" defined

"Proper county" means the county where the corporation's principal office in this state is located or, if the corporation has no such office, the County of Sacramento.

Ca. Corp. Code § 5068
Amended by Stats. 1979, Ch. 724.

Section 5069 - "Proxy" defined

"Proxy" means a written authorization signed by a member or the member's attorney in fact giving another person or persons power to vote on behalf of such member. "Signed" for the purpose of this section means the placing of the member's name on the proxy (whether by manual signature, typewriting, telegraphic transmission or otherwise) by the member or such member's attorney in fact.

Ca. Corp. Code § 5069
Added by Stats. 1978, Ch. 567.

Section 5070 - "Proxyholder" defined

"Proxyholder" means the person or persons to whom a proxy is given.

Ca. Corp. Code § 5070
Added by Stats. 1978, Ch. 567.

Section 5071 - "Shareholder" defined

"Shareholder," as used in Part 3 (commencing with Section 7110), means one who is a holder of record of shares.
   Ca. Corp. Code § 5071
Amended by Stats. 1983, Ch. 101, Sec. 25.

Section 5072 - "Shares" defined

"Shares," as used in Part 3 (commencing with Section 7110), means the units into which the proprietary interests in a business corporation or foreign business corporation are divided in the articles.
   Ca. Corp. Code § 5072
Amended by Stats. 1983, Ch. 101, Sec. 26.

Section 5073 - "Subsidiary" defined

(a) Except as provided in subdivision (b), "subsidiary" of a specified corporation means a corporation more than 50 percent of the voting power of which is owned directly, or indirectly through one or more subsidiaries, by the specified corporation.
(b) For the purpose of Section 7315, "subsidiary" of a specified corporation means a corporation more than 25 percent of the voting power of which is owned directly, or indirectly through one or more subsidiaries as defined in subdivision (a), by the specified corporation.
   Ca. Corp. Code § 5073
Amended by Stats. 1979, Ch. 724.

Section 5074 - "Surviving corporation" defined

"Surviving corporation" means a corporation into which one or more other corporations are merged.
   Ca. Corp. Code § 5074
Added by Stats. 1978, Ch. 567.

Section 5075 - "Vacancy" defined

"Vacancy" when used with respect to the board means any authorized position of director which is not then filled, whether the vacancy is caused by death, resignation, removal, change in the number of directors authorized in the articles or bylaws (by the board or the members) or otherwise.

Ca. Corp. Code § 5075
Amended by Stats. 1979, Ch. 724.

Section 5076 - "Verified" defined

"Verified" means that the statements contained in a certificate or other document are declared to be true of the own knowledge of the persons executing the same in either:
(a) An affidavit signed by them under oath before an officer authorized by the laws of this state or of the place where it is executed to administer oaths; or
(b) A declaration in writing executed by them under penalty of perjury and stating the date and place (whether within or without this state) of execution. Any affidavit sworn to without this state before a notary public or a judge or clerk of a court of record having an official seal need not be further authenticated.
Ca. Corp. Code § 5076
Added by Stats. 1978, Ch. 567.

Section 5077 - "Vote" defined

"Vote" includes, but is not limited to, authorization by written consent pursuant to subdivision (b) of Section 5211, subdivision (b) of Section 7211, or subdivision (b) of Section 9211 and authorization by written ballot pursuant to Section 5513, Section 7513, or Section 9413.
Ca. Corp. Code § 5077
Added by Stats. 1978, Ch. 567.

Section 5078 - "Voting power" defined

"Voting power" means the power to vote for the election of directors at the time any determination of voting power is made and does not include the right to vote upon the happening of some condition or event which has not yet occurred. In any case where different classes of memberships are entitled to vote as separate classes for different members of the board, the determination of percentage of voting power shall be made on the basis of the percentage of the total number of authorized directors which the memberships in question (whether of one or more classes) have the power to elect in an election at which all memberships then entitled to vote for the election of any directors are voted.
Ca. Corp. Code § 5078
Amended by Stats. 1979, Ch. 724.

Section 5079 - "Written" or "in writing" defined

"Written" or "in writing" includes facsimile, telegraphic, and other electronic communication as authorized by this code, including an electronic transmission by a corporation that satisfies the requirements of Section 20.

Ca. Corp. Code § 5079
Amended by Stats 2004 ch 254 (SB 1306),s 13, eff. 1/1/2005

Section 5080 - "Written ballot" defined

"Written ballot" does not include a ballot distributed at a special or regular meeting of members.
   Ca. Corp. Code § 5080
Added by Stats. 1978, Ch. 567.

Part 2 - NONPROFIT PUBLIC BENEFIT CORPORATIONS

Chapter 1 - ORGANIZATION AND BYLAWS

Article 1 - TITLE AND PURPOSES

Section 5110 - Short title

This part shall be known and may be cited as the Nonprofit Public Benefit Corporation Law.
   Ca. Corp. Code § 5110
Added by Stats. 1978, Ch. 567.

Section 5111 - Formation of corporation for public or charitable purposes

Subject to any other provisions of law of this state applying to the particular class of corporation or line of activity, a corporation may be formed under this part for any public or charitable purposes.
   Ca. Corp. Code § 5111
Amended by Stats. 1979, Ch. 724.

Article 2 - FORMATION

Section 5120 - Formation

(a) One or more persons may form a corporation under this part by executing and filing articles of incorporation.
(b) If initial directors are named in the articles, each director named in the articles shall sign and acknowledge the articles; if initial directors are not named in the articles, the articles shall be signed by one or more persons who thereupon are the incorporators of the corporation.
(c) The corporate existence begins upon the filing of the articles and continues perpetually, unless otherwise expressly provided by law or in the articles.
(d) At the time of filing pursuant to this section, the Secretary of State shall make available the filed articles of incorporation to the Attorney General.

(e) If the corporation was created by the elected legislative body in order to exercise authority that may lawfully be delegated by the elected governing body to a private corporation or other entity, the Secretary of State shall forward a copy of the filed articles of incorporation to the Controller.

Ca. Corp. Code § 5120
Amended by Stats 2022 ch 617 (SB 1202),s 45, eff. 1/1/2023.
Amended by Stats 2014 ch 834 (SB 1041),s 10, eff. 1/1/2015.
Amended by Stats 2007 ch 343 (SB 144),s 2, eff. 1/1/2008.

Section 5121 - Change of status of existing unincorporated association to corporation

(a) In the case of an existing unincorporated association, the association may change its status to that of a corporation upon a proper authorization for such by the association in accordance with its rules and procedures.

(b) In addition to the matters required to be set forth in the articles pursuant to Section 5130, the articles in the case of an incorporation authorized by subdivision (a) shall set forth that an existing unincorporated association, stating its name, is being incorporated by the filing of the articles.

(c) The articles filed pursuant to this section shall be accompanied by a verified statement of any two officers or governing board members of the association stating that the incorporation of the association by means of the articles to which the verified statement is attached has been approved by the association in accordance with its rules and procedures.

(d) Upon the change of status of an unincorporated association to a corporation pursuant to subdivision (a), the property of the association becomes the property of the corporation and the members of the association who had any voting rights of the type referred to in Section 5056 become members of the corporation.

(e) The filing for record in the office of the county recorder of any county in this state in which any of the real property of the association is located of a copy of the articles of incorporation filed pursuant to this section, certified by the Secretary of State shall evidence record ownership in the corporation of all interests of the association in and to the real property located in that county.

(f) All rights of creditors and all liens upon the property of the association shall be preserved unimpaired. Any action or proceeding pending by or against the unincorporated association may be prosecuted to judgment, which shall bind the corporation, or the corporation may be proceeded against or substituted in its place.

(g) If a corporation is organized by a person who is or was an officer, director or member of an unincorporated association and such corporation is not organized pursuant to subdivision (a), the unincorporated association may continue to use its name and the corporation may not use a name which is the same as or similar to the name of the unincorporated association.

Ca. Corp. Code § 5121
Amended by Stats. 1981, Ch. 587, Sec. 3.

Section 5122 - Name of corporation

(a) The Secretary of State shall not file articles setting forth a name in which "bank," "trust," "trustee," or related words appear, unless the certificate of approval of the Commissioner of Financial Protection and Innovation is attached thereto.

(b) The name of a corporation shall not be a name that the Secretary of State determines is likely to mislead the public and shall be distinguishable in the records of the Secretary of State from all of the following:

    (1) The name of any corporation.

    (2) The name of any foreign corporation authorized to transact intrastate business in this state.

    (3) Each name that is under reservation pursuant to this title.

    (4) The name of a foreign corporation that has registered its name pursuant to Section 2101.

    (5) An alternate name of a foreign corporation under subdivision (b) of Section 2106.

    (6)A name that will become the record name of a domestic or foreign corporation upon a corporate instrument when there is a delayed effective or file date.

(c) The use by a corporation of a name in violation of this section may be enjoined notwithstanding the filing of its articles by the Secretary of State.

(d) Any applicant may, upon payment of the fee prescribed therefor in the Government Code, obtain from the Secretary of State a certificate of reservation of any name not prohibited by subdivision (b), and upon the issuance of the certificate the name stated therein shall be reserved for a period of 60 days. The Secretary of State shall not, however, issue certificates reserving the same name for two or more consecutive 60-day periods to the same applicant or for the use or benefit of the same person; nor shall consecutive reservations be made by or for the use or benefit of the same person of names so similar as to fall within the prohibitions of subdivision (b).

Ca. Corp. Code § 5122

Amended by Stats 2022 ch 617 (SB 1202),s 46, eff. 1/1/2023.
Amended by Stats 2022 ch 452 (SB 1498),s 53, eff. 1/1/2023.
Amended by Stats 2020 ch 361 (SB 522),s 5, eff. 1/1/2021.
Amended by Stats 2014 ch 401 (AB 2763),s 20, eff. 1/1/2015.
Amended by Stats 2011 ch 740 (SB 201),s 13, eff. 1/1/2012.

Section 5122.5 - Corporate name or file articles using the name Golden State Energy

The Secretary of State shall not reserve a corporate name or file articles using the name Golden State Energy unless those articles are for Golden State Energy, incorporated and operating pursuant to this part and Division 1.7 (commencing with Section 3400) of the Public Utilities Code.

Ca. Corp. Code § 5122.5
Added by Stats 2021 ch 115 (AB 148),s 2, eff. 7/22/2021.

Article 3 - ARTICLES OF INCORPORATION

Section 5130 - Articles of incorporation

The articles of incorporation of a corporation formed under this part shall set forth:
(a) The name of the corporation.
(b)

(1) Except as provided in paragraph (2), the following statement: "This corporation is a nonprofit public benefit corporation and is not organized for the private gain of any person. It is organized under the Nonprofit Public Benefit Corporation Law for (public or charitable [insert one or both]) purposes."
[If the purposes include "public" purposes, the articles shall, and in all other cases the articles may, include a further description of the corporation's purposes.]

(2) If the corporation is a public bank, as defined in Section 57600 of the Government Code, the articles shall set forth a statement of purpose that is prescribed in subdivision (b) of Section 57601 of the Government Code.
(c) The name and street address in this state of the corporation's initial agent for service of process in accordance with subdivision (b) of Section 6210.
(d) The initial street address of the corporation.
(e) The initial mailing address of the corporation, if different from the initial street address.

Ca. Corp. Code § 5130
Amended by Stats 2019 ch 442 (AB 857),s 2, eff. 1/1/2020.
Amended by Stats 2012 ch 494 (SB 1532),s 13, eff. 1/1/2013.

Section 5131 - Statement limiting purposes or powers of corporation

The articles of incorporation may set forth a further statement limiting the purposes or powers of the corporation.

Ca. Corp. Code § 5131
Added by Stats. 1978, Ch. 567.

Section 5132 - Provisions in articles of incorporation

(a) The articles of incorporation may set forth any or all of the following provisions, which shall not be effective unless expressly provided in the articles:

(1) A provision limiting the duration of the corporation's existence to a specified date.

(2) In the case of a subordinate corporation instituted or created under the authority of a head organization, a provision setting forth either or both of the following:

(A) That the subordinate corporation shall dissolve whenever its charter is surrendered to, taken away by, or revoked by the head organization granting it.

(B) That in the event of its dissolution pursuant to an article provision allowed by subparagraph (A) or in the event of its dissolution for any reason, any assets of the corporation after compliance with the applicable provisions of Chapters 15 (commencing with Section 6510), 16 (commencing with Section 6610) and 17 (commencing with Section 6710) shall be distributed to the head organization.
(b) Nothing contained in subdivision (a) shall affect the enforceability, as between the parties thereto, of any lawful agreement not otherwise contrary to public policy.
(c) The articles of incorporation may set forth any or all of the following provisions:

(1) The names and addresses of the persons appointed to act as initial directors.

(2) The classes of members, if any, and if there are two or more classes, the rights, privileges, preferences, restrictions and conditions attaching to each class.

(3) A provision that would allow any member to have more or less than one vote in any election or other matter presented to the members for a vote.

(4) A provision that requires an amendment to the articles, as provided in subdivision (a) of Section 5812, or to the bylaws, and any amendment or repeal of that amendment, to be approved in writing by a specified person or persons other than the board or the members. However, this approval requirement, unless the articles specify otherwise, shall not apply if any of the following circumstances exist:

(A) The specified person or persons have died or ceased to exist.

(B) If the right of the specified person or persons to approve is in the capacity of an officer, trustee, or other status and the office, trust, or status has ceased to exist.

(C) If the corporation has a specific proposal for amendment or repeal, and the corporation has provided written notice of that proposal, including a copy of the proposal, to the specified person or persons at the most recent address for each of them, based on the corporation's records, and the corporation has not received written approval or nonapproval within the period specified in the notice, which shall not be less than 10 nor more than 30 days commencing at least 20 days after the notice has been provided.

(5) Any other provision, not in conflict with law, for the management of the activities and for the conduct of the affairs of the corporation, including any provision that is required or permitted by this part to be stated in the bylaws.

Ca. Corp. Code § 5132

Amended by Stats 2009 ch 631 (AB 1233),s 6, eff. 1/1/2010.

Section 5133 - Prima facie evidence of corporate existence

For all purposes other than an action in the nature of quo warranto, a copy of the articles of a corporation duly certified by the Secretary of State is conclusive evidence of the formation of the corporation and prima facie evidence of its corporate existence.

Ca. Corp. Code § 5133

Added by Stats. 1978, Ch. 567.

Section 5134 - Authority of incorporators

If initial directors have not been named in the articles, the incorporator or incorporators, until the directors are elected, may do whatever is necessary and proper to perfect the organization of the corporation, including the adoption and amendment of bylaws of the corporation and the election of directors and officers.

Ca. Corp. Code § 5134

Added by Stats. 1978, Ch. 567.

Article 4 - POWERS

Section 5140 - Powers

Subject to any limitations contained in the articles or bylaws and to compliance with other provisions of this division and any other applicable laws, a corporation, in carrying out its activities, shall have all of the powers of a natural person, including, without limitation, the power to:

(a) Adopt, use, and at will alter a corporate seal, but failure to affix a seal does not affect the validity of any instrument.

(b) Adopt, amend, and repeal bylaws.

(c) Qualify to conduct its activities in any other state, territory, dependency, or foreign country.

(d) Issue, purchase, redeem, receive, take or otherwise acquire, own, sell, lend, exchange, transfer or otherwise dispose of, pledge, use, and otherwise deal in and with its own bonds, debentures, notes, and debt securities.

(e) Issue memberships.

(f) Pay pensions, and establish and carry out pension, deferred compensation, saving, thrift, and other retirement, incentive, and benefit plans, trusts, and provisions for any or all of its directors, officers, employees, and persons providing services to it or any of its subsidiary or related or associated corporations, and to indemnify and purchase and maintain insurance on behalf of any fiduciary of such plans, trusts, or provisions.

(g) Levy dues, assessments, and admission fees.

(h) Make donations for the public welfare or for community funds, hospital, charitable, educational, scientific, civic, religious, or similar purposes.

(i) Assume obligations, enter into contracts, including contracts of guaranty or suretyship, incur liabilities, borrow or lend money or otherwise use its credit, and secure any of its obligations, contracts, or liabilities by mortgage, pledge, or other encumbrance of all or any part of its property and income.

(j) Participate with others in any partnership, joint venture, or other association, transaction, or arrangement of any kind whether or not such participation involves sharing or delegation of control with or to others.

(k) Act as trustee under any trust incidental to the principal objects of the corporation, and receive, hold, administer, exchange, and expend funds and property subject to such trust.

(l) Carry on a business at a profit and apply any profit that results from the business activity to any activity in which it may lawfully engage.

(m) Pay the reasonable value of services rendered in this state to the corporation before January 1, 1975, and not previously paid, by any person who performed such services on a full-time basis under the direction of a religious organization in connection with the religious tenets of the organization. Such person shall have relied solely on the religious organization for their financial support for a minimum of five years. A payment shall not be made if such person or religious organization waives the payment or receipt of compensation for such services in writing. Payment may be made to such religious organization to reimburse it for maintenance of any person who rendered such services and to assist it in providing future support and maintenance; however, payment shall not be made from any funds or assets acquired with funds donated by or traceable to gifts made to the corporation by any person, organization, or governmental agency other than the members, immediate families of members, and affiliated religious organizations of the religious organization under whose direction the services were performed.

(n)

    (1) In anticipation of or during an emergency, take either or both of the following actions necessary to conduct the corporation's business operations and affairs, unless emergency bylaws provide otherwise pursuant to subdivision (g) of Section 5151:

(A) Modify lines of succession to accommodate the incapacity of any director, officer, employee, or agent resulting from the emergency.

(B) Relocate the principal office, designate alternative principal offices or regional offices, or authorize the officers to do so.

(2) During an emergency, take either or both of the following actions necessary to conduct the corporation's business operations and affairs, unless emergency bylaws provide otherwise pursuant to subdivision (g) of Section 5151:

(A) Give notice to a director or directors in any practicable manner under the circumstances, including, but not limited to, by publication and radio, when notice of a meeting of the board cannot be given to that director or directors in the manner prescribed by the bylaws or Section 5211.

(B) Deem that one or more officers of the corporation present at a board meeting is a director, in order of rank and within the same rank in order of seniority, as necessary to achieve a quorum for that meeting.

(3) In anticipation of or during an emergency, the board may take any action that it determines to be necessary or appropriate to respond to the emergency, mitigate the effects of the emergency, or comply with lawful federal and state government orders, but shall not take any action that requires the vote of the members, unless the required vote of the members was obtained prior to the emergency.

(4) Any actions taken in good faith in anticipation of or during an emergency under this subdivision bind the corporation and shall not be used to impose liability on a corporate director, officer, employee, or agent.

(5) For purposes of this subdivision, "emergency" means any of the following events or circumstances as a result of which, and only so long as, a quorum of the corporation's board of directors cannot be readily convened for action:

(A) A natural catastrophe, including, but not limited to, a hurricane, tornado, storm, high water, wind-driven water, tidal wave, tsunami, earthquake, volcanic eruption, landslide, mudslide, snowstorm, drought, epidemic, pandemic, or disease outbreak, or, regardless of cause, any fire, flood, or explosion.

(B) An attack on or within this state or on the public security of its residents by an enemy of this state or on the nation by an enemy of the United States of America, or upon receipt by this state of a warning from the federal government indicating that any such enemy attack is probable or imminent.

(C) An act of terrorism or other manmade disaster that results in extraordinary levels of casualties or damage or disruption severely affecting the infrastructure, environment, economy, government functions, or population, including, but not limited to, mass evacuations.

(D) A state of emergency proclaimed by the Governor of this state, including any person serving as Governor in accordance with Section 10 of Article V of the California Constitution and Section 12058 of the Government Code, or by the President of the United States of America.

Ca. Corp. Code § 5140
Amended by Stats 2021 ch 523 (AB 663),s 5, eff. 1/1/2022.
Amended by Stats 2013 ch 255 (AB 491),s 3, eff. 1/1/2014.

Section 5141 - Assertion of limitation as between corporation or member, officer, or director and third person

Subject to Section 5142:
(a) No limitation upon the activities, purposes, or powers of the corporation or upon the powers of the members, officers, or directors, or the manner of exercise of such powers, contained in or implied by the articles or by Chapters 15 (commencing with Section 6510), 16 (commencing with Section 6610), and 17 (commencing with Section 6710) shall be asserted as between the corporation or member, officer or director and any third person, except in a proceeding:

(1) by a member or the state to enjoin the doing or continuation of unauthorized activities by the corporation or its officers, or both, in cases where third parties have not acquired rights thereby,

(2) to dissolve the corporation, or

(3) by the corporation or by a member suing in a representative suit against the officers or directors of the corporation for violation of their authority.
(b) Any contract or conveyance made in the name of a corporation which is authorized or ratified by the board or is done within the scope of authority, actual or apparent, conferred by the board or within the agency power of the officer executing it, except as the board's authority is limited by law other than this part, binds the corporation, and the corporation acquires rights thereunder whether the contract is executed or wholly or in part executory.

Ca. Corp. Code § 5141
Amended by Stats. 1979, Ch. 724.

Section 5142 - Action to enjoin, correct, obtain damages for or otherwise remedy breach of charitable trust

(a) Notwithstanding Section 5141, any of the following may bring an action to enjoin, correct, obtain damages for or to otherwise remedy a breach of a charitable trust:

(1) The corporation, or a member in the name of the corporation pursuant to Section 5710.

(2) An officer of the corporation.

(3) A director of the corporation.

(4) A person with a reversionary, contractual, or property interest in the assets subject to such charitable trust.

(5) The Attorney General, or any person granted relator status by the Attorney General. The Attorney General shall be given notice of any action brought by the persons specified in paragraphs (1) through (4), and may intervene.
(b) In an action under this section, the court may not rescind or enjoin the performance of a contract unless:

(1) All of the parties to the contract are parties to the action;

(2) No party to the contract has, in good faith, and without actual notice of the trust restriction, parted with value under the contract or in reliance upon it; and

(3) It is equitable to do so.
Ca. Corp. Code § 5142
Amended by Stats. 1979, Ch. 724.

Article 5 - BYLAWS

Section 5150 - Adoption, amendment, or repeal of bylaws

(a) Except as provided in subdivision (c), and Sections 5151, 5220, 5224, 5512, 5613, and 5616, bylaws may be adopted, amended or repealed by the board unless the action would materially and adversely affect the rights of members as to voting or transfer.
(b) Bylaws may be adopted, amended or repealed by approval of members (Section 5034); provided, however, that such adoption, amendment or repeal also requires approval by the members of a class if that action would materially and adversely affect the rights of that class as to voting or transfer in a manner different than that action affects another class.
(c) The articles or bylaws may restrict or eliminate the power of the board to adopt, amend or repeal any or all bylaws, subject to subdivision (e) of Section 5151.
(d) Bylaws may also provide that repeal or amendment of those bylaws, or the repeal or amendment of specified portions of those bylaws, may occur only with the approval

in writing of a specified person or persons other than the board or members. However, this approval requirement, unless the bylaws specify otherwise, shall not apply if any of the following circumstances exist:

(1) The specified person or persons have died or ceased to exist.

(2) If the right of the specified person or persons to approve is in the capacity of an officer, trustee, or other status and the office, trust, or status has ceased to exist.

(3) If the corporation has a specific proposal for amendment or repeal, and the corporation has provided written notice of that proposal, including a copy of the proposal, to the specified person or persons at the most recent address for each of them, based on the corporation's records, and the corporation has not received written approval or nonapproval within the period specified in the notice, which shall not be less than 10 nor more than 30 days commencing at least 20 days after the notice has been provided.

Ca. Corp. Code § 5150
Amended by Stats 2009 ch 631 (AB 1233),s 7, eff. 1/1/2010.

Section 5151 - Number of directors; management of corporation; members; corporate actions

(a) The bylaws shall set forth (unless that provision is contained in the articles, in which case it may only be changed by an amendment of the articles) the number of directors of the corporation, or the method of determining the number of directors of the corporation, or that the number of directors shall be not less than a stated minimum nor more than a stated maximum with the exact number of directors to be fixed, within the limits specified, by approval of the board or the members (Section 5034), in the manner provided in the bylaws, subject to subdivision (e). The number or minimum number of directors may be one or more.
(b) Once members have been admitted, a bylaw specifying or changing a fixed number of directors or the maximum or minimum number or changing from a fixed to a variable board or vice versa may only be adopted by approval of the members (Section 5034).
(c) The bylaws may contain any provision, not in conflict with law or the articles, for the management of the activities and for the conduct of the affairs of the corporation, including, but not limited to:

(1) Any provision referred to in subdivision (c) of Section 5132.

(2) The time, place, and manner of calling, conducting, and giving notice of members', directors', and committee meetings, or of conducting mail ballots.

(3) The qualifications, duties, and compensation of directors; the time of their

election; and the requirements of a quorum for directors' and committee meetings.

(4) The appointment and authority of committees.

(5) The appointment, duties, compensation, and tenure of officers.

(6) The mode of determination of members of record.

(7) The making of reports and financial statements to members.

(8) Setting, imposing, and collecting dues, assessments, and admission fees.
(d) The bylaws may provide for the manner of admission, withdrawal, suspension, and expulsion of members, consistent with the requirements of Section 5341.
(e) The bylaws may require, for any or all corporate actions (except as provided in paragraphs (1) and (2) of subdivision (a) of Section 5222, subdivision (c) of Section 5616, and Section 6610), the vote of a larger proportion of, or all of, the members or the members of any class, unit, or grouping of members, or the vote of a larger proportion of, or all of, the directors, than is otherwise required by this part. Such a provision in the bylaws requiring such greater vote shall not be altered, amended, or repealed except by such greater vote, unless otherwise provided in the bylaws.
(f) The bylaws may contain a provision limiting the number of members, in total or of any class, which the corporation is authorized to admit.
(g)

(1) The bylaws may contain any provision, not in conflict with the articles, to manage and conduct the business affairs of the corporation effective only in an emergency as defined in Section 5140, including, but not limited to, procedures for calling a board meeting, quorum requirements for a board meeting, and designation of additional or substitute directors.

(2) During an emergency, the board may take any action that it determines to be necessary or appropriate to respond to the emergency, mitigate the effects of the emergency, or comply with lawful federal and state government orders, but shall not take any action that requires the vote of the members, unless the required vote of the members was obtained prior to the emergency.

(3) All provisions of the regular bylaws consistent with the emergency bylaws shall remain effective during the emergency, and the emergency bylaws shall not be effective after the emergency ends.

(4) Corporate action taken in good faith in accordance with the emergency bylaws binds the corporation, and shall not be used to impose liability on a corporate director, officer, employee, or agent.
Ca. Corp. Code § 5151

Amended by Stats 2021 ch 523 (AB 663),s 6, eff. 1/1/2022.
Amended by Stats 2013 ch 255 (AB 491),s 4, eff. 1/1/2014.
Amended by Stats 2009 ch 631 (AB 1233),s 8, eff. 1/1/2010.

Section 5152 - Authority of delegates

A corporation may provide in its bylaws for delegates having some or all of the authority of members. Where delegates are provided for, the bylaws shall set forth delegates' terms of office, any reasonable method for delegates' selection and removal, and any reasonable method for calling, noticing, and holding meetings of delegates, may set forth the manner in which delegates may act by written ballot similar to Section 5513 for written ballot of members, and may set forth the manner in which delegates may participate in meetings of delegates similar to paragraph (6) of subdivision (a) of Section 5211 for meetings of directors. Each delegate shall have one vote on each matter presented for action. A delegate shall not vote by proxy. Delegates may be given a name other than "delegates."

Ca. Corp. Code § 5152

Amended by Stats 2021 ch 523 (AB 663),s 7, eff. 1/1/2022.
Amended by Stats. 1983, Ch. 1085, Sec. 2.

Section 5153 - Voting by members or delegates on basis of chapter or by region

A corporation may provide in its bylaws for voting by its members or delegates on the basis of chapter or other organizational unit, or by region or other geographic grouping.

Ca. Corp. Code § 5153

Added by Stats. 1979, Ch. 724.

Article 6 - LOCATION AND INSPECTION OF ARTICLES AND BYLAWS

Section 5160 - Location of articles and bylaws; inspection

Every corporation shall keep at its principal office in this state the original or a copy of its articles and bylaws as amended to date, which shall be open to inspection by the members at all reasonable times during office hours. If the corporation has no office in this state, it shall upon the written request of any member furnish to such member a copy of the articles or bylaws as amended to date.

Ca. Corp. Code § 5160

Added by Stats. 1978, Ch. 567.

Chapter 2 - DIRECTORS AND MANAGEMENT

Article 1 - GENERAL PROVISIONS

Section 5210 - Board of directors

Each corporation shall have a board of directors. Subject to the provisions of this part and any limitations in the articles or bylaws relating to action required to be approved by the members (Section 5034), or by a majority of all members (Section 5033), the activities and affairs of a corporation shall be conducted and all corporate powers shall be exercised by or under the direction of the board. The board may delegate the management of the activities of the corporation to any person or persons, management company, or committee however composed, provided that the activities and affairs of the corporation shall be managed and all corporate powers shall be exercised under the ultimate direction of the board.

Ca. Corp. Code § 5210

Amended by Stats. 1996, Ch. 589, Sec. 4. Effective January 1, 1997.

Section 5211 - Board meetings; quorum

(a) Unless otherwise provided in the articles or in the bylaws, all of the following apply:

(1) Meetings of the board may be called by the chair of the board or the president or any vice president or the secretary or any two directors.

(2) Regular meetings of the board may be held without notice if the time and place of the meetings are fixed by the bylaws or the board. Special meetings of the board shall be held upon four days' notice by first-class mail or 48 hours' notice delivered personally or by telephone, including a voice messaging system or by electronic transmission by the corporation (Section 20). The articles or bylaws may not dispense with notice of a special meeting. A notice, or waiver of notice, need not specify the purpose of any regular or special meeting of the board.

(3) Notice of a meeting need not be given to a director who provides a waiver of notice or consent to holding the meeting or an approval of the minutes thereof in writing, whether before or after the meeting, or who attends the meeting without protesting, prior thereto or at its commencement, the lack of notice to that director. These waivers, consents, and approvals shall be filed with the corporate records or made a part of the minutes of the meetings.

(4) A majority of the directors present, whether or not a quorum is present, may adjourn any meeting to another time and place. If the meeting is adjourned for more than 24 hours, notice of an adjournment to another time or place shall be given prior to the time of the adjourned meeting to the directors who were not present at the time of the adjournment.

(5) Meetings of the board may be held at a place within or without the state that has been designated in the notice of the meeting or, if not stated in the notice or there is no notice, designated in the bylaws or by resolution of the board.

(6) Directors may participate in a meeting through use of conference telephone, electronic video screen communication, or electronic transmission by and to the corporation (Sections 20 and 21). Participation in a meeting through use of conference telephone or electronic video screen communication pursuant to this subdivision constitutes presence in person at that meeting as long as all directors participating in the meeting are able to hear one another. Participation in a meeting through use of electronic transmission by and to the corporation, other than conference telephone and electronic video screen communication, pursuant to this subdivision constitutes presence in person at that meeting if both of the following apply:

(A) Each director participating in the meeting can communicate with all of the other directors concurrently.

(B) Each director is provided the means of participating in all matters before the board, including, without limitation, the capacity to propose, or to interpose an objection to, a specific action to be taken by the corporation.

(7) A majority of the number of directors authorized in or pursuant to the articles or bylaws constitutes a quorum of the board for the transaction of business. The articles or bylaws may require the presence of one or more specified directors in order to constitute a quorum of the board to transact business, as long as the death or nonexistence of a specified director or the death or nonexistence of the person or persons otherwise authorized to appoint or designate that director does not prevent the corporation from transacting business in the normal course of events. The articles or bylaws may not provide that a quorum shall be less than one-fifth the number of directors authorized in or pursuant to the articles or bylaws, or less than two, whichever is larger, unless the number of directors authorized in or pursuant to the articles or bylaws is one, in which case one director constitutes a quorum.

(8) Subject to the provisions of Sections 5212, 5233, 5234, 5235, and subdivision (e) of Section 5238, an act or decision done or made by a majority of the directors present at a meeting duly held at which a quorum is present is the act of the board. The articles or bylaws may not provide that a lesser vote than a majority of the directors present at a meeting is the act of the board. A meeting at which a quorum is initially present may continue to transact business notwithstanding the withdrawal of directors, if any action taken is approved by at least a majority of the required quorum

for that meeting, or a greater number required by this division, the articles, or the bylaws.

(b) An action required or permitted to be taken by the board may be taken without a meeting if all directors individually or collectively consent in writing to that action and if, subject to subdivision (a) of Section 5224, the number of directors then in office constitutes a quorum. The written consent or consents shall be filed with the minutes of the proceedings of the board. The action by written consent shall have the same force and effect as a unanimous vote of the directors. For purposes of this subdivision only, "all directors" does not include an "interested director" as defined in subdivision (a) of Section 5233 or a "common director" as described in Section 5234 who abstains in writing from providing consent, if (1) the facts described in paragraph (2) or (3) of subdivision (d) of Section 5233 are established or the provisions of paragraph (1) or (2) of subdivision (a) of Section 5234 are satisfied, as appropriate, at or prior to execution of the written consent or consents; (2) the establishment of those facts or satisfaction of those provisions, as applicable, is included in the written consent or consents executed by the noninterested or noncommon directors or in other records of the corporation; and (3) the noninterested or noncommon directors, as applicable, approve the action by a vote that is sufficient without counting the votes of the interested directors or common directors.

(c) Each director shall have one vote on each matter presented to the board of directors for action. A director shall not vote by proxy.

(d) The provisions of this section apply also to incorporators, to committees of the board, and to action by those incorporators or committees mutatis mutandis.

　　Ca. Corp. Code § 5211

Amended by Stats 2019 ch 497 (AB 991),s 32, eff. 1/1/2020.
Amended by Stats 2018 ch 322 (AB 2557),s 1, eff. 1/1/2019.
Amended by Stats 2011 ch 442 (AB 1211),s 2, eff. 1/1/2012.
Amended by Stats 2009 ch 631 (AB 1233),s 9, eff. 1/1/2010.
Amended by Stats 2005 ch 102 (SB 119),s 3, eff. 1/1/2006
Amended by Stats 2004 ch 254 (SB 1306),s 14, eff. 1/1/2005
Amended by Stats 2003 ch 168 (SB 735),s 3, eff. 1/1/2004.
Amended by Stats 2002 ch 1008 (AB 3028),s 9, eff. 1/1/2003.

Section 5212 - Committees

(a) The board may, by resolution adopted by a majority of the number of directors then in office, provided that a quorum is present, create one or more committees, each consisting of two or more directors, to serve at the pleasure of the board. Appointments to such committees shall be by a majority vote of the directors then in office, unless the articles or bylaws require a majority vote of the number of directors authorized in or pursuant to the articles or bylaws. The bylaws may authorize one or more such committees, each consisting of two or more directors, and may provide that a specified officer or officers who are also directors of the corporation shall be a member or members of such committee or committees. The board may appoint one or more directors as alternate members of such committee, who may replace any absent member at any meeting of the committee. Such committee, to the extent provided in the resolution of the board or in the bylaws, shall have all the authority of the board, except with respect to:

(1) The approval of any action for which this part also requires approval of the members (Section 5034) or approval of a majority of all members (Section 5033), regardless of whether the corporation has members.

(2) The filling of vacancies on the board or in any committee which has the authority of the board.

(3) The fixing of compensation of the directors for serving on the board or on any committee.

(4) The amendment or repeal of bylaws or the adoption of new bylaws.

(5) The amendment or repeal of any resolution of the board which by its express terms is not so amendable or repealable.

(6) The appointment of committees of the board or the members thereof.

(7) The expenditure of corporate funds to support a nominee for director after there are more people nominated for director than can be elected.

(8) The approval of any self-dealing transaction except as provided in paragraph (3) of subdivision (d) of Section 5233.

(b) A committee exercising the authority of the board shall not include as members persons who are not directors. However, the board may create other committees that do not exercise the authority of the board and these other committees may include persons regardless of whether they are directors.

(c) Unless the bylaws otherwise provide, the board may delegate to any committee powers as authorized by Section 5210, but may not delegate the powers set forth in paragraphs (1) to (8), inclusive, of subdivision (a).

(d) If required by subdivision (e) of Section 12586 of the Government Code, the board shall appoint an audit committee in accordance with that subdivision and for the purposes set forth therein.

Ca. Corp. Code § 5212

Amended by Stats 2011 ch 442 (AB 1211),s 3, eff. 1/1/2012.
Amended by Stats 2009 ch 631 (AB 1233),s 10, eff. 1/1/2010.

Section 5213 - Officers

(a)A corporation shall have (1) a chair of the board, who may be given the title chair, chairperson, chair of the board, or chairperson of the board, or a president or both, (2) a secretary, (3) a treasurer or a chief financial officer or both, and (4) any other officers with any titles and duties as shall be stated in the bylaws or determined by the board and as may be necessary to enable it to sign instruments. The president, or if there is no president the chair of the board, is the general manager and chief executive officer of the corporation, unless otherwise provided in the articles or bylaws. Unless otherwise specified in the articles or the bylaws, if there is no chief financial officer, the treasurer is the chief financial officer of the corporation. Any number of offices may be held by the same person unless the articles or bylaws provide otherwise, except that no person serving as the secretary, the treasurer, or the chief financial officer may serve concurrently as the president or chair of the board. Any compensation of the president or chief executive officer and the chief financial officer or treasurer shall be determined in accordance with subdivision (g) of Section 12586 of the Government Code, if applicable.

(b) Except as otherwise provided by the articles or bylaws, officers shall be chosen by the board and serve at the pleasure of the board, subject to the rights, if any, of an officer under any contract of employment. Any officer may resign at any time upon written notice to the corporation without prejudice to the rights, if any, of the corporation under any contract to which the officer is a party.

(c) If the articles or bylaws provide for the election of any officers by the members, the term of office of the elected officer shall be one year unless the articles or bylaws provide for a different term which shall not exceed three years.

   Ca. Corp. Code § 5213

Amended by Stats 2022 ch 617 (SB 1202),s 47, eff. 1/1/2023.
Amended by Stats 2015 ch 98 (SB 351),s 11, eff. 1/1/2016.
Amended by Stats 2011 ch 442 (AB 1211),s 4, eff. 1/1/2012.
Amended by Stats 2009 ch 631 (AB 1233),s 11, eff. 1/1/2010.

Section 5214 - Authority of signing officers

Subject to the provisions of subdivision (a) of Section 5141 and Section 5142, any note, mortgage, evidence of indebtedness, contract, conveyance or other instrument in writing, and any assignment or endorsement thereof, executed or entered into between any corporation and any other person, when signed by any one of the chairperson of the board, the president or any vice president and by any one of the secretary, any assistant secretary, the chief financial officer or any assistant treasurer of such corporation, is not invalidated as to the corporation by any lack of authority of the signing officers in the absence of actual knowledge on the part of the other person that the signing officers had no authority to execute the same.

   Ca. Corp. Code § 5214

Amended by Stats 2022 ch 617 (SB 1202),s 48, eff. 1/1/2023.
Amended by Stats. 1996, Ch. 589, Sec. 5. Effective January 1, 1997.

Section 5215 - Bylaws, minutes, resolutions

The original or a copy in writing or in any other form capable of being converted into clearly legible tangible form of the bylaws or of the minutes of any incorporators', members', directors', committee or other meeting or of any resolution adopted by the board or a committee thereof, or members, certified to be a true copy by a person purporting to be the secretary or an assistant secretary of the corporation, is prima facie evidence of the adoption of such bylaws or resolution or of the due holding of such meeting and of the matters stated therein.

Ca. Corp. Code § 5215
Amended by Stats 2004 ch 254 (SB 1306),s 15, eff. 1/1/2005

Article 2 - SELECTION, REMOVAL AND RESIGNATION OF DIRECTORS

Section 5220 - Term of directors

(a) Except as provided in subdivision (d), (e), or (f), directors shall be elected for terms of not longer than four years, as fixed in the articles or bylaws. However, the terms of directors of a corporation without members may be up to six years. In the absence of any provision in the articles or bylaws, the term shall be one year. The articles or bylaws may provide for staggering the terms of directors by dividing the total number of directors into groups of one or more directors. The terms of office of the several groups and the number of directors in each group need not be uniform. An amendment of the articles or bylaws may not extend the term of a director beyond that for which the director was elected, and any bylaw provision increasing the terms of directors may not be adopted without approval of the members (Section 5034).
(b) Unless otherwise provided in the articles or bylaws, each director, including a director elected to fill a vacancy, shall hold office until the expiration of the term for which elected and until a successor has been elected and qualified, unless the director has been removed from office.
(c) The articles or bylaws may provide for the election of one or more directors by the members of any class voting as a class.
(d) For the purposes of this subdivision, "designator" means one or more designators. Notwithstanding subdivisions (a) to (c), inclusive, all or any portion of the directors authorized in the articles or bylaws of a corporation may hold office by virtue of designation or selection by a specified designator as provided by the articles or bylaws rather than by election. Those directors shall continue in office for the term prescribed by the governing article or bylaw provision, or, if there is no term prescribed, until the governing article or bylaw provision is duly amended or repealed, except as provided in subdivision (e) of Section 5222. A bylaw provision authorized by this subdivision may be adopted, amended, or repealed only by approval of the members (Section 5034) except as provided in subdivision (d) of Section 5150. Unless otherwise provided in the articles or bylaws, the entitlement to designate or select a director or directors shall cease if any of the following circumstances exist:

(1) The specified designator of that director or directors has died or ceased to exist.

(2) If the entitlement of the specified designator of that director or directors to designate is in the capacity of an officer, trustee, or other status and the office, trust, or status has ceased to exist.

(e) If a corporation has not issued memberships and (1) all the directors resign, die, or become incompetent, or (2) a corporation's initial directors have not been named in the articles and all incorporators resign, die, or become incompetent before the election of the initial directors, the superior court of any county may appoint directors of the corporation upon application by any party in interest.

(f) If authorized in the articles or bylaws of a corporation, all or any portion of the directors may hold office ex officio by virtue of occupying a specified position within the corporation or outside the corporation. The term of office of an ex officio director shall coincide with that director's respective term of office in the specified position entitling him or her to serve on the board of directors. Upon an ex officio director's resignation or removal from that position, or resignation or removal from the board for any reason, the term of office as a director of the corporation shall immediately cease. At that time, the successor in office shall become an ex officio director of the corporation, occupying the place of the former director.

Ca. Corp. Code § 5220

Amended by Stats 2018 ch 322 (AB 2557),s 2, eff. 1/1/2019.
Amended by Stats 2009 ch 631 (AB 1233),s 12, eff. 1/1/2010.
Amended by Stats 2006 ch 567 (AB 2303),s 17, eff. 1/1/2007.
Amended by Stats 2000 ch 485 (AB 1895), s 10, eff. 1/1/2001.

Section 5221 - Vacancy based on unsound mind, felony conviction, breach of duty, or failure to attend meetings; qualifications of directors

(a) The board may declare vacant the office of a director who has been declared of unsound mind by a final order of court, or convicted of a felony, or been found by a final order or judgment of any court to have breached any duty under Article 3 (commencing with Section 5230), or, if at the time a director is elected, the bylaws provide that a director may be removed for missing a specified number of board meetings, fails to attend the specified number of meetings.

(b) As provided in paragraph (3) of subdivision (c) of Section 5151, the articles or bylaws may prescribe the qualifications of directors. The board, by a majority vote of the directors who meet all of the required qualifications to be a director, may declare vacant the office of any director who fails or ceases to meet any required qualification that was in effect at the beginning of that director's current term of office.

Ca. Corp. Code § 5221

Amended by Stats. 1996, Ch. 589, Sec. 7. Effective January 1, 1997.

Section 5222 - Removal of director

(a) Subject to subdivisions (b) and (f), any or all directors may be removed without cause if:

(1) In a corporation with fewer than 50 members, the removal is approved by a majority of all members (Section 5033).

(2) In a corporation with 50 or more members, the removal is approved by the members (Section 5034).

(3) In a corporation with no members, the removal is approved by a majority of the directors then in office.

(b) Except for a corporation having no members pursuant to Section 5310:

(1) In a corporation in which the articles or bylaws authorize members to cumulate their votes pursuant to subdivision (a) of Section 5616, no director may be removed (unless the entire board is removed) if the votes cast against removal, or not consenting in writing to the removal, would be sufficient to elect the director if voted cumulatively at an election at which the same total number of votes were cast (or, if the action is taken by written ballot, all memberships entitled to vote were voted) and the entire number of directors authorized at the time of the director's most recent election were then being elected.

(2) If by the provisions of the articles or bylaws the members of any class, voting as a class, are entitled to elect one or more directors, any director so elected may be removed only by the applicable vote of the members of that class.

(3) If by the provisions of the articles or bylaws the members within a chapter or other organizational unit, or region or other geographic grouping, voting as such, are entitled to elect one or more directors, any director so elected may be removed only by the applicable vote of the members within the organizational unit or geographic grouping.

(c) Any reduction of the authorized number of directors or any amendment reducing the number of classes of directors does not remove any director prior to the expiration of the director's term of office unless the reduction or any amendment also provides for the removal of one or more specified directors.

(d) Except as provided in this section and Sections 5221, 5223, and 5227, a director may not be removed prior to the expiration of the director's term of office.

(e) If a director removed under this section, Section 5221, Section 5223, or Section 5227 was chosen by designation pursuant to subdivision (d) of Section 5220, then:

(1) If a different person may be designated pursuant to a governing article or bylaw provision, the new designation shall be made.

(2) If the governing article or bylaw provision contains no provision under which a different person may be designated, the governing article or bylaw provision shall be deemed repealed.

(f) For the purposes of this subdivision, "designator" means one or more designators. If by the provisions of the articles or bylaws a designator is entitled to designate one or more directors, then:

(1) Unless otherwise provided in the articles or bylaws at the time of designation, any director so designated may be removed without cause by the designator of that director.

(2) Any director so designated may only be removed under subdivision (a) with the written consent of the designator of that director.

(3) Unless otherwise provided in the articles or bylaws, the right to remove shall not apply if any of the following circumstances exist:

(A) The designator entitled to that right has died or ceased to exist.

(B) If that right is in the capacity of an officer, trustee, or other status, and the office, trust, or status has ceased to exist.

Ca. Corp. Code § 5222
Amended by Stats 2011 ch 442 (AB 1211),s 5, eff. 1/1/2012.
Amended by Stats 2009 ch 631 (AB 1233),s 13, eff. 1/1/2010.
Amended by Stats 2000 ch 135 (AB 2539), s 22, eff. 1/1/2001.
Amended September 21, 1999 (Bill Number: AB 1687) (Chapter 453).

Section 5223 - Removal in case of fraudulent or dishonest acts, gross abuse of authority or discretion, or breach of duty

(a) The superior court of the proper county may, at the suit of a director, or twice the authorized number (Section 5036) of members or 20 members, whichever is less, remove from office any director in case of fraudulent or dishonest acts or gross abuse of authority or discretion with reference to the corporation or breach of any duty arising under Article 3 (commencing with Section 5230) of this chapter, and may bar from reelection any director so removed for a period prescribed by the court. The corporation shall be made a party to such action.
(b) The Attorney General may bring an action under subdivision (a), may intervene in such an action brought by any other party and shall be given notice of any such action brought by any other party.

Ca. Corp. Code § 5223
Amended by Stats. 1981, Ch. 587, Sec. 6.

Section 5224 - Filling vacancies

(a) Unless otherwise provided in the articles or bylaws and except for a vacancy created by the removal of a director, vacancies on the board may be filled by approval of the board (Section 5032) or, if the number of directors then in office is less than a quorum, by (1) the unanimous written consent of the directors then in office, (2) the affirmative vote of a majority of the directors then in office at a meeting held pursuant to notice or waivers of notice complying with Section 5211, or (3) a sole remaining director. Unless the articles or a bylaw approved by the members (Section 5034) provide that the board may fill vacancies occurring in the board by reason of the removal of directors, or unless the corporation has no members pursuant to Section 5310, such vacancies may be filled only by approval of the members (Section 5034).

(b) The members may elect a director at any time to fill any vacancy not filled by the directors.

(c) Any director may resign effective upon giving written notice to the chairperson of the board, the president, the secretary or the board of directors of the corporation, unless the notice specifies a later time for the effectiveness of such resignation. If the resignation is effective at a future time, a successor may be elected to take office when the resignation becomes effective.

Ca. Corp. Code § 5224

Amended by Stats 2022 ch 617 (SB 1202),s 49, eff. 1/1/2023.

Amended by Stats. 1985, Ch. 329, Sec. 2.

Section 5225 - Provisional director

(a) If a corporation has an even number of directors who are equally divided and cannot agree as to the management of its affairs, so that its activities can no longer be conducted to advantage or so that there is danger that its property, activities, or business will be impaired or lost, the superior court of the proper county may, notwithstanding any provisions of the articles or bylaws and whether or not an action is pending for an involuntary winding up or dissolution of the corporation, appoint a provisional director pursuant to this section. Action for such appointment may be brought by any director or by members holding not less than 33 $^1/_3$ percent of the voting power.

(b) If the members of a corporation are deadlocked so that they cannot elect the directors to be elected at the time prescribed therefor, the superior court of the proper county may, notwithstanding any provisions of the articles or bylaws, upon petition of members holding 50 percent of the voting power, appoint a provisional director or directors pursuant to this section or order such other equitable relief as the court deems appropriate.

(c) Any person bringing an action under subdivision (a) or (b) shall give notice to the Attorney General, who may intervene.

(d) The Attorney General may bring an action under subdivision (a) or (b).

(e) A provisional director shall be an impartial person, who is neither a member nor a creditor of the corporation, nor related by consanguinity or affinity within the third degree according to the common law to any of the other directors of the corporation or to any judge of the court by which such provisional director is appointed. A provisional director shall have all the rights and powers of a director until the deadlock in the board or among members is broken or until such provisional director is removed by order of the court or by approval of a majority of all members (Section 5033). Such person shall be entitled to such compensation as shall be fixed by the court unless otherwise agreed with the corporation.

Ca. Corp. Code § 5225
Amended by Stats. 1995, Ch. 154, Sec. 12. Effective January 1, 1996.

Section 5226 - Resignation

Except upon notice to the Attorney General, no director may resign where the corporation would then be left without a duly elected director or directors in charge of its affairs.

Ca. Corp. Code § 5226
Added by Stats. 1978, Ch. 567.

Section 5227 - Interested persons

(a) Any other provision of this part notwithstanding, not more than 49 percent of the persons serving on the board of any corporation may be interested persons.
(b) For the purpose of this section, "interested persons" means either:

(1) Any person currently being compensated by the corporation for services rendered to it within the previous 12 months, whether as a full- or part-time employee, independent contractor, or otherwise, excluding any reasonable compensation paid to a director as director; or

(2) Any brother, sister, ancestor, descendant, spouse, brother-in-law, sister-in-law, son-in-law, daughter-in-law, mother-in-law, or father-in-law of any such person.
(c) A person with standing under Section 5142 may bring an action to correct any violation of this section. The court may enter any order which shall provide an equitable and fair remedy to the corporation, including, but not limited to, an order for the election of additional directors, an order to enlarge the size of the board, or an order for the removal of directors.
(d) The provisions of this section shall not affect the validity or enforceability of any transaction entered into by a corporation.

Ca. Corp. Code § 5227
Amended by Stats. 1996, Ch. 589, Sec. 8. Effective January 1, 1997.

Article 3 - STANDARDS OF CONDUCT

Section 5230 - Duties and liabilities

(a) Any duties and liabilities set forth in this article shall apply without regard to whether a director is compensated by the corporation.

(b) Part 4 (commencing with Section 16000) of Division 9 of the Probate Code does not apply to the directors of any corporation.

Ca. Corp. Code § 5230

Amended by Stats. 1987, Ch. 923, Sec. 1.2. Operative January 1, 1988, by Sec. 103 of Ch. 923.

Section 5231 - Good faith; best interests of corporation; care of ordinarily prudent person

(a) A director shall perform the duties of a director, including duties as a member of any committee of the board upon which the director may serve, in good faith, in a manner that director believes to be in the best interests of the corporation and with such care, including reasonable inquiry, as an ordinarily prudent person in a like position would use under similar circumstances.

(b) In performing the duties of a director, a director shall be entitled to rely on information, opinions, reports or statements, including financial statements and other financial data, in each case prepared or presented by:

(1) One or more officers or employees of the corporation whom the director believes to be reliable and competent in the matters presented;

(2) Counsel, independent accountants or other persons as to matters which the director believes to be within that person's professional or expert competence; or

(3) A committee upon which the director does not serve that is composed exclusively of any or any combination of directors, persons described in paragraph (1), or persons described in paragraph (2), as to matters within the committee's designated authority, which committee the director believes to merit confidence, so long as, in any case, the director acts in good faith, after reasonable inquiry when the need therefor is indicated by the circumstances and without knowledge that would cause that reliance to be unwarranted.

(c) Except as provided in Section 5233, a person who performs the duties of a director in accordance with subdivisions (a) and (b) shall have no liability based upon any alleged failure to discharge the person's obligations as a director, including, without limiting the generality of the foregoing, any actions or omissions which exceed or defeat a public or charitable purpose to which a corporation, or assets held by it, are dedicated.

Ca. Corp. Code § 5231

Amended by Stats 2009 ch 631 (AB 1233),s 14, eff. 1/1/2010.

Section 5232 - Acts or omissions in connection with election, selection, or

nomination of directors

(a) Section 5231 governs the duties of directors as to any acts or omissions in connection with the election, selection, or nomination of directors.
(b) This section shall not be construed to limit the generality of Section 5231.
    Ca. Corp. Code § 5232
Added by Stats. 1978, Ch. 567.

Section 5233 - Self-dealing transaction

(a) Except as provided in subdivision (b), for the purpose of this section, a self-dealing transaction means a transaction to which the corporation is a party and in which one or more of its directors has a material financial interest and which does not meet the requirements of paragraph (1), (2), or (3) of subdivision (d). Such a director is an "interested director" for the purpose of this section.
(b) The provisions of this section do not apply to any of the following:

    (1) An action of the board fixing the compensation of a director as a director or officer of the corporation.

    (2) A transaction which is part of a public or charitable program of the corporation if it:

        (i) is approved or authorized by the corporation in good faith and without unjustified favoritism; and

        (ii) results in a benefit to one or more directors or their families because they are in the class of persons intended to be benefited by the public or charitable program.

    (3) A transaction, of which the interested director or directors have no actual knowledge, and which does not exceed the lesser of 1 percent of the gross receipts of the corporation for the preceding fiscal year or one hundred thousand dollars ($100,000).
(c) The Attorney General or, if the Attorney General is joined as an indispensable party, any of the following may bring an action in the superior court of the proper county for the remedies specified in subdivision (h):

    (1) The corporation, or a member asserting the right in the name of the corporation pursuant to Section 5710.

    (2) A director of the corporation.

    (3) An officer of the corporation.

(4) Any person granted relator status by the Attorney General.

(d) In any action brought under subdivision (c) the remedies specified in subdivision (h) shall not be granted if:

(1) The Attorney General, or the court in an action in which the Attorney General is an indispensable party, has approved the transaction before or after it was consummated; or

(2) The following facts are established:

(A) The corporation entered into the transaction for its own benefit;

(B) The transaction was fair and reasonable as to the corporation at the time the corporation entered into the transaction;

(C) Prior to consummating the transaction or any part thereof the board authorized or approved the transaction in good faith by a vote of a majority of the directors then in office without counting the vote of the interested director or directors, and with knowledge of the material facts concerning the transaction and the director's interest in the transaction. Except as provided in paragraph (3) of this subdivision, action by a committee of the board shall not satisfy this paragraph; and

(D)

(i) Prior to authorizing or approving the transaction the board considered and in good faith determined after reasonable investigation under the circumstances that the corporation could not have obtained a more advantageous arrangement with reasonable effort under the circumstances or

(ii) the corporation in fact could not have obtained a more advantageous arrangement with reasonable effort under the circumstances; or

(3) The following facts are established:

(A) A committee or person authorized by the board approved the transaction in a manner consistent with the standards set forth in paragraph (2) of this subdivision;

(B) It was not reasonably practicable to obtain approval of the board prior to entering into the transaction; and

(C) The board, after determining in good faith that the conditions of subparagraphs (A) and (B) of this paragraph were satisfied, ratified the transaction at its next meeting by a vote of the majority of the directors then in office without counting the vote of the interested director or directors.

(e) Except as provided in subdivision (f), an action under subdivision (c) must be filed within two years after written notice setting forth the material facts of the transaction and the director's interest in the transaction is filed with the Attorney General in accordance with such regulations, if any, as the Attorney General may adopt or, if no such notice is filed, within three years after the transaction occurred, except for the Attorney General, who shall have 10 years after the transaction occurred within which to file an action.

(f) In any action for breach of an obligation of the corporation owed to an interested director, where the obligation arises from a self-dealing transaction which has not been approved as provided in subdivision (d), the court may, by way of offset only, make any order authorized by subdivision (h), notwithstanding the expiration of the applicable period specified in subdivision (e).

(g) Interested directors may be counted in determining the presence of a quorum at a meeting of the board which authorizes, approves or ratifies a contract or transaction.

(h) If a self-dealing transaction has taken place, the interested director or directors shall do such things and pay such damages as in the discretion of the court will provide an equitable and fair remedy to the corporation, taking into account any benefit received by the corporation and whether the interested director or directors acted in good faith and with intent to further the best interest of the corporation. Without limiting the generality of the foregoing, the court may order the director to do any or all of the following:

(1) Account for any profits made from such transaction, and pay them to the corporation;

(2) Pay the corporation the value of the use of any of its property used in such transaction; and

(3) Return or replace any property lost to the corporation as a result of such transaction, together with any income or appreciation lost to the corporation by reason of such transaction, or account for any proceeds of sale of such property, and pay the proceeds to the corporation together with interest at the legal rate. The court may award prejudgment interest to the extent allowed in Section 3287 or 3288 of the Civil Code. In addition, the court may, in its discretion, grant exemplary damages for a fraudulent or malicious violation of this section.

Ca. Corp. Code § 5233
Amended by Stats. 1981, Ch. 587, Sec. 7.

Section 5234 - Contract or other transaction not void or voidable

(a) No contract or other transaction between a corporation and any domestic or foreign corporation, firm or association of which one or more of its directors are directors is either void or voidable because such director or directors are present at the meeting of the board or a committee thereof which authorizes, approves or ratifies the contract or transaction, if:

(1) The material facts as to the transaction and as to such director's other directorship are fully disclosed or known to the board or committee, and the board or committee authorizes, approves or ratifies the contract or transaction in good faith by a vote sufficient without counting the vote of the common director or directors; or

(2) As to contracts or transactions not approved as provided in paragraph (1) of this subdivision, the contract or transaction is just and reasonable as to the corporation at the time it is authorized, approved or ratified.
(b) This section does not apply to transactions covered by Section 5233.

Ca. Corp. Code § 5234
Added by Stats. 1978, Ch. 567.

Section 5235 - Compensation

(a) The board may fix the compensation of a director, as director or officer, and no obligation, otherwise valid, to pay such compensation shall be voidable merely because the persons receiving the compensation participated in the decision to pay it, unless it was not just and reasonable as to the corporation at the time it was authorized, ratified or approved. The board shall take other actions that are required by subdivision (g) of Section 12586 of the Government Code, if applicable.
(b) In the absence of fraud, any liability under this section shall be limited to the amount by which the compensation exceeded what was just and reasonable, plus interest from the date of payment.

Ca. Corp. Code § 5235
Amended by Stats 2011 ch 442 (AB 1211),s 6, eff. 1/1/2012.

Section 5236 - Loan of money or property or guarantee of obligation of director or officer prohibited

(a) A corporation shall not make any loan of money or property to or guarantee the obligation of any director or officer, unless approved by the Attorney General; provided, however, that a corporation may advance money to a director or officer of the corporation or of its parent or any subsidiary for expenses reasonably anticipated to be incurred in the performance of the duties of such officer or director, provided that in the absence of such advance, such director or officer would be entitled to be reimbursed for such expenses by such corporation, its parent, or any subsidiary.
(b) The provisions of subdivision (a) do not apply to the payment of premiums in whole or in part by a corporation on a life insurance policy on the life of a director or officer so long as repayment to the corporation of the amount paid by it is secured by either the policy's death benefit proceeds or its cash surrender value, or both.

(c) When repayment of a loan, entered into under subdivision (b), to a corporation is secured by only the policy's death benefit, the contract between the corporation and director or officer that secures the loan shall include terms sufficient to ensure that any policy fees and charges, withdrawals of the cash value, or loans taken against it do not impair the value of the death benefit to repay the cost of the loan, for the life of the policy.

(d) When repayment of a loan, entered into under subdivision (b), to a corporation is secured by only the policy's cash surrender value, the contract between the corporation and the director or officer that secures the loan shall include terms sufficient to ensure that the cash surrender value is sufficient to repay the cost of the loan, for the life of the policy.

(e) The provisions of subdivision (a) do not apply to a loan of money to or for the benefit of an officer in circumstances where the loan is necessary, in the judgment of the board, to provide financing for the purchase of the principal residence of the officer in order to secure the services or continued services of the officer and the loan is secured by real property located in the state.

Ca. Corp. Code § 5236
Amended by Stats 2019 ch 250 (SB 540),s 1, eff. 1/1/2020.

Section 5237 - Joint and several liability of directors who approve certain corporate actions

(a) Subject to the provisions of Section 5231, directors of a corporation who approve any of the following corporate actions shall be jointly and severally liable to the corporation for:

(1) The making of any distribution.

(2) The distribution of assets after institution of dissolution proceedings of the corporation, without paying or adequately providing for all known liabilities of the corporation, excluding any claims not filed by creditors within the time limit set by the court in a notice given to creditors under Chapters 15 (commencing with Section 6510), 16 (commencing with Section 6610) and 17 (commencing with Section 6710).

(3) The making of any loan or guaranty contrary to Section 5236.

(b) A director who is present at a meeting of the board, or any committee thereof, at which action specified in subdivision (a) is taken and who abstains from voting shall be considered to have approved the action.

(c) Suit may be brought in the name of the corporation to enforce the liability:

(1) Under paragraph (1) of subdivision (a) against any or all directors liable by the persons entitled to sue under subdivision (b) of Section 5420;

(2) Under paragraph (2) or (3) of subdivision (a) against any or all directors liable by any one or more creditors of the corporation whose debts or claims arose prior to the time of the corporate action who have not consented to the corporate action, whether or not they have reduced their claims to judgment;

(3) Under paragraph (1), (2) or (3) of subdivision (a), by the Attorney General.

(d) The damages recoverable from a director under this section shall be the amount of the illegal distribution, or if the illegal distribution consists of property, the fair market value of that property at the time of the illegal distribution, plus interest thereon from the date of the distribution at the legal rate on judgments until paid, together with all reasonably incurred costs of appraisal or other valuation, if any, of that property, or the loss suffered by the corporation as a result of the illegal loan or guaranty.

(e) Any director sued under this section may implead all other directors liable and may compel contribution, either in that action or in an independent action against directors not joined in that action.

(f) Directors liable under this section shall also be entitled to be subrogated to the rights of the corporation:

(1) With respect to paragraph (1) of subdivision (a), against the persons who received the distribution.

(2) With respect to paragraph (2) of subdivision (a), against the persons who received the distribution.

(3) With respect to paragraph (3) of subdivision (a), against the person who received the loan or guaranty. Any director sued under this section may file a cross-complaint against the person or persons who are liable to the director as a result of the subrogation provided for in this subdivision or may proceed against them in an independent action.

Ca. Corp. Code § 5237

Added 9/21/1999 (Bill Number: AB 1687) (Chapter 453).

Section 5238 - Indemnification

(a) For the purposes of this section, "agent" means any person who is or was a director, officer, employee or other agent of the corporation, or is or was serving at the request of the corporation as a director, officer, employee or agent of another foreign or domestic corporation, partnership, joint venture, trust or other enterprise, or was a director, officer, employee or agent of a foreign or domestic corporation that was a predecessor corporation of the corporation or of another enterprise at the request of the predecessor corporation; "proceeding" means any threatened, pending or completed action or proceeding, whether civil, criminal, administrative or investigative; and "expenses" includes without limitation attorneys' fees and any expenses of establishing a right to indemnification under subdivision (d) or paragraph

(3) of subdivision (e).

(b) A corporation shall have power to indemnify any person who was or is a party or is threatened to be made a party to any proceeding (other than an action by or in the right of the corporation to procure a judgment in its favor, an action brought under Section 5233, or an action brought by the Attorney General or a person granted relator status by the Attorney General for any breach of duty relating to assets held in charitable trust) by reason of the fact that the person is or was an agent of the corporation, against expenses, judgments, fines, settlements and other amounts actually and reasonably incurred in connection with the proceeding if the person acted in good faith and in a manner the person reasonably believed to be in the best interests of the corporation and, in the case of a criminal proceeding, had no reasonable cause to believe the conduct of the person was unlawful. The termination of any proceeding by judgment, order, settlement, conviction or upon a plea of nolo contendere or its equivalent shall not, of itself, create a presumption that the person did not act in good faith and in a manner which the person reasonably believed to be in the best interests of the corporation or that the person had reasonable cause to believe that the person's conduct was unlawful.

(c) A corporation shall have power to indemnify any person who was or is a party or is threatened to be made a party to any threatened, pending or completed action by or in the right of the corporation, or brought under Section 5233, or brought by the Attorney General or a person granted relator status by the Attorney General for breach of duty relating to assets held in charitable trust, to procure a judgment in its favor by reason of the fact that the person is or was an agent of the corporation, against expenses actually and reasonably incurred by the person in connection with the defense or settlement of the action if the person acted in good faith, in a manner the person believed to be in the best interests of the corporation and with such care, including reasonable inquiry, as an ordinarily prudent person in a like position would use under similar circumstances. No indemnification shall be made under this subdivision:

(1) In respect of any claim, issue or matter as to which the person shall have been adjudged to be liable to the corporation in the performance of the person's duty to the corporation, unless and only to the extent that the court in which the proceeding is or was pending shall determine upon application that, in view of all the circumstances of the case, the person is fairly and reasonably entitled to indemnity for the expenses which the court shall determine;

(2) Of amounts paid in settling or otherwise disposing of a threatened or pending action, with or without court approval; or

(3) Of expenses incurred in defending a threatened or pending action which is settled or otherwise disposed of without court approval unless it is settled with the approval of the Attorney General.

(d) To the extent that an agent of a corporation has been successful on the merits in defense of any proceeding referred to in subdivision (b) or (c) or in defense of any claim, issue or matter therein, the agent shall be indemnified against expenses actually and reasonably incurred by the agent in connection therewith.

(e) Except as provided in subdivision (d), any indemnification under this section shall be made by the corporation only if authorized in the specific case, upon a determination that indemnification of the agent is proper in the circumstances because the agent has met the applicable standard of conduct set forth in subdivision (b) or (c), by:

(1) A majority vote of a quorum consisting of directors who are not parties to the proceeding;

(2) Approval of the members (Section 5034), with the persons to be indemnified not being entitled to vote thereon; or

(3) The court in which the proceeding is or was pending upon application made by the corporation or the agent or the attorney or other person rendering services in connection with the defense, whether or not the application by the agent, attorney, or other person is opposed by the corporation.

(f) Expenses incurred in defending any proceeding may be advanced by the corporation prior to the final disposition of the proceeding upon receipt of an undertaking by or on behalf of the agent to repay the amount unless it shall be determined ultimately that the agent is entitled to be indemnified as authorized in this section. The provisions of subdivision (a) of Section 5236 do not apply to advances made pursuant to this subdivision.

(g) No provision made by a corporation to indemnify its or its subsidiary's directors or officers for the defense of any proceeding, whether contained in the articles, bylaws, a resolution of members or directors, an agreement or otherwise, shall be valid unless consistent with this section. Nothing contained in this section shall affect any right to indemnification to which persons other than the directors and officers may be entitled by contract or otherwise.

(h) No indemnification or advance shall be made under this section, except as provided in subdivision (d) or paragraph (3) of subdivision (e), in any circumstance where it appears:

(1) That it would be inconsistent with a provision of the articles, bylaws, a resolution of the members or an agreement in effect at the time of the accrual of the alleged cause of action asserted in the proceeding in which the expenses were incurred or other amounts were paid, which prohibits or otherwise limits indemnification; or

(2) That it would be inconsistent with any condition expressly imposed by a court in approving a settlement.

(i) A corporation shall have power to purchase and maintain insurance on behalf of any agent of the corporation against any liability asserted against or incurred by the agent in such capacity or arising out of the agent's status as such whether or not the corporation would have the power to indemnify the agent against that liability under the provisions of this section; provided, however, that a corporation shall have no power to purchase and maintain that insurance to indemnify any agent of the corporation for a violation of Section 5233.

(j) This section does not apply to any proceeding against any trustee, investment manager, or other fiduciary of a pension, deferred compensation, saving, thrift, or other retirement, incentive, or benefit plan, trust, or provision for any or all of the corporation's directors, officers, employees, and persons providing services to the corporation or any of its subsidiary or related or affiliated corporations, in that person's capacity as such, even though the person may also be an agent as defined in subdivision (a) of the employer corporation. A corporation shall have power to indemnify the trustee, investment manager or other fiduciary to the extent permitted by subdivision (f) of Section 5140.

   Ca. Corp. Code § 5238
Amended by Stats 2012 ch 61 (AB 2668),s 1, eff. 1/1/2013.

Section 5239 - No personal liability to third party for monetary damages on part of volunteer director or volunteer executive officer caused by negligent act or omission

(a) There shall be no personal liability to a third party for monetary damages on the part of a volunteer director or volunteer executive officer of a nonprofit corporation subject to this part, caused by the director's or officer's negligent act or omission in the performance of that person's duties as a director or officer, if all of the following conditions are met:

   (1) The act or omission was within the scope of the director's or executive officer's duties.

   (2) The act or omission was performed in good faith.

   (3) The act or omission was not reckless, wanton, intentional, or grossly negligent.

   (4) Damages caused by the act or omission are covered pursuant to a liability insurance policy issued to the corporation, either in the form of a general liability policy or a director's and officer's liability policy, or personally to the director or executive officer. In the event that the damages are not covered by a liability insurance policy, the volunteer director or volunteer executive officer shall not be personally liable for the damages if the board of directors of the corporation and the person had made all reasonable efforts in good faith to obtain available liability insurance.

(b) "Volunteer" means the rendering of services without compensation. "Compensation" means remuneration whether by way of salary, fee, or other consideration for services rendered. However, the payment of per diem, mileage, or other reimbursement expenses to a director or executive officer does not affect that person's status as a volunteer within the meaning of this section.

(c) "Executive officer" means the president, vice president, secretary, or treasurer of a corporation, or such other individual who serves in like capacity, who assists in establishing the policy of the corporation.

(d) Nothing in this section shall limit the liability of the corporation for any damages caused by acts or omissions of the volunteer director or volunteer executive officer.

(e) This section does not eliminate or limit the liability of a director or officer for any of the following:

(1) As provided in Section 5233 or 5237.

(2) In any action or proceeding brought by the Attorney General.

(f) Nothing in this section creates a duty of care or basis of liability for damage or injury caused by the acts or omissions of a director or officer.

(g) This section is only applicable to causes of action based upon acts or omissions occurring on or after January 1, 1988.

(h) As used in this section as applied to nonprofit public benefit corporations which have an annual budget of less than twenty-five thousand dollars ($25,000) and that are exempt from federal income taxation under Section 501(c)(3)(c)(3) of the Internal Revenue Code, the condition of making "all reasonable efforts in good faith to obtain available liability insurance" shall be satisfied by the corporation if it makes at least one inquiry per year to purchase a general liability insurance policy and that insurance was not available at a cost of less than 5 percent of the previous year's annual budget of the corporation. If the corporation is in its first year of operation, this subdivision shall apply for as long as the budget of the corporation does not exceed twenty-five thousand dollars ($25,000) in its first year of operation. An inquiry pursuant to this subdivision shall obtain premium costs for a general liability policy with an amount of coverage of at least five hundred thousand dollars ($500,000).

Ca. Corp. Code § 5239
Amended by Stats. 1993, Ch. 634, Sec. 1. Effective January 1, 1994.

Article 4 - INVESTMENTS

Section 5240 - Investments

(a) This section applies to all assets held by the corporation for investment. Assets which are directly related to the corporation's public or charitable programs are not subject to this section.

(b) Except as provided in subdivision (c), in investing, reinvesting, purchasing, acquiring, exchanging, selling and managing the corporation's investments, the board shall do the following:

(1) Avoid speculation, looking instead to the permanent disposition of the funds, considering the probable income, as well as the probable safety of the corporation's capital.

(2) Comply with additional standards, if any, imposed by the articles, bylaws or express terms of an instrument or agreement pursuant to which the assets were contributed to the corporation.

(c) No investment violates this section where it conforms to provisions authorizing the investment contained in an instrument or agreement pursuant to which the assets were contributed to the corporation. No investment violates this section or Section 5231 where it conforms to provisions requiring the investment contained in an instrument or agreement pursuant to which the assets were contributed to the corporation.

(d) In carrying out duties under this section, each director shall act as required by subdivision (a) of Section 5231, may rely upon others as permitted by subdivision (b) of Section 5231, and shall have the benefit of subdivision (c) of Section 5231, and the board may delegate its investment powers as permitted by Section 5210.

(e) Compliance with the Uniform Prudent Management of Institutional Funds Act (Part 7 (commencing with Section 18501) of Division 9 of the Probate Code), if that act would be applicable, will be deemed to be compliance with subdivision (b).

   Ca. Corp. Code § 5240

Amended by Stats 2015 ch 56 (AB 792),s 1, eff. 1/1/2016.

Amended by Stats 2008 ch 715 (SB 1329),s 1, eff. 1/1/2009.

Section 5241 - Deviation from terms of trust or agreement regarding making or retention of investments

Nothing in Section 5240 shall abrogate or restrict the power of the appropriate court in proper cases to direct or permit a corporation to deviate from the terms of a trust or agreement regarding the making or retention of investments. Notice of such action or proceeding shall be given to the Attorney General who may intervene.

   Ca. Corp. Code § 5241

Amended by Stats. 1979, Ch. 724.

Article 5 - EXAMINATION BY ATTORNEY GENERAL

Section 5250 - Examination by attorney general

A corporation is subject at all times to examination by the Attorney General, on behalf of the state, to ascertain the condition of its affairs and to what extent, if at all, it fails to comply with trusts which it has assumed or has departed from the purposes for which it is formed. In case of any such failure or departure the Attorney General may institute, in the name of the state, the proceeding necessary to correct the noncompliance or departure.

Ca. Corp. Code § 5250
Added by Stats. 1978, Ch. 567.

Article 6 - COMPLIANCE WITH INTERNAL REVENUE CODE

Section 5260 - Corporation deemed "private foundation"

Notwithstanding any other law, every corporation, during any period or periods that corporation is deemed to be a "private foundation" as defined in Section 509 of the Internal Revenue Code of 1986, shall distribute its income for each taxable year (and principal, if necessary) at the time and in a manner so as not to subject that corporation to tax under Section 4942 of that code, and the corporation shall not engage in any act of self-dealing as defined in subsection (d) of Section 4941 of that code, retain any excess business holdings as defined in subsection (c) of Section 4943 of that code, make any investments in a manner that subjects the corporation to tax under Section 4944 of that code, or make any taxable expenditure as defined in subsection (d) of Section 4945 of that code.

This section shall apply to any corporation, and any provision contained in its articles of incorporation or other governing instrument inconsistent with, or contrary to, this section shall be without effect.

Ca. Corp. Code § 5260
Amended by Stats 2017 ch 516 (SB 363),s 1, eff. 1/1/2018.

Chapter 3 - MEMBERS

Article 1 - ISSUANCE OF MEMBERSHIPS

Section 5310 - Admission to membership; corporation which has no members

(a) A corporation may admit persons to membership, as provided in its articles or bylaws, or may provide in its articles or bylaws that it shall have no members. In the absence of any provision in its articles or bylaws providing for members, a corporation shall have no members.

(b) In the case of a corporation which has no members, any action for which there is no specific provision of this part applicable to a corporation which has no members and which would otherwise require approval by a majority of all members (Section 5033) or approval by the members (Section 5034) shall require only approval of the board, any provision of this part or the articles or bylaws to the contrary notwithstanding.

(c) Reference in this part to a corporation which has no members includes a corporation in which the directors are the only members.

Ca. Corp. Code § 5310
Amended by Stats. 1984, Ch. 812, Sec. 1.7.

Section 5311 - Consideration

Subject to the articles or bylaws, memberships may be issued by a corporation for no consideration or for such consideration as is determined by the board.

Ca. Corp. Code § 5311

Amended by Stats. 1981, Ch. 587, Sec. 10.

Section 5312 - One membership; no fractional memberships

No person may hold more than one membership, and no fractional memberships may be held, provided, however, that:

(a) Two or more persons may have an indivisible interest in a single membership when authorized by, and in such manner or under the circumstances prescribed by, the articles or bylaws subject to Section 5612; and

(b) If the articles or bylaws provide for classes of membership and if the articles or bylaws permit a person to be a member of more than one class, a person may hold a membership in one or more classes.

Ca. Corp. Code § 5312

Amended by Stats. 1979, Ch. 724.

Section 5313 - Admission of any person

Except as provided in its articles or bylaws, a corporation may admit any person to membership.

Ca. Corp. Code § 5313

Added by Stats. 1978, Ch. 567.

Article 2 - TRANSFER OF MEMBERSHIPS

Section 5320 - Transfer of membership; member's death or dissolution

(a) Subject to Section 5613, and unless otherwise provided in the corporation's articles or bylaws:

(1) No member may transfer a membership or any right arising therefrom.

(2) All rights of membership cease upon the member's death or dissolution.

(b) Notwithstanding subdivision (a), no member may transfer for value a membership or any right arising therefrom.

(c) Notwithstanding subdivisions (a) and (b), this section does not prohibit or restrict the transfer, purchase, or sale of a membership in a limited equity housing cooperative, provided that the transfer, purchase, or sale is consistent with Section 33007.5 of the Health and Safety Code.

Ca. Corp. Code § 5320
Amended by Stats. 1992, Ch. 250, Sec. 1. Effective January 1, 1993.

Article 3 - TYPES OF MEMBERSHIPS

Section 5330 - Memberships having different rights, privileges, preferences, restrictions, or conditions as authorized by articles or bylaws

A corporation may issue memberships having different rights, privileges, preferences, restrictions or conditions, as authorized by its articles or bylaws.
Ca. Corp. Code § 5330
Amended by Stats. 1979, Ch. 724.

Section 5331 - Memberships with same rights, privileges, preferences, restrictions, and conditions

Except as provided in or authorized by the articles or bylaws, all memberships shall have the same rights, privileges, preferences, restrictions and conditions.
Ca. Corp. Code § 5331
Amended by Stats. 1979, Ch. 724.

Section 5332 - References to members

(a) A corporation may refer to persons associated with it as "members" even though such persons are not members within the meaning of Section 5056; but references to members in this part mean members as defined in Section 5056.
(b) A corporation may benefit, serve, or assist persons who are not members within the meaning of Section 5056 for such consideration, if any, as the board may determine or as is authorized or provided for in the articles or bylaws.
Ca. Corp. Code § 5332
Amended by Stats. 1979, Ch. 724.

Article 4 - TERMINATION OF MEMBERSHIPS

Section 5340 - Resignation; expiration

(a) A member may resign from membership at any time.
(b) This section shall not relieve the resigning member from any obligation for charges incurred, services or benefits actually rendered, dues, assessments or fees, or arising from contract or otherwise, and this section shall not diminish any right of the corporation to enforce any such obligation or obtain damages for its breach.
(c) A membership issued for a period of time shall expire when such period of time has elapsed unless the membership is renewed.

Ca. Corp. Code § 5340
Amended by Stats. 1979, Ch. 724.

Section 5341 - Expulsion, termination, or suspension

(a) No member may be expelled or suspended, and no membership or membership rights may be terminated or suspended, except according to procedures satisfying the requirements of this section. An expulsion, termination or suspension not in accord with this section shall be void and without effect.

(b) Any expulsion, suspension or termination must be done in good faith and in a fair and reasonable manner. Any procedure which conforms to the requirements of subdivision (c) is fair and reasonable, but a court may also find other procedures to be fair and reasonable when the full circumstances of the suspension, termination, or expulsion are considered.

(c) A procedure is fair and reasonable when:

(1) The provisions of the procedure have been set forth in the articles or bylaws, or copies of such provisions are sent annually to all the members as required by the articles or bylaws;

(2) It provides the giving of 15 days prior notice of the expulsion, suspension or termination and the reasons therefor; and

(3) It provides an opportunity for the member to be heard, orally or in writing, not less than five days before the effective date of the expulsion, suspension or termination by a person or body authorized to decide that the proposed expulsion, termination or suspension not take place.

(d) Any notice required under this section may be given by any method reasonably calculated to provide actual notice. Any notice given by mail must be given by first-class or registered mail sent to the last address of the member shown on the corporation's records.

(e) Any action challenging an expulsion, suspension or termination of membership, including any claim alleging defective notice, must be commenced within one year after the date of the expulsion, suspension or termination. In the event such an action is successful the court may order any relief, including reinstatement, it finds equitable under the circumstances, but no vote of the members or of the board may be set aside solely because a person was at the time of the vote wrongfully excluded by virtue of the challenged expulsion, suspension or termination, unless the court finds further that the wrongful expulsion, suspension or termination was in bad faith and for the purpose, and with the effect, of wrongfully excluding the member from the vote or from the meeting at which the vote took place, so as to affect the outcome of the vote.

(f) This section governs only the procedures for expulsion, suspension or termination and not the substantive grounds therefor. An expulsion, suspension or termination based upon substantive grounds which violate contractual or other rights of the member or are otherwise unlawful, is not made valid by compliance with this section.

(g) A member who is expelled or suspended or whose membership is terminated shall be liable for any charges incurred, services or benefits actually rendered, dues, assessments or fees incurred before the expulsion, suspension or termination or arising from contract or otherwise.

Ca. Corp. Code § 5341

Amended by Stats. 1996, Ch. 589, Sec. 9. Effective January 1, 1997.

Section 5342 - Amendment of articles and bylaws which would terminate all memberships or class of memberships

(a) An amendment of the articles or bylaws which would terminate all memberships or any class of memberships shall meet the requirements of this part and this section.

(b) Before such an amendment is adopted the corporation shall give written notice to members not less than 45 nor more than 90 days prior to any vote by the members on the amendment. The written notice shall describe the effect of the amendment on the corporation and the members. However, written notice need not be given at least 45 days prior to any vote by the members on the amendment if all members entitled to vote receive a written notice prior to the vote setting forth the information described in the preceding sentence and sign a written waiver of 45 days notice.

(c) Any such amendment shall be approved by the members (Section 5034).

(d) The articles or bylaws may impose additional requirements regarding termination of all memberships or any class of memberships.

(e) Upon request of a member the corporation shall provide at its option the rights set forth in either paragraph (1) or (2) of subdivision (a) of Section 6330 as soon as reasonably possible to allow the member to communicate with other members regarding the proposed amendment.

(f) Any such amendment shall terminate the rights members have pursuant to this part as members (Section 5056).

(g) The provisions of Section 5341 shall not apply to termination of all memberships or any class of memberships pursuant to an amendment of the articles or bylaws.

Ca. Corp. Code § 5342

Amended by Stats. 1986, Ch. 766, Sec. 29.

Article 5 - RIGHTS AND OBLIGATIONS OF MEMBERS AND CREDITORS

Section 5350 - Liability of member

(a) A member of a corporation is not, as such, personally liable for the debts, liabilities, or obligations of the corporation.

(b) No person is liable for any obligation arising from membership unless the person was admitted to membership upon the person's application or with the person's consent.

Ca. Corp. Code § 5350
Added by Stats. 1978, Ch. 567.

Section 5351 - Dues, assessments, or fees

A corporation may levy dues, assessments or fees upon its members pursuant to its articles or bylaws, but a member upon learning of them may avoid liability for them by promptly resigning from membership, except where the member is, by contract or otherwise, liable for them. Article or bylaw provisions authorizing such dues, assessments or fees do not, of themselves, create such liability.
 Ca. Corp. Code § 5351
Added by Stats. 1978, Ch. 567.

Section 5352 - Creditor's action

(a) No action shall be brought by or on behalf of any creditor to reach and apply the liability, if any, of a member to the corporation to pay the amount due on such member's membership or otherwise due to the corporation unless final judgment has been rendered in favor of the creditor against the corporation and execution has been returned unsatisfied in whole or in part or unless such proceedings would be useless.
(b) All creditors of the corporation, with or without reducing their claims to judgment, may intervene in any such creditor's action to reach and apply unpaid amounts due the corporation and any or all members who owe amounts to the corporation may be joined in such action. Several judgments may be rendered for and against the parties to the action or in favor of a receiver for the benefit of the respective parties thereto.
(c) All amounts paid by any member in any such action shall be credited on the unpaid balance due the corporation by such member.
 Ca. Corp. Code § 5352
Added by Stats. 1978, Ch. 567.

Section 5353 - No derogation of rights or remedies of creditor or member because of fraud or illegality

Nothing in this part shall be construed as in derogation of any rights or remedies which any creditor or member may have against any promoter, member, director, officer or the corporation because of participation in any fraud or illegality practiced upon such creditor or member by any such person or by the corporation in connection with the issue or sale of memberships or securities or in derogation of any rights which the corporation may have by rescission, cancellation or otherwise because of any fraud or illegality practiced on it by any such person in connection with the issue or sale of memberships or securities.
 Ca. Corp. Code § 5353
Added by Stats. 1978, Ch. 567.

Section 5354 - Liability of person holding membership in representative or fiduciary capacity

A person holding a membership as executor, administrator, guardian, trustee, receiver or in any representative or fiduciary capacity is not personally liable for any unpaid balance of the purchase price of the membership, or for any amounts owing to the corporation by the member, because the membership is so held; but the estate and funds in the hands of such fiduciary are liable therefor.

Ca. Corp. Code § 5354
Added by Stats. 1978, Ch. 567.

Chapter 4 - DISTRIBUTIONS

Article 1 - LIMITATIONS

Section 5410 - Distribution prohibited

No corporation shall make any distribution. This section shall not apply to the purchase of a membership in a limited-equity housing cooperative, as defined in Section 33007.5 of the Health and Safety Code, which is organized as a public benefit corporation.

Ca. Corp. Code § 5410
Amended by Stats. 1992, Ch. 250, Sec. 2. Effective January 1, 1993.

Article 2 - LIABILITY OF MEMBERS

Section 5420 - Liability of person who receives distribution

(a) Any person who receives any distribution is liable to the corporation for the amount so received by such person with interest thereon at the legal rate on judgments until paid.

(b) Suit may be brought in the name of a corporation by a creditor, a director, the Attorney General, or, subject to meeting the requirements of Section 5710, a member. In any such action in addition to the remedy provided in subdivision (a), the court may award punitive damages for the benefit of the corporation against any director, officer, member or other person who with intent to defraud the corporation caused, received or aided and abetted in the making of any distribution.

(c) Any person sued under this section may implead all other persons liable under this section and may in the absence of fraud by a moving party compel contribution, either in that action or in an independent action against persons not joined in the action.

(d) This section shall not affect any liability which any person may have under the Uniform Voidable Transactions Act (Chapter 1 (commencing with Section 3439) of Title 2 of Part 2 of Division 4 of the Civil Code).

Ca. Corp. Code § 5420
Amended by Stats 2015 ch 44 (SB 161),s 19, eff. 1/1/2016.

Chapter 5 - MEETINGS AND VOTING

Article 1 - GENERAL PROVISIONS

Section 5510 - Meetings of members

(a) Meetings of members may be held at a place within or without this state as may be stated in or fixed in accordance with the bylaws. If no other place is stated or so fixed, meetings of members shall be held at the principal office of the corporation. Subject to any limitations in the articles or the bylaws of the corporation, if authorized by the board of directors in its sole discretion, and subject to those guidelines and procedures as the board of directors may adopt, members not physically present in person (or, if proxies are allowed, by proxy) at a meeting of members may, by electronic transmission by and to the corporation (Sections 20 and 21), electronic video screen communication, conference telephone, or other means of remote communication, participate in a meeting of members, be deemed present in person (or, if proxies are allowed, by proxy), and vote at a meeting of members, subject to subdivision (f).

(b)A regular meeting of members shall be held on a date, time, and with the frequency stated in or fixed in accordance with the bylaws, but in any event in each year in which directors are to be elected at that meeting for the purpose of conducting such election, and to transact any other proper business which may be brought before the meeting.

(c) If a corporation with members is required by subdivision (b) to hold a regular meeting and fails to hold the regular meeting for a period of 60 days after the date designated therefor or, if no date has been designated, for a period of 15 months after the formation of the corporation, or after its last regular meeting, or if the corporation fails to hold a written ballot for a period of 60 days after the date designated therefor, then the superior court of the proper county may summarily order the meeting to be held or the ballot to be conducted upon the application of a member or the Attorney General, after notice to the corporation giving it an opportunity to be heard.

(d) The votes represented, either in person (or, if proxies are allowed, by proxy), at a meeting called or by written ballot ordered pursuant to subdivision (c), and entitled to be cast on the business to be transacted shall constitute a quorum, notwithstanding any provision of the articles or bylaws or in this part to the contrary. The court may issue such orders as may be appropriate including, without limitation, orders designating the time and place of the meeting, the record date for determination of members entitled to vote, and the form of notice of the meeting.

(e) Special meetings of members for any lawful purpose may be called by the board, the chairperson of the board, the president, or such other persons, if any, as are specified in the bylaws. In addition, special meetings of members for any lawful purpose may be called by 5 percent or more of the members.

(f)A meeting of the members may be conducted, in whole or in part, by electronic transmission by and to the corporation, electronic video screen communication, conference telephone, or other means of remote communication if the corporation implements reasonable measures:

(1) to provide members and proxyholders, if proxies are allowed, a reasonable opportunity to participate in the meeting and to vote on matters submitted to the members, including an opportunity to read or hear the proceedings of the meeting substantially concurrently with those proceedings,

(2) if any member or proxyholder, if proxies are allowed, votes or takes other action at the meeting by means of electronic transmission to the corporation, electronic video screen communication, conference telephone, or other means of remote communication, to maintain a record of that vote or action in its books and records, and

(3) to verify that each person participating remotely is a member or proxyholder, if proxies are allowed. A corporation shall not conduct a meeting of members solely by electronic transmission by and to the corporation, electronic video screen communication, conference telephone, or other means of remote communication unless one or more of the following conditions apply:

(A) all of the members consent; or

(B) the board determines it is necessary or appropriate because of an emergency, as defined in paragraph (5) of subdivision (n) of Section 5140; or

(C) the meeting is conducted on or before June 30, 2022.
Ca. Corp. Code § 5510
Amended by Stats 2022 ch 617 (SB 1202),s 50, eff. 1/1/2023.
Amended by Stats 2022 ch 12 (AB 769),s 2, eff. 3/25/2022.
Amended by Stats 2021 ch 523 (AB 663),s 8, eff. 1/1/2022.
Amended by Stats 2004 ch 254 (SB 1306),s 16, eff. 1/1/2005

Section 5511 - Notice of members' meeting or report

(a) Whenever members are required or permitted to take any action at a meeting, a written notice of the meeting shall be given not less than 10 nor more than 90 days before the date of the meeting to each member who, on the record date for notice of the meeting, is entitled to vote thereat; provided, however, that if notice is given by mail, and the notice is not mailed by first-class, registered, or certified mail, that notice shall be given not less than 20 days before the meeting. Subject to subdivision (f), and subdivision (b) of Section 5512, that notice shall state the place, date and time of the meeting, the means of electronic transmission by and to the corporation (Sections 20 and 21), electronic video screen communication, conference telephone, or other means of remote communication, if any, by which members may participate in that meeting, and (1) in the case of a special meeting, the general nature of the business to be transacted, and no other business may be transacted, or (2) in the case of the regular meeting, those matters which the board, at the time the notice is given, intends to present for action by the members, but, except as provided in subdivision (b) of Section 5512, any proper matter may be presented at the meeting for such action. The notice of any meeting at which directors are to be elected shall include the names of all those who are nominees at the time the notice is given to members.

(b)

(1) Notice of a members' meeting or any report shall be given personally, by electronic transmission by the corporation, or by mail or other means of written communication, addressed to the member at the address of such member appearing on the books of the corporation or given by the member to the corporation for purpose of notice, or if no such address appears or is given, at the place where the principal office of the corporation is located or by publication at least once in a newspaper of general circulation in the county in which the principal office is located. Notwithstanding the foregoing, the notice of a members' meeting or any report may be sent by electronic communication or other means of remote communication if the board determines it is necessary or appropriate because of an emergency, as defined in paragraph (5) of subdivision (n) of Section 5140. An affidavit of giving of any notice or report as permitted because of an emergency or otherwise in accordance with the provisions of this part, executed by the secretary, assistant secretary, or any transfer agent, shall be prima facie evidence of the giving of the notice or report.

(2) If any notice or report addressed to a member at the address of such member appearing on the books of the corporation is returned to the corporation by the United States Postal Service marked to indicate that the United States Postal Service is unable to deliver the notice or report to the member at such address, all future notices or reports shall be deemed to have been duly given without further mailing if the same shall be available for the member upon written demand of the member at the principal office of the corporation for a period of one year from the date of the giving of the notice or report to all other members.

(3)

(A) Notice given by electronic transmission by the corporation under this subdivision shall be valid only if it complies with Section 20. Notwithstanding the foregoing, notice shall not be given by electronic transmission by the corporation under this subdivision after either of the following:

(i) The corporation is unable to deliver two consecutive notices to the member by that means.

(ii) The inability to so deliver the notices to the member becomes known to the secretary, any assistant secretary, the transfer agent, or other person responsible for the giving of the notice.

(B) This paragraph shall not apply if notices are provided by electronic communication or other means of remote communication as permitted because of an emergency.

(c) Upon request in writing to the corporation addressed to the attention of the chairperson of the board, president, vice president, or secretary by any person (other than the board) entitled to call a special meeting of members, the officer forthwith shall cause notice to be given to the members entitled to vote that a meeting will be held at a time fixed by the board, not less than 35 nor more than 90 days after the receipt of the request. If the notice is not given within 20 days after receipt of the request, the persons entitled to call the meeting may give the notice or the superior court of the proper county shall summarily order the giving of the notice, after notice to the corporation giving it an opportunity to be heard. The court may issue such orders as may be appropriate, including, without limitation, orders designating the time and place of the meeting, the record date for determination of members entitled to vote, and the form of notice.

(d) When a members' meeting is adjourned to another time or place, unless the bylaws otherwise require and except as provided in this subdivision, notice need not be given of the adjourned meeting if the time and place thereof (or the means of electronic transmission by and to the corporation, conference telephone, or other means of remote communication, or electronic video screen communication, if any, by which members may participate) are announced at the meeting at which the adjournment is taken. No meeting may be adjourned for more than 45 days. At the adjourned meeting the corporation may transact any business which might have been transacted at the original meeting. If after the adjournment a new record date is fixed for notice or voting, a notice of the adjourned meeting shall be given to each member who, on the record date for notice of the meeting, is entitled to vote at the meeting.

(e) The transactions of any meeting of members, however called and noticed, and wherever held, are as valid as though had at a meeting duly held after regular call and notice, if a quorum is present either in person or by proxy, and if, either before or after the meeting, each of the persons entitled to vote, not present in person or by proxy, provides a waiver of notice or consent to the holding of the meeting, or an approval of the minutes thereof in writing. All such waivers, consents, and approvals shall be filed with the corporate records or made a part of the minutes of the meeting. Attendance of a person at a meeting shall constitute a waiver of notice of and presence at such meeting, except when the person objects, at the beginning of the meeting, to the transaction of any business because the meeting is not lawfully called or convened and except that attendance at a meeting is not a waiver of any right to object to the consideration of matters required by this part to be included in the notice but not so included, if such objection is expressly made at the meeting. Neither the business to be transacted at nor the purpose of any regular or special meeting of members need be specified in any written waiver of notice, consent to the holding of the meeting, or approval of the minutes thereof, unless otherwise provided in the articles or bylaws, except as provided in subdivision (f).

(f) Any approval of the members required under Section 5222, 5224, 5812, or 6610, other than unanimous approval by those entitled to vote, shall be valid only if the general nature of the proposal so approved was stated in the notice of meeting, or in any written waiver of notice.

(g) A court may find that notice not given in conformity with this section is still valid, if it was given in a fair and reasonable manner.

Ca. Corp. Code § 5511

Amended by Stats 2022 ch 617 (SB 1202),s 51, eff. 1/1/2023.
Amended by Stats 2021 ch 523 (AB 663),s 9, eff. 1/1/2022.
Amended by Stats 2004 ch 254 (SB 1306),s 17, eff. 1/1/2005

Section 5512 - Quorum at meeting of members

(a) One-third of the voting power, represented in person or by proxy, shall constitute a quorum at a meeting of members, but, subject to subdivisions (b) and (c), a bylaw may set a different quorum. Any bylaw amendment to increase the quorum may be adopted only by approval of the members (Section 5034). If a quorum is present, the affirmative vote of the majority of the voting power represented at the meeting, entitled to vote, and voting on any matter shall be the act of the members, unless the vote of a greater number or voting by classes is required by this part or the articles or bylaws.

(b) Where a bylaw authorizes a corporation to conduct a meeting with a quorum of less than one-third of the voting power, then the only matters that may be voted upon at any regular meeting actually attended, in person or by proxy, by less than one-third of the voting power are matters notice of the general nature of which was given, pursuant to the first sentence of subdivision (a) of Section 5511.

(c) Subject to subdivision (b), the members present at a duly called or held meeting at which a quorum is present may continue to transact business until adjournment notwithstanding the withdrawal of enough members to leave less than a quorum, if any action taken (other than adjournment) is approved by at least a majority of the members required to constitute a quorum or, if required by this division or the articles or the bylaws, the vote of a greater number or voting by classes.

(d) In the absence of a quorum, any meeting of members may be adjourned from time to time by the vote of a majority of the votes represented either in person or by proxy, but no other business may be transacted, except as provided in subdivision (c).

Ca. Corp. Code § 5512

Amended by Stats 2000 ch 485 (AB 1895), s 11, eff. 1/1/2001.

Section 5513 - Approval by written ballot

(a) Subject to subdivision (e), and unless prohibited in the articles or bylaws, any action which may be taken at any regular or special meeting of members may be taken without a meeting if the corporation distributes a written ballot to every member entitled to vote on the matter. Unless otherwise provided by the articles or bylaws and if approved by the board of directors, that ballot and any related material may be sent by electronic transmission by the corporation (Section 20) and responses may be returned to the corporation by electronic transmission to the corporation (Section 21). That ballot shall set forth the proposed action, provide an opportunity to specify approval or disapproval of any proposal, and provide a reasonable time within which to return the ballot to the corporation.

(b) Approval by written ballot pursuant to this section shall be valid only when the number of votes cast by ballot within the time period specified equals or exceeds the quorum required to be present at a meeting authorizing the action, and the number of approvals equals or exceeds the number of votes that would be required to approve at a meeting at which the total number of votes cast was the same as the number of votes cast by ballot.

(c) Ballots shall be solicited in a manner consistent with the requirements of subdivision (b) of Section 5511, and Section 5514. All such solicitations shall indicate the number of responses needed to meet the quorum requirement and, with respect to ballots other than for the election of directors, shall state the percentage of approvals necessary to pass the measure submitted. The solicitation must specify the time by which the ballot must be received in order to be counted.

(d) Unless otherwise provided in the articles or bylaws, a written ballot may not be revoked.

(e) Directors may be elected by written ballot under this section, where authorized by the articles or bylaws, except that election by written ballot may not be authorized where the directors are elected by cumulative voting pursuant to Section 5616.

(f) When directors are to be elected by written ballot and the articles or bylaws prescribe a nomination procedure, the procedure may provide for a date for the close of nominations prior to the printing and distributing of the written ballots.

Ca. Corp. Code § 5513
Amended by Stats 2004 ch 254 (SB 1306),s 18, eff. 1/1/2005

Section 5514 - Form of proxy or written ballot

(a) Any form of proxy or written ballot distributed to 10 or more members of a corporation with 100 or more members shall afford an opportunity on the proxy or form of written ballot to specify a choice between approval and disapproval of each matter or group of related matters intended, at the time the written ballot or proxy is distributed, to be acted upon at the meeting for which the proxy is solicited or by such written ballot, and shall provide, subject to reasonable specified conditions, that where the person solicited specifies a choice with respect to any such matter the vote shall be cast in accordance therewith.

(b) In any election of directors, any form of proxy or written ballot in which the directors to be voted upon are named therein as candidates and which is marked by a member "withhold" or otherwise marked in a manner indicating that the authority to vote for the election of directors is withheld shall not be voted either for or against the election of a director.

(c) Failure to comply with this section shall not invalidate any corporate action taken, but may be the basis for challenging any proxy at a meeting or written ballot and the superior court may compel compliance therewith at the suit of any member.

    Ca. Corp. Code § 5514

Amended by Stats. 1979, Ch. 724.

Section 5515 - Order providing for method of notice reasonably designed to give actual notice

(a) If for any reason it is impractical or unduly difficult for any corporation to call or conduct a meeting of its members, delegates, or directors, or otherwise obtain their consent, in the manner prescribed by its articles or bylaws, or this part, then the superior court of the proper county, upon petition of a director, officer, delegate, member or the Attorney General, may order that such a meeting be called or that a written ballot or other form of obtaining the vote of members, delegates, or directors be authorized, in such a manner as the court finds fair and equitable under the circumstances.

(b) The court shall, in an order issued pursuant to this section, provide for a method of notice reasonably designed to give actual notice to all parties who would be entitled to notice of a meeting held pursuant to the articles, bylaws and this part, whether or not the method results in actual notice to every such person, or conforms to the notice requirements that would otherwise apply. In a proceeding under this section the court may determine who the members or directors are.

(c) The order issued pursuant to this section may dispense with any requirement relating to the holding of and voting at meetings or obtaining of votes, including any requirement as to quorums or as to the number or percentage of votes needed for approval, that would otherwise be imposed by the articles, bylaws, or this part.

(d) Wherever practical any order issued pursuant to this section shall limit the subject matter of the meetings or other forms of consent authorized to items, including amendments to the articles or bylaws, the resolution of which will or may enable the corporation to continue managing its affairs without further resort to this section; provided, however, that an order under this section may also authorize the obtaining of whatever votes and approvals are necessary for the dissolution, merger, sale of assets or reorganization of the corporation.

(e) Any meeting or other method of obtaining the vote of members, delegates, or directors conducted pursuant to an order issued under this section, and which complies with all the provisions of such order, is for all purposes a valid meeting or vote, as the case may be, and shall have the same force and effect as if it complied with every requirement imposed by the articles, bylaws and this part.

    Ca. Corp. Code § 5515

Amended by Stats. 1986, Ch. 766, Sec. 30.

Section 5516 - Action by written consent

Any action required or permitted to be taken by the members may be taken without a meeting, if all members shall individually or collectively consent in writing to the action. The written consent or consents shall be filed with the minutes of the proceedings of the members. The action by written consent shall have the same force and effect as the unanimous vote of the members.

    Ca. Corp. Code § 5516

Added by Stats. 1980, Ch. 1155.

Section 5517 - Name signed on ballot, consent, waiver, or proxy appointment

(a) If the name signed on a ballot, consent, waiver, or proxy appointment corresponds to the name of a member, the corporation if acting in good faith is entitled to accept the ballot, consent, waiver, or proxy appointment and give it effect as the act of the member.

(b) If the name signed on a ballot, consent, waiver, or proxy appointment does not correspond to the record name of a member, the corporation if acting in good faith is nevertheless entitled to accept the ballot, consent, waiver, or proxy appointment and give it effect as the act of the member if any of the following occur:

    (1) The member is an entity and the name signed purports to be that of an officer or agent of the entity.

    (2) The name signed purports to be that of an attorney-in-fact of the member and if the corporation requests, evidence acceptable to the corporation of the signatory's authority to sign for the member has been presented with respect to the ballot, consent, waiver, or proxy appointment.

    (3) Two or more persons hold the membership as cotenants or fiduciaries and the name signed purports to be the name of at least one of the coholders and the person signing appears to be acting on behalf of all the coholders.

(c) The corporation is entitled to reject a ballot, consent, waiver, or proxy appointment if the secretary or other officer or agent authorized to tabulate votes, acting in good faith, has a reasonable basis for doubt concerning the validity of the signature or the signatory's authority to sign for the member.

(d) The corporation and any officer or agent thereof who accepts or rejects a ballot, consent, waiver, or proxy appointment in good faith and in accordance with the standards of this section shall not be liable in damages to the member for the consequences of the acceptance or rejection.

(e) Corporate action based on the acceptance or rejection of a ballot, consent, waiver, or proxy appointment under this section is valid unless a court of competent jurisdiction determines otherwise.

Ca. Corp. Code § 5517

Added by Stats. 1996, Ch. 589, Sec. 11. Effective January 1, 1997.

Article 2 - ADDITIONAL PROVISIONS RELATING TO ELECTION OF DIRECTORS

Section 5520 - Reasonable nomination and election procedures

(a) As to directors elected by members, there shall be available to the members reasonable nomination and election procedures given the nature, size and operations of the corporation.

(b) If a corporation complies with all of the provisions of Sections 5521, 5522, 5523, and 5524 applicable to a corporation with the same number of members, the nomination and election procedures of that corporation shall be deemed reasonable. However, those sections do not prescribe the exclusive means of making available to the members reasonable procedures for nomination and election of directors. A corporation may make available to the members other reasonable nomination and election procedures given the nature, size, and operations of the corporation.

Ca. Corp. Code § 5520

Amended by Stats. 1996, Ch. 589, Sec. 12. Effective January 1, 1997.

Section 5521 - Corporation with 500 or more members

A corporation with 500 or more members may provide that, except for directors who are elected as authorized by Section 5152 or 5153, and except as provided in Section 5522, any person who is qualified to be elected to the board of directors of the corporation may be nominated:

(a) By any method authorized by the bylaws, or if no method is set forth in the bylaws by any method authorized by the board.

(b) By petition delivered to an officer of the corporation, signed within 11 months preceding the next time directors will be elected, by members representing the following number of votes:

Number of Votes Eligible to be Cast for Director Disregarding any Provision for Cumulative Voting	Number of Votes
Under 5,000	2 percent of voting power
5,000 or more	one-twentieth of 1 percent of

voting power but not less than
100, nor more than 500.

(c) If there is a meeting to elect directors, by any member present at the meeting in person or by proxy if proxies are permitted.

Ca. Corp. Code § 5521

Amended by Stats. 1996, Ch. 589, Sec. 13. Effective January 1, 1997.

Section 5522 - Corporation with 5,000 or more members

A corporation with 5,000 or more members may provide that, in any election of a director or directors by members of the corporation except for an election authorized by Section 5152 or 5153.

(a) The corporation's articles or bylaws shall set a date for the close of nominations for the board. The date shall not be less than 50 nor more than 120 days before the day directors are to be elected. No nominations for the board can be made after the date set for the close of nominations.

(b) If more people are nominated for the board than can be elected, the election shall take place by means of a procedure which allows all nominees a reasonable opportunity to solicit votes and all members a reasonable opportunity to choose among the nominees.

(c) A nominee shall have a reasonable opportunity to communicate to the members the nominee's qualifications and the reasons for the nominee's candidacy.

(d) If after the close of nominations the number of people nominated for the board is not more than the number of directors to be elected, the corporation may without further action declare that those nominated and qualified to be elected have been elected.

Ca. Corp. Code § 5522

Amended by Stats. 1996, Ch. 589, Sec. 14. Effective January 1, 1997.

Section 5523 - Equal space for nominees in election material distributed by corporation with 500 or more members

A corporation with 500 or more members may provide that where it distributes any written election material soliciting a vote for any nominee for director at the corporation's expense, it shall make available, at the corporation's expense to each other nominee, in or with the same material, the same amount of space that is provided any other nominee, with equal prominence, to be used by the nominee for a purpose reasonably related to the election.

Ca. Corp. Code § 5523

Amended by Stats. 1996, Ch. 589, Sec. 15. Effective January 1, 1997.

Section 5524 - Request by nominee and payment

A corporation with 500 or more members may provide that upon written request by any nominee for election to the board and the payment with such request of the reasonable costs of mailing (including postage) the corporation shall within 10 business days after such request (provided payment has been made) mail to all members, or such portion of them as the nominee may reasonably specify, any material, which the nominee may furnish and which is reasonably related to the election, unless the corporation within five business days after the request allows the nominee, at the corporation's option, the rights set forth in either paragraph (1) or (2) of subdivision (a) of Section 6330.

   Ca. Corp. Code § 5524
Amended by Stats. 1996, Ch. 589, Sec. 16. Effective January 1, 1997.

Section 5525 - Corporations publishing or mailing materials on behalf of nominee

(a) This section shall apply to corporations publishing or mailing materials on behalf of any nominee in connection with procedures for the nomination and election of directors.

(b) Neither the corporation, nor its agents, officers, directors, or employees, may be held criminally liable, liable for any negligence (active or passive) or otherwise liable for damages to any person on account of any material which is supplied by a nominee for director and which it mails or publishes in procedures intended to comply with Section 5520 or pursuant to Section 5523 or 5524, but the nominee on whose behalf such material was published or mailed shall be liable and shall indemnify and hold the corporation, its agents, officers, directors and employees and each of them harmless from all demands, costs, including reasonable legal fees and expenses, claims, damages and causes of action arising out of such material or any such mailing or publication.

(c) Nothing in this section shall prevent a corporation or any of its agents, officers, directors, or employees from seeking a court order providing that the corporation need not mail or publish material tendered by or on behalf of a nominee under this article on the ground the material will expose the moving party to liability.

   Ca. Corp. Code § 5525
Amended by Stats. 1996, Ch. 589, Sec. 17. Effective January 1, 1997.

Section 5526 - Expenditure of corporate funds to support nominee

Without authorization of the board, no corporate funds may be expended to support a nominee for director after there are more people nominated for director than can be elected.

   Ca. Corp. Code § 5526
Added by Stats. 1978, Ch. 567.

Section 5527 - Action challenging validity of any election, appointment or

removal of director or directors

An action challenging the validity of any election, appointment or removal of a director or directors must be commenced within nine months after the election, appointment or removal. If no such action is commenced, in the absence of fraud, any election, appointment or removal of a director is conclusively presumed valid nine months thereafter.

Ca. Corp. Code § 5527
Amended by Stats. 1981, Ch. 587, Sec. 14.

Chapter 6 - VOTING OF MEMBERSHIPS

Section 5610 - One vote

Except as provided in a corporation's articles or bylaws or Section 5616, each member shall be entitled to one vote on each matter submitted to a vote of the members. Single memberships in which two or more persons have an indivisible interest shall be voted as provided in Section 5612.

Ca. Corp. Code § 5610
Amended by Stats. 1979, Ch. 724.

Section 5611 - Record date

(a) The bylaws may provide or, in the absence of such provision, the board may fix, in advance, a date as the record date for the purpose of determining the members entitled to notice of any meeting of members. Such record date shall not be more than 90 nor less than 10 days before the date of the meeting. If no record date is fixed, members at the close of business on the business day preceding the day on which notice is given or, if notice is waived, at the close of business on the business day preceding the day on which the meeting is held are entitled to notice of a meeting of members. A determination of members entitled to notice of a meeting of members shall apply to any adjournment of the meeting unless the board fixes a new record date for the adjourned meeting.

(b) The bylaws may provide or, in the absence of such provision, the board may fix, in advance, a date as the record date for the purpose of determining the members entitled to vote at a meeting of members. Such record date shall not be more than 60 days before the date of the meeting. Such record date shall also apply in the case of an adjournment of the meeting unless the board fixes a new record date for the adjourned meeting. If no record date is fixed, members on the day of the meeting who are otherwise eligible to vote are entitled to vote at the meeting of members or, in the case of an adjourned meeting, members on the day of the adjourned meeting who are otherwise eligible to vote are entitled to vote at the adjourned meeting of members.

(c) The bylaws may provide or, in the absence of such provision, the board may fix, in advance, a date as the record date for the purpose of determining the members entitled to cast written ballots (Section 5513). Such record date shall not be more than 60 days before the day on which the first written ballot is mailed or solicited. If no record date is fixed, members on the day the first written ballot is mailed or solicited who are otherwise eligible to vote are entitled to cast written ballots.

(d) The bylaws may provide or, in the absence of such provision, the board may fix, in advance, a date as the record date for the purpose of determining the members entitled to exercise any rights in respect of any other lawful action. Such record date shall not be more than 60 days prior to such other action. If no record date is fixed, members at the close of business on the day on which the board adopts the resolution relating thereto, or the 60th day prior to the date of such other action, whichever is later, are entitled to exercise such rights.

Ca. Corp. Code § 5611
Amended by Stats. 1981, Ch. 587, Sec. 15.

Section 5612 - Membership in names of two or more persons

If a membership stands of record in the names of two or more persons, whether fiduciaries, members of a partnership, joint tenants, tenants in common, spouses as community property, tenants by the entirety, or otherwise, or if two or more persons (including proxyholders) have the same fiduciary relationship respecting the same membership, unless the secretary of the corporation is given written notice to the contrary and is furnished with a copy of the instrument or order appointing them or creating the relationship wherein it is so provided, their acts with respect to voting shall have the following effect:

(a) If only one votes, such act binds all;

(b) If more than one vote, the act of the majority so voting binds all.

Ca. Corp. Code § 5612
Amended by Stats 2016 ch 50 (SB 1005),s 22, eff. 1/1/2017.

Section 5613 - Proxy

(a) Any member may authorize another person or persons to act by proxy with respect to such membership, except that this right may be limited or withdrawn by the articles or bylaws, subject to subdivision (e). Any proxy purported to be executed in accordance with the provisions of this part shall be presumptively valid.

(b) No proxy shall be valid after the expiration of 11 months from the date thereof unless otherwise provided in the proxy, except that the maximum term of any proxy shall be three years from the date of execution. Every proxy continues in full force and effect until revoked by the person executing it prior to the vote pursuant thereto. Such revocation may be effected by a writing delivered to the corporation stating that the proxy is revoked or by a subsequent proxy executed by the person executing the prior proxy and presented to the meeting, or as to any meeting by attendance at such meeting and voting in person by the person executing the proxy. The dates contained on the forms of proxy presumptively determine the order of execution, regardless of the postmark dates on the envelopes in which they are mailed.

(c) A proxy is not revoked by the death or incapacity of the maker or the termination of a membership as a result thereof unless, before the vote is counted, written notice of such death or incapacity is received by the corporation.

(d) The proxy of a member may not be irrevocable.

(e) Subdivision (a) notwithstanding, no amendment of the articles or bylaws repealing, restricting, creating or expanding proxy rights may be adopted without approval by the members (Section 5034).

(f) Anything to the contrary notwithstanding, any proxy covering matters requiring a vote of the members pursuant to Section 5222, Section 5224, subdivision (e) of this section, Section 5812, paragraph (2) of subdivision (a) of Section 5911, Section 6012, subdivision (a) of Section 6015, or Section 6610 is not valid as to such matters unless it sets forth the general nature of the matter to be voted on, or, in the event of a vote pursuant to Section 5220, unless the proxy lists those nominated at the time the notice of the vote is given to members.

Ca. Corp. Code § 5613

Amended by Stats. 1981, Ch. 587, Sec. 16.

Section 5614 - Voting agreement or voting trust agreement

A voting agreement or voting trust agreement entered into by a member or members of a corporation shall not be enforced.

Ca. Corp. Code § 5614

Amended by Stats. 1979, Ch. 724.

Section 5615 - Inspectors of election

(a) In advance of any meeting of members the board may appoint inspectors of election to act at the meeting and any adjournment thereof. If inspectors of election are not so appointed, or if any persons so appointed fail to appear or refuse to act, the chairperson of any meeting of members may, and on the request of any member or a member's proxy shall, appoint inspectors of election (or persons to replace those who so fail or refuse) at the meeting. The number of inspectors shall be either one or three. If appointed at a meeting on the request of one or more members or proxies, the majority of members represented in person or by proxy shall determine whether one or three inspectors are to be appointed. In the case of any action by written ballot (Section 5513), the board may similarly appoint inspectors of election to act with powers and duties as set forth in this section.

(b) The inspectors of election shall determine the number of memberships outstanding and the voting power of each, the number represented at the meeting, the existence of a quorum and the authenticity, validity and effect of proxies, receive votes, ballots or consents, hear and determine all challenges and questions in any way arising in connection with the right to vote, count and tabulate all votes or consents, determine when the polls shall close, determine the result and do such acts as may be proper to conduct the election or vote with fairness to all members.

(c) The inspectors of election shall perform their duties impartially, in good faith, to the best of their ability and as expeditiously as is practical. If there are three inspectors of election, the decision, act or certificate of a majority is effective in all respects as the decision, act or certificate of all. Any report or certificate made by the inspectors of election is prima facie evidence of the facts stated therein.

Ca. Corp. Code § 5615

Amended by Stats 2022 ch 617 (SB 1202),s 52, eff. 1/1/2023.

Amended by Stats. 1984, Ch. 812, Sec. 2.

Section 5616 - Cumulative voting

(a) If the articles or bylaws authorize cumulative voting, but not otherwise, every member entitled to vote at any election of directors may cumulate the member's votes and give one candidate a number of votes equal to the number of directors to be elected multiplied by the number of votes to which the member is entitled, or distribute the member's votes on the same principle among as many candidates as the member thinks fit. An article or bylaw provision authorizing cumulative voting may be repealed or amended only by approval of the members (Section 5034), except that the governing article or bylaw provision may require the vote of a greater proportion of the members, or of the members of any class, for its repeal.

(b) No member shall be entitled to cumulate votes for a candidate or candidates unless the candidate's name or candidates' names have been placed in nomination prior to the voting and a member has given notice at the meeting prior to the voting of the member's intention to cumulate votes. If any one member has given this notice, all members may cumulate their votes for candidates in nomination.

(c) In any election of directors by cumulative voting, the candidates receiving the highest number of votes are elected, subject to any lawful provision specifying election by classes.

(d) In any election of directors not governed by subdivision (c), unless otherwise provided in the articles or bylaws, the candidates receiving the highest number of votes are elected.

(e) Elections for directors need not be by ballot unless a member demands election by ballot at the meeting and before the voting begins or unless the bylaws so require.

Ca. Corp. Code § 5616

Amended by Stats. 1984, Ch. 812, Sec. 3.

Section 5617 - Action to determine validity of election or appointment of director

(a) Upon the filing of an action therefor by any director or member, or by any person who had the right to vote in the election at issue, the superior court of the proper county shall determine the validity of any election or appointment of any director of any corporation.

(b) Any person bringing an action under this section shall give notice of the action to the Attorney General, who may intervene.

(c) Upon the filing of the complaint, and before any further proceedings are had, the court shall enter an order fixing a date for the hearing, which shall be within five days unless for good cause shown a later date is fixed, and requiring notice of the date for the hearing and a copy of the complaint to be served upon the corporation and upon the person whose purported election or appointment is questioned and upon any person (other than the plaintiff) whom the plaintiff alleges to have been elected or appointed, in the manner in which a summons is required to be served, or, if the court so directs, by registered mail; and the court may make such further requirements as to notice as appear to be proper under the circumstances.

(d) The court, consistent with the provisions of this part and in conformity with the articles and bylaws to the extent feasible, may determine the person entitled to the office of director or may order a new election to be held or appointment to be made, may determine the validity of the issuance of memberships and the right of persons to vote and may direct such other relief as may be just and proper.

Ca. Corp. Code § 5617
Added by Stats. 1978, Ch. 567.

Chapter 7 - MEMBERS' DERIVATIVE ACTIONS

Section 5710 - Members' derivative action

(a) Subdivisions (c) through (f) notwithstanding, no motion to require a bond shall be granted in an action brought by 100 members or the authorized number (Section 5036), whichever is less.

(b) No action may be instituted or maintained in the right of any corporation by any member of such corporation unless both of the following conditions exist:

  (1) The plaintiff alleges in the complaint that plaintiff was a member at the time of the transaction or any part thereof of which plaintiff complains; and

  (2) The plaintiff alleges in the complaint with particularity plaintiff's efforts to secure from the board such action as plaintiff desires, or the reasons for not making such effort, and alleges further that plaintiff has either informed the corporation or the board in writing of the ultimate facts of each cause of action against each defendant or delivered to the corporation or the board a true copy of the complaint which plaintiff proposes to file.

(c) Subject to subdivision (a), in any action referred to in subdivision (b), at any time within 30 days after service of summons upon the corporation or upon any defendant who is an officer or director of the corporation, or held such office at the time of the acts complained of, the corporation or such defendant may move the court for an order, upon notice and hearing, requiring the plaintiff to furnish a bond as hereinafter provided. The motion shall be based upon one or both of the following grounds:

(1) That there is no reasonable possibility that the prosecution of the cause of action alleged in the complaint against the moving party will benefit the corporation or its members, economically or otherwise.

(2) That the moving party, if other than the corporation, did not participate in the transaction complained of in any capacity. The court on application of the corporation or any defendant may, for good cause shown, extend the 30-day period for an additional period or periods not exceeding 60 days.

(d) At the hearing upon any motion pursuant to subdivision (c), the court shall consider such evidence, written or oral, by witnesses or affidavit, as may be material (1) to the ground or grounds upon which the motion is based, or (2) to a determination of the probable reasonable expenses, including attorneys' fees, of the corporation and the moving party which will be incurred in the defense of the action. If the court determines, after hearing the evidence adduced by the parties, that the moving party has established a probability in support of any of the grounds upon which the motion is based, the court shall fix the amount of the bond, not to exceed fifty thousand dollars ($50,000), to be furnished by the plaintiff for reasonable expenses, including attorneys' fees, which may be incurred by the moving party and the corporation in connection with the action, including expenses for which the corporation may become liable pursuant to Section 5238. A ruling by the court on the motion shall not be a determination of any issue in the action or of the merits thereof. If the court, upon the motion, makes a determination that a bond shall be furnished by the plaintiff as to any one or more defendants, the action shall be dismissed as to such defendant or defendants, unless the bond required by the court has been furnished within such reasonable time as may be fixed by the court.

(e) If the plaintiff shall, either before or after a motion is made pursuant to subdivision (c), or any order or determination pursuant to the motion, furnish a bond or bonds in the aggregate amount of fifty thousand dollars ($50,000) to secure the reasonable expenses of the parties entitled to make the motion, the plaintiff has complied with the requirements of this section and with any order for a bond theretofore made, and any such motion then pending shall be dismissed and no further or additional bond shall be required.

(f) If a motion is filed pursuant to subdivision (c), no pleadings need be filed by the corporation or any other defendant and the prosecution of the action shall be stayed until 10 days after the motion has been disposed of.

Ca. Corp. Code § 5710

Amended by Stats. 1982, Ch. 517, Sec. 187.

Chapter 8 - AMENDMENT OF ARTICLES

Section 5810 - Amendment of articles

(a) By complying with the provisions of this chapter, a corporation may amend its articles from time to time, in any and as many respects as may be desired, so long as its articles as amended contain only such provisions as it would be lawful to insert in original articles filed at the time of the filing of the amendment or as authorized by Section 5813.5 and, if a change in the rights of members or an exchange, reclassification or cancellation of memberships is to be made, such provisions as may be necessary to effect such change, exchange, reclassification or cancellation. It is the intent of the Legislature in adopting this section to exercise to the fullest extent the reserve power of the state over corporations and to authorize any amendment of the articles covered by the preceding sentence regardless of whether any provision contained in the amendment was permissible at the time of the original incorporation of the corporation.

(b) A corporation shall not amend its articles to add any statement or to alter any statement which may appear in the original articles of the initial street address and initial mailing address of the corporation, the names and addresses of the first directors, or the name and address of the initial agent, except to correct an error in the statement or to delete the information after the corporation has filed a statement under Section 6210.

Ca. Corp. Code § 5810
Amended by Stats 2012 ch 494 (SB 1532),s 14, eff. 1/1/2013.

Section 5811 - Adoption by writing signed by majority of incorporators

Except as provided in Section 5813.5, any amendment of the articles may be adopted by a writing signed by a majority of the incorporators, so long as:

(a) No directors were named in the original articles;

(b) No directors have been elected; and

(c) The corporation has no members.

Ca. Corp. Code § 5811
Amended by Stats. 1979, Ch. 724.

Section 5812 - Approval by board, members, and other persons

(a) Except as provided in this section or Section 5813.5, amendments may be adopted if approved by the board and approved by the members (Section 5034) and approved by such other person or persons, if any, as required by the articles. The approval by the members or other person or persons may be before or after the approval by the board.

(b) Notwithstanding subdivision (a), the following amendments may be adopted by approval of the board alone:

(1) An amendment extending the corporate existence or making the corporate existence perpetual, if the corporation was organized prior to August 14, 1929.

(2) An amendment deleting the initial street address and initial mailing address of

the corporation, the names and addresses of the first directors, or the name and address of the initial agent.

(3) Any amendment, at a time the corporation has no members; provided, however, that if the articles require approval by any person for an amendment, that an amendment may not be adopted without such approval.

(4) An amendment adopted pursuant to Section 9913.

(c) Whenever the articles require for corporate action the approval of a particular class of members or of a larger proportion of, or all of, the votes of any class, or of a larger proportion of, or all of, the directors, than is otherwise required by this part, the provision in the articles requiring such greater vote shall not be altered, amended or repealed except by such class or such greater vote, unless otherwise provided in the articles.

Ca. Corp. Code § 5812
Amended by Stats 2012 ch 494 (SB 1532),s 15, eff. 1/1/2013.

Section 5813 - Approval by members of class

An amendment must also be approved by the members (Section 5034) of a class, whether or not such class is entitled to vote thereon by the provisions of the articles or bylaws, if the amendment would materially and adversely affect the rights of that class as to voting or transfer in a manner different than such action affects another class.

Ca. Corp. Code § 5813
Amended by Stats. 1981, Ch. 587, Sec. 17.

Section 5813.5 - Public benefit corporation changing status to mutual benefit corporation, religious corporation, business corporation, or cooperative corporation

(a) A public benefit corporation may amend its articles to change its status to that of a mutual benefit corporation, a social purpose corporation, a religious corporation, a business corporation, or a cooperative corporation by complying with this section and the other sections of this chapter. The Secretary of State shall notify the Franchise Tax Board, in the manner and at the times agreed upon by the Secretary of State and the Franchise Tax Board, of any amendments to a public benefit corporation's articles.

(b) If the public benefit corporation has any assets, an amendment to change its status to a mutual benefit corporation, business corporation, social purpose corporation, or cooperative corporation shall be approved in advance in writing by the Attorney General. If the public benefit corporation has no assets, the Attorney General shall be given a copy of the amendment at least 20 days before the amendment is filed.

(c) Amended articles authorized by this section shall include the provisions which would have been required (other than the initial street address and initial mailing address of the corporation and the name of the initial agent for service of process if a statement has been filed pursuant to Section 6210), and may in addition only include those provisions which would have been permitted, in original articles filed by the type of corporation (mutual benefit, religious, business, social purpose, or cooperative) into which the public benefit corporation is changing its status.

(d) In the case of a change of status to a business corporation, social purpose corporation, or cooperative corporation, if the Franchise Tax Board has issued a determination exempting the corporation from tax as provided in Section 23701 of the Revenue and Taxation Code, the corporation shall be subject to Section 23221 of the Revenue and Taxation Code upon filing the certificate of amendment.

Ca. Corp. Code § 5813.5
Amended by Stats 2014 ch 694 (SB 1301),s 68, eff. 1/1/2015.
Amended by Stats 2012 ch 494 (SB 1532),s 16, eff. 1/1/2013.

Section 5814 - Certificate of amendment

(a) Except for amendments adopted by the incorporators pursuant to Section 5811, upon adoption of an amendment, the corporation shall file a certificate of amendment, which shall consist of an officers' certificate stating:

(1) The wording of the amendment or amended articles in accordance with Section 5816;

(2) That the amendment has been approved by the board;

(3) If the amendment is one for which the approval of the members (Section 5034) is required, that the amendment was approved by the required vote of members; and

(4) If the amendment is one which may be adopted with approval by the board alone, a statement of the facts entitling the board alone to adopt the amendment.

(5) If the amendment is one for which the approval of a person or persons other than the incorporators, directors, or members is required, that the approval of such person or persons has been obtained.

(b) In the event of an amendment of the articles pursuant to a merger, the filing of the officers' certificate and agreement pursuant to Section 6014 shall be in lieu of any filing required under this chapter.

Ca. Corp. Code § 5814
Amended by Stats. 1979, Ch. 724.

Section 5815 - Certificate of amendment signed and verified by majority of incorporators

In the case of amendments adopted by the incorporators under Section 5811, the corporation shall file a certificate of amendment signed and verified by a majority of the incorporators which shall state that the signers thereof constitute at least a majority of the incorporators, that directors were not named in the original articles and have not been elected, that the corporation has no members and that they adopt the amendment or amendments therein set forth.

Ca. Corp. Code § 5815
Amended by Stats. 1979, Ch. 724.

Section 5816 - Wording of amendment or amended articles

The certificate of amendment shall establish the wording of the amendment or amended articles by one or more of the following means:
(a) By stating that the articles shall be amended to read as therein set forth in full.
(b) By stating that any provision of the articles, which shall be identified by the numerical or other designation given it in the articles or by stating the wording thereof, shall be stricken from the articles or shall be amended to read as set forth in the certificate.
(c) By stating that the provisions set forth therein shall be added to the articles. If the purpose of the amendment is to reclassify, cancel, exchange, or otherwise change outstanding memberships, the amended articles shall state the effect thereof on outstanding memberships.

Ca. Corp. Code § 5816
Added by Stats. 1978, Ch. 567.

Section 5817 - Amendment and change, reclassification, or cancellation of memberships effected

Upon the filing of the certificate of amendment, the articles shall be amended in accordance with the certificate and any change, reclassification, or cancellation of memberships shall be effected, and a copy of the certificate, certified by the Secretary of State, is prima facie evidence of the performance of the conditions necessary to the adoption of the amendment. The Secretary of State shall make available the filed certificate of amendment to the Attorney General.

Ca. Corp. Code § 5817
Amended by Stats 2022 ch 617 (SB 1202),s 53, eff. 1/1/2023.
Amended by Stats 2014 ch 834 (SB 1041),s 11, eff. 1/1/2015.

Section 5818 - Extension of term of existence

A corporation formed for a limited period may at any time subsequent to the expiration of the term of its corporate existence, extend the term of its existence by an amendment to its articles removing any provision limiting the term of its existence and providing for perpetual existence. If the filing of the certificate of amendment providing for perpetual existence would be prohibited if it were original articles by the provisions of Section 5122, the Secretary of State shall not file such certificate unless, by the same or a concurrently filed certificate of amendment, the articles of such corporation are amended to adopt a new available name. For the purpose of the adoption of any such amendment, persons who have been functioning as directors of such corporation shall be considered to have been validly elected even though their election may have occurred after the expiration of the original term of the corporate existence.

Ca. Corp. Code § 5818
Added by Stats. 1978, Ch. 567.

Section 5819 - Restated articles of incorporation

(a) A corporation may restate in a single certificate the entire text of its articles as amended by filing an officers' certificate or, in circumstances where incorporators or the board may amend a corporation's articles pursuant to Sections 5811 and 5815, a certificate signed and verified by a majority of the incorporators or the board, as applicable, entitled "Restated Articles of Incorporation of (insert name of corporation)" that shall set forth the articles as amended to the date of filing of the certificate, except that the signatures and acknowledgments of the articles by the incorporators and any statements regarding the effect of any prior amendment upon memberships and any provisions of agreements of merger (other than amendments to the articles of the surviving corporation), and the initial street address and initial mailing address of the corporation and the names and addresses of the first directors and of the initial agent for service of process shall be omitted (except that the initial street address and initial mailing address of the corporation and the names and addresses of the initial agent for service of process and, if previously set forth in the articles, the initial directors, shall not be omitted prior to the time that the corporation has filed a statement under Section 6210). Those omissions are not alterations or amendments of the articles. The certificate may also itself alter or amend the articles in any respect, in which case the certificate must comply with Section 5814 or 5815, as the case may be, and Section 5816.
(b) If the certificate does not itself alter or amend the articles in any respect, it shall be approved by the board or, prior to the issuance of any memberships and the naming and election of directors, by a majority of the incorporators, and shall be subject to the provisions of this chapter relating to an amendment of the articles not requiring approval of the members (Section 5034). If the certificate does itself alter or amend the articles, it shall be subject to the provisions of this chapter relating to the amendment or amendments so made.
(c) Restated articles of incorporation filed pursuant to this section shall supersede for all purposes the original articles and all amendments filed prior thereto.

Ca. Corp. Code § 5819
Amended by Stats 2012 ch 494 (SB 1532),s 17, eff. 1/1/2013.
Amended September 21, 1999 (Bill Number: AB 1687) (Chapter 453).

Section 5820 - Effect of amendment; attorney general rulings

(a) Amendment of the articles of a corporation, pursuant to this chapter, does not, of itself, abrogate any requirement or limitation imposed upon the corporation, or any property held by it, by virtue of the trust under which such property is held by the corporation.

(b) The Attorney General may, at the corporation's request, and pursuant to such regulations as the Attorney General may issue, give rulings as to whether the Attorney General will or may oppose a proposed action, or article amendment, as inconsistent with or proscribed by the requirements of a charitable trust.

Ca. Corp. Code § 5820
Added by Stats. 1978, Ch. 567.

Chapter 9 - SALES OF ASSETS

Article 1 - GENERAL PROVISIONS

Section 5910 - Approval of mortgage, deed of trust, pledge, or other hypothecation of corporation's property

Any mortgage, deed of trust, pledge or other hypothecation of all or any part of the corporation's property, real or personal, for the purpose of securing the payment or performance of any contract or obligation may be approved by the board. Unless the articles or bylaws otherwise provide, no approval of the members (Section 5034) shall be necessary for such action.

Ca. Corp. Code § 5910
Added by Stats. 1978, Ch. 567.

Section 5911 - Sale or other disposal of assets

(a) Subject to the provisions of Section 5142, a corporation may sell, lease, convey, exchange, transfer or otherwise dispose of all or substantially all of its assets when the principal terms are:

(1) Approved by the board; and

(2) Unless the transaction is in the usual and regular course of its activities, approved by the members (Section 5034) and by any other person or persons whose approval is required by the articles, either before or after approval by the board and before or after the transaction.

(b) Notwithstanding approval by the members (Section 5034) or such other person, the board may abandon the proposed transaction without further action by the members, subject to the contractual rights, if any, of third parties.

(c) Subject to the provisions of Section 5142, such sale, lease, conveyance, exchange, transfer or other disposition may be made upon such terms and conditions and for such consideration as the board may deem in the best interests of the corporation. The consideration may be money, property, or securities of any domestic corporation, foreign corporation, or foreign business corporation or any of them.

Ca. Corp. Code § 5911
Amended by Stats. 1981, Ch. 587, Sec. 18.

Section 5912 - Certificate annexed to deed or instrument conveying or otherwise transferring assets

Any deed or instrument conveying or otherwise transferring any assets of a corporation may have annexed to it the certificate of the secretary or an assistant secretary of the corporation, setting forth that the transaction has been validly approved by the board, that the notice, if any, required by Section 5913 has been given and (a) stating that the property described in such deed or instrument is less than substantially all of the assets of the corporation or that the transfer is in the usual and regular course of the business of the corporation, if such be the case, or (b) if such property constitutes all or substantially all of the assets of the corporation and the transfer is not in the usual and regular course of the business of the corporation, stating the fact of approval thereof by the members (Section 5034). Such certificate is prima facie evidence of the existence of the facts authorizing such conveyance or other transfer of the assets and conclusive evidence in favor of any purchaser or encumbrancer for value who, without notice of any trust restriction applicable to the property or any failure to comply therewith, in good faith parted with value.

Ca. Corp. Code § 5912
Added by Stats. 1978, Ch. 567.

Section 5913 - Written notice to attorney general

Except for an agreement or transaction subject to Section 5914 or 5920, a corporation shall give written notice to the Attorney General 20 days before it sells, leases, conveys, exchanges, transfers or otherwise disposes of all or substantially all of its assets unless the transaction is in the usual and regular course of its activities or unless the Attorney General has given the corporation a written waiver of this section as to the proposed transaction. This section shall not apply to a public benefit corporation that is exempt from the supervisory authority of the Attorney General pursuant to Sections 12581 and 12583 of the Government Code by virtue of being a committee, as defined in Section 82013 of the Government Code, that is required to and does file any statement pursuant to the provisions of Article 2 (commencing with Section 84200) of Chapter 4 of Title 9 of the Government Code.

Ca. Corp. Code § 5913
Amended by Stats 2011 ch 442 (AB 1211),s 7, eff. 1/1/2012.
Amended October 10, 1999 (Bill Number: AB 254) (Chapter 850).

Article 2 - HEALTH FACILITIES

Section 5914 - Notice and consent of attorney general for agreement or transaction between nonprofit corporation and for-profit corporation or mutual benefit corporation or entity

(a)

(1) Any nonprofit corporation that is defined in Section 5046 and operates or controls a health facility, as defined in Section 1250 of the Health and Safety Code, or operates or controls a facility that provides similar health care, regardless of whether it is currently operating or providing health care services or has a suspended license, shall be required to provide written notice to, and to obtain the written consent of, the Attorney General prior to entering into any agreement or transaction to do either of the following:

(A) Sell, transfer, lease, exchange, option, convey, or otherwise dispose of, its assets to a for-profit corporation or entity or to a mutual benefit corporation or entity when a material amount of the assets of the nonprofit corporation are involved in the agreement or transaction.

(B) Transfer control, responsibility, or governance of a material amount of the assets or operations of the nonprofit corporation to any for-profit corporation or entity or to any mutual benefit corporation or entity.

(2) The substitution of a new corporate member or members that transfers the control of, responsibility for, or governance of the nonprofit corporation shall be deemed a transfer for purposes of this article. The substitution of one or more members of the governing body, or any arrangement, written or oral, that would transfer voting control of the members of the governing body, shall also be deemed a transfer for purposes of this article.

(b) The notice to the Attorney General provided for in this section shall include and contain the information the Attorney General determines is required. The notice, including any other information provided to the Attorney General under this article, and that is in the public file, shall be made available by the Attorney General to the public in written form, as soon as is practicable after it is received by the Attorney General. The notice shall include a list of the primary languages spoken at the facility and the threshold languages for Medi-Cal beneficiaries, as determined by the State Department of Health Care Services for the county in which the facility is located. The Attorney General may require the nonprofit corporation to provide certain components of the notice in any of these languages.

(c) This section shall not apply to a nonprofit corporation if the agreement or transaction is in the usual and regular course of its activities or if the Attorney General has given the corporation a written waiver of this section as to the proposed agreement or transaction.

(d) This section shall apply to any foreign nonprofit corporation that operates or controls a health facility, as defined in Section 1250 of the Health and Safety Code, or a facility that provides similar health care, regardless of whether it is currently operating or providing health care services or has a suspended license.

Ca. Corp. Code § 5914

Amended by Stats 2017 ch 782 (AB 651),s 1, eff. 1/1/2018.

Amended by Stats 2002 ch 427 (AB 890),s 1, eff. 1/1/2003.

Previously Amended October 10, 1999 (Bill Number: AB 254) (Chapter 850).

Section 5915 - Notification of attorney general's decision

Within 90 days of the receipt of the written notice required by Section 5914, the Attorney General shall notify the public benefit corporation in writing of the decision to consent to, give conditional consent to, or not consent to the agreement or transaction. The Attorney General may extend this period for one additional 45-day period if any of the following conditions are satisfied:

(a) The extension is necessary to obtain information pursuant to subdivision (a) of Section 5919.

(b) The proposed agreement or transaction is substantially modified after the first public meeting conducted by the Attorney General in accordance with Section 5916.

(c) The proposed agreement or transaction involves a multifacility health system serving multiple communities, rather than a single facility.

Ca. Corp. Code § 5915

Amended by Stats 2017 ch 782 (AB 651),s 2, eff. 1/1/2018.

Amended 10/10/1999 (Bill Number: AB 254) (Chapter 850).

Section 5916 - Public meetings

Prior to issuing any written decision referred to in Section 5915, or giving a written waiver under subdivision (c) of Section 5914, the Attorney General shall conduct one or more public meetings, one of which shall be in the county in which the facility is located, to hear comments from interested parties. At least 14 days before conducting the public meeting, the Attorney General shall provide written notice of the time and place of the meeting through publication in one or more newspapers of general circulation in the affected community and to the board of supervisors of the county in which the facility is located. This notice shall be provided in English and in the primary languages spoken at the facility and the threshold languages for Medi-Cal beneficiaries, as determined by the State Department of Health Care Services for the county in which the facility is located. If a substantive change in the proposed agreement or transaction is submitted to the Attorney General after the initial public meeting, the Attorney General may conduct an additional public meeting to hear comments from interested parties with respect to that change.

Ca. Corp. Code § 5916

Amended by Stats 2017 ch 782 (AB 651),s 3, eff. 1/1/2018.
Amended 10/10/1999 (Bill Number: AB 254) (Chapter 850).

Section 5917 - Attorney general's discretion; consideration of factors

The Attorney General shall have discretion to consent to, give conditional consent to, or not consent to any agreement or transaction described in subdivision (a) of Section 5914. In making the determination, the Attorney General shall consider any factors that the Attorney General deems relevant, including, but not limited to, whether any of the following apply:

(a) The terms and conditions of the agreement or transaction are fair and reasonable to the nonprofit corporation.

(b) The agreement or transaction will result in inurement to any private person or entity.

(c) Any agreement or transaction that is subject to this article is at fair market value. In this regard, "fair market value" means the most likely price that the assets being sold would bring in a competitive and open market under all conditions requisite to a fair sale, the buyer and seller, each acting prudently, knowledgeably and in their own best interest, and a reasonable time being allowed for exposure in the open market.

(d) The market value has been manipulated by the actions of the parties in a manner that causes the value of the assets to decrease.

(e) The proposed use of the proceeds from the agreement or transaction is consistent with the charitable trust on which the assets are held by the health facility or by the affiliated nonprofit health system.

(f) The agreement or transaction involves or constitutes any breach of trust.

(g) The Attorney General has been provided, pursuant to Section 5250, with sufficient information and data by the nonprofit corporation to evaluate adequately the agreement or transaction or the effects thereof on the public.

(h) The agreement or transaction may create a significant effect on the availability or accessibility of health care services to the affected community.

(i) The proposed agreement or transaction is in the public interest.

(j) The agreement or transaction may create a significant effect on the availability and accessibility of cultural interests provided by the facility in the affected community.

Ca. Corp. Code § 5917

Amended by Stats 2017 ch 782 (AB 651),s 4, eff. 1/1/2018.
Amended by Stats 2002 ch 427 (AB 890),s 2, eff. 1/1/2003.

Section 5917.5 - No consent to agreement or transaction in which seller restricts type or level of medical services that may be provided

The Attorney General shall not consent to a health facility agreement or transaction pursuant to Section 5914 or Section 5920 in which the seller restricts the type or level of medical services that may be provided at the health facility that is the subject of the agreement or transaction.

Ca. Corp. Code § 5917.5
Added by Stats 2003 ch 65 (SB 932),s 1, eff. 1/1/2004.

Section 5918 - Regulations

The Attorney General may adopt regulations implementing this article.
  Ca. Corp. Code § 5918
Added by Stats. 1996, Ch. 1105, Sec. 4. Effective January 1, 1997.

Section 5919 - Contracts; contract costs; reimbursement

(a) Within the time periods designated in Section 5915 and relating to those factors specified in Section 5917, the Attorney General may do the following:

  (1) Contract with, consult, and receive advice from any state agency on those terms and conditions that the Attorney General deems appropriate.

  (2) In his or her sole discretion, contract with experts or consultants to assist in reviewing the proposed agreement or transaction.
(b) Contract costs shall not exceed an amount that is reasonable and necessary to conduct the review and evaluation. Any contract entered into under this section shall be on a noncompetitive bid basis and shall be exempt from Chapter 2 (commencing with Section 10290) of Part 2 of Division 2 of the Public Contract Code. The nonprofit corporation, upon request, shall pay the Attorney General promptly for all contract costs.
(c) The Attorney General shall be entitled to reimbursement from the nonprofit corporation for all actual, reasonable, direct costs incurred in reviewing, evaluating, and making the determination referred to in this article, including administrative costs. The nonprofit corporation shall promptly pay the Attorney General, upon request, for all of those costs.
(d)

  (1) In order to monitor effectively ongoing compliance with the terms and conditions of any sale or transfer of assets subject to Section 5914, including, but not limited to, the ongoing use of the charitable assets in a manner consistent with the trust pursuant to which they are held, the Attorney General may, in his or her sole discretion, contract with experts and consultants to assist in this regard.

  (2) Contract costs shall not exceed an amount that is reasonable and necessary to conduct the review and evaluation. Any contract entered into under this section shall be on a noncompetitive bid basis and shall be exempt from Chapter 2 (commencing with Section 10290) of Part 2 of Division 2 of the Public Contract Code. The nonprofit corporation shall pay the Attorney General promptly for all contract costs.

(3) The Attorney General shall be entitled to reimbursement from either the selling or the acquiring corporation, depending upon which one the burden of compliance falls, for all actual, reasonable, and direct costs incurred in monitoring ongoing compliance with the terms and conditions of the sale or transfer of assets, including contract and administrative costs. The Attorney General may bill either the selling or the acquiring corporation and the corporation billed by the Attorney General shall promptly pay for all of those costs.

Ca. Corp. Code § 5919

Amended by Stats 2002 ch 427 (AB 890),s 3, eff. 1/1/2003.

Previously Amended October 10, 1999 (Bill Number: AB 254) (Chapter 850).

Section 5920 - Notice and consent of attorney general of agreement or transaction between nonprofit corporation and another nonprofit corporation or entity

(a)

(1) Any nonprofit corporation that is defined in Section 5046 and operates or controls a health care facility, as defined in Section 1250 of the Health and Safety Code, or operates or controls a facility that provides similar health care, regardless of whether it is currently operating or providing health care services or has a suspended license, shall be required to provide written notice to, and to obtain the written consent of, the Attorney General prior to entering into any agreement or transaction to do either of the following:

(A) Sell, transfer, lease, exchange, option, convey, or otherwise dispose of, its assets to another nonprofit corporation or entity when a material amount of the assets of the nonprofit corporation are involved in the agreement or transaction.

(B) Transfer control, responsibility, or governance of a material amount of the assets or operations of the nonprofit corporation to another nonprofit corporation or entity.

(2) The substitution of a new corporate member or members that transfers the control of, responsibility for, or governance of the nonprofit corporation, the substitution of one or more members of the governing body that would transfer voting control of the members of the governing body, or any arrangement, written or oral, that would transfer voting control of the entity shall be deemed a transfer for purposes of this article.

(b) The notice to the Attorney General provided for in this section shall contain the information the Attorney General determines is required. The notice, including any other information provided to the Attorney General under this article, and that is the public file, shall be made available by the Attorney General to the public in written form, as soon as is practicable after it is received by the Attorney General. The notice to the Attorney General shall include a list of the primary languages spoken at the facility and the threshold languages for Medi-Cal beneficiaries as determined by the State Department of Health Care Services for the county in which the facility is located. The Attorney General may require the nonprofit corporation to provide certain components of the notice in any of those languages.

(c) This section shall not apply to a nonprofit corporation if the agreement or transaction is in the usual and regular course of its activities or if the Attorney General has given the corporation a written waiver of this section as to the proposed agreement or transaction.

(d) This section shall apply to any foreign nonprofit corporation that operates or controls a health facility, as defined in Section 1250 of the Health and Safety Code, or a facility that provides similar health care, regardless of whether it is currently operating or providing health care services or has a suspended license.

(e) This section shall not apply to an agreement or transaction if the other party to the agreement or transaction is an affiliate, as defined in Section 5031, of the transferring nonprofit corporation or entity, and the corporation or entity has given the Attorney General 20 days advance notice of the agreement or transaction.

Ca. Corp. Code § 5920

Amended by Stats 2017 ch 782 (AB 651),s 5, eff. 1/1/2018.

Amended by Stats 2002 ch 427 (AB 890),s 4, eff. 1/1/2003.

Added October 10, 1999 (Bill Number: AB 254) (Chapter 850).

Section 5921 - Notification of attorney general's decision

Within 90 days of the receipt of the written notice required by Section 5920, the Attorney General shall notify the nonprofit corporation in writing of the decision to consent to, give conditional consent to, or not consent to the agreement or transaction. The Attorney General may extend this period for one additional 45-day period if any of the following conditions are satisfied:

(a) The extension is necessary to obtain relevant information from any state agency, experts, or consultants.

(b) The proposed agreement or transaction is substantially modified after the first public meeting conducted by the Attorney General in accordance with Section 5922.

(c) The proposed agreement or transaction involves a multifacility health system serving multiple communities, rather than a single facility.

Ca. Corp. Code § 5921

Amended by Stats 2017 ch 782 (AB 651),s 6, eff. 1/1/2018.

Amended by Stats 2002 ch 427 (AB 890),s 5, eff. 1/1/2003.

Added October 10, 1999 (Bill Number: AB 254) (Chapter 850).

Section 5922 - Public meetings

Prior to issuing any written decision referred to in Section 5921, or giving a written waiver under subdivision (c) of Section 5920, the Attorney General shall conduct one or more public meetings, one of which shall be in the county in which the facility is located, to hear comments from interested parties. At least 14 days before conducting the public meeting, the Attorney General shall provide written notice of the time and place of the meeting through publication in one or more newspapers of general circulation in the affected community and to the board of supervisors of the county in which the facility is located. This notice shall be provided in English and in the primary languages spoken at the facility and the threshold languages for Medi-Cal beneficiaries as determined by the State Department of Health Care Services for the county in which the facility is located. If a substantive change in the proposed agreement or transaction is submitted to the Attorney General after the initial public meeting, the Attorney General may conduct an additional public meeting to hear comments from interested parties with respect to that change.

Ca. Corp. Code § 5922
Amended by Stats 2019 ch 795 (AB 174),s 1, eff. 1/1/2020.
Amended by Stats 2017 ch 782 (AB 651),s 7, eff. 1/1/2018.
Added 10/10/1999 (Bill Number: AB 254) (Chapter 850).

Section 5923 - Attorney general's discretion; consideration of factors

The Attorney General shall have discretion to consent to, give conditional consent to, or not consent to any agreement or transaction described in subdivision (a) of Section 5920. In making the determination, the Attorney General shall consider any factors that the Attorney General deems relevant, including, but not limited to, whether any of the following apply:

(a) The terms and conditions of the agreement or transaction are fair and reasonable to the nonprofit corporation.

(b) The agreement or transaction will result in inurement to any private person or entity.

(c) Fair market value of the agreement or transaction, meaning the most likely price that the assets being sold would bring in a competitive and open market under all conditions requisite to a fair sale, the buyer and seller, each acting prudently, knowledgeably, and in their own best interest, and a reasonable time being allowed for exposure in the open market.

(d) The market value has been manipulated by the actions of the parties in a manner that causes the value of the assets to decrease.

(e) The proposed use of the proceeds from the agreement or transaction is consistent with the charitable trust on which the assets are held by the health facility or by the affiliated nonprofit health system.

(f) The agreement or transaction involves or constitutes any breach of trust.

(g) The Attorney General has been provided, pursuant to Section 5250, with sufficient information and data by the nonprofit public benefit corporation to evaluate adequately the agreement or transaction or the effects thereof on the public.

(h) The agreement or transaction may create a significant effect on the availability or accessibility of health care services to the affected community.

(i) The proposed agreement or transaction is in the public interest.

(j) The agreement or transaction may create a significant effect on the availability and accessibility of cultural interests provided by the facility in the affected community.

Ca. Corp. Code § 5923

Amended by Stats 2017 ch 782 (AB 651),s 8, eff. 1/1/2018.

Amended by Stats 2002 ch 427 (AB 890),s 6, eff. 1/1/2003.

Added October 10, 1999 (Bill Number: AB 254) (Chapter 850).

Section 5924 - Contracts; contract costs; reimbursement

(a) Within the time periods designated in Section 5921 and relating to those factors specified in Section 5923, the Attorney General may do the following:

(1) Contract with, consult, and receive advice from any state agency on those terms and conditions that the Attorney General deems appropriate.

(2) In his or her sole discretion, contract with experts or consultants to assist in reviewing the proposed agreement or transaction.

(b) Contract costs shall not exceed an amount that is reasonable and necessary to conduct the review and evaluation. Any contract entered into under this section shall be on a noncompetitive bid basis and shall be exempt from Chapter 2 (commencing with Section 10290) of Part 2 of Division 2 of the Public Contract Code. The selling nonprofit corporation, upon request, shall pay the Attorney General promptly for all contract costs.

(c) The Attorney General shall be entitled to reimbursement from the selling nonprofit corporation for all actual, reasonable, direct costs incurred in reviewing, evaluating, and making the determination referred to in Section 5921, including administrative costs. The selling nonprofit corporation shall promptly pay the Attorney General, upon request, for all of those costs.

(d)

(1) In order to effectively monitor ongoing compliance with the terms and conditions of any sale or transfer of assets subject to Section 5920, including, but not limited to, the ongoing use of the charitable assets in a manner consistent with the trust pursuant to which they are held, the Attorney General may, in his or her sole discretion, contract with experts and consultants to assist in this regard.

(2) Contract costs shall not exceed an amount that is reasonable and necessary to conduct the review and evaluation. Any contract entered into under this section shall be on a noncompetitive bid basis and shall be exempt from Chapter 2 (commencing with Section 10290) of Part 2 of Division 2 of the Public Contract Code. The selling nonprofit corporation shall pay the Attorney General promptly for all contract costs.

(3) The Attorney General shall be entitled to reimbursement from either the selling or the acquiring nonprofit corporation, depending upon which one the burden of compliance falls, for all actual, reasonable, and direct costs incurred in monitoring ongoing compliance with the terms and conditions of the sale or transfer of assets, including contract and administrative costs. The Attorney General shall be entitled to this reimbursement for a period of time not to exceed two years after any time period specified in the terms or conditions of sale or transfer of assets. The Attorney General may bill either the selling or the acquiring corporation and the corporation billed by the Attorney General shall promptly pay for all of those costs.

Ca. Corp. Code § 5924
Amended by Stats 2002 ch 427 (AB 890),s 7, eff. 1/1/2003.
Added October 10, 1999 (Bill Number: AB 254) (Chapter 850).

Section 5925 - Regulations

The Attorney General may adopt regulations implementing Sections 5920 to 5924, inclusive.

Ca. Corp. Code § 5925
Added 10/10/1999 (Bill Number: AB 254) (Chapter 850).

Section 5926 - Enforcement of conditions imposed on Attorney General's consent to agreement or transaction

The Attorney General may enforce conditions imposed on the Attorney General's consent to an agreement or transaction pursuant to Section 5914 or 5920 to the fullest extent provided by law. In addition to any legal remedies the Attorney General may have, the Attorney General shall be entitled to specific performance, injunctive relief, and other equitable remedies a court deems appropriate for breach of any of the conditions and shall be entitled to recover its attorney's fees and costs incurred in remedying each violation.

Ca. Corp. Code § 5926
Added by Stats 2017 ch 782 (AB 651),s 9, eff. 1/1/2018.

Section 5930 - Plan for evaluation of whether additional standards should be established

(a) The Attorney General shall prepare a plan for an evaluation of whether additional standards for charitable care and community benefits should be established for private, not-for-profit corporations that operate or control a general acute care hospital as defined in Section 1250 of the Health and Safety Code.
(b) In preparing the plan, the Attorney General shall consult with representatives of interested parties, including, but not limited to, all of the following:

(1) Health facility associations.

(2) Physician organizations.

(3) Consumer groups.

(4) Health care employee organizations.

(5) Community groups.

(6) The Office of Statewide Health Planning and Development.
(c) The plan shall provide for the evaluation of all of the following:

(1) The degree to which private, not-for-profit hospitals provide charitable care and community benefits, including the nature of the benefits, the definition of the community, and a comparison of the cost of providing the benefit with the value of the benefits given to the community.

(2) The implications of the relationships among private not-for-profit hospitals and affiliated entities, as defined in Section 5031 of the Corporations Code, for purposes of determining community benefits.

(3) The role of the board of directors of private, not-for-profit hospitals in ensuring benefit to the community.
(d) The plan shall be submitted to the appropriate policy and fiscal committees of the Legislature by March 1, 2001.
Ca. Corp. Code § 5930
Added by Stats 2000 ch 801 (AB 2276), s 1, eff. 1/1/2001.

Chapter 10 - MERGERS

Article 1 - MERGER

Section 6010 - Merger with domestic corporation, foreign corporation, or other business entity

(a) A public benefit corporation may merge with any domestic corporation, foreign corporation (Section 171), or other business entity (Section 5063.5). However, without the prior written consent of the Attorney General, a public benefit corporation may only merge with another public benefit corporation or a religious corporation or a foreign nonprofit corporation or an unincorporated association the governing documents of which provide that its assets are irrevocably dedicated to charitable, religious, or public purposes. In addition, a public benefit corporation that is exempt from the supervisory authority of the Attorney General pursuant to Sections 12581 and 12583 of the Government Code by virtue of being a committee, as defined in Section 82013 of the Government Code, that is required to and does file any statement pursuant to the provisions of Article 2 (commencing with Section 84200) of Chapter 4 of Title 9 of the Government Code, may merge with another public benefit corporation similarly exempt without having to obtain the Attorney General's consent.

(b) At least 20 days prior to consummation of any merger allowed by subdivision (a), the Attorney General must be provided with a copy of the proposed agreement of merger.

(c) Without the prior written consent of the Attorney General, when a merger occurs pursuant to subdivision (a), each member of a constituent corporation may only receive or keep a membership in the surviving corporation for or as a result of the member's membership in the constituent corporation.

   Ca. Corp. Code § 6010

Amended by Stats 2011 ch 442 (AB 1211),s 8, eff. 1/1/2012.

Amended September 21, 1999 (Bill Number: AB 198) (Chapter 437).

Section 6011 - Agreement of merger

The board of each corporation which desires to merge shall approve an agreement of merger. The constituent corporations shall be parties to the agreement of merger and other persons may be parties to the agreement of merger. The agreement shall state:

(a) The terms and conditions of the merger;

(b) The amendments, subject to Sections 5810 and 5816, to the articles of the surviving corporation to be effected by the merger, if any; if any amendment changes the name of the surviving corporation, the new name may be the same as or similar to the name of a disappearing corporation, subject to subdivision (b) of Section 5122;

(c) The amendments to the bylaws of the surviving corporation to be effected by the merger, if any;

(d) The name and place of incorporation of each constituent corporation and which of the constituent corporations is the surviving corporation;

(e) The manner, if any, of converting memberships of the constituent corporations into memberships of the surviving corporation; and

(f) Such other details or provisions as are desired, if any.

   Ca. Corp. Code § 6011

Amended by Stats. 1979, Ch. 724.

Section 6012 - Approval of principal terms of merger by members and other persons

The principal terms of the merger shall be approved by the members (Section 5034) of each constituent corporation and by each other person or persons whose approval of an amendment of articles is required by the articles; and the approval by the members (Section 5034) or such other person or persons required by this section may be given before or after the approval by the board.

   Ca. Corp. Code § 6012

Amended by Stats. 1981, Ch. 587, Sec. 20.

Section 6013 - Signing agreement

Each constituent corporation shall sign the agreement by the chairperson of its board, president or a vice president, and secretary or an assistant secretary acting on behalf of their respective corporations.

Ca. Corp. Code § 6013
Amended by Stats 2022 ch 617 (SB 1202),s 54, eff. 1/1/2023.
Added by Stats. 1978, Ch. 567.

Section 6014 - Filing of agreement of merger

After approval of a merger by the board and any approval by the members (Section 5034) or other person or persons required by Section 6012, the surviving corporation shall file a copy of the agreement of merger with an officers' certificate of each constituent corporation attached stating the total number of memberships of each class entitled to vote on the merger, identifying any other person or persons whose approval is required, and stating that the principal terms of the agreement in the form attached were duly approved by the required vote of the members and (if applicable) such other person or persons. The merger and any amendment of the articles of the surviving corporation contained in the merger agreement shall thereupon be effective (subject to subdivision (c) of Section 5008 and subject to the provisions of Section 6018) and the several parties thereto shall be one surviving corporation. The Secretary of State may certify a copy of the merger agreement separate from the officers' certificates attached thereto.

Ca. Corp. Code § 6014
Amended by Stats 2006 ch 773 (AB 2341),s 15, eff. 9/29/2006.

Section 6015 - Amendment to agreement

(a) Any amendment to the agreement may be adopted and the agreement so amended may be approved by the board and, if it changes any of the principal terms of the agreement, by the members (Section 5034) or other person or persons, as required by Section 6012, of any constituent corporation in the same manner as the original agreement.
(b) If the agreement so amended is approved as provided in subdivision (a), the agreement so amended shall then constitute the agreement of merger.

Ca. Corp. Code § 6015
Amended by Stats. 1981, Ch. 587, Sec. 21.

Section 6016 - Abandonment of merger

The board may, in its discretion, abandon a merger, subject to the contractual rights, if any, of third parties, including other constituent corporations, without further approval by the members (Section 5034) or other persons entitled to approve the merger at any time before the merger is effective.

Ca. Corp. Code § 6016
Added by Stats. 1978, Ch. 567.

Section 6017 - Certified copy of agreement of merger

A copy of an agreement of merger certified on or after the effective date by an official having custody thereof has the same force in evidence as the original and, except as against the state, is conclusive evidence of the performance of all conditions precedent to the merger, the existence on the effective date of the surviving corporation and the performance of the conditions necessary to the adoption of any amendment to the articles contained in the agreement of merger.

Ca. Corp. Code § 6017
Added by Stats. 1978, Ch. 567.

Section 6018 - Merger of corporations with foreign corporations

(a) Subject to the provisions of Section 6010, the merger of any number of corporations with any number of foreign corporations may be effected if the foreign corporations are authorized by the laws under which they are formed to effect the merger. The surviving corporation may be any one of the constituent corporations and shall continue to exist under the laws of the state or place of its incorporation.

(b) If the surviving corporation is a public benefit corporation or a religious corporation, the merger proceedings with respect to that corporation and any disappearing corporation shall conform to the provisions of this chapter governing the merger of corporations, but if the surviving corporation is a foreign corporation, then, subject to the requirements of subdivision (d) and Section 6012, the merger proceedings may be in accordance with the laws of the state or place of incorporation of the surviving corporation.

(c) If the surviving corporation is a public benefit corporation or a religious corporation, the agreement and the officers' certificate of each constituent corporation shall be filed as provided in Section 6014 and thereupon, subject to subdivision (c) of Section 5008, the merger shall be effective as to each corporation; and each foreign disappearing corporation that is qualified for the transaction of intrastate business shall by virtue of the filing automatically surrender its right to transact intrastate business.

(d) If the surviving corporation is a foreign corporation, the merger shall become effective in accordance with the law of the jurisdiction in which it is organized, but shall be effective as to any disappearing corporation as of the time of effectiveness in the foreign jurisdiction upon the filing in this state as required by this subdivision. There shall be filed as to the domestic disappearing corporation or corporations the documents described in any one of the following paragraphs:

(1) A copy of the agreement, certificate, or other document filed by the surviving foreign corporation in the state or place of its incorporation for the purpose of effecting the merger, which copy shall be certified by the public officer having official custody of the original.

(2) An executed counterpart of the agreement, certificate, or other document filed by the surviving corporation in the state or place of its incorporation for the purpose of effecting the merger.

(3) A copy of the agreement of merger with an officers' certificate of the surviving foreign corporation and of each constituent domestic corporation attached, which officers' certificates shall conform to the requirements of Section 6014.
(e) If the date of the filing in this state pursuant to subdivision (d) is more than six months after the time of the effectiveness in the foreign jurisdiction, or if the powers of the domestic corporation are suspended at the time of effectiveness in the foreign jurisdiction, the merger shall be effective as to the domestic disappearing corporation or corporations as of the date of filing in this state. Each foreign disappearing corporation that is qualified for the transaction of intrastate business shall automatically by the filing pursuant to subdivision (d) surrender its right to transact intrastate business as of the date of filing in this state regardless of the time of effectiveness as to a domestic disappearing corporation.

    Ca. Corp. Code § 6018
Amended by Stats 2006 ch 773 (AB 2341),s 16, eff. 9/29/2006.
Amended September 21, 1999 (Bill Number: AB 1687) (Chapter 453).

Section 6019 - Agreement of merger between nonprofit corporation and business corporation

If an agreement of merger is entered into between a nonprofit corporation and a business corporation:
(i) Sections 6011, 6012, 6014, and 6015 shall apply to any constituent public benefit corporation;
(ii) Sections 8011, 8011.5, 8012, 8014, and 8015 shall apply to any constituent mutual benefit corporation;
(iii) Sections 6014 and 6015 and subdivisions (c) and (d) of Section 9640 shall apply to any constituent religious corporation; and
(iv) Sections 1101, 1101.1, 1103, and 1104 shall apply to any constituent business corporation.

    Ca. Corp. Code § 6019
Added by Stats. 1981, Ch. 587, Sec. 22.

Section 6019.1 - Merger with other business entities

(a) Subject to the provisions of Sections 6010 and 9640, any one or more corporations may merge with one or more other business entities (Section 5063.5). One or more other domestic corporations and foreign corporations (Section 5053) may be parties to the merger. Notwithstanding the provisions of this section, such a merger may be effected only if:

(1) In a merger in which a domestic corporation or domestic other business entity is a party, it is authorized by the laws under which it is organized to effect the merger.

(2) In a merger in which a foreign corporation is a party, it is authorized by the laws under which it is organized to effect the merger.

(3) In a merger in which a foreign other business entity is a party, it is authorized by the laws under which it is organized to effect the merger.

(b) Each corporation and each other party which desires to merge shall approve an agreement of merger. The board and the members (Section 5034) of each corporation which desires to merge, and each other person or persons, if any, whose approval of an amendment of the articles of that corporation is required by the articles or bylaws shall approve the agreement of merger. The agreement of merger shall be approved on behalf of each other party by those persons authorized or required to approve the merger by the laws under which it is organized. The parties desiring to merge shall be parties to the agreement of merger and other persons, including a parent party (Section 5064.5), may be parties to the agreement of merger. The agreement of merger shall state all of the following:

(1) The terms and conditions of the merger.

(2) The name and place of incorporation or organization of each party and the identity of the surviving party.

(3) The amendments, if any, subject to Sections 5810 and 5816, to the articles of the surviving corporation, if applicable, to be effected by the merger. The name of the surviving corporation may be, subject to subdivision (b) of Section 5122 and subdivision (b) of Section 9122, the same as, or similar to, the name of a disappearing party to the merger.

(4) The manner, if any, of converting the memberships of each of the constituent corporations into shares, memberships, interests, or other securities of the surviving party; and, if any memberships of any of the constituent corporations are not to be converted solely into shares, memberships, interests, or other securities of the surviving party, the cash, rights, securities, or other property which the holders of those memberships are to receive in exchange for the memberships, which cash, rights, securities, or other property may be in addition to, or in lieu of, shares, memberships, interests, or other securities of the surviving corporation or surviving other business entity.

(5) Any other details or provisions required by the laws under which any party to the merger is organized, including, if an unincorporated association is a party to the merger, Section 18370, or if a domestic limited partnership is a party to the merger, subdivision (a) of Section 15911.12, if a domestic general partnership is a party to the merger, subdivision (a) of Section 16911, or, if a domestic limited liability company is a party to the merger, subdivision (a) of Section 17710.12.

(6) Any other details or provisions as are desired.

(c) Notwithstanding its prior approval, an agreement of merger may be amended prior to the filing of the agreement of merger if the amendment is approved by each constituent corporation in the same manner as the original agreement of merger. If the agreement of merger as so amended and approved is also approved by each of the other parties to the agreement of merger, as so amended it shall then constitute the agreement of merger.

(d) The board of a constituent corporation may, in its discretion, abandon a merger, subject to the contractual rights, if any, of third parties, including other parties to the agreement of merger, without further approval by the members (Section 5034) or other persons, at any time before the merger is effective.

(e) Each constituent corporation shall sign the agreement of merger by its chairperson of the board, president or a vice president, and also by its secretary or an assistant secretary acting on behalf of their respective corporations.

(f) After required approvals of the merger by each constituent corporation and each other party to the merger, the surviving party shall file a copy of the agreement of merger with an officers' certificate of each constituent domestic and foreign corporation attached stating the total number of outstanding shares or membership interests of each class, if any, entitled to vote on the merger (and identifying any other person or persons whose approval is required), that the agreement of merger in the form attached or its principal terms, as required, were approved by that corporation by a vote of a number of shares or membership interests of each class entitled to vote, if any, which equaled or exceeded the vote required, specifying each class entitled to vote and the percentage vote required of each class, and, if applicable, by that other person or persons whose approval is required. If equity securities of a parent party (Section 5064.5) are to be issued in the merger, the officers' certificate or certificate of merger of the controlled party shall state either that no vote of the shareholders of the parent party was required or that the required vote was obtained. The merger and any amendment of the articles of the surviving corporation, if applicable, contained in the agreement of merger shall be effective upon the filing of the agreement of merger, subject to the provisions of subdivision (h). If a domestic reciprocal insurer organized after 1974 to provide medical malpractice insurance is a party to the merger, the agreement of merger or certificate of merger shall not be filed until there has been filed the certificate issued by the Insurance Commissioner approving the merger pursuant to Section 1555 of the Insurance Code.

In lieu of an officers' certificate, a certificate of merger, on a form prescribed by the

Secretary of State, shall be filed for each constituent other business entity. The certificate of merger shall be executed and acknowledged by each domestic constituent limited liability company by all of the managers of the limited liability company (unless a lesser number is specified in its articles of organization or operating agreement) and by each domestic constituent limited partnership by all general partners (unless a lesser number is provided in its certificate of limited partnership or partnership agreement) and by each domestic constituent general partnership by two partners (unless a lesser number is provided in its partnership agreement) and by each foreign constituent limited liability company by one or more managers and by each foreign constituent general partnership or foreign constituent limited partnership by one or more general partners, and by each constituent reciprocal insurer by the chairperson of the board, president, or vice president, and also by the secretary or assistant secretary, or, if a constituent reciprocal insurer has not appointed such officers, by the chairperson of the board, president, or vice president, and also by the secretary or assistant secretary of the constituent reciprocal insurer's attorney-in-fact, and by each other party to the merger by those persons required or authorized to execute the certificate of merger by the laws under which that party is organized, specifying for such party the provision of law or other basis for the authority of the signing persons.

The certificate of merger shall set forth, if a vote of the shareholders, members, partners, or other holders of interests of a constituent other business entity was required, a statement setting forth the total number of outstanding interests of each class entitled to vote on the merger and that the agreement of merger or its principal terms, as required, were approved by a vote of the number of interests of each class which equaled or exceeded the vote required, specifying each class entitled to vote and the percentage vote required of each class, and any other information required to be set forth under the laws under which the constituent other business entity is organized, including, if a domestic limited partnership is a party to the merger, subdivision (a) of Section 15911.14, if a domestic general partnership is a party to the merger, subdivision (b) of Section 16915, and, if a domestic limited liability company is a party to the merger, subdivision (a) of Section 17710.14. The certificate of merger for each constituent foreign other business entity, if any, shall also set forth the statutory or other basis under which that foreign other business entity is authorized by the laws under which it is organized to effect the merger.

The Secretary of State may certify a copy of the agreement of merger separate from the officers' certificates and certificates of merger attached thereto.

(g) A copy of an agreement of merger certified on or after the effective date by an official having custody thereof has the same force in evidence as the original and, except as against the state, is conclusive evidence of the performance of all conditions precedent to the merger, the existence on the effective date of the surviving party to the merger, the performance of the conditions necessary to the adoption of any amendment to the articles, if applicable, contained in the agreement of merger, and the merger of the constituent corporations, either by themselves or together with other constituent parties, into the surviving party to the merger.

(h)

(1) The merger of domestic corporations with foreign corporations or foreign other business entities in a merger in which one or more other business entities is a party shall comply with subdivisions (a) and (f) and this subdivision.

(2) Subject to subdivision (c) of Section 5008 and paragraph (3), the merger shall be effective as to each domestic constituent corporation and domestic constituent other business entity upon filing of the agreement of merger with attachments as provided in subdivision (f).

(3) If the surviving party is a foreign corporation or foreign other business entity, except as provided in paragraph (4), the merger shall be effective as to any domestic disappearing corporation as of the time of effectiveness in the foreign jurisdiction upon the filing in this state of a copy of the agreement of merger with an officers' certificate of the surviving foreign corporation and of each constituent foreign and domestic corporation and a certificate of merger of each constituent other business entity attached, which officers' certificates and certificates of merger shall conform to the requirements of subdivision (f). If one or more domestic other business entities is a disappearing party in a merger pursuant to this subdivision in which a foreign other business entity is the surviving entity, a certificate of merger required by the laws under which each domestic other business entity is organized, including subdivision (a) of Section 15911.14, subdivision (b) of Section 16915, or subdivision (a) of Section 17710.14, if applicable, shall also be filed at the same time as the filing of the agreement of merger.

(4) If the date of the filing in this state pursuant to this subdivision is more than six months after the time of the effectiveness in the foreign jurisdiction, or if the powers of a domestic disappearing corporation are suspended at the time of effectiveness in the foreign jurisdiction, the merger shall be effective as to the domestic disappearing corporation as of the date of filing in this state.

(5) Each foreign disappearing corporation that is qualified for the transaction of intrastate business shall automatically by the filing pursuant to subdivision (f) surrender its right to transact intrastate business as of the date of filing in this state or, if later, the effective date of the merger. With respect to each foreign disappearing other business entity previously registered for the transaction of intrastate business in this state, the filing of the agreement of merger pursuant to subdivision (f) automatically has the effect of a cancellation of registration for that foreign other business entity as of the date of filing in this state or, if later, the effective date of the merger, without the necessity of the filing of a certificate of cancellation.

Ca. Corp. Code § 6019.1

Amended by Stats 2012 ch 419 (SB 323),s 11, eff. 1/1/2013, op. 1/1/2014.

Amended by Stats 2011 ch 442 (AB 1211),s 9, eff. 1/1/2012.
Amended by Stats 2006 ch 773 (AB 2341),s 17, eff. 9/29/2006.
Amended by Stats 2006 ch 773 (AB 2341),s 17.5, eff. 9/29/2006.
Amended by Stats 2006 ch 495 (AB 339),s 11, eff. 1/1/2007.
Added September 21, 1999 (Bill Number: AB 198) (Chapter 437).

Article 2 - EFFECT OF MERGER

Section 6020 - Surviving party; rights of creditors and liens and trusts; pending action or proceeding

(a) Upon merger pursuant to this chapter the separate existences of the disappearing parties to the merger cease and the surviving party to the merger shall succeed, without other transfer, to all the rights and property of each of the disappearing parties to the merger and shall be subject to all the debts and liabilities of each and trust obligations upon the property of a disappearing party in the same manner as if incurred by the surviving party to the merger.
(b) All rights of creditors and all liens and trusts upon or arising from the property of each of the constituent corporations and other parties to the merger shall be preserved unimpaired, provided that the liens and trust obligations upon property of a disappearing party shall be limited to the property affected thereby immediately prior to the time the merger is effective.
(c) Any action or proceeding pending by or against any disappearing corporation or other party to the merger may be prosecuted to judgment, which shall bind the surviving party to the merger, or the surviving party to the merger may be proceeded against or substituted in its place.
  Ca. Corp. Code § 6020
Amended 9/21/1999 (Bill Number: AB 198) (Chapter 437).

Section 6020.5 - Assumption of liability

(a) Upon merger pursuant to this chapter, a surviving domestic or foreign corporation or other business entity shall be deemed to have assumed the liability of each disappearing domestic or foreign corporation or other business entity that is taxed under Part 10 (commencing with Section 17001) of, or under Part 11 (commencing with Section 23001) of, Division 2 of the Revenue and Taxation Code for the following:

  (1) To prepare and file, or to cause to be prepared and filed, tax and information returns otherwise required of that disappearing entity as specified in Chapter 2 (commencing with Section 18501) of Part 10.2 of Division 2 of the Revenue and Taxation Code.

  (2) To pay any tax liability determined to be due.

(b) If the surviving entity is a domestic limited liability company, domestic corporation, or registered limited liability partnership or a foreign limited liability company, foreign limited liability partnership, or foreign corporation that is registered or qualified to do business in California, the Secretary of State shall notify the Franchise Tax Board of the merger.

    Ca. Corp. Code § 6020.5
Amended by Stats 2006 ch 495 (AB 339),s 12, eff. 1/1/2007.
Amended by Stats 2006 ch 773 (AB 2341),s 18, eff. 9/29/2006.
Added by Stats 2005 ch 286 (AB 241),s 2, eff. 1/1/2006.

Section 6021 - Real property

Whenever a domestic or foreign corporation or other business entity (Section 5063.5) having any real property in this state merges with another domestic or foreign corporation or other business entity pursuant to the laws of this state or of the state or place in which any constituent party to the merger was organized, and the laws of the state or place of organization (including this state) of any disappearing party to the merger provide substantially that the making and filing of the agreement of merger vests in the surviving party to the merger all the real property of any disappearing party to the merger, the filing for record in the office of the county recorder of any county in this state in which any of the real property of the disappearing party to the merger is located of either (a) a certificate prescribed by the Secretary of State, or (b) a copy of the agreement of merger or certificate of merger, certified by the Secretary of State or an authorized public official of the state or place pursuant to the laws of which the merger is effected, shall evidence record ownership in the surviving party to the merger of all interest of that disappearing party to the merger in and to the real property located in that county.

    Ca. Corp. Code § 6021
Amended 9/21/1999 (Bill Number: AB 198) (Chapter 437).

Section 6022 - Bequest, devise, gift, grant, or promise contained in will or other instrument of donation, subscription, or conveyance

Any bequest, devise, gift, grant, or promise contained in a will or other instrument of donation, subscription, or conveyance, which is made to a constituent corporation and which takes effect or remains payable after the merger, inures to the surviving party to the merger.

    Ca. Corp. Code § 6022
Amended 9/21/1999 (Bill Number: AB 198) (Chapter 437).

Chapter 11 - BANKRUPTCY REORGANIZATIONS AND ARRANGEMENTS

Section 6110 - Law governing reorganization of corporations

Any proceeding, initiated with respect to a corporation, under any applicable statute of the United States, as now existing or hereafter enacted, relating to reorganizations of corporations, shall be governed by the provisions of Chapter 14 (commencing with Section 1400) of Division 1 of Title 1, and for this purpose the reference in Chapter 14 to "shareholders" shall be deemed to be a reference to members and the reference to "this division" shall be deemed to be a reference to this part.

Ca. Corp. Code § 6110
Amended by Stats 2009 ch 500 (AB 1059),s 19, eff. 1/1/2010.

Chapter 12 - REQUIRED FILINGS BY CORPORATION OR ITS AGENT

Section 6210 - Statement

(a) Every corporation shall, within 90 days after the filing of its original articles and biennially thereafter during the applicable filing period, file, on a form prescribed by the Secretary of State, a statement containing:

(1) the name of the corporation and the Secretary of State's file number;

(2) the names and complete business or residence addresses of its chief executive officer, secretary, and chief financial officer;

(3) the street address of its principal office in California, if any;

(4) the mailing address of the corporation, if different from the street address of its principal office or if the corporation has no principal office address in California; and

(5) if the corporation chooses to receive renewal notices and any other notifications from the Secretary of State by electronic mail instead of by United States mail, a valid electronic mail address for the corporation or for the corporation's designee to receive those notices.

(b) The statement required by subdivision (a) shall also designate, as the agent of the corporation for the purpose of service of process, a natural person residing in this state or any domestic or foreign or foreign business corporation that has complied with Section 1505 and whose capacity to act as an agent has not terminated. If a natural person is designated, the statement shall set forth the person's complete business or residence street address. If a corporate agent is designated, no address for it shall be set forth.

(c) For the purposes of this section, the applicable filing period for a corporation shall be the calendar month during which its original articles were filed and the immediately preceding five calendar months. The Secretary of State shall provide a notice to each corporation to comply with this section approximately three months before the close of the applicable filing period. The notice shall state the due date for compliance and shall be sent to the last address of the corporation according to the records of the Secretary of State or to the last electronic mail address according to the records of the Secretary of State if the corporation has elected to receive notices from the Secretary of State by electronic mail. Neither the failure of the Secretary of State to send the notice nor the failure of the corporation to receive it is an excuse for failure to comply with this section.

(d) Whenever any of the information required by subdivision (a) is changed, the corporation may file a current statement containing all the information required by subdivisions (a) and (b). In order to change its agent for service of process or the address of the agent, the corporation must file a current statement containing all the information required by subdivisions (a) and (b). Whenever any statement is filed pursuant to this section, it supersedes any previously filed statement and the statement in the articles as to the agent for service of process and the address of the agent.

(e) The Secretary of State may destroy or otherwise dispose of any statement filed pursuant to this section after it has been superseded by the filing of a new statement.

(f) This section does not place any person dealing with the corporation on notice of, or under any duty to inquire about, the existence or content of a statement filed pursuant to this section.

Ca. Corp. Code § 6210

Amended by Stats 2022 ch 617 (SB 1202),s 55, eff. 1/1/2023.
Amended by Stats 2012 ch 162 (SB 1171),s 20, eff. 1/1/2013.
Amended by Stats 2011 ch 204 (AB 657),s 7, eff. 1/1/2012.
Amended by Stats 2007 ch 101 (SB 998),s 3, eff. 1/1/2008.
Amended October 10, 1999 (Bill Number: SB 284) (Chapter 1000).

Section 6211 - Resignation of agent

(a) An agent designated for service of process pursuant to Section 6210 may deliver to the Secretary of State, on a form prescribed by the Secretary of State for filing, a signed and acknowledged written statement of resignation as an agent for service of process containing the name of the corporation, the Secretary of State's file number of the corporation, the name of the resigning agent for service of process, and a statement that the agent is resigning. Thereupon the authority of the agent to act in that capacity shall cease and the Secretary of State forthwith shall mail or otherwise provide written notice of the filing of the statement of resignation to the corporation at its principal office.

(b) The resignation of an agent may be effective if, on a form prescribed by the Secretary of State containing the name of the corporation, the Secretary of State's file number for the corporation, and the name of the agent for service of process, the agent disclaims having been properly appointed as the agent. Similarly, a person named as an officer or director may indicate that the person was never properly appointed as the officer or director.

(c) The Secretary of State may destroy or otherwise dispose of any resignation filed pursuant to this section after a new form is filed pursuant to Section 6210 replacing the agent for service of process that has resigned.

    Ca. Corp. Code § 6211

Amended by Stats 2014 ch 834 (SB 1041),s 12, eff. 1/1/2015.

Amended September 21, 1999 (Bill Number: AB 1687) (Chapter 453).

Section 6212 - Designation of new agent

If a natural person who has been designated agent for service of process pursuant to Section 6210 dies or resigns or no longer resides in the state or if the corporate agent for such purpose resigns, dissolves, withdraws from the state, forfeits its right to transact intrastate business, has its corporate rights, powers and privileges suspended or ceases to exist, the corporation shall forthwith file a designation of a new agent conforming to the requirements of Section 6210.

    Ca. Corp. Code § 6212

Added by Stats. 1978, Ch. 567.

Section 6214 - Business records available to assessor

Upon request of an assessor, a corporation owning, claiming, possessing or controlling property in this state subject to local assessment shall make available at the corporation's principal office in California or at a place mutually acceptable to the assessor and the corporation a true copy of business records relevant to the amount, cost and value of all property that it owns, claims, possesses or controls within the county.

    Ca. Corp. Code § 6214

Amended by Stats. 1979, Ch. 724.

Section 6215 - Joint and several liability of officers, directors, employees, or agents

Any officers, directors, employees or agents of a corporation who do any of the following are liable jointly and severally for all the damages resulting therefrom to the corporation or any person injured thereby who relied thereupon or to both:

(a) Make, issue, deliver or publish any report, circular, certificate, financial statement, balance sheet, public notice or document respecting the corporation or its memberships, assets, liabilities, business, earnings or accounts which is false in any material respect, knowing it to be false, or participate in the making, issuance, delivery or publication thereof with knowledge that the same is false in a material respect.

(b) Make or cause to be made in the books, minutes, records or accounts of a corporation any entry which is false in any material particular knowing such entry is false.

(c) Remove, erase, alter or cancel any entry in any books or records of the corporation, with intent to deceive.

Ca. Corp. Code § 6215
Added by Stats. 1978, Ch. 567.

Section 6216 - Action by attorney general

(a) The Attorney General, upon complaint of a member, director or officer, that a corporation is failing to comply with the provisions of this chapter, Chapter 5 (commencing with Section 5510), Chapter 6 (commencing with Section 5610) or Chapter 13 (commencing with Section 6310), may, in the name of the people of the State of California, send to the principal office of such corporation, (or, if there is no such office, to the office or residence of the chief executive officer or secretary, of the corporation, as set forth in the most recent statement filed pursuant to Section 6210) notice of the complaint. If the answer is not satisfactory, or if there is no answer within 30 days, the Attorney General may institute, maintain or intervene in such suits, actions, or proceedings of any type in any court or tribunal of competent jurisdiction or before any administrative agency for such relief by way of injunction, the dissolution of entities, the appointment of receivers or any other temporary, preliminary, provisional or final remedies as may be appropriate to protect the rights of members or to undo the consequences of failure to comply with such requirements. In any such action, suit or proceeding there may be joined as parties all persons and entities responsible for or affected by such activity.
(b) The Attorney General may bring an action under subdivision (a) without having received a complaint, and without first giving notice of a complaint.

Ca. Corp. Code § 6216
Added by Stats. 1978, Ch. 567.

Chapter 13 - RECORDS, REPORTS, AND RIGHTS OF INSPECTION

Article 1 - GENERAL PROVISIONS

Section 6310 - Availability of record in written form

If any record subject to inspection pursuant to this chapter is not maintained in written form, a request for inspection is not complied with unless and until the corporation at its expense makes such record available in written form. For the purposes of this chapter "written" or "in writing" also includes cathode ray tube and similar electronic communications methods.

Ca. Corp. Code § 6310
Amended by Stats. 1982, Ch. 662, Sec. 9.

Section 6311 - Inspection

Any inspection under this chapter may be made in person or by agent or attorney and

the right of inspection includes the right to copy and make extracts.
Ca. Corp. Code § 6311
Added by Stats. 1978, Ch. 567.

Section 6312 - Inspection of records of subsidiary

Any right of inspection created by this chapter extends to the records of each subsidiary of a corporation.
Ca. Corp. Code § 6312
Added by Stats. 1978, Ch. 567.

Section 6313 - Limitation of rights of members prohibited

The rights of members provided in this chapter may not be limited by contract or the articles or bylaws.
Ca. Corp. Code § 6313
Added by Stats. 1978, Ch. 567.

Article 2 - REQUIRED RECORDS, REPORTS TO DIRECTORS AND MEMBERS

Section 6320 - Keeping records

(a) Each corporation shall keep:

(1) Adequate and correct books and records of account;

(2) Minutes of the proceedings of its members, board and committees of the board; and

(3) A record of its members giving their names and addresses and the class of membership held by each.
(b) Those minutes and other books and records shall be kept either in written form or in any other form capable of being converted into clearly legible tangible form or in any combination of the foregoing. When minutes and other books and records are kept in a form capable of being converted into clearly legible paper form, the clearly legible paper form into which those minutes and other books and records are converted shall be admissible in evidence, and accepted for all other purposes, to the same extent as an original paper record of the same information would have been, provided that the paper form accurately portrays the record.
Ca. Corp. Code § 6320
Amended by Stats 2004 ch 254 (SB 1306),s 19, eff. 1/1/2005

Section 6321 - Members' report

(a) Except as provided in subdivision (c), (d), or (f), the board shall cause an annual report to be sent to the members not later than 120 days after the close of the corporation's fiscal year. Unless otherwise provided by the articles or bylaws and if approved by the board of directors, that report and any accompanying material sent pursuant to this section may be sent by electronic transmission by the corporation (Section 20). That report shall contain in appropriate detail the following:

(1) The assets and liabilities, including the trust funds, of the corporation as of the end of the fiscal year.

(2) The principal changes in assets and liabilities, including trust funds, during the fiscal year.

(3) The revenue or receipts of the corporation, both unrestricted and restricted to particular purposes, for the fiscal year.

(4) The expenses or disbursements of the corporation, for both general and restricted purposes, during the fiscal year.

(5) Any information required by Section 6322.
(b) The report required by subdivision (a) shall be accompanied by any report thereon of independent accountants, or, if there is no such report, the certificate of an authorized officer of the corporation that such statements were prepared without audit from the books and records of the corporation. The report shall be prepared, audited, and made available in the manner required by paragraph (1) of subdivision (e) of Section 12586 of the Government Code, if applicable.
(c) Subdivision (a) does not apply to any corporation which receives less than twenty-five thousand dollars ($25,000) in gross revenues or receipts during the fiscal year.
(d) Where a corporation has provided, pursuant to Section 5510, for regular meetings of members less often than annually, then the report required by subdivision (a) need be made to members only with the frequency with which regular membership meetings are required, unless the articles or bylaws require a report more often.
(e) Subdivisions (c) and (d) notwithstanding, a report with the information required by subdivision (a) shall be furnished annually to all of the following:

(1) All directors of the corporation.

(2) Any member who requests it in writing.
(f) A corporation which in writing solicits contributions from 500 or more persons need not send the report otherwise required by subdivision (a) if it does all of the following:

(1) Includes with any written material used to solicit contributions a written statement that its latest annual report will be mailed upon request and that such request may be sent to the corporation at a name and address which is set forth in the statement. The term "annual report" as used in this subdivision refers to the report required by subdivision (a).

(2) Promptly mails a copy of its latest annual report to any person who requests a copy thereof.

(3) Causes its annual report to be published not later than 120 days after the close of its fiscal year in a newspaper of general circulation in the county in which its principal office is located.

Ca. Corp. Code § 6321
Amended by Stats 2011 ch 442 (AB 1211),s 10, eff. 1/1/2012.
Amended by Stats 2004 ch 254 (SB 1306),s 20, eff. 1/1/2005

Section 6322 - Statement of transaction or indemnification

(a) Any provision of the articles or bylaws notwithstanding, every corporation shall furnish annually to its members and directors a statement of any transaction or indemnification of a kind described in subdivision (d) or (e), if any such transaction or indemnification took place. If the corporation issues an annual report to all members, this subdivision shall be satisfied by including the required information in the annual report. A corporation which does not issue an annual report to all members, pursuant to subdivision (c) or (d) of Section 6321, shall satisfy this section by mailing or delivering to its members the required statement within 120 days after the close of the corporation's fiscal year. Unless otherwise provided by the articles or bylaws and if approved by the board of directors, that statement may be sent by electronic transmission by the corporation (Section 20).

(b) Except as provided in subdivision (c), a covered transaction under this section is a transaction in which the corporation, its parent, or its subsidiary was a party, and in which either of the following had a direct or indirect material financial interest:

(1) Any director or officer of the corporation, or its parent or subsidiary.

(2) Any holder of more than 10 percent of the voting power of the corporation, its parent or its subsidiary. For the purpose of subdivision (d), an "interested person" is any person described in paragraph (1) or (2) of this subdivision.

(c) For the purpose of subdivision (b), a mere common directorship is not a material financial interest.

(d) The statement required by subdivision (a) shall describe briefly:

(1) Any covered transaction during the previous fiscal year involving more than fifty thousand dollars ($50,000), or which was one of a number of covered transactions in which the same interested person had a direct or indirect material financial interest, and which transactions in the aggregate involved more than fifty thousand dollars ($50,000).

(2) The names of the interested persons involved in such transactions, stating such person's relationship to the corporation, the nature of such person's interest in the transaction and, where practicable, the amount of such interest; provided, that in the case of a transaction with a partnership of which such person is a partner, only the interest of the partnership need be stated.

(e) The statement required by subdivision (a) shall describe briefly the amount and circumstances of any indemnifications or advances aggregating more than ten thousand dollars ($10,000) paid during the fiscal year to any officer or director of the corporation pursuant to Section 5238; provided that no such report need be made in the case of indemnification approved by the members (Section 5034) under paragraph (2) of subdivision (e) of Section 5238.

  Ca. Corp. Code § 6322
Amended by Stats 2004 ch 254 (SB 1306),s 21, eff. 1/1/2005

Section 6323 - Enforcement of duty of making and mailing or delivering information and financial statements

(a) The superior court of the proper county shall enforce the duty of making and mailing or delivering the information and financial statements required by this article and, for good cause shown, may extend the time therefor.

(b) In any action or proceeding under this section, if the court finds the failure of the corporation to comply with the requirements of this article to have been without justification, the court may award the member reasonable expenses, including attorneys' fees, in connection with such action or proceeding.

  Ca. Corp. Code § 6323
Added by Stats. 1978, Ch. 567.

Section 6324 - Furnishing copy of report to attorney general in lieu of annual report

(a) Nothing in this part relieves a corporation from the requirements of Article 7 (commencing with Section 12580) of Chapter 6 of Part 2 of Division 3 of the Government Code including, without limitation, subdivision (a) of Section 12586. If a report sent to the Attorney General in compliance with the requirements of Article 7 (commencing with Section 12580) of Chapter 6 of Part 2 of Division 3 of the Government Code includes the information required in the annual report, then the corporation may furnish a copy of its report to the Attorney General in lieu of the annual report, whenever it is required to furnish an annual report.

(b) A corporation shall furnish any member who so requests a copy of any report filed by the corporation pursuant to Article 7 (commencing with Section 12580) of Chapter

6 of Part 2 of Division 3 of the Government Code. The corporation may impose reasonable charges for copying and mailing a report furnished under this subdivision.

Ca. Corp. Code § 6324

Amended by Stats 2011 ch 442 (AB 1211),s 11, eff. 1/1/2012.

Section 6325 - Report on vote

For a period of 60 days following the conclusion of an annual, regular, or special meeting of members, a corporation shall, upon written request from a member, forthwith inform the member of the result of any particular vote of members taken at the meeting, including the number of memberships voting for, the number of memberships voting against, and the number of memberships abstaining or withheld from voting. If the matter voted on was the election of directors, the corporation shall report the number of memberships, or votes if voted cumulatively, cast for each nominee for director. If more than one class or series of memberships voted, the report shall state the appropriate numbers by class and series of memberships.

Ca. Corp. Code § 6325

Added 9/21/1999 (Bill Number: AB 1687) (Chapter 453).

Article 3 - RIGHTS OF INSPECTION

Section 6330 - Right to inspect and copy record of members' names, addresses, and voting rights or obtain list of names, addresses, and voting rights of members entitled to vote for election of directors

(a) Subject to Sections 6331 and 6332, and unless the corporation provides a reasonable alternative pursuant to subdivision (c), a member may do either or both of the following as permitted by subdivision (b):

(1) Inspect and copy the record of all the members' names, addresses and voting rights, at reasonable times, upon five business days' prior written demand upon the corporation which demand shall state the purpose for which the inspection rights are requested; or

(2) Obtain from the secretary of the corporation, upon written demand and tender of a reasonable charge, an alphabetized list of the names, addresses, and voting rights of those members entitled to vote for the election of directors, as of the most recent record date for which it has been compiled or as of a date specified by the member subsequent to the date of demand. The demand shall state the purpose for which the list is requested. The membership list shall be made available on or before the later of 10 business days after the demand is received or after the date specified therein as the date as of which the list is to be compiled.

(b) The rights set forth in subdivision (a) may be exercised by:

(1) Any member, for a purpose reasonably related to the person's interest as a member. Where the corporation reasonably believes that the information will be used for another purpose, or where it provides a reasonable alternative pursuant to subdivision (c), it may deny the member access to the list. In any subsequent action brought by the member under Section 6336, the court shall enforce the rights set forth in subdivision (a) unless the corporation proves that the member will allow use of the information for purposes unrelated to the person's interest as a member or that the alternative method offered reasonably achieves the proper purpose set forth in the demand.

(2) The authorized number of members for a purpose reasonably related to the members' interest as members.

(c) The corporation may, within 10 business days after receiving a demand under subdivision (a), deliver to the person or persons making the demand a written offer of an alternative method of achieving the purpose identified in the demand without providing access to or a copy of the membership list. An alternative method which reasonably and in a timely manner accomplishes the proper purpose set forth in a demand made under subdivision (a) shall be deemed a reasonable alternative, unless within a reasonable time after acceptance of the offer the corporation fails to do those things which it offered to do. Any rejection of the offer shall be in writing and shall indicate the reasons the alternative proposed by the corporation does not meet the proper purpose of the demand made pursuant to subdivision (a).

Ca. Corp. Code § 6330

Amended by Stats. 1989, Ch. 451, Sec. 1.

Section 6331 - Petition for order setting aside demand

(a) Where the corporation, in good faith, and with a substantial basis, believes that the membership list, demanded under Section 6330 by the authorized number (Section 5036), will be used for a purpose not reasonably related to the interests as members of the person or persons making the demand (hereinafter called the requesting parties) as members or provides a reasonable alternative pursuant to subdivision (c) of Section 6330, it may petition the superior court of the proper county for an order setting aside the demand.

(b) Except as provided in subdivision (c), a petition for an order to show cause why a protective order pursuant to subdivision (d) should not issue shall be filed within 10 business days after the demand by the authorized number under Section 6330 or receipt of a written rejection by the authorized number of an offer made pursuant to subdivision (c) of Section 6330, whichever is later. The petition shall be accompanied by an application for a hearing on the petition. Upon the filing of the petition, the court shall issue a protective order staying production of the list demanded until the hearing on the order to show cause. The court shall set the hearing on the order to show cause not more than 20 days from the date of the filing of the petition. The order to show cause shall be granted unless the court finds that there is no reasonable probability that the corporation will make the showing required under subdivision (f).

(c) A corporation may file a petition under this section more than 10 business days after the demand or rejection under Section 6330, but only upon a showing the delay was caused by excusable neglect. In no event, however, may any petition under this section be considered if filed more than 30 days after the requesting parties' demand or rejection, whichever is later.

(d) Upon the return day of the order to show cause, the court may issue a protective order staying production of the list demanded until final adjudication of the petition filed pursuant to this section. No protective order shall issue under this subdivision unless the court finds that the rights of the requesting parties can reasonably be preserved and that the corporation is likely to make the showing required by subdivision (f) or the court is likely to issue a protective order pursuant to subdivision (g).

(e) If the corporation fails to file a petition within the time allowed by subdivision (b) or (c), whichever is applicable, or fails to obtain a protective order under subdivision (d), then the corporation shall comply with the demand, and no further action may be brought by the corporation under this section.

(f) The court shall issue the final order setting aside the demand only if the corporation proves:

    (1) That there is a reasonable probability that the requesting parties will permit use of the membership list for a purpose unrelated to their interests as members; or

    (2) That the method offered by the corporation is a reasonable alternative in that it reasonably achieves the proper purpose set forth in the requesting parties' demand and that the corporation intends and is able to effectuate the reasonable alternative.

(g) In the final order, the court may, in its discretion, order an alternative mechanism for achieving the proper purposes of the requesting parties, or impose just and proper conditions upon the use of the membership list which reasonably assures compliance with Sections 6330 and 6338.

(h) The court shall award reasonable costs and expenses, including reasonable attorneys' fees, to requesting parties who successfully oppose any petition or application filed pursuant to this section.

(i) Where the corporation has neither, within the time allowed, complied with a demand by the authorized number (Section 5036) under Section 6330, nor obtained a protective order staying production of the list, or a final order setting aside the demand, which is then in effect, the requesting parties may petition the superior court of the proper county for a writ of mandamus pursuant to Section 1085 of the Code of Civil Procedure compelling the corporation to comply with the demand. At the hearing, the court shall hear the parties summarily, by affidavit or otherwise, and shall issue a peremptory writ of mandamus unless it appears that the demand was not made by an authorized number (Section 5036), that the demand has been complied with, that the corporation, pursuant to subdivision (c) of Section 6330, made an offer which was not rejected in writing within a reasonable time, or that a protective or final order properly issued under subdivision (d), (f) or (g) is then in effect. No inquiry may be made in such proceeding into the use for which the authorized number seek the list. The court shall award reasonable costs and expenses, including reasonable attorneys' fees, to persons granted an order under this subdivision.

(j) Nothing in this section shall be construed to limit the right of the corporation to obtain damages for any misuse of a membership list obtained under Section 6330, or otherwise, or to obtain injunctive relief necessary to restrain misuse of a member list. A corporation shall be entitled to recover reasonable costs and expenses, including reasonable attorneys' fees, incurred in successfully bringing any such action.

Ca. Corp. Code § 6331

Amended by Stats. 1979, Ch. 724.

Section 6332 - Limitation or restriction of rights

(a) Upon petition of the corporation or any member, the superior court of the proper county may limit or restrict the rights set forth in Section 6330 where, and only where such limitation or restriction is necessary to protect the rights of any member under the Constitution of the United States or the Constitution of the State of California. An order issued pursuant to this subdivision shall provide, insofar as possible, for alternative mechanisms by which the persons seeking to exercise rights under Section 6330 may communicate with members for purposes reasonably related to their interests as members.

(b) Upon the filing of a petition under subdivision (a), the court may, if requested by the person making the petition, issue a temporary order suspending the running of any time limit specified in Section 6330 for compliance with that section. Such an order may be extended, after notice and hearing, until final adjudication of the petition, wherever it appears that the petitioner may prevail on the merits, and it is otherwise equitable to do so.

Ca. Corp. Code § 6332

Added by Stats. 1978, Ch. 567.

Section 6333 - Accounting books and records and minutes

The accounting books and records and minutes of proceedings of the members and the board and committees of the board shall be open to inspection upon the written demand on the corporation of any member at any reasonable time, for a purpose reasonably related to such person's interests as a member.

Ca. Corp. Code § 6333

Added by Stats. 1978, Ch. 567.

Section 6334 - Inspection by director

Every director shall have the absolute right at any reasonable time to inspect and copy all books, records and documents of every kind and to inspect the physical properties of the corporation of which such person is a director.

Ca. Corp. Code § 6334

Added by Stats. 1978, Ch. 567.

Section 6335 - Frustration of proper purpose of person making demand

Where the proper purpose of the person or persons making a demand pursuant to Section 6330 is frustrated by (1) any delay by the corporation in complying with a demand under Section 6330 beyond the time limits specified therein, or (2) any delay caused by the filing of a petition under Section 6331 or Section 6332, or (3) any delay caused by the alternative proposed under subdivision (c) of Section 6330, the person or persons properly making the demand shall have, in the discretion of the court, a right to obtain from the superior court an order postponing any members' meeting previously noticed for a period equal to the period of such delay. The members may obtain such an order in a proceeding brought pursuant to Section 6331 upon the filing of a verified complaint in the proper county and after a hearing, notice of which shall be given to such persons and in such manner as the court may direct. Such right shall be in addition to any other legal or equitable remedies to which the member may be entitled.

Ca. Corp. Code § 6335

Amended by Stats. 1979, Ch. 724.

Section 6336 - Enforcement of demand or right of inspection

(a) Upon refusal of a lawful demand for inspection under this chapter, or a lawful demand pursuant to Section 6330 or Section 6333, the superior court of the proper county, or the county where the books or records in question are kept, may enforce the demand or right of inspection with just and proper conditions or may, for good cause shown, appoint one or more competent inspectors or independent accountants to audit the financial statements kept in this state and investigate the property, funds and affairs of any corporation and of any subsidiary corporation thereof, domestic or foreign, keeping records in this state and to report thereon in such manner as the court may direct.

(b) All officers and agents of the corporation shall produce to the inspectors or accountants so appointed all books and documents in their custody or power, under penalty of punishment for contempt of court.

(c) All expenses of the investigation or audit shall be defrayed by the applicant unless the court orders them to be paid or shared by the corporation.

Ca. Corp. Code § 6336

Amended by Stats. 1979, Ch. 724.

Section 6337 - Award of reasonable costs and expenses

In any action or proceeding under this article, and except as required by Section 6331, if the court finds the failure of the corporation to comply with a proper demand thereunder was without justification, the court may award the member reasonable costs and expenses, including reasonable attorneys' fees, in connection with such action or proceeding.

Ca. Corp. Code § 6337
Added by Stats. 1978, Ch. 567.

Section 6338 - Membership list

(a) A membership list is a corporate asset. Without consent of the board a membership list or any part thereof may not be obtained or used by any person for any purpose not reasonably related to a member's interest as a member. Without limiting the generality of the foregoing, without the consent of the board a membership list or any part thereof may not be:

(1) Used to solicit money or property unless such money or property will be used solely to solicit the vote of the members in an election to be held by their corporation.

(2) Used for any purpose which the user does not reasonably and in good faith believe will benefit the corporation.

(3) Used for any commercial purpose or purpose in competition with the corporation.

(4) Sold to or purchased by any person.
(b) Any person who violates the provisions of subdivision (a) shall be liable for any damage such violation causes the corporation and shall account for and pay to the corporation any profit derived as a result of such violation. In addition, a court in its discretion may award exemplary damages for a fraudulent or malicious violation of subdivision (a).
(c) Nothing in this article shall be construed to limit the right of a corporation to obtain injunctive relief necessary to restrain misuse of a membership list or any part thereof.
(d) In any action or proceeding under this section, a court may award the corporation reasonable costs and expenses, including reasonable attorneys' fees, in connection with such action or proceeding.
(e) As used in this section, the term "membership list" means the record of the members' names and addresses.

Ca. Corp. Code § 6338
Amended by Stats. 1996, Ch. 589, Sec. 18. Effective January 1, 1997.

Chapter 14 - SERVICE OF PROCESS

Section 6410 - Law governing service of process

Service of process upon a corporation shall be governed by Chapter 17 (commencing with Section 1700) of Division 1 of Title 1.

Ca. Corp. Code § 6410

Added by Stats. 1978, Ch. 567.

Chapter 15 - INVOLUNTARY DISSOLUTION

Section 6510 - Complaint for involuntary dissolution; grounds

(a) A complaint for involuntary dissolution of a corporation on any one or more of the grounds specified in subdivision (b) may be filed in the superior court of the proper county by any of the following persons:

(1) One-half or more of the directors in office.

(2) A person or persons holding or authorized in writing by persons holding not less than $33^1/_3$ percent of the voting power exclusive of memberships held by persons who have personally participated in any of the transactions enumerated in paragraph (5) of subdivision (b).

(3) Any member if the ground for dissolution is that the period for which the corporation was formed has terminated without extension thereof.

(4) Any other person expressly authorized to do so in the articles.

(5) The Attorney General.

(6) The head organization under whose authority the corporation was created, where the corporation's articles include the provision authorized by subdivision (a), paragraph (2), clause (i), of Section 5132.

(b) The grounds for involuntary dissolution are that:

(1) The corporation has abandoned its activity for more than one year.

(2) The corporation has an even number of directors who are equally divided and cannot agree as to the management of its affairs, so that its activities can no longer be conducted to advantage or so that there is danger that its property will be impaired or lost or its activities impaired and the members are so divided into factions that they cannot elect a board consisting of an uneven number.

(3) There is internal dissension and two or more factions of members in the corporation are so deadlocked that its activities can no longer be conducted with advantage.

(4) When during any four-year period or when all voting power has been exercised at two consecutive meetings or in two written ballots for the election of directors, whichever period is shorter, the members have failed to elect successors to directors whose terms have expired or would have expired upon election of their successors.

(5) Those in control of the corporation have been guilty of or have knowingly countenanced persistent and pervasive fraud, mismanagement or abuse of authority or the corporation's property is being misapplied or wasted by its directors or officers.

(6) Liquidation is reasonably necessary as the corporation is failing and has continuously failed to carry out its purposes.

(7) The period for which the corporation was formed has terminated without extension of such period.

(8) The corporation is required to dissolve under the terms of any article provision adopted pursuant to subdivision (a), paragraph (2), clause (i), of Section 5132.
(c) At any time prior to the trial of the action any creditor or the authorized number (Section 5036) of members may intervene therein.
(d) In any action brought pursuant to subdivision (a), the Attorney General shall be an indispensable party.
Ca. Corp. Code § 6510
Amended by Stats. 1979, Ch. 724.

Section 6511 - Action by attorney general to procure judgment dissolving corporation; grounds

(a) The Attorney General may bring an action against any corporation or purported corporation in the name of the people of this state, upon the Attorney General's own information or upon complaint of a private party, to procure a judgment dissolving the corporation and annulling, vacating or forfeiting its corporate existence upon any of the following grounds:

(1) The corporation has seriously offended against any provision of the statutes regulating corporations or charitable organizations.

(2) The corporation has fraudulently abused or usurped corporate privileges or powers.

(3) The corporation has violated any provision of law by any act or default which under the law is a ground for forfeiture of corporate existence.

(4) The corporation has failed to pay to the Franchise Tax Board for a period of five years any tax imposed upon it by the Bank and Corporation Tax Law.

(b) If the ground of the action is a matter or act which the corporation has done or omitted to do that can be corrected by amendment of its articles or by other corporate action, such suit shall not be maintained unless (1) the Attorney General, at least 30 days prior to the institution of suit, has given the corporation written notice of the matter or act done or omitted to be done and (2) the corporation has failed to institute proceedings to correct it within the 30-day period or thereafter fails to duly and properly make such amendment or take the corrective corporate action.

(c) In any such action the court may order dissolution or such other or partial relief as it deems just and expedient. The court also may appoint a receiver for winding up the affairs of the corporation or may order that the corporation be wound up by its board subject to the supervision of the court.

(d) Service of process on the corporation may be made pursuant to Chapter 17 (commencing with Section 1700) of Division 1 or by written notice to the president or secretary of the corporation at the address indicated in the corporation's last tax return filed pursuant to the Bank and Corporation Tax Law. The Attorney General shall also publish one time in a newspaper of general circulation in the proper county a notice to the members of the corporation.

 Ca. Corp. Code § 6511
Added by Stats. 1978, Ch. 567.

Section 6512 - Appointment of provisional director

If the ground for the complaint for involuntary dissolution of the corporation is a deadlock in the board as set forth in paragraph (2) of subdivision (b) of Section 6510, the court may appoint a provisional director. The provisions of subdivision (e) of Section 5225 apply to any such provisional director so appointed.

 Ca. Corp. Code § 6512
Added by Stats. 1978, Ch. 567.

Section 6513 - Appointment of receiver

If, at the time of the filing of a complaint for involuntary dissolution or at any time thereafter, the court has reasonable grounds to believe that unless a receiver of the corporation is appointed the interests of the corporation or the public or charitable purpose of the corporation will suffer pending the hearing and determination of the complaint, upon the application of the plaintiff, and after a hearing upon such notice to the corporation as the court may direct and upon the giving of security pursuant to Sections 566 and 567 of the Code of Civil Procedure, the court may appoint a receiver to take over and manage the affairs of the corporation and to preserve its property pending the hearing and determination of the complaint for dissolution.

 Ca. Corp. Code § 6513
Amended by Stats. 1982, Ch. 517, Sec. 188.

Section 6514 - Orders and decrees

After hearing the court may decree a winding up and dissolution of the corporation if cause therefor is shown or, with or without winding up and dissolution, may make such orders and decrees and issue such injunctions in the case as justice and equity require.

Ca. Corp. Code § 6514
Added by Stats. 1978, Ch. 567.

Section 6515 - Commencement of involuntary proceedings for winding up

(a) Involuntary proceedings for winding up a corporation commence when the order for winding up is entered under Section 6514.

(b) When an involuntary proceeding for winding up has commenced, the board shall conduct the winding up of the affairs of the corporation, subject to the supervision of the court, unless other persons are appointed by the court, on good cause shown, to conduct the winding up. The directors or such other persons may, subject to any restrictions imposed by the court, exercise all their powers through the executive officers without any order of court.

(c) When an involuntary proceeding for winding up has commenced, the corporation shall cease to conduct its activities except to the extent necessary for the beneficial winding up thereof and except during such period as the board may deem necessary to preserve the corporation's goodwill or going concern value, pending a sale or other disposition of its assets, or both, in whole or in part. The directors shall cause written notice of the commencement of the proceeding for involuntary winding up to be given by mail to all members and to all known creditors and claimants whose addresses appear on the records of the corporation, unless the order for winding up has been stayed by appeal therefrom or otherwise or the proceeding or the execution of the order has been enjoined.

Ca. Corp. Code § 6515
Added by Stats. 1978, Ch. 567.

Section 6516 - Jurisdiction of court

When an involuntary proceeding for winding up has been commenced, the jurisdiction of the court includes:

(a) The requirement of the proof of all claims and demands against the corporation, whether due or not yet due, contingent, unliquidated or sounding only in damages, and the barring from participation of creditors and claimants failing to make and present claims and proof as required by any order.

(b) The determination or compromise of all claims of every nature against the corporation or any of its property, and the determination of the amount of money or assets required to be retained to pay or provide for the payment of claims.

(c) The presentation and filing of intermediate and final accounts of the directors or other persons appointed to conduct the winding up and hearing thereon, the allowance, disallowance or settlement thereof and the discharge of the directors or such other persons from their duties and liabilities.

(d) The appointment of a commissioner to hear and determine any or all matters, with such power or authority as the court may deem proper.

(e) The filling of any vacancies on the board which the directors or members are unable to fill.

(f) The removal of any director if it appears that the director has been guilty of dishonesty, misconduct, neglect or breach of trust in conducting the winding up or if the director is unable to act. The court may order an election to fill the vacancy so caused, and may enjoin, for such time as it considers proper, the reelection of the director so removed; or the court, in lieu of ordering an election, may appoint a director to fill the vacancy caused by such removal. Any director so appointed by the court shall serve until the next regular meeting of members or until a successor is elected or appointed.

(g) The staying of the prosecution of any suit, proceeding or action against the corporation and requiring the parties to present and prove their claims in the manner required of other creditors.

(h) The determination of whether adequate provision has been made for payment or satisfaction of all debts and liabilities not actually paid.

(i) The making of orders for the withdrawal or termination of proceedings, to windup and dissolve, subject to conditions for the protection of creditors.

(j) The making of an order, upon the allowance or settlement of the final accounts of the directors or such other persons, that the corporation has been duly wound up and is dissolved. Upon the making of such order, the corporate existence shall cease except for purposes of further winding up if needed.

(k) The making of orders for the bringing in of new parties as the court deems proper for the determination of all questions and matters.

(l) The disposition of assets held in charitable trust.

Ca. Corp. Code § 6516

Added by Stats. 1978, Ch. 567.

Section 6517 - Creditors and claimants

(a) All creditors and claimants may be barred from participation in any distribution of the general assets if they fail to make and present claims and proofs within such time as the court may direct, which shall not be less than four nor more than six months after the first publication of notice to creditors unless it appears by affidavit that there are no claims, in which case the time limit may be three months. If it is shown that a claimant did not receive notice because of absence from the state or other cause, the court may allow a claim to be filed or presented at any time before distribution is completed.

(b) Such notice to creditors shall be published not less than once a week for three consecutive weeks in a newspaper of general circulation published in the county in which the proceeding is pending or, if there is no such newspaper published in that county, in such newspaper as may be designated by the court, directing creditors and claimants to make and present claims and proofs to the person, at the place and within the time specified in the notice. A copy of the notice shall be mailed to each person shown as a creditor or claimant on the books of the corporation, at such person's last known address.

(c) Holders of secured claims may prove for the whole debt in order to realize any deficiency. If such creditors fail to present their claims they shall be barred only as to any right to claim against the general assets for any deficiency in the amount realized on their security.

(d) Before any distribution is made the amount of any unmatured, contingent or disputed claim against the corporation which has been presented and has not been disallowed, or such part of any such claim as the holder would be entitled to if the claim were due, established or absolute, shall be paid into court and there remain to be paid over to the party when the party becomes entitled thereto or, if the party fails to establish a claim, to be paid over or distributed with the other assets of the corporation to those entitled thereto; or such other provision for the full payment of such claim, if and when established, shall be made as the court may deem adequate. A creditor whose claim has been allowed but is not yet due shall be entitled to its present value upon distribution.

(e) Suits against the corporation on claims which have been rejected shall be commenced within 30 days after written notice of rejection thereof is given to the claimant.

Ca. Corp. Code § 6517
Added by Stats. 1978, Ch. 567.

Section 6518 - Order declaring corporation duly wound up and dissolved

(a) Upon the final settlement of the accounts of the directors or other persons appointed pursuant to Section 6515 and the determination that the corporation's affairs are in condition for it to be dissolved, the court may make an order declaring the corporation duly wound up and dissolved. The order shall declare:

(1) That the corporation has been duly wound up, that a final franchise tax return, as described by Section 23332 of the Revenue and Taxation Code, has been filed with the Franchise Tax Board, as required under Part 10.2 (commencing with Section 18401) of Division 2 of the Revenue and Taxation Code and that its known debts and liabilities have been paid or adequately provided for, or that those debts and liabilities have been paid as far as its assets permitted, as the case may be. If there are known debts or liabilities for payment of which adequate provision has been made, the order shall state what provision has been made, setting forth the name and address of the corporation, person or governmental agency that has assumed or guaranteed the payment, or the name and address of the depositary with which deposit has been made or such other information as may be necessary to enable the creditor or other person to whom payment is to be made to appear and claim payment of the debt or liability.

(2) That its known assets have been distributed to the persons entitled thereto or that it acquired no known assets, as the case may be.

(3) That the accounts of directors or such other persons have been settled and that they are discharged from their duties and liabilities to creditors and members.

(4) That the corporation is dissolved.

(b) In an action brought by, and at the request of, the Attorney General, the court may make an order declaring that a corporation is wound up and dissolved without meeting the requirements in subdivision (a), upon a finding by the court that it is impossible or impracticable to meet some or all of those requirements.

(c) The court may make such additional orders and grant such further relief as it deems proper upon the evidence submitted.

(d) Upon the making of the order declaring the corporation dissolved, corporate existence shall cease except for the purposes of further winding up if needed; and the directors or such other persons shall be discharged from their duties and liabilities, except as otherwise ordered by the court and in respect to completion of the winding up.

Ca. Corp. Code § 6518

Amended by Stats 2008 ch 715 (SB 1329),s 2, eff. 1/1/2009.
Amended by Stats 2006 ch 773 (AB 2341),s 19, eff. 9/29/2006.

Section 6519 - Filing of order, decree, or judgment; notification of Franchise Tax Board

Whenever a corporation is dissolved or its existence forfeited by order, decree or judgment of a court, a copy of the order, decree or judgment, certified by the clerk of court, shall forthwith be filed. The Secretary of State shall notify the Franchise Tax Board of the dissolution.

Ca. Corp. Code § 6519

Amended by Stats 2006 ch 773 (AB 2341),s 20, eff. 9/29/2006.

Chapter 16 - VOLUNTARY DISSOLUTION

Section 6610 - Voluntary election to wind up and dissolve

(a) Any corporation may elect voluntarily to wind up and dissolve (1) by approval of a majority of all members (Section 5033) or (2) by approval of the board and approval of the members (Section 5034).

(b) Any corporation which comes within one of the following descriptions may elect by approval of the board to wind up and dissolve:

(1) A corporation which has been the subject of an order for relief in bankruptcy.

(2) A corporation which has disposed of all of its assets and has not conducted any activity for a period of five years immediately preceding the adoption of the resolution electing to dissolve the corporation.

(3) A corporation which has no members.

(4) A corporation which is required to dissolve under provisions of its articles adopted pursuant to subparagraph (A) of paragraph (2) of subdivision (a), of Section 5132.
(c) If a corporation comes within one of the descriptions in subdivision (b) and the number of directors then in office is less than a quorum, the corporation may elect to voluntarily wind up and dissolve by any of the following:

(1) The unanimous consent of the directors then in office.

(2) The affirmative vote of a majority of the directors then in office at a meeting held pursuant to waiver of notice by those directors complying with subdivision (a) of Section 5211.

(3) The vote of a sole remaining director.
(d) If a corporation elects to voluntarily wind up and dissolve pursuant to subdivision (c), references to the board in this chapter and Chapter 17 (commencing with Section 6710) shall be deemed to be to a board consisting solely of those directors or that sole director and action by the board shall require at least the same consent or vote as would be required under subdivision (c) for an election to wind up and dissolve.
Ca. Corp. Code § 6610
Amended by Stats 2009 ch 631 (AB 1233),s 15, eff. 1/1/2010.
Amended by Stats 2009 ch 500 (AB 1059),s 20, eff. 1/1/2010.

Section 6610.5 - Verification of certificate of dissolution of nonprofit

(a) Notwithstanding any other provision of this division, when a corporation has not issued any memberships, a majority of the directors, or, if no directors have been named in the articles or have been elected, the incorporator or a majority of the incorporators, may sign and verify a certificate of dissolution stating all of the following:

(1) That the certificate of dissolution is being filed within 24 months from the date the articles of incorporation were filed.

(2) That the corporation does not have any debts or other liabilities, except as provided in paragraph (3) and subdivision (d).

(3) That the tax liability will be satisfied on a taxes-paid basis or that a person or corporation or other business entity assumes the tax liability, if any, of the dissolving corporation and is responsible for additional corporate taxes, if any, that are assessed and that become due after the date of the assumption of the tax liability.

(4) That a final franchise tax return, as described by Section 23332 of the Revenue and Taxation Code, has been or will be filed with the Franchise Tax Board as required under Part 10.2 (commencing with Section 18401) of Division 2 of the Revenue and Taxation Code.

(5) That the corporation was created in error.

(6) That the known assets of the corporation remaining after payment of, or adequately providing for, known debts and liabilities have been distributed as required by law or that the corporation acquired no known assets, as the case may be.

(7) That a majority of the directors, or, if no directors have been named in the articles or have been elected, the incorporator or a majority of the incorporators authorized the dissolution and elected to dissolve the corporation.

(8) That the corporation has not issued any memberships, and if the corporation has received payments for memberships, those payments have been returned to those making the payments.

(9) That the corporation is dissolved.
(b) A certificate of dissolution signed and verified pursuant to subdivision (a) shall be filed with the Secretary of State. The Secretary of State shall notify the Franchise Tax Board and the Attorney General's Registry of Charitable Trusts of the dissolution.
(c) Upon filing a certificate of dissolution pursuant to subdivision (b), a corporation shall be dissolved and its powers, rights, and privileges shall cease.
(d) Notwithstanding the dissolution of a corporation pursuant to this section, its liability to creditors, if any, is not discharged. The liability of the directors of, or other persons related to, the dissolved corporation is not discharged. The dissolution of a corporation pursuant to this section shall not diminish or adversely affect the ability of the Attorney General to enforce liabilities as otherwise provided by law.
Ca. Corp. Code § 6610.5
Added by Stats 2015 ch 363 (AB 557),s 3, eff. 1/1/2016.

Section 6611 - Certificate evidencing election

(a) Whenever a corporation has elected to wind up and dissolve a certificate evidencing that election shall forthwith be filed and a copy thereof filed with the Attorney General.

(b) The certificate shall be an officers' certificate or shall be signed and verified by at least a majority of the directors then in office or by one or more members authorized to do so by approval of a majority of all members (Section 5033) and shall set forth:

(1) That the corporation has elected to wind up and dissolve.

(2) If the election was made by the vote of members alone, the number of votes for the election and that the election was made by a majority of all members (Section 5033).

(3) If the election was made by the board and members pursuant to paragraph (2) of subdivision (a) of Section 6610, or subparagraph (B) of paragraph (1) of subdivision (b) of Section 9680, the certificate shall state that it was made by the board and the members in accordance with Section 5034.

(4) If the certificate is executed by a member or members, that the subscribing person or persons were authorized to execute the certificate by a majority of all members (Section 5033).

(5) If the election was made by the board pursuant to subdivision (b) of Section 6610, or paragraph (2) of subdivision (b) of Section 9680, the circumstances showing the corporation to be within one of the categories described in that subdivision.

(c) If an election to dissolve made pursuant to subdivision (a) of Section 6610 or paragraph (1) of subdivision (b) of Section 9680 is made by the vote of all the members of a corporation with members or by all members of the board of a corporation without members pursuant to subdivision (b) of Section 6610, or paragraph (2) of subdivision (b) of Section 9680 and a statement to that effect is added to the certificate of dissolution pursuant to Section 6615, the separate filing of the certificate of election pursuant to this section is not required.

Ca. Corp. Code § 6611

Amended by Stats 2014 ch 834 (SB 1041),s 13, eff. 1/1/2015.

Amended September 21, 1999 (Bill Number: AB 1687) (Chapter 453).

Section 6612 - Revocation of voluntary election to wind up and dissolve

(a) A voluntary election to wind up and dissolve may be revoked prior to distribution of any assets:

(1) if the election was made pursuant to paragraph (1) of subdivision (a) of Section 6610, by the vote of a majority of all members (Section 5033); or

(2) if the election was made pursuant to paragraph (2) of subdivision (a) of

Section 6610, by the approval of the board and the members (Section 5034); or

(3) if the election was by the board pursuant to subdivision (b) of Section 6610, by approval of the board. Thereupon a certificate evidencing the revocation shall be signed, verified and filed in the manner prescribed by Section 6611 and a copy thereof filed with the Attorney General.
(b) The certificate shall set forth:

(1) That the corporation has revoked its election to wind up and dissolve.

(2) That no assets have been distributed pursuant to the election.

(3) If the revocation was made by the vote of members alone, the number of votes for the revocation and that the revocation was made by a majority of all members (Section 5033).

(4) If the revocation was made by the board and members pursuant to paragraph (2) of subdivision (a) of Section 6612, the certificate shall so state.

(5) If the revocation was made by the board alone, the certificate shall so state.
Ca. Corp. Code § 6612
Amended by Stats. 1979, Ch. 724.

Section 6613 - Commencement of voluntary proceedings for winding up

(a) Voluntary proceedings for winding up the corporation commence upon the adoption of the resolution required by Section 6610 by the members, by the board and members, or by the board alone, electing to wind up and dissolve.
(b) When a voluntary proceeding for winding up has commenced, the board shall continue to act as a board and shall have full powers to wind up and settle its affairs, both before and after the filing of the certificate of dissolution.
(c) When a voluntary proceeding for winding up has commenced, the corporation shall cease to conduct its activities except to the extent necessary for the beneficial winding up thereof, to the extent necessary to carry out its purposes and except during such period as the board may deem necessary to preserve the corporation's goodwill or going-concern value pending a sale or other disposition of its assets, or both, in whole or in part. The board shall cause written notice of the commencement of the proceeding for voluntary winding up to be given by mail to all its members (except no notice need be given to the members who voted in favor of winding up and dissolving the corporation), to all known creditors and claimants whose addresses appear on the records of the corporation, and to the Attorney General.
Ca. Corp. Code § 6613
Added by Stats. 1978, Ch. 567.

Section 6614 - Assumption of jurisdiction by superior court

If a corporation is in the process of voluntary winding up, the superior court of the proper county, upon the petition of (a) the corporation, or (b) the authorized number (Section 5036), or (c) the Attorney General, or (d) three or more creditors, and upon such notice to the corporation and to other persons interested in the corporation as members and creditors as the court may order, may take jurisdiction over such voluntary winding up proceeding if that appears necessary for the protection of any parties in interest or if it appears necessary to protect the purpose or purposes served by the corporation. The court, if it assumes jurisdiction, may make such orders as to any and all matters concerning the winding up of the affairs of the corporation and the protection of its creditors, its assets and its purpose or purposes as justice and equity may require. The provisions of Chapter 15 (commencing with Section 6510) (except Sections 6510 and 6511) shall apply to such court proceedings.

Ca. Corp. Code § 6614
Added by Stats. 1978, Ch. 567.

Section 6615 - Certificate of dissolution

(a) When a corporation has been completely wound up without court proceedings, a majority of the directors then in office shall sign and verify a certificate of dissolution stating:

(1) That the corporation has been completely wound up.

(2) That its known debts and liabilities have been actually paid, or adequately provided for, or paid or adequately provided for as far as its assets permitted, or that it has incurred no known debts or liabilities, as the case may be. If there are known debts or liabilities for payment of which adequate provision has been made, the certificate shall state what provision has been made, setting forth the name and address of the corporation, person or governmental agency that has assumed or guaranteed the payment, or the name and address of the depositary with which deposit has been made or other information as may be necessary to enable the creditor or other person to whom payment is to be made to appear and claim payment of the debt or liability.

(3) That the corporation is dissolved.

(4) That all final returns required under the Revenue and Taxation Code have been or will be filed with the Franchise Tax Board.

(5) That the corporation, if applicable, is a committee, as defined in Section 82013 of the Government Code, that is required to and does file any statement pursuant to the provisions of Article 2 (commencing with Section 84200) of Chapter 4 of Title 9 of the Government Code and is exempt from the supervisory authority of the Attorney General pursuant to Sections 12581 and 12583 of the Government Code and is exempt from and not required to file the attachment specified in subdivision (b).

(b) Except as provided in subdivision (c), one of the following documents issued by the Attorney General shall be attached to the certificate of dissolution:

(1) A written waiver of objections to the distribution of the corporation's assets pursuant to subdivision (c) of Section 6716.

(2) A written confirmation that the corporation has no assets.

(c) The certificate of dissolution and attachment described in subdivision (b) shall be filed with the Secretary of State. The Secretary of State shall not accept a certificate of dissolution for filing without this attachment unless the attachment is not required as specified in paragraph (5) of subdivision (a). The corporate existence shall cease upon the acceptance of the filing of the certificate of dissolution and, if required, the attachment, by the Secretary of State, except for the purpose of further winding up if needed. The Secretary of State shall notify the Franchise Tax Board of the dissolution.

Ca. Corp. Code § 6615

Amended by Stats 2011 ch 442 (AB 1211),s 12, eff. 1/1/2012.
Amended by Stats 2006 ch 773 (AB 2341),s 21, eff. 9/29/2006.
Amended by Stats 2002 ch 112 (AB 2519),s 1, eff. 1/1/2003.

Section 6616 - Expiration of term of existence without renewal or extension

Except as otherwise provided by law, if the term of existence for which any corporation was organized expires without renewal or extension thereof, the board shall terminate its activities and wind up its affairs; and when the affairs of the corporation have been wound up a majority of the directors shall execute and file a certificate conforming to the requirements of Section 6615.

Ca. Corp. Code § 6616

Added by Stats. 1978, Ch. 567.

Section 6617 - Petition for order declaring corporation duly wound up and dissolved

(a) The board, in lieu of filing the certificate of dissolution, may petition the superior court of the proper county for an order declaring the corporation duly wound up and dissolved. Such petition shall be filed in the name of the corporation.

(b) Upon the filing of the petition, the court shall make an order requiring all persons, including the Attorney General, interested to show cause why an order shall not be made declaring the corporation duly wound up and dissolved and shall direct that the order be served by notice to all creditors, claimants and members in the same manner as the notice given under subdivision (b) of Section 6517. Notice shall be served upon the Attorney General.

(c) Any person claiming to be interested as creditor or otherwise may appear in the proceeding at any time before the expiration of 30 days from the completion of publication of the order to show cause and contest the petition, and upon failure to appear such person's claim shall be barred.

(d) Thereafter an order shall be entered and filed and have the effect as prescribed in Sections 6518 and 6519.

Ca. Corp. Code § 6617

Added by Stats. 1978, Ch. 567.

Section 6618 - Disposal of known claims

(a) A corporation in the process of voluntary winding up may dispose of the known claims against it by following the procedure described in this section.

(b) The written notice to known creditors and claimants required by subdivision (c) of Section 6613 shall comply with all of the following requirements:

(1) Describe any information that must be included in a claim.

(2) Provide a mailing address where a claim may be sent.

(3) State the deadline, which may not be fewer than 120 days from the effective date of the written notice, by which the corporation must receive the claim.

(4) State that the claim will be barred if not received by the deadline.

(c) A claim against the corporation is barred if any of the following occur:

(1) A claimant who has been given the written notice under subdivision (b) does not deliver the claim to the corporation by the deadline.

(2) A claimant whose claim was rejected by the corporation does not commence a proceeding to enforce the claim within 90 days from the effective date of the rejection notice.

(d) For purposes of this section "claim" does not include a contingent liability or a claim based on an event occurring after the effective date of dissolution.

Ca. Corp. Code § 6618

Added by Stats. 1996, Ch. 589, Sec. 19. Effective January 1, 1997.

Chapter 17 - GENERAL PROVISIONS RELATING TO DISSOLUTION

Section 6710 - Powers and duties of directors and officers

The powers and duties of the directors (or other persons appointed by the court pursuant to Section 6515) and officers after commencement of a dissolution proceeding include, but are not limited to, the following acts in the name and on behalf of the corporation:

(a) To elect officers and to employ agents and attorneys to liquidate or wind up its affairs.

(b) To continue the conduct of the affairs of the corporation insofar as necessary for the disposal or winding up thereof.

(c) To carry out contracts and collect, pay, compromise and settle debts and claims for or against the corporation.

(d) To defend suits brought against the corporation.

(e) To sue, in the name of the corporation, for all sums due or owing to the corporation or to recover any of its property.

(f) To collect any amounts remaining unpaid on memberships or to recover unlawful distributions.

(g) Subject to the provisions of Section 5142, to sell at public or private sale, exchange, convey or otherwise dispose of all or any part of the assets of the corporation for an amount deemed reasonable by the board without compliance with the provisions of Section 5911, and to execute bills of sale and deeds of conveyance in the name of the corporation.

(h) In general, to make contracts and to do any and all things in the name of the corporation which may be proper or convenient for the purposes of winding up, settling and liquidating the affairs of the corporation.

Ca. Corp. Code § 6710
Amended by Stats. 1979, Ch. 724.

Section 6711 - Vacancy on board

A vacancy on the board may be filled during a winding up proceeding in the manner provided in Section 5224.

Ca. Corp. Code § 6711
Added by Stats. 1978, Ch. 567.

Section 6712 - Petition to determine identity of directors or to appoint directors to wind up

When the identity of the directors or their right to hold office is in doubt, or if they are dead or unable to act, or they fail or refuse to act or their whereabouts cannot be ascertained, any interested person, including the Attorney General, may petition the superior court of the proper county to determine the identity of the directors or, if there are no directors, to appoint directors to wind up the affairs of the corporation, after hearing upon such notice to such persons as the court may direct.

Ca. Corp. Code § 6712
Added by Stats. 1978, Ch. 567.

Section 6713 - Distribution of remaining corporate assets

(a) After determining that all the known debts and liabilities of a corporation in the process of winding up have been paid or adequately provided for, the board shall distribute all the remaining corporate assets in the manner provided in Sections 6715 and 6716.

(b) If the winding up is by court proceeding or subject to court supervision, the distribution shall not be made until after the expiration of any period for the presentation of claims that has been prescribed by order of the court.

(c) Anything to the contrary notwithstanding, assets, if any, which are not subject to attachment, execution or sale for the corporation's debts and liabilities may be distributed pursuant to Sections 6715 and 6716 even though all debts and liabilities have not been paid or adequately provided for.

Ca. Corp. Code § 6713
Added by Stats. 1978, Ch. 567.

Section 6714 - Payment of debt or liability

The payment of a debt or liability, whether the whereabouts of the creditor is known or unknown, has been adequately provided for if the payment has been provided for by either of the following means:

(a) Payment thereof has been assumed or guaranteed in good faith by one or more financially responsible persons or by the United States government or any agency thereof, and the provision (including the financial responsibility of such persons) was determined in good faith and with reasonable care by the board to be adequate at the time of any distribution of the assets by the board pursuant to this chapter.

(b) The amount of the debt or liability has been deposited as provided in Section 6718. This section does not prescribe the exclusive means of making adequate provision for debts and liabilities.

Ca. Corp. Code § 6714
Amended by Stats. 1979, Ch. 724.

Section 6715 - Assets held upon valid condition requiring return, transfer, or conveyance

After complying with the provisions of Section 6713, assets held by a corporation upon a valid condition requiring return, transfer, or conveyance, which condition has occurred or will occur by reason of the dissolution, shall be returned, transferred, or conveyed in accordance with the condition.

Ca. Corp. Code § 6715
Added by Stats. 1978, Ch. 567.

Section 6716 - Disposal of assets

After complying with the provisions of Section 6713:

(a) Except as provided in Section 6715, all of a corporation's assets shall be disposed of on dissolution in conformity with its articles or bylaws subject to complying with the provisions of any trust under which such assets are held.

(b) Except as provided in subdivision (c), the disposition required in subdivision (a) shall be made by decree of the superior court of the proper county in proceedings to which the Attorney General is a party. The decree shall be made upon petition therefor by the Attorney General or, upon 30 days' notice to the Attorney General, by any person concerned in the dissolution.

(c) The disposition required in subdivision (a) may be made without the decree of the superior court, subject to the rights of persons concerned in the dissolution, if the Attorney General makes a written waiver of objections to the disposition.

(d) Subdivisions (b) and (c) shall not be applicable to any corporation as described in paragraph (5) of subdivision (a) of Section 6615.

Ca. Corp. Code § 6716
Amended by Stats 2011 ch 442 (AB 1211),s 13, eff. 1/1/2012.

Section 6717 - Manner of distribution

Subject to the provisions of any trust under which assets to be distributed are held, distribution may be made either in money or in property or securities and either in installments from time to time or as a whole, if this can be done fairly and ratably and in conformity with the provisions of the articles and bylaws and shall be made as soon as reasonably consistent with the beneficial liquidation of the corporation's assets.

Ca. Corp. Code § 6717
Added by Stats. 1978, Ch. 567.

Section 6718 - Deposit with Controller in trust

(a) If any creditors or other persons are unknown or fail or refuse to accept their payment or distribution in cash or property or their whereabouts cannot be ascertained after diligent inquiry, or the existence or amount of a claim of a creditor or other person is contingent, contested, or not determined, the corporation may deposit any such payment, distribution, or the maximum amount of the claim with the Controller in trust for the benefit of those lawfully entitled to the payment, distribution, or the amount of the claim. The payment or distribution shall be paid over by the depositary to the lawful owners, their representatives or assigns, upon satisfactory proof of title.

(b) For the purpose of providing for the transmittal, receipt, accounting for, claiming, management, and investment of all money or other property deposited with the Controller under subdivision (a), the money or other property shall be deemed to be paid or delivered for deposit with the Controller under Chapter 7 (commencing with Section 1500) of Title 10 of Part 3 of the Code of Civil Procedure, and may be recovered in the manner prescribed in that chapter.

Ca. Corp. Code § 6718

Amended by Stats. 1996, Ch. 860, Sec. 2. Effective January 1, 1997.

Section 6719 - Recovery of improper distribution

(a) Whenever in the process of winding up a corporation any distribution of assets has been made, otherwise than under an order of court, without prior payment or adequate provision for payment of any of the debts and liabilities of the corporation, any amount so improperly distributed to any person may be recovered by the corporation. Any of such persons may be joined as defendants in the same action or be brought in on the motion of any other defendant.

(b) Suit may be brought in the name of the corporation to enforce the liability under subdivision (a) against any or all persons receiving the distribution by the Attorney General or by any one or more creditors of the corporation, whether or not they have reduced their claims to judgment.

(c) As used in this section, "process of winding up" includes proceedings under Chapters 15 (commencing with Section 6510) and 16 (commencing with Section 6610) and also any other distribution of assets to persons made in contemplation of termination or abandonment of the corporate business.

Ca. Corp. Code § 6719

Added by Stats. 1978, Ch. 567.

Section 6720 - Continued existence of dissolved corporation

(a) A corporation which is dissolved nevertheless continues to exist for the purpose of winding up its affairs, prosecuting and defending actions by or against it and enabling it to collect and discharge obligations, dispose of and convey its property and collect and divide its assets, but not for the purpose of continuing its activities except so far as necessary for the winding up thereof.

(b) No action or proceeding to which a corporation is a party abates by the dissolution of the corporation or by reason of proceedings for winding up and dissolution thereof.

(c) Any assets inadvertently or otherwise omitted from the winding up continue in the dissolved corporation for the benefit of the persons entitled thereto upon dissolution of the corporation and on realization shall be distributed accordingly.

Ca. Corp. Code § 6720

Added by Stats. 1978, Ch. 567.

Section 6721 - Suing person to whom assets were distributed upon dissolution

(a) In all cases where a corporation has been dissolved, any person to whom assets were distributed upon dissolution may be sued in the corporate name upon any cause of action against the corporation arising prior to its dissolution. Notice of such action shall be given to the Attorney General who may intervene. This section is procedural in nature and is not intended to determine liability.

(b) Summons or other process against such a corporation may be served by delivering a copy thereof to an officer, director or person having charge of its assets or, if no such person can be found, to any agent upon whom process might be served at the time of dissolution. If none of such persons can be found with due diligence and it is so shown by affidavit to the satisfaction of the court, then the court may make an order that summons or other process be served upon the dissolved corporation by personally delivering a copy thereof, together with a copy of the order, to the Secretary of State or an assistant or deputy secretary of state. Service in this manner is deemed complete on the 10th day after the delivery of process to the Secretary of State. A copy of any summons or other process shall be served on the Attorney General.

(c) Every such corporation shall survive and continue to exist indefinitely for the purpose of being sued in any quiet title action. Any judgment rendered in any such action shall bind each and every person having an interest in such corporation, to the extent of their interest therein, and such action shall have the same force and effect as an action brought under the provisions of Sections 410.50 and 410.60 of the Code of Civil Procedure. Service of summons or other process in any such action may be made as provided in Chapter 4 (commencing with Section 413.10) of Title 5 of Part 2 of the Code of Civil Procedure or as provided in subdivision (b).

(d) Upon receipt of such process and the fee therefor, the Secretary of State forthwith shall give notice to the corporation as provided in Section 1702.

 Ca. Corp. Code § 6721

Amended by Stats. 1979, Ch. 724.

Chapter 18 - CRIMES AND PENALTIES

Section 6810 - Failure to file statement

(a) Upon the failure of a corporation to file the statement required by Section 6210, the Secretary of State shall provide a notice of that delinquency to the corporation. The notice shall also contain information concerning the application of this section, and advise the corporation of the penalty imposed by Section 19141 of the Revenue and Taxation Code for failure to timely file the required statement after notice of delinquency has been provided by the Secretary of State. If, within 60 days after providing the notice of delinquency, a statement pursuant to Section 6210 has not been filed by the corporation, the Secretary of State shall certify the name of the corporation to the Franchise Tax Board.

(b) Upon certification pursuant to subdivision (a), the Franchise Tax Board shall assess against the corporation a penalty of fifty dollars ($50) pursuant to Section 19141 of the Revenue and Taxation Code.

(c) The penalty herein provided shall not apply to a corporation that on or prior to the date of certification pursuant to subdivision (a) has dissolved, has converted to another type of business entity, or has been merged into another corporation or other business entity.

(d) The penalty herein provided shall not apply and the Secretary of State need not provide a notice of the delinquency to a corporation the corporate powers, rights, and privileges of which have been suspended by the Franchise Tax Board pursuant to Section 23301, 23301.5, or 23775 of the Revenue and Taxation Code on or prior to, and remain suspended on, the last day of the filing period pursuant to Section 6210. The Secretary of State need not provide notice of the filing requirement pursuant to Section 6210 to a corporation the corporate powers, rights, and privileges of which have been so suspended by the Franchise Tax Board on or prior to, and remain suspended on, the day the Secretary of State prepares the notice for sending.

(e) If, after certification pursuant to subdivision (a), the Secretary of State finds the required statement was filed before the expiration of the 60-day period after providing notice of the delinquency, the Secretary of State shall promptly decertify the name of the corporation to the Franchise Tax Board. The Franchise Tax Board shall then promptly abate any penalty assessed against the corporation pursuant to Section 19141 of the Revenue and Taxation Code.

(f) If the Secretary of State determines that the failure of a corporation to file a statement required by Section 6210 is excusable because of reasonable cause or unusual circumstances that justify the failure, the Secretary of State may waive the penalty imposed by this section and by Section 19141 of the Revenue and Taxation Code, in which case the Secretary of State shall not certify the name of the corporation to the Franchise Tax Board, or if already certified, the Secretary of State shall promptly decertify the name of the corporation.

Ca. Corp. Code § 6810
Amended by Stats 2014 ch 834 (SB 1041),s 14, eff. 1/1/2015.
Amended by Stats 2011 ch 204 (AB 657),s 8, eff. 1/1/2012.
Amended by Stats 2000 ch 415 (AB 2897), s 1, eff. 1/1/2001.
Amended by Stats 2001 ch 159 (SB 662), s 45, eff. 1/1/2002.

Section 6811 - Unlawful distribution

Any director of any corporation who concurs in any vote or act of the directors of the corporation or any of them, knowingly and with dishonest or fraudulent purpose, to make any distribution with the design of defrauding creditors, members, or the corporation, is guilty of a crime. Each such crime is punishable by imprisonment pursuant to subdivision (h) of Section 1170 of the Penal Code or by a fine of not more than one thousand dollars ($1,000) or imprisonment in a county jail for not more than one year, or both that fine and imprisonment.

Ca. Corp. Code § 6811
Amended by Stats 2011 ch 39 (AB 117),s 68, eff. 6/30/2011.
Amended by Stats 2011 ch 15 (AB 109),s 40, eff. 4/4/2011, but operative no earlier than October 1, 2011, and only upon creation of a community corrections grant

program to assist in implementing this act and upon an appropriation to fund the grant program.

Section 6812 - Unlawful acts related to reports and statements

(a) Every director or officer of any corporation is guilty of a crime if such director or officer knowingly concurs in making or publishing, either generally or privately, to members or other persons (1) any materially false report or statement as to the financial condition of the corporation, or (2) any willfully or fraudulently exaggerated report, account or statement of operations or financial condition, intended to induce and having a tendency to induce, contributions or donations to the corporation by members or other persons.

(b) Every director or officer of any corporation is guilty of a crime who refuses to make or direct to be made any book entry or the posting of any notice required by law in the manner required by law.

(c) A violation of subdivision (a) or (b) of this section shall be punishable by imprisonment in state prison or by a fine of not more than one thousand dollars ($1,000) or imprisonment in the county jail for not more than one year or both such fine and imprisonment.

   Ca. Corp. Code § 6812

Added by Stats. 1978, Ch. 567.

Section 6813 - Unlawful possession of corporate property; unlawful alteration or falsification or omission

(a) Every director, officer or agent of any corporation, who knowingly receives or acquires possession of any property of the corporation, otherwise than in payment of a just demand, and, with intent to defraud, omits to make, or to cause or direct to be made, a full and true entry thereof in the books or accounts of the corporation is guilty of a crime.

(b) Every director, officer, agent or member of any corporation who, with intent to defraud, destroys, alters, mutilates or falsifies any of the books, papers, writings or securities belonging to the corporation or makes or concurs in omitting to make any material entry in any book of accounts or other record or document kept by the corporation is guilty of a crime.

(c) Each crime specified in this section is punishable by imprisonment in state prison, or by imprisonment in a county jail for not exceeding one year, or a fine not exceeding one thousand dollars ($1,000), or by both such fine and imprisonment.

   Ca. Corp. Code § 6813

Added by Stats. 1978, Ch. 567.

Section 6814 - Unlawful exhibition of false, forged, or altered instrument of evidence to public officer or board

Every director, officer or agent of any corporation, or any person proposing to organize such a corporation, who knowingly exhibits any false, forged or altered book, paper, voucher, security or other instrument of evidence to any public officer or board authorized by law to examine the organization of such corporation or to investigate its affairs, with intent to deceive such officer or board in respect thereto, is punishable by imprisonment pursuant to subdivision (h) of Section 1170 of the Penal Code, or by imprisonment in a county jail for not more than one year.

Ca. Corp. Code § 6814
Amended by Stats 2011 ch 39 (AB 117),s 68, eff. 6/30/2011.
Amended by Stats 2011 ch 15 (AB 109),s 41, eff. 4/4/2011, but operative no earlier than October 1, 2011, and only upon creation of a community corrections grant program to assist in implementing this act and upon an appropriation to fund the grant program.

Section 6815 - No limitation of power of state to punish

Nothing in this chapter limits the power of the state to punish any person for any conduct which constitutes a crime under any other statute.

Ca. Corp. Code § 6815
Added by Stats. 1978, Ch. 567.

Chapter 19 - FOREIGN CORPORATIONS

Section 6910 - Foreign corporations transacting intrastate business

Foreign corporations transacting intrastate business shall comply with Chapter 21 (commencing with Section 2100) of Division 1, except as to matters specifically otherwise provided for in this part and except that Section 2115 shall not be applicable.

Ca. Corp. Code § 6910
Amended by Stats. 1997, Ch. 187, Sec. 8. Effective January 1, 1998.

Part 3 - NONPROFIT MUTUAL BENEFIT CORPORATIONS

Chapter 1 - ORGANIZATION AND BYLAWS

Article 1 - TITLE AND PURPOSES

Section 7110 - Short title

This part shall be known and may be cited as the Nonprofit Mutual Benefit Corporation Law.

Ca. Corp. Code § 7110
Added by Stats. 1978, Ch. 567.

Section 7111 - Formation of corporation under this part

Subject to any other provision of law of this state applying to the particular class of corporation or line of activity, a corporation may be formed under this part for any lawful purpose; provided that a corporation all of the assets of which are irrevocably dedicated to charitable, religious, or public purposes and which as a matter of law or according to its articles or bylaws must, upon dissolution, distribute its assets to a person or persons carrying on a charitable, religious, or public purpose or purposes may not be formed under this part.

Ca. Corp. Code § 7111

Amended by Stats. 1981, Ch. 587, Sec. 25.

Article 2 - FORMATION

Section 7120 - Formation

(a) One or more persons may form a corporation under this part by executing and filing articles of incorporation.

(b) If initial directors are named in the articles, each director named in the articles shall sign and acknowledge the articles; if initial directors are not named in the articles, the articles shall be signed by one or more persons who thereupon are the incorporators of the corporation.

(c) The corporate existence begins upon the filing of the articles and continues perpetually, unless otherwise expressly provided by law or in the articles.

Ca. Corp. Code § 7120

Amended by Stats. 1983, Ch. 1085, Sec. 3.

Section 7121 - Unincorporated association changing status to corporation

(a) In the case of an existing unincorporated association, the association may change its status to that of a corporation upon a proper authorization for such by the association in accordance with its rules and procedures.

(b) In addition to the matters required to be set forth in the articles pursuant to Section 7130, the articles in the case of an incorporation authorized by subdivision (a) shall set forth that an existing unincorporated association, stating its name, is being incorporated by the filing of the articles.

(c) The articles filed pursuant to this section shall be accompanied by a verified statement of any two officers or governing board members of the association stating that the incorporation of the association by means of the articles to which the verified statement is attached has been approved by the association in accordance with its rules and procedures.

(d) Upon the change of status of an unincorporated association to a corporation pursuant to subdivision (a), the property of the association becomes the property of the corporation and the members of the association who had any voting rights of the type referred to in Section 5056 become members of the corporation.

(e) The filing for record in the office of the county recorder of any county in this state in which any of the real property of the association is located, of a copy of the articles of incorporation filed pursuant to this section, certified by the Secretary of State, shall evidence record ownership in the corporation of all interests of the association in and to the real property located in that county.

(f) All rights of creditors and all liens upon the property of the association shall be preserved unimpaired. Any action or proceeding pending by or against the unincorporated association may be prosecuted to judgment, which shall bind the corporation, or the corporation may be proceeded against or substituted in its place.

(g) If a corporation is organized by a person who is or was an officer, director or member of an unincorporated association and such corporation is not organized pursuant to subdivision (a), the unincorporated association may continue to use its name and the corporation may not use a name which is the same as or similar to the name of the unincorporated association.

Ca. Corp. Code § 7121
Amended by Stats. 1981, Ch. 587, Sec. 26.

Section 7122 - Name

(a) The Secretary of State shall not file articles setting forth a name in which "bank," "trust," "trustee," or related words appear, unless the certificate of approval of the Commissioner of Financial Protection and Innovation is attached thereto.

(b) The Secretary of State shall not file articles pursuant to this part setting forth a name that may create the impression that the purpose of the corporation is public, charitable, or religious or that it is a charitable foundation.

(c) The name of a corporation shall not be a name that the Secretary of State determines is likely to mislead the public and shall be distinguishable in the records of the Secretary of State from all of the following:

(1) The name of any corporation.

(2) The name of any foreign corporation authorized to transact intrastate business in this state.

(3) Each name that is under reservation pursuant to this title.

(4) The name of a foreign corporation that has registered its name pursuant to Section 2101.

(5) An alternate name of a foreign corporation under subdivision (b) of Section 2106.

(6) A name that will become the record name of a domestic or foreign corporation upon a corporate instrument when there is a delayed effective or file date.

(d) The use by a corporation of a name in violation of this section may be enjoined notwithstanding the filing of its articles by the Secretary of State.

(e) Any applicant may, upon payment of the fee prescribed therefor in the Government Code, obtain from the Secretary of State a certificate of reservation of any name not prohibited by subdivision (c), and upon the issuance of the certificate the name stated therein shall be reserved for a period of 60 days. The Secretary of State shall not, however, issue certificates reserving the same name for two or more consecutive 60-day periods to the same applicant or for the use or benefit of the same person; nor shall consecutive reservations be made by or for the use or benefit of the same person of names so similar as to fall within the prohibitions of subdivision (c).

Ca. Corp. Code § 7122

Amended by Stats 2022 ch 617 (SB 1202),s 56, eff. 1/1/2023.
Amended by Stats 2022 ch 452 (SB 1498),s 54, eff. 1/1/2023.
Amended by Stats 2020 ch 361 (SB 522),s 6, eff. 1/1/2021.
Amended by Stats 2014 ch 401 (AB 2763),s 21, eff. 1/1/2015.
Amended by Stats 2011 ch 740 (SB 201),s 14, eff. 1/1/2012.

Section 7122.3 - Restriction on names under Financial Code

The Secretary of State shall not file articles for a corporation the name of which would fall within the prohibitions of Section 18104 of the Financial Code. This section shall not apply to articles filed for a corporation organized in accordance with Section 18100 of the Financial Code.

Ca. Corp. Code § 7122.3

Added 9/21/1999 (Bill Number: AB 1687) (Chapter 453).

Article 3 - ARTICLES OF INCORPORATION

Section 7130 - Articles of incorporation

The articles of incorporation of a corporation formed under this part shall set forth the following:

(a) The name of the corporation.

(b)

(1) Except as provided in paragraph (2) or (3), the following statement: "This corporation is a nonprofit mutual benefit corporation organized under the Nonprofit Mutual Benefit Corporation Law. The purpose of this corporation is to engage in any lawful act or activity, other than credit union business, for which a corporation may be organized under such law."

(2) In the case of a corporation formed under this part that is subject to the California Credit Union Law (Chapter 1 (commencing with Section 14000) of Division 5 of the Financial Code), the articles shall set forth a statement of purpose that is prescribed in the applicable provisions of the California Credit Union Law.

(3) In the case of a corporation formed under this part that is a public bank, as defined in Section 57600 of the Government Code, the articles shall set forth a statement of purpose that is prescribed in subdivision (a) of Section 57601 of the Government Code.

(4) The articles may include a further definition of the corporation's purposes.
(c) The name and street address in this state of the corporation's initial agent for service of process in accordance with subdivision (b) of Section 8210.
(d) The initial street address of the corporation.
(e) The initial mailing address of the corporation, if different from the initial street address.

Ca. Corp. Code § 7130
Amended by Stats 2019 ch 442 (AB 857),s 3, eff. 1/1/2020.
Amended by Stats 2012 ch 494 (SB 1532),s 18, eff. 1/1/2013.
Amended by Stats 2002 ch 734 (AB 2157),s 1, eff. 9/20/2002.

Section 7131 - Statement limiting purposes or powers of corporation

The articles of incorporation may set forth a further statement limiting the purposes or powers of the corporation.

Ca. Corp. Code § 7131
Added by Stats. 1978, Ch. 567.

Section 7132 - Provisions in articles of incorporation

(a) The articles of incorporation may set forth any or all of the following provisions, which shall not be effective unless expressly provided in the articles:

(1) A provision limiting the duration of the corporation's existence to a specified date.

(2) A provision conferring upon the holders of any evidences of indebtedness, issued or to be issued by a corporation the right to vote in the election of directors and on any other matters on which members may vote under this part even if the corporation does not have members.

(3) A provision conferring upon members the right to determine the consideration for which memberships shall be issued.

(4) In the case of a subordinate corporation instituted or created under the authority of a head organization, a provision setting forth either or both of the following:

(A) That the subordinate corporation shall dissolve whenever its charter is surrendered to, taken away by, or revoked by the head organization granting it.

(B) That in the event of its dissolution pursuant to an article provision allowed by subparagraph (A) or in the event of its dissolution for any reason, any assets of the corporation after compliance with the applicable provisions of Chapters 15 (commencing with Section 8510), 16 (commencing with Section 8610), and 17 (commencing with Section 8710) shall be distributed to the head organization.
(b) Nothing contained in subdivision (a) shall affect the enforceability, as between the parties thereto, of any lawful agreement not otherwise contrary to public policy.
(c) The articles of incorporation may set forth any or all of the following provisions:

(1) The names and addresses of the persons appointed to act as initial directors.

(2) Provisions concerning the transfer of memberships, in accordance with Section 7320.

(3) The classes of members, if any, and if there are two or more classes, the rights, privileges, preferences, restrictions and conditions attaching to each class.

(4) A provision which would allow any member to have more or less than one vote in any election or other matter presented to the members for a vote.

(5) A provision that requires an amendment to the articles, as provided in subdivision (a) of Section 7812, or to the bylaws, and any amendment or repeal of that amendment, to be approved in writing by a specified person or persons other than the board or the members. However, this approval requirement, unless the articles specify otherwise, shall not apply if any of the following circumstances exist:

(A) The specified person or persons have died or ceased to exist.

(B) If the right of the specified person or persons to approve is in the capacity of an officer, trustee, or other status and the office, trust, or status has ceased to exist.

(C) If the corporation has a specific proposal for amendment or repeal, and the corporation has provided written notice of that proposal, including a copy of the proposal, to the specified person or persons at the most recent address for each of them, based on the corporation's records, and the corporation has not received written approval or nonapproval within the period specified in the notice, which shall not be less than 10 nor more than 30 days commencing at least 20 days after the notice has been provided.

(6) Any other provision, not in conflict with law, for the management of the activities and for the conduct of the affairs of the corporation, including any provision which is required or permitted by this part to be stated in the bylaws.

Ca. Corp. Code § 7132

Amended by Stats 2009 ch 631 (AB 1233),s 16, eff. 1/1/2010.

Section 7133 - Certified copy of articles

For all purposes other than an action in the nature of quo warranto, a copy of the articles of a corporation duly certified by the Secretary of State is conclusive evidence of the formation of the corporation and prima facie evidence of its corporate existence.

Ca. Corp. Code § 7133

Added by Stats. 1978, Ch. 567.

Section 7134 - Perfection of organization of corporation by incorporators

If initial directors have not been named in the articles, the incorporator or incorporators, until the directors are elected, may do whatever is necessary and proper to perfect the organization of the corporation, including the adoption and amendment of bylaws of the corporation and the election of directors and officers.

Ca. Corp. Code § 7134

Added by Stats. 1978, Ch. 567.

Section 7135 - No limitation on equitable power of court

Nothing in Section 7130 or 7131 or in any provision of the articles of a mutual benefit corporation shall be construed to limit the equitable power of a court to impress a charitable trust upon any or all of the assets of a mutual benefit corporation or otherwise treat it as a public benefit corporation.

Ca. Corp. Code § 7135

Added by Stats. 1978, Ch. 567.

Article 4 - POWERS

Section 7140 - Powers

Subject to any limitations contained in the articles or bylaws and to compliance with other provisions of this division and any other applicable laws, a corporation, in carrying out its activities, shall have all of the powers of a natural person, including, without limitation, the power to:

(a) Adopt, use, and at will alter a corporate seal, but failure to affix a seal does not affect the validity of any instrument.

(b) Adopt, amend, and repeal bylaws.

(c) Qualify to conduct its activities in any other state, territory, dependency, or foreign country.

(d) Issue, purchase, redeem, receive, take or otherwise acquire, own, sell, lend, exchange, transfer or otherwise dispose of, pledge, use, and otherwise deal in and with its own memberships, bonds, debentures, notes, and debt securities.

(e) Pay pensions, and establish and carry out pension, deferred compensation, saving, thrift, and other retirement, incentive, and benefit plans, trusts, and provisions for any or all of its directors, officers, employees, and persons providing services to it or any of its subsidiary or related or associated corporations, and to indemnify and purchase and maintain insurance on behalf of any fiduciary of such plans, trusts, or provisions.

(f) Issue certificates evidencing membership in accordance with the provisions of Section 7313 and issue identity cards.

(g) Levy dues, assessments, and admission and transfer fees.

(h) Make donations for the public welfare or for community funds, hospital, charitable, educational, scientific, civic, religious, or similar purposes.

(i) Assume obligations, enter into contracts, including contracts of guarantee or suretyship, incur liabilities, borrow or lend money or otherwise use its credit, and secure any of its obligations, contracts, or liabilities by mortgage, pledge, or other encumbrance of all or any part of its property and income.

(j) Participate with others in any partnership, joint venture, or other association, transaction, or arrangement of any kind whether or not such participation involves sharing or delegation of control with or to others.

(k) Act as trustee under any trust incidental to the principal objects of the corporation, and receive, hold, administer, exchange, and expend funds and property subject to such trust.

(l) Carry on a business at a profit and apply any profit that results from the business activity to any activity in which it may lawfully engage.

(m)

(1) In anticipation of or during an emergency, take either or both of the following actions necessary to conduct the corporation's business operations and affairs, unless emergency bylaws provide otherwise pursuant to subdivision (g) of Section 7151:

(A) Modify lines of succession to accommodate the incapacity of any director, officer, employee, or agent resulting from the emergency.

(B) Relocate the principal office, designate alternative principal offices or regional offices, or authorize the officers to do so.

(2) During an emergency, take either or both of the following actions necessary to conduct the corporation's business operations and affairs, unless emergency bylaws provide otherwise pursuant to subdivision (g) of Section 7151:

(A) Give notice to a director or directors in any practicable manner under the circumstances, including, but not limited to, by publication and radio, when notice of a meeting of the board cannot be given to that director or directors in the manner prescribed by the bylaws or Section 7211.

(B) Deem that one or more officers of the corporation present at a board meeting is a director, in order of rank and within the same rank in order of seniority, as necessary to achieve a quorum for that meeting.

(3) In anticipation of or during an emergency, the board may take any action that it determines to be necessary or appropriate to respond to the emergency, mitigate the effects of the emergency, or comply with lawful federal and state government orders, but shall not take any action that requires the vote of the members, unless the required vote of the members was obtained prior to the emergency.

(4) Any actions taken in good faith in anticipation of or during an emergency under this subdivision bind the corporation and shall not be used to impose liability on a corporate director, officer, employee, or agent.

(5) For purposes of this subdivision, "emergency" means any of the following events or circumstances as a result of which, and only so long as, a quorum of the corporation's board of directors cannot be readily convened for action:

(A) A natural catastrophe, including, but not limited to, a hurricane, tornado, storm, high water, wind-driven water, tidal wave, tsunami, earthquake, volcanic eruption, landslide, mudslide, snowstorm, drought, epidemic, pandemic, or disease outbreak, or, regardless of cause, any fire, flood, or explosion.

(B) An attack on or within this state or on the public security of its residents by an enemy of this state or on the nation by an enemy of the United States of America, or upon receipt by this state of a warning from the federal government indicating that any such enemy attack is probable or imminent.

(C) An act of terrorism or other manmade disaster that results in extraordinary levels of casualties or damage or disruption severely affecting the infrastructure, environment, economy, government functions, or population, including, but not limited to, mass evacuations.

(D) A state of emergency proclaimed by the Governor of this state, including any person serving as Governor in accordance with Section 10 of Article V of the California Constitution and Section 12058 of the Government Code, or by the President of the United States of America.

Ca. Corp. Code § 7140
Amended by Stats 2021 ch 523 (AB 663),s 10, eff. 1/1/2022.
Amended by Stats 2013 ch 255 (AB 491),s 5, eff. 1/1/2014.

Section 7141 - Assertion of limitation upon activities, purposes, or powers; contract or conveyance

Subject to Section 7142:

(a) No limitation upon the activities, purposes, or powers of the corporation or upon the powers of the members, officers, or directors, or the manner of exercise of such powers, contained in or implied by the articles or by Chapters 15 (commencing with Section 8510), 16 (commencing with Section 8610), and 17 (commencing with Section 8710) shall be asserted as between the corporation or member, officer or director and any third person, except in a proceeding:

(1) by a member or the state to enjoin the doing or continuation of unauthorized activities by the corporation or its officers, or both, in cases where third parties have not acquired rights thereby,

(2) to dissolve the corporation, or

(3) by the corporation or by a member suing in a representative suit against the officers or directors of the corporation for violation of their authority.

(b) Any contract or conveyance made in the name of a corporation which is authorized or ratified by the board, or is done within the scope of authority, actual or apparent, conferred by the board or within the agency power of the officer executing it, except as the board's authority is limited by law other than this part, binds the corporation, and the corporation acquires rights thereunder whether the contract is executed or wholly or in part executory.

Ca. Corp. Code § 7141
Amended by Stats. 1979, Ch. 724.

Section 7142 - Action to enjoin, correct, obtain damages for or to otherwise remedy breach of charitable trust

(a) Notwithstanding Section 7141, in the case of a corporation holding assets in charitable trust, any of the following may bring an action to enjoin, correct, obtain damages for or to otherwise remedy a breach of the charitable trust:

(1) The corporation, or a member in the name of the corporation pursuant to Section 7710.

(2) An officer of the corporation.

(3) A director of the corporation.

(4) A person with a reversionary, contractual, or property interest in the assets subject to such charitable trust.

(5) The Attorney General, or any person granted relator status by the Attorney General. The Attorney General shall be given notice of any action brought by the persons specified in paragraphs (1) through (4), and may intervene.
(b) In an action under this section, the court may not rescind or enjoin the performance of a contract unless:

(1) All of the parties to the contract are parties to the action; or

(2) No party to the contract has, in good faith, and without actual notice of the trust restriction, parted with value, under the contract or in reliance upon it; and

(3) It is equitable to do so.
Ca. Corp. Code § 7142
Amended by Stats. 1979, Ch. 724.

Article 5 - BYLAWS

Section 7150 - Adoption, amendment, or repeal of bylaws

(a) Except as provided in subdivision (c) and Sections 7151, 7220, 7224, 7512, 7613, and 7615, bylaws may be adopted, amended or repealed by the board unless the action would:

(1) Materially and adversely affect the rights of members as to voting, dissolution, redemption, or transfer;

(2) Increase or decrease the number of members authorized in total or for any class;

(3) Effect an exchange, reclassification or cancellation of all or part of the memberships; or

(4) Authorize a new class of membership.
(b) Bylaws may be adopted, amended or repealed by approval of the members (Section 5034); provided, however, that such adoption, amendment or repeal also requires approval by the members of a class if such action would:

(1) Materially and adversely affect the rights, privileges, preferences, restrictions or conditions of that class as to voting, dissolution, redemption, or transfer in a manner different than such action affects another class;

(2) Materially and adversely affect such class as to voting, dissolution, redemption, or transfer by changing the rights, privileges, preferences, restrictions or conditions of another class;

(3) Increase or decrease the number of memberships authorized for such class;

(4) Increase the number of memberships authorized for another class;

(5) Effect an exchange, reclassification or cancellation of all or part of the memberships of such class; or

(6) Authorize a new class of memberships.
(c) The articles or bylaws may restrict or eliminate the power of the board to adopt, amend or repeal any or all bylaws, subject to subdivision (e) of Section 7151.
(d) Bylaws may also provide that the repeal or amendment of those bylaws, or the repeal or amendment of specified portions of those bylaws, may occur only with the approval in writing of a specified person or persons other than the board or members. However, this approval requirement, unless the bylaws specify otherwise, shall not apply if any of the following circumstances exist:

(1) The specified person or persons have died or ceased to exist.

(2) If the right of the specified person or persons to approve is in the capacity of an officer, trustee, or other status and the office, trust, or status has ceased to exist.

(3) If the corporation has a specific proposal for amendment or repeal, and the corporation has provided written notice of that proposal, including a copy of the proposal, to the specified person or persons at the most recent address for each of them, based on the corporation's records, and the corporation has not received written approval or nonapproval within the period specified in the notice, which shall not be less than 10 nor more than 30 days commencing at least 20 days after the notice has been provided.
Ca. Corp. Code § 7150
Amended by Stats 2009 ch 631 (AB 1233),s 17, eff. 1/1/2010.

Section 7151 - Number of directors; management of corporation; members; voting

(a) The bylaws shall set forth (unless such provision is contained in the articles, in which case it may only be changed by an amendment of the articles) the number of directors of the corporation, or the method of determining the number of directors of the corporation, or that the number of directors shall be not less than a stated minimum nor more than a stated maximum with the exact number of directors to be fixed, within the limits specified, by approval of the board or the members (Section 5034), in the manner provided in the bylaws, subject to subdivision (e). The number or minimum number of directors may be one or more.

(b) Once members have been admitted, a bylaw specifying or changing a fixed number of directors or the maximum or minimum number or changing from a fixed to a variable board or vice versa may only be adopted by approval of the members (Section 5034).

(c) The bylaws may contain any provision, not in conflict with law or the articles, for the management of the activities and for the conduct of the affairs of the corporation, including but not limited to:

(1) Any provision referred to in subdivision (c) of Section 7132.

(2) The time, place, and manner of calling, conducting, and giving notice of members', directors', and committee meetings, or of conducting mail ballots.

(3) The qualifications, duties, and compensation of directors; the time of their election; and the requirements of a quorum for directors' and committee meetings.

(4) The appointment of committees, composed of directors or nondirectors, or both, by the board or any officer and the authority of any such committees.

(5) The appointment, duties, compensation, and tenure of officers.

(6) The mode of determination of members of record.

(7) The making of reports and financial statements to members.

(8) Setting, imposing, and collecting dues, assessments, and admission and transfer fees.

(d) The bylaws may provide for the manner of admission, withdrawal, suspension, and expulsion of members, consistent with the requirements of Section 7341.

(e) The bylaws may require, for any or all corporate actions (except as provided in paragraphs (1) and (2) of subdivision (a) of Section 7222, subdivision (c) of Section 7615, and Section 8610) the vote of a larger proportion of, or all of, the members or the members of any class, unit, or grouping of members or the vote of a larger proportion of, or all of, the directors, than is otherwise required by this part. Such a provision in the bylaws requiring such greater vote shall not be altered, amended, or repealed except by such greater vote, unless otherwise provided in the bylaws.

(f) The bylaws may contain a provision limiting the number of members, in total or of any class, which the corporation is authorized to admit.

(g)

(1) The bylaws may contain any provision, not in conflict with the articles, to manage and conduct the business affairs of the corporation effective only in an emergency as defined in Section 7140, including, but not limited to, procedures for calling a board meeting, quorum requirements for a board meeting, and designation of additional or substitute directors.

(2) During an emergency, the board may take any action that it determines to be necessary or appropriate to respond to the emergency, mitigate the effects of the emergency, or comply with lawful federal and state government orders, but shall not take any action that requires the vote of the members, unless the required vote of the members was obtained prior to the emergency.

(3) All provisions of the regular bylaws consistent with the emergency bylaws shall remain effective during the emergency, and the emergency bylaws shall not be effective after the emergency ends.

(4) Corporate action taken in good faith in accordance with the emergency bylaws binds the corporation, and shall not be used to impose liability on a corporate director, officer, employee, or agent.

Ca. Corp. Code § 7151
Amended by Stats 2021 ch 523 (AB 663),s 11, eff. 1/1/2022.
Amended by Stats 2013 ch 255 (AB 491),s 6, eff. 1/1/2014.
Amended by Stats 2009 ch 631 (AB 1233),s 18, eff. 1/1/2010.

Section 7152 - Delegates

A corporation may provide in its bylaws for delegates having some or all of the authority of members. Where delegates are provided for, the bylaws shall set forth delegates' terms of office, any reasonable method for delegates' selection and removal, and any reasonable method for calling, noticing, and holding meetings of delegates, may set forth the manner in which delegates may act by written ballot similar to Section 7513 for written ballot of members, and may set forth the manner in which delegates may participate in meetings of delegates similar to paragraph (6) of subdivision (a) of Section 7211. Each delegate shall have one vote on each matter presented for action. A delegate shall not vote by proxy. Delegates may be given a name other than "delegates."

Ca. Corp. Code § 7152
Amended by Stats 2021 ch 523 (AB 663),s 12, eff. 1/1/2022.
Amended by Stats. 1983, Ch. 1085, Sec. 4.

Section 7153 - Voting by members or delegates

A corporation may provide in its bylaws for voting by its members or delegates on the basis of chapter or other organizational unit, or by region or other geographic grouping.

Ca. Corp. Code § 7153
Added by Stats. 1979, Ch. 724.

Article 6 - LOCATION AND INSPECTION OF ARTICLES AND BYLAWS

Section 7160 - Location and inspection of articles and bylaws

Every corporation shall keep at its principal office in this state the original or a copy of its articles and bylaws as amended to date, which shall be open to inspection by the members at all reasonable times during office hours. If the corporation has no office in this state, it shall upon the written request of any member furnish to such member a copy of the articles or bylaws as amended to date.

Ca. Corp. Code § 7160
Added by Stats. 1978, Ch. 567.

Chapter 2 - DIRECTORS AND MANAGEMENT

Article 1 - GENERAL PROVISIONS

Section 7210 - Board of directors

Each corporation shall have a board of directors. Subject to the provisions of this part and any limitations in the articles or bylaws relating to action required to be approved by the members (Section 5034), or by a majority of all members (Section 5033), the activities and affairs of a corporation shall be conducted and all corporate powers shall be exercised by or under the direction of the board. The board may delegate the management of the activities of the corporation to any person or persons, management company, or committee however composed, provided that the activities and affairs of the corporation shall be managed and all corporate powers shall be exercised under the ultimate direction of the board.

Ca. Corp. Code § 7210
Amended by Stats. 1996, Ch. 589, Sec. 23. Effective January 1, 1997.

Section 7211 - Meetings

(a) Unless otherwise provided in the articles or in the bylaws, all of the following apply:

(1) Meetings of the board may be called by the chair of the board or the president or any vice president or the secretary or any two directors.

(2) Regular meetings of the board may be held without notice if the time and place of the meetings are fixed by the bylaws or the board. Special meetings of the board shall be held upon four days' notice by first-class mail or 48 hours' notice delivered personally or by telephone, including a voice messaging system or by electronic transmission by the corporation (Section 20). The articles or bylaws may not dispense with notice of a special meeting. A notice, or waiver of notice, need not specify the purpose of any regular or special meeting of the board.

(3) Notice of a meeting need not be given to a director who provided a waiver of notice or consent to holding the meeting or an approval of the minutes thereof in writing, whether before or after the meeting, or who attends the meeting without protesting, prior thereto or at its commencement, the lack of notice to that director. These waivers, consents and approvals shall be filed with the corporate records or made a part of the minutes of the meetings.

(4) A majority of the directors present, whether or not a quorum is present, may adjourn any meeting to another time and place. If the meeting is adjourned for more than 24 hours, notice of an adjournment to another time or place shall be given prior to the time of the adjourned meeting to the directors who were not present at the time of the adjournment.

(5) Meetings of the board may be held at a place within or without the state that has been designated in the notice of the meeting or, if not stated in the notice or if there is no notice, designated in the bylaws or by resolution of the board.

(6) Directors may participate in a meeting through use of conference telephone, electronic video screen communication, or electronic transmission by and to the corporation (Sections 20 and 21). Participation in a meeting through use of conference telephone or electronic video screen communication pursuant to this subdivision constitutes presence in person at that meeting as long as all directors participating in the meeting are able to hear one another. Participation in a meeting through use of electronic transmission by and to the corporation, other than conference telephone and electronic video screen communication, pursuant to this subdivision constitutes presence in person at that meeting if both of the following apply:

(A) Each director participating in the meeting can communicate with all of the other directors concurrently.

(B) Each director is provided the means of participating in all matters before the board, including, without limitation, the capacity to propose, or to interpose an objection to, a specific action to be taken by the corporation.

(7) A majority of the number of directors authorized in or pursuant to the articles or bylaws constitutes a quorum of the board for the transaction of business. The articles or bylaws may require the presence of one or more specified directors in order to constitute a quorum of the board to transact business, as long as the death or

nonexistence of a specified director or the death or nonexistence of the person or persons otherwise authorized to appoint or designate that director does not prevent the corporation from transacting business in the normal course of events. The articles or bylaws may not provide that a quorum shall be less than one-fifth the number of directors authorized in or pursuant to the articles or bylaws, or less than two, whichever is larger, unless the number of directors authorized in or pursuant to the articles or bylaws is one, in which case one director constitutes a quorum.

(8) Subject to the provisions of Sections 7212, 7233, 7234, and subdivision (e) of Section 7237 and Section 5233, insofar as it is made applicable pursuant to Section 7238, an act or decision done or made by a majority of the directors present at a meeting duly held at which a quorum is present is the act of the board. The articles or bylaws may not provide that a lesser vote than a majority of the directors present at a meeting is the act of the board. A meeting at which a quorum is initially present may continue to transact business notwithstanding the withdrawal of directors, if any action taken is approved by at least a majority of the required quorum for that meeting, or a greater number required by this division, the articles or the bylaws.
(b) An action required or permitted to be taken by the board may be taken without a meeting if all directors individually or collectively consent in writing to that action and if, subject to subdivision (a) of Section 7224, the number of directors then in office constitutes a quorum. The written consent or consents shall be filed with the minutes of the proceedings of the board. The action by written consent shall have the same force and effect as a unanimous vote of the directors. For purposes of this subdivision only, "all directors" does not include an "interested director" as defined in subdivision (a) of Section 5233, insofar as it is made applicable pursuant to Section 7238 or described in subdivision (a) of Section 7233, or a "common director" as described in subdivision (b) of Section 7233 who abstains in writing from providing consent, where (1) the facts described in paragraph (2) or (3) of subdivision (d) of Section 5233 are established or the provisions of paragraph (1) or (2) of subdivision (a) of Section 7233 or in paragraph (1) or (2) of subdivision (b) of Section 7233 are satisfied, as appropriate, at or prior to execution of the written consent or consents; (2) the establishment of those facts or satisfaction of those provisions, as applicable, is included in the written consent or consents executed by the noninterested directors or noncommon directors or in other records of the corporation; and (3) the noninterested directors or noncommon directors, as applicable, approve the action by a vote that is sufficient without counting the votes of the interested directors or common directors.
(c) Each director shall have one vote on each matter presented to the board of directors for action. A director shall not vote by proxy.
(d) This section applies also to incorporators, to committees of the board, and to action by those incorporators or committees mutatis mutandis.
    Ca. Corp. Code § 7211
Amended by Stats 2020 ch 370 (SB 1371),s 38, eff. 1/1/2021.
Amended by Stats 2011 ch 442 (AB 1211),s 14, eff. 1/1/2012.

Amended by Stats 2009 ch 631 (AB 1233),s 19, eff. 1/1/2010.

Amended by Stats 2005 ch 102 (SB 119),s 4, eff. 1/1/2006

Amended by Stats 2004 ch 254 (SB 1306),s 22, eff. 1/1/2005

Amended by Stats 2003 ch 168 (SB 735),s 5, eff. 1/1/2004.

Amended by Stats 2002 ch 1008 (AB 3028),s 11, eff. 1/1/2003.

Repealed by Stats 2002 ch 1008 (AB 3028),s 11, eff. 1/1/2004.

Section 7212 - Committees

(a) The board may, by resolution adopted by a majority of the number of directors then in office, provided that a quorum is present, create one or more committees, each consisting of two or more directors, to serve at the pleasure of the board. Appointments to such committees shall be by a majority vote of the directors then in office, unless the articles or bylaws require a majority vote of the number of directors authorized in or pursuant to the articles or bylaws. The bylaws may authorize one or more such committees, each consisting of two or more directors, and may provide that a specified officer or officers who are also directors of the corporation shall be a member or members of such committee or committees. The board may appoint one or more directors as alternate members of such committee, who may replace any absent member at any meeting of the committee. Such committee, to the extent provided in the resolution of the board or in the bylaws, shall have all the authority of the board, except with respect to:

(1) The approval of any action for which this part also requires approval of the members (Section 5034) or approval of a majority of all members (Section 5033), regardless of whether the corporation has members.

(2) The filling of vacancies on the board or in any committee which has the authority of the board.

(3) The fixing of compensation of the directors for serving on the board or on any committee.

(4) The amendment or repeal of bylaws or the adoption of new bylaws.

(5) The amendment or repeal of any resolution of the board which by its express terms is not so amendable or repealable.

(6) The appointment of committees of the board or the members thereof.

(7) The expenditure of corporate funds to support a nominee for director after there are more people nominated for director than can be elected.

(8) With respect to any assets held in charitable trust, the approval of any self-dealing transaction except as provided in paragraph (3) of subdivision (d) of Section 5233.

(b) A committee exercising the authority of the board shall not include as members persons who are not directors. However, the board may create other committees that do not exercise the authority of the board and these other committees may include persons regardless of whether they are directors.

(c) Unless the bylaws otherwise provide, the board may delegate to any committee, appointed pursuant to paragraph (4) of subdivision (c) of Section 7151 or otherwise, powers as authorized by Section 7210, but may not delegate the powers set forth in paragraphs (1) to (8), inclusive, of subdivision (a).

   Ca. Corp. Code § 7212

Amended by Stats 2011 ch 442 (AB 1211),s 15, eff. 1/1/2012.

Amended by Stats 2009 ch 631 (AB 1233),s 20, eff. 1/1/2010.

Section 7213 - Officers

(a) A corporation shall have (1) a chair of the board, who may be given the title chair, chairperson, chair of the board, or chairperson of the board, or a president or both, (2) a secretary, (3) a treasurer or a chief financial officer or both, and (4) any other officers with any titles and duties as shall be stated in the bylaws or determined by the board and as may be necessary to enable it to sign instruments. The president, or if there is no president the chair of the board, is the general manager and chief executive officer of the corporation, unless otherwise provided in the articles or bylaws. Unless otherwise specified in the articles or the bylaws, if there is no chief financial officer, the treasurer is the chief financial officer of the corporation. Any number of offices may be held by the same person unless the articles or bylaws provide otherwise. Where a corporation holds assets in charitable trust, any compensation of the president or chief executive officer and the chief financial officer or treasurer shall be determined in accordance with subdivision (g) of Section 12586 of the Government Code, if applicable.

(b) Except as otherwise provided by the articles or bylaws, officers shall be chosen by the board and serve at the pleasure of the board, subject to the rights, if any, of an officer under any contract of employment. Any officer may resign at any time upon written notice to the corporation without prejudice to the rights, if any, of the corporation under any contract to which the officer is a party.

   Ca. Corp. Code § 7213

Amended by Stats 2022 ch 617 (SB 1202),s 57, eff. 1/1/2023.

Amended by Stats 2015 ch 98 (SB 351),s 12, eff. 1/1/2016.

Amended by Stats 2011 ch 442 (AB 1211),s 16, eff. 1/1/2012.

Amended by Stats 2009 ch 631 (AB 1233),s 21, eff. 1/1/2010.

Section 7214 - Authority of signing officers

Subject to the provisions of subdivision (a) of Section 7141 and Section 7142, any note, mortgage, evidence of indebtedness, contract, conveyance or other instrument in writing, and any assignment or endorsement thereof, executed or entered into between any corporation and any other person, when signed by any one of the chairperson of the board, the president or any vice president and by any one of the secretary, any assistant secretary, the chief financial officer, or any assistant treasurer of such corporation, is not invalidated as to the corporation by any lack of authority of the signing officers in the absence of actual knowledge on the part of the other person that the signing officers had no authority to execute the same.

Ca. Corp. Code § 7214
Amended by Stats 2022 ch 617 (SB 1202),s 58, eff. 1/1/2023.
Amended by Stats. 1996, Ch. 589, Sec. 24. Effective January 1, 1997.

Section 7215 - Prima facie evidence

The original or a copy in writing or in any other form capable of being converted into clearly legible tangible form of the bylaws or of the minutes of any incorporators', members', directors', committee or other meeting or of any resolution adopted by the board or a committee thereof, or members, certified to be a true copy by a person purporting to be the secretary or an assistant secretary of the corporation, is prima facie evidence of the adoption of such bylaws or resolution or of the due holding of such meeting and of the matters stated therein.

Ca. Corp. Code § 7215
Amended by Stats 2004 ch 254 (SB 1306),s 23, eff. 1/1/2005

Article 2 - SELECTION, REMOVAL AND RESIGNATION OF DIRECTORS

Section 7220 - Terms of directors

(a) Except as provided in subdivision (d), (e), or (f), directors shall be elected for terms of not longer than four years, as fixed in the articles or bylaws. However, the terms of directors of a corporation without members may be up to six years. In the absence of any provision in the articles or bylaws, the term shall be one year. The articles or bylaws may provide for staggering the terms of directors by dividing the total number of directors into groups of one or more directors. The terms of office of the several groups and the number of directors in each group need not be uniform. No amendment of the articles or bylaws may extend the term of a director beyond that for which the director was elected, nor may any bylaw provision increasing the terms of directors be adopted without approval of the members (Section 5034).
(b) Except as otherwise provided in the articles or bylaws, each director, including a director elected to fill a vacancy, shall hold office until the expiration of the term for which elected and until a successor has been elected and qualified, unless the director has been removed from office.
(c) The articles or bylaws may provide for the election of one or more directors by the members of any class voting as a class.

(d) For the purposes of this subdivision, "designator" means one or more designators. Notwithstanding subdivisions (a) to (c), inclusive, all or any portion of the directors authorized in the articles or bylaws of a corporation may hold office by virtue of designation or selection by a specified designator as provided by the articles or bylaws rather than by election. Those directors shall continue in office for the term prescribed by the governing article or bylaw provision, or, if there is no term prescribed, until the governing article or bylaw provision is duly amended or repealed, except as provided in subdivision (e) of Section 7222. A bylaw provision authorized by this subdivision may be adopted, amended, or repealed only by approval of the members (Section 5034), except as provided in subdivision (d) of Section 7150. Unless otherwise provided in the articles or bylaws, the entitlement to designate or select a director or directors shall cease if any of the following circumstances exist:

(1) The specified designator of that director or directors has died or ceased to exist.

(2) If the entitlement of the specified designator of that director or directors to designate is in the capacity of an officer, trustee, or other status and the office, trust, or status has ceased to exist.

(e) If a corporation has not issued memberships and (1) all the directors resign, die, or become incompetent, or (2) a corporation's initial directors have not been named in the articles and all incorporators resign, die, or become incompetent before the election of the initial directors, the superior court of any county may appoint directors of the corporation upon application by any party in interest.

(f) If authorized in the articles or bylaws of a corporation, all or any portion of the directors may hold office ex officio by virtue of occupying a specified position within the corporation or outside the corporation. The term of office of an ex officio director shall coincide with that director's respective term of office in the specified position entitling him or her to serve on the board of directors. Upon an ex officio director's resignation or removal from that position, or resignation or removal from the board for any reason, the term of office as a director of the corporation shall immediately cease. At that time, the successor in office shall become an ex officio director of the corporation, occupying the place of the former director.

Ca. Corp. Code § 7220

Amended by Stats 2018 ch 322 (AB 2557),s 3, eff. 1/1/2019.
Amended by Stats 2009 ch 631 (AB 1233),s 22, eff. 1/1/2010.
Amended by Stats 2000 ch 485 (AB 1895), s 12, eff. 1/1/2001.

Section 7221 - Declaration of vacancy; qualifications of directors

(a) The board may declare vacant the office of a director who has been declared of unsound mind by a final order of court, or convicted of a felony, or, in the case of a corporation holding assets in charitable trust, has been found by a final order or judgment of any court to have breached any duty arising as a result of Section 7238, or, if at the time a director is elected, the bylaws provide that a director may be removed for missing a specified number of board meetings, fails to attend the specified number of meetings.

(b) As provided in paragraph (3) of subdivision (c) of Section 7151, the articles or bylaws may prescribe the qualifications of the directors. The board, by a majority vote of the directors who meet all of the required qualifications to be a director, may declare vacant the office of any director who fails or ceases to meet any required qualification that was in effect at the beginning of that director's current term of office.

Ca. Corp. Code § 7221

Amended by Stats. 1996, Ch. 589, Sec. 26. Effective January 1, 1997.

Section 7222 - Removal

(a) Subject to subdivisions (b) and (f), any or all directors may be removed without cause if:

(1) In a corporation with fewer than 50 members, the removal is approved by a majority of all members (Section 5033).

(2) In a corporation with 50 or more members, the removal is approved by the members (Section 5034).

(3) In a corporation with no members, the removal is approved by a majority of the directors then in office.

(b) Except for a corporation having no members, pursuant to Section 7310:

(1) In a corporation in which the articles or bylaws authorize members to cumulate their votes pursuant to subdivision (a) of Section 7615, no director may be removed (unless the entire board is removed) when the votes cast against removal, or not consenting in writing to the removal, would be sufficient to elect the director if voted cumulatively at an election at which the same total number of votes were cast (or, if the action is taken by written ballot, all memberships entitled to vote were voted) and the entire number of directors authorized at the time of the director's most recent election were then being elected.

(2) When by the provisions of the articles or bylaws the members of any class, voting as a class, are entitled to elect one or more directors, any director so elected may be removed only by the applicable vote of the members of that class.

(3) When by the provisions of the articles or bylaws the members within a chapter or other organizational unit, or region or other geographic grouping, voting as such, are entitled to elect one or more directors, any director so elected may be removed only by the applicable vote of the members within the organizational unit or geographic grouping.

(c) Any reduction of the authorized number of directors or any amendment reducing the number of classes of directors does not remove any director prior to the expiration of the director's term of office unless the reduction or amendment also provides for the removal of one or more specified directors.

(d) Except as provided in this section and Sections 7221 and 7223, a director may not be removed prior to the expiration of the director's term of office.

(e) Where a director removed under this section or Section 7221 or 7223 was chosen by designation pursuant to subdivision (d) of Section 7220, then:

(1) Where a different person may be designated pursuant to the governing article or bylaw provision, the new designation shall be made.

(2) Where the governing article or bylaw provision contains no provision under which a different person may be designated, the governing article or bylaw provision shall be deemed repealed.

(f) For the purposes of this subdivision, "designator" means one or more designators. If by the provisions of the articles or bylaws a designator is entitled to designate one or more directors, then:

(1) Unless otherwise provided in the articles or bylaws at the time of designation, any director so designated may be removed without cause by the designator of that director.

(2) Any director so designated may only be removed under subdivision (a) with the written consent of the designator of that director.

(3) Unless otherwise provided in the articles or bylaws, the right to remove shall not apply if any of the following circumstances exist:

(A) The designator entitled to that right has died or ceased to exist.

(B) If that right is in the capacity of an officer, trustee, or other status, and the office, trust, or status has ceased to exist.

Ca. Corp. Code § 7222

Amended by Stats 2009 ch 631 (AB 1233),s 23, eff. 1/1/2010.
Amended September 21, 1999 (Bill Number: AB 1687) (Chapter 453).

Section 7223 - Action to remove director

(a) The superior court of the proper county may, at the suit of one of the parties specified in subdivision (b), remove from office any director in case of fraudulent or dishonest acts or gross abuse of authority or discretion with reference to the corporation or breach of any duty arising as a result of Section 7238 and may bar from reelection any director so removed for a period prescribed by the court. The corporation shall be made a party to such action.

(b) An action under subdivision (a) may be instituted by any of the following:

(1) A director.

(2) In the case of a corporation where the total number of votes entitled to be cast for a director is less than 5,000, twice the authorized number (Section 5036) of members, or 20 members, whichever is less.

(3) In the case of a corporation where the total number of votes entitled to be cast for a director is 5,000 or more, twice the authorized number (Section 5036) of members, or 100 members, whichever is less.

(c) In the case of a corporation holding assets in charitable trust, the Attorney General may bring an action under subdivision (a), may intervene in such an action brought by any other party and shall be given notice of any such action brought by any other party.

Ca. Corp. Code § 7223
Amended by Stats. 1981, Ch. 587, Sec. 29.

Section 7224 - Filling vacancies

(a) Unless otherwise provided in the articles or bylaws and except for a vacancy created by the removal of a director, vacancies on the board may be filled by approval of the board (Section 5032) or, if the number of directors then in office is less than a quorum, by (1) the unanimous written consent of the directors then in office, (2) the affirmative vote of a majority of the directors then in office at a meeting held pursuant to notice or waivers of notice complying with Section 7211, or (3) a sole remaining director. Unless the articles or a bylaw approved by the members (Section 5034) provide that the board may fill vacancies occurring in the board by reason of the removal of directors, or unless the corporation has no members pursuant to Section 7310, such vacancies may be filled only by approval of the members (Section 5034).

(b) The members may elect a director at any time to fill any vacancy not filled by the directors.

(c) Any director may resign effective upon giving written notice to the chairperson of the board, the president, the secretary, or the board of directors of the corporation, unless the notice specifies a later time for the effectiveness of such resignation. If the resignation is effective at a future time, a successor may be elected to take office when the resignation becomes effective.

Ca. Corp. Code § 7224
Amended by Stats 2022 ch 617 (SB 1202),s 59, eff. 1/1/2023.
Amended by Stats. 1985, Ch. 329, Sec. 3.

Section 7225 - Provisional director

(a) If a corporation has an even number of directors who are equally divided and cannot agree as to the management of its affairs, so that its activities can no longer be conducted to advantage or so that there is danger that its property, activities, or business will be impaired or lost, the superior court of the proper county may, notwithstanding any provisions of the articles or bylaws and whether or not an action is pending for an involuntary winding up or dissolution of the corporation, appoint a provisional director pursuant to this section. Action for such appointment may be brought by any director or by members holding not less than $33^1/_3$ percent of the voting power.

(b) If the members of a corporation are deadlocked so that they cannot elect the directors to be elected at the time prescribed therefor, the superior court of the proper county may, notwithstanding any provisions of the articles or bylaws, upon petition of members holding 50 percent of the voting power, appoint a provisional director or directors pursuant to this section or order such other equitable relief as the court deems appropriate.

(c) In the case of a corporation holding assets in charitable trust:

   (1) Any person bringing an action under subdivision (a) or (b) shall give notice to the Attorney General, who may intervene; and

   (2) The Attorney General may bring an action under subdivision (a) or (b).

(d) A provisional director shall be an impartial person, who is neither a member nor a creditor of the corporation, nor related by consanguinity or affinity within the third degree according to the common law to any of the other directors of the corporation or to any judge of the court by which such provisional director is appointed. A provisional director shall have all the rights and powers of a director until the deadlock in the board or among members is broken or until such provisional director is removed by order of the court or by approval of a majority of all members (Section 5033). Such person shall be entitled to such compensation as shall be fixed by the court unless otherwise agreed with the corporation.

   Ca. Corp. Code § 7225

Amended by Stats. 1995, Ch. 154, Sec. 16. Effective January 1, 1996.

Article 3 - STANDARDS OF CONDUCT

Section 7230 - Duties and liabilities applicable without regard to compensation

(a) Any duties and liabilities set forth in this article shall apply without regard to whether a director is compensated by the corporation.

(b) Part 4 (commencing with Section 16000) of Division 9 of the Probate Code does not apply to the directors of any corporation.

   Ca. Corp. Code § 7230

Amended by Stats. 1987, Ch. 923, Sec. 1.3. Operative January 1, 1988, by Sec. 103 of Ch. 923.

Section 7231 - Good faith; best interests of corporation; care of ordinarily prudent person

(a) A director shall perform the duties of a director, including duties as a member of any committee of the board upon which the director may serve, in good faith, in a manner such director believes to be in the best interests of the corporation and with such care, including reasonable inquiry, as an ordinarily prudent person in a like position would use under similar circumstances.

(b) In performing the duties of a director, a director shall be entitled to rely on information, opinions, reports or statements, including financial statements and other financial data, in each case prepared or presented by:

(1) One or more officers or employees of the corporation whom the director believes to be reliable and competent in the matters presented;

(2) Counsel, independent accountants or other persons as to matters which the director believes to be within such person's professional or expert competence; or

(3) A committee upon which the director does not serve that is composed exclusively of any or any combination of directors, persons described in paragraph (1), or persons described in paragraph (2), as to matters within the committee's designated authority, which committee the director believes to merit confidence, so long as, in any case, the director acts in good faith, after reasonable inquiry when the need therefor is indicated by the circumstances and without knowledge that would cause such reliance to be unwarranted.

(c) A person who performs the duties of a director in accordance with subdivisions (a) and (b) shall have no liability based upon any alleged failure to discharge the person's obligations as a director, including, without limiting the generality of the foregoing, any actions or omissions which exceed or defeat a public or charitable purpose to which assets held by a corporation are dedicated.

Ca. Corp. Code § 7231

Amended by Stats 2009 ch 631 (AB 1233),s 24, eff. 1/1/2010.

Section 7231.5 - Volunteer director or volunteer executive office of nonprofit corporation

(a) Except as provided in Section 7233 or 7236, there is no monetary liability on the part of, and no cause of action for damages shall arise against, any volunteer director or volunteer executive officer of a nonprofit corporation subject to this part based upon any alleged failure to discharge the person's duties as a director or officer if the duties are performed in a manner that meets all of the following criteria:

(1) The duties are performed in good faith.

(2) The duties are performed in a manner such director or officer believes to be in the best interests of the corporation.

(3) The duties are performed with such care, including reasonable inquiry, as an ordinarily prudent person in a like position would use under similar circumstances.
(b) "Volunteer" means the rendering of services without compensation. "Compensation" means remuneration whether by way of salary, fee, or other consideration for services rendered. However, the payment of per diem, mileage, or other reimbursement expenses to a director or executive officer does not affect that person's status as a volunteer within the meaning of this section.
(c) "Executive officer" means the president, vice president, secretary, or treasurer of a corporation or other individual serving in like capacity who assists in establishing the policy of the corporation.
(d) This section shall apply only to trade, professional, and labor organizations incorporated pursuant to this part which operate exclusively for fraternal, educational, and other nonprofit purposes, and under the provisions of Section 501(c)(c) of the United States Internal Revenue Code.
(e) This section shall not be construed to limit the provisions of Section 7231.
  Ca. Corp. Code § 7231.5
Amended by Stats. 1990, Ch. 107, Sec. 5.

Section 7232 - Acts or omissions in connection with election, selection, or nomination of directors

(a) Section 7231 governs the duties of directors as to any acts or omissions in connection with the election, selection, or nomination of directors.
(b) This section shall not be construed to limit the generality of Section 7231.
  Ca. Corp. Code § 7232
Added by Stats. 1978, Ch. 567.

Section 7233 - Effect of interested or common directors on contract or transaction

(a) No contract or other transaction between a corporation and one or more of its directors, or between a corporation and any domestic or foreign corporation, firm or association in which one or more of its directors has a material financial interest, is either void or voidable because such director or directors or such other corporation, business corporation, firm or association are parties or because such director or directors are present at the meeting of the board or a committee thereof which authorizes, approves or ratifies the contract or transaction, if:

(1) The material facts as to the transaction and as to such director's interest are fully disclosed or known to the members and such contract or transaction is approved by the members (Section 5034) in good faith, with any membership owned by any interested director not being entitled to vote thereon;

(2) The material facts as to the transaction and as to such director's interest are fully disclosed or known to the board or committee, and the board or committee authorizes, approves or ratifies the contract or transaction in good faith by a vote sufficient without counting the vote of the interested director or directors and the contract or transaction is just and reasonable as to the corporation at the time it is authorized, approved or ratified; or

(3) As to contracts or transactions not approved as provided in paragraph (1) or (2) of this subdivision, the person asserting the validity of the contract or transaction sustains the burden of proving that the contract or transaction was just and reasonable as to the corporation at the time it was authorized, approved or ratified. A mere common directorship does not constitute a material financial interest within the meaning of this subdivision. A director is not interested within the meaning of this subdivision in a resolution fixing the compensation of another director as a director, officer or employee of the corporation, notwithstanding the fact that the first director is also receiving compensation from the corporation.

(b) No contract or other transaction between a corporation and any corporation, business corporation or association of which one or more of its directors are directors is either void or voidable because such director or directors are present at the meeting of the board or a committee thereof which authorizes, approves or ratifies the contract or transaction, if:

(1) The material facts as to the transaction and as to such director's other directorship are fully disclosed or known to the board or committee, and the board or committee authorizes, approves or ratifies the contract or transaction in good faith by a vote sufficient without counting the vote of the common director or directors or the contract or transaction is approved by the members (Section 5034) in good faith; or

(2) As to contracts or transactions not approved as provided in paragraph (1) of this subdivision, the contract or transaction is just and reasonable as to the corporation at the time it is authorized, approved or ratified. This subdivision does not apply to contracts or transactions covered by subdivision (a).

Ca. Corp. Code § 7233
Amended by Stats. 1979, Ch. 724.

Section 7234 - Counting of interested or common directors in determining quorum

Interested or common directors may be counted in determining the presence of a quorum at a meeting of the board or a committee thereof which authorizes, approves or ratifies a contract or transaction as provided in Section 7233.

Ca. Corp. Code § 7234
Added by Stats. 1978, Ch. 567.

Section 7235 - Loan to, or guarantee of obligation of, director or officer

(a) Unless prohibited by the articles or bylaws, a corporation may loan money or property to, or guarantee the obligation of, any director or officer of the corporation or of its parent, affiliate or subsidiary, provided:

(1) The board determines the loan or guaranty may reasonably be expected to benefit the corporation.

(2) Prior to consummating the transaction or any part thereof, the loan or guaranty is either:

(A) Approved by the members (Section 5034), without counting the vote of the director or officer, if a member, or

(B) Approved by the vote of a majority of the directors then in office, without counting the vote of the director who is to receive the loan or the benefit of the guaranty.

(b) Notwithstanding subdivision (a), a corporation may advance money to a director or officer of the corporation or of its parent, affiliate or subsidiary, for any expenses reasonably anticipated to be incurred in the performance of the duties of the director or officer of the corporation or of its parent, affiliate or subsidiary, provided that in the absence of such an advance the director or officer would be entitled to be reimbursed for these expenses by the corporation, its parent, affiliate, or subsidiary.

(c) The provisions of subdivisions (a) and (b) do not apply to credit unions, or to the payment of premiums in whole or in part by a corporation on a life insurance policy on the life of a director or officer so long as repayment to the corporation of the amount paid by it is secured by the proceeds of the policy and its cash surrender value, or to loans permitted under any statute regulating any special class of corporations.

Ca. Corp. Code § 7235
Amended by Stats. 1983, Ch. 1085, Sec. 5.

Section 7236 - Joint and several liability of directors who approve certain corporate actions

(a) Subject to the provisions of Section 7231, directors of a corporation who approve any of the following corporate actions shall be jointly and severally liable to the corporation for the benefit of all of the creditors entitled to institute an action under paragraph (1) or (2) of subdivision (c) or to the corporation in an action by the head organization or members under paragraph (1) or (3) of subdivision (c):

(1) The making of any distribution contrary to Chapter 4 (commencing with Section 7410).

(2) The distribution of assets after institution of dissolution proceedings of the corporation, without paying or adequately providing for all known liabilities of the corporation, excluding any claims not filed by creditors within the time limit set by the court in a notice given to creditors under Chapter 15 (commencing with Section 8510), Chapter 16 (commencing with Section 8610), and Chapter 17 (commencing with Section 8710).

(3) The making of any loan or guaranty contrary to Section 7235.
(b) A director who is present at a meeting of the board, or any committee thereof, at which an action specified in subdivision (a) is taken and who abstains from voting shall be considered to have approved the action.
(c) Suit may be brought in the name of the corporation to enforce the liability:

(1) Under paragraph (1) of subdivision (a), against any or all directors liable by the persons entitled to sue under subdivision (c) of Section 7420.

(2) Under paragraph (2) or (3) of subdivision (a), against any or all directors liable by any one or more creditors of the corporation whose debts or claims arose prior to the time of the corporate action who have not consented to the corporate action, whether or not they have reduced their claims to judgment.

(3) Under paragraph (3) of subdivision (a), against any or all directors liable by any one or more members at the time of any corporate action specified in paragraph (3) of subdivision (a) who have not consented to the corporate action, without regard to the provisions of Section 7710.
(d) The damages recoverable from a director under this section shall be the amount of the illegal distribution, or if the illegal distribution consists of property, the fair market value of that property at the time of the illegal distribution, plus interest thereon from the date of the distribution at the legal rate on judgments until paid, together with all reasonably incurred costs of appraisal or other valuation, if any, of that property, or the loss suffered by the corporation as a result of the illegal loan or guaranty, but not exceeding, in the case of an action for the benefit of creditors, the liabilities of the corporation owed to nonconsenting creditors at the time of the violation.
(e) Any director sued under this section may implead all other directors liable and may compel contribution, either in that action or in an independent action against directors not joined in that action.
(f) Directors liable under this section shall also be entitled to be subrogated to the

rights of the corporation:

(1) With respect to paragraph (1) of subdivision (a), against the persons who received the distribution.

(2) With respect to paragraph (2) of subdivision (a), against the persons who received the distribution.

(3) With respect to paragraph (3) of subdivision (a), against the person who received the loan or guaranty. Any director sued under this section may file a cross-complaint against the person or persons who are liable to the director as a result of the subrogation provided for in this subdivision or may proceed against them in an independent action.

Ca. Corp. Code § 7236
Amended by Stats 2000 ch 135 (AB 2539), s 23, eff. 1/1/2001.
Amended September 21, 1999 (Bill Number: AB 1687) (Chapter 453).

Section 7237 - Indemnification

(a) For purposes of this section, "agent" means a person who is or was a director, officer, employee, or other agent of the corporation, or is or was serving at the request of the corporation as a director, officer, employee, or agent of another foreign or domestic corporation, partnership, joint venture, trust or other enterprise, or was a director, officer, employee, or agent of a foreign or domestic corporation that was a predecessor corporation of the corporation or of another enterprise at the request of the predecessor corporation; "proceeding" means any threatened, pending, or completed action or proceeding, whether civil, criminal, administrative, or investigative; and "expenses" includes, without limitation, attorneys' fees and any expenses of establishing a right to indemnification under subdivision (d) or paragraph (3) of subdivision (e).

(b) A corporation shall have power to indemnify a person who was or is a party or is threatened to be made a party to any proceeding (other than an action by or in the right of the corporation to procure a judgment in its favor, an action brought under Section 5233 of Part 2 (commencing with Section 5110) made applicable pursuant to Section 7238, or an action brought by the Attorney General or a person granted relator status by the Attorney General for any breach of duty relating to assets held in charitable trust) by reason of the fact that the person is or was an agent of the corporation, against expenses, judgments, fines, settlements, and other amounts actually and reasonably incurred in connection with the proceeding if the person acted in good faith and in a manner the person reasonably believed to be in the best interests of the corporation and, in the case of a criminal proceeding, had no reasonable cause to believe the conduct of the person was unlawful. The termination of any proceeding by judgment, order, settlement, conviction, or upon a plea of nolo contendere or its equivalent shall not, of itself, create a presumption that the person did not act in good faith and in a manner which the person reasonably believed to be in the best interests of the corporation or that the person had reasonable cause to believe that the person's conduct was unlawful.

(c) A corporation shall have power to indemnify a person who was or is a party or is threatened to be made a party to any threatened, pending, or completed action by or in the right of the corporation, or brought under Section 5233 of Part 2 (commencing with Section 5110) made applicable pursuant to Section 7238, or brought by the Attorney General or a person granted relator status by the Attorney General for breach of duty relating to assets held in charitable trust, to procure a judgment in its favor by reason of the fact that the person is or was an agent of the corporation, against expenses actually and reasonably incurred by the person in connection with the defense or settlement of the action if the person acted in good faith, in a manner the person believed to be in the best interests of the corporation and with such care, including reasonable inquiry, as an ordinarily prudent person in a like position would use under similar circumstances. No indemnification shall be made under this subdivision:

(1) With respect to any claim, issue, or matter as to which the person shall have been adjudged to be liable to the corporation in the performance of the person's duty to the corporation, unless and only to the extent that the court in which the proceeding is or was pending shall determine upon application that, in view of all the circumstances of the case, the person is fairly and reasonably entitled to indemnity for the expenses which the court shall determine;

(2) Of amounts paid in settling or otherwise disposing of a threatened or pending action, with or without court approval; or

(3) Of expenses incurred in defending a threatened or pending action that is settled or otherwise disposed of without court approval unless the action concerns assets held in charitable trust and is settled with the approval of the Attorney General.

(d) To the extent that an agent of a corporation has been successful on the merits in defense of any proceeding referred to in subdivision (b) or (c) or in defense of any claim, issue, or matter therein, the agent shall be indemnified against expenses actually and reasonably incurred by the agent in connection therewith.

(e) Except as provided in subdivision (d), any indemnification under this section shall be made by the corporation only if authorized in the specific case, upon a determination that indemnification of the agent is proper in the circumstances because the agent has met the applicable standard of conduct set forth in subdivision (b) or (c), by:

(1) A majority vote of a quorum consisting of directors who are not parties to the proceeding;

(2) Approval of the members (Section 5034), with the persons to be indemnified

not being entitled to vote thereon; or

(3) The court in which the proceeding is or was pending upon application made by the corporation or the agent or the attorney, or other person rendering services in connection with the defense, whether or not the application by the agent, attorney or other person is opposed by the corporation.

(f) Expenses incurred in defending any proceeding may be advanced by the corporation before the final disposition of the proceeding upon receipt of an undertaking by or on behalf of the agent to repay the amount unless it shall be determined ultimately that the agent is entitled to be indemnified as authorized in this section. The provisions of subdivision (a) of Section 7235 do not apply to advances made pursuant to this subdivision.

(g) A provision made by a corporation to indemnify its or its subsidiary's directors or officers for the defense of any proceeding, whether contained in the articles, bylaws, a resolution of members or directors, an agreement, or otherwise, shall not be valid unless consistent with this section. Nothing contained in this section shall affect any right to indemnification to which persons other than the directors and officers may be entitled by contract or otherwise.

(h) No indemnification or advance shall be made under this section, except as provided in subdivision (d) or paragraph (3) of subdivision (e), in any circumstance where it appears:

(1) That it would be inconsistent with a provision of the articles, bylaws, a resolution of the members, or an agreement in effect at the time of the accrual of the alleged cause of action asserted in the proceeding in which the expenses were incurred or other amounts were paid, which prohibits or otherwise limits indemnification; or

(2) That it would be inconsistent with any condition expressly imposed by a court in approving a settlement.

(i) A corporation shall have power to purchase and maintain insurance on behalf of an agent of the corporation against any liability asserted against or incurred by the agent in that capacity or arising out of the agent's status as such whether or not the corporation would have the power to indemnify the agent against that liability under the provisions of this section.

(j) This section does not apply to any proceeding against a trustee, investment manager, or other fiduciary of a pension, deferred compensation, saving, thrift, or other retirement, incentive, or benefit plan, trust, or provision for any or all of the corporation's directors, officers, employees, and persons providing services to the corporation or any of its subsidiary or related or affiliated corporations, in that person's capacity as such, even though the person may also be an agent as defined in subdivision (a) of the employer corporation. A corporation shall have power to indemnify the trustee, investment manager, or other fiduciary to the extent permitted by subdivision (e) of Section 7140.

Ca. Corp. Code § 7237

Amended by Stats 2013 ch 76 (AB 383),s 25, eff. 1/1/2014.
Amended by Stats 2012 ch 61 (AB 2668),s 2, eff. 1/1/2013.

Section 7238 - Standards of conduct where corporation holds assets in charitable trust

Where a corporation holds assets in charitable trust, the conduct of its directors or of any person performing functions similar to those performed by a director, shall, in respect to the assets held in charitable trust, be governed by the standards of conduct set forth in Article 3 (commencing with Section 5230) of Chapter 2 of Part 2 for directors of nonprofit public benefit corporations. This does not limit any additional requirements which may be specifically set forth in this part regarding corporations holding assets in charitable trust.

Ca. Corp. Code § 7238
Added by Stats. 1978, Ch. 567.

Article 4 - EXAMINATION BY ATTORNEY GENERAL

Section 7240 - Examination by attorney general

A corporation holding assets in charitable trust is subject at all times to examination by the Attorney General, on behalf of the state, to ascertain to what extent, if at all, it has failed or is failing to comply with trusts it has assumed. In case of any such failure the Attorney General, in the name of the state, may institute against any person or persons the proceedings necessary to correct the failure.

Ca. Corp. Code § 7240
Amended by Stats. 1979, Ch. 724.

Chapter 3 - MEMBERS

Article 1 - ISSUANCE OF MEMBERSHIPS

Section 7310 - Admission of members; no members

(a) A corporation may admit persons to membership, as provided in its articles or bylaws, or may provide in its articles or bylaws that it shall have no members. In the absence of any provision in its articles or bylaws providing for members, a corporation shall have no members.

(b) In the case of a corporation which has no members:

(1) Any action for which there is no specific provision of this part applicable to a corporation which has no members and which would otherwise require approval by a majority of all members (Section 5033) or approval by the members (Section 5034) shall require only approval of the board, any provision of this part or the articles or bylaws to the contrary notwithstanding.

(2) All rights which would otherwise vest in the members to share in a distribution upon dissolution shall vest in the directors.

(c) Reference in this part to a corporation which has no members includes a corporation in which the directors are the only members.

Ca. Corp. Code § 7310

Amended by Stats. 1984, Ch. 812, Sec. 6.5.

Section 7311 - Consideration

Subject to the articles or bylaws, memberships may be issued by a corporation for no consideration or for such consideration as is determined by the board.

Ca. Corp. Code § 7311

Amended by Stats. 1981, Ch. 587, Sec. 30.

Section 7312 - One membership; fractional memberships

No person may hold more than one membership, and no fractional memberships may be held, except as follows:

(a) Two or more persons may have an indivisible interest in a single membership when authorized by, and in a manner or under the circumstances prescribed by, the articles or bylaws subject to Section 7612.

(b) If the articles or bylaws provide for classes of membership and if the articles or bylaws permit a person to be a member of more than one class, a person may hold a membership in one or more classes.

(c) Any branch, division, or office of any person, which is not formed primarily to be a member, may hold a separate membership.

(d) In the case of membership in an owners' association, created in connection with any of the forms of development referred to in Section 11004.5 of the Business and Professions Code, the articles or bylaws may permit a person who owns an interest, or who has a right of exclusive occupancy, in more than one lot, parcel, area, apartment, or unit to hold a separate membership in the owners' association for each lot, parcel, area, apartment, or unit.

(e) In the case of membership in a mutual water company, as defined in Section 14300, the articles or bylaws may permit a person entitled to membership by reason of the ownership, lease, or right of occupancy of more than one lot, parcel, or other service unit to hold a separate membership in the mutual water company for each lot, parcel, or other service unit.

(f) In the case of membership in a mobilehome park acquisition corporation, as described in Section 11010.8 of the Business and Professions Code, a bona fide secured party who has, pursuant to a security interest in a membership, taken title to the membership by way of foreclosure, repossession, or voluntary repossession, and who is actively attempting to resell the membership to a prospective homeowner or resident of the mobilehome park, may own more than one membership.

Ca. Corp. Code § 7312
Amended by Stats 2006 ch 538 (SB 1852),s 79, eff. 1/1/2007.

Section 7313 - Membership certificates

(a) A corporation may, but is not required to, issue membership certificates. Nothing in this section shall restrict a corporation from issuing identity cards or similar devices to members which serve to identify members qualifying to use facilities or services of the corporation.

(b) Membership certificates issued by corporations shall state the following on the certificate:

(1) The corporation is a nonprofit mutual benefit corporation which may not make distributions to its members except upon dissolution, or, if the articles or bylaws so provide, that it may not make distributions to its members during its life or upon dissolution.

(2) If there are restrictions upon the transferability, a statement that a copy of the restrictions are on file with the secretary of the corporation and are open for inspection by a member on the same basis as the records of the corporation.

(c) If the membership certificates are transferable only with consent of the corporation, or if there are no membership certificates, then instead of complying with paragraph (2) of subdivision (b) the corporation may, or if there are no membership certificates, shall, give notice to the transferee, within a reasonable time after the corporation is first notified of the proposed transfer, and before the membership is transferred on the books and records of the corporation, of the information that would otherwise be provided by the legends required by paragraph (2) of subdivision (b).

(d) If the articles or bylaws are amended so that any statement required by subdivision (b) upon outstanding membership certificates is no longer accurate, then the board may cancel the outstanding certificates and issue in their place new certificates conforming to the articles or bylaw amendments.

(e) Where new membership certificates are issued in accordance with subdivision (d), the board may order holders of outstanding certificates to surrender and exchange them for new certificates within a reasonable time fixed by the board. The board may further provide that the holder of a certificate so ordered to be surrendered shall not be entitled to exercise any of the rights of membership until the certificate is surrendered and exchanged, but rights shall be suspended only after notice of such order is given to the holder of the certificate and only until the certificate is exchanged. The duty of surrender of any outstanding certificates may also be enforced by civil action.

Ca. Corp. Code § 7313
Amended by Stats. 1985, Ch. 378, Sec. 4.

Section 7314 - Issuance of new membership certificate or new certificate for security

(a) A corporation may issue a new membership certificate or a new certificate for any security in the place of any certificate theretofore issued by it, alleged to have been lost, stolen or destroyed, and the corporation may require the owner of the lost, stolen or destroyed certificate or the owner's legal representative to give the corporation a bond (or other adequate security) sufficient to indemnify it against any claim that may be made against it (including any expense or liability) on account of the alleged loss, theft or destruction of any such certificate or the issuance of such new certificate.
(b) If a corporation refuses to issue a new membership certificate or other certificate in place of one theretofore issued by it, or by any corporation of which it is the lawful successor, alleged to have been lost, stolen or destroyed, the owner of the lost, stolen or destroyed certificate or the owner's legal representative may bring an action in the superior court of the proper county for an order requiring the corporation to issue a new certificate in place of the one lost, stolen or destroyed.

Ca. Corp. Code § 7314
Added by Stats. 1978, Ch. 567.

Section 7315 - Admission of any person except subsidiary

(a) Except as provided in subdivision (b), or in its articles or bylaws, a corporation may admit any person to membership.
(b) A corporation may not admit its subsidiary (Section 5073) to membership.

Ca. Corp. Code § 7315
Amended by Stats. 1979, Ch. 724.

Article 2 - TRANSFER OF MEMBERSHIPS

Section 7320 - Transfer of membership; member's death or dissolution

Subject to Section 7613:
(a) Unless the articles or bylaws otherwise provide:

    (1) No member may transfer a membership or any right arising therefrom; and

    (2) Subject to the provisions of subdivision (b), all rights as a member of the corporation cease upon the member's death or dissolution.
(b) The articles or bylaws may provide for, or may authorize the board to provide for, the transfer of memberships, or of memberships within any class or classes, with or without restriction or limitation, including transfer upon the death, dissolution, merger, or reorganization of a member.
(c) Where transfer rights have been provided, no restriction of them shall be binding

with respect to memberships issued prior to the adoption of the restriction, unless the holders of such memberships voted in favor of the restriction.

Ca. Corp. Code § 7320
Added by Stats. 1978, Ch. 567.

Article 3 - TYPES OF MEMBERSHIPS

Section 7330 - Memberships having different rights, privileges, preferences, restrictions, or conditions

A corporation may issue memberships having different rights, privileges, preferences, restrictions, or conditions, as authorized by its articles or bylaws.

Ca. Corp. Code § 7330
Amended by Stats. 1979, Ch. 724.

Section 7331 - Memberships having same rights, privileges, preferences, restrictions, or conditions

Except as provided in or authorized by the articles or bylaws, all memberships shall have the same rights, privileges, preferences, restrictions and conditions.

Ca. Corp. Code § 7331
Amended by Stats. 1979, Ch. 724.

Section 7332 - Classes of membership

(a) A corporation may provide in its articles for one or more classes of memberships which are redeemable, in whole or in part, at the option of the corporation, or the member for such consideration within such time or upon the happening of one or more specified events and upon such terms and conditions as are stated in the articles. However, no membership shall actually be redeemed if prohibited by Chapter 4 (commencing with Section 7410).
(b) Nothing in this section shall prevent a corporation from creating a sinking fund or similar provision for, or entering into an agreement for, the redemption or purchase of its memberships to the extent permitted by Chapter 4 (commencing with Section 7410).

Ca. Corp. Code § 7332
Added by Stats. 1978, Ch. 567.

Section 7333 - Referral to persons associated with corporation as "members"; assisting persons who are not members

(a) A corporation may refer to persons associated with it as "members" even though such persons are not members within the meaning of Section 5056; but references to members in this part mean members as defined in Section 5056.

(b) A corporation may benefit, serve, or assist persons who are not members within the meaning of Section 5056 for such consideration, if any, as the board may determine or as is authorized or provided for in the articles or bylaws.

Ca. Corp. Code § 7333
Amended by Stats. 1979, Ch. 724.

Article 4 - TERMINATION OF MEMBERSHIPS

Section 7340 - Resignation; expiration

(a) A member may resign from membership at any time, although the articles or bylaws may require reasonable notice before the resignation is effective.
(b) This section shall not relieve the resigning member from any obligation for charges incurred, services or benefits actually rendered, dues, assessments or fees, or arising from contract, a condition to ownership of land, an obligation arising out of the ownership of land, or otherwise, and this section shall not diminish any right of the corporation to enforce any such obligation or obtain damages for its breach.
(c) A membership issued for a period of time shall expire when such period of time has elapsed unless the membership is renewed.

Ca. Corp. Code § 7340
Amended by Stats. 1979, Ch. 724.

Section 7341 - Expulsion, suspension, or termination

(a) No member may be expelled or suspended, and no membership or memberships may be terminated or suspended, except according to procedures satisfying the requirements of this section. An expulsion, termination or suspension not in accord with this section shall be void and without effect.
(b) Any expulsion, suspension, or termination must be done in good faith and in a fair and reasonable manner. Any procedure which conforms to the requirements of subdivision (c) is fair and reasonable, but a court may also find other procedures to be fair and reasonable when the full circumstances of the suspension, termination, or expulsion are considered.
(c) A procedure is fair and reasonable when:

(1) The provisions of the procedure have been set forth in the articles or bylaws, or copies of such provisions are sent annually to all the members as required by the articles or bylaws;

(2) It provides the giving of 15 days' prior notice of the expulsion, suspension or termination and the reasons therefor; and

(3) It provides an opportunity for the member to be heard, orally or in writing, not less than five days before the effective date of the expulsion, suspension or

termination by a person or body authorized to decide that the proposed expulsion, termination or suspension not take place.

(d) Any notice required under this section may be given by any method reasonably calculated to provide actual notice. Any notice given by mail must be given by first-class or registered mail sent to the last address of the members shown on the corporation's records.

(e) Any action challenging an expulsion, suspension or termination of membership, including any claim alleging defective notice, must be commenced within one year after the date of the expulsion, suspension or termination. In the event such an action is successful the court may order any relief, including reinstatement, it finds equitable under the circumstances, but no vote of the members or of the board may be set aside solely because a person was at the time of the vote wrongfully excluded by virtue of the challenged expulsion, suspension or termination, unless the court finds further that the wrongful expulsion, suspension or termination was in bad faith and for the purpose, and with the effect, of wrongfully excluding the member from the vote or from the meeting at which the vote took place, so as to affect the outcome of the vote.

(f) This section governs only the procedures for expulsion, suspension or termination and not the substantive grounds therefor. An expulsion, suspension or termination based upon substantive grounds which violate contractual or other rights of the member or are otherwise unlawful is not made valid by compliance with this section.

(g) A member who is expelled or suspended or whose membership is terminated shall be liable for any charges incurred, services or benefits actually rendered, dues, assessments or fees incurred before the expulsion, suspension or termination or arising from contract or otherwise.

Ca. Corp. Code § 7341
Amended by Stats. 1996, Ch. 589, Sec. 27. Effective January 1, 1997.

Article 5 - RIGHTS AND OBLIGATIONS OF MEMBERS AND CREDITORS

Section 7350 - Liability; consent to membership

(a) A member of a corporation is not, as such, personally liable for the debts, liabilities, or obligations of the corporation.

(b) No person is liable for any obligation arising from membership unless the person was admitted to membership upon the person's application or with the person's consent.

(c) The ownership of an interest in real property, when a condition of its ownership is membership in a corporation, shall be considered consent to such membership for the purpose of this section.

Ca. Corp. Code § 7350
Added by Stats. 1978, Ch. 567.

Section 7351 - Dues, assessments, or fees

A corporation may levy dues, assessments, or fees upon its members pursuant to its articles or bylaws, but a member upon learning of them may avoid liability for them by promptly resigning from membership, except where the member is liable for them by contract, as a condition to ownership of an interest in real property, as an obligation arising out of the ownership of an interest in real property, or otherwise. Article or bylaw provisions authorizing such dues, assessments or fees do not, of themselves, create such liability.

Ca. Corp. Code § 7351
Amended by Stats. 1979, Ch. 724.

Section 7352 - Membership as pledgee or membership in representative or fiduciary capacity

A person holding a membership as pledgee or a membership as executor, administrator, guardian, trustee, receiver or in any representative or fiduciary capacity is not personally liable for any unpaid balance of the purchase price of the membership, or for any amount owing to the corporation by the member, because the membership is so held, but the estate and funds in the hands of such fiduciary or representative are liable and the membership subject to sale therefor.

Ca. Corp. Code § 7352
Amended by Stats. 1983, Ch. 1085, Sec. 5.1.

Section 7353 - Creditor's action

(a) No action shall be brought by or on behalf of any creditor to reach and apply the liability, if any, of a member to the corporation to pay the amount due on such member's membership or otherwise due to the corporation unless final judgment has been rendered in favor of the creditor against the corporation and execution has been returned unsatisfied in whole or in part or unless such proceedings would be useless.
(b) All creditors of the corporation, with or without reducing their claims to judgment, may intervene in any such creditor's action to reach and apply unpaid amounts due the corporation and any or all members who owe amounts to the corporation may be joined in such action. Several judgments may be rendered for and against the parties to the action or in favor of a receiver for the benefit of the respective parties thereto.
(c) All amounts paid by any member in any such action shall be credited on the unpaid balance due the corporation by such member.

Ca. Corp. Code § 7353
Added by Stats. 1978, Ch. 567.

Section 7354 - No derogation of rights or remedies of creditor or member because of fraud or illegality

Nothing in this part shall be construed as in derogation of any rights or remedies which any creditor or member may have against any promoter, member, director, officer or the corporation because of participation in any fraud or illegality practiced upon such creditor or member by any such person or by the corporation in connection with the issue or sale of memberships or securities or in derogation of any rights which the corporation may have by rescission, cancellation or otherwise because of any fraud or illegality practiced on it by any such person in connection with the issue or sale of memberships or securities.

Ca. Corp. Code § 7354
Added by Stats. 1978, Ch. 567.

Chapter 4 - DISTRIBUTIONS

Article 1 - LIMITATIONS

Section 7410 - Applicability

This chapter does not apply to any proceeding for winding up and dissolution of corporations under Chapters 15 (commencing with Section 8510), 16 (commencing with Section 8610), and 17 (commencing with Section 8710).

Ca. Corp. Code § 7410
Added by Stats. 1978, Ch. 567.

Section 7411 - Distribution upon dissolution; purchase or redemption of membership

(a) Except as provided in subdivision (b), no corporation shall make any distribution except upon dissolution.
(b) A corporation may, subject to meeting the requirements of Sections 7412 and 7413 and any additional restrictions authorized by Section 7414, purchase or redeem memberships.

Ca. Corp. Code § 7411
Amended by Stats. 1979, Ch. 724.

Section 7412 - No distribution if unable to meet liabilities

Neither a corporation nor any of its subsidiaries shall make a distribution if the corporation or the subsidiary making the distribution is, or as a result thereof would be, likely to be unable to meet its liabilities (except those whose payment is otherwise adequately provided for) as they mature.

Ca. Corp. Code § 7412
Added by Stats. 1978, Ch. 567.

Section 7413 - No purchase or redemption of membership if unable to meet liabilities

Neither a corporation nor any of its subsidiaries shall purchase or redeem a membership of the parent or subsidiary if the articles of the corporation contain a provision authorized by subparagraph (B) of paragraph (4) of subdivision (a) of Section 7132 and such corporation or the subsidiary making the purchase or redemption is, or as a result thereof would be, likely to be unable to meet the obligations resulting from such article provision.

Ca. Corp. Code § 7413

Amended by Stats 2022 ch 617 (SB 1202),s 60, eff. 1/1/2023.

Amended by Stats. 1979, Ch. 724.

Section 7414 - No prohibition of additional restrictions upon purchase or redemption of membership

Nothing in this chapter prohibits additional restrictions upon the purchase or redemption of a membership by provision in a corporation's articles or bylaws or agreement entered into by the corporation.

Ca. Corp. Code § 7414

Added by Stats. 1978, Ch. 567.

Article 2 - LIABILITY OF MEMBERS

Section 7420 - Liability upon receipt of improper distribution

(a) Any person who with knowledge of facts indicating the impropriety thereof receives any distribution, including a payment in redemption of a membership, prohibited by this chapter is liable to the corporation for the amount so received by the person with interest thereon at the legal rate on judgments until paid.

(b) Any person who with knowledge of facts indicating the impropriety thereof receives any distribution, including a payment in redemption of a membership, prohibited by this chapter is liable to the corporation for the benefit of the head organization, or of all of the creditors entitled to institute an action under subdivision (c), for the amount so received by the person with interest thereon at the legal rate on judgments until paid, but not exceeding the obligations of the corporation owed to the head organization at the time of the violation, or the liabilities of the corporation owed to nonconsenting creditors at the time of the violation, as the case may be.

(c) Suit may be brought in the name of the corporation to enforce the liability (1) to creditors arising under subdivision (b) for a violation of Section 7411 or 7412 against any or all persons liable by any one or more creditors of the corporation whose debts or claims arose prior to the time of the distribution and who have not consented thereto, whether or not they have reduced their claims to judgment, or (2) to the head organization arising under subdivision (b) for a violation of Section 7413 against any or all persons liable by any head organization which pursuant to the corporation's articles is entitled to a distribution of assets upon dissolution.

(d) Any person sued under subdivision (b) may implead all other persons liable under subdivision (b) and may in the absence of fraud by the moving party compel contribution, either in that action or in an independent action against persons not joined in that action.

(e) Nothing contained in this section affects any liability which any person may have under the Uniform Voidable Transactions Act (Chapter 1 (commencing with Section 3439) of Title 2 of Part 2 of Division 4 of the Civil Code).

Ca. Corp. Code § 7420

Amended by Stats 2015 ch 44 (SB 161),s 20, eff. 1/1/2016.

Chapter 5 - MEETINGS AND VOTING

Article 1 - GENERAL PROVISIONS

Section 7510 - Meetings of members

(a) Meetings of members may be held at a place within or without this state as may be stated in or fixed in accordance with the bylaws. If no other place is stated or so fixed, meetings of members shall be held at the principal office of the corporation. Subject to any limitations in the articles or bylaws of the corporation, if authorized by the board of directors in its sole discretion, and subject to those guidelines and procedures as the board of directors may adopt, members not physically present in person (or, if proxies are allowed, by proxy) at a meeting of members may, by electronic transmission by and to the corporation (Sections 20 and 21), electronic video screen communication, conference telephone, or other means of remote communication, participate in a meeting of members, be deemed present in person (or, if proxies are allowed, by proxy), and vote at a meeting of members, subject to subdivision (f).

(b)A regular meeting of members shall be held on a date and time, and with the frequency stated in or fixed in accordance with the bylaws, but in any event in each year in which directors are to be elected at that meeting for the purpose of conducting such election, and to transact any other proper business which may be brought before the meeting.

(c) If a corporation with members is required by subdivision (b) to hold a regular meeting and fails to hold the regular meeting for a period of 60 days after the date designated therefor or, if no date has been designated, for a period of 15 months after the formation of the corporation or after its last regular meeting, or if the corporation fails to hold a written ballot for a period of 60 days after the date designated therefor, then the superior court of the proper county may summarily order the meeting to be held or the ballot to be conducted upon the application of a member or the Attorney General, after notice to the corporation giving it an opportunity to be heard.

(d) The votes represented, either in person (or, if proxies are allowed, by proxy), at a meeting called or by written ballot ordered pursuant to subdivision (c), and entitled to be cast on the business to be transacted shall constitute a quorum, notwithstanding any provision of the articles or bylaws or in this part to the contrary. The court may issue such orders as may be appropriate including, without limitation, orders designating the time and place of the meeting, the record date for determination of members entitled to vote, and the form of notice of the meeting.

(e) Special meetings of members for any lawful purpose may be called by the board, the chairperson of the board, the president, or such other persons, if any, as are specified in the bylaws. In addition, special meetings of members for any lawful purpose may be called by 5 percent or more of the members.

(f)A meeting of the members may be conducted, in whole or in part, by electronic transmission by and to the corporation, electronic video screen communication, conference telephone, or other means of remote communication if the corporation implements reasonable measures:

(1) to provide members and proxyholders, if proxies are allowed, a reasonable opportunity to participate in the meeting and to vote on matters submitted to the members, including an opportunity to read or hear the proceedings of the meeting substantially concurrently with those proceedings,

(2) if any member or proxyholder, if proxies are allowed, votes or takes other action at the meeting by means of electronic transmission to the corporation, electronic video screen communication, conference telephone, or other means of remote communication, to maintain a record of that vote or action in its books and records, and

(3) to verify that each person participating remotely is a member or proxyholder, if proxies are allowed. A corporation shall not conduct a meeting of members solely by electronic transmission by and to the corporation, electronic video screen communication, conference telephone, or other means of remote communication unless one or more of the following conditions apply:

(A) all of the members consent; or

(B) the board determines it is necessary or appropriate because of an emergency, as defined in paragraph (5) of subdivision (m) of Section 7140; or

(C) the meeting is conducted on or before June 30, 2022.

Ca. Corp. Code § 7510

Amended by Stats 2022 ch 617 (SB 1202),s 61, eff. 1/1/2023.
Amended by Stats 2022 ch 12 (AB 769),s 3, eff. 3/25/2022.
Amended by Stats 2021 ch 523 (AB 663),s 13, eff. 1/1/2022.
Amended by Stats 2004 ch 254 (SB 1306),s 24, eff. 1/1/2005

Section 7511 - Notice of members' meeting or report

(a) Whenever members are required or permitted to take any action at a meeting, a written notice of the meeting shall be given not less than 10 nor more than 90 days before the date of the meeting to each member who, on the record date for notice of the meeting, is entitled to vote thereat; provided, however, that if notice is given by mail, and the notice is not mailed by first-class, registered, or certified mail, that notice shall be given not less than 20 days before the meeting. Subject to subdivision (f), and subdivision (b) of Section 7512, the notice shall state the place, date and time of the meeting, the means of electronic transmission by and to the corporation (Sections 20 and 21), electronic video screen communication, conference telephone, or other means of remote communication, if any, by which members may participate in that meeting, and (1)in the case of a special meeting, the general nature of the business to be transacted, and no other business may be transacted, or (2)in the case of the regular meeting, those matters which the board, at the time the notice is given, intends to present for action by the members, but, except as provided in subdivision (b) of Section 7512, any proper matter may be presented at the meeting for the action. The notice of any meeting at which directors are to be elected shall include the names of all those who are nominees at the time the notice is given to members.

(b)

(1)Notice of a members' meeting or any report shall be given personally, by electronic transmission by a corporation, or by mail or other means of written communication, addressed to a member at the address of the member appearing on the books of the corporation or given by the member to the corporation for purpose of notice, or if no such address appears or is given, at the place where the principal office of the corporation is located or by publication at least once in a newspaper of general circulation in the county in which the principal office is located. Notwithstanding the foregoing, the notice of a members' meeting or any report may be sent by electronic communication or other means of remote communication if the board determines it is necessary or appropriate because of an emergency, as defined in paragraph (5) of subdivision (m) of Section 7140. An affidavit of giving of any notice or report as permitted because of an emergency or otherwise in accordance with the provisions of this part, executed by the secretary, assistant secretary, or any transfer agent, shall be prima facie evidence of the giving of the notice or report.

(2)If any notice or report addressed to the member at the address of the member appearing on the books of the corporation is returned to the corporation by the United States Postal Service marked to indicate that the United States Postal Service is unable to deliver the notice or report to the member at the address, all future notices or reports shall be deemed to have been duly given without further mailing if the same shall be available for the member upon written demand of the member at the principal office of the corporation for a period of one year from the date of the giving of the notice or report to all other members.

(3)

(A) Notice given by electronic transmission by the corporation under this subdivision shall be valid only if it complies with Section 20. Notwithstanding the foregoing, notice shall not be given by electronic transmission by the corporation under this subdivision after either of the following:

(i) The corporation is unable to deliver two consecutive notices to the member by that means.

(ii) The inability to so deliver the notices to the member becomes known to the secretary, any assistant secretary, the transfer agent, or other person responsible for the giving of the notice.

(B) This paragraph shall not apply if notices are provided by electronic communication or other means of remote communication as permitted because of an emergency.

(c) Upon request in writing to the corporation addressed to the attention of the chairperson of the board, president, vice president, or secretary by any person (other than the board) entitled to call a special meeting of members, the officer forthwith shall cause notice to be given to the members entitled to vote that a meeting will be held at a time fixed by the board not less than 35 nor more than 90 days after the receipt of the request. If the corporation is a common interest development, as defined in Section 4100 of the Civil Code, the corporation shall cause notice to be given to the members entitled to vote that a meeting will be held at a time fixed by the board not less than 35 nor more than 150 days after receipt of the request. If the notice is not given within 20 days after receipt of the request, the persons entitled to call the meeting may give the notice or the superior court of the proper county shall summarily order the giving of the notice, after notice to the corporation giving it an opportunity to be heard. The court may issue such orders as may be appropriate, including, without limitation, orders designating the time and place of the meeting, the record date for determination of members entitled to vote, and the form of notice.

(d) When a members' meeting is adjourned to another time or place, unless the bylaws otherwise require and except as provided in this subdivision, notice need not be given of the adjourned meeting if the time and place thereof (or the means of electronic transmission by and to the corporation or electronic video screen communication, conference telephone, or other means of remote communication, if any, by which members may participate) are announced at the meeting at which the adjournment is taken. No meeting may be adjourned for more than 45 days. At the adjourned meeting the corporation may transact any business which might have been transacted at the original meeting. If after the adjournment a new record date is fixed for notice or voting, a notice of the adjourned meeting shall be given to each member who, on the record date for notice of the meeting, is entitled to vote at the meeting.

(e) The transactions of any meeting of members however called and noticed, and wherever held, are as valid as though had at a meeting duly held after regular call and notice, if a quorum is present either in person or by proxy, and if, either before or after the meeting, each of the persons entitled to vote, not present in person (or, if proxies are allowed, by proxy), provides a waiver of notice or consent to the holding of the meeting or an approval of the minutes thereof in writing. All such waivers, consents, and approvals shall be filed with the corporate records or made a part of the minutes of the meeting. Attendance of a person at a meeting shall constitute a waiver of notice of and presence at the meeting, except when the person objects, at the beginning of the meeting, to the transaction of any business because the meeting is not lawfully called or convened and except that attendance at a meeting is not a waiver of any right to object to the consideration of matters required by this part to be included in the notice but not so included, if the objection is expressly made at the meeting. Neither the business to be transacted at nor the purpose of any regular or special meeting of members need be specified in any written waiver of notice, consent to the holding of the meeting or approval of the minutes thereof, unless otherwise provided in the articles or bylaws, except as provided in subdivision (f).

(f) Any approval of the members required under Section 7222, 7224, 7233, 7812, 8610, or 8719, other than unanimous approval by those entitled to vote, shall be valid only if the general nature of the proposal so approved was stated in the notice of meeting or in any written waiver of notice.

(g)A court may find that notice not given in conformity with this section is still valid, if it was given in a fair and reasonable manner.

Ca. Corp. Code § 7511

Amended by Stats 2022 ch 617 (SB 1202),s 62, eff. 1/1/2023.
Amended by Stats 2021 ch 642 (SB 432),s 5.5, eff. 1/1/2022.
Amended by Stats 2021 ch 523 (AB 663),s 14, eff. 1/1/2022.
Amended by Stats 2004 ch 254 (SB 1306),s 25, eff. 1/1/2005

Section 7512 - Quorum

(a) One-third of the voting power, represented in person or by proxy, shall constitute a quorum at a meeting of members, but, subject to subdivisions (b) and (c), a bylaw may set a different quorum. Any bylaw amendment to increase the quorum may be adopted only by approval of the members (Section 5034). If a quorum is present, the affirmative vote of the majority of the voting power represented at the meeting, entitled to vote, and voting on any matter shall be the act of the members unless the vote of a greater number or voting by classes is required by this part or the articles or bylaws.

(b) Where a bylaw authorizes a corporation to conduct a meeting with a quorum of less than one-third of the voting power, then the only matters that may be voted upon at any regular meeting actually attended, in person or by proxy, by less than one-third of the voting power are matters notice of the general nature of which was given, pursuant to the first sentence of subdivision (a) of Section 7511.

(c) Subject to subdivision (b), the members present at a duly called or held meeting at which a quorum is present may continue to transact business until adjournment notwithstanding the withdrawal of enough members to leave less than a quorum, if any action taken (other than adjournment) is approved by at least a majority of the members required to constitute a quorum or, if required by this division, or by the articles or the bylaws, the vote of the greater number or voting by classes.

(d) In the absence of a quorum, any meeting of members may be adjourned from time to time by the vote of a majority of the votes represented either in person or by proxy, but no other business may be transacted, except as provided in subdivision (c).

   Ca. Corp. Code § 7512

Amended by Stats 2000 ch 485 (AB 1895), s 13, eff. 1/1/2001.

Section 7513 - Approval by written ballot

(a) Subject to subdivision (e), and unless prohibited in the articles or bylaws, any action which may be taken at any regular or special meeting of members may be taken without a meeting if the corporation distributes a written ballot to every member entitled to vote on the matter. Unless otherwise provided by the articles or bylaws and if approved by the board of directors, that ballot and any related material may be sent by electronic transmission by the corporation (Section 20) and responses may be returned to the corporation by electronic transmission to the corporation (Section 21). That ballot shall set forth the proposed action, provide an opportunity to specify approval or disapproval of any proposal, and provide a reasonable time within which to return the ballot to the corporation.

(b) Approval by written ballot pursuant to this section shall be valid only when the number of votes cast by ballot within the time period specified equals or exceeds the quorum required to be present at a meeting authorizing the action, and the number of approvals equals or exceeds the number of votes that would be required to approve at a meeting at which the total number of votes cast was the same as the number of votes cast by ballot.

(c) Ballots shall be solicited in a manner consistent with the requirements of subdivision (b) of Section 7511 and Section 7514. All such solicitations shall indicate the number of responses needed to meet the quorum requirement and, with respect to ballots other than for the election of directors, shall state the percentage of approvals necessary to pass the measure submitted. The solicitation must specify the time by which the ballot must be received in order to be counted.

(d) Unless otherwise provided in the articles or bylaws, a written ballot may not be revoked.

(e) Directors may be elected by written ballot under this section, where authorized by the articles or bylaws, except that election by written ballot may not be authorized where the directors are elected by cumulative voting pursuant to Section 7615.

(f) When directors are to be elected by written ballot and the articles or bylaws prescribe a nomination procedure, the procedure may provide for a date for the close of nominations prior to the printing and distributing of the written ballots.

Ca. Corp. Code § 7513
Amended by Stats 2004 ch 254 (SB 1306),s 26, eff. 1/1/2005

Section 7514 - Form of proxy or written ballot

(a) Any form of proxy or written ballot distributed to 10 or more members of a corporation with 100 or more members shall afford an opportunity on the proxy or form of written ballot to specify a choice between approval and disapproval of each matter or group of related matters intended, at the time the written ballot or proxy is distributed, to be acted upon at the meeting for which the proxy is solicited or by such written ballot, and shall provide, subject to reasonable specified conditions, that where the person solicited specifies a choice with respect to any such matter the vote shall be cast in accordance therewith.

(b) In any election of directors, any form of proxy or written ballot in which the directors to be voted upon are named therein as candidates and which is marked by a member "withhold" or otherwise marked in a manner indicating that the authority to vote for the election of directors is withheld shall not be voted either for or against the election of a director.

(c) Failure to comply with this section shall not invalidate any corporate action taken, but may be the basis for challenging any proxy at a meeting or written ballot and the superior court may compel compliance therewith at the suit of any member.

Ca. Corp. Code § 7514
Amended by Stats. 1979, Ch. 724.

Section 7515 - Impractical or difficult to call or conduct meeting or otherwise obtain consent; petition; order

(a) If for any reason it is impractical or unduly difficult for any corporation to call or conduct a meeting of its members, delegates or directors, or otherwise obtain their consent, in the manner prescribed by its articles or bylaws, or this part, then the superior court of the proper county, upon petition of a director, officer, delegate or member, may order that such a meeting be called or that a written ballot or other form of obtaining the vote of members, delegates or directors be authorized, in such a manner as the court finds fair and equitable under the circumstances.

(b) The court shall, in an order issued pursuant to this section, provide for a method of notice reasonably designed to give actual notice to all parties who would be entitled to notice of a meeting held pursuant to the articles, bylaws and this part, whether or not the method results in actual notice to every such person, or conforms to the notice requirements that would otherwise apply. In a proceeding under this section the court may determine who the members or directors are.

(c) The order issued pursuant to this section may dispense with any requirement relating to the holding of and voting at meetings or obtaining of votes, including any requirement as to quorums or as to the number or percentage of votes needed for approval, that would otherwise be imposed by the articles, bylaws, or this part.

(d) Wherever practical any order issued pursuant to this section shall limit the subject matter of the meetings or other forms of consent authorized to items, including amendments to the articles or bylaws, the resolution of which will or may enable the corporation to continue managing its affairs without further resort to this section; provided, however, that an order under this section may also authorize the obtaining of whatever votes and approvals are necessary for the dissolution, merger, sale of assets or reorganization of the corporation.

(e) Any meeting or other method of obtaining the vote of members, delegates or directors conducted pursuant to an order issued under this section, and which complies with all the provisions of such order, is for all purposes a valid meeting or vote, as the case may be, and shall have the same force and effect as if it complied with every requirement imposed by the articles, bylaws, and this part.

Ca. Corp. Code § 7515
Amended by Stats. 1986, Ch. 766, Sec. 31.

Section 7516 - Action by written consent

Any action required or permitted to be taken by the members may be taken without a meeting, if all members shall individually or collectively consent in writing to the action. The written consent or consents shall be filed with the minutes of the proceedings of the members. The action by written consent shall have the same force and effect as the unanimous vote of the members.

Ca. Corp. Code § 7516
Added by Stats. 1981, Ch. 587, Sec. 33.

Section 7517 - Name signed on ballot, consent, waiver, or proxy appointment

(a) If the name signed on a ballot, consent, waiver, or proxy appointment corresponds to the name of a member, the corporation if acting in good faith is entitled to accept the ballot, consent, waiver or proxy appointment and give it effect as the act of the member.

(b) If the name signed on a ballot, consent, waiver, or proxy appointment does not correspond to the record name of a member, the corporation if acting in good faith is nevertheless entitled to accept the ballot, consent, waiver, or proxy appointment and give it effect as the act of the member if any of the following occur:

(1) The member is an entity and the name signed purports to be that of an officer or agent of the entity.

(2) The name signed purports to be that of an attorney-in-fact of the member and if the corporation requests, evidence acceptable to the corporation of the signatory's authority to sign for the member has been presented with respect to the ballot, consent, waiver, or proxy appointment.

503

(3) Two or more persons hold the membership as cotenants or fiduciaries and the name signed purports to be the name of at least one of the coholders and the person signing appears to be acting on behalf of all the coholders.

(4) The name signed purports to be that of an administrator, executor, guardian, or conservator representing the member and, if the corporation requests, evidence of fiduciary status acceptable to the corporation has been presented with respect to the ballot, consent, waiver, or proxy appointment.

(5) The name signed purports to be that of a receiver or trustee in bankruptcy of the member, and, if the corporation requests, evidence of this status acceptable to the corporation has been presented with respect to the ballot, consent, waiver, or proxy appointment.
(c) The corporation is entitled to reject a ballot, consent, waiver, or proxy appointment if the secretary or other officer or agent authorized to tabulate votes, acting in good faith, has a reasonable basis for doubt concerning the validity of the signature or the signatory's authority to sign for the member.
(d) The corporation and any officer or agent thereof who accepts or rejects a ballot, consent, waiver, or proxy appointment in good faith and in accordance with the standards of this section shall not be liable in damages to the member for the consequences of the acceptance or rejection.
(e) Corporate action based on the acceptance or rejection of a ballot, consent, waiver, or proxy appointment under this section is valid unless a court of competent jurisdiction determines otherwise.
 Ca. Corp. Code § 7517
Added by Stats. 1996, Ch. 589, Sec. 29. Effective January 1, 1997.

Article 2 - ADDITIONAL PROVISIONS RELATING TO ELECTION OF DIRECTORS

Section 7520 - Reasonable nomination and election procedures

(a) As to directors elected by members, there shall be available to the members reasonable nomination and election procedures given the nature, size and operations of the corporation.
(b) If a corporation complies with all of the provisions of Sections 7521, 7522, 7523, and 7524 applicable to a corporation with the same number of members, the nomination and election procedures of that corporation, shall be deemed reasonable. However, those sections do not prescribe the exclusive means of making available to the members reasonable procedures for nomination and election of directors. A corporation may make available to the members other reasonable nomination and election procedures given the nature, size, and operations of the corporation.
(c) Subject to the provisions of subdivisions (a), (b), and (d) of Section 7616, the

superior court of the proper county shall enforce the provisions of this section.

  Ca. Corp. Code § 7520

Amended by Stats. 1996, Ch. 589, Sec. 30. Effective January 1, 1997.

Section 7521 - Corporation with 500 or more members

A corporation with 500 or more members may provide that, except for directors who are elected as authorized by Section 7152 or 7153, and except as provided in Section 7522, any person who is qualified to be elected to the board of directors of the corporation may be nominated:

(a) By any method authorized by the bylaws, or if no method is set forth in the bylaws by any method authorized by the board.

(b) By petition delivered to an officer of the corporation, signed within 11 months preceding the next time directors will be elected, by members representing the following number of votes:

Number of Votes Eligible to be Cast for Director Disregarding any Provision for Cumulative Voting	Number of Votes
Under 5,000	2 percent of voting power
5,000 or more	one-twentieth of 1 percent of voting power but not less than 100.

This subdivision does not apply to a corporation described in subdivision (c).

(c) In corporations with one million or more members engaged primarily in the business of retail merchandising of consumer goods, by petition delivered to an officer of the corporation, signed within 11 months preceding the next time directors will be elected, by such reasonable number of members as is set forth in the bylaws, or if no number is set forth in the bylaws, by such reasonable number of members as is determined by the directors.

(d) If there is a meeting to elect directors, by any member present at the meeting in person or by proxy if proxies are permitted.

  Ca. Corp. Code § 7521

Amended by Stats. 1996, Ch. 589, Sec. 31. Effective January 1, 1997.

Section 7522 - Corporation with 5,000 or more members

A corporation with 5,000 or more members may provide that, in any election of a director or directors by members of the corporation except for an election authorized by Section 7152 or 7153:

(a) The corporation's articles or bylaws shall set a date for the close of nominations for the board. The date shall not be less than 50 nor more than 120 days before the day directors are to be elected. No nominations for the board can be made after the date set for the close of nominations.

(b) If more people are nominated for the board than can be elected, the election shall take place by means of a procedure which allows all nominees a reasonable opportunity to solicit votes and all members a reasonable opportunity to choose among the nominees.

(c) A nominee shall have a reasonable opportunity to communicate to the members the nominee's qualifications and the reasons for the nominee's candidacy.

(d) If after the close of nominations the number of people nominated for the board is not more than the number of directors to be elected, the corporation may without further action declare that those nominated and qualified to be elected have been elected.

(e)

(1) Notwithstanding subdivision (d), for a common interest development subject to this part, if, after the close of nominations of directors for the board of directors of the common interest development, the number of director nominees is not more than the number of vacancies to be elected, as determined by the inspector or inspectors of elections selected pursuant to Section 5110 of the Civil Code, the director nominees shall be considered elected by acclamation if the association provided individual notice of the election and the procedure for nominating candidates at least 30 days before the close of nominations.

(2) For purposes of this subdivision:

(A) "Common interest development" has the same meaning as that term is defined in Section 4100 of the Civil Code.

(B) "Individual notice" has the same meaning as that term is defined in Section 4153 of the Civil Code.

Ca. Corp. Code § 7522
Amended by Stats 2019 ch 858 (SB 754),s 2, eff. 1/1/2020.

Section 7523 - Publication of material soliciting vote for nominee

Where a corporation with 500 or more members publishes any material soliciting a vote for any nominee for director in any publication owned or controlled by the corporation, the corporation may provide that it shall make available to all other nominees, in the same issue of the publication, an equal amount of space, with equal prominence, to be used by the nominee for a purpose reasonably related to the election.

Ca. Corp. Code § 7523
Amended by Stats. 1996, Ch. 589, Sec. 33. Effective January 1, 1997.

Section 7524 - Request by nominee and payment

A corporation with 500 or more members may provide that upon written request by any nominee for election to the board and the payment of the reasonable costs of mailing (including postage), the corporation shall within 10 business days after such request (provided payment has been made) mail to all members, or such portion of them as the nominee may reasonably specify, any material, which the nominee may furnish and which is reasonably related to the election, unless the corporation within five business days after the request allows the nominee, at the corporation's option, the rights set forth in either paragraph (1) or (2) of subdivision (a) of Section 8330.

Ca. Corp. Code § 7524
Amended by Stats. 1996, Ch. 589, Sec. 34. Effective January 1, 1997.

Section 7525 - Liability of corporation, agents, officers, directors, or employees

(a) This section shall apply to corporations publishing or mailing materials on behalf of any nominee in connection with procedures for the nomination and election of directors.
(b) Neither the corporation, nor its agents, officers, directors, or employees, may be held criminally liable, liable for any negligence (active or passive) or otherwise liable for damages to any person on account of any material which is supplied by a nominee for director and which it mails or publishes in procedures intended to comply with Section 7520 or pursuant to Section 7523 or 7524 but the nominee on whose behalf such material was published or mailed shall be liable and shall indemnify and hold the corporation, its agents, officers, directors, and employees and each of them harmless from all demands, costs, including reasonable legal fees and expenses, claims, damages and causes of action arising out of such material or any such mailing or publication.
(c) Nothing in this section shall prevent a corporation or any of its agents, officers, directors, or employees from seeking a court order providing that the corporation need not mail or publish material tendered by or on behalf of a nominee under this article on the ground the material will expose the moving party to liability.

Ca. Corp. Code § 7525
Amended by Stats. 1996, Ch. 589, Sec. 35. Effective January 1, 1997.

Section 7526 - Expenditure of corporate funds

Without authorization of the board, no corporation funds may be expended to support a nominee for director after there are more people nominated for director than can be elected.

Ca. Corp. Code § 7526
Added by Stats. 1978, Ch. 567.

Section 7527 - Action challenging validity of election, appointment, or removal of director

An action challenging the validity of any election, appointment or removal of a director or directors must be commenced within nine months after the election, appointment or removal. If no such action is commenced, in the absence of fraud, any election, appointment or removal of a director is conclusively presumed valid nine months thereafter.

    Ca. Corp. Code § 7527
Amended by Stats. 1981, Ch. 587, Sec. 35.

Chapter 6 - VOTING OF MEMBERSHIPS

Section 7610 - One vote

Except as provided in a corporation's articles or bylaws or Section 7615, each member shall be entitled to one vote on each matter submitted to a vote of the members. Single memberships in which two or more persons have an indivisible interest shall be voted as provided in Section 7612.

    Ca. Corp. Code § 7610
Added by Stats. 1978, Ch. 567.

Section 7611 - Record date

(a) The bylaws may provide or, in the absence of such provision, the board may fix, in advance, a date as the record date for the purpose of determining the members entitled to notice of any meeting of members. Such record date shall not be more than 90 nor less than 10 days before the date of the meeting. If no record date is fixed, members at the close of business on the business day preceding the day on which notice is given or, if notice is waived, at the close of business on the business day preceding the day on which the meeting is held are entitled to notice of a meeting of members. A determination of members entitled to notice of a meeting of members shall apply to any adjournment of the meeting unless the board fixes a new record date for the adjourned meeting.

(b) The bylaws may provide or, in the absence of such provision, the board may fix, in advance, a date as the record date for the purpose of determining the members entitled to vote at a meeting of members. Such record date shall not be more than 60 days before the date of the meeting. Such record date shall also apply in the case of an adjournment of the meeting unless the board fixes a new record date for the adjourned meeting. If no record date is fixed, members on the day of the meeting who are otherwise eligible to vote are entitled to vote at the meeting of members or, in the case of an adjourned meeting, members on the day of the adjourned meeting who are otherwise eligible to vote are entitled to vote at the adjourned meeting of members.

(c) The bylaws may provide or, in the absence of such provision, the board may fix, in advance, a date as the record date for the purpose of determining the members entitled to cast written ballots (Section 7513). Such record date shall not be more than 60 days before the day on which the first written ballot is mailed or solicited. If no record date is fixed, members on the day the first written ballot is mailed or solicited who are otherwise eligible to vote are entitled to cast written ballots.

(d) The bylaws may provide or, in the absence of such provision, the board may fix, in advance, a date as the record date for the purpose of determining the members entitled to exercise any rights in respect of any other lawful action. Such record date shall not be more than 60 days prior to such other action. If no record date is fixed, members at the close of business on the day on which the board adopts the resolution relating thereto, or the 60th day prior to the date of such other action, whichever is later, are entitled to exercise such rights.

Ca. Corp. Code § 7611

Amended by Stats. 1981, Ch. 587, Sec. 36.

Section 7612 - Single memberships in which two or more persons have indivisible interest

If a membership stands of record in the names of two or more persons, whether fiduciaries, members of a partnership, joint tenants, tenants in common, spouses as community property, tenants by the entirety, persons entitled to vote under a voting agreement or otherwise, or if two or more persons (including proxyholders) have the same fiduciary relationship respecting the same membership, unless the secretary of the corporation is given written notice to the contrary and is furnished with a copy of the instrument or order appointing them or creating the relationship wherein it is so provided, their acts with respect to voting shall have the following effect:

(a) If only one votes, such act binds all; or

(b) If more than one vote, the act of the majority so voting binds all.

Ca. Corp. Code § 7612

Amended by Stats 2016 ch 50 (SB 1005),s 23, eff. 1/1/2017.

Section 7613 - Proxy

(a) Any member may authorize another person or persons to act by proxy with respect to such membership except that this right may be limited or withdrawn by the articles or bylaws, subject to subdivision (f). Any proxy purported to be executed in accordance with the provisions of this part shall be presumptively valid.

(b) No proxy shall be valid after the expiration of 11 months from the date thereof unless otherwise provided in the proxy, except that the maximum term of any proxy shall be three years from the date of execution. Every proxy continues in full force and effect until revoked by the person executing it prior to the vote pursuant thereto, except as otherwise provided in this section. Such revocation may be effected by a writing delivered to the corporation stating that the proxy is revoked or by a subsequent proxy executed by the person executing the prior proxy and presented to the meeting, or as to any meeting by attendance at such meeting and voting in person by the person executing the proxy. The dates contained on the forms of proxy presumptively determine the order of execution, regardless of the postmark dates on the envelopes in which they are mailed.

(c) A proxy is not revoked by the death or incapacity of the maker or the termination of a membership as a result thereof unless, before the vote is counted, written notice of such death or incapacity is received by the corporation.

(d) Unless otherwise provided in the articles or bylaws, the proxy of a member which states that it is irrevocable is irrevocable for the period specified therein (notwithstanding subdivisions (b) and (c)) when it is held by any of the following or a nominee of any of the following:

(1) A person who has purchased or who has agreed to purchase the membership;

(2) A creditor or creditors of the corporation or the member who extended or continued credit to the corporation or the member in consideration of the proxy if the proxy states that it was given in consideration of such extension or continuation of credit and the name of the person extending or continuing the credit; or

(3) A person who has contracted to perform services as an employee of the corporation, if the proxy is required by the contract of employment and if the proxy states that it was given in consideration of such contract of employment, the name of the employee and the period of employment contracted for. Notwithstanding the period of irrevocability specified, the proxy becomes revocable when the agreement to purchase is terminated; the debt of the corporation or the member is paid; or the period of employment provided for in the contract of employment has terminated. In addition to the foregoing paragraphs (1) through (3), a proxy of a member may be made irrevocable (notwithstanding subdivision (c)) if it is given to secure the performance of a duty or to protect a title, either legal or equitable, until the happening of events which, by its terms, discharge the obligations secured by it.

(e) A proxy may be revoked, notwithstanding a provision making it irrevocable, by a transferee of a membership without knowledge of the existence of the provision unless the existence of the proxy and its irrevocability appears on the certificate representing the membership.

(f) Subdivision (a) notwithstanding:

(1) No amendment of the articles or bylaws repealing, restricting, creating or expanding proxy rights may be adopted without approval by the members (Section 5034); and

(2) No amendment of the articles or bylaws restricting or limiting the use of proxies may affect the validity of a previously issued irrevocable proxy during the term of its irrevocability, so long as it complied with applicable provisions, if any, of the articles or bylaws at the time of its issuance, and is otherwise valid under this section.

(g) Anything to the contrary notwithstanding, any revocable proxy covering matters requiring a vote of the members pursuant to Section 7222; Section 7224; Section 7233; paragraph (1) of subdivision (f) of this section; Section 7812; paragraph (2) of subdivision (a) of Section 7911; Section 8012; subdivision (a) of Section 8015; Section 8610; or subdivision (a) of Section 8719 is not valid as to such matters unless it sets forth the general nature of the matter to be voted on.

   Ca. Corp. Code § 7613
Amended by Stats. 1981, Ch. 587, Sec. 37.

Section 7614 - Inspectors of election

(a) In advance of any meeting of members, the board may appoint inspectors of election to act at the meeting and any adjournment thereof. If inspectors of election are not so appointed, or if any persons so appointed fail to appear or refuse to act, the chairperson of any meeting of members may, and on the request of any member or a member's proxy shall, appoint inspectors of election (or persons to replace those who so fail or refuse) at the meeting. The number of inspectors shall be either one or three. If appointed at a meeting on the request of one or more members or proxies, the majority of members represented in person or by proxy shall determine whether one or three inspectors are to be appointed. In the case of any action by written ballot (Section 7513), the board may similarly appoint inspectors of election to act with powers and duties as set forth in this section.

(b) The inspectors of election shall determine the number of memberships outstanding and the voting power of each, the number represented at the meeting, the existence of a quorum, and the authenticity, validity and effect of proxies, receive votes, ballots or consents, hear and determine all challenges and questions in any way arising in connection with the right to vote, count and tabulate all votes or consents, determine when the polls shall close, determine the result and do such acts as may be proper to conduct the election or vote with fairness to all members.

(c) The inspectors of election shall perform their duties impartially, in good faith, to the best of their ability and as expeditiously as is practical. If there are three inspectors of election, the decision, act or certificate of a majority is effective in all respects as the decision, act, or certificate of all. Any report or certificate made by the inspectors of election is prima facie evidence of the facts stated therein.

   Ca. Corp. Code § 7614
Amended by Stats 2022 ch 617 (SB 1202),s 63, eff. 1/1/2023.
Amended by Stats. 1984, Ch. 812, Sec. 9.

Section 7615 - Cumulative voting

(a) If the articles or bylaws authorize cumulative voting, but not otherwise, every member entitled to vote at any election of directors may cumulate the member's votes and give one candidate a number of votes equal to the number of directors to be elected multiplied by the number of votes to which the member is entitled, or distribute the member's votes on the same principle among as many candidates as the member thinks fit. An article or bylaw provision authorizing cumulative voting may be repealed or amended only by approval of the members (Section 5034), except that the governing article or bylaw provision may require the vote of a greater proportion of the members, or of the members of any class, for its repeal.

(b) No member shall be entitled to cumulate votes for a candidate or candidates unless the candidate's name or candidates' names have been placed in nomination prior to the voting and the member has given notice at the meeting prior to the voting of the member's intention to cumulate votes. If any one member has given this notice, all members may cumulate their votes for candidates in nomination.

(c) In any election of directors by cumulative voting, the candidates receiving the highest number of votes are elected, subject to any lawful provision specifying election by classes.

(d) In any election of directors not governed by subdivision (c), unless otherwise provided in the articles or bylaws, the candidates receiving the highest number of votes are elected.

(e) Elections for directors need not be by ballot unless a member demands election by ballot at the meeting and before the voting begins or unless the bylaws so require.

Ca. Corp. Code § 7615

Amended by Stats. 1984, Ch. 812, Sec. 10.

Section 7616 - Action to determine validity of election or appointment of director

(a) Upon the filing of an action therefor by any director or member or by any person who had the right to vote in the election at issue, the superior court of the proper county shall determine the validity of any election or appointment of any director of any corporation.

(b) In the case of a corporation holding assets in charitable trust, any person bringing an action under this section shall give notice of the action to the Attorney General, who may intervene.

(c) Upon the filing of the complaint, and before any further proceedings are had, the court shall enter an order fixing a date for the hearing, which shall be within five days unless for good cause shown a later date is fixed, and requiring notice of the date for the hearing and a copy of the complaint to be served upon the corporation and upon the person whose purported election or appointment is questioned and upon any person (other than the plaintiff) whom the plaintiff alleges to have been elected or appointed, in the manner in which a summons is required to be served, or, if the court so directs, by registered mail; and the court may make such further requirements as to notice as appear to be proper under the circumstances.

(d) The court, consistent with the provisions of this part and in conformity with the articles and bylaws to the extent feasible, may determine the person entitled to the office of director or may order a new election to be held or appointment to be made, may determine the validity, effectiveness and construction of voting agreements and voting trusts, the validity of the issuance of memberships and the right of persons to vote and may direct such other relief as may be just and proper.

Ca. Corp. Code § 7616
Added by Stats. 1978, Ch. 567.

Chapter 7 - MEMBERS' DERIVATIVE ACTIONS

Section 7710 - Members' derivative actions

(a) Subdivisions (c) through (f) notwithstanding, no motion to require a bond shall be granted in an action brought by 100 members or the authorized number (Section 5036), whichever is less.

(b) No action may be instituted or maintained in the right of any corporation by any member of such corporation unless both of the following conditions exist:

(1) The plaintiff alleges in the complaint that plaintiff was a member at the time of the transaction or any part thereof of which plaintiff complains, or that plaintiff's membership thereafter devolved upon plaintiff by operation of law from a holder who was a holder at the time of transaction or any part thereof complained of; and

(2) The plaintiff alleges in the complaint with particularity plaintiff's efforts to secure from the board such action as plaintiff desires, or the reasons for not making such effort, and alleges further that plaintiff has either informed the corporation or the board in writing of the ultimate facts of each cause of action against each defendant or delivered to the corporation or the board a true copy of the complaint which plaintiff proposes to file.

(c) Subject to subdivision (a), in any action referred to in subdivision (b), at any time within 30 days after service of summons upon the corporation or upon any defendant who is an officer or director of the corporation, or held such office at the time of the acts complained of, the corporation or such defendant may move the court for an order, upon notice and hearing, requiring the plaintiff to furnish a bond as hereinafter provided. The motion shall be based upon one or both of the following grounds:

(1) That there is no reasonable possibility that the prosecution of the cause of action alleged in the complaint against the moving party will benefit the corporation or its members economically or otherwise.

(2) That the moving party, if other than the corporation, did not participate in the transaction complained of in any capacity. The court on application of the corporation or any defendant may, for good cause shown, extend the 30-day period for an additional period or periods not exceeding 60 days.

(d) At the hearing upon any motion pursuant to subdivision (c), the court shall consider such evidence, written or oral, by witnesses or affidavit, as may be material (1) to the ground or grounds upon which the motion is based, or (2) to a determination of the probable reasonable expenses, including attorneys' fees, of the corporation and the moving party which will be incurred in the defense of the action. If the court determines, after hearing the evidence adduced by the parties, that the moving party has established a probability in support of any of the grounds upon which the motion is based, the court shall fix the amount of the bond, not to exceed fifty thousand dollars ($50,000), to be furnished by the plaintiff for reasonable expenses, including attorneys' fees, which may be incurred by the moving party and the corporation in connection with the action, including expenses for which the corporation may become liable pursuant to Section 7237. A ruling by the court on the motion shall not be a determination of any issue in the action or of the merits thereof. If the court, upon any such motion, makes a determination that a bond shall be furnished by the plaintiff as to any one or more defendants, the action shall be dismissed as to such defendant or defendants, unless the bond required by the court has been furnished within such reasonable time as may be fixed by the court.

(e) If the plaintiff shall, either before or after a motion is made pursuant to subdivision (c), or any order or determination pursuant to such motion, furnish a bond or bonds in the aggregate amount of fifty thousand dollars ($50,000) to secure the reasonable expenses of the parties entitled to make the motion, the plaintiff has complied with the requirements of this section and with any order for a bond theretofore made, and any such motion then pending shall be dismissed and no further or additional bond shall be required.

(f) If a motion is filed pursuant to subdivision (c), no pleadings need be filed by the corporation or any other defendant and the prosecution of the action shall be stayed until 10 days after the motion has been disposed of.

Ca. Corp. Code § 7710

Amended by Stats. 1982, Ch. 517, Sec. 189.

Chapter 8 - AMENDMENT OF ARTICLES

Section 7810 - Amendment of articles

(a) By complying with the provisions of this chapter, a corporation may amend its articles from time to time, in any and as many respects as may be desired, so long as its articles as amended contain only such provisions as it would be lawful to insert in original articles filed at the time of the filing of the amendment or as authorized by Section 7813.5 and, if a change in the rights of members or an exchange, reclassification or cancellation of memberships is to be made, such provisions as may be necessary to effect such change, exchange, reclassification or cancellation. It is the intent of the Legislature in adopting this section to exercise to the fullest extent the reserve power of the state over corporations and to authorize any amendment of the articles covered by the preceding sentence regardless of whether any provision contained in the amendment was permissible at the time of the original incorporation of the corporation.

(b) A corporation shall not amend its articles to add any statement or to alter any statement which may appear in the original articles of the initial street address and initial mailing address of the corporation, the names and addresses of the first directors, or the name and address of the initial agent, except to correct an error in the statement or to delete the information after the corporation has filed a statement under Section 8210.

Ca. Corp. Code § 7810

Amended by Stats 2012 ch 494 (SB 1532),s 19, eff. 1/1/2013.

Section 7811 - Adoption by incorporators

Any amendment of the articles may be adopted by a writing signed by a majority of the incorporators, so long as:

(a) No directors were named in the original articles;

(b) No directors have been elected; and

(c) The corporation has no members.

Ca. Corp. Code § 7811

Added by Stats. 1978, Ch. 567.

Section 7812 - Adoption by approval of board, members, and other persons

(a) Except as provided in this section or Section 7813, amendments may be adopted if approved by the board and approved by the members (Section 5034) and approved by such other person or persons, if any, as required by the articles. The approval by the members or other person or persons may be before or after the approval by the board.

(b) Notwithstanding subdivision (a), the following amendments may be adopted by approval of the board alone:

(1) An amendment extending the corporate existence or making the corporate existence perpetual, if the corporation was organized prior to August 14, 1929.

(2) An amendment deleting the initial street address and initial mailing address of the corporation, the names and addresses of the first directors, or the name and address of the initial agent.

(3) Any amendment, at a time the corporation has no members; provided, however, that if the articles require approval by any person for an amendment, an amendment may not be adopted without such approval.

(4) An amendment adopted pursuant to Section 9913.

(c) Whenever the articles require for corporate action the approval of a particular class of members or of a larger proportion of, or all of, the votes of any class, or of a larger proportion of, or all of, the directors, than is otherwise required by this part, the provision in the articles requiring such greater vote shall not be altered, amended or repealed except by such class or such greater vote, unless otherwise provided in the articles.

Ca. Corp. Code § 7812

Amended by Stats 2012 ch 494 (SB 1532),s 20, eff. 1/1/2013.

Section 7813 - Approval by members of class

An amendment must also be approved by the members (Section 5034) of a class, whether or not such class is entitled to vote thereon by the provisions of the articles or bylaws, if the amendment would:

(a) Materially and adversely affect the rights, privileges, preferences, restrictions or conditions of that class as to voting, dissolution, redemption or transfer in a manner different than such action affects another class;

(b) Materially and adversely affect such class as to voting, dissolution, redemption or transfer by changing the rights, privileges, preferences, restrictions or conditions of another class;

(c) Increase or decrease the number of memberships authorized for such class;

(d) Increase the number of memberships authorized for another class;

(e) Effect an exchange, reclassification or cancellation of all or part of the memberships of such class; or

(f) Authorize a new class of memberships.

Ca. Corp. Code § 7813

Amended by Stats. 1981, Ch. 587, Sec. 38.

Section 7813.5 - Mutual benefit corporation changing status to public benefit corporation, religious corporation, business corporation, or cooperative corporation

(a) A mutual benefit corporation may amend its articles to change its status to that of a public benefit corporation, a religious corporation, a business corporation, a social purpose corporation, or a cooperative corporation by complying with this section and the other sections of this chapter.

(b) Except as authorized by Section 7811 or unless the corporation has no members, an amendment to change its status to a public benefit corporation or religious corporation shall:

(1) be approved by the members (Section 5034), and the fairness of the amendment to the members shall be approved by the Commissioner of Financial Protection and Innovation pursuant to Section 25142;

(2) be approved by the members (Section 5034) in an election conducted by written ballot pursuant to Section 7513 in which no negative votes are cast; or

(3) be approved by 100 percent of the voting power.

(c) Amended articles authorized by this section shall include the provisions which would have been required (other than the initial street address and initial mailing address of the corporation and the name of the initial agent for service of process if a statement has been filed pursuant to Section 8210), and may in addition only include those provisions which would have been permitted, in original articles filed by the type of corporation (public benefit, religious, business, social purpose, or cooperative) into which the mutual benefit corporation is changing its status.

(d) At the time of filing a certificate of amendment to change status to a public benefit corporation, the Secretary of State shall make available the filed certificate to the Attorney General.

(e) In the case of a change of status to a business corporation, social purpose corporation, or a cooperative corporation, if the Franchise Tax Board has issued a determination exempting the corporation from tax as provided in Section 23701 of the Revenue and Taxation Code, the corporation shall be subject to Section 23221 of the Revenue and Taxation Code upon filing the certificate of amendment.

Ca. Corp. Code § 7813.5

Amended by Stats 2022 ch 617 (SB 1202),s 64, eff. 1/1/2023.
Amended by Stats 2022 ch 452 (SB 1498),s 55, eff. 1/1/2023.
Amended by Stats 2019 ch 143 (SB 251),s 28, eff. 1/1/2020.
Amended by Stats 2014 ch 694 (SB 1301),s 69, eff. 1/1/2015.
Amended by Stats 2012 ch 494 (SB 1532),s 21, eff. 1/1/2013.

Section 7814 - Certificate of amendment

(a) Except for amendments adopted by the incorporators pursuant to Section 7811, upon adoption of an amendment, the corporation shall file a certificate of amendment, which shall consist of an officers' certificate stating:

(1) The wording of the amendment or amended articles in accordance with Section 7816;

(2) That the amendment has been approved by the board;

(3) If the amendment is one for which the approval of the members (Section 5034) or the approval of 100 percent of the voting power is required, that the amendment was approved by the required vote of members; and

(4) If the amendment is one which may be adopted with approval by the board alone, a statement of the facts entitling the board alone to adopt the amendment.

(5) If the amendment is one for which the approval of a person or persons other than the incorporators, directors or members is required, that the approval of such person or persons has been obtained.

(b) In the event of an amendment of the articles pursuant to a merger, the filing of the officers' certificate and agreement pursuant to Section 8014 shall be in lieu of any filing required under this chapter.

Ca. Corp. Code § 7814

Amended by Stats. 1979, Ch. 724.

Section 7815 - Certificate of amendment signed by incorporators

In the case of amendments adopted by the incorporators under Section 7811, the corporation shall file a certificate of amendment signed and verified by a majority of the incorporators which shall state that the signers thereof constitute at least a majority of the incorporators, that directors were not named in the original articles and have not been elected, that the corporation has no members and that they adopt the amendment or amendments therein set forth.

Ca. Corp. Code § 7815

Amended by Stats. 1979, Ch. 724.

Section 7816 - Wording of amendment or amended articles

The certificate of amendment shall establish the wording of the amendment or amended articles by one or more of the following means:

(a) By stating that the articles shall be amended to read as therein set forth in full.

(b) By stating that any provision of the articles, which shall be identified by the numerical or other designation given it in the articles or by stating the wording thereof, shall be stricken from the articles or shall be amended to read as set forth in the certificate.

(c) By stating that the provisions set forth therein shall be added to the articles. If the purpose of the amendment is to reclassify, cancel, exchange, or otherwise change outstanding memberships the amended articles shall state the effect thereof on outstanding memberships.

Ca. Corp. Code § 7816

Added by Stats. 1978, Ch. 567.

Section 7817 - Amendment and change, reclassification, or cancellation of memberships effected

Upon the filing of the certificate of amendment, the articles shall be amended in accordance with the certificate and any change, reclassification or cancellation of memberships shall be effected, and a copy of the certificate, certified by the Secretary of State, is prima facie evidence of the performance of the conditions necessary to the adoption of the amendment.

Ca. Corp. Code § 7817

Added by Stats. 1978, Ch. 567.

Section 7818 - Extension of term of existence

A corporation formed for a limited period may at any time subsequent to the expiration of the term of its corporate existence, extend the term of its existence by an amendment to its articles removing any provision limiting the term of its existence and providing for perpetual existence. If the filing of the certificate of amendment providing for perpetual existence would be prohibited if it were original articles by the provisions of Section 7122, the Secretary of State shall not file such certificate unless, by the same or a concurrently filed certificate of amendment, the articles of such corporation are amended to adopt a new available name. For the purpose of the adoption of any such amendment, persons who have been functioning as directors of such corporation shall be considered to have been validly elected even though their election may have occurred after the expiration of the original term of the corporate existence.

Ca. Corp. Code § 7818
Added by Stats. 1978, Ch. 567.

Section 7819 - Restated articles of incorporation

(a) A corporation may restate in a single certificate the entire text of its articles as amended by filing an officers' certificate or, in circumstances where incorporators or the board may amend a corporation's articles pursuant to Sections 7811 and 7815, a certificate signed and verified by a majority of the incorporators or the board, as applicable, entitled "Restated Articles of Incorporation of (insert name of corporation)" which shall set forth the articles as amended to the date of filing of the certificate, except that the signatures and acknowledgments of the articles by the incorporators and any statements regarding the effect of any prior amendment upon memberships and any provisions of agreements of merger (other than amendments to the articles of the surviving corporation), and the initial street address and initial mailing address of the corporation, and the names and addresses of the first directors and of the initial agent for service of process shall be omitted (except that the initial street address and initial mailing address of the corporation and the names and addresses of the initial agent for service of process and, if previously set forth in the articles, the initial directors, shall not be omitted prior to the time that the corporation has filed a statement under Section 8210). Such omissions are not alterations or amendments of the articles. The certificate may also itself alter or amend the articles in any respect, in which case the certificate must comply with Section 7814 or 7815, as the case may be, and Section 7816.
(b) If the certificate does not itself alter or amend the articles in any respect, it shall be approved by the board or, prior to the issuance of any memberships and the naming and election of directors, by a majority of the incorporators, and shall be subject to the provisions of this chapter relating to an amendment of the articles not requiring approval of the members (Section 5034). If the certificate does itself alter or

amend the articles, it shall be subject to the provisions of this chapter relating to the amendment or amendments so made.

(c) Restated articles of incorporation filed pursuant to this section shall supersede for all purposes the original articles and all amendments filed prior thereto.

Ca. Corp. Code § 7819

Amended by Stats 2012 ch 494 (SB 1532),s 22, eff. 1/1/2013.

Section 7820 - Amendment of articles of corporation holding property in charitable trust

(a) Amendment of the articles of a corporation holding property in charitable trust, pursuant to this chapter, does not, of itself, abrogate any requirement or limitation imposed upon the corporation, or any property held by it, by virtue of the trust under which such property is held by the corporation.

(b) The Attorney General may, at the corporation's request, and pursuant to such regulations as the Attorney General may issue, give rulings as to whether the Attorney General will or may oppose a proposed action, or article amendment, as inconsistent with or proscribed by the requirements of a charitable trust.

Ca. Corp. Code § 7820

Added by Stats. 1978, Ch. 567.

Chapter 9 - SALES OF ASSETS

Section 7910 - Mortgage, deed of trust, pledge, or other hypothecation of corporation's property

Any mortgage, deed of trust, pledge or other hypothecation of all or any part of the corporation's property, real or personal, for the purpose of securing the payment or performance of any contract or obligation may be approved by the board. Unless the articles or bylaws otherwise provide, no approval of the members (Section 5034) shall be necessary for such action.

Ca. Corp. Code § 7910

Added by Stats. 1978, Ch. 567.

Section 7911 - Sale or other disposal of assets

(a) Subject to the provisions of Section 7142, a corporation may sell, lease, convey, exchange, transfer or otherwise dispose of all or substantially all of its assets when the principal terms are:

(1) Approved by the board; and

(2) Unless the transaction is in the usual and regular course of its activities, approved by the members (Section 5034), either before or after approval by the board

and before or after the transaction.

(b) Notwithstanding approval by the members (Section 5034), the board may abandon the proposed transaction without further action by the members, subject to the contractual rights, if any, of third parties.

(c) Subject to the provisions of Section 7142, such sale, lease, conveyance, exchange, transfer or other disposition may be made upon such terms and conditions and for such consideration as the board may deem in the best interests of the corporation. The consideration may be money, property, or securities of any domestic corporation, foreign corporation, or foreign business corporation or any of them.

Ca. Corp. Code § 7911
Amended by Stats. 1981, Ch. 587, Sec. 39.

Section 7912 - Certificated annexed to deed or instrument conveying or otherwise transferring assets

Any deed or instrument conveying or otherwise transferring any assets of a corporation may have annexed to it the certificate of the secretary or an assistant secretary of the corporation, setting forth that the transaction has been validly approved by the board and (a) stating that the property described in such deed or instrument is less than substantially all of the assets of the corporation or that the transfer is in the usual and regular course of the business of the corporation, if such be the case, or (b) if such property constitutes all or substantially all of the assets of the corporation and the transfer is not in the usual and regular course of the business of the corporation, stating the fact of approval thereof by the members (Section 5034) or all the members pursuant to this chapter. Such certificate is prima facie evidence of the existence of the facts authorizing such conveyance or other transfer of the assets and conclusive evidence in favor of any purchaser or encumbrancer for value who, without notice of any trust restriction applicable to the property or any failure to comply therewith, in good faith parted with value.

Ca. Corp. Code § 7912
Added by Stats. 1978, Ch. 567.

Section 7913 - Notice to attorney general

A corporation holding assets in charitable trust must give written notice to the Attorney General 20 days before it sells, leases, conveys, exchanges, transfers or otherwise disposes of any or all of the assets held in trust unless the Attorney General has given the corporation a written waiver of this section as to the proposed transaction.

Ca. Corp. Code § 7913
Added by Stats. 1978, Ch. 567.

Section 7914 - Applicable statutes

The provisions of Article 2 (commencing with Section 5914) of Chapter 9 of Part 2 apply to mutual benefit corporations to the extent provided therein.

   Ca. Corp. Code § 7914
Added by Stats 2011 ch 442 (AB 1211),s 17, eff. 1/1/2012.

Chapter 10 - MERGERS

Article 1 - MERGER

Section 8010 - Merger

A mutual benefit corporation may merge with any domestic corporation, foreign corporation, foreign business corporation, or other business entity (Section 5063.5). However, a merger with a public benefit corporation, or a religious corporation, or an unincorporated association, the governing documents of which provide that its assets are irrevocably dedicated to charitable, religious, or public purposes, must have the prior written consent of the Attorney General.

   Ca. Corp. Code § 8010
Amended by Stats 2011 ch 442 (AB 1211),s 18, eff. 1/1/2012.
Amended September 21, 1999 (Bill Number: AB 198) (Chapter 437).

Section 8011 - Agreement of merger

The board of each corporation that desires to merge shall approve an agreement of merger. The constituent corporations shall be parties to the agreement of merger and other persons may be parties to the agreement of merger. The agreement shall state all of the following:

(a) The terms and conditions of the merger.

(b) The amendments, subject to Sections 7810 and 7816, to the articles of the surviving corporation to be effected by the merger, if any; if any amendment changes the name of the surviving corporation, the new name may be the same as or similar to the name of a disappearing corporation, subject to subdivision (c) of Section 7122.

(c) The amendments to the bylaws of the surviving corporation to be effected by the merger, if any.

(d) The name and place of incorporation of each constituent corporation and which of the constituent corporations is the surviving corporation.

(e) The manner, if any, of converting memberships or securities of the constituent corporations into memberships or securities of the surviving corporation and, if any memberships or securities of any of the constituent corporations are not to be converted solely into memberships or securities of the surviving corporation, the cash, property, rights or securities of any corporation that the holders of those memberships or securities are to receive in exchange for the memberships or securities, which cash, property, rights or securities of any corporation may be in addition to or in lieu of memberships or securities of the surviving corporation, or that the memberships are to be canceled without consideration.

(f) Other details or provisions as are desired, if any, including, without limitation, if not prohibited by this chapter, a provision for the payment of cash in lieu of fractional memberships or for any other arrangement with respect thereto.

Ca. Corp. Code § 8011

Amended 9/21/1999 (Bill Number: AB 1687) (Chapter 453).

Section 8011.5 - Treatment of each membership of same class of constituent corporation

Each membership of the same class of any constituent corporation (other than the cancellation of memberships held by a surviving corporation or its parent or a wholly owned subsidiary of either in a constituent corporation) shall be treated equally with respect to any distribution of cash, property, rights or securities unless:

(a) all members of the class consent or

(b) the Commissioner of Financial Protection and Innovation has approved the terms and conditions of the transaction and the fairness of the terms pursuant to Section 25142.

Ca. Corp. Code § 8011.5

Amended by Stats 2022 ch 452 (SB 1498),s 56, eff. 1/1/2023.

Amended by Stats 2019 ch 143 (SB 251),s 29, eff. 1/1/2020.

Section 8012 - Approval of principal terms of merger

The principal terms of the merger shall be approved by the members (Section 5034) of each class of each constituent corporation and by each other person or persons whose approval of an amendment of articles is required by the articles; and the approval by the members (Section 5034) or such other person or persons required by this section may be given before or after the approval by the board.

Ca. Corp. Code § 8012

Amended by Stats. 1981, Ch. 587, Sec. 41.

Section 8013 - Signing agreement

Each constituent corporation shall sign the agreement by the chairperson of its board, president or a vice president, and secretary or an assistant secretary acting on behalf of their respective corporations.

Ca. Corp. Code § 8013

Amended by Stats 2022 ch 617 (SB 1202),s 65, eff. 1/1/2023.

Added by Stats. 1978, Ch. 567.

Section 8014 - Filing agreement of merger

After approval of a merger by the board and any approval by the members (Section

5034) required by Section 8012, the surviving corporation shall file a copy of the agreement of merger with an officers' certificate of each constituent corporation attached stating the total number of memberships of each class entitled to vote on the merger, identifying any other person or persons whose approval is required, and that the principal terms of the agreement in the form attached were duly approved by the required vote of the members and, if applicable, any other person or persons. The merger and any amendment of the articles of the surviving corporation contained in the merger agreement shall thereupon be effective (subject to subdivision (c) of Section 5008 and subject to the provisions of Section 8018) and the several parties thereto shall be one corporation. The Secretary of State may certify a copy of the merger agreement separate from the officers' certificates attached thereto.

Ca. Corp. Code § 8014
Amended by Stats 2006 ch 773 (AB 2341),s 22, eff. 9/29/2006.

Section 8015 - Amendment to agreement

(a) Any amendment to the agreement may be adopted and the agreement so amended may be approved by the board and, if it changes any of the principal terms of the agreement, by the members (Section 5034) or other person or persons, as required by Section 8012, of any constituent corporation in the same manner as the original agreement.

(b) If the agreement so amended is approved as provided in subdivision (a), the agreement so amended shall then constitute the agreement of merger.

Ca. Corp. Code § 8015
Amended by Stats. 1981, Ch. 587, Sec. 42.

Section 8016 - Abandonment of merger

The board may, in its discretion, abandon a merger, subject to the contractual rights, if any, of third parties, including other constituent corporations, without further approval by the members (Section 5034) or other persons entitled to approve the merger at any time before the merger is effective.

Ca. Corp. Code § 8016
Amended by Stats. 1982, Ch. 662, Sec. 18.

Section 8017 - Certified copy of agreement of merger

A copy of an agreement of merger certified on or after the effective date by an official having custody thereof has the same force in evidence as the original and, except as against the state, is conclusive evidence of the performance of all conditions precedent to the merger, the existence on the effective date of the surviving corporation and the performance of the conditions necessary to the adoption of any amendment to the articles contained in the agreement of merger.

Ca. Corp. Code § 8017
Added by Stats. 1978, Ch. 567.

Section 8018 - Merger of corporations with foreign corporations

(a) Subject to the provisions of Section 8010, the merger of any number of corporations with any number of foreign corporations, foreign business corporations or domestic corporations may be effected if the foreign corporations are authorized by the laws under which they are formed to effect the merger. The surviving corporation may be any one of the constituent corporations and shall continue to exist under the laws of the state or place of its incorporation.

(b) If the surviving corporation is a mutual benefit corporation, the merger proceedings with respect to that corporation and any domestic disappearing corporation shall conform to the provisions of this chapter and other applicable laws of this state, but if the surviving corporation is a foreign corporation, then, subject to the requirements of subdivision (d) and Section 8012 the merger proceedings may be in accordance with the laws of the state or place of incorporation of the surviving corporation.

(c) If the surviving corporation is a mutual benefit corporation, the agreement and the officers' certificate of each constituent corporation shall be filed as provided in Section 8014 and thereupon, subject to subdivision (c) of Section 5008, the merger shall be effective as to each corporation; and each foreign disappearing corporation that is qualified for the transaction of intrastate business shall, by virtue of the filing, automatically surrender its right to transact intrastate business.

(d) If the surviving corporation is a foreign corporation, or foreign business corporation, the merger shall become effective in accordance with the law of the jurisdiction in which it is organized, but shall be effective as to any disappearing corporation as of the time of effectiveness in the foreign jurisdiction upon the filing in this state as required by this subdivision. There shall be filed as to the domestic disappearing corporation or corporations the documents described in any one of the following paragraphs:

(1) A copy of the agreement, certificate, or other document filed by the surviving foreign corporation in the state or place of its incorporation for the purpose of effecting the merger, which copy shall be certified by the public officer having official custody of the original.

(2) An executed counterpart of the agreement, certificate, or other document filed by the surviving corporation in the state or place of its incorporation for the purpose of effecting the merger.

(3) A copy of the agreement of merger with an officers' certificate of the surviving foreign corporation and of each constituent domestic corporation attached, which officers' certificates shall conform to the requirements of Section 8014.

(e) If the date of the filing in this state pursuant to subdivision (d) is more than six months after the time of the effectiveness in the foreign jurisdiction, or if the powers of the domestic corporation are suspended at the time of effectiveness in the foreign jurisdiction, the merger shall be effective as to the domestic disappearing corporation or corporations as of the date of filing in this state. Each foreign disappearing corporation that is qualified for the transaction of intrastate business shall automatically by the filing pursuant to subdivision (d) surrender its right to transact intrastate business as of the date of filing in this state regardless of the time of effectiveness as to a domestic disappearing corporation.

Ca. Corp. Code § 8018

Amended by Stats 2006 ch 773 (AB 2341),s 23, eff. 9/29/2006.
Amended September 21, 1999 (Bill Number: AB 1687) (Chapter 453).

Section 8019 - Agreement of merger between nonprofit corporation and business corporation

If an agreement of merger is entered into between a nonprofit corporation and a business corporation:

(a) Sections 6011, 6012, 6014, and 6015 shall apply to any constituent public benefit corporation;

(b) Sections 8011, 8011.5, 8012, 8014, and 8015 shall apply to any constituent mutual benefit corporation;

(c) Sections 6014 and 6015 and subdivisions (c) and

(d) of Section 9640 shall apply to any constituent religious corporation; and (d) Sections 1101, 1101.1, 1103, and 1104 shall apply to any constituent business corporation.

Ca. Corp. Code § 8019

Amended by Stats. 1981, Ch. 587, Sec. 44.

Section 8019.1 - Merger of corporations with other business entities

(a) Subject to the provisions of Section 8010, any one or more corporations may merge with one or more other business entities (Section 5063.5). One or more other domestic corporations, foreign corporations (Section 5053), and foreign business corporations (Section 5052) may be parties to the merger. Notwithstanding the provisions of this section, such a merger may be effected only if:

(1) In a merger in which a domestic corporation or domestic other business entity is a party, it is authorized by the laws under which it is organized to effect the merger.

(2) In a merger in which a foreign corporation or foreign business corporation is a party, it is authorized by the laws under which it is organized to effect the merger.

(3) In a merger in which a foreign other business entity is a party, it is authorized by the laws under which it is organized to effect the merger.

(b) Each corporation and each other party which desires to merge shall approve an agreement of merger. The board and the members (Section 5034) of each corporation which desires to merge, and each other person or persons, if any, whose approval of an amendment of the articles of that corporation is required by the articles or bylaws shall approve the agreement of merger. The agreement of merger shall be approved on behalf of each other constituent party by those persons authorized or required to approve the merger by the laws under which it is organized. The parties desiring to merge shall be parties to the agreement of merger and other persons, including a parent party (Section 5064.5), may be parties to the agreement of merger. The agreement of merger shall state all of the following:

(1) The terms and conditions of the merger.

(2) The name and place of incorporation or organization of each party and the identity of the surviving party.

(3) The amendments, if any, subject to Sections 7810 and 7816, to the articles of the surviving corporation, if applicable, to be effected by the merger. The name of the surviving corporation may be, subject to subdivisions (b) and (c) of Section 7122, the same as or similar to the name of a disappearing party to the merger.

(4) The manner, if any, of converting the memberships or securities of each of the constituent corporations into shares, memberships, interests, or other securities of the surviving party; and, if any memberships or securities of any of the constituent corporations are not to be converted solely into shares, memberships, interests, or other securities of the surviving party, cash, rights, securities, or other property which the holders of those memberships or securities are to receive in exchange for the memberships or securities, which cash, rights, securities, or other property may be in addition to or in lieu of shares, memberships, interests, or other securities of the surviving party.

(5) Any other details or provisions required by the laws under which any party to the merger is organized, including, if an unincorporated association is a party to the merger, Section 18370, or if a domestic limited partnership is a party to the merger, subdivision (a) of Section 15911.12, or, if a domestic general partnership is a party to the merger, subdivision (a) of Section 16911, or, if a domestic limited liability company is a party to the merger, subdivision (a) of Section 17710.12.

(6) Any other details or provisions as are desired.

(c) Each membership of the same class of any constituent corporation (other than the cancellation of memberships held by a party to the merger or its parent or a wholly owned subsidiary of either in another constituent corporation) shall be treated equally with respect to any distribution of cash, property, rights, or securities unless (i) all members of the class consent or (ii) the commissioner has approved the terms and conditions of the transaction and the fairness of those terms pursuant to Section 25142.

(d) Notwithstanding its prior approval, an agreement of merger may be amended prior to the filing of the agreement of merger if the amendment is approved by each constituent corporation in the same manner as the original agreement of merger. If the agreement of merger as so amended and approved is also approved by each of the other parties to the agreement of merger, as so amended it shall then constitute the agreement of merger.

(e) The board of a constituent corporation may, in its discretion, abandon a merger, subject to the contractual rights, if any, of third parties, including other parties to the agreement of merger, without further approval by the members (Section 5034) or other persons, at any time before the merger is effective.

(f) Each constituent corporation shall sign the agreement of merger by its chairperson of the board, president, or a vice president and also by its secretary or an assistant secretary acting on behalf of their respective corporations.

(g) After required approvals of the merger by each constituent corporation and each other party to the merger, the surviving party shall file a copy of the agreement of merger with an officers' certificate of each constituent domestic corporation, foreign corporation, and foreign business corporation attached stating the total number of outstanding shares or membership interests of each class entitled to vote on the merger (and identifying any other person or persons whose approval is required), that the agreement of merger in the form attached or its principal terms, as required, were approved by that corporation by a vote of a number of shares or membership interests of each class which equaled or exceeded the vote required, specifying each class entitled to vote required of each class, and, if applicable, by such other person or persons whose approval is required. If equity securities of a parent party (Section 5064.5) are to be issued in the merger, the officers' certificate or certificate of merger of the controlled party shall state either that no vote of the shareholders of the parent party was required or that the required vote was obtained. The merger and any amendment of the articles of the surviving corporation, if applicable, contained in the agreement of merger shall be effective upon the filing of the agreement of merger, subject to the provisions of subdivision (i). If a domestic reciprocal insurer organized after 1974 to provide medical malpractice insurance is a party to the merger, the agreement of merger or certificate of merger shall not be filed until there has been filed the certificate issued by the Insurance Commissioner approving the merger pursuant to Section 1555 of the Insurance Code.

In lieu of an officers' certificate, a certificate of merger, on a form prescribed by the Secretary of State, shall be filed for each constituent other business entity. The certificate of merger shall be executed and acknowledged by each domestic constituent limited liability company by all of the managers of the limited liability company (unless a lesser number is specified in its articles of organization or operating agreement) and by each domestic constituent limited partnership by all general partners (unless a lesser number is provided in its certificate of limited partnership or partnership agreement) and by each domestic constituent general partnership by two partners (unless a lesser number is provided in its partnership agreement) and by each foreign constituent limited liability company by one or more managers and by each foreign constituent general partnership or foreign constituent limited partnership by one or more general partners, and by each constituent reciprocal insurer by the chairperson of the board, president, or vice president, and by the secretary or assistant secretary, or, if a constituent reciprocal insurer has not appointed such officers, by the chairperson of the board, president, or vice president, and by the secretary or assistant secretary of the constituent reciprocal insurer's attorney-in-fact, and by each other party to the merger by those persons required or authorized to execute the certificate of merger by the laws under which that party is organized, specifying for such party the provision of law or other basis for the authority of the signing persons.

The certificate of merger shall set forth, if a vote of the shareholders, members, partners, or other holders of interests of a constituent other business entity was required, a statement setting forth the total number of outstanding interests of each class entitled to vote on the merger and that the principal terms of the agreement of merger were approved by a vote of the number of interests of each class which equaled or exceeded the vote required, specifying each class entitled to vote and the percentage vote required of each class, and any other information required to be set forth under the laws under which the constituent other business entity is organized, including, if a domestic limited partnership is a party to the merger, subdivision (a) of Section 15911.14, if a domestic general partnership is a party to the merger, subdivision (b) of Section 16915 and, if a domestic limited liability company is a party to the merger, subdivision (a) of Section 17710.14. The certificate of merger for each constituent foreign other business entity, if any, shall also set forth the statutory or other basis under which that foreign other business entity is authorized by the laws under which it is organized to effect the merger.

The Secretary of State may certify a copy of the agreement of merger separate from the officers' certificates and certificates of merger attached thereto.

(h) A copy of an agreement of merger certified on or after the effective date by an official having custody thereof has the same force in evidence as the original and, except as against the state, is conclusive evidence of the performance of all conditions precedent to the merger, the existence on the effective date of the surviving party to the merger, the performance of the conditions necessary to the adoption of any amendment to the articles, if applicable, contained in the agreement of merger, and of the merger of the constituent corporations, either by themselves or together with other constituent parties, into the surviving party to the merger.

(i)

(1) The merger of domestic corporations with foreign corporations or foreign other business entities in a merger in which one or more other business entities is a party shall comply with subdivisions (a) and (g) and this subdivision.

(2) Subject to subdivision (c) of Section 5008 and paragraph (3), the merger shall be effective as to each domestic constituent corporation and domestic constituent other business entity upon filing of the agreement of merger with attachments as provided in subdivision (g).

(3) If the surviving party is a foreign corporation or foreign business corporation or foreign other business entity, except as provided in paragraph (4), the merger shall be effective as to any domestic disappearing corporation as of the time of effectiveness in the foreign jurisdiction upon the filing in this state of a copy of the agreement of merger with an officers' certificate of the surviving foreign corporation or foreign business corporation and of each constituent foreign and domestic corporation and a certificate of merger of each constituent other business entity attached, which officers' certificates and certificates of merger shall conform to the requirements of subdivision (g). If one or more domestic other business entities is a disappearing party in a merger pursuant to this subdivision in which a foreign other business entity is the surviving entity, a certificate of merger required by the laws under which each domestic other business entity is organized, including subdivision (a) of Section 15911.14, subdivision (b) of Section 16915, or subdivision (a) of Section 17710.14, if applicable, shall also be filed at the same time as the filing of the agreement of merger.

(4) If the date of the filing in this state pursuant to this subdivision is more than six months after the time of the effectiveness in the foreign jurisdiction, or if the powers of a domestic disappearing corporation are suspended at the time of effectiveness in the foreign jurisdiction, the merger shall be effective as to the domestic disappearing corporation as of the date of filing in this state.

(5) Each foreign disappearing corporation that is qualified for the transaction of intrastate business shall automatically by the filing pursuant to subdivision (g) surrender its right to transact intrastate business as of the date of filing in this state or, if later, the effective date of the merger. With respect to each foreign disappearing other business entity previously registered for the transaction of intrastate business in this state, the filing of the agreement of merger pursuant to subdivision (g) automatically has the effect of a cancellation of registration for that foreign other business entity as of the date of filing in this state or, if later, the effective date of the merger, without the necessity of the filing of a certificate of cancellation.

Ca. Corp. Code § 8019.1

Amended by Stats 2012 ch 419 (SB 323),s 12, eff. 1/1/2013, op. 1/1/2014.
Amended by Stats 2011 ch 442 (AB 1211),s 19, eff. 1/1/2012.
Amended by Stats 2006 ch 773 (AB 2341),s 24.5, eff. 9/29/2006.
Amended by Stats 2006 ch 495 (AB 339),s 13, eff. 1/1/2007.
Amended by Stats 2006 ch 773 (AB 2341),s 24, eff. 9/29/2006.
Added September 21, 1999 (Bill Number: AB 198) (Chapter 437).

Article 2 - EFFECT OF MERGER

Section 8020 - Effect of merger

(a) Upon merger pursuant to this chapter the separate existences of the disappearing parties to the merger cease and the surviving party to the merger shall succeed, without other transfer, to all the rights and property of each of the disappearing parties to the merger and shall be subject to all the debts and liabilities of each and trust obligations upon the property of a disappearing party in the same manner as if incurred by the surviving party to the merger.

(b) All rights of creditors and all liens and trusts upon or arising from the property of each of the constituent corporations and other parties to the merger shall be preserved unimpaired, provided that the liens and trust obligations upon property of a disappearing party shall be limited to the property affected thereby immediately prior to the time the merger is effective.

(c) Any action or proceeding pending by or against any disappearing corporation or other party to the merger may be prosecuted to judgment, which shall bind the surviving party to the merger, or the surviving party to the merger may be proceeded against or substituted in its place.

Ca. Corp. Code § 8020
Amended 9/21/1999 (Bill Number: AB 198) (Chapter 437).

Section 8020.5 - Assumption of liability

(a) Upon merger pursuant to this chapter, a surviving domestic or foreign corporation or other business entity shall be deemed to have assumed the liability of each disappearing domestic or foreign corporation or other business entity that is taxed under Part 10 (commencing with Section 17001) of, or under Part 11 (commencing with Section 23001) of, Division 2 of the Revenue and Taxation Code for the following:

(1) To prepare and file, or to cause to be prepared and filed, tax and information returns otherwise required of that disappearing entity as specified in Chapter 2 (commencing with Section 18501) of Part 10.2 of Division 2 of the Revenue and Taxation Code.

(2) To pay any tax liability determined to be due.

(b) If the surviving entity is a domestic limited liability company, domestic corporation, or registered limited liability partnership or a foreign limited liability company, foreign limited liability partnership, or foreign corporation that is registered or qualified to do business in California, the Secretary of State shall notify the Franchise Tax Board of the merger.

Ca. Corp. Code § 8020.5
Amended by Stats 2006 ch 495 (AB 339),s 14, eff. 1/1/2007.

Amended by Stats 2006 ch 773 (AB 2341),s 25, eff. 9/29/2006.
Added by Stats 2005 ch 286 (AB 241),s 3, eff. 1/1/2006.

Section 8021 - Real property

Whenever a domestic or foreign or foreign business corporation or other business entity (Section 5063.5) having any real property in this state merges with another domestic or foreign or foreign business corporation or other business entity pursuant to the laws of this state or of the state or place in which any constituent party to the merger was organized, and the laws of the state or place of organization (including this state) of any disappearing party to the merger provide substantially that the making and filing of the agreement of merger vests in the surviving party to the merger all the real property of any disappearing party to the merger, the filing for record in the office of the county recorder of any county in this state in which any of the real property of the disappearing party to the merger is located of either (a) a certificate prescribed by the Secretary of State, or (b) a copy of the agreement of merger or certificate of merger, certified by the Secretary of State or an authorized public official of the state or place pursuant to the laws of which the merger is effected, shall evidence record ownership in the surviving party to the merger of all interest of such disappearing party to the merger in and to the real property located in that county.

Ca. Corp. Code § 8021
Amended 9/21/1999 (Bill Number: AB 198) (Chapter 437).

Section 8022 - Bequest, devise, gift, grant, or promise contained in will or other instrument of donation, subscription, or conveyance

Any bequest, devise, gift, grant, or promise contained in a will or other instrument of donation, subscription, or conveyance, which is made to a constituent corporation and which takes effect or remains payable after the merger, inures to the surviving party to the merger.

Ca. Corp. Code § 8022
Amended 9/21/1999 (Bill Number: AB 198) (Chapter 437).

Chapter 11 - BANKRUPTCY REORGANIZATIONS AND ARRANGEMENTS

Section 8110 - Law governing reorganizations of corporations

Any proceeding, initiated with respect to a corporation, under any applicable statute of the United States, as now existing or hereafter enacted, relating to reorganizations of corporations, shall be governed by the provisions of Chapter 14 (commencing with Section 1400) of Division 1 of Title 1, and for this purpose the reference in Chapter 14 to "shareholders" shall be deemed to be a reference to members and the reference to "this division" shall be deemed to be a reference to this part.

Ca. Corp. Code § 8110
Amended by Stats 2009 ch 500 (AB 1059),s 21, eff. 1/1/2010.

Chapter 12 - REQUIRED FILINGS BY CORPORATION OR ITS AGENT

Section 8210 - Statement

(a) Every corporation shall, within 90 days after the filing of its original articles and biennially thereafter during the applicable filing period, file, on a form prescribed by the Secretary of State, a statement containing:

(1) the name of the corporation and the Secretary of State's file number;

(2) the names and complete business or residence addresses of its chief executive officer, secretary, and chief financial officer;

(3) the street address of its principal office in California, if any;

(4) the mailing address of the corporation, if different from the street address of its principal office or if the corporation has no principal office address in California and

(5) if the corporation chooses to receive renewal notices and any other notifications from the Secretary of State by electronic mail instead of by United States mail, a valid electronic mail address for the corporation or for the corporation's designee to receive those notices.

(b) The statement required by subdivision (a) shall also designate, as the agent of the corporation for the purpose of service of process, a natural person residing in this state or any domestic or foreign or foreign business corporation that has complied with Section 1505 and whose capacity to act as an agent has not terminated. If a natural person is designated, the statement shall set forth the person's complete business or residence street address. If a corporate agent is designated, no address for it shall be set forth.

(c) For the purposes of this section, the applicable filing period for a corporation shall be the calendar month during which its original articles were filed and the immediately preceding five calendar months. The Secretary of State shall provide a notice to each corporation to comply with this section approximately three months before the close of the applicable filing period. The notice shall state the due date for compliance and shall be sent to the last address of the corporation according to the records of the Secretary of State or to the last electronic mail address according to the records of the Secretary of State if the corporation has elected to receive notices from the Secretary of State by electronic mail. Neither the failure of the Secretary of State to send the notice nor the failure of the corporation to receive it is an excuse for failure to comply with this section.

(d) Whenever any of the information required by subdivision (a) is changed, the corporation may file a current statement containing all the information required by subdivisions (a) and (b). In order to change its agent for service of process or the address of the agent, the corporation must file a current statement containing all the information required by subdivisions (a) and (b). Whenever any statement is filed pursuant to this section, it supersedes any previously filed statement and the statement in the articles as to the agent for service of process and the address of the agent.

(e) The Secretary of State may destroy or otherwise dispose of any statement filed pursuant to this section after it has been superseded by the filing of a new statement.

(f) This section does not place any person dealing with the corporation on notice of, or under any duty to inquire about, the existence or content of a statement filed pursuant to this section.

 Ca. Corp. Code § 8210

Amended by Stats 2022 ch 617 (SB 1202),s 66, eff. 1/1/2023.
Amended by Stats 2012 ch 162 (SB 1171),s 21, eff. 1/1/2013.
Amended by Stats 2011 ch 204 (AB 657),s 9, eff. 1/1/2012.
Amended by Stats 2009 ch 140 (AB 1164),s 40, eff. 1/1/2010.
Amended by Stats 2007 ch 101 (SB 998),s 4, eff. 1/1/2008.
Amended October 10, 1999 (Bill Number: SB 284) (Chapter 1000).

Section 8211 - Resignation of agent

(a) An agent designated for service of process pursuant to Section 8210 may deliver to the Secretary of State, on a form prescribed by the Secretary of State for filing, a signed and acknowledged written statement of resignation as an agent for service of process containing the name of the corporation, the Secretary of State's file number of the corporation, the name of the resigning agent for service of process, and a statement that the agent is resigning. Thereupon the authority of the agent to act in that capacity shall cease and the Secretary of State forthwith shall mail or otherwise provide written notice of the filing of the statement of resignation to the corporation at its principal office.

(b) The resignation of an agent may be effective if, on a form prescribed by the Secretary of State containing the name of the corporation, the Secretary of State's file number for the corporation, and the name of the agent for service of process, the agent disclaims having been properly appointed as the agent. Similarly, a person named as an officer or director may indicate that the person was never properly appointed as the officer or director.

(c) The Secretary of State may destroy or otherwise dispose of any statement of resignation filed pursuant to this section after a new form is filed pursuant to Section 8210 replacing the agent for service of process that has resigned.

 Ca. Corp. Code § 8211

Amended by Stats 2014 ch 834 (SB 1041),s 15, eff. 1/1/2015.
Amended September 21, 1999 (Bill Number: AB 1687) (Chapter 453).

Section 8212 - Designation of new agent

If a natural person who has been designated agent for service of process pursuant to Section 8210 dies or resigns or no longer resides in the state or if the corporate agent for such purpose resigns, dissolves, withdraws from the state, forfeits its right to transact intrastate business, has its corporate rights, powers and privileges suspended or ceases to exist, the corporation shall forthwith file a designation of a new agent conforming to the requirements of Section 8210.

Ca. Corp. Code § 8212
Added by Stats. 1978, Ch. 567.

Section 8214 - Availability of business records to assessor

Upon request of an assessor, a corporation owning, claiming, possessing or controlling property in this state subject to local assessment shall make available at the corporation's principal office in California or at a place mutually acceptable to the assessor and the corporation a true copy of business records relevant to the amount, cost and value of all property that it owns, claims, possesses or controls within the county.

Ca. Corp. Code § 8214
Amended by Stats. 1979, Ch. 724.

Section 8215 - Joint and several liability of officers, directors, employees or agents

Any officers, directors, employees or agents of a corporation who do any of the following are liable jointly and severally for all the damages resulting therefrom to the corporation or any person injured thereby who relied thereupon or to both:

(a) Make, issue, deliver or publish any prospectus, report, circular, certificate, financial statement, balance sheet, public notice or document respecting the corporation or its memberships, assets, liabilities, capital, dividends, business, earnings or accounts which is false in any material respect, knowing it to be false, or participate in the making, issuance, delivery or publication thereof with knowledge that the same is false in a material respect.

(b) Make or cause to be made in the books, minutes, records or accounts of a corporation any entry which is false in any material particular knowing such entry is false.

(c) Remove, erase, alter or cancel any entry in any books or records of the corporation, with intent to deceive.

Ca. Corp. Code § 8215
Added by Stats. 1978, Ch. 567.

Section 8216 - Action by attorney general

(a) The Attorney General, upon complaint of a member, director or officer, that a corporation is failing to comply with the provisions of this chapter, Chapter 5 (commencing with Section 7510), Chapter 6 (commencing with Section 7610) or Chapter 13 (commencing with Section 8310), may, in the name of the people of the State of California, send to the principal office of such corporation, (or, if there is no such office, to the office or residence of the chief executive officer or secretary, of the corporation, as set forth in the most recent statement filed pursuant to Section 8210) notice of the complaint. If the answer is not satisfactory, or if there is no answer within 30 days, the Attorney General may institute, maintain or intervene in such suits, actions, or proceedings of any type in any court or tribunal of competent jurisdiction or before any administrative agency for such relief by way of injunction, the dissolution of entities, the appointment of receivers or any other temporary, preliminary, provisional or final remedies as may be appropriate to protect the rights of members or to undo the consequences of failure to comply with such requirements. In any such action, suit or proceeding there may be joined as parties all persons and entities responsible for or affected by such activity.

(b) In the case of a corporation where the action concerns assets held in charitable trust, the Attorney General may bring an action under subdivision (a) without having received a complaint, and without first giving notice of a complaint.

   Ca. Corp. Code § 8216
Added by Stats. 1978, Ch. 567.

Section 8217 - Corporation formed for sole purpose of operating single ridesharing vanpool vehicle

(a) No corporation formed under this part for the sole purpose of operating a single ridesharing vanpool vehicle designed for transporting at least seven persons, including the driver, under an arrangement in which ridesharing is incidental to another purpose of the driver shall be subject to the payment of any fee under provisions of the Government Code for any filing required by this part.

(b) For purposes of this section, "ridesharing" shall have the meaning specified in Section 522 of the Vehicle Code.

   Ca. Corp. Code § 8217
Amended by Stats. 1984, Ch. 1563, Sec. 1. Effective September 30, 1984.

Chapter 13 - RECORDS, REPORTS, AND RIGHTS OF INSPECTION

Article 1 - GENERAL PROVISIONS

Section 8310 - Record available in written form

If any record subject to inspection pursuant to this chapter is not maintained in written form, a request for inspection is not complied with unless and until the corporation at its expense makes such record available in written form. For the purposes of this chapter "written" or "in writing" also includes cathode ray tube and similar electronic communications methods.

   Ca. Corp. Code § 8310
Amended by Stats. 1982, Ch. 662, Sec. 19.

Section 8311 - Inspection

Any inspection under this chapter may be made in person or by agent or attorney and the right of inspection includes the right to copy and make extracts.

   Ca. Corp. Code § 8311
Added by Stats. 1978, Ch. 567.

Section 8312 - Records of subsidiary

Any right of inspection created by this chapter extends to the records of each subsidiary of a corporation.

   Ca. Corp. Code § 8312
Added by Stats. 1978, Ch. 567.

Section 8313 - Limitation of rights of members prohibited

The rights of members provided in this chapter may not be limited by contract or the articles or bylaws.

   Ca. Corp. Code § 8313
Added by Stats. 1978, Ch. 567.

Article 2 - REQUIRED RECORDS, REPORTS TO DIRECTORS AND MEMBERS

Section 8320 - Keeping records

(a) Each corporation shall keep:

   (1) Adequate and correct books and records of account:

   (2) Minutes of the proceedings of its members, board and committees of the board; and

   (3) A record of its members giving their names and addresses and the class of membership held by each.
(b) Those minutes and other books and records shall be kept either in written form or in any other form capable of being converted into clearly legible tangible form or in any combination of the foregoing. When minutes and other books and records are

kept in a form capable of being converted into clearly legible paper form, the clearly legible paper form into which those minutes and other books and records are converted shall be admissible in evidence, and accepted for all other purposes, to the same extent as an original paper record of the same information would have been, provided that the paper form accurately portrays the record.

Ca. Corp. Code § 8320
Amended by Stats 2004 ch 254 (SB 1306),s 27, eff. 1/1/2005

Section 8321 - Right to receive financial report

(a) A corporation shall notify each member yearly of the member's right to receive a financial report pursuant to this subdivision. Except as provided in subdivision (c), upon written request of a member, the board shall promptly cause the most recent annual report to be sent to the requesting member. An annual report shall be prepared not later than 120 days after the close of the corporation's fiscal year. Unless otherwise provided by the articles or bylaws and if approved by the board of directors, that report and any accompanying material may be sent by electronic transmission by the corporation (Section 20). That report shall contain in appropriate detail the following:

(1) A balance sheet as of the end of that fiscal year and an income statement and a statement of cashflows for that fiscal year.

(2) A statement of the place where the names and addresses of the current members are located.

(3) Any information required by Section 8322.
(b) The report required by subdivision (a) shall be accompanied by any report thereon of independent accountants, or, if there is no report, the certificate of an authorized officer of the corporation that the statements were prepared without audit from the books and records of the corporation.
(c) Subdivision (a) does not apply to any corporation that receives less than ten thousand dollars ($10,000) in gross revenues or receipts during the fiscal year.

Ca. Corp. Code § 8321
Amended by Stats 2006 ch 214 (AB 1959),s 6, eff. 1/1/2007.
Amended by Stats 2004 ch 254 (SB 1306),s 28, eff. 1/1/2005

Section 8322 - Statement of transaction or indemnification

(a) Any provision of the articles or bylaws notwithstanding, every corporation shall furnish annually to its members and directors a statement of any transaction or indemnification of a kind described in subdivision (d) or (e), if any such transaction or indemnification took place. If the corporation issues an annual report to all members, this subdivision shall be satisfied by including the required information in the annual report. A corporation which does not issue an annual report to all members, pursuant to subdivision (c) of Section 8321, shall satisfy this section by mailing or delivering to its members the required statement within 120 days after the close of the corporation's fiscal year. Unless otherwise provided by the articles or bylaws and if approved by the board of directors, that statement may be sent by electronic transmission by the corporation (Section 20).

(b) Except as provided in subdivision (c), a covered transaction under this section is a transaction in which the corporation, its parent, or its subsidiary was a party, and in which either of the following had a direct or indirect material financial interest:

(1) Any director or officer of the corporation, or its parent or subsidiary.

(2) Any holder of more than 10 percent of the voting power of the corporation, its parent or its subsidiary. For the purpose of subdivision (d), an "interested person" is any person described in paragraph (1) or (2) of this subdivision.

(c) Transactions approved by the members of a corporation (Section 5034), under subdivision (a) of Section 7233, are not covered transactions. For the purpose of subdivision (b), a mere common directorship is not a material financial interest.

(d) The statement required by subdivision (a) shall describe briefly:

(1) Any covered transaction (excluding compensation of officers and directors) during the previous fiscal year involving more than fifty thousand dollars ($50,000), or which was one of a number of covered transactions in which the same interested person had a direct or indirect material financial interest, and which transactions in the aggregate involved more than fifty thousand dollars ($50,000).

(2) The names of the interested persons involved in such transactions, stating such person's relationship to the corporation, the nature of such person's interest in the transaction and, where practicable, the amount of such interest; provided, that in the case of a transaction with a partnership of which such person is a partner, only the interest of the partnership need be stated.

(e) The statement required by subdivision (a) shall describe briefly the amount and circumstances of any loans, guaranties, indemnifications or advances aggregating more than ten thousand dollars ($10,000) paid or made during the fiscal year to any officer or director of the corporation pursuant to Section 7237; provided that no such report need be made in the case of a loan, guaranty, or indemnification approved by the members (Section 5034) or a loan or guaranty not subject to the provisions of subdivision (a) of Section 7235.

Ca. Corp. Code § 8322
Amended by Stats 2004 ch 254 (SB 1306),s 29, eff. 1/1/2005

Section 8323 - Enforcement of duty of making and mailing or delivering information and financial statements

(a) The superior court of the proper county shall enforce the duty of making and mailing or delivering the information and financial statements required by this article and, for good cause shown, may extend the time therefor.

(b) In any action or proceeding under this section, if the court finds the failure of the corporation to comply with the requirements of this article to have been without justification, the court may award the member reasonable expenses, including attorneys' fees, in connection with such action or proceeding.

 Ca. Corp. Code § 8323

Added by Stats. 1978, Ch. 567.

Section 8324 - Furnishing copy of report to attorney general in lieu of annual report

(a) Nothing in this part relieves a corporation from the requirements of Article 7 (commencing with Section 12580) of Chapter 6 of Part 2 of Division 3 of the Government Code as to any assets held in charitable trust including, without limitation, subdivision (a) of Section 12586. If a report sent to the Attorney General in compliance with the requirements of Article 7 (commencing with Section 12580) of Chapter 6 of Part 2 of Division 3 of the Government Code includes the information required in the annual report, then the corporation may furnish a copy of its report to the Attorney General in lieu of the annual report, whenever it is required to furnish an annual report.

(b) A corporation shall furnish any member who so requests a copy of any report filed by the corporation pursuant to Article 7 (commencing with Section 12580) of Chapter 6 of Part 2 of Division 3 of the Government Code. The corporation may impose reasonable charges for copying and mailing a report furnished under this subdivision.

 Ca. Corp. Code § 8324

Amended by Stats 2011 ch 442 (AB 1211),s 20, eff. 1/1/2012.

Section 8325 - Report on voting

For a period of 60 days following the conclusion of an annual, regular, or special meeting of members, a corporation shall, upon written request from a member, forthwith inform the member of the result of any particular vote of members taken at the meeting, including the number of memberships voting for, the number of memberships voting against, and the number of memberships abstaining or withheld from voting. If the matter voted on was the election of directors, the corporation shall report the number of memberships, or votes if voted cumulatively, cast for each nominee for director. If more than one class or series of memberships voted, the report shall state the appropriate numbers by class and series of memberships.

 Ca. Corp. Code § 8325

Added 9/21/1999 (Bill Number: AB 1687) (Chapter 453).

Article 3 - RIGHTS OF INSPECTION

Section 8330 - Inspection of record of members' names, addresses, and voting rights or list of names, addresses, and voting rights of members

(a) Subject to Sections 8331 and 8332, and unless the corporation provides a reasonable alternative pursuant to subdivision (c), a member may do either or both of the following as permitted by subdivision (b):

   (1) Inspect and copy the record of all the members' names, addresses and voting rights, at reasonable times, upon five business days' prior written demand upon the corporation which demand shall state the purpose for which the inspection rights are requested; or

   (2) Obtain from the secretary of the corporation, upon written demand and tender of a reasonable charge, a list of the names, addresses and voting rights of those members entitled to vote for the election of directors, as of the most recent record date for which it has been compiled or as of a date specified by the member subsequent to the date of demand. The demand shall state the purpose for which the list is requested. The membership list shall be made available on or before the later of ten business days after the demand is received or after the date specified therein as the date as of which the list is to be compiled.

(b) The rights set forth in subdivision (a) may be exercised by:

   (1) Any member, for a purpose reasonably related to such person's interest as a member. Where the corporation reasonably believes that the information will be used for another purpose, or where it provides a reasonable alternative pursuant to subdivision (c), it may deny the member access to the list. In any subsequent action brought by the member under Section 8336, the court shall enforce the rights set forth in subdivision (a) unless the corporation proves that the member will allow use of the information for purposes unrelated to the person's interest as a member or that the alternative method offered reasonably achieves the proper purpose set forth in the demand.

   (2) The authorized number of members for a purpose reasonably related to the members' interest as members.

(c) The corporation may, within ten business days after receiving a demand under subdivision (a), deliver to the person or persons making the demand a written offer of an alternative method of achieving the purpose identified in said demand without providing access to or a copy of the membership list. An alternative method which reasonably and in a timely manner accomplishes the proper purpose set forth in a demand made under subdivision (a) shall be deemed a reasonable alternative, unless within a reasonable time after acceptance of the offer the corporation fails to do those things which it offered to do. Any rejection of the offer shall be in writing and shall indice the reasons the alternative proposed by the corporation does not meet the proper purpose of the demand made pursuant to subdivision (a).

Ca. Corp. Code § 8330

Added by Stats. 1978, Ch. 567.

Section 8331 - Petition for order setting aside demand

(a) Where the corporation, in good faith, and with a substantial basis, believes that the membership list, demanded under Section 8330 by the authorized number (Section 5036), will be used for a purpose not reasonably related to the interests as members of the person or persons making the demand (hereinafter called the requesting parties) as members or provides a reasonable alternative pursuant to subdivision (c) of Section 8330, it may petition the superior court of the proper county for an order setting aside the demand.

(b) Except as provided in subdivision (c), a petition for an order to show cause why a protective order pursuant to subdivision (d) should not issue shall be filed within 10 business days after the demand by the authorized number under Section 8330 or receipt of a written rejection by the authorized number of an offer made pursuant to subdivision (c) of Section 8330, whichever is later. The petition shall be accompanied by an application for a hearing on the petition. Upon the filing of the petition, the court shall issue a protective order staying production of the list demanded until the hearing on the order to show cause. The court shall set the hearing on the order to show cause not more than 20 days from the date of the filing of the petition. The order to show cause shall be granted unless the court finds that there is no reasonable probability that the corporation will make the showing required under subdivision (f).

(c) A corporation may file a petition under this section more than 10 business days after the demand or rejection under Section 8330, but only upon a showing the delay was caused by excusable neglect. In no event, however, may any petition under this section be considered if filed more than 30 days after the requesting parties' demand or rejection, whichever is later.

(d) Upon the return day of the order to show cause, the court may issue a protective order staying production of the list demanded until final adjudication of the petition filed pursuant to this section. No protective order shall issue under this subdivision unless the court finds that the rights of the requesting parties can reasonably be preserved and that the corporation is likely to make the showing required by subdivision (f) or the court is likely to issue a protective order pursuant to subdivision (g).

(e) If the corporation fails to file a petition within the time allowed by subdivision (b) or (c), whichever is applicable, or fails to obtain a protective order under subdivision (d), then the corporation shall comply with the demand, and no further action may be brought by the corporation under this section.

(f) The court shall issue the final order setting aside the demand only if the corporation proves:

(1) That there is a reasonable probability that the requesting parties will permit use of the membership list for a purpose unrelated to their interests as members; or

(2) That the method offered by the corporation is a reasonable alternative in that it reasonably achieves the proper purpose set forth in the requesting parties' demand and that the corporation intends and is able to effectuate the reasonable alternative.

(g) In the final order, the court may, in its discretion, order an alternate mechanism for achieving the proper purposes of the requesting parties, or impose just and proper conditions upon the use of the membership list which reasonably assures compliance with Section 8330 and Section 8338.

(h) The court shall award reasonable costs and expenses including reasonable attorneys' fees, to requesting parties who successfully oppose any petition or application filed pursuant to this section.

(i) Where the corporation has neither, within the time allowed, complied with a demand by the authorized number (Section 5036) under Section 8330, nor obtained a protective order staying production of the list, or a final order setting aside the demand, which is then in effect, the requesting parties may petition the superior court of the proper county for a writ of mandamus pursuant to Section 1085 of the Code of Civil Procedure compelling the corporation to comply with the demand. At the hearing, the court shall hear the parties summarily, by affidavit or otherwise, and shall issue a peremptory writ of mandamus unless it appears that the demand was not made by an authorized number (Section 5036), that the demand has been complied with, that the corporation, pursuant to subdivision (c) of Section 8330, made an offer which was not rejected in writing within a reasonable time, or that a protective or final order properly issued under subdivision (d), (f) or (g) is then in effect. No inquiry may be made in such proceeding into the use for which the authorized number seek the list. The court shall award reasonable costs and expenses, including reasonable attorneys' fees, to persons granted an order under this subdivision.

(j) Nothing in this section shall be construed to limit the right of the corporation to obtain damages for any misuse of a membership list obtained under Section 8330, or otherwise, or to obtain injunctive relief necessary to restrain misuse of a member list. A corporation shall be entitled to recover reasonable costs and expenses, including reasonable attorneys' fees, incurred in successfully bringing any such action.

Ca. Corp. Code § 8331
Amended by Stats. 1979, Ch. 724.

Section 8332 - Limitation or restriction of rights

(a) Upon petition of the corporation or any member, the superior court of the proper county may limit or restrict the rights set forth in Section 8330 where, and only where, such limitation or restriction is necessary to protect the rights of any member under the Constitution of the United States or the Constitution of the State of California. An order issued pursuant to this subdivision shall provide, insofar as possible, for alternative mechanisms by which the persons seeking to exercise rights under Section 8330 may communicate with members for purposes reasonably related to their interests as members.

(b) Upon the filing of a petition under subdivision (a), the court may, if requested by the person making the petition, issue a temporary order suspending the running of any time limit specified in Section 8330 for compliance with that section. Such an order may be extended, after notice and hearing, until final adjudication of the petition, wherever it appears that the petitioner may prevail on the merits, and it is otherwise equitable to do so.

Ca. Corp. Code § 8332
Added by Stats. 1978, Ch. 567.

Section 8333 - Accounting books and records and minutes of proceedings

The accounting books and records and minutes of proceedings of the members and the board and committees of the board shall be open to inspection upon the written demand on the corporation of any member at any reasonable time, for a purpose reasonably related to such person's interests as a member.

Ca. Corp. Code § 8333
Added by Stats. 1978, Ch. 567.

Section 8334 - Inspection by director

Every director shall have the absolute right at any reasonable time to inspect and copy all books, records and documents of every kind and to inspect the physical properties of the corporation of which such person is a director.

Ca. Corp. Code § 8334
Added by Stats. 1978, Ch. 567.

Section 8335 - Frustration of proper purpose of person making demand

Where the proper purpose of the person or persons making a demand pursuant to Section 8330 is frustrated by (1) any delay by the corporation in complying with a demand under Section 8330 beyond the time limits specified therein, or (2) any delay caused by the filing of a petition under Section 8331 or Section 8332, or (3) any delay caused by the alternative proposed under subdivision (c) of Section 8330, the person or persons properly making the demand shall have, in the discretion of the court, a right to obtain from the superior court an order postponing any members' meeting previously noticed for a period equal to the period of such delay. The members may obtain such an order in a proceeding brought pursuant to Section 8331 upon the filing of a verified complaint in the proper county and after a hearing, notice of which shall be given to such persons and in such manner as the court may direct. Such right shall be in addition to any other legal or equitable remedies to which the member may be entitled.

Ca. Corp. Code § 8335
Amended by Stats. 1979, Ch. 724.

Section 8336 - Enforcement of demand or right of inspection

(a) Upon refusal of a lawful demand for inspection under this chapter, or a lawful demand pursuant to Section 8330 or Section 8333, the superior court of the proper county, or the county where the books or records in question are kept, may enforce the demand or right of inspection with just and proper conditions or may, for good cause shown, appoint one or more competent inspectors or independent accountants to audit the financial statements kept in this state and investigate the property, funds and affairs of any corporation and of any subsidiary corporation thereof, domestic or foreign, keeping records in this state and to report thereon in such manner as the court may direct.

(b) All officers and agents of the corporation shall produce to the inspectors or accountants so appointed all books and documents in their custody or power, under penalty of punishment for contempt of court.

(c) All expenses of the investigation or audit shall be defrayed by the applicant unless the court orders them to be paid or shared by the corporation.

Ca. Corp. Code § 8336
Amended by Stats. 1979, Ch. 724.

Section 8337 - Award of reasonable costs and expenses

In any action or proceeding under this article, and except as required by Section 8331, if the court finds the failure of the corporation to comply with a proper demand thereunder was without justification, the court may award the member reasonable costs and expenses, including reasonable attorneys' fees, in connection with such action or proceeding.

Ca. Corp. Code § 8337
Added by Stats. 1978, Ch. 567.

Section 8338 - Membership list

(a) A membership list is a corporate asset. Without consent of the board a membership list or any part thereof may not be obtained or used by any person for any purpose not reasonably related to a member's interest as a member. Without limiting the generality of the foregoing, without the consent of the board a membership list or any part thereof may not be:

(1) Used to solicit money or property unless such money or property will be used solely to solicit the vote of the members in an election to be held by their corporation.

(2) Used for any purpose which the user does not reasonably and in good faith believe will benefit the corporation.

(3) Used for any commercial purpose or purpose in competition with the corporation.

(4) Sold to or purchased by any person.

(b) Any person who violates the provisions of subdivision (a) shall be liable for any damage such violation causes the corporation and shall account for and pay to the corporation any profit derived as a result of said violation. In addition, a court in its discretion may award exemplary damages for a fraudulent or malicious violation of subdivision (a).

(c) Nothing in this article shall be construed to limit the right of a corporation to obtain injunctive relief necessary to restrain misuse of a membership list or any part thereof.

(d) In any action or proceeding under this section, a court may award the corporation reasonable costs and expenses, including reasonable attorneys' fees, in connection with such action or proceeding.

(e) As used in this section, the term "membership list" means the record of the members' names and addresses.

Ca. Corp. Code § 8338

Amended by Stats. 1996, Ch. 589, Sec. 36. Effective January 1, 1997.

Chapter 14 - SERVICE OF PROCESS

Section 8410 - Service of process

Service of process upon a corporation shall be governed by Chapter 17 (commencing with Section 1700) of Division 1 of Title 1.

Ca. Corp. Code § 8410

Added by Stats. 1978, Ch. 567.

Chapter 15 - INVOLUNTARY DISSOLUTION

Section 8510 - Complaint for involuntary dissolution; grounds

(a) A complaint for involuntary dissolution of a corporation on any one or more of the grounds specified in subdivision (b) may be filed in the superior court of the proper county by any of the following persons:

(1) One-half or more of the directors in office.

(2) A person or persons holding or authorized in writing by persons holding not less than $33^{1}/_{3}$ percent of the voting power exclusive of memberships held by persons who have personally participated in any of the transactions enumerated in paragraph

(5) of subdivision (b).

(3) Any member if the ground for dissolution is that the period for which the corporation was formed has terminated without extension thereof.

(4) Any other person expressly authorized to do so in the articles.

(5) In the case of a corporation holding assets in charitable trust, the Attorney General.

(6) The head organization under whose authority the corporation was created, where the corporation's articles include the provision authorized by subdivision (a), paragraph (4), clause (i), of Section 7132.
(b) The grounds for involuntary dissolution are that:

(1) The corporation has abandoned its activity for more than one year.

(2) The corporation has an even number of directors who are equally divided and cannot agree as to the management of its affairs, so that its activities can no longer be conducted to advantage or so that there is danger that its property will be impaired or lost or its activities impaired and the members are so divided into factions that they cannot elect a board consisting of an uneven number.

(3) There is internal dissension and two or more factions of members in the corporation are so deadlocked that its activities can no longer be conducted with advantage.

(4) When during any four-year period or when all voting power has been exercised at two consecutive meetings or in two written ballots for the election of directors, whichever period is shorter, the members have failed to elect successors to directors whose terms have expired or would have expired upon election of their successors.

(5) Those in control of the corporation have been guilty of or have knowingly countenanced persistent and pervasive fraud, mismanagement or abuse of authority or persistent unfairness toward any member or the corporation's property is being misapplied or wasted by its directors or officers.

(6) In the case of any corporation with 35 or fewer members, liquidation is reasonably necessary for the protection of the rights or interests of a complaining member or members.

(7) The period for which the corporation was formed has terminated without extension of such period.

(8) The corporation is required to dissolve under the terms of any article provision adopted pursuant to subdivision (a), paragraph (4), clause (i) of Section 7132.
(c) At any time prior to the trial of the action any member or creditor may intervene therein.
(d) This section does not apply to any corporation subject to:

(1) The Public Utilities Act (Part 1 (commencing with Section 201) of Division 1 of the Public Utilities Code) unless an order is obtained from the Public Utilities Commission authorizing the corporation either (a) to dispose of its assets as provided in Section 851 of the Public Utilities Code or (b) to dissolve.

(2) The provisions of Article 14 (commencing with Section 1010) of Chapter 1 of Part 2 of Division 1 of the Insurance Code when the application authorized by Section 1011 of the Insurance Code has been filed by the Insurance Commissioner unless the consent of the Insurance Commissioner has been obtained.

(3) The California Credit Union Law (Chapter 1 (commencing with Section 14000) of Division 5 of the Financial Code).
(e) In the case of a corporation holding assets in charitable trust at the time of the filing of the complaint pursuant to subdivision (a), a copy thereof shall be served on the Attorney General who may intervene.
Ca. Corp. Code § 8510
Amended by Stats. 1982, Ch. 662, Sec. 22.

Section 8511 - Action by attorney general

(a) The Attorney General may bring an action against any corporation or purported corporation in the name of the people of this state, upon the Attorney General's own information or upon complaint of a private party, to procure a judgment dissolving the corporation and annulling, vacating or forfeiting its corporate existence upon any of the following grounds:

(1) The corporation has seriously offended against any provision of the statutes regulating corporations.

(2) The corporation has fraudulently abused or usurped corporate privileges or powers.

(3) The corporation has violated any provision of law by any act or default which under the law is a ground for forfeiture of corporate existence.

(4) The corporation has failed to pay to the Franchise Tax Board for a period of five years any tax imposed upon it by the Bank and Corporation Tax Law.
(b) If the ground of the action is a matter or act which the corporation has done or

omitted to do that can be corrected by amendment of its articles or by other corporate action, such suit shall not be maintained unless (1) the Attorney General, at least 30 days prior to the institution of suit, has given the corporation written notice of the matter or act done or omitted to be done and (2) the corporation has failed to institute proceedings to correct it within the 30-day period or thereafter fails to duly and properly make such amendment or take the corrective corporate action.

(c) In any such action the court may order dissolution or such other or partial relief as it deems just and expedient. The court also may appoint a receiver for winding up the affairs of the corporation or may order that the corporation be wound up by its board subject to the supervision of the court.

(d) Service of process on the corporation may be made pursuant to Chapter 17 (commencing with Section 1700) of Division 1 or by written notice to the president or secretary of the corporation at the address indicated in the corporation's last tax return filed pursuant to the Bank and Corporation Tax Law. The Attorney General shall also publish one time in a newspaper of general circulation in the proper county a notice to the members of the corporation.

Ca. Corp. Code § 8511
Added by Stats. 1978, Ch. 567.

Section 8512 - Appointment of provisional director

If the ground for the complaint for involuntary dissolution of the corporation is a deadlock in the board as set forth in paragraph (2) of subdivision (b) of Section 8510, the court may appoint a provisional director. The provisions of subdivision (d) of Section 7225 apply to any such provisional director so appointed.

Ca. Corp. Code § 8512
Added by Stats. 1978, Ch. 567.

Section 8513 - Appointment of receiver

If, at the time of the filing of a complaint for involuntary dissolution or at any time thereafter, the court has reasonable grounds to believe that unless a receiver of the corporation is appointed the interests of the corporation or its members will suffer pending the hearing and determination of the complaint, upon the application of the plaintiff, and after a hearing upon such notice to the corporation as the court may direct and upon the giving of security pursuant to Sections 566 and 567 of the Code of Civil Procedure, the court may appoint a receiver to take over and manage the affairs of the corporation and to preserve its property pending the hearing and determination of the complaint for dissolution.

Ca. Corp. Code § 8513
Amended by Stats. 1982, Ch. 517, Sec. 190.

Section 8514 - Orders and decrees

After hearing the court may decree a winding up and dissolution of the corporation if cause therefor is shown or, with or without winding up and dissolution, may make such orders and decrees and issue such injunctions in the case as justice and equity require.

    Ca. Corp. Code § 8514

Added by Stats. 1978, Ch. 567.

Section 8515 - Commencement of involuntary proceedings for winding up

(a) Involuntary proceedings for winding up a corporation commence when the order for winding up is entered under Section 8514.

(b) When an involuntary proceeding for winding up has commenced, the board shall conduct the winding up of the affairs of the corporation, subject to the supervision of the court, unless other persons are appointed by the court, on good cause shown, to conduct the winding up. The directors or such other persons may, subject to any restrictions imposed by the court, exercise all their powers through the executive officers without any order of court.

(c) When an involuntary proceeding for winding up has commenced, the corporation shall cease to conduct its activities except to the extent necessary for the beneficial winding up thereof and except during such period as the board may deem necessary to preserve the corporation's goodwill or going-concern value, pending a sale or other disposition of its assets, or both, in whole or in part. The directors shall cause written notice of the commencement of the proceeding for involuntary winding up to be given by mail to all members and to all known creditors and claimants whose addresses appear on the records of the corporation, unless the order for winding up has been stayed by appeal therefrom or otherwise or the proceeding or the execution of the order has been enjoined.

    Ca. Corp. Code § 8515

Added by Stats. 1978, Ch. 567.

Section 8516 - Jurisdiction of court

When an involuntary proceeding for winding up has been commenced, the jurisdiction of the court includes:

(a) The requirement of the proof of all claims and demands against the corporation, whether due or not yet due, contingent, unliquidated or sounding only in damages, and the barring from participation of creditors and claimants failing to make and present claims and proof as required by any order.

(b) The determination or compromise of all claims of every nature against the corporation or any of its property, and the determination of the amount of money or assets required to be retained to pay or provide for the payment of claims.

(c) The determination of the rights of members and of all classes of members in and to the assets of the corporation.

(d) The presentation and filing of intermediate and final accounts of the directors or other persons appointed to conduct the winding up and hearing thereon, the allowance, disallowance or settlement thereof and the discharge of the directors or such other persons from their duties and liabilities.

(e) The appointment of a commissioner to hear and determine any or all matters, with such power or authority as the court may deem proper.

(f) The filling of any vacancies on the board which the directors or the members are unable to fill.

(g) The removal of any director if it appears that the director has been guilty of dishonesty, misconduct, neglect or breach of trust in conducting the winding up or if the director is unable to act. The court may order an election to fill the vacancy so caused, and may enjoin, for such time as it considers proper, the reelection of the director so removed; or the court, in lieu of ordering an election, may appoint a director to fill the vacancy caused by such removal. Any director so appointed by the court shall serve until the next regular meeting of members or until a successor is elected or appointed.

(h) The staying of the prosecution of any suit, proceeding or action against the corporation and requiring the parties to present and prove their claims in the manner required of other creditors.

(i) The determination of whether adequate provision has been made for payment or satisfaction of all debts and liabilities not actually paid.

(j) The making of orders for the withdrawal or termination of proceedings, to wind up and dissolve, subject to conditions for the protection of members and creditors.

(k) The making of an order, upon the allowance or settlement of the final accounts of the directors or such other persons, that the corporation has been duly wound up and is dissolved. Upon the making of such order, the corporate existence shall cease except for purposes of further winding up if needed.

(l) The making of orders for the bringing in of new parties as the court deems proper for the determination of all questions and matters.

(m) The disposition of assets held in charitable trust.

Ca. Corp. Code § 8516

Added by Stats. 1978, Ch. 567.

Section 8517 - Creditors and claimants

(a) All creditors and claimants may be barred from participation in any distribution of the general assets if they fail to make and present claims and proofs within such time as the court may direct, which shall not be less than four nor more than six months after the first publication of notice to creditors unless it appears by affidavit that there are no claims, in which case the time limit may be three months. If it is shown that a claimant did not receive notice because of absence from the state or other cause, the court may allow a claim to be filed or presented at any time before distribution is completed.

(b) Such notice to creditors shall be published not less than once a week for three consecutive weeks in a newspaper of general circulation published in the county in which the proceeding is pending or, if there is no such newspaper published in that county, in such newspaper as may be designated by the court, directing creditors and claimants to make and present claims and proofs to the person, at the place and within the time specified in the notice. A copy of the notice shall be mailed to each person shown as a creditor or claimant on the books of the corporation, at such person's last known address.

(c) Holders of secured claims may prove for the whole debt in order to realize any deficiency. If such creditors fail to present their claims they shall be barred only as to any right to claim against the general assets for any deficiency in the amount realized on their security.

(d) Before any distribution is made the amount of any unmatured, contingent or disputed claim against the corporation which has been presented and has not been disallowed, or such part of any such claim as the holder would be entitled to if the claim were due, established or absolute, shall be paid into court and there remain to be paid over to the party when the party becomes entitled thereto or, if the party fails to establish a claim, to be paid over or distributed with the other assets of the corporation to those entitled thereto; or such other provision for the full payment of such claim, if and when established, shall be made as the court may deem adequate. A creditor whose claim has been allowed but is not yet due shall be entitled to its present value upon distribution.

(e) Suits against the corporation on claims which have been rejected shall be commenced within 30 days after written notice of rejection thereof is given to the claimant.

Ca. Corp. Code § 8517
Added by Stats. 1978, Ch. 567.

Section 8518 - Order declaring corporation duly wound up and dissolved

(a) Upon the final settlement of the accounts of the directors or other persons appointed pursuant to Section 8515 and the determination that the corporation's affairs are in condition for it to be dissolved, the court may make an order declaring the corporation duly wound up and dissolved. The order shall declare:

(1) That the corporation has been duly wound up, that a final franchise tax return, as described by Section 23332 of the Revenue and Taxation Code, has been filed with the Franchise Tax Board, as required under Part 10.2 (commencing with Section 18401) of Division 2 of the Revenue and Taxation Code and that its known debts and liabilities have been paid or adequately provided for, or that those debts and liabilities have been paid as far as its assets permitted, as the case may be. If there are known debts or liabilities for payment of which adequate provision has been made, the order shall state what provision has been made, setting forth the name and address of the corporation, person or governmental agency that has assumed or guaranteed the payment, or the name and address of the depositary with which deposit has been made or such other information as may be necessary to enable the creditor or other person to whom payment is to be made to appear and claim payment of the debt or liability.

(2) That its known assets have been distributed to the persons entitled thereto or that it acquired no known assets, as the case may be.

(3) That the accounts of directors or such other persons have been settled and that they are discharged from their duties and liabilities to creditors and members.

(4) That the corporation is dissolved.
(b) The court may make such additional orders and grant such further relief as it deems proper upon the evidence submitted.
(c) Upon the making of the order declaring the corporation dissolved, corporate existence shall cease except for the purposes of further winding up if needed; and the directors or such other persons shall be discharged from their duties and liabilities, except in respect to completion of the winding up.
Ca. Corp. Code § 8518
Amended by Stats 2006 ch 773 (AB 2341),s 26, eff. 9/29/2006.

Section 8519 - Filing of order, decree, or judgment; notification of Franchise Tax Board

Whenever a corporation is dissolved or its existence forfeited by order, decree or judgment of a court, a copy of the order, decree or judgment, certified by the clerk of court, shall forthwith be filed. The Secretary of State shall notify the Franchise Tax Board of the dissolution.
Ca. Corp. Code § 8519
Amended by Stats 2006 ch 773 (AB 2341),s 27, eff. 9/29/2006.

Chapter 16 - VOLUNTARY DISSOLUTION

Section 8610 - Voluntary election to wind up and dissolve

(a) Any corporation may elect voluntarily to wind up and dissolve (1) by approval of a majority of all members (Section 5033), or (2) by approval of the board and approval of the members (Section 5034).
(b) Any corporation which comes within one of the following descriptions may elect by approval of the board to wind up and dissolve:

(1) A corporation which has been the subject of an order for relief in bankruptcy.

(2) A corporation which has disposed of all of its assets and has not conducted any activity for a period of five years immediately preceding the adoption of the resolution electing to dissolve the corporation.

(3) A corporation which has no members.

(4) A corporation which is required to dissolve under provisions of its articles adopted pursuant to subparagraph (A) of paragraph (4) of subdivision (a) of Section 7132.

(c) If a corporation comes within one of the descriptions in subdivision (b) and if the number of directors then in office is less than a quorum, it may elect to voluntarily wind up and dissolve by any of the following:

(1) The unanimous consent of the directors then in office.

(2) The affirmative vote of a majority of the directors then in office at a meeting held pursuant to waiver of notice by those directors complying with paragraph (3) of subdivision (a) of Section 7211.

(3) The vote of a sole remaining director.

(d) If a corporation elects to voluntarily wind up and dissolve pursuant to subdivision (c), references to the board in this chapter and Chapter 17 (commencing with Section 8710) shall be deemed to be to a board consisting solely of those directors or that sole director and action by the board shall require at least the same consent or vote as would be required under subdivision (c) for an election to wind up and dissolve.

Ca. Corp. Code § 8610

Amended by Stats 2009 ch 631 (AB 1233),s 25, eff. 1/1/2010.
Amended by Stats 2009 ch 500 (AB 1059),s 22, eff. 1/1/2010.

Section 8610.5 - Verification of certificate of dissolution of nonprofit

(a) Notwithstanding any other provision of this division, when a corporation has not issued any memberships, a majority of the directors, or, if no directors have been named in the articles or have been elected, the incorporator or a majority of the incorporators, may sign and verify a certificate of dissolution stating the following:

(1) That the certificate of dissolution is being filed within 24 months from the date the articles of incorporation were filed.

(2) That the corporation does not have any debts or other liabilities, except as provided in paragraph (3) and subdivision (d).

(3) That the tax liability will be satisfied on a taxes-paid basis, or that a person or corporation or other business entity assumes the tax liability, if any, of the dissolving corporation and is responsible for additional corporate taxes, if any, that are assessed and that become due after the date of the assumption of the tax liability.

(4) That a final franchise tax return, as described by Section 23332 of the Revenue and Taxation Code, has been or will be filed with the Franchise Tax Board as required under Part 10.2 (commencing with Section 18401) of Division 2 of the Revenue and Taxation Code.

(5) That the corporation was created in error.

(6) That the known assets of the corporation remaining after payment of, or adequately providing for, known debts and liabilities have been distributed as required by law or that the corporation acquired no known assets, as the case may be.

(7) That a majority of the directors, or, if no directors have been named in the articles or have been elected, the incorporator or a majority of the incorporators authorized the dissolution and elected to dissolve the corporation.

(8) That the corporation has not issued any memberships, and if the corporation has received payments for memberships, those payments have been returned to those making the payments.

(9) That the corporation is dissolved.
(b) A certificate of dissolution signed and verified pursuant to subdivision (a) shall be filed with the Secretary of State. The Secretary of State shall notify the Franchise Tax Board and the Attorney General's Registry of Charitable Trusts of the dissolution.
(c) Upon filing a certificate of dissolution pursuant to subdivision (b), a corporation shall be dissolved and its powers, rights, and privileges shall cease.
(d) Notwithstanding the administrative dissolution of a corporation pursuant to this section, its liability to creditors, if any, is not discharged. The liability of the directors of, or other persons related to, the administratively dissolved corporation is not discharged. The dissolution of a corporation pursuant to this section shall not diminish or adversely affect the ability of the Attorney General to enforce liabilities as otherwise provided by law.

Ca. Corp. Code § 8610.5
Added by Stats 2015 ch 363 (AB 557),s 4, eff. 1/1/2016.

Section 8611 - Certificate evidencing election

(a) Whenever a corporation has elected to wind up and dissolve a certificate evidencing that election shall forthwith be filed. A copy of that certificate shall be filed with the Attorney General if the corporation holds assets in charitable trust or has a charitable dissolution clause.
(b) The certificate shall be an officers' certificate or shall be signed and verified by at least a majority of the directors then in office or by one or more members authorized to do so by approval of a majority of all members (Section 5033) and shall set forth:

(1) That the corporation has elected to wind up and dissolve.

(2) If the election was made by the vote of members alone, the number of votes for the election and that the election was made by a majority of all members (Section 5033).

(3) If the election was made by the board and the members pursuant to paragraph (2) of subdivision (a) of Section 8610, the certificate shall state that it was made by the board and the members in accordance with Section 5034.

(4) If the certificate is executed by a member or members, that the subscribing person or persons were authorized to execute the certificate a majority of all members (Section 5033).

(5) If the election was made by the board pursuant to subdivision (b) of Section 8610, the circumstances showing the corporation to be within one of the categories described in that subdivision.
(c) If an election to dissolve made pursuant to subdivision (a) of Section 8610 is made by the vote of all the members of a corporation with members or by a vote of all members of the board of a corporation without members pursuant to subdivision (b) of Section 8610 and a statement to that effect is added to the certificate of dissolution pursuant to Section 8615, the separate filing of the certificate of election pursuant to this section is not required.
  Ca. Corp. Code § 8611
Amended by Stats 2014 ch 834 (SB 1041),s 16, eff. 1/1/2015.
Amended September 21, 1999 (Bill Number: AB 1687) (Chapter 453).

Section 8612 - Revocation

(a) A voluntary election to wind up and dissolve may be revoked prior to distribution of any assets:

(1) if the election was made pursuant to subdivision (a) of Section 8610, by the vote of members representing a majority of the voting power; or

(2) if the election was by the board pursuant to subdivision (b) of Section 8610, by approval of the board. Thereupon a certificate evidencing the revocation shall be signed, verified and filed in the manner prescribed by Section 8611 and a copy thereof filed with the Attorney General.
(b) The certificate shall set forth:

(1) That the corporation has revoked its election to wind up and dissolve.

(2) That no assets have been distributed pursuant to the election.

(3) If the revocation was made by the vote of members alone, the number of votes for the revocation and that the revocation was made by persons representing at least a majority of the voting power.

(4) If the revocation was made by the board alone, the certificate shall so state.
Ca. Corp. Code § 8612
Added by Stats. 1978, Ch. 567.

Section 8613 - Commencement of voluntary proceedings for winding up

(a) Voluntary proceedings for winding up the corporation commence upon the adoption of the resolution required by Section 8610 by the members, by the board and members, or by the board alone, electing to wind up and dissolve.
(b) When a voluntary proceeding for winding up has commenced, the board shall continue to act as a board and shall have full powers to wind up and settle its affairs, both before and after the filing of the certificate of dissolution.
(c) When a voluntary proceeding for winding up has commenced, the corporation shall cease to conduct its activities except to the extent necessary for the beneficial winding up thereof, to the extent necessary to carry out its purposes, and except during such period as the board may deem necessary to preserve the corporation's goodwill or going-concern value pending a sale or other disposition of its assets, or both, in whole or in part. The board shall cause written notice of the commencement of the proceeding for voluntary winding up to be given by mail to all its members (except no notice need be given to the members who voted in favor of winding up and dissolving the corporation), to all known creditors and claimants whose addresses appear on the records of the corporation, and in the case of a corporation holding assets in charitable trust to the Attorney General.
Ca. Corp. Code § 8613
Amended by Stats. 1984, Ch. 812, Sec. 13.

Section 8614 - Assumption of jurisdiction by superior court

If a corporation is in the process of voluntary winding up, the superior court of the proper county, upon the petition of (a) the corporation, or (b) the authorized number (Section 5036), or (c) in the case of a corporation holding assets in charitable trust, the Attorney General, or (d) three or more creditors, and upon such notice to the corporation and to other persons interested in the corporation as members and creditors as the court may order, may take jurisdiction over such voluntary winding up proceeding if that appears necessary for the protection of any parties in interest or in the case of a corporation holding assets in charitable trust, for the protection of such assets. The court, if it assumes jurisdiction, may make such orders as to any and all matters concerning the winding up of the affairs of the corporation and the protection of its members, creditors and in the case of a corporation holding assets in charitable trust, for the protection of such assets, as justice and equity may require. The provisions of Chapter 15 (commencing with Section 8510) (except Sections 8510 and 8511) shall apply to such court proceedings.

Ca. Corp. Code § 8614
Added by Stats. 1978, Ch. 567.

Section 8615 - Certificate of dissolution

(a) When a corporation has been completely wound up without court proceedings therefor, a majority of the directors then in office shall sign and verify a certificate of dissolution stating:

(1) That the corporation has been completely wound up.

(2) That its known debts and liabilities have been actually paid, or adequately provided for, or paid or adequately provided for as far as its assets permitted, or that it has incurred no known debts or liabilities, as the case may be. If there are known debts or liabilities for payment of which adequate provision has been made, the certificate shall state what provision has been made, setting forth the name and address of the corporation, person or governmental agency that has assumed or guaranteed the payment, or the name and address of the depositary with which deposit has been made or such other information as may be necessary to enable the creditor or other person to whom payment is to be made to appear and claim payment of the debt or liability.

(3) That its known assets have been distributed to the persons entitled thereto or that it acquired no known assets, as the case may be.

(4) That the corporation is dissolved.

(5) That all final returns required under the Revenue and Taxation Code, have been or will be filed with the Franchise Tax Board.
(b) The certificate of dissolution shall be filed and thereupon the corporate existence shall cease, except for the purpose of further winding up if needed. The Secretary of State shall notify the Franchise Tax Board of the dissolution.

Ca. Corp. Code § 8615
Amended by Stats 2011 ch 442 (AB 1211),s 21, eff. 1/1/2012.
Amended by Stats 2006 ch 773 (AB 2341),s 28, eff. 9/29/2006.

Section 8616 - Expiration of term of existence without renewal or extension

Except as otherwise provided by law, if the term of existence for which any corporation was organized expires without renewal or extension thereof, the board shall terminate its activities and wind up its affairs; and when the affairs of the corporation have been wound up a majority of the directors shall execute and file a certificate conforming to the requirements of Section 8615.

Ca. Corp. Code § 8616

Added by Stats. 1978, Ch. 567.

Section 8617 - Petition for order declaring corporation duly wound up and dissolved

(a) The board, in lieu of filing the certificate of dissolution, may petition the superior court of the proper county for an order declaring the corporation duly wound up and dissolved. Such petition shall be filed in the name of the corporation.

(b) Upon the filing of the petition, the court shall make an order requiring all interested persons, including the Attorney General in the case of a corporation holding assets in charitable trust, to show cause why an order shall not be made declaring the corporation duly wound up and dissolved and shall direct that the order be served by notice to all creditors, claimants, and members in the same manner as the notice given under subdivision (b) of Section 8517.

(c) Any person claiming to be interested as member, creditor or otherwise may appear in the proceeding at any time before the expiration of 30 days from the completion of publication of the order to show cause and contest the petition, and upon failure to appear such person's claim shall be barred.

(d) Thereafter an order shall be entered and filed and have the effect as prescribed in Sections 8518 and 8519.

Ca. Corp. Code § 8617

Amended by Stats. 1979, Ch. 724.

Section 8618 - Disposal of known claims

(a) A corporation in the process of voluntary winding up may dispose of the known claims against it by following the procedure described in this section.

(b) The written notice to known creditors and claimants required by subdivision (c) of Section 8613 shall comply with all of the following requirements:

(1) Describe any information that must be included in a claim.

(2) Provide a mailing address where a claim may be sent.

(3) State the deadline, which may not be fewer than 120 days from the effective date of the written notice, by which the corporation must receive the claim.

(4) State that the claim will be barred if not received by the deadline.

(c) A claim against the corporation is barred if any of the following occur:

(1) A claimant who has been given the written notice under subdivision (b) does not deliver the claim to the corporation by the deadline.

(2) A claimant whose claim was rejected by the corporation does not commence a proceeding to enforce the claim within 90 days from the effective date of the rejection notice.

(d) For purposes of this section "claim" does not include a contingent liability or a claim based on an event occurring after the effective date of dissolution.

Ca. Corp. Code § 8618

Added by Stats. 1996, Ch. 589, Sec. 37. Effective January 1, 1997.

Chapter 17 - GENERAL PROVISIONS RELATING TO DISSOLUTION

Section 8710 - Powers and duties of directors and officers

The powers and duties of the directors (or other persons appointed by the court pursuant to Section 8515) and officers after commencement of a dissolution proceeding include, but are not limited to, the following acts in the name and on behalf of the corporation:

(a) To elect officers and to employ agents and attorneys to liquidate or wind up its affairs.

(b) To continue the conduct of the affairs of the corporation insofar as necessary for the disposal or winding up thereof.

(c) To carry out contracts and collect, pay, compromise and settle debts and claims for or against the corporation.

(d) To defend suits brought against the corporation.

(e) To sue, in the name of the corporation, for all sums due or owing to the corporation or to recover any of its property.

(f) To collect any amounts remaining unpaid on memberships or to recover unlawful distributions.

(g) To sell at public or private sale, exchange, convey or otherwise dispose of all or any part of the assets of the corporation for an amount deemed reasonable by the board without compliance with the provisions of Section 7911 and to execute bills of sale and deeds of conveyance in the name of the corporation.

(h) In general, to make contracts and to do any and all things in the name of the corporation which may be proper or convenient for the purposes of winding up, settling and liquidating the affairs of the corporation.

Ca. Corp. Code § 8710

Amended by Stats. 1979, Ch. 724.

Section 8711 - Vacancy on board

A vacancy on the board may be filled during a winding up proceeding in the manner provided in Section 7224.

Ca. Corp. Code § 8711
Added by Stats. 1978, Ch. 567.

Section 8712 - Petition to determine identity of directors or to appoint directors

When the identity of the directors or their right to hold office is in doubt, or if they are dead or unable to act, or they fail or refuse to act or their whereabouts cannot be ascertained, any interested person, including the Attorney General in the case of corporations holding assets in charitable trust, may petition the superior court of the proper county to determine the identity of the directors or, if there are no directors, to appoint directors to wind up the affairs of the corporation, after hearing upon such notice to such persons as the court may direct.

Ca. Corp. Code § 8712
Added by Stats. 1978, Ch. 567.

Section 8713 - Distribution of remaining corporate assets

(a) After determining that all the known debts and liabilities of a corporation in the process of winding up have been paid or adequately provided for, the board shall distribute all the remaining corporate assets in the manner provided in Sections 8715 to 8717, inclusive.

(b) If the winding up is by court proceeding or subject to court supervision, the distribution shall not be made until after the expiration of any period for the presentation of claims that has been prescribed by order of the court.

(c) Anything to the contrary notwithstanding, assets, if any, which are not subject to attachment, execution or sale for the corporation's debts and liabilities may be distributed pursuant to Sections 8715 to 8717, inclusive, even though all debts and liabilities have not been paid or adequately provided for.

Ca. Corp. Code § 8713
Added by Stats. 1978, Ch. 567.

Section 8714 - Payment of debt or liability

The payment of a debt or liability, whether the whereabouts of the creditor is known or unknown, has been adequately provided for if the payment has been provided for by either of the following means:

(a) Payment thereof has been assumed or guaranteed in good faith by one or more financially responsible persons or by the United States government or any agency thereof, and the provision (including the financial responsibility of such persons) was determined in good faith and with reasonable care by the board to be adequate at the time of any distribution of the assets by the board pursuant to this chapter.

(b) The amount of the debt or liability has been deposited as provided in Section 8720. This section does not prescribe the exclusive means of making adequate

provision for debts and liabilities.
Ca. Corp. Code § 8714
Amended by Stats. 1979, Ch. 724.

Section 8715 - Assets held upon condition requiring return, transfer, or conveyance

After complying with the provisions of Section 8713, assets held by a corporation upon a valid condition requiring return, transfer, or conveyance, which condition has occurred or will occur, shall be returned, transferred, or conveyed in accordance with the condition.
Ca. Corp. Code § 8715
Added by Stats. 1978, Ch. 567.

Section 8716 - Assets held in charitable trust

After complying with the provisions of Section 8713:
(a) Except as provided in Section 8715 those assets held by a corporation in a charitable trust shall be disposed of on dissolution in conformity with its articles or bylaws subject to complying with the provisions of any trust under which such assets are held.
(b) Except as provided in subdivision (c), the disposition required in subdivision (a) shall be made by decree of the superior court of the proper county in proceedings to which the Attorney General is a party. The decree shall be made upon petition therefor by the Attorney General or, upon 30 days' notice to the Attorney General, by any person concerned in the dissolution.
(c) The disposition required in subdivision (a) may be made without the decree of the superior court, subject to the rights of persons concerned in the dissolution, if the Attorney General makes a written waiver of objections to the disposition.
Ca. Corp. Code § 8716
Added by Stats. 1978, Ch. 567.

Section 8717 - Disposal of assets on dissolution

After complying with the provisions of Section 8713 and except as otherwise provided in Sections 8715 and 8716, assets held by a corporation shall be disposed of on dissolution as follows:
(a) If the articles or bylaws provide the manner of disposition, the assets shall be disposed of in that manner.
(b) If the articles or bylaws do not provide the manner of disposition, the assets shall be distributed among the members in accordance with their respective rights therein.
Ca. Corp. Code § 8717
Added by Stats. 1978, Ch. 567.

Section 8718 - Manner of distribution

Subject to the provisions of any trust under which assets to be distributed are held, distribution may be made either in money or in property or securities and either in installments from time to time or as a whole, if this can be done fairly and ratably and in conformity with the provisions of the articles and bylaws and shall be made as soon as reasonably consistent with the beneficial liquidation of the corporation assets.

Ca. Corp. Code § 8718
Added by Stats. 1978, Ch. 567.

Section 8719 - Plan of distribution if corporation has more than one class of membership

(a) If a corporation in process of winding up has more than one class of memberships outstanding, a plan of distribution of the memberships, obligations or securities of any other corporation, domestic or foreign, or assets other than money which is not in accordance with the liquidation rights of any class or classes as specified in the articles or bylaws may nevertheless be adopted if approved by (1) the board and (2) by approval by the members (Section 5034) of each class. The plan may provide that such distribution is in complete or partial satisfaction of the rights of any of such members upon distribution and liquidation of the assets.
(b) A plan of distribution so approved shall be binding upon all the members. The board shall cause notice of the adoption of the plan to be given by mail within 20 days after its adoption to all holders of memberships having a liquidation preference.

Ca. Corp. Code § 8719
Amended by Stats. 1979, Ch. 724.

Section 8720 - Deposit with controller in trust

(a) If any members, creditors, or other persons are unknown or fail or refuse to accept their payment or distribution in cash or property or their whereabouts cannot be ascertained after diligent inquiry, or the existence or amount of a claim of a creditor, member or other person is contingent, contested, or not determined, or if the ownership of any memberships is in dispute, the corporation may deposit any such payment, distribution, or the maximum amount of the claim with the Controller in trust for the benefit of those lawfully entitled to the payment, distribution, or the amount of the claim. The payment or distribution shall be paid over by the depositary to the lawful owners, their representatives or assigns, upon satisfactory proof of title.
(b) For the purpose of providing for the transmittal, receipt, accounting for, claiming, management, and investment of all money or other property deposited with the Controller under subdivision (a), the money or other property shall be deemed to be paid or delivered for deposit with the Controller under Chapter 7 (commencing with Section 1500) of Title 10 of Part 3 of the Code of Civil Procedure, and may be

recovered in the manner prescribed in that chapter.

Ca. Corp. Code § 8720

Amended by Stats. 1996, Ch. 860, Sec. 3. Effective January 1, 1997.

Section 8721 - Recovery of improper distribution

(a) Whenever in the process of winding up a corporation any distribution of assets has been made, otherwise than under an order of court, without prior payment or adequate provision for payment of any of the debts and liabilities of the corporation, any amount so improperly distributed to any person may be recovered by the corporation. Any of such persons may be joined as defendants in the same action or be brought in on the motion of any other defendant.

(b) Suit may be brought in the name of the corporation to enforce the liability under subdivision (a) against any or all persons receiving the distribution by any one or more creditors of the corporation, whether or not they have reduced their claims to judgment.

(c) Members who satisfy any liability under this section shall have the right of ratable contribution from other distributees similarly liable. Any member who has been compelled to return to the corporation more than the member's ratable share of the amount needed to pay the debts and liabilities of the corporation may require that the corporation recover from any or all of the other distributees such proportion of the amounts received by them upon the improper distribution as to give contribution to those held liable under this section and make the distribution of the assets fair and ratable, according to the respective rights and preferences of the memberships, after payment or adequate provision for payment of all the debts and liabilities of the corporation.

(d) As used in this section, "process of winding up" includes proceedings under Chapters 15 (commencing with Section 8510) and 16 (commencing with Section 8610) and also any other distribution of assets to persons made in contemplation of termination or abandonment of the corporate business.

Ca. Corp. Code § 8721

Amended by Stats. 1979, Ch. 724.

Section 8722 - Continued existence

(a) A corporation which is dissolved nevertheless continues to exist for the purpose of winding up its affairs, prosecuting and defending actions by or against it and enabling it to collect and discharge obligations, dispose of and convey its property and collect and divide its assets, but not for the purpose of continuing its activities except so far as necessary for the winding up thereof.

(b) No action or proceeding to which a corporation is a party abates by the dissolution of the corporation or by reason of proceedings for winding up and dissolution thereof.

(c) Any assets inadvertently or otherwise omitted from the winding up continue in the dissolved corporation for the benefit of the persons entitled thereto upon dissolution of the corporation and on realization shall be distributed accordingly.

Ca. Corp. Code § 8722

Added by Stats. 1978, Ch. 567.

Section 8723 - Causes of action against dissolved corporation or against person to whom assets were distributed

(a)

(1) Causes of action against a dissolved corporation, whether arising before or after the dissolution of the corporation, may be enforced against any of the following:

(A) Against the dissolved corporation, to the extent of its undistributed assets, including, without limitation, any insurance assets held by the corporation that may be available to satisfy claims.

(B) If any of the assets of the dissolved corporation have been distributed to other persons, against those persons to the extent of their pro rata share of the claim or to the extent of the corporate assets distributed to them upon dissolution of the corporation, whichever is less. The total liability of a person under this section may not exceed the total amount of assets of the dissolved corporation distributed to that person upon dissolution of the corporation.

(2) Except as set forth in subdivision (c), all causes of action against a person to whom assets were distributed arising under this section are extinguished unless the claimant commences a proceeding to enforce the cause of action against that person prior to the earlier of the following:

(A) The expiration of the statute of limitations applicable to the cause of action.

(B) Four years after the effective date of the dissolution of the corporation.

(3) As a matter of procedure only, and not for purposes of determining liability, persons to whom assets of a dissolved corporation are distributed may be sued in the name of the corporation upon any cause of action against the corporation. This section does not affect the rights of the corporation or its creditors under Section 2009, or the rights, if any, of creditors under the Uniform Voidable Transactions Act, which may arise against persons to whom those assets are distributed.

(4) This subdivision applies to corporations dissolved on or after January 1, 2000. Corporations dissolved prior to that date are subject to the law in effect prior to that date.

(b) Summons or other process against the corporation may be served by delivering a copy thereof to an officer, director, or person having charge of its assets or, if none of these persons can be found, to any agent upon whom process might be served at the time of dissolution. If none of those persons can be found with due diligence and it is so shown by affidavit to the satisfaction of the court, then the court may make an order that summons or other process be served upon the dissolved corporation by personally delivering a copy thereof, together with a copy of the order, to the Secretary of State or an assistant or deputy secretary of state, with an additional copy of the summons or other process and order being delivered to the Attorney General in the case of a corporation that at the commencement of the dissolution proceedings held assets in charitable trust. Service in this manner is deemed complete on the 10th day after delivery of the process to the Secretary of State, or in the case of a corporation that at the commencement of the dissolution proceedings held assets in charitable trust, upon the 10th day after the later of delivery of process to the Secretary of State or Attorney General.

(c) The corporation shall survive and continue to exist indefinitely for the purpose of being sued in any quiet title action. Any judgment rendered in that action shall bind each of its members or other persons having any equity or other interest in the corporation, to the extent of their interest therein, and that action shall have the same force and effect as an action brought under the provisions of Sections 410.50 and 410.60 of the Code of Civil Procedure. Service of summons or other process in that action may be made as provided in Chapter 4 (commencing with Section 413.10) of Title 5 of Part 2 of the Code of Civil Procedure or as provided in subdivision (b).

(d) Upon receipt of that process and the fee therefor, the Secretary of State forthwith shall give notice to the corporation as provided in Section 1702.

Ca. Corp. Code § 8723

Amended by Stats 2019 ch 143 (SB 251),s 30, eff. 1/1/2020.
Amended 9/21/1999 (Bill Number: AB 1687) (Chapter 453).

Section 8724 - Owners' association

Without the approval of 100 percent of the members, any contrary provision in this part or the articles or bylaws notwithstanding, so long as there is any lot, parcel, area, apartment, or unit for which an owners' association, created in connection with any of the forms of development referred to in Section 11004.5 of the Business and Professions Code, is obligated to provide management, maintenance, preservation, or control, the following shall apply:

(a) The owners' association or any person acting on its behalf shall not do either of the following:

(1) Transfer all or substantially all of its assets.

(2) File a certificate of dissolution.

(b) No court shall enter an order declaring the owners' association duly wound up and dissolved.

Ca. Corp. Code § 8724

Amended by Stats 2006 ch 538 (SB 1852),s 80, eff. 1/1/2007.

Chapter 18 - CRIMES AND PENALTIES

Section 8810 - Failure to file statement

(a) Upon the failure of a corporation to file the statement required by Section 8210, the Secretary of State shall provide a notice of such delinquency to the corporation. The notice shall also contain information concerning the application of this section, and advise the corporation of the penalty imposed by Section 19141 of the Revenue and Taxation Code for failure to timely file the required statement after notice of delinquency has been provided by the Secretary of State. If, within 60 days after providing notice of the delinquency, a statement pursuant to Section 8210 has not been filed by the corporation, the Secretary of State shall certify the name of the corporation to the Franchise Tax Board.

(b) Upon certification pursuant to subdivision (a), the Franchise Tax Board shall assess against the corporation a penalty of fifty dollars ($50) pursuant to Section 19141 of the Revenue and Taxation Code.

(c) The penalty herein provided shall not apply to a corporation which on or prior to the date of certification pursuant to subdivision (a) has dissolved, has converted to another type of business entity, or has been merged into another corporation or other business entity.

(d) The penalty herein provided shall not apply and the Secretary of State need not provide a notice of the delinquency to a corporation the corporate powers, rights, and privileges of which have been suspended by the Franchise Tax Board pursuant to Section 23301, 23301.5, or 23775 of the Revenue and Taxation Code on or prior to, and remain suspended on, the last day of the filing period pursuant to Section 8210. The Secretary of State need not provide notice of the filing requirement pursuant to Section 8210, to a corporation the corporate powers, rights, and privileges of which have been so suspended by the Franchise Tax Board on or prior to, and remain suspended on, the day the Secretary of State prepares the notice for sending.

(e) If, after certification pursuant to subdivision (a) the Secretary of State finds the required statement was filed before the expiration of the 60-day period after providing the notice of delinquency, the Secretary of State shall promptly decertify the name of the corporation to the Franchise Tax Board. The Franchise Tax Board shall then promptly abate any penalty assessed against the corporation pursuant to Section 19141 of the Revenue and Taxation Code.

(f) If the Secretary of State determines that the failure of a corporation to file a statement required by Section 8210 is excusable because of reasonable cause or unusual circumstances which justify the failure, the Secretary of State may waive the penalty imposed by this section and by Section 19141 of the Revenue and Taxation Code, in which case the Secretary of State shall not certify the name of the corporation to the Franchise Tax Board, or if already certified, the Secretary of State shall promptly decertify the name of the corporation.

Ca. Corp. Code § 8810

Amended by Stats 2014 ch 834 (SB 1041),s 17, eff. 1/1/2015.

Amended by Stats 2012 ch 494 (SB 1532),s 23, eff. 1/1/2013.

Amended by Stats 2011 ch 204 (AB 657),s 10, eff. 1/1/2012.

Section 8811 - Unlawful issuance of memberships or membership certificates

Any promoter, director, or officer of a corporation who knowingly and willfully issues or consents to the issuance of memberships or membership certificates with intent to defraud present or future members or creditors is guilty of a misdemeanor punishable by a fine of not more than one thousand dollars ($1,000) or by imprisonment in county jail for not more than one year or by both such fine and imprisonment.

Ca. Corp. Code § 8811

Added by Stats. 1978, Ch. 567.

Section 8812 - Unlawful distribution of assets

Any director of any corporation who concurs in any vote or act of the directors of the corporation or any of them, knowingly and with dishonest or fraudulent purpose, to make any distribution of assets, except in the case and in the manner allowed by this part, either with the design of defrauding creditors or members or of giving a false appearance to the value of the membership and thereby defrauding purchasers is guilty of a crime. Each such crime is punishable by imprisonment pursuant to subdivision (h) of Section 1170 of the Penal Code, or by a fine of not more than one thousand dollars ($1,000) or imprisonment in a county jail for not more than one year, or by both that fine and imprisonment.

Ca. Corp. Code § 8812

Amended by Stats 2011 ch 39 (AB 117),s 68, eff. 6/30/2011.

Amended by Stats 2011 ch 15 (AB 109),s 42, eff. 4/4/2011, but operative no earlier than October 1, 2011, and only upon creation of a community corrections grant program to assist in implementing this act and upon an appropriation to fund the grant program.

Section 8813 - False report or statement as to financial condition; refusal to make book entry or post notice

(a) Every director or officer of any corporation is guilty of a crime if such director or officer knowingly concurs in making or publishing, either generally or privately, to members or other persons (1) any materially false report or statement as to the financial condition of the corporation, or (2) any willfully or fraudulently exaggerated report, prospectus, account or statement of operations, financial condition or prospects, or (3) any other paper intended to give, and having a tendency to give, a membership in such corporation a greater or lesser value than it really possesses.

(b) Every director or officer of any corporation is guilty of a crime who refuses to make or direct to be made any book entry or the posting of any notice required by law in the manner required by law.

(c) A violation of subdivision (a) or (b) of this section shall be punishable by imprisonment in state prison or by a fine of not more than one thousand dollars ($1,000) or imprisonment in the county jail for not more than one year or both such fine and imprisonment.

Ca. Corp. Code § 8813
Added by Stats. 1978, Ch. 567.

Section 8814 - Unlawful possession of corporate property; unlawful destruction or falsification; unlawful making or omitting to make entry

(a) Every director, officer or agent of any corporation, who knowingly receives or acquires possession of any property of the corporation, otherwise than in payment of a just demand, and, with intent to defraud, omits to make, or to cause or direct to be made, a full and true entry thereof in the books or accounts of the corporation is guilty of a crime.

(b) Every director, officer, agent or member of any corporation who, with intent to defraud, destroys, alters, mutilates or falsifies any of the books, papers, writings or securities belonging to the corporation or makes or concurs in omitting to make any material entry in any book of accounts or other record or document kept by the corporation is guilty of a crime.

(c) Each crime specified in this section is punishable by imprisonment in state prison, or by imprisonment in a county jail for not exceeding one year, or a fine not exceeding one thousand dollars ($1,000), or both such fine and imprisonment.

Ca. Corp. Code § 8814
Added by Stats. 1978, Ch. 567.

Section 8815 - Unlawful exhibition of instrument of evidence to public officer or board

Every director, officer or agent of any corporation, or any person proposing to organize such a corporation who knowingly exhibits any false, forged or altered book, paper, voucher, security or other instrument of evidence to any public officer or board authorized by law to examine the organization of such corporation or to investigate its affairs, with intent to deceive such officer or board in respect thereto, is punishable by imprisonment pursuant to subdivision (h) of Section 1170 of the Penal Code, or by imprisonment in a county jail for not exceeding one year.

Ca. Corp. Code § 8815
Amended by Stats 2011 ch 39 (AB 117),s 68, eff. 6/30/2011.
Amended by Stats 2011 ch 15 (AB 109),s 43, eff. 4/4/2011, but operative no earlier

than October 1, 2011, and only upon creation of a community corrections grant program to assist in implementing this act and upon an appropriation to fund the grant program.

Section 8816 - Unlawful subscribing of name of another

Every person who, without being authorized so to do, subscribes the name of another to or inserts the name of another in any prospectus, circular or other advertisement or announcement of any corporation, whether existing or intended to be formed, with intent to permit the document to be published and thereby to lead persons to believe that the person whose name is so subscribed is an officer, agent or promoter of such corporation, when in fact no such relationship exists to the knowledge of such person, is guilty of a misdemeanor.
   Ca. Corp. Code § 8816
Added by Stats. 1978, Ch. 567.

Section 8817 - No limitation of power of state to punish

Nothing in this chapter limits the power of the state to punish any person for any conduct which constitutes a crime under any other statute.
   Ca. Corp. Code § 8817
Added by Stats. 1978, Ch. 567.

Chapter 19 - FOREIGN CORPORATIONS

Section 8910 - Foreign corporations transacting intrastate business

Foreign corporations transacting intrastate business shall comply with Chapter 21 (commencing with Section 2100) of Division 1, except as to matters specifically otherwise provided for in this part and except that Section 2115 shall not be applicable.
   Ca. Corp. Code § 8910
Amended by Stats. 1997, Ch. 187, Sec. 9. Effective January 1, 1998.

Part 4 - NONPROFIT RELIGIOUS CORPORATIONS

Chapter 1 - ORGANIZATION AND BYLAWS

Article 1 - TITLE AND PURPOSES

Section 9110 - Short title

This part shall be known and may be cited as the Nonprofit Religious Corporation Law.

Ca. Corp. Code § 9110
Added by Stats. 1978, Ch. 567.

Section 9111 - Formation under this part

Subject to any other provision of law of this state applying to the particular class of corporation or line of activity, a corporation may be formed under this part primarily or exclusively for any religious purposes.

Ca. Corp. Code § 9111
Added by Stats. 1978, Ch. 567.

Article 2 - FORMATION

Section 9120 - Formation

(a) One or more persons may form a corporation under this part by executing and filing articles of incorporation.

(b) If initial directors are named in the articles, each director named in the articles shall sign and acknowledge the articles; if initial directors are not named in the articles, the articles shall be signed by one or more persons who thereupon are the incorporators of the corporation.

(c) The corporate existence begins upon the filing of the articles and continues perpetually, unless otherwise expressly provided by law or in the articles.

Ca. Corp. Code § 9120
Amended by Stats. 1983, Ch. 1085, Sec. 6.

Section 9121 - Unincorporated association changing status to that of corporation

(a) In the case of an existing unincorporated association, the association may change its status to that of a corporation upon a proper authorization for such by the association in accordance with its rules and procedures.

(b) In addition to the matters required to be set forth in the articles pursuant to Section 9130, the articles in the case of an incorporation authorized by subdivision (a) shall set forth that an existing unincorporated association, stating its name, is being incorporated by the filing of the articles.

(c) The articles filed pursuant to this section shall be accompanied by a verified statement of any two officers or governing board members of the association stating that the incorporation of the association by means of the articles to which the verified statement is attached has been approved by the association in accordance with its rules and procedures.

(d) Upon the change of status of an unincorporated association to a corporation pursuant to subdivision (a), the property of the association becomes the property of the corporation and the members of the association who had any voting rights of the type referred to in Section 5056 become members of the corporation.

(e) The filing for records in the office of the county recorder of any county in this state in which any of the real property of the association is located of a copy of the articles of incorporation filed pursuant to this section, certified by the Secretary of State, shall evidence record ownership in the corporation of all interests of the association in and to the real property located in that county.

(f) All rights of creditors and all liens upon the property of the association shall be preserved unimpaired. Any action or proceeding pending by or against the unincorporated association may be prosecuted to judgment, which shall bind the corporation, or the corporation may be proceeded against or substituted in its place.

(g) If a corporation is organized by a person who is or was an officer, director or member of an unincorporated association and such corporation is not organized pursuant to subdivision (a), the unincorporated association may continue to use its name and the corporation may not use a name which is the same as or similar to the name of the unincorporated association.

Ca. Corp. Code § 9121
Amended by Stats. 1981, Ch. 587, Sec. 48.

Section 9122 - Names

(a) The Secretary of State shall not file articles setting forth a name in which "bank," "trust," "trustee," or related words appear, unless the certificate of approval of the Commissioner of Financial Protection and Innovation is attached thereto.

(b) The name of a corporation shall not be a name that the Secretary of State determines is likely to mislead the public and shall be distinguishable in the records of the Secretary of State from all of the following:

(1)The name of any corporation.

(2)The name of any foreign corporation authorized to transact intrastate business in this state.

(3)Each name that is under reservation pursuant to this title.

(4)The name of a foreign corporation that has registered its name pursuant to Section 2101.

(5)An alternate name of a foreign corporation under subdivision (b) of Section 2106.

(6)A name that will become the record name of a domestic or foreign corporation upon a corporate instrument when there is a delayed effective or file date.

(c) The use by a corporation of a name in violation of this section may be enjoined notwithstanding the filing of its articles by the Secretary of State.

(d) Any applicant may, upon payment of the fee prescribed therefor in the Government Code, obtain from the Secretary of State a certificate of reservation of any name not prohibited by subdivision (b), and upon the issuance of the certificate the name stated therein shall be reserved for a period of 60 days. The Secretary of State shall not, however, issue certificates reserving the same name for two or more consecutive 60-day periods to the same applicant or for the use or benefit of the same person; nor shall consecutive reservations be made by or for the use or benefit of the same person of names so similar as to fall within the prohibitions of subdivision (b).

Ca. Corp. Code § 9122
Amended by Stats 2022 ch 617 (SB 1202),s 67, eff. 1/1/2023.
Amended by Stats 2022 ch 452 (SB 1498),s 57, eff. 1/1/2023.
Amended by Stats 2020 ch 361 (SB 522),s 7, eff. 1/1/2021.
Amended by Stats 2014 ch 401 (AB 2763),s 22, eff. 1/1/2015.
Amended by Stats 2011 ch 740 (SB 201),s 15, eff. 1/1/2012.

Article 3 - ARTICLES OF INCORPORATION

Section 9130 - Articles of incorporation

The articles of incorporation of a corporation formed under this part shall set forth:
(a) The name of the corporation.
(b) The following statement: "This corporation is a religious corporation and is not organized for the private gain of any person. It is organized under the Nonprofit Religious Corporation Law (primarily or exclusively [insert one or both]) for religious purposes." [The articles may include a further description of the corporation's purpose.]
(c) The name and street address in this state of the corporation's initial agent for service of process in accordance with subdivision (b) of Section 6210 (made applicable pursuant to Section 9660).
(d) The initial street address of the corporation.
(e) The initial mailing address of the corporation, if different from the initial street address.

Ca. Corp. Code § 9130
Amended by Stats 2012 ch 494 (SB 1532),s 24, eff. 1/1/2013.

Section 9131 - Statement limiting purpose or powers of corporation

The articles of incorporation may set forth a further statement limiting the purposes or powers of the corporation.

Ca. Corp. Code § 9131
Added by Stats. 1978, Ch. 567.

Section 9132 - Additional provisions

(a) The articles of incorporation may set forth any or all of the following provisions, which shall not be effective unless expressly provided in the articles:

(1) A provision limiting the duration of the corporation's existence to a specified date.

(2) In the case of a subordinate corporation instituted or created under the authority of a head organization, a provision setting forth either or both of the following:

(A) That the subordinate corporation shall dissolve whenever its charter is surrendered to, taken away by, or revoked by the head organization granting it.

(B) That in the event of its dissolution pursuant to an article provision allowed by subparagraph (A) or in the event of its dissolution for any reason, any assets of the corporation after compliance with the applicable provisions of Chapters 16 (commencing with Section 6610) and 17 (commencing with Section 6710) (made applicable pursuant to Section 9680) shall be distributed to the head organization.
(b) Nothing contained in subdivision (a) shall affect the enforceability, as between the parties thereto, of any lawful agreement not otherwise contrary to public policy.
(c) The articles of incorporation may set forth any or all of the following provisions:

(1) The names and addresses of the persons appointed to act as initial directors.

(2) The classes of members, if any, and if there are two or more classes, the rights, privileges, preferences, restrictions and conditions attaching to each class.

(3) A provision which would allow any member to have more or less than one vote in any election or other matter presented to the members for a vote.

(4) A provision that requires an amendment to the articles or to the bylaws, and any amendment or repeal of that amendment, to be approved in writing by a specified person or persons other than the board or the members. However, this approval requirement, unless the articles or the bylaws specify otherwise, shall not apply if any of the following circumstances exist:

(A) The specified person or persons have died or ceased to exist.

(B) If the right of the specified person or persons to approve is in the capacity of an officer, trustee, or other status and the office, trust, or status has ceased to exist.

(C) If the corporation has a specific proposal for amendment or repeal, and the corporation has provided written notice of that proposal, including a copy of the proposal, to the specified person or persons at the most recent address for each of them, based on the corporation's records, and the corporation has not received written approval or nonapproval within the period specified in the notice, which shall not be less than 10 nor more than 30 days commencing at least 20 days after the notice has been provided.

(5) Any other provision, not in conflict with law, for the management of the activities and for the conduct of the affairs of the corporation, including any provision which is required or permitted by this part to be stated in the bylaws.

   Ca. Corp. Code § 9132
Amended by Stats 2009 ch 631 (AB 1233),s 26, eff. 1/1/2010.

Section 9133 - Certified copy of articles of incorporation

For all purposes other than an action in the nature of quo warranto, a copy of the articles of a corporation duly certified by the Secretary of State is conclusive evidence of the formation of the corporation and prima facie evidence of its corporate existence.

   Ca. Corp. Code § 9133
Added by Stats. 1978, Ch. 567.

Section 9134 - Perfection of organization of corporation by incorporators

If initial directors have not been named in the articles, the incorporator or incorporators, until the directors are elected, may do whatever is necessary and proper to perfect the organization of the corporation, including the adoption and amendment of bylaws of the corporation and the election of directors and officers.

   Ca. Corp. Code § 9134
Amended by Stats. 1979, Ch. 724.

Article 4 - POWERS

Section 9140 - Powers

Subject to any limitations contained in the articles or bylaws and to compliance with other provisions of this division and any other applicable laws, a corporation, in carrying out its activities, shall have all of the powers of a natural person, including, without limitation, the power to:
(a) Adopt, use, and at will alter a corporate seal, but failure to affix a seal does not affect the validity of any instrument.
(b) Adopt, amend, and repeal bylaws.
(c) Qualify to conduct its activities in any other state, territory, dependency, or foreign country.
(d) Issue, purchase, redeem, receive, take or otherwise acquire, own, sell, lend, exchange, transfer or otherwise dispose of, pledge, use, and otherwise deal in and with

its own bonds, debentures, notes, and debt securities.

(e) Issue memberships.

(f) Pay pensions, and establish and carry out pension, deferred compensation, saving, thrift, and other retirement, incentive, and benefit plans, trusts, and provisions for any or all of its directors, officers, employees, and persons providing services to it or any of its subsidiary or related or associated corporations, and to indemnify and purchase and maintain insurance on behalf of any fiduciary of such plans, trusts, or provisions.

(g) Levy dues, assessments, and fees.

(h) Make donations for the public welfare or for community funds, hospital, charitable, educational, scientific, civic, religious, or similar purposes.

(i) Assume obligations, enter into contracts, including contracts of guarantee or suretyship, incur liabilities, borrow or lend money or otherwise use its credit, and secure any of its obligations, contracts, or liabilities by mortgage, pledge, or other encumbrance of all or any part of its property and income.

(j) Participate with others in any partnership, joint venture, or other association, transaction, or arrangement of any kind whether or not such participation involves sharing or delegation of control with or to others.

(k) Act as trustee under any trust incidental to the principal objects of the corporation, and receive, hold, administer, exchange, and expend funds and property subject to such trust.

(l) Carry on a business at a profit and apply any profit that results from the business activity to any activity in which it may lawfully engage.

(m) Pay the reasonable value of services rendered in this state to the corporation before January 1, 1975, and not previously paid, by any person who performed such services on a full-time basis under the direction of a religious organization in connection with the religious tenets of the organization. Such person shall have relied solely on the religious organization for their financial support for a minimum of five years. A payment shall not be made if such person or religious organization waives the payment or receipt of compensation for such services in writing. Payment may be made to such religious organization to reimburse it for maintenance of any person who rendered such services and to assist it in providing future support and maintenance; however, payment shall not be made from any funds or assets acquired with funds donated by or traceable to gifts made to the corporation by any person, organization, or governmental agency other than the members, immediate families of members, and affiliated religious organizations of the religious organization under whose direction the services were performed.

(n)

(1) In anticipation of or during an emergency, take either or both of the following actions necessary to conduct the corporation's business operations and affairs, unless emergency bylaws provide otherwise pursuant to subdivision (g) of Section 9151:

(A) Modify lines of succession to accommodate the incapacity of any director, officer, employee, or agent resulting from the emergency.

(B) Relocate the principal office, designate alternative principal offices or regional offices, or authorize the officers to do so.

(2) During an emergency, take either or both of the following actions necessary to conduct the corporation's business operations and affairs, unless emergency bylaws provide otherwise pursuant to subdivision (g) of Section 9151:

(A) Give notice to a director or directors in any practicable manner under the circumstances, including, but not limited to, by publication and radio, when notice of a meeting of the board cannot be given to that director or directors in the manner prescribed by the bylaws or Section 9211.

(B) Deem that one or more officers of the corporation present at a board meeting is a director, in order of rank and within the same rank in order of seniority, as necessary to achieve a quorum for that meeting.

(3) In anticipation of or during an emergency, the board may take any action that it determines to be necessary or appropriate to respond to the emergency, mitigate the effects of the emergency, or comply with lawful federal and state government orders, but shall not take any action that requires the vote of the members, unless the required vote of the members was obtained prior to the emergency.

(4) Any actions taken in good faith in anticipation of or during an emergency under this subdivision bind the corporation and shall not be used to impose liability on a corporate director, officer, employee, or agent.

(5) For purposes of this subdivision, "emergency" means any of the following events or circumstances as a result of which, and only so long as, a quorum of the corporation's board of directors cannot be readily convened for action:

(A) A natural catastrophe, including, but not limited to, a hurricane, tornado, storm, high water, wind-driven water, tidal wave, tsunami, earthquake, volcanic eruption, landslide, mudslide, snowstorm, drought, epidemic, pandemic, or disease outbreak, or, regardless of cause, any fire, flood, or explosion.

(B) An attack on or within this state or on the public security of its residents by an enemy of this state or on the nation by an enemy of the United States of America, or upon receipt by this state of a warning from the federal government indicating that any such enemy attack is probable or imminent.

(C) An act of terrorism or other manmade disaster that results in extraordinary levels of casualties or damage or disruption severely affecting the infrastructure, environment, economy, government functions, or population, including, but not limited to, mass evacuations.

(D) A state of emergency proclaimed by the Governor of this state, including any person serving as Governor in accordance with Section 10 of Article V of the California Constitution and Section 12058 of the Government Code or by the President of the United States of America.

Ca. Corp. Code § 9140
Amended by Stats 2021 ch 523 (AB 663),s 15, eff. 1/1/2022.
Amended by Stats 2013 ch 255 (AB 491),s 7, eff. 1/1/2014.

Section 9141 - No assertion of limitation; binding contract or conveyance

Subject to Section 9142:
(a) No limitation upon the activities, purposes, or powers of the corporation or upon the powers of the members, officers, or directors, or the manner of exercise of such powers, contained in or implied by the articles or by Chapters 16 (commencing with Section 6610), and 17 (commencing with Section 6710) (made applicable pursuant to Section 9680) shall be asserted as between the corporation or member, officer or director and any third person, except in a proceeding:

(1) by the authorized number of members (Section 5036), by any person authorized by the articles or bylaws to bring an action, or by the state to enjoin the doing or continuation of unauthorized activities by the corporation or its officers, or both, in cases where third parties have not acquired rights thereby, or

(2) by the authorized number of members (Section 5036), by any person authorized by the articles or bylaws to bring an action, by any member suing in a representative suit, or by the corporation, against the officers or directors of the corporation for violation of their authority.
(b) Any contract or conveyance made in the name of a corporation which is authorized or ratified by the board or is done within the scope of authority, actual or apparent, conferred by the board or within the agency power of the officer executing it, except as the board's authority is limited by law other than this part, binds the corporation, and the corporation acquires rights thereunder whether the contract is executed or wholly or in part executory.

Ca. Corp. Code § 9141
Amended by Stats. 1979, Ch. 724.

Section 9142 - Action to enjoin, correct, obtain damages for or to otherwise remedy breach of trust under which assets corporate held

(a) Notwithstanding Section 9141, any of the following may bring an action to enjoin, correct, obtain damages for or to otherwise remedy a breach of a trust under which any or all of the assets of a corporation are held:

(1) The corporation, a member, or a former member asserting the right in the name of the corporation, provided that for the purpose of this paragraph the provisions of Section 5710 shall apply to such action.

(2) An officer of the corporation.

(3) A director of the corporation.

(4) A person with a reversionary, contractual, or property interest in the assets subject to such trust.

(b) In an action under this section, the court may not rescind or enjoin the performance of a contract unless:

(1) All of the parties to the contract are parties to the action;

(2) No party to the contract has, in good faith and without actual notice of the restriction, parted with value under the contract or in reliance upon it; and

(3) It is equitable to do so.

(c) No assets of a religious corporation are or shall be deemed to be impressed with any trust, express or implied, statutory or at common law unless one of the following applies:

(1) Unless, and only to the extent that, the assets were received by the corporation with an express commitment by resolution of its board of directors to so hold those assets in trust.

(2) Unless, and only to the extent that, the articles or bylaws of the corporation, or the governing instruments of a superior religious body or general church of which the corporation is a member, so expressly provide.

(3) Unless, and only to the extent that, the donor expressly imposed a trust, in writing, at the time of the gift or donation.

(d) Trusts created by paragraph (2) of subdivision (c) may be amended or dissolved by amendment from time to time to the articles, bylaws, or governing instruments creating the trusts. However, nothing in this subdivision shall be construed to permit the amendment of the articles to delete or to amend provisions required by Section 214.01 of the Revenue and Taxation Code to a greater extent than otherwise allowable by law.

Ca. Corp. Code § 9142
Amended by Stats. 1982, Ch. 242, Sec. 1.

Section 9143 - Action by contributor

(a) Notwithstanding any other provision of this part to the contrary, when property, received by a corporation, covered by this part from a person directly affiliated with that corporation has been contributed based upon an affirmative representation that it would be used for a specific purpose other than the general support of the corporation's activities and has been used in a manner contrary to the specific purpose for which the property was contributed, an action may be brought by the contributor or by any person listed in paragraph (1), (2), or (3) of subdivision (a) of Section 9142, if that person, before bringing an action, notifies the corporation, in writing, that an action will be brought unless the corporation takes immediate steps to correct any improper diversion of funds.

(b) In the event that it becomes impractical or impossible for the corporation to devote the property to the specific purpose for which it was contributed, or that the directors or members of the corporation in good faith expressly conclude and record in writing that the stated purpose for which the property was contributed is no longer in accord with the policies or best interests of the corporation, the directors or members of the corporation may, in good faith, approve or ratify the use of the property for the general purposes of the corporation rather than for the specific purpose for which it was contributed.

(c) A public officer may not bring an action in an official capacity under this section even on behalf of a private person.

Ca. Corp. Code § 9143

Added by Stats. 1982, Ch. 242, Sec. 2.

Article 5 - BYLAWS

Section 9150 - Adoption, amendment, or repeal of bylaws

(a) "Bylaws," as used in this part means the code or codes of rules used, adopted, or recognized for the regulation or management of the affairs of the corporation irrespective of the name or names by which such rules are designated.

(b) Bylaws may be adopted, amended or repealed as provided in the articles or bylaws and absent any provision, bylaws may be adopted, amended or repealed by approval of the members (Section 5034) or the board, except as provided in subdivision (c). The articles or bylaws may restrict or eliminate the power of the board to adopt, amend or repeal any or all bylaws subject to subdivision (e) of Section 9151.

(c) Subject to any provision in the articles or bylaws, the power of the board to adopt, amend or repeal bylaws is subject to the powers of members set forth in Section 9151.

Ca. Corp. Code § 9150

Amended by Stats. 1979, Ch. 724.

Section 9151 - Number of directors

(a) The bylaws shall set forth (unless such provision is contained in the articles, in which case it may only be changed by an amendment of the articles) the number of directors of the corporation, or the method of determining the number of directors of the corporation, or that the number of directors shall be not less than a stated minimum nor more than a stated maximum with the exact number of directors to be fixed, within the limits specified, by approval of the board or the members (Section 5034), in the manner provided in the bylaws, subject to subdivision (e) of Section 9151. The number or minimum number of directors may be one or more.

(b) Except as otherwise provided in the articles or bylaws, once members have been admitted, a bylaw specifying or changing a fixed number of directors or the maximum or minimum number or changing from a fixed to a variable board or vice versa may only be adopted by approval of the members (Section 5034).

(c) The bylaws may contain any provision, not in conflict with law or the articles, for the management of the activities and for the conduct of the affairs of the corporation, including, but not limited to:

(1) Any provision referred to in subdivision (c) of Section 9132.

(2) The time, place, and manner of calling, conducting, and giving notice of members', directors', and committee meetings, or of conducting mail ballots.

(3) The qualifications, duties, and compensation of directors; the time of their election; and the requirements of a quorum for directors' and committee meetings.

(4) The appointment of committees, composed of directors or nondirectors, or both, by the board or any officer and the authority of any such committees.

(5) The appointment, duties, compensation, and tenure of officers.

(6) The mode of determination of members of record.

(7) The making of reports and financial statements to members.

(8) Setting, imposing, and collecting dues, assessments, and admissions and transfer fees.

(d) The bylaws may provide for the manner of admission, withdrawal, suspension, and expulsion of members.

(e) The bylaws may require, for any or all corporate actions (except as provided in Section 9222 and subdivision (b) of Section 9680), the vote of a larger proportion of, or all of, the members or the members of any class, unit, or grouping of members, or the vote of a larger proportion of, or all of, the directors than is otherwise required by this part. Such a provision in the bylaws requiring such greater vote shall not be altered, amended, or repealed except by such greater vote, unless otherwise provided in the bylaws.

(f) The bylaws may contain a provision limiting the number of members, in total or of any class, which the corporation is authorized to admit.

(g)

    (1) The bylaws may contain any provision, not in conflict with the articles, to manage and conduct the business affairs of the corporation effective only in an emergency as defined in Section 9140, including, but not limited to, procedures for calling a board meeting, quorum requirements for a board meeting, and designation of additional or substitute directors.

    (2) During an emergency, the board may take any action that it determines to be necessary or appropriate to respond to the emergency, mitigate the effects of the emergency, or comply with lawful federal and state government orders, but shall not take any action that requires the vote of the members, unless the required vote of the members was obtained prior to the emergency.

    (3) All provisions of the regular bylaws consistent with the emergency bylaws shall remain effective during the emergency, and the emergency bylaws shall not be effective after the emergency ends.

    (4) Corporate action taken in good faith in accordance with the emergency bylaws binds the corporation, and shall not be used to impose liability on a corporate director, officer, employee, or agent.

    Ca. Corp. Code § 9151
Amended by Stats 2021 ch 523 (AB 663),s 16, eff. 1/1/2022.
Amended by Stats 2013 ch 255 (AB 491),s 8, eff. 1/1/2014.
Amended by Stats 2009 ch 631 (AB 1233),s 27, eff. 1/1/2010.

Section 9152 - Delegates

Any corporation may provide in its bylaws for delegates having some or all of the authority of members. Where delegates are provided for, the bylaws shall set forth delegates' terms of office, any reasonable method for delegates' selection and removal, and any reasonable method for calling, noticing, and holding meetings of delegates, may set forth the manner in which delegates may act by written ballot similar to Section 9413 for written ballot of members, and may set forth the manner in which delegates may participate in meetings of delegates similar to paragraph (6) of subdivision (a) of Section 9211. Each delegate shall have one vote on each matter presented for action. A delegate shall not vote by proxy. Delegates may be given a name other than "delegates."

    Ca. Corp. Code § 9152
Amended by Stats 2021 ch 523 (AB 663),s 17, eff. 1/1/2022.
Amended by Stats. 1983, Ch. 1085, Sec. 7.

Section 9153 - Voting by members or delegates

A corporation may provide in its bylaws for voting by its members or delegates on the basis of chapter or other organizational unit, or by region or other geographic grouping.

Ca. Corp. Code § 9153
Added by Stats. 1979, Ch. 724.

Article 6 - LOCATION AND INSPECTION OF ARTICLES AND BYLAWS

Section 9160 - Location and inspection of articles and bylaws

Every corporation shall keep at its principal office in this state the original or a copy of its articles and bylaws as amended to date, which shall be open to inspection by the members at all reasonable times during office hours. If the corporation has no office in this state, it shall upon the written request of any member furnish to such member a copy of the articles or bylaws as amended to date.

Ca. Corp. Code § 9160
Added by Stats. 1978, Ch. 567.

Chapter 2 - DIRECTORS AND MANAGEMENT

Article 1 - GENERAL PROVISIONS

Section 9210 - Board of directors; delegation of management

Subject to the provisions of this part and any provision in the articles or bylaws:
(a) Each corporation shall have a board of directors. The activities and affairs of a corporation shall be conducted and all corporate powers shall be exercised by or under the direction of the board.
(b) The board may delegate the management of the activities of the corporation to any person or persons provided that the activities and affairs of the corporation shall be managed and all corporate powers shall be exercised under the ultimate direction of the board.

Ca. Corp. Code § 9210
Amended by Stats. 1996, Ch. 589, Sec. 40. Effective January 1, 1997.

Section 9211 - Meetings of board

(a) Unless otherwise provided in the articles or in the bylaws, all of the following apply:

(1) Meetings of the board may be called by the chair of the board or the president or any vice president or the secretary or any two directors.

(2) Regular meetings of the board may be held without notice if the time and place of the meetings are fixed by the bylaws or the board. Special meetings of the board shall be held upon four days' notice by first-class mail or 48 hours' notice delivered personally or by telephone, including a voice messaging system or by electronic transmission by a corporation (Section 20). The articles or bylaws may not dispense with notice of a special meeting. A notice, or waiver of notice, need not specify the purpose of any regular or special meeting of the board.

(3) Notice of a meeting need not be given to a director who provided a waiver of notice or consent to holding the meeting or an approval of the minutes thereof in writing, whether before or after the meeting, or who attends the meeting without protesting, prior thereto or at its commencement, the lack of notice to that director. These waivers, consents and approvals shall be filed with the corporate records or made a part of the minutes of the meetings.

(4) A majority of the directors present, whether or not a quorum is present, may adjourn any meeting to another time and place.

(5) Meetings of the board may be held at a place within or without the state that has been designated in the notice of the meeting or, if not stated in the notice or there is no notice, designated in the bylaws or by resolution of the board.

(6) Directors may participate in a meeting through use of conference telephone, electronic video screen communication, or electronic transmission by and to the corporation. Participation in a meeting through use of conference telephone or electronic video screen communication pursuant to this subdivision constitutes presence in person at that meeting as long as all directors participating in the meeting are able to hear one another. Participation in a meeting through use of electronic transmission by and to the corporation, other than conference telephone and electronic video screen communication pursuant to this subdivision constitutes presence in person at that meeting, if both of the following apply:

(A) Each director participating in the meeting can communicate with all of the other directors concurrently.

(B) Each director is provided the means of participating in all matters before the board, including, without limitation, the capacity to propose, or to interpose an objection to, a specific action to be taken by the corporation.

(7) A majority of the number of directors authorized in or pursuant to the articles or bylaws constitutes a quorum of the board for the transaction of business. The articles or bylaws may require the presence of one or more specified directors in order to constitute a quorum of the board to transact business, as long as the death or nonexistence of a specified director or the death or nonexistence of the person or persons otherwise authorized to appoint or designate that director does not prevent the corporation from transacting business in the normal course of events.

(8) An act or decision done or made by a majority of the directors present at a meeting duly held at which a quorum is present is the act of the board. The articles or bylaws may not provide that a lesser vote than a majority of the directors present at a meeting is the act of the board. A meeting at which a quorum is initially present may continue to transact business notwithstanding the withdrawal of directors if any action taken is approved by at least a majority of the required quorum for that meeting, or a greater number required by this division, the articles or the bylaws.

(b) An action required or permitted to be taken by the board may be taken without a meeting if all directors shall individually or collectively consent in writing to that action and if, subject to subdivision (a) of Section 9224, the number of directors then in office constitutes a quorum. The written consent or consents shall be filed with the minutes of the proceedings of the board. The action by written consent shall have the same force and effect as a unanimous vote of the directors. For purposes of this subdivision only, "all directors" does not include an "interested director" as defined in subdivision (a) of Section 9243 or a "common director" as described in subdivision (a) of Section 9244 who abstains in writing from providing consent, where (1) the facts described in paragraph (2) or (3) of subdivision (d) of Section 9243 are established or the provisions of paragraph (1) of subdivision (a) of Section 9244 are satisfied, as appropriate, at or prior to execution of the written consent or consents; (2) the establishment of those facts or satisfaction of those provisions, as applicable, is included in the written consent or consents executed by the noninterested or noncommon directors or in other records of the corporation; and (3) the noninterested directors or noncommon directors, as applicable, approve the action by a vote that is sufficient without counting the votes of the interested directors or common directors.

(c) Each director shall have one vote on each matter presented to the board of directors for action. A director shall not vote by proxy.

(d) This section applies also to incorporators, to committees of the board, and to action by those incorporators or committees mutatis mutandis.

Ca. Corp. Code § 9211

Amended by Stats 2020 ch 370 (SB 1371),s 39, eff. 1/1/2021.
Amended by Stats 2011 ch 442 (AB 1211),s 22, eff. 1/1/2012.
Amended by Stats 2009 ch 631 (AB 1233),s 28, eff. 1/1/2010.
Amended by Stats 2005 ch 102 (SB 119),s 5, eff. 1/1/2006
Amended by Stats 2004 ch 254 (SB 1306),s 30, eff. 1/1/2005
Amended by Stats 2003 ch 168 (SB 735),s 7, eff. 1/1/2004.
Amended by Stats 2002 ch 1008 (AB 3028),s 13, eff. 1/1/2003.

Section 9212 - Quorum; committees

(a) Subject to any provision in the articles or bylaws:

(i) the board may, by resolution adopted by a majority of the number of directors then in office, provided that a quorum is present, create one or more committees, each consisting of two or more directors, to serve at the pleasure of the board; and

(ii) appointments to such committees shall be by a majority vote of the directors then in office. The bylaws may authorize one or more such committees, each consisting of two or more directors, and may provide that a specified officer or officers who are also directors of the corporation shall be a member or members of such committee or committees. The board may appoint one or more directors as alternate members of such committee, who may replace any absent member at any meeting of the committee. Such committee, to the extent provided in the resolution of the board or in the bylaws, shall have all the authority of the board, except with respect to:

(1) The approval of any action for which this part also requires approval of the members (Section 5034) or approval of a majority of all members (Section 5033) regardless of whether the corporation has members.

(2) The filling of vacancies on the board or in any committee which has the authority of the board.

(3) The fixing of compensation of the directors for serving on the board or on any committee.

(4) The amendment or repeal of bylaws or the adoption of new bylaws.

(5) The amendment or repeal of any resolution of the board which by its express terms is not so amendable or repealable.

(6) The appointment of committees of the board or the members thereof.
(b) A committee exercising the authority of the board shall not include as members persons who are not directors. However, the board may create other committees that do not exercise the authority of the board and these other committees may include persons regardless of whether they are directors.
(c) Unless the bylaws otherwise provide, the board may delegate to any committee powers as authorized by Section 9210, but may not delegate the powers set forth in paragraphs (1) to (6), inclusive, of subdivision (a).
(d) The board shall take the actions regarding audit committees that are required by subdivision (e) of Section 12586 of the Government Code, if applicable.
Ca. Corp. Code § 9212
Amended by Stats 2011 ch 442 (AB 1211),s 23, eff. 1/1/2012.
Amended by Stats 2009 ch 631 (AB 1233),s 29, eff. 1/1/2010.

Section 9213 - Officers

(a)A corporation shall have (1) a chair of the board, who may be given the title chair, chairperson, chair of the board, or chairperson of the board, or a president or both, (2) a secretary, (3) a treasurer or a chief financial officer or both and (4) any other officers with any titles and duties as are stated in the bylaws or determined by the board and as may be necessary to enable it to sign instruments. The president, or if there is no president, the chair of the board, is the general manager and chief executive officer of the corporation, unless otherwise provided in the articles or bylaws. Unless otherwise specified in the articles or the bylaws, if there is no chief financial officer, the treasurer is the chief financial officer of the corporation. Any number of offices may be held by the same person unless the articles or bylaws provide otherwise, except that no person serving as the secretary, the treasurer, or the chief financial officer may serve concurrently as the president or chair of the board. Any compensation of the president or chief executive officer and the chief financial officer or treasurer shall be determined in accordance with subdivision (g) of Section 12586 of the Government Code, if applicable.
(b) Except as otherwise provided by the articles or bylaws, officers shall be chosen by the board and serve at the pleasure of the board, subject to the rights, if any, of an officer under any contract of employment. Any officer may resign at any time upon written notice to the corporation without prejudice to the rights, if any, of the corporation under any contract to which the officer is a party.

Ca. Corp. Code § 9213
Amended by Stats 2022 ch 617 (SB 1202),s 68, eff. 1/1/2023.
Amended by Stats 2015 ch 98 (SB 351),s 13, eff. 1/1/2016.
Amended by Stats 2011 ch 442 (AB 1211),s 24, eff. 1/1/2012.
Amended by Stats 2010 ch 212 (AB 2767),s 4, eff. 1/1/2011.
Amended by Stats 2009 ch 631 (AB 1233),s 30, eff. 1/1/2010.

Section 9214 - Authority of signing officers

Subject to the provisions of subdivision (a) of Section 9141 and Section 9142, any note, mortgage, evidence of indebtedness, contract, conveyance or other instrument in writing, and any assignment or endorsement thereof, executed or entered into between any corporation and any other person, when signed by any one of the chairperson of the board, the president, or any vice president and by any one of the secretary, any assistant secretary, the chief financial officer, or any assistant treasurer of such corporation, is not invalidated as to the corporation by any lack of authority of the signing officers in the absence of actual knowledge on the part of the other person that the signing officers had no authority to execute the same.

Ca. Corp. Code § 9214
Amended by Stats 2022 ch 617 (SB 1202),s 69, eff. 1/1/2023.
Amended by Stats. 1996, Ch. 589, Sec. 41. Effective January 1, 1997.

Section 9215 - Certified copy as prima facie evidence

The original or a copy in writing or in any other form capable of being converted into clearly legible tangible form of the bylaws or of the minutes of any incorporators', members', directors', committee or other meeting or of any resolution adopted by the board or a committee thereof, or members, certified to be a true copy by a person purporting to be the secretary or an assistant secretary of the corporation, is prima facie evidence of the adoption of such bylaws or resolution or of the due holding of such meeting and of the matters stated therein.

Ca. Corp. Code § 9215

Amended by Stats 2004 ch 254 (SB 1306),s 31, eff. 1/1/2005

Article 2 - SELECTION, REMOVAL AND RESIGNATION OF DIRECTORS

Section 9220 - Term of directors

(a) The articles or bylaws may provide for the tenure, election, selection, designation, removal, and resignation of directors.

(b) In the absence of any provision in the articles or bylaws, the term of directors shall be one year.

(c) Unless the articles or bylaws otherwise provide, each director, including a director elected to fill a vacancy, shall hold office until the expiration of the term for which elected and until a successor has been elected and qualified, unless the director has been removed from office.

(d) If a corporation has not issued memberships and (1) all the directors resign, die, or become incompetent, or (2) a corporation's initial directors have not been named in the articles and all incorporators resign, die, or become incompetent before the election of the initial directors, the superior court of any county may appoint directors of the corporation upon application by any party in interest.

(e) If authorized in the articles or bylaws of a corporation, all or any portion of the directors may hold office ex officio by virtue of occupying a specified position within the corporation or outside the corporation. The term of office of an ex officio director shall coincide with that director's respective term of office in the specified position entitling him or her to serve on the board of directors. Upon an ex officio director's resignation or removal from that position, or resignation or removal from the board for any reason, the term of office as a director of the corporation shall immediately cease. At that time, the successor in office shall become an ex officio director of the corporation, occupying the place of the former director.

Ca. Corp. Code § 9220

Amended by Stats 2018 ch 322 (AB 2557),s 4, eff. 1/1/2019.

Amended by Stats 2009 ch 631 (AB 1233),s 31, eff. 1/1/2010.

Amended by Stats 2000 ch 485 (AB 1895), s 14, eff. 1/1/2001.

Section 9221 - Declaration of vacancy; qualifications of directors

(a) The board may declare vacant the office of a director who has been declared of unsound mind by a final order of court, or convicted of a felony, or, if at the time a director is elected, the bylaws provide that a director may be removed for missing a specified number of board meetings, fails to attend the specified number of meetings.

(b) As provided in paragraph (3) of subdivision (c) of Section 9151, the articles or bylaws may prescribe the qualifications of the directors. Unless otherwise provided by the articles or bylaws, the board, by a majority vote of the directors who meet all of the required qualifications to be a director, may declare vacant the office of any director who fails or ceases to meet any required qualification that was in effect at the beginning of that director's current term of office.

Ca. Corp. Code § 9221
Amended by Stats. 1996, Ch. 589, Sec. 42. Effective January 1, 1997.

Section 9222 - Removal of directors

(a) Except as provided in the articles or bylaws and subject to subdivision (b) of this section, any or all directors may be removed without cause if the removal is approved by the members (Section 5034).

(b) Except for a corporation having no members pursuant to Section 9310:

(1) When by the provisions of the articles or bylaws the members of any class, voting as a class, are entitled to elect one or more directors, any director so elected may be removed only by the applicable vote of the members of that class.

(2) When by the provisions of the articles or bylaws the members within a chapter or other organizational unit, or region or other geographic grouping, voting as such, are entitled to elect one or more directors, any director so elected may be removed only by the applicable vote of the members within the organizational unit or geographic grouping.

(c) Any reduction of the authorized number of directors or any amendment reducing the number of classes of directors does not remove any director prior to the expiration of the director's term of office, unless the reduction or the amendment also provides for the removal of one or more specified directors.

Ca. Corp. Code § 9222
Amended by Stats 2009 ch 631 (AB 1233),s 32, eff. 1/1/2010.
Amended September 21, 1999 (Bill Number: AB 1687) (Chapter 453).

Section 9223 - Action to remove director

(a) The superior court of the proper county may, at the suit of a director, or twice the authorized number (Section 5036) of members, remove from office any director in case of fraudulent acts and may bar from reelection any director so removed for a period prescribed by the court. The corporation shall be made a party to such action.

(b) The Attorney General may bring an action under subdivision (a), may intervene in such an action brought by any other party and shall be given notice of any such action brought by any other party.

Ca. Corp. Code § 9223

Added by Stats. 1978, Ch. 567.

Section 9224 - Filling vacancies

(a) Unless otherwise provided in the articles or bylaws and except for a vacancy created by the removal of a director by the members, vacancies on the board may be filled by approval of the board (Section 5032) or, if the number of directors then in office is less than a quorum, by (1) the unanimous written consent of the directors then in office, (2) the affirmative vote of a majority of the directors then in office at a meeting held pursuant to notice or waivers of notice complying with Section 9211, or (3) a sole remaining director.

(b) Subject to any provision in the articles or bylaws, the members may elect a director at any time to fill any vacancy not filled by the directors.

(c) Any director may resign effective upon giving written notice to the chairperson of the board, the president, the secretary or the board of directors of the corporation, unless the notice specifies a later time for the effectiveness of such resignation. If the resignation is effective at a future time, a successor may be elected to take office when the resignation becomes effective.

Ca. Corp. Code § 9224

Amended by Stats 2022 ch 617 (SB 1202),s 70, eff. 1/1/2023.

Amended by Stats. 1985, Ch. 329, Sec. 4.

Section 9226 - Resignation of director

No director may resign where the corporation would then be left without a duly elected director or directors in charge of its affairs.

Ca. Corp. Code § 9226

Added by Stats. 1978, Ch. 567.

Article 3 - EXAMINATION BY ATTORNEY GENERAL

Section 9230 - Authority of attorney general

(a) Except as the Attorney General is empowered to act in the enforcement of the criminal laws of this state, and except as the Attorney General is expressly empowered by subdivisions (b), (c) and (d), the Attorney General shall have no powers with respect to any corporation incorporated or classified as a religious corporation under or pursuant to this code.

(b) The Attorney General shall have authority to institute an action or proceeding under Section 803 of the Code of Civil Procedure, to obtain judicial determination that a corporation is not properly qualified or classified as a religious corporation under the provisions of this part.

(c) The Attorney General shall have the authority (1) expressly granted with respect to any subject or matter covered by Sections 9660 to 9690, inclusive; (2) to initiate criminal procedures to prosecute violations of the criminal laws, and upon conviction seek restitution as punishment; and (3) to represent as legal counsel any other agency or department of the State of California expressly empowered to act with respect to the status of religious corporations, or expressly empowered to regulate activities in which religious corporations, as well as other entities, may engage.

(d) Where property has been solicited and received from the general public, based on a representation that it would be used for a specific charitable purpose other than general support of the corporation's activities, and has been used in a manner contrary to that specific charitable purpose for which the property was solicited, the Attorney General may institute an action to enforce the specific charitable purpose for which the property was solicited; provided (1) that before bringing such action the Attorney General shall notify the corporation that an action will be brought unless the corporation takes immediate steps to correct the improper diversion of funds, and (2) that in the event it becomes impractical or impossible for the corporation to devote the property to the specified charitable purpose, or that the directors or members of the corporation in good faith expressly conclude and record in writing that the stated purpose for which the property was contributed is no longer in accord with the policies of the corporation, then the directors or members of the corporation may approve or ratify in good faith the use of such property for the general purposes of the corporation rather than for the specific purpose for which it was contributed. As used in this section, "solicited from the general public" means solicitations directed to the general public, or to any individual or group of individuals who are not directly affiliated with the soliciting organization and includes, but is not limited to, instances where property has been solicited on an individual basis, such as door to door, direct mail, face to face, or similar solicitations, as well as solicitations on a more general level to the general public, or a portion thereof, such as through the media, including newspapers, television, radio, or similar solicitations.

(e) Nothing in this section shall be construed to affect any individual rights of action which were accorded under law in existence prior to the enactment of Chapter 1324 of the Statutes of 1980. As used in this section, "individual rights of action" include only rights enforceable by private individuals and do not include any right of action of a public officer in an official capacity regardless of whether the officer brings the action on behalf of a private individual.

(f) Nothing in this section shall be construed to require express statutory authorization by the California Legislature of any otherwise lawful and duly authorized action by any agency of local government.

Ca. Corp. Code § 9230

Amended by Stats. 1981, Ch. 797, Sec. 1.

Article 4 - STANDARDS OF CONDUCT

Section 9240 - Duties and liabilities

(a) Any duties and liabilities set forth in this article shall apply without regard to whether a director is compensated by the corporation.

(b) Part 4 (commencing with Section 16000) of Division 9 of the Probate Code does not apply to the directors of any corporation.

(c) A director, in making a good faith determination, may consider what the director believes to be:

  (1) The religious purposes of the corporation; and

  (2) Applicable religious tenets, canons, laws, policies, and authority.
  Ca. Corp. Code § 9240

Amended by Stats. 1987, Ch. 923, Sec. 1.4. Operative January 1, 1988, by Sec. 103 of Ch. 923.

Section 9241 - Good faith; best interests of corporation

(a) A director shall perform the duties of a director, including duties as a member of any committee of the board upon which the director may serve, in good faith, in a manner such director believes to be in the best interests of the corporation and with such care, including reasonable inquiry, as is appropriate under the circumstances.

(b) In performing the duties of a director, a director shall be entitled to rely on information, opinions, reports, or statements, including financial statements and other financial data, in each case prepared or presented by:

  (1) One or more officers or employees of the corporation whom the director believes to be reliable and competent in the matters presented;

  (2) Counsel, independent accountants, or other persons as to matters which the director believes to be within that person's professional or expert competence;

  (3) A committee upon which the director does not serve that is composed exclusively of any or any combination of directors, persons described in paragraph (1), or persons described in paragraph (2), as to matters within the committee's designated authority, which committee the director believes to merit confidence; or

  (4) Religious authorities and ministers, priests, rabbis, or other persons whose position or duties in the religious organization the director believes justify reliance and confidence and whom the director believes to be reliable and competent in the matters presented, so long as, in any case, the director acts in good faith, after reasonable inquiry when the need therefor is indicated by the circumstances, and without knowledge that would cause that reliance to be unwarranted.

(c) The provisions of this section, and not Section 9243, shall govern any action or omission of a director in regard to the compensation of directors, as directors or officers, or any loan of money or property to or guaranty of the obligation of any director or officer. No obligation, otherwise valid, shall be voidable merely because directors who benefited by a board resolution to pay such compensation or to make such loan or guaranty participated in making such board resolution.

(d) Except as provided in Section 9243, a person who performs the duties of a director in accordance with subdivisions (a) and (b) shall have no liability based upon any alleged failure to discharge his or her obligations as a director, including, without limiting the generality of the foregoing, any actions or omissions which exceed or defeat any purpose to which the corporation, or assets held by it, may be dedicated.

  Ca. Corp. Code § 9241
Amended by Stats 2009 ch 631 (AB 1233),s 33, eff. 1/1/2010.

Section 9242 - Acts or omissions in connection with election, selection, or nomination of directors

(a) Section 9241 governs the duties of directors as to any acts or omissions in connection with the election, selection, or nomination of directors.

(b) This section shall not be construed to limit the provisions of Section 9241.

  Ca. Corp. Code § 9242
Added by Stats. 1979, Ch. 681.

Section 9243 - Self-dealing transaction

(a) Except as provided in subdivision (b), for the purpose of this section, a self-dealing transaction means a transaction to which the corporation is a party and in which one or more of its directors has a material financial interest and which does not meet the requirements of paragraph (1), (2), (3), or (4) of subdivision (d). Such a director is an "interested director" for the purpose of this section.

(b) This section does not apply to any of the following:

  (1) An action of the board fixing the compensation of a director as a director or officer of the corporation or making any loan of money or property to, or guaranteeing the obligation of, any director or officer.

  (2) A transaction which is part of a public, charitable or religious program of the corporation if it (A) is approved or authorized by the corporation in good faith and without unjustified favoritism, and (B) results in a benefit to one or more directors or their families because they are in the class of persons intended to be benefited by the public, charitable or religious program.

  (3) A transaction, of which the interested director or directors have no actual knowledge, and which does not exceed the lesser of 1 percent of the gross receipts of the corporation for the preceding fiscal year or one hundred thousand dollars ($100,000).

(c) Any of the following may bring an action in the superior court of the proper county for the remedies specified in subdivision (h):

(1) The corporation, or a member asserting the right in the name of the corporation; however, for the purpose of this paragraph the provisions of Section 5710 shall apply to the action.

(2) A director of the corporation.

(3) An officer of the corporation.

(4) Any person authorized by the bylaws to bring an action.

(d) In any action brought under subdivision (c) the remedies specified in subdivision (h) shall not be granted if:

(1) The Attorney General, or the court in an action in which the Attorney General is an indispensable party, has approved the transaction before or after it was consummated; or

(2) The transaction is approved or ratified in good faith by the members (Section 5034) other than the directors, after notice and disclosure to the members of the material facts concerning the transaction and the director's interest in the transaction; or

(3) The following facts are established:

(A) The corporation entered into the transaction for its own benefit or for the benefit of the religious organization;

(B) The transaction was fair and reasonable as to the corporation or was in furtherance of its religious purposes at the time the corporation entered into the transaction;

(C) Prior to consummating the transaction or any part thereof, the board authorized or approved the transaction in good faith by a vote of a majority of the directors then in office without counting the vote of the interested director or directors, and with knowledge of the material facts concerning the transaction and the director's interest in the transaction. Except as provided in paragraph (4), action by a committee of the board shall not satisfy this paragraph; and

(D)

(i) Prior to authorizing or approving the transaction, the board considered and in good faith determined after reasonable investigation under the circumstances that either the corporation could not have obtained a more advantageous arrangement with reasonable effort under the circumstances or the transaction was in furtherance of the corporation's religious purposes or

(ii) in fact, either the corporation could not have obtained a more advantageous arrangement with reasonable effort under the circumstances or the transaction was in furtherance of the corporation's religious purposes; or

(4) The following facts are established:

(A) A committee or person authorized by the board approved the transaction in a manner consistent with the standards set forth in paragraph (3).

(B) It was not reasonably practicable to obtain approval of the board prior to entering into the transaction; and

(C) The board, after determining in good faith that the conditions of subparagraphs (A) and (B) were satisfied, ratified the transaction at its next meeting by a vote of the majority of the directors then in office without counting the vote of the interested director or directors.

(e) Except as provided in subdivision (f), an action under subdivision (c) or Section 9230 shall be commenced within two years after written notice setting forth the material facts of the transaction is filed with the Attorney General in accordance with such regulations, if any, as the Attorney General may adopt or if no such notice is filed, five years after the cause of action has accrued.

(f) In any action for breach of an obligation of the corporation owed to an interested director, where the obligation arises from a self-dealing transaction which has not been approved as provided in subdivision (d), the court may, by way of offset only, make any order authorized by subdivision (h), notwithstanding the expiration of the applicable period specified in subdivision (e).

(g) Interested directors may be counted in determining the presence of a quorum at a meeting of the board which authorizes, approves or ratifies a contract or transaction.

(h) If a self-dealing transaction has taken place, the interested director or directors shall do such things and pay such damages as in the discretion of the court will provide an equitable and fair remedy to the corporation, taking into account any benefit received by the corporation and whether the interested director or directors acted in good faith and with intent to further the best interest of the corporation. Without limiting the generality of the foregoing, the court may order the director to do any or all of the following:

(1) Account for any profits made from the transaction, and pay them to the corporation.

(2) Pay the corporation the value of the use of any of its property used in the transactions.

(3) Return or replace any property lost to the corporation as a result of the transaction, together with any income or appreciation lost to the corporation by reason of the transaction, or account for any proceeds of sale of the property, and pay the proceeds to the corporation together with interest at the legal rate. The court may award prejudgment interest to the extent allowed in Sections 3287 and 3288 of the Civil Code. In addition, the court may, in its discretion, grant exemplary damages for a fraudulent or malicious violation of this section.

Ca. Corp. Code § 9243
Amended by Stats. 1984, Ch. 812, Sec. 14.

Section 9244 - Effect of common director

(a) No contract or other transaction between a corporation and any domestic or foreign corporation, firm or association of which one or more of its directors are directors is either void or voidable because such director or directors are present at the meeting of the board or a committee thereof which authorizes, approves or ratifies the contract or transaction, if:

(1) The material facts as to the transaction and as to such director's other directorship are fully disclosed or known to the board or committee, and the board or committee authorizes, approves or ratifies the contract or transaction in good faith by a vote sufficient without counting the vote of the common director or directors; or

(2) As to contracts or transactions not approved as provided in paragraph (1) of this subdivision, the contract or transaction is just and reasonable as to the corporation, taking into account its religious purposes, or is in furtherance of its religious purposes at the time it is authorized, approved or ratified.

(b) This section does not apply to transactions covered by Section 9243.

Ca. Corp. Code § 9244
Added by Stats. 1979, Ch. 681.

Section 9245 - Joint and several liability of directors who approve certain corporate actions

(a) Subject to the provisions of Section 9241, directors of a corporation who approve any of the following corporate actions shall be jointly and severally liable to the corporation for:

(1) The making of any distribution.

(2) The distribution of assets after institution of dissolution proceedings of the corporation, without paying or adequately providing for all known liabilities of the corporation, excluding any claims not filed by creditors within the time limit set by the court in a notice given to creditors under Section 9680 and those sections made applicable to this part by Section 9680.

(3) The making of any loan or guaranty contrary to Section 9241.

(b) Suit may be brought in the name of the corporation to enforce the liability:

(1) Under paragraph (1) of subdivision (a) against any or all directors liable by the persons entitled to sue under subdivision (b) of Section 9610;

(2) Under paragraph (2) or (3) of subdivision (a) against any or all directors liable by any one or more creditors of the corporation whose debts or claims arose prior to the time of the corporate action who have not consented to the corporate action, whether or not they have reduced their claims to judgment.

(c) The damages recoverable from a director under this section shall be the amount of the illegal distribution, or if the illegal distribution consists of property, the fair market value of that property at the time of the illegal distribution, plus interest thereon from the date of the distribution at the legal rate on judgments until paid, together with all reasonably incurred costs of appraisal or other valuation, if any, of that property, or the loss suffered by the corporation as a result of the illegal loan or guaranty.

(d) Any director sued under this section may implead all other directors liable and may compel contribution, either in that action or in an independent action against directors not joined in that action.

(e) Directors liable under this section shall also be entitled to be subrogated to the rights of the corporation as follows:

(1) With respect to paragraph (1) of subdivision (a), against members who received the distribution.

(2) With respect to paragraph (2) of subdivision (a), against the members who received the distribution.

(3) With respect to paragraph (3) of subdivision (a), against the person who received the loan or guaranty. Any director sued under this section may file a cross-complaint against the person or persons who are liable to the director as a result of the subrogation provided for in this subdivision or may proceed against them in an independent action.

Ca. Corp. Code § 9245
Amended 9/21/1999 (Bill Number: AB 1687) (Chapter 453).

Section 9246 - Indemnification

(a) For the purposes of this section, "agent" means any person who is or was a director, officer, employee or other agent of the corporation, or is or was serving at the request of the corporation as a director, officer, employee, or agent of another foreign or domestic corporation, partnership, joint venture, trust, or other enterprise, or was a director, officer, employee, or agent of a foreign or domestic corporation which was a predecessor corporation of the corporation or of another enterprise at the request of that predecessor corporation; "proceeding" means any threatened, pending, or completed action or proceeding, whether civil, criminal, administrative or investigative; and "expenses" includes without limitation attorneys' fees and any expenses of establishing a right to indemnification under subdivision (d) or paragraph (3) of subdivision (e).

(b) A corporation shall have power to indemnify any person who was or is a party or is threatened to be made a party to any proceeding (other than an action by or in the right of the corporation to procure a judgment in its favor, an action brought under Section 9243, or an action brought by the Attorney General pursuant to Section 9230) by reason of the fact that the person is or was an agent of the corporation, against expenses, judgments, fines, settlements and other amounts actually and reasonably incurred in connection with the proceeding if the person acted in good faith and in a manner the person believed to be in the best interests of the corporation and, in the case of a criminal proceeding, had no reasonable cause to believe the conduct of the person was unlawful. The termination of any proceeding by judgment, order, settlement, conviction or upon a plea of nolo contendere or its equivalent shall not, of itself, create a presumption that the person did not act in good faith and in a manner which the person believed to be in the best interests of the corporation or that the person had reasonable cause to believe that the person's conduct was unlawful.

(c) A corporation shall have power to indemnify any person who was or is a party or is threatened to be made a party to any threatened, pending or completed action by or in the right of the corporation, or brought under Section 9243, or brought by the Attorney General pursuant to Section 9230, to procure a judgment in its favor by reason of the fact that the person is or was an agent of the corporation, against expenses actually and reasonably incurred by the person in connection with the defense or settlement of the action if the person acted in good faith, in a manner in which the person believed to be in the best interests of the corporation and with that care, including reasonable inquiry, as an ordinary prudent person in a like position would use under similar circumstances. No indemnification shall be made under this subdivision:

(1) In respect of any claim, issue, or matter as to which the person shall have been adjudged to be liable to the corporation in the performance of the person's duty to the corporation, unless and only to the extent that the court in which the proceeding is or was pending shall determine upon application that, in view of all the circumstances of

the case, the person is fairly and reasonably entitled to indemnity for the expenses which the court shall determine;

(2) Of amounts paid in settling or otherwise disposing of a threatened or pending action, with or without court approval; or

(3) Of expenses incurred in defending a threatened or pending action which is settled or otherwise disposed of without court approval unless it is settled with the approval of the Attorney General.

(d) To the extent that an agent of a corporation has been successful on the merits in defense of any proceeding referred to in subdivision (b) or (c) or in defense of any claim, issue or matter therein, the agent shall be indemnified against expenses actually and reasonably incurred by the agent in connection therewith.

(e) Except as provided in subdivision (d), any indemnification under this section shall be made by the corporation only if authorized in the specific case, upon a determination that indemnification of the agent is proper in the circumstances because the agent has met the applicable standard of conduct set forth in either subdivision (b) or (c) by:

(1) A majority vote of a quorum consisting of directors who are not parties to the proceeding;

(2) Approval of the members (Section 5034), with the persons to be indemnified not being entitled to vote thereon; or

(3) The court in which the proceeding is or was pending upon application made by the corporation or the agent or the attorney or other person rendering services in connection with the defense, whether or not the application by the agent, attorney, or other person is opposed by the corporation.

(f) Expenses incurred in defending any proceeding may be advanced by the corporation prior to the final disposition of the proceeding upon receipt of an undertaking by or on behalf of the agent to repay the amount unless it shall be determined ultimately that the agent is entitled to be indemnified as authorized in this section.

(g) No provision made by a corporation to indemnify its or its subsidiary's directors or officers for the defense of any proceeding, whether contained in the articles, bylaws, a resolution of members or directors, an agreement or otherwise, shall be valid unless consistent with this section. Nothing contained in this section shall affect any right to indemnification to which persons other than the directors and officers may be entitled by contract or otherwise.

(h) No indemnification or advance shall be made under this section, except as provided in subdivision (d) or paragraph (3) of subdivision (e), in any circumstance where it appears that:

(1) It would be inconsistent with a provision of the articles, bylaws, a resolution of the members or an agreement in effect at the time of the accrual of the alleged cause of action asserted in the proceeding in which the expenses were incurred or other amounts were paid, which prohibits or otherwise limits indemnification; or

(2) It would be inconsistent with any condition expressly imposed by a court in approving a settlement.

(i) A corporation shall have power to purchase and maintain insurance on behalf of any agent of the corporation against any liability asserted against or incurred by the agent in that capacity or arising out of the agent's status as such whether or not the corporation would have the power to indemnify the agent against that liability under the provisions of this section; provided, however, that a corporation shall have no power to purchase and maintain insurance to indemnify any agent of the corporation for a violation of Section 9243.

(j) This section does not apply to any proceeding against any trustee, investment manager, or other fiduciary of a pension, deferred compensation, saving, thrift, or other retirement, incentive, or benefit plan, trust, or provision for any or all of the corporation's directors, officers, employees, and persons providing services to the corporation or any of its subsidiary or related or affiliated corporations, in the person's capacity as such, even though the person may also be an agent as defined in subdivision (a) of the employer corporation. A corporation shall have power to indemnify the trustee, investment manager or other fiduciary to the extent permitted by subdivision (f) of Section 9140.

Ca. Corp. Code § 9246
Amended by Stats 2012 ch 61 (AB 2668),s 3, eff. 1/1/2013.

Section 9247 - Liability of volunteer director or volunteer executive officer of nonprofit corporation

(a) There shall be no personal liability for monetary damages to a third party on the part of a volunteer director or volunteer executive officer of a nonprofit corporation subject to this part, caused by the director's or officer's negligent act or omission in the performance of that person's duties as a director or officer, if all of the following conditions are met:

(1) The act or omission was within the scope of the director's or executive officer's duties.

(2) The act or omission was performed in good faith.

(3) The act or omission was not reckless, wanton, intentional, or grossly negligent.

(4) Damages caused by the act or omission are covered pursuant to a liability insurance policy issued to the corporation, either in the form of a general liability policy or a director's or officer's liability policy, or personally to the director or executive officer. In the event that the damages are not covered by a liability insurance policy, the volunteer director or volunteer executive officer shall not be personally liable for the damages if the board of directors of the corporation and the person had made all reasonable efforts in good faith to obtain available liability insurance.

(b) "Volunteer" means the rendering of services without compensation. "Compensation" means remuneration whether by way of salary, fee, or other consideration for services rendered. However, the payment of per diem, mileage, or other reimbursement expenses to a director or executive officer does not affect that person's status as a volunteer within the meaning of this section.

(c) "Executive officer" means the president, vice president, secretary, or treasurer of a corporation, or other individual serving in like capacity, who assists in establishing the policy of the corporation.

(d) Nothing in this section shall limit the liability of the corporation for any damages caused by acts or omissions of the volunteer director or volunteer executive officer.

(e) This section does not eliminate or limit the liability of a director or officer for any of the following:

(1) As provided in Section 9243 or 9245.

(2) In any action or proceeding brought by the Attorney General.

(f) Nothing in this section creates a duty of care or basis of liability for damage or injury caused by the acts or omissions of a director or officer.

(g) This section is only applicable to causes of action based upon acts or omissions occurring on or after January 1, 1988.

Ca. Corp. Code § 9247

Amended by Stats. 1990, Ch. 107, Sec. 6.

Article 5 - INVESTMENTS

Section 9250 - Standards for investments

(a) In investing, reinvesting, purchasing, acquiring, exchanging, selling, and managing a corporation's investments, the board shall meet the standards set forth in Section 9241.

(b) Compliance with the Uniform Prudent Management of Institutional Funds Act (Part 7 (commencing with Section 18501) of Division 9 of the Probate Code), if that act would be applicable, will be deemed to be compliance with subdivision (a).

Ca. Corp. Code § 9250

Amended by Stats 2015 ch 56 (AB 792),s 2, eff. 1/1/2016.

Amended by Stats 2011 ch 442 (AB 1211),s 25, eff. 1/1/2012.

Section 9251 - Power of court to permit corporation to deviate from terms

of trust or agreement

Nothing in Section 9250 shall abrogate or restrict the power of a court in proper cases to direct or permit a corporation to deviate from the terms of a trust or agreement regarding the making or retention of investments.

    Ca. Corp. Code § 9251
Added by Stats. 1979, Ch. 681.

Article 6 - COMPLIANCE WITH INTERNAL REVENUE CODE

Section 9260 - Corporation deemed "private foundation"

Notwithstanding any other law, every corporation, during any period or periods that corporation is deemed to be a "private foundation" as defined in Section 509 of the Internal Revenue Code of 1986, shall be subject to the requirements of Section 5260.

    Ca. Corp. Code § 9260
Amended by Stats 2017 ch 516 (SB 363),s 2, eff. 1/1/2018.
Added by Stats 2009 ch 631 (AB 1233),s 34, eff. 1/1/2010.

Chapter 3 - MEMBERS

Article 1 - ISSUANCE OF MEMBERSHIPS

Section 9310 - Admission to membership; no members

(a) A corporation may admit persons to membership, as provided in its articles or bylaws, or may provide in its articles or bylaws that it shall have no members. In the absence of any provision in its articles or bylaws providing for members, a corporation shall have no members.
(b) Subject to the articles or bylaws, in the case of a corporation which has no members:

    (1) Any action for which there is no specific provision of this part applicable to a corporation which has no members and which would otherwise require approval by a majority of all members (Section 5033) or approval by the members (Section 5034) shall require only approval of the board.

    (2) All rights which would otherwise vest under this part in the members shall vest in the directors.
(c) Reference in this part to a corporation which has no members includes a corporation in which the directors are the only members.

    Ca. Corp. Code § 9310
Amended by Stats. 1984, Ch. 812, Sec. 14.5.

Section 9311 - Consideration

Subject to the articles or bylaws, memberships may be issued by a corporation for no consideration or for such consideration as is determined by the board.

Ca. Corp. Code § 9311

Amended by Stats. 1979, Ch. 724.

Section 9312 - One membership; fractional memberships

No person may hold more than one membership, and no fractional memberships may be held, provided, however, that:

(a) Two or more persons may have an indivisible interest in a single membership when authorized by, and in such manner or under the circumstances prescribed by, the articles or bylaws; and

(b) If the articles or bylaws provide for classes of membership in which the differences are not merely the number of votes entitled to be cast by members of the class, and if the articles or bylaws permit a person to be a member of more than one class, a person may hold a membership in one or more classes.

Ca. Corp. Code § 9312

Amended by Stats. 1979, Ch. 724.

Section 9313 - Admission of any person

Except as provided in its articles or bylaws, a corporation may admit any person to membership.

Ca. Corp. Code § 9313

Added by Stats. 1978, Ch. 567.

Article 2 - TRANSFER OF MEMBERSHIPS

Section 9320 - No transfer for value; membership rights cease upon member's death or dissolution

Subject to Section 9417:

(a) No member may transfer for value a membership or any right arising therefrom; and

(b) Unless otherwise provided in the corporation's articles or bylaws, all rights of membership cease upon the member's death or dissolution.

Ca. Corp. Code § 9320

Amended by Stats. 1981, Ch. 587, Sec. 50.

Article 3 - TYPES OF MEMBERSHIPS

Section 9330 - Different rights privileges preferences restrictions or conditions

A corporation may issue memberships having different rights, privileges, preferences, restrictions, or conditions, as authorized by its articles or bylaws.

Ca. Corp. Code § 9330

Amended by Stats. 1979, Ch. 724.

Section 9331 - Same rights, privileges, preferences, restrictions, and conditions

Except as provided in or authorized by the articles or bylaws, all memberships shall have the same rights, privileges, preferences, restrictions, and conditions.

Ca. Corp. Code § 9331

Amended by Stats. 1979, Ch. 724.

Section 9332 - References to members; assisting persons who are not members

(a) A corporation may refer to persons associated with it as "members" even though such persons are not members within the meaning of Section 5056; but references to members in this part mean members as defined in Section 5056.

(b) A corporation may benefit, serve, or assist persons who are not members within the meaning of Section 5056 for such consideration, if any, as the board may determine or as is authorized or provided for in the articles or bylaws.

Ca. Corp. Code § 9332

Amended by Stats. 1979, Ch. 724.

Article 4 - TERMINATION OF MEMBERSHIPS

Section 9340 - Resignation

(a) A member may resign from membership at any time.

(b) This section shall not relieve the resigning member from any obligation for charges incurred, services or benefits actually rendered, dues, assessments or fees, or arising from contract or otherwise, and this section shall not diminish any right of the corporation to enforce any such obligation or obtain damages for its breach.

(c) Except as provided in subdivision (b) of Section 9320 or in subdivision (a) of this section, a membership issued for a period of time shall expire when such period of time has elapsed unless the membership is renewed.

(d) A membership may be terminated as provided in the articles or bylaws of the corporation.

Ca. Corp. Code § 9340

Amended by Stats. 1979, Ch. 724.

Article 5 - RIGHTS AND OBLIGATIONS OF MEMBERS AND CREDITORS

Section 9350 - Liability

(a) A member of a corporation is not, as such, personally liable for the debts, liabilities, or obligations of the corporation.

(b) No person is liable for any obligation arising from membership unless the person was admitted to membership upon the person's application or with the person's consent.

Ca. Corp. Code § 9350
Added by Stats. 1978, Ch. 567.

Section 9351 - Dues, assessments, or fees

A corporation may levy dues, assessments, or fees upon its members pursuant to its articles or bylaws, but a member upon learning of them may avoid liability for them by promptly resigning from membership, except where the member is, by contract or otherwise, liable for them. Article or bylaw provisions authorizing such dues, assessments, or fees do not, of themselves, create such liability.

Ca. Corp. Code § 9351
Added by Stats. 1978, Ch. 567.

Section 9352 - Actions by creditors

(a) No action shall be brought by or on behalf of any creditor to reach and apply the liability, if any, of a member to the corporation to pay any amount due to the corporation unless final judgment has been rendered in favor of the creditor against the corporation and execution has been returned unsatisfied in whole or in part or unless such proceedings would be useless.

(b) All creditors of the corporation, with or without reducing their claims to judgment, may intervene in any such creditor's action to reach and apply unpaid amounts due the corporation and any or all members who owe amounts to the corporation may be joined in such action. Several judgments may be rendered for and against the parties to the action or in favor of a receiver for the benefit of the respective parties thereto.

(c) All amounts paid by any member in any such action shall be credited on the unpaid balance due the corporation by such member.

Ca. Corp. Code § 9352
Added by Stats. 1978, Ch. 567.

Section 9353 - No derogation of rights or remedies of creditor or member against promoter, member, director, officer, or corporation because of fraud or illegality

Nothing in this part shall be construed as in derogation of any rights or remedies which any creditor or member may have against any promoter, member, director, officer or the corporation because of participation in any fraud or illegality practiced upon such creditor or member by any such person or by the corporation in connection with the issue or sale of memberships or securities or in derogation of any rights which the corporation may have by rescission, cancellation or otherwise because of any fraud or illegality practiced on it by any such person in connection with the issue or sale of memberships or securities.

Ca. Corp. Code § 9353
Added by Stats. 1978, Ch. 567.

Chapter 4 - MEETINGS AND VOTING

Section 9410 - Applicability

(a) In the absence of a contrary provision in the articles or bylaws, the provisions of this chapter shall apply to any regular or special meeting of members or obtaining approval of members (Section 5034) or approval of a majority of members (Section 5033). The articles or bylaws may provide any reasonable method of calling, noticing, and holding such meetings or obtaining such approvals.

(b) Anything in subdivision (a) to the contrary notwithstanding, the articles or bylaws may not vary the provisions of subdivision (e) of Section 9411, subdivision (e) of Section 9417 (if proxies are authorized), or Section 9418.

Ca. Corp. Code § 9410
Amended by Stats. 1981, Ch. 587, Sec. 51.

Section 9411 - Meetings of members

(a) Subject to the provisions of this chapter, regular and special meetings of members shall be called, noticed, and held as may be ordered by the board. Notwithstanding the foregoing, the notice of a members' meeting or any report may be sent by electronic communication or other means of remote communication if the board determines it is necessary or appropriate because of an emergency, as defined in paragraph (5) of subdivision (n) of Section 9140. Subject to any limitations in the articles or bylaws of the corporation, if authorized by the board of directors in its sole discretion, and subject to those guidelines and procedures as the board of directors may adopt, members not physically present in person (or, if proxies are allowed, by proxy) at a meeting of members may, by electronic transmission by and to the corporation (Sections 20 and 21), electronic video screen communication, conference telephone, or other means of remote communication, participate in a meeting of members, be deemed present in person (or, if proxies are allowed, by proxy), and vote at a meeting of members, subject to subdivision (f).

(b) Special meetings of members for any lawful purpose may be called by the board or the chairperson of the board or the president. In addition, special meetings of members for any lawful purpose may be called by 5 percent or more of the members.

(c) Upon request in writing to the chairperson of the board, president, vice president, or secretary by any person (other than the board) entitled to call a special meeting of members, the board shall expeditiously set a reasonable time and place for the meeting and the officer forthwith shall cause notice to be given to the members entitled to vote of the time and place of the meeting. If the notice is not given within 20 days after receipt of the request, the persons entitled to call the meeting may give the notice or the superior court of the proper county shall summarily order the giving of the notice, after notice to the corporation giving it an opportunity to be heard. The court may issue such orders as may be appropriate, including, without limitation, orders designating the time and place of the meeting, the record date for determination of members entitled to vote, and the form of notice.

(d) The transactions of any meeting of members, however called and noticed, and wherever held, are as valid as though had at a meeting duly held after regular call and notice, if a quorum is present either in person (or, if proxies are allowed, by proxy), and if, either before or after the meeting, each of the persons entitled to vote, not present in person or by proxy, signs a written waiver of notice or a consent to the holding of the meeting or an approval of the minutes thereof. All such waivers, consents, and approvals shall be filed with the corporate records or made a part of the minutes of the meeting. Attendance of a person at a meeting shall constitute a waiver of notice of and presence at such meeting, except when the person objects, at the beginning of the meeting, to the transaction of any business because the meeting is not lawfully called or convened and except that attendance at a meeting is not a waiver of any right to object to the consideration of matters required by this part to be included in the notice but not so included, if such objection is expressly made at the meeting. Neither the business to be transacted at nor the purpose of any regular or special meeting of members need be specified in any written waiver of notice, consent to the holding of the meeting, or approval of the minutes thereof except as provided in subdivision (e).

(e) Any member approval required under subdivision (b) of Section 9150, Section 9222, Section 5812 (made applicable pursuant to Section 9620), subdivision (a) of Section 9631, subdivision (c) of Section 9640, subdivision (a) of Section 6015 (made applicable pursuant to Section 9640), or subdivision (b) of Section 9680, other than unanimous approval by those entitled to vote, shall be valid only if the general nature of the proposal so approved was stated in the notice of meeting or in any written waiver of notice.

(f)A meeting of the members may be conducted, in whole or in part, by electronic transmission by and to the corporation or by electronic video screen communication, conference telephone, or other means of remote communication if the corporation implements reasonable measures:

(1) to provide members and proxyholders (if proxies are allowed) a reasonable opportunity to participate in the meeting and to vote on matters submitted to the members, including an opportunity to read or hear the proceedings of the meeting substantially concurrently with those proceedings,

(2) if any member or proxyholder (if proxies are allowed) votes or takes other action at the meeting by means of electronic transmission to the corporation, electronic video screen communication, conference telephone, or other means of remote communication, to maintain a record of that vote or action in its books and records, and

(3) to verify that each person participating remotely is a member or proxyholder (if proxies are allowed). A corporation shall not conduct a meeting of members solely by electronic transmission by and to the corporation, electronic video screen communication, conference telephone, or other means of remote communication unless one or more of the following conditions apply:

(A) all of the members consent, or

(B) the board determines it is necessary or appropriate because of an emergency, as defined in paragraph (5) of subdivision (n) of Section 9140; or

(C) the meeting is conducted on or before June 30, 2022.
Ca. Corp. Code § 9411
Amended by Stats 2022 ch 617 (SB 1202),s 71, eff. 1/1/2023.
Amended by Stats 2022 ch 12 (AB 769),s 4, eff. 3/25/2022.
Amended by Stats 2021 ch 523 (AB 663),s 18, eff. 1/1/2022.
Amended by Stats 2004 ch 254 (SB 1306),s 32, eff. 1/1/2005

Section 9412 - Quorum

(a) One-third of the voting power, represented in person, by written ballot, or by proxy, shall constitute a quorum at a meeting of members. If a quorum is present, the affirmative vote of the majority of the voting power represented at the meeting, entitled to vote, and voting on any matter shall be the act of the members.
(b) The members present at a duly called or held meeting at which a quorum is present may continue to transact business until adjournment notwithstanding the withdrawal of enough members to leave less than a quorum, if any action taken (other than adjournment) is approved by at least a majority of the members required to constitute a quorum or, if required by this division, or by the articles or the bylaws, the vote of the greater number or voting by classes.
(c) In the absence of a quorum, any meeting of members may be adjourned from time to time by the vote of a majority of the votes represented either in person or by proxy, but no other business may be transacted, except as provided in subdivision (b).
Ca. Corp. Code § 9412
Amended by Stats 2000 ch 485 (AB 1895), s 15, eff. 1/1/2001.

Section 9413 - Approval by written ballot

(a) Any action which may be taken at any regular or special meeting of members may be taken without a meeting if the written ballot of every member is solicited, if the required number of signed approvals in writing, setting forth the action so taken, is received, and if the requirements of subdivision (c) are satisfied. Unless otherwise provided by the articles or bylaws and if approved by the board of directors, that ballot and any related material may be sent by electronic transmission by the corporation (Section 20) and responses may be returned to the corporation by electronic transmission to the corporation (Section 21).

(b) All solicitations of ballots shall indicate the time by which the ballot must be returned to be counted.

(c) Approval by written ballot pursuant to this section shall be valid only when the number of ballots cast on or before the time the ballot must be returned to be counted equals or exceeds the quorum required to be present at a meeting authorizing the action, and the number of approvals equals or exceeds the number of votes that would be required to approve at a meeting at which the total number of votes cast was the same as the number of ballots cast.

(d) A written ballot may not be revoked.

(e) Directors may be elected by written ballot under this section, where authorized by the articles or bylaws, except that election by written ballot may not be authorized where the directors are elected by cumulative voting pursuant to Section 9415.

Ca. Corp. Code § 9413
Amended by Stats 2004 ch 254 (SB 1306),s 33, eff. 1/1/2005

Section 9414 - Court order

(a) If for any reason it is impractical or unduly difficult for any corporation to call or conduct a meeting of its members, delegates or directors, or otherwise obtain their consent, in the manner prescribed by its articles or bylaws, or this part, then the superior court of the proper county, upon petition of a director, officer, delegate, or member, may order that such a meeting be called or that a written ballot or other form of obtaining the vote of members, delegates or directors be authorized, in such a manner as the court finds fair and equitable under the circumstances.

(b) The court shall, in an order issued pursuant to this section, provide for a method of notice reasonably designed to give actual notice to all parties who would be entitled to notice of a meeting held pursuant to the articles, bylaws and this part, whether or not the method results in actual notice to every such person, or conforms to the notice requirements that would otherwise apply. In a proceeding under this section the court may determine who the members or directors are.

(c) The order issued pursuant to this section may dispense with any requirement relating to the holding of and voting at meetings or obtaining of votes, including any requirement as to quorums or as to the number or percentage of votes needed for approval, that would otherwise be imposed by the articles, bylaws, or this part.

(d) Wherever practical any order issued pursuant to this section shall limit the subject matter of the meetings or other forms of consent authorized to items, including amendments to the articles or bylaws, the resolution of which will or may enable the corporation to continue managing its affairs without further resort to this section; provided, however, that an order under this section may also authorize the obtaining of whatever votes and approvals are necessary for the dissolution, merger, sale of assets or reorganization of the corporation.

(e) Any meeting or other method of obtaining the vote of members, delegates or directors conducted pursuant to an order issued under this section, and which complies with all the provisions of such order, is for all purposes a valid meeting or vote, as the case may be, and shall have the same force and effect as if it complied with every requirement imposed by the articles, bylaws and this part.

Ca. Corp. Code § 9414

Amended by Stats. 1986, Ch. 766, Sec. 32.

Section 9415 - Cumulative voting

(a) If the articles or bylaws authorize cumulative voting, but not otherwise, every member entitled to vote at any election of directors may cumulate such member's votes and give one candidate a number of votes equal to the number of directors to be elected multiplied by the number of votes to which the member is entitled, or distribute the member's votes on the same principle among as many candidates as the member thinks fit.

(b) No member shall be entitled to cumulate votes for a candidate or candidates unless such candidate's name or candidates' names have been placed in nomination prior to the voting and the member has given notice at the meeting prior to the voting of the member's intention to cumulate votes. If any one member has given such notice, all members may cumulate their votes for candidates in nomination.

(c) In any election of directors, the candidates receiving the highest number of votes are elected, subject to any lawful provision specifying election by classes.

(d) Elections for directors need not be by ballot unless a member demands election by ballot at the meeting and before the voting begins or unless the bylaws so require.

Ca. Corp. Code § 9415

Repealed and added by Stats. 1981, Ch. 570, Sec. 10.

Section 9417 - Proxy

(a) Any member may authorize another person or persons to act by proxy with respect to such membership, except that this right may be limited or withdrawn by the articles or bylaws. Any proxy purported to be executed in accordance with the provisions of this part shall be presumptively valid.

(b) No proxy shall be valid after the expiration of 11 months from the date thereof unless otherwise provided in the proxy, except that the maximum term of any proxy shall be three years from the date of execution. Every proxy continues in full force and effect until revoked by the person executing it prior to the vote pursuant thereto. Such revocation may be effected by a writing delivered to the corporation stating that the proxy is revoked or by a subsequent proxy executed by the person executing the prior proxy and presented to the meeting, or as to any meeting by attendance at such meeting and voting in person by the person executing the proxy.

(c) A proxy is not revoked by the death or incapacity of the maker or the termination of a membership as a result thereof unless, before the vote is counted, written notice of such death or incapacity is received by the corporation.

(d) The proxy of a member may not be irrevocable.

(e) Any proxy covering matters requiring a vote of the members pursuant to Section 5812 (made applicable pursuant to Section 9620), subdivision (a) of Section 9631, subdivision (c) of Section 9640, subdivision (a) of Section 6015 (made applicable pursuant to Section 9640), or subdivision (b) of Section 9680 is not valid unless it sets forth the general nature of the matter to be voted on.

Ca. Corp. Code § 9417

Amended by Stats. 1981, Ch. 587, Sec. 53.

Section 9418 - Action to determine validity of election or appointment of director

(a) Upon the filing of an action therefor by any director or member, or by any person who had the right to vote in the election at issue after such director, member, or person has exhausted any remedies provided in the articles or bylaws, the superior court of the proper county shall determine the validity of any election or appointment of any director of any corporation.

(b) Upon the filing of the complaint, and before any further proceedings are had, the court shall enter an order fixing a date for the hearing, which shall be within five days unless for good cause shown a later date is fixed, and requiring notice of the date for the hearing and a copy of the complaint to be served upon the corporation and upon the person whose purported election or appointment is questioned and upon any person (other than the plaintiff) whom the plaintiff alleges to have been elected or appointed, in the manner in which a summons is required to be served, or, if the court so directs, by registered mail; and the court may make such further requirements as to notice as appear to be proper under the circumstances.

(c) The court, consistent with the provisions of this part and in conformity with the articles and bylaws to the extent feasible, may determine the person entitled to the office of director or may order a new election to be held or appointment to be made, may determine the validity of the issuance of memberships and the right of persons to vote and may direct such other relief as may be just and proper.

Ca. Corp. Code § 9418

Added by Stats. 1978, Ch. 567.

Section 9419 - Presumption of validity of appointment or removal of

director

In the absence of fraud, any election, appointment or removal of a director is conclusively presumed valid nine months thereafter if the only defect in the election, appointment or removal is the failure to give notice as provided in this part or in the corporation's articles or bylaws.

    Ca. Corp. Code § 9419
Added by Stats. 1979, Ch. 724.

Section 9420 - Action by written consent

Any action required or permitted to be taken by the members may be taken without a meeting, if all members shall individually or collectively consent in writing to the action. The written consent or consents shall be filed with the minutes of the proceedings of the members. The action by written consent shall have the same force and effect as the unanimous vote of the members.

    Ca. Corp. Code § 9420
Added by Stats. 1981, Ch. 587, Sec. 54.

Section 9421 - Signature on ballot, consent, waiver, or proxy appointment

(a) If the name signed on a ballot, consent, waiver, or proxy appointment corresponds to the name of a member, the corporation if acting in good faith is entitled to accept the ballot, consent, waiver, or proxy appointment and give it effect as the act of the member.

(b) If the name signed on a ballot, consent, waiver, or proxy appointment does not correspond to the record name of a member, the corporation if acting in good faith is nevertheless entitled to accept the ballot, consent, waiver, or proxy appointment and give it effect as the act of the member if any of the following occur:

    (1) The member is an entity and the name signed purports to be that of an officer or agent of the entity.

    (2) The name signed purports to be that of an attorney-in-fact of the member and if the corporation requests, evidence acceptable to the corporation of the signatory's authority to sign for the member has been presented with respect to the ballot, consent, waiver, or proxy appointment.

    (3) Two or more persons hold the membership as cotenants or fiduciaries and the name signed purports to be the name of at least one of the coholders and the person signing appears to be acting on behalf of all the coholders.

(c) The corporation is entitled to reject a ballot, consent, waiver, or proxy appointment if the secretary or other officer or agent authorized to tabulate votes, acting in good faith, has a reasonable basis for doubt concerning the validity of the signature or the signatory's authority to sign for the member.

(d) The corporation and any officer or agent thereof who accepts or rejects a ballot, consent, waiver, or proxy appointment in good faith and in accordance with the standards of this section shall not be liable in damages to the member for the consequences of the acceptance or rejection.

(e) Corporate action based on the acceptance or rejection of a ballot, consent, waiver, or proxy appointment under this section is valid unless a court of competent jurisdiction determines otherwise.

   Ca. Corp. Code § 9421

Added by Stats. 1996, Ch. 589, Sec. 44. Effective January 1, 1997.

Chapter 5 - RECORDS, REPORTS AND RIGHTS OF INSPECTION

Section 9510 - Keeping records

(a) Each corporation shall keep:

   (1) Adequate and correct books and records of account.

   (2) Minutes of the proceedings of its members, board and committees of the board.

   (3) A record of its members giving their names and addresses and the class of membership held by each.

(b) Those minutes and other books and records shall be kept either in written form or in any other form capable of being converted into clearly legible tangible form or in any combination of the foregoing. When minutes and other books and records are kept in a form capable of being converted into clearly legible paper form, the clearly legible paper form into which those minutes and other books and records are converted shall be admissible in evidence, and accepted for all other purposes, to the same extent as an original paper record of the same information would have been, provided that the paper form accurately portrays the record.

   Ca. Corp. Code § 9510

Amended by Stats 2004 ch 254 (SB 1306),s 34, eff. 1/1/2005

Section 9511 - Inspection of record of members' names, addresses, and voting rights

Except as otherwise provided in the articles or bylaws, a member may inspect and copy the record of all the members' names, addresses and voting rights, at reasonable times, upon five business days' prior written demand upon the corporation for a purpose reasonably related to the member's interest as a member.

   Ca. Corp. Code § 9511

Amended by Stats. 1979, Ch. 724.

Section 9512 - Accounting books and records and minutes

Except as otherwise provided in the articles or bylaws, the accounting books and records and minutes of proceedings of the members and the board and committees of the board shall be open to inspection upon the written demand on the corporation of any member at any reasonable time, for a purpose reasonably related to such person's interests as a member.

 Ca. Corp. Code § 9512
Added by Stats. 1978, Ch. 567.

Section 9513 - Director's right to inspect

Every director shall have the right at any reasonable time to inspect and copy all books, records and documents of every kind and to inspect the physical properties of the corporation of which such person is a director for a purpose reasonably related to such person's interests as a director.

 Ca. Corp. Code § 9513
Amended by Stats. 1981, Ch. 587, Sec. 55.

Section 9514 - Enforcement of demand for inspection or right of inspection

(a) Upon refusal of a lawful demand for inspection under this chapter, the superior court of the proper county, or the county where the books or records in question are kept, may enforce the demand or right of inspection with just and proper conditions or may, for good cause shown, appoint one or more competent inspectors or independent accountants to audit the financial statements kept in this state and investigate the property and funds of any corporation and of any subsidiary corporation thereof, domestic or foreign, keeping records in this state and to report thereon in such manner as the court may direct.
(b) All officers and agents of the corporation shall produce to the inspectors or accountants so appointed all books and documents in their custody or power, under penalty of punishment for contempt of court.
(c) All expenses of the investigation or audit shall be defrayed by the applicant unless the court orders them to be paid or shared by the corporation.

 Ca. Corp. Code § 9514
Amended by Stats. 1979, Ch. 724.

Chapter 6 - MISCELLANEOUS PROVISIONS

Article 1 - DISTRIBUTIONS

Section 9610 - Applicable provisions; suit

(a) The provisions of Chapter 4 (commencing with Section 5410) of Part 2 apply to religious corporations except for subdivision (b) of Section 5420.

(b) Suit may be brought in the name of the corporation by a creditor, a director, or the authorized number of members. In any such action in addition to the remedy provided in subdivision (a) of Section 5420, the court may award punitive damages for the benefit of the corporation against any director, officer, member or other person who with intent to defraud the corporation caused, received or aided and abetted in the making of any distribution.

 Ca. Corp. Code § 9610
Repealed and added by Stats. 1978, Ch. 567.

Article 2 - AMENDMENT OF ARTICLES

Section 9620 - Applicable provisions; extension of term of existence

(a) The provisions of Chapter 8 (commencing with Section 5810) of Part 2 apply to religious corporations except for Section 5813.5, the second sentence of Section 5817, and Section 5818.

(b) A corporation formed for a limited period may at any time subsequent to the expiration of the term of its corporate existence, extend the term of its existence by an amendment to its articles removing any provision limiting the term of its existence and providing for perpetual existence. If the filing of the certificate of amendment providing for perpetual existence would be prohibited if it were original articles by the provisions of Section 9122 the Secretary of State shall not file such certificate unless, by the same or a concurrently filed certificate of amendment, the articles of such corporation are amended to adopt a new available name. For the purpose of the adoption of any such amendment, persons who have been functioning as directors of such corporation shall be considered to have been validly elected even though their election may have occurred after the expiration of the original term of the corporate existence.

 Ca. Corp. Code § 9620
Amended by Stats. 1981, Ch. 587, Sec. 56.

Section 9621 - Amendment of articles to change status of religious corporation

(a) A religious corporation may amend its articles to change its status to that of (1), a public benefit corporation, by complying with this section and the other sections of Chapter 8 (commencing with Section 5810) of Part 2 (made applicable pursuant to Section 9620) or (2), a mutual benefit corporation, business corporation, a social purpose corporation, or cooperative corporation by complying with Chapter 8 (commencing with Section 5810) of Part 2.

(b) Amended articles authorized by this section shall include the provisions which would have been required (other than the initial street address and initial mailing address of the corporation and the name of the initial agent for service of process if a statement has been filed pursuant to Section 6210, made applicable pursuant to Section 9660) and may in addition only include those provisions which would have been permitted, in original articles filed by the type of corporation (public benefit, mutual benefit, business, social purpose, or cooperative) into which the religious corporation is changing its status.

Ca. Corp. Code § 9621
Amended by Stats 2014 ch 694 (SB 1301),s 70, eff. 1/1/2015.
Amended by Stats 2012 ch 494 (SB 1532),s 25, eff. 1/1/2013.

Article 3 - SALE OF ASSETS

Section 9630 - Mortgage, deed of trust, pledge, or other hypothecation of property

Any mortgage, deed of trust, pledge or other hypothecation of all or any part of the corporation's property, real or personal, for the purpose of securing the payment or performance of any contract or obligation may be approved by the board. Unless the articles or bylaws otherwise provide, no approval of the members (Section 5034) or of any other person or persons shall be necessary for such action.

Ca. Corp. Code § 9630
Amended by Stats. 1979, Ch. 724.

Section 9631 - Sale or other disposal of assets

(a) Subject to the provisions of Section 9142, a corporation may sell, lease, convey, exchange, transfer or otherwise dispose of all or substantially all of its assets when the principal terms are:

(1) Approved by the board; and

(2) Unless the transaction is in the usual and regular course of its activities, approved by the members (Section 5034) and by any other person or persons whose approval is required by the articles or bylaws either before or after approval by the board and before or after the transaction.

(b) Subject to any provision in the articles or bylaws, the board may, notwithstanding approval by the members (Section 5034) or such other person, abandon the proposed transaction without further action by the members, subject to the contractual rights, if any, of third parties.

(c) Subject to the provisions of Section 9142, such sale, lease, conveyance, exchange, transfer or other disposition may be made upon such terms and conditions and for such consideration as the board may deem in the best interests of the corporation. The consideration may be money, property, or securities of any domestic corporation,

foreign corporation, or foreign business corporation or any of them.
Ca. Corp. Code § 9631
Amended by Stats. 1981, Ch. 587, Sec. 57.

Section 9632 - Certificate annexed to deed or instrument conveying or transferring assets

Any deed or instrument conveying or otherwise transferring any assets of a corporation may have annexed to it the certificate of the secretary or an assistant secretary of the corporation, setting forth that the transaction has been validly approved by the board, that the notice, if any, required by Section 9633 has been given and (a) stating that the property described in such deed or instrument is less than substantially all of the assets of the corporation or that the transfer is in the usual and regular course of the business of the corporation, if such be the case, or (b) if such property constitutes all or substantially all of the assets of the corporation and the transfer is not in the usual and regular course of the business of the corporation, stating the fact of approval thereof by the members (Section 5034). Such certificate is prima facie evidence of the existence of the facts authorizing such conveyance or other transfer of the assets and conclusive evidence in favor of any purchaser or encumbrancer for value who, without notice of any trust restriction applicable to the property or any failure to comply therewith, in good faith parted with value.
Ca. Corp. Code § 9632
Added by Stats. 1979, Ch. 724.

Section 9633 - Notice to attorney general

A corporation must give written notice to the Attorney General 20 days before it sells, leases, conveys, exchanges, transfers or otherwise disposes of all or substantially all of its assets unless the Attorney General has given the corporation a written waiver of this section as to the proposed transaction.
Ca. Corp. Code § 9633
Added by Stats. 1979, Ch. 724.

Section 9634 - Applicable provisions

The provisions of Article 2 (commencing with Section 5914) of Chapter 9 of Part 2 apply to religious corporations to the extent provided therein.
Ca. Corp. Code § 9634
Added by Stats 2011 ch 442 (AB 1211),s 26, eff. 1/1/2012.

Article 4 - MERGERS

Section 9640 - Applicable provisions; merger

(a) The provisions of Chapter 10 (commencing with Section 6010) of Part 2 apply to religious corporations except subdivision (a) of Section 6010 and Sections 6011 and 6012.

(b) A corporation may merge with any domestic corporation, foreign corporation, or other business entity (Section 5063.5). However, without the prior written consent of the Attorney General, a religious corporation may only merge with another religious corporation or with a public benefit corporation or a foreign nonprofit corporation or an unincorporated association, the governing documents of which provide that its assets are irrevocably dedicated to charitable, religious, or public purposes.

(c) The principal terms of the merger shall be approved by the members (Section 5034) of each class of each constituent corporation and by each other person or persons whose approval of an amendment of the articles is required by the articles or bylaws; and the approval by the members (Section 5034) or any other person or persons required by this section may be given before or after the approval by the board.

(d) The board of each corporation that desires to merge shall approve an agreement of merger. The constituent corporations shall be parties to the agreement of merger and other persons may be parties to the agreement of merger. The agreement shall state all of the following:

(1) The terms and conditions of the merger.

(2) The amendments, subject to Sections 5810 and 5816, to the articles of the surviving corporation to be effected by the merger, if any. If any amendment changes the name of the surviving corporation, the new name may be the same as or similar to the name of a disappearing corporation, subject to subdivision (b) of Section 9122.

(3) The amendments to the bylaws of the surviving corporation to be effected by the merger, if any.

(4) The name and place of incorporation of each constituent corporation and which of the constituent corporations is the surviving corporation.

(5) The manner, if any, of converting memberships of the constituent corporations into memberships of the surviving corporation.

(6) Any other details or provisions as are desired, if any.
Ca. Corp. Code § 9640
Amended by Stats 2011 ch 442 (AB 1211),s 27, eff. 1/1/2012.
Amended September 21, 1999 (Bill Number: AB 198) (Chapter 437).

Article 5 - BANKRUPTCY REORGANIZATIONS AND ARRANGEMENTS

Section 9650 - Law governing reorganization

Any proceeding, initiated with respect to a corporation, under any applicable statute of the United States, as now existing or hereafter enacted, relating to reorganizations of corporations, shall be governed by the provisions of Chapter 14 (commencing with Section 1400) of Division 1 of Title 1, and for this purpose the reference in Chapter 14 to "shareholders" shall be deemed to be a reference to members and the reference to "this division" shall be deemed to be a reference to this part.

Ca. Corp. Code § 9650
Amended by Stats 2009 ch 500 (AB 1059),s 23, eff. 1/1/2010.

Article 6 - FILINGS

Section 9660 - Applicable provisions; action to compel compliance

(a) The provisions of Chapter 12 (commencing with Section 6210) of Part 2 apply to religious corporations except for Section 6216.
(b) The Attorney General may bring an action in the proper county to compel compliance with Chapter 12 (commencing with Section 6210) made applicable to religious corporations by this section.

Ca. Corp. Code § 9660
Added by Stats. 1978, Ch. 567.

Article 7 - SERVICE OF PROCESS

Section 9670 - Service of process

Service of process upon a corporation shall be governed by Chapter 17 (commencing with Section 1700) of Division 1 of Title 1.

Ca. Corp. Code § 9670
Added by Stats. 1978, Ch. 567.

Article 8 - DISSOLUTION

Section 9680 - Applicable provisions; voluntary election to wind up and dissolve

(a) Chapters 16 (commencing with Section 6610) and 17 (commencing with Section 6710) of Part 2 apply to religious corporations except for Sections 6610, 6614, 6710, 6711 and 6716.
(b)

(1) Any corporation may elect voluntarily to wind up and dissolve (A) by approval of a majority of all the members (Section 5033) or (B) by approval of the board and approval of the members (Section 5034).

(2) Any corporation which comes within one of the following descriptions may elect by approval of the board to wind up and dissolve:

(A) A corporation which has been the subject of an order for relief in bankruptcy.

(B) A corporation which has disposed of all its assets and has not conducted any activity for a period of five years immediately preceding the adoption of the resolution electing to dissolve the corporation.

(C) A corporation which has no members.

(D) A corporation which is required to dissolve under provisions of its articles adopted pursuant to subparagraph (i) of paragraph (2) of subdivision (a) of Section 9132.

(3) If a corporation comes within one of the descriptions in paragraph (2) and if the number of directors then in office is less than a quorum, it may elect to voluntarily wind up and dissolve by any of the following:

(A) The unanimous consent of the directors then in office.

(B) The affirmative vote of a majority of the directors then in office at a meeting held pursuant to waiver of notice by those directors complying with paragraph (3) of subdivision (a) of Section 9211.

(C) The vote of a sole remaining director.

(4) If a corporation elects to voluntarily wind up and dissolve pursuant to paragraph (3), references to the board in this chapter shall be deemed to be to a board consisting solely of those directors or that sole director and action by the board shall require at least the same consent or vote as would be required under paragraph (3) for an election to wind up and dissolve.

(c) If a corporation is in the process of voluntary winding up, the superior court of the proper county, upon the petition of (1) the corporation, or (2) the authorized number (Section 5036), or (3) the Attorney General, or (4) three or more creditors, and upon such notice to the corporation and members and creditors as the court may order, may take jurisdiction over the voluntary winding up proceeding if that appears necessary for the protection of the assets of the corporation. The court, if it assumes jurisdiction, may make such orders as to any and all matters concerning the winding up of the affairs of the corporation and the protection of its creditors and its assets as justice and equity may require. Chapter 15 (commencing with Section 6510) (except Sections 6510 and 6511) shall apply to those court proceedings.

(d) The powers and duties of the directors (or other persons appointed by the court pursuant to Section 6515) and officers after commencement of a dissolution proceeding include, but are not limited to, the following acts in the name and on behalf of the corporation:

(1) To elect officers and to employ agents and attorneys to liquidate or wind up its affairs.

(2) To continue the conduct of the affairs of the corporation insofar as necessary for the disposal or winding up thereof.

(3) To carry out contracts and collect, pay, compromise, and settle debts and claims for or against the corporation.

(4) To defend suits brought against the corporation.

(5) To sue, in the name of the corporation, for all sums due or owing to the corporation or to recover any of its property.

(6) To collect any amounts remaining unpaid on memberships or to recover unlawful distributions.

(7) Subject to the provisions of Section 9142, to sell at public or private sale, exchange, convey, or otherwise dispose of all or any part of the assets of the corporation in an amount deemed reasonable by the board without compliance with Section 9631, and to execute bills of sale and deeds of conveyance in the name of the corporation.

(8) In general, to make contracts and to do any and all things in the name of the corporation which may be proper or convenient for the purposes of winding up, settling and liquidating the affairs of the corporation.
(e) After complying with Section 6713:

(1) Except as provided in Section 6715, all of a corporation's assets shall be disposed of on dissolution in conformity with its articles or bylaws subject to complying with the provisions of any trust under which such assets are held.

(2) Except as provided in subdivision (3), the disposition required in subdivision (1) shall be made by decree of the superior court of the proper county. The decree shall be made upon petition therefor, upon 30 days' notice to the Attorney General, by any person concerned in the dissolution.

(3) The disposition required in subdivision (1) may be made without the decree of the superior court, subject to the rights of persons concerned in the dissolution, if the Attorney General makes a written waiver of objections to the disposition.

(f) A vacancy on the board may be filled during a winding up proceeding in the manner provided in Section 9224.

(g) Chapter 15 (commencing with Section 6510) does not apply to religious corporations except to the extent its provisions apply under subdivision (d) of Section 6617, subdivision (c) of Section 6719, or subdivision (c) or (d) of this section.

Ca. Corp. Code § 9680

Amended by Stats 2009 ch 631 (AB 1233),s 35, eff. 1/1/2010.

Amended by Stats 2009 ch 500 (AB 1059),s 24, eff. 1/1/2010.

Section 9680.5 - Verification of certificate of dissolution of nonprofit

(a) Notwithstanding any other provision of this division, when a corporation has not issued any memberships, a majority of the directors, or, if no directors have been named in the articles or been elected, the incorporator or a majority of the incorporators, may sign and verify a certificate of dissolution stating the following:

(1) That the certificate of dissolution is being filed within 24 months from the date the articles of incorporation were filed.

(2) That the corporation does not have any debts or other liabilities, except as provided in paragraph (3) and subdivision (d).

(3) That the tax liability will be satisfied on a taxes-paid basis or that a person or corporation or other business entity assumes the tax liability, if any, of the dissolving corporation and is responsible for additional corporate taxes, if any, that are assessed and that become due after the date of the assumption of the tax liability.

(4) That a final franchise tax return, as described by Section 23332 of the Revenue and Taxation Code, has been or will be filed with the Franchise Tax Board as required under Part 10.2 (commencing with Section 18401) of Division 2 of the Revenue and Taxation Code.

(5) That the corporation was created in error.

(6) That the known assets of the corporation remaining after payment of, or adequately providing for, known debts and liabilities have been distributed as required by law or that the corporation acquired no known assets, as the case may be.

(7) That a majority of the directors, or, if no directors have been named in the articles or been elected, the incorporator or a majority of the incorporators authorized the dissolution and elected to dissolve the corporation.

(8) That the corporation has not issued any memberships, and if the corporation has received payments for memberships, those payments have been returned to those making the payments.

(9) That the corporation is dissolved.

(b) A certificate of dissolution signed and verified pursuant to subdivision (a) shall be filed with the Secretary of State. The Secretary of State shall notify the Franchise Tax Board of the dissolution.

(c) Upon filing a certificate of dissolution pursuant to subdivision (b), a corporation shall be dissolved and its powers, rights, and privileges shall cease.

(d) Notwithstanding the dissolution of a nonprofit corporation pursuant to this section, its liability to creditors, if any, is not discharged. The liability of the directors of, or other persons related to, the dissolved corporation is not discharged. The dissolution of a nonprofit corporation pursuant to this section shall not diminish or adversely affect the ability of the Attorney General to enforce liabilities as otherwise provided by law.

    Ca. Corp. Code § 9680.5

Added by Stats 2015 ch 363 (AB 557),s 5, eff. 1/1/2016.

Article 9 - CRIMES AND PENALTIES

Section 9690 - Applicable provisions; restitution

The provisions of Chapter 18 (commencing with Section 6810) of Part 2 apply to religious corporations. In so providing, the Legislature encourages the criminal courts of this state in sentencing persons convicted of fraudulent activities in the guise of religious activity to exercise their authority to impose restitution as a means of compensating the victims.

    Ca. Corp. Code § 9690

Amended by Stats. 1980, Ch. 1324.

Part 5 - TRANSITION PROVISIONS

Section 9910 - Definitions

As used in Sections 9910 to 9927 of this part:

(a) "New public benefit, mutual benefit and religious corporation law" means Part 1 (commencing with Section 5002), Part 2 (commencing with Section 5110), Part 3 (commencing with Section 7110), Part 4 (commencing with Section 9110) and Part 5 (commencing with Section 9910), of Division 2 of Title 1 of the Corporations Code enacted by the California Legislature during the 1977-1978 Regular Session and, except as required by Section 9912, operative January 1, 1980.

(b) "New public benefit corporation law" means Part 2 of the new public benefit, mutual benefit and religious corporation law.

(c) "New mutual benefit corporation law" means Part 3 of the new public benefit, mutual benefit, and religious corporation law.

(d) "New religious corporation law" means Part 4 of the new public benefit, mutual benefit and religious corporation law.

(e) "Prior nonprofit law" means Part 1, Division 2 (commencing with Section 9000) of Title 1 of the Corporations Code in effect on December 31, 1979.

(f) "Subject corporation" means any corporation described in paragraphs (3) through (5), inclusive, of subdivision (a) of Section 5003 and subject to the prior nonprofit law.

Ca. Corp. Code § 9910
Added by Stats. 1978, Ch. 567.

Section 9911 - Application of new laws

(a) The new public benefit corporation law applies to all corporations which are incorporated on or after January 1, 1980, under Part 2 of this division or which are expressly governed by Part 2 pursuant to a particular provision of this division, Division 3 (commencing with Section 12000) or other specific statutory provision.

(b) The new mutual benefit corporation law applies to all corporations which are incorporated on or after January 1, 1980, under Part 3 of this division or which are expressly governed by Part 3 pursuant to a particular provision of this division or Division 3 (commencing with Section 12000) or other specific statutory provision.

(c) The new religious corporation law applies to all corporations which are incorporated on or after January 1, 1980, under Part 4 of this division or which are expressly governed by Part 4 pursuant to a particular provision of this division, Division 3 (commencing with Section 12000) or other specific statutory provision.

(d) Notwithstanding subdivisions (a) through (c), if articles of incorporation intended to and in fact meeting the requirements of the prior nonprofit law have been initially received by the Secretary of State prior to January 1, 1980, and the matter is still pending on that date, then the entity may be incorporated pursuant to the prior nonprofit law if its articles are filed prior to May 1, 1980.

(e) Except as otherwise expressly provided in this part, (i) the new public benefit corporation law applies to all subject corporations referred to in Section 5060 and to all actions taken by the directors, officers or members of such corporation on or after January 1, 1980; (ii) the new mutual benefit corporation law applies to all subject corporations referred to in Section 5059 and to all actions taken by the directors, officers or members of such corporations on or after January 1, 1980; and (iii) the new religious corporation law applies to all subject corporations referred to in Section 5061 and to all actions taken by the directors, officers or members of such corporations on or after January 1, 1980.

(f) Except as otherwise expressly provided in this part, all of the sections of the new public benefit, mutual benefit and religious corporation law governing acts, contracts or other transactions by a corporation or its directors, officers or members, apply only to acts, contracts, or transactions occurring on or after January 1, 1980; and the prior nonprofit law governs acts, contracts or transactions occurring before January 1, 1980.

(g) Except as otherwise expressly provided in this part, any vote or consent by the directors or members of a corporation prior to January 1, 1980, in accordance with the prior nonprofit law shall be effective in accordance with that law; and if any certificate or document is required to be filed in any public office of this state relating to such vote or consent, it may be filed on or after January 1, 1980, in accordance with the prior nonprofit law.

Ca. Corp. Code § 9911
Added by Stats. 1978, Ch. 567.

Section 9912 - Corporations subject to prior nonprofit law

(a) Each corporation which is subject (pursuant to the terms of the prior nonprofit law or some other specific statutory provision) to the prior nonprofit law shall, on and after January 1, 1980, be subject to the new public benefit corporation law, the new mutual benefit corporation law, or the new religious corporation law based on the following:

(1) Any corporation of a type designated by statute as being subject to the new public benefit corporation law, the new mutual benefit corporation law, or the new religious corporation law, shall be subject to such law.

(2) Any corporation organized primarily or exclusively for religious purposes shall be subject to the new religious corporation law.

(3) Any corporation which does not come within paragraphs 1 or 2 of this subdivision but which has received an exemption under Section 23701d of the Revenue and Taxation Code, shall be subject to the new public benefit corporation law.

(4) Any corporation which does not come within paragraphs 1, 2, or 3 of this subdivision and all of the assets of which are irrevocably dedicated to charitable or public purposes and which according to its articles or bylaws must upon dissolution distribute its assets to a person or persons carrying on a similar purpose or purposes shall be subject to the new public benefit corporation law.

(5) Any corporation which does not come within paragraphs 1, 2, 3 or 4 of this subdivision and which permits distribution of assets to its members upon dissolution shall be subject to the new mutual benefit corporation law.

(6) Any corporation not otherwise described in this subdivision shall be subject to the new mutual benefit corporation law.

(b) Prior to January 1, 1980, the Secretary of State's office shall send a nonbinding, advisory notice to each corporation covered by subdivision (a) indicating the type of corporation it is, based on the rules set forth in subdivision (a) of this section.

(c) Notwithstanding subdivision (a), assets held by a mutual benefit corporation in charitable trust shall be administered in compliance with the provisions of the trust and in accordance with any standards applicable pursuant to Section 7238.

(d) A corporation may petition the superior court of the proper county to determine its status as a public benefit, mutual benefit or religious corporation in accordance with subdivision (a). Notice of the proceeding shall be given as the court may direct. Any member may intervene. Notice of the proceeding shall be served on the Attorney General who may intervene. A certified copy of any final judgment in any such proceeding shall be filed with the Secretary of State.

(e) The Secretary of State may, in carrying out any obligation arising under this article, require any information necessary on existing corporations from the Franchise Tax Board or other state agency.

Ca. Corp. Code § 9912
Amended by Stats. 1979, Ch. 724.

Section 9913 - Provisions relating to contents of articles of incorporation

(a) The provisions of Sections 5130, 5131 and 5132 of the new Public Benefit Corporation Law relating to the contents of articles of incorporation do not apply to subject corporations designated as public benefit corporations unless and until an amendment of the articles is filed stating that the corporation elects to be governed by all of the provisions of the new law not otherwise applicable to it under this part.

(b) The provisions of Sections 7130, 7131, and 7132 of the new Mutual Benefit Corporation Law relating to the contents of articles of incorporation do not apply to subject corporations governed by the Mutual Benefit Corporation Law unless and until an amendment of the articles of incorporation is filed stating that the corporation elects to be governed by all of the provisions of the new law not otherwise applicable to it under this part.

(c) The provisions of Sections 9130, 9131, and 9132 of the new Religious Corporation Law relating to the contents of articles of incorporation do not apply to subject corporations governed by the Religious Corporation Law unless and until an amendment of the articles is filed stating that the corporation elects to be governed by all of the provisions of the new law not otherwise applicable to it under this part.

(d) The amendment described in subdivision (a) may be adopted by the board alone, except that if such amendment makes any change in the articles other than conforming the statement of purposes of the public benefit corporation to Section 5130 and the deletion of any references to the location of principal office and deleting any statement regarding the number of directors or conforming any such statement to Section 5151 (subject to Section 9915), it shall also be approved by the members (Section 5034) if such approval is otherwise required for the changes made.

(e) The amendment described in subdivision (b) may be adopted by the board alone, except that if such amendment makes any change in the articles other than conforming the statement of purposes of the mutual benefit corporation to subdivisions (a) and (b) of Section 7130 and the deletion of any references to the location of principal office and deleting any statement regarding the number of directors or conforming any such statement to Section 7151 (subject to Section 9915), it shall also be approved by the members (Section 5034) if such approval is otherwise required for the changes made.

(f) The amendment described in subdivision (c) may be adopted by the board alone, except that if such amendment makes any change in the articles other than conforming the statement of purposes of the religious corporation to Section 9130 and the deletion of any references to the location of principal office and deleting any statement regarding the number of directors or conforming any such statement to Section 9151 (subject to Section 9915), it shall also be approved by the members (Section 5034) if such approval is otherwise required for the changes made.

(g) The amendment shall not contain the initial street address or initial mailing address of the corporation or name the corporation's initial agent for service of process if a statement required by Section 6210, 8210, or 6210 (made applicable by Section 9660), as the case may be, has been filed.

Ca. Corp. Code § 9913
Amended by Stats 2012 ch 494 (SB 1532),s 26, eff. 1/1/2013.

Section 9914 - Provisions relating to powers of corporation

Section 5140 of the new public benefit corporation law applies to subject corporations governed by the public benefit corporation law, and Section 7140 of the new mutual benefit corporation law applies to subject corporations governed by the mutual benefit corporation law and Section 9140 of the new religious corporation law applies to subject corporations governed by the religious corporation law; but any statement in the articles of such corporations prior to an amendment thereof pursuant to Section 9913, relating to the powers of the corporation shall not be construed as a limitation unless it is expressly stated as such.

Ca. Corp. Code § 9914
Added by Stats. 1978, Ch. 567.

Section 9915 - Provisions relating to number of directors

(a) Subdivision (a) of Section 5151 of the new public benefit corporation law does not apply to subject corporations governed by the public benefit corporation law, subdivision (a) of Section 7151 of the new mutual benefit corporation law does not apply to subject corporations governed by the mutual benefit corporation law, and subdivision (a) of Section 9151 of the new religious corporation law does not apply to subject corporations governed by the religious corporation law, but those corporations shall continue to be governed by the prior nonprofit law unless and until an amendment of the articles is filed pursuant to Section 9913. If an amendment makes any change in the number of directors or the maximum or minimum number of directors or makes change from a fixed to a variable board or vice versa, it shall also be approved by the members (Section 5034).

(b) Notwithstanding subdivision (a), the new public benefit corporation law, the new mutual benefit corporation law, or the new religious corporation law, as appropriate, rather than the provisions of the prior nonprofit law apply with the respect to determining the limits on the number of directors.

Ca. Corp. Code § 9915

Amended by Stats. 1988, Ch. 919, Sec. 12.

Section 9916 - Provisions relating to officers

Subdivision (a) of Section 5213 of the new public benefit corporation law applies to subject corporations governed by the public benefit corporation law, subdivision (a) of Section 7213 of the new mutual benefit corporation law apply to subject corporations governed by the mutual benefit corporation law, and subdivision (a) of Section 9213 of the new religious corporation law applies to subject corporations governed by the religious corporation law; but the "treasurer" of those corporations shall be deemed to be the "chief financial officer," unless otherwise provided in the articles or bylaws.

Ca. Corp. Code § 9916

Amended by Stats 2009 ch 631 (AB 1233),s 36, eff. 1/1/2010.

Section 9916.5 - Provisions relating to term of director

Subdivisions (a) and (d) of Section 5220 apply to subject corporations governed by the nonprofit public benefit corporation law and subdivisions (a) and (d) of Section 7220 apply to subject corporations governed by the nonprofit mutual benefit corporation law, provided that:

(a) If a director on January 1, 1980, is serving a term in excess of three years in duration, the director may continue to serve until December 31, 1982, or until the expiration of the term whichever is earlier.

(b) If, on January 1, 1980, more than one-third of the directors of a corporation hold office by virtue of designation or selection, they may continue to do so until December 31, 1982.

Ca. Corp. Code § 9916.5

Amended by Stats. 1984, Ch. 144, Sec. 23.

Section 9917 - Provisions relating to indemnification

Section 5238 governs any proposed indemnification by a public benefit corporation, Section 7237 governs any proposed indemnification by a mutual benefit corporation, and Section 9246 governs any proposed indemnification by a religious corporation, after January 1, 1980, whether the events upon which the indemnification is based occurred before or after January 1, 1980. Any statement relating to indemnification contained in the articles or bylaws of a subject corporation shall not be construed as limiting the indemnification permitted by Section 5238, Section 7237, or Section 9246 unless it is expressly stated as so intended.

Ca. Corp. Code § 9917
Amended by Stats. 1980, Ch. 1155.

Section 9918 - Provision relating to membership certificates

Section 7313 of the new mutual benefit corporation law relating to membership certificates applies to the membership certificates of a subject corporation if the certificates are issued on or after January 1, 1980, and the prior nonprofit law shall continue to govern certificates representing memberships issued prior to January 1, 1980, unless and until an amendment of the articles is filed pursuant to Section 9913.
    Ca. Corp. Code § 9918
Added by Stats. 1978, Ch. 567.

Section 9920 - Provisions relating to meetings of members

(a) The provisions of Chapter 5 (commencing with Section 5510) and Chapter 6 (commencing with Section 5610) of the new Public Benefit Corporation Law apply to any meeting of members of a public benefit corporation, the provisions of Chapter 5 (commencing with Section 7510) and Chapter 6 (commencing with Section 7610) of the new Mutual Benefit Corporation Law apply to any meeting of members of a mutual benefit corporation, and the provisions of Chapter 4 (commencing with Section 9410) of the new Religious Corporation Law apply to any meeting of members of a religious corporation, held on or after January 1, 1980, and to any action by such members pursuant to a written ballot, which becomes effective on or after January 1, 1980, and to any vote cast at such a meeting or ballot, given for such action (whether or not a proxy or ballot was executed by the member prior to January 1, 1980).
(b) Notwithstanding subdivision (a):

    (1) The prior nonprofit law shall apply to any such meeting of members and to any vote cast at such a meeting if such meeting was initially called for a date prior to January 1, 1980, and notice thereof was given to members entitled to vote thereat; and

    (2) Where a proxy would be valid under the prior nonprofit law but would not be valid for a public benefit corporation under the new Public Benefit Corporation Law, for a mutual benefit corporation under the new Mutual Benefit Corporation Law, or for a religious corporation under the new Religious Corporation Law, and where the proxy by its terms expires during or after 1980, such proxy may be voted at meetings of members during 1980 (prior to its expiration date) but not thereafter.

    (3) Action taken by the board or the members after December 31, 1979, and before January 1, 1982, shall be valid if such action was taken in compliance with the prior nonprofit law and the articles and bylaws as they then existed, subject to the rights of any person who acted in detrimental reliance upon the invalidity of such action prior to Janaury 1, 1982. This subdivision does not validate any provision in the articles or bylaws after December 31, 1981, which does not comply with the then existing provisions of the new public benefit, mutual benefit, or religious corporation law, as the case may be.

Ca. Corp. Code § 9920
Amended by Stats. 1981, Ch. 587, Sec. 61.

Section 9921 - Provisions applying to actions

Section 5710 of the new public benefit corporation law applies to actions commenced on or after January 1, 1980, with respect to a public benefit corporation, and Section 7710 of the new mutual benefit corporation law applies to actions commenced on or after January 1, 1980, with respect to a mutual benefit corporation. The prior nonprofit law governs actions commenced prior to but still pending on January 1, 1980.

Ca. Corp. Code § 9921
Added by Stats. 1978, Ch. 567.

Section 9922 - Provisions relating to transactions

Chapters 9 (commencing with Section 5910) and 10 (commencing with Section 6010) of the new public benefit corporation law apply to transactions consummated on or after January 1, 1980, by a public benefit corporation or, subject to Sections 9630 and 9640, by a religious corporation, and Chapters 9 (commencing with Section 7910) and 10 (commencing with Section 8010) of the new mutual benefit corporation law apply to transactions consummated on or after January 1, 1980, by a mutual benefit corporation, unless the approval required by the prior nonprofit law has been given prior to January 1, 1980, or has been given on or after January 1, 1980, but at a meeting of members initially called for a date prior to January 1, 1980, in which case the transaction shall be governed by the prior nonprofit law.

Ca. Corp. Code § 9922
Added by Stats. 1978, Ch. 567.

Section 9923 - Provisions relating to involuntary dissolution

Chapters 15 (commencing with Section 6510) and 17 (commencing with Section 6710) of the new public benefit corporation law apply to acts for involuntary dissolution of a public benefit corporation commenced on or after January 1, 1980, and Chapters 15 (commencing with Section 8510) and 17 (commencing with Section 8710) of the new mutual benefit corporation law apply to acts for involuntary dissolution of a mutual benefit corporation commenced on or after January 1, 1980; but the prior nonprofit law governs any such actions commenced prior to but still pending on January 1, 1980.

Ca. Corp. Code § 9923
Added by Stats. 1978, Ch. 567.

Section 9924 - Provisions relating to voluntary dissolution

Chapters 16 (commencing with Section 6610) and 17 (commencing with Section 6710) of the new public benefit corporation law apply to any voluntary dissolution proceeding initiated with respect to a public benefit corporation or, subject to Section 9680, with respect to a religious corporation, by the filing on or after January 1, 1980, of an election to wind up and dissolve, and Chapters 16 (commencing with Section 8610) and 17 (commencing with Section 8710) of the new mutual benefit corporation law apply to any voluntary dissolution proceeding initiated with respect to a mutual benefit corporation by the filing on or after January 1, 1980, of an election to wind up and dissolve; but the prior nonprofit law governs any such proceeding so initiated prior to January 1, 1980.

Ca. Corp. Code § 9924
Added by Stats. 1978, Ch. 567.

Section 9925 - Provisions relating to agent for service of process

When any corporate agent for service of process has been designated prior to January 1, 1980, and such designation of agent included a name of a city, town or village wherein the corporate agent maintained an office, service on such agent may be effected at any office of the agent set forth in the certificate of the corporate agent filed pursuant to Section 6213 of the new public benefit corporation law (applicable to public benefit corporations and, subject to Section 9660, to religious corporations), Section 8213 of the new mutual benefit corporation law, Section 1505 of the Corporations Code, or filed pursuant to Section 3301.5, 3301.6, 6403.5, or 6403.6 of the Corporations Code as in effect prior to January 1, 1977.

Ca. Corp. Code § 9925
Added by Stats. 1978, Ch. 567.

Section 9926 - Election to continue existence

Any subject corporation that existed on the first day of January, 1873, and was formed under the laws of this state, which corporation has not already elected to continue its existence under the prior nonprofit law, may at any time elect to continue its existence under the provisions of this code applicable thereto by the unanimous vote of all its directors, or such election may be made at any annual meeting of the members, or at any meeting called by the directors especially for considering the subject, if voted by members representing a majority of the voting power, or may be made by the directors upon the written consent of that number of the members.

A certificate of the action of the directors, signed by them and their secretary, when the election is made by their unanimous votes or upon the written consent of the members, or a certificate of the proceedings of the meeting of the members when the election is made at any such meeting, signed by the chairperson and secretary of the meeting and a majority of the directors, shall be filed in the office of the Secretary of State, and thereafter the corporation continues its existence under the provisions of this code which are applicable thereto, and possesses all the rights, and powers, and is subject to all the obligations, restrictions, and limitations prescribed thereby.

 Ca. Corp. Code § 9926

Amended by Stats 2022 ch 617 (SB 1202),s 72, eff. 1/1/2023.
Added by Stats. 1978, Ch. 567.

Section 9927 - Suspension of corporate rights, privileges, and powers of corporation

If the corporate rights, privileges and powers of a corporation have been suspended and are still suspended immediately prior to January 1, 1980, pursuant to the prior nonprofit law as a result of its incorporation of Sections 5700 through 5908 of the prior law (Section 2300), such sections and provisions continue to apply to such a corporation until restoration by the Controller pursuant to such sections.

 Ca. Corp. Code § 9927

Added by Stats. 1978, Ch. 567.

Section 9928 - Corporation subject to suspension

(a) A corporation which was organized prior to January 1, 1971, under any statutory provisions other than the General Corporation Law as then in effect (Division 1 (commencing with Section 100) of Title 1 of the Corporations Code or predecessor statutory provisions), has never filed a statement pursuant to Section 6210 or 8210, has never filed a statement pursuant to former Section 3301 and is not under suspension by the Franchise Tax Board, shall be subject to suspension by the Secretary of State pursuant to this section.

(b) Prior to taking action to suspend, the Secretary of State shall, in accordance with Section 6061 of the Government Code, publish a notice one time in a newspaper of general circulation published in the county in which the articles require the principal office of the corporation to be located. The notice shall identify the corporation by name and corporate number and shall state that the corporation shall be subject to suspension without further notice if a statement pursuant to Section 6210 or 8210 is not filed within 60 days after the date of publication of the notice.

(c) Not less than 61 days and not more than 180 days after the date of the publication, the Secretary of State may act to suspend the corporation in accordance with subdivisions (a) and (b).

(d) The Secretary of State shall notify the Franchise Tax Board of the suspension and thereupon, except for the purpose of amending the articles to set forth a new name, the corporate powers, rights, and privileges of the corporation are suspended.

(e) A statement pursuant to Section 6210 or 8210 may be filed notwithstanding suspension of the corporate powers, rights and privileges pursuant to this section or Section 23301, 23301.5, or 23775 of the Revenue and Taxation Code. Upon the filing of a statement pursuant to Section 6210 or 8210 by a corporation which has suffered suspension pursuant to this section, the Secretary of State shall certify that fact to the Franchise Tax Board and the corporation may thereupon, in accordance with Section 23305a of the Revenue and Taxation Code, be relieved from suspension unless the corporation is held in suspension by the Franchise Tax Board by reason of Section 23301, 23301.5, or 23775 of the Revenue and Taxation Code.

Ca. Corp. Code § 9928
Added by Stats. 1989, Ch. 440, Sec. 1.

Part 6 - CORPORATIONS SOLE

Section 10000 - Applicable provisions

The provisions of this part apply to all corporations sole organized either before or after March 30, 1878, whether or not the corporations organized before have elected to continue their existence under the Civil Code or elect to continue their existence under this code, except that Sections 10002, and 10012 to 10015, inclusive, do not apply to corporations sole formed before March 30, 1878, unless they have elected to continue their existence under the Civil Code or under this code.

Ca. Corp. Code § 10000
Enacted by Stats. 1947, Ch. 1038.

Section 10001 - Election to continue existence

Any corporation sole formed prior to March 30, 1878, and existing under the laws of this State may elect to continue its existence under this part by filing a certificate to that effect, under its corporate seal, if any, signed by its chief officer, or by filing amended articles of incorporation in the form required in this part.

Ca. Corp. Code § 10001
Enacted by Stats. 1947, Ch. 1038.

Section 10002 - Formation of corporation sole

A corporation sole may be formed under this part by the bishop, chief priest, presiding elder, or other presiding officer of any religious denomination, society, or church, for the purpose of administering and managing the affairs, property, and temporalities thereof.

Ca. Corp. Code § 10002
Enacted by Stats. 1947, Ch. 1038.

Section 10003 - Articles of incorporation

The articles of incorporation shall state:

(a) The name of the corporation.

(b) That the officer forming the corporation is duly authorized by the rules, regulations, or discipline of the religious denomination, society, or church to take such action.

(c) The county in this State where the principal office for the transaction of the business of the corporation is located.

(d) The manner in which any vacancy occurring in the office of the bishop, chief priest, presiding elder, or other presiding officer is required to be filled by the rules, regulations, or constitution of the denomination, society, or church.

Ca. Corp. Code § 10003

Enacted by Stats. 1947, Ch. 1038.

Section 10004 - Provision for regulation of affairs of corporation

The articles of incorporation may state any desired provision for the regulation of the affairs of the corporation in a manner not in conflict with law, including restrictions upon the power to amend all or any part of the articles of incorporation.

Ca. Corp. Code § 10004

Enacted by Stats. 1947, Ch. 1038.

Section 10005 - Signing and filing of articles

The articles shall be signed and verified by the bishop, chief priest, presiding elder, or other presiding officer forming the corporation and shall be submitted to the Secretary of State for filing in his office. If they conform to law he shall file them and endorse the date of filing thereon. Upon the filing of the articles with the Secretary of State the corporation sole is formed.

Ca. Corp. Code § 10005

Enacted by Stats. 1947, Ch. 1038.

Section 10007 - Powers

Every corporation sole may:

(a) Sue and be sued, and defend, in all courts and places, in all matters and proceedings whatever.

(b) Contract in the same manner and to the same extent as a natural person, for the purposes of the trust.

(c) Borrow money, and give promissory notes therefor, and secure the payment thereof by mortgage or other lien upon property, real or personal.

(d) Buy, sell, lease, mortgage, and in every way deal in real and personal property in the same manner that a natural person may, without the order of any court.

(e) Receive bequests and devises for its own use or upon trusts to the same extent as natural persons may, subject, however, to the laws regulating the transfer of property by will.

(f) Appoint attorneys in fact.

Ca. Corp. Code § 10007

Enacted by Stats. 1947, Ch. 1038.

Section 10008 - Perpetual existence and continuity of existence

Every corporation sole has perpetual existence and also has continuity of existence, notwithstanding vacancies in the incumbency thereof. During the period of any such vacancy, the corporation sole has the same capacity and right to receive and take any gift, bequest, devise, or conveyance of property, either as grantee for its own use, or as trustee, and to be or be made the beneficiary of a trust, as though there were no vacancy. No agency created by a corporation sole by a written instrument which in express terms provides that the agency thereby created shall not be terminated by a vacancy in the incumbency of the corporation is terminated or affected by the death of the incumbent of the corporation or by a vacancy in the incumbency thereof, however caused.

Ca. Corp. Code § 10008

Enacted by Stats. 1947, Ch. 1038.

Section 10009 - Access to books

Any judge of the superior court in the county in which a corporation sole has its principal office shall at all times have access to the books of the corporation.

Ca. Corp. Code § 10009

Enacted by Stats. 1947, Ch. 1038.

Section 10010 - Amendment of articles of incorporation

The chief officer of a corporation sole may at any time amend the articles of incorporation of the corporation changing its name, the term of its existence, its territorial jurisdiction, or the manner of filling any vacancy in the office thereof, and may by amended articles of incorporation make provision for any act or thing for which provision is authorized in original articles of incorporation of corporations sole. The chief officer of the corporation shall sign and verify a statement setting forth the provisions of the amendment and stating that it has been duly authorized by the religious organization governed by the corporation.

The amendment shall include the Secretary of State entity number and be submitted to the Secretary of State's office for filing. If it conforms to law, the Secretary shall file it and endorse the date of filing thereon. Thereupon the articles are amended in the manner set forth in the statement.

Ca. Corp. Code § 10010

Amended by Stats 2020 ch 361 (SB 522),s 8, eff. 1/1/2021.

Section 10012 - Dissolution

A corporation sole may be dissolved and its affairs wound up voluntarily by filing with the Secretary of State a declaration of dissolution executed, signed, and verified by the chief officer of the corporation.

Ca. Corp. Code § 10012
Enacted by Stats. 1947, Ch. 1038.

Section 10013 - Declaration of dissolution

The declaration of dissolution shall set forth all of the following:
(a) The name and entity number of the corporation as they exist on the Secretary of State's records.
(b) The reason for its dissolution or winding up.
(c) That dissolution of the corporation has been duly authorized by the religious organization governed by the corporation sole.
(d) The names and addresses of the persons who are to supervise the winding up of the affairs of the corporation.

Ca. Corp. Code § 10013
Amended by Stats 2020 ch 361 (SB 522),s 9, eff. 1/1/2021.

Section 10014 - Filing of declaration

The declaration shall be submitted to the Secretary of State for filing in his office. If it conforms to law he shall file it and endorse the date of filing thereon. Thereupon the corporation shall cease to carry on business, except for the purpose of adjusting and winding up its affairs.

Ca. Corp. Code § 10014
Amended by Stats. 1982, Ch. 662, Sec. 28.

Section 10015 - Payment of debts and obligation; transfer or disposal of remaining assets

After the debts and obligations of the corporation are paid or adequately provided for, any assets remaining shall be transferred to the religious organization governed by the corporation sole, or to trustees in its behalf, or disposed of as may be decreed by the superior court of the county in which the dissolved corporation had its principal office upon petition therefor by the Attorney General or any person connected with the organization.

Ca. Corp. Code § 10015
Enacted by Stats. 1947, Ch. 1038.

Part 7 - CORPORATIONS FOR CHARITABLE OR ELEEMOSYNARY PURPOSES

Section 10200 - Corporation deemed nonprofit public benefit corporation organized for charitable purpose or nonprofit religious corporation

Every corporation organized or existing under Part 3 (commencing with Section 10200) of Division 2 in effect on December 31, 1979, is subject to and deemed to be a nonprofit public benefit corporation organized for charitable purposes under Part 2 (commencing with Section 5110) of the Nonprofit Corporation Law (Division 2 (commencing with Section 5000) of this title) except if the corporation is organized primarily or exclusively for religious purposes, in which case it is subject to and deemed to be a nonprofit religious corporation under Part 4 (commencing with Section 9110) of the Nonprofit Corporation Law.

Ca. Corp. Code § 10200
Amended by Stats. 1980, Ch. 1155.

Part 8 - TRUST FUNDS

Section 10250 - Common trust funds

(a) Any corporation organized under the provisions of or for the purposes set forth in Part 6 (commencing with Section 10000) of this division or organized on or prior to December 31, 1979, under the provisions of or for purposes set forth in Part 3 (commencing with Section 10200) of this division, then in effect, or organized under or subject to Part 2 (commencing with Section 5110), or organized under or subject to Part 4 (commencing with Section 9110), may, if authorized so to do by its articles of incorporation, establish one or more common trust funds for the purpose of furnishing investments to such corporation or to any church, parish, congregation, society, chapel, mission, religious, beneficial, charitable or educational institution affiliated with it, or to any organization, society or corporation holding funds or property for the benefit of any of the foregoing, or holding funds for the purpose of supporting a bishop, priest, religious pastor, or teacher or any building or buildings used by or owned by any of the foregoing, whether holding such funds or property as fiduciary or otherwise. Notwithstanding the provisions of any general or special law in any way limiting the right of any of the foregoing or the officers or directors thereof, as fiduciary or otherwise, to invest funds held by them, it shall be lawful for any of the foregoing to invest any or all of their funds or property in shares or interests of such common trust fund or trust funds; provided, that, in the case of funds or property held as fiduciary, such investment is not prohibited by the wording of the will, deed or other instrument creating such fiduciary relationship.
(b) The directors or trustees of any such common trust fund, or trust funds, so organized, may employ such officers or agents as they think best, define their duties, and fix their compensation. They may also appoint a trust company or bank as

custodian of the trust estate and may employ an investment adviser or advisers, define their duties, and fix their compensation. Securities which constitute part or all of the trust estate may be deposited in a securities depository, as defined in Section 30004 of the Financial Code, which is licensed under Section 30200 of the Financial Code or exempted from licensing thereunder by Section 30005 or 30006 of the Financial Code, and such securities may be held by such securities depository in the manner authorized by Section 775 of the Financial Code.

(c) The directors or trustees of any such common trust fund, or trust funds, shall pay ratably among the holders of shares or beneficial certificates then outstanding, semiannual dividends which shall approximately equal, in each fiscal year, the net income of the trust, or trusts.

(d) The provisions of the Corporate Securities Law (Division 1 (commencing with Section 25000) of Title 4) shall not apply to the creation, administration, or termination of common trust funds created hereunder, nor to participation therein.

   Ca. Corp. Code § 10250
Amended by Stats. 1981, Ch. 570, Sec. 14.

Section 10251 - Educational institution

(a) "Educational institution," as used in this section, means any nonprofit corporation organized under Chapter 4 (commencing with Section 94400) or Chapter 7 (commencing with Section 94700) of Part 59 of the Education Code or organized under Part 1 (commencing with Section 9000) of this division in effect on December 31, 1979, and designated on or after January 1, 1980, as a nonprofit public benefit corporation, or organized for charitable or eleemosynary purposes under Part 2 (commencing with Section 5110) of this division, or Part 3 (commencing with Section 10200) of this division in effect on December 31, 1979, and designated on or after January 1, 1980, as a nonprofit public benefit corporation for the purpose of establishing, conducting or maintaining an institution offering courses beyond high school and issuing or conferring a diploma or for the purpose of offering or conducting private school instruction on the high school or elementary school level and any charitable trust organized for such purpose or purposes. "Educational institution," as used in this section, also means the University of California, the California State University, the California Community Colleges, and any auxiliary organization, as defined in Section 89901 of the Education Code, established for the purpose of receiving gifts, property and funds to be used for the benefit of a state college.

(b) It shall be lawful for any educational institution to become a member of a nonprofit corporation incorporated under the laws of any state for the purpose of maintaining a common trust fund or similar common fund in which nonprofit organizations may commingle their funds and property for investment and to invest any and all of its funds, whenever and however acquired, in the common fund or funds; provided that, in the case of funds or property held as fiduciary, the investment is not prohibited by the wording of the will, deed, or other instrument creating the fiduciary relationship.

(c) An educational institution electing to invest in a common fund or funds under this section may elect to receive distributions from each fund in an amount not to exceed for each fiscal year the greater of the income, as determined under the Uniform Principal and Income Act, Chapter 3 (commencing with Section 16320) of Part 4 of Division 9 of the Probate Code, accrued on its interest in the fund or 10 percent of the value of its interest in the fund as of the last day of its next preceding fiscal year. The educational institution may expend the distribution or distributions for any lawful purpose notwithstanding any general or special law characterizing the distribution, or any part thereof, as principal or income; provided that, in the case of funds or property invested as fiduciary, the expenditure is not prohibited by the wording of the will, deed, or other instrument creating the fiduciary relationship. No such prohibition of expenditure shall be deemed to exist solely because a will, deed, or other instrument, whether executed or in effect before or after the effective date of this section, directs or authorizes the use of only the "income," or "interest," or "dividends" or "rents, issues or profits," or contains words of similar import.

(d) The Corporate Securities Law of 1968 shall not apply to the creation, administration, or termination of common trust funds authorized under this section, or to participation therein.

(e) This section shall become operative on January 1, 1997.

Ca. Corp. Code § 10251

EFFECTIVE 1/1/2000. Amended July 22, 1999 (Bill Number: AB 846) (Chapter 145).

Part 9 - SOCIETIES FOR PREVENTION OF CRUELTY TO ANIMALS

Section 10400 - Formation

Corporations for the prevention of cruelty to animals may be formed under the Nonprofit Public Benefit Corporation Law (Part 2 (commencing with Section 5110)) by 20 or more persons, who shall be citizens and residents of this state. If the corporation is formed on or after January 1, 2011, its articles of incorporation shall specifically state that the corporation is being formed pursuant to this section.

Ca. Corp. Code § 10400

Amended by Stats 2011 ch 296 (AB 1023),s 43, eff. 1/1/2012.
Part heading amended by Stats 2011 ch 296 (AB 1023),s 42, eff. 1/1/2012.
Amended by Stats 2010 ch 652 (SB 1417),s 1, eff. 1/1/2011.

Section 10401 - [Repealed]

Ca. Corp. Code § 10401

Repealed by Stats 2010 ch 652 (SB 1417),s 2, eff. 1/1/2011.

Section 10402 - [Repealed]

Ca. Corp. Code § 10402
Repealed by Stats 2010 ch 652 (SB 1417),s 3, eff. 1/1/2011.

Section 10403 - Property

Every such corporation may take by gift, purchase, devise, or bequest, any property, real or personal, and hold it or dispose thereof at its pleasure; but no such corporation shall hold real property the annual income of which exceeds fifty thousand dollars ($50,000).

Ca. Corp. Code § 10403
Enacted by Stats. 1947, Ch. 1038.

Section 10404 - Complaint for violation of law relating to or affecting animals

Any such corporation, or humane officer thereof, may proffer a complaint against any person, before any court or magistrate having jurisdiction, for the violation of any law relating to or affecting animals and may aid in the prosecution of the offender before the court or magistrate.

Ca. Corp. Code § 10404
Amended by Stats 2011 ch 296 (AB 1023),s 44, eff. 1/1/2012.
Amended by Stats 2010 ch 652 (SB 1417),s 4, eff. 1/1/2011.

Section 10405 - Enforcement of laws

All magistrates, sheriffs, and officers of police shall, as occasion may require, aid any such corporation, its officers, members, and agents, in the enforcement of all laws relating to or affecting animals.

Ca. Corp. Code § 10405
Amended by Stats 2010 ch 652 (SB 1417),s 5, eff. 1/1/2011.

Section 10406 - Applicability

This part applies to all corporations for the prevention of cruelty to animals, whether formed prior to or after May 20, 1905, but does not apply to any association, society, or corporation that uses or specifies a name or style the same, or substantially the same, as that of any previously existing society or corporation in this state organized for a like purpose.

Ca. Corp. Code § 10406
Amended by Stats 2010 ch 652 (SB 1417),s 6, eff. 1/1/2011.

Part 10 - PORT AND TERMINAL PROTECTION AND DEVELOPMENT CORPORATIONS

Section 10700 - "Public agency" defined

As used in this part, "public agency" includes every port district, river port district, municipal port district, harbor district, harbor improvement district, joint harbor improvement district, Board of State Harbor Commissioners, board of harbor commissioners, city, county, and city and county in this state.

Ca. Corp. Code § 10700
Repealed and added by Stats. 1978, Ch. 1305.

Section 10701 - Association with other public agencies, private corporations, or individuals

Every public agency owning or operating any port or marine terminal and every public agency organized for such purposes may associate itself with other public agencies, private corporations or individuals owning or operating, or organized for the purpose of owning or operating, ports or marine terminals located on the same harbor, bay, or other waterway or on communicating or related waterways, of this state and with other public agencies and with private corporations and individuals, or any of them, in the formation under the Nonprofit Mutual Benefit Corporation Law, Part 3 (commencing with Section 7110) of this division, and may become and remain a member of a nonprofit corporation organized under the Nonprofit Mutual Benefit Corporation Law for the purpose of, or the principal powers and purposes of which include carrying on a program of nonregulatory activities in the common interests of its members, including but not limited to any or all of the following activities: studies and research into traffic conditions, cargo volume, rate structures, cost factors, commercial transportation practices, and similar fields; the acquisition and dissemination of information relative to the said and similar subjects; the representation of the common interests of its members before federal, state, and local legislative and administrative authorities; and service as a facility for the cooperation of its members and the coordination of their activities toward the maintenance and improvement of the commercial welfare and competitive position of the ports and terminals owned or operated by its members, the maintenance of equitable and nondiscriminatory rate structures, and the elimination of inequitable, unfair, or discriminatory trade practices adversely affecting the interests of its members; and the undertaking or coordination of any other program of related activities or in related fields for the mutual benefit of its members as may be desired by the membership. Every such public agency may pay the dues and assessments required of its members by such nonprofit mutual benefit corporation out of any funds available to it for that purpose or for its support; may make contracts; may enter into agreements; may appoint an individual as its representative to such nonprofit mutual benefit corporation to exercise the voting power of such public agency and to act in its behalf with respect to such nonprofit mutual benefit corporation; and may do or perform all acts necessary and proper to carry out the purposes of this part; but no public agency shall become or remain a member of any such nonprofit mutual benefit corporation unless the articles of incorporation or the bylaws of the nonprofit mutual benefit corporation include at all times a provision limiting the liability of members to assessments to a specified or ascertainable amount.

 Ca. Corp. Code § 10701
Repealed and added by Stats. 1978, Ch. 1305.

Section 10702 - Person; legal capacity to act as incorporator and member

For the purposes of this part, of the Nonprofit Mutual Benefit Corporation Law, and of the General Corporation Law of this state, every public agency and private corporation qualifying under this part shall be deemed to be a "person" and shall have the legal capacity to act as incorporator and as member of any nonprofit mutual benefit corporation formed under the provisions of this part.

 Ca. Corp. Code § 10702
Repealed and added by Stats. 1978, Ch. 1305.

Section 10703 - Applicability of corporate securities law; exemption from taxation

If, when, and during such times as public agencies or individuals duly authorized to represent them and act in their behalf constitute a majority of the incorporators or of the directors and are entitled to exercise a majority of the voting power of a nonprofit mutual benefit corporation pursuant to this part:

(a) The Corporate Securities Law (Division 1 (commencing with Section 25000) of Title 4) shall not apply to memberships nor to membership certificates issued by the corporation; and

(b) The corporation shall be exempt from payment of any taxes under the Bank and Corporation Tax Law (Part 11 of Division 2 of the Revenue and Taxation Code), except as provided in Article 2 of Chapter 4 thereof.

 Ca. Corp. Code § 10703
Repealed and added by Stats. 1978, Ch. 1305.

Part 11 - NONPROFIT MEDICAL, HOSPITAL, OR LEGAL SERVICES CORPORATIONS

Article 1 - NONPROFIT CORPORATIONS FOR MEDICAL SERVICES

Section 10810 - Formation for purposes of defraying or assuming cost of professional services of licentiates or of rendering any such services

A nonprofit corporation may be formed under Part 2 (commencing with Section 5110) or Part 3 (commencing with Section 7110) of this division for the purposes of defraying or assuming the cost of professional services of licentiates under any chapter of Division 2 (commencing with Section 500) of the Business and Professions Code or of rendering any such services, but it may not engage directly or indirectly in the performance of the corporate purposes or objects unless all of the following requirements are met:

(a) At least one-fourth of all licentiates of the particular profession residing in California become members.

(b) Membership in the corporation and an opportunity to render professional services upon a uniform basis are available to all licensed members of the particular profession.

(c) Voting by proxy and cumulative voting are prohibited.

(d) A certificate is issued to the corporation by the particular professional board whose licentiates have become members, finding compliance with the requirements of subdivisions (a), (b), and (c). Any such corporation shall be subject to supervision by the particular professional board under which its members are licensed and shall also be subject to the part under which it is formed, either Part 2 (commencing with Section 5110) or Part 3 (commencing with Section 7110) of this division, except as to matters specifically otherwise provided for in this article.

Ca. Corp. Code § 10810
Added by Stats. 1978, Ch. 1305.

Section 10811 - Equal opportunity to render professional services upon uniform basis to all licentiates

Any nonprofit corporation described in Section 10810 which defrays or assumes some portion or all of the costs of refractions or eye appliances shall offer an equal opportunity to render professional services upon a uniform basis to all licentiates expressly authorized by law to render such services.

Ca. Corp. Code § 10811
Added by Stats. 1978, Ch. 1305.

Section 10812 - Applicability

The provisions of Sections 10810 and 10811 of this article apply to corporations formed on or after January 1, 1980, under Part 2 or Part 3 of this division and pursuant to this article and to corporations existing on December 31, 1979, and formed under Section 9201 or 9201.1 of the Corporations Code then in effect.

Ca. Corp. Code § 10812
Added by Stats. 1978, Ch. 1305.

Article 2 - NONPROFIT HEALTH CARE SERVICE PLANS

Section 10820 - Formation of health care services plan

(a) "Health care service plan," as used in this section means a corporation which is a health care service plan defined in the Knox-Keene Health Care Service Plan Act of 1975 (Chapter 2.2 (commencing with Section 1340) of Division 2 of the Health and Safety Code), other than a corporation which is exempted from that act by subdivision (d) of Section 1343 of the Health and Safety Code.

(b) A health care service plan may be formed under or subject to Part 2 (commencing with Section 5110) of this division or Part 3 (commencing with Section 7110) of this division.

 Ca. Corp. Code § 10820

Amended by Stats. 1983, Ch. 1085, Sec. 8.5.

Section 10821 - References to attorney general

Notwithstanding any other provision of this division, as to a health care service plan which is formed under or subject to Part 2 (commencing with Section 5110) or Part 3 (commencing with Section 7110) of this division, all references to the Attorney General contained in Part 2 or Part 3 of this division shall, in the case of health care service plans, be deemed to refer to the Director of the Department of Managed Health Care.

 Ca. Corp. Code § 10821

Amended by Stats 2000 ch 857 (AB 2903), s 6, eff. 1/1/2001.

Previously Amended September 28, 1999 (Bill Number: AB 78) (Chapter 525).

Article 3 - NONPROFIT CORPORATION TO ADMINISTER SYSTEM OF DEFRAYING COST OF PROFESSIONAL SERVICES OF ATTORNEYS

Section 10830 - Formation for purposes of administering system of defraying cost of professional services of attorneys

A nonprofit corporation may be formed under Part 3 (commencing with Section 7110) of this division for the purposes of administering a system or systems of defraying the cost of professional services of attorneys, but any such corporation may not engage directly or indirectly in the performance of the corporate purposes or objects unless all of the following requirements are met:

(a) The attorneys furnishing professional services pursuant to such system or systems are acting in compliance with the Rules of Professional Conduct of the State Bar of California concerning such system or systems.

(b) Membership in the corporation and an opportunity to render professional services upon a uniform basis are available to all active members of the State Bar.

(c) Voting by proxy and cumulative voting are prohibited.

(d) A certificate is issued to the corporation by the State Bar of California, finding compliance with the requirements of subdivisions (a), (b) and (c). Any such corporation shall be subject to supervision by the State Bar of California and shall also be subject to Part 3 (commencing with Section 7110) of this division except as to matters specifically otherwise provided for in this article.

Ca. Corp. Code § 10830
Added by Stats. 1978, Ch. 1305.

Section 10831 - Applicability

The provisions of this article apply to corporations formed on or after January 1, 1980, under Part 3 of this division and pursuant to this article and to corporations existing on December 31, 1979, and formed under Section 9201.2 of the Corporations Code then in effect.

Ca. Corp. Code § 10831
Added by Stats. 1978, Ch. 1305.

Article 4 - HOSPITAL SERVICE PLANS

Section 10840 - Formation of hospital service plan

(a) "Hospital service plan," as used in this section means a corporation which is a nonprofit hospital service plan defined in Chapter 11a (commencing with Section 11491) of Part 2 of Division 2 of the Insurance Code.
(b) A hospital service plan may be formed under or subject to Part 2 (commencing with Section 5110) or Part 3 (commencing with Section 7110).

Ca. Corp. Code § 10840
Amended by Stats. 1983, Ch. 1085, Sec. 14.5.

Section 10841 - References to attorney general

Notwithstanding any other provision of this division, as to a hospital service plan which is formed under or subject to Part 2 (commencing with Section 5110) or Part 3 (commencing with Section 7110) of this division, all references to the Attorney General contained in Part 2 or Part 3 of this division shall, in the case of hospital service plans, be deemed to refer to the Insurance Commissioner.

Ca. Corp. Code § 10841
Repealed and added by Stats. 1983, Ch. 1085, Sec. 16.

Division 3 - CORPORATIONS FOR SPECIFIC PURPOSES

Part 1 - CHAMBERS OF COMMERCE, BOARDS OF TRADE, MECHANICS' INSTITUTES, ETC

Section 12000 - Organization

Every corporation organized or existing under Part 1 (commencing with Section 12000) in effect on December 31, 1979, is subject to and deemed to be organized under:

(a) The General Corporation Law (Division 1 (commencing with Section 100) of this title), if the corporation is organized with capital stock.

(b) The Nonprofit Mutual Benefit Corporation Law (Part 3 (commencing with Section 7110) of Division 2 of this title) if the corporation is organized without capital stock.

Ca. Corp. Code § 12000
Repealed and added by Stats. 1978, Ch. 1305.

Part 2 - COOPERATIVE CORPORATIONS

Chapter 1 - GENERAL PROVISIONS, ORGANIZATION AND BYLAWS

Article 1 - TITLE, PURPOSE AND APPLICATION OF PART

Section 12200 - Short title; applicability

This part shall be known as the Cooperative Corporation Law. This part is intended primarily to apply to the organization and operation of cooperatives, including, but not limited to, consumer cooperatives, worker cooperatives, and cooperatives formed for the purpose of recycling or treating hazardous waste that elect to incorporate under its provisions.

Ca. Corp. Code § 12200
Amended by Stats 2015 ch 192 (AB 816),s 3, eff. 1/1/2016.
Part heading amended by Stats 2015 ch 192 (AB 816),s 2, eff. 1/1/2016.

Section 12201 - Formation

Subject to any other provision of law of this state applying to the particular class of corporation or line of activity, a corporation may be formed under this part for any lawful purpose provided that it shall be organized and shall conduct its business primarily for the mutual benefit of its members as patrons of the corporation. The earnings, savings, or benefits of the corporation shall be used for the general welfare of the members or shall be proportionately and equitably distributed to some or all of its members or its patrons, based upon their patronage (Section 12243) of the corporation, in the form of cash, property, evidences of indebtedness, capital credits, memberships, or services.

Such corporations are democratically controlled and are not organized to make a profit for themselves, as such, or for their members, as such, but primarily for their members as patrons (Section 12243).

Ca. Corp. Code § 12201
Repealed and added by Stats. 1982, Ch. 1625, Sec. 3. Operative January 1, 1984.

Section 12201.5 - Apportionment of net earnings and losses of worker cooperative

(a) Notwithstanding Section 12201, the net earnings and losses of a worker cooperative shall be apportioned and distributed at the time and in the manner specified in the articles of incorporation or bylaws.

(b) Net earnings declared as patronage distributions with respect to a period of time, and paid to a creditor or member, shall be apportioned among the members in accordance with the ratio that each member's patronage during the period bears to total patronage by all members during the period.

(c) The apportionment, distribution, and payment of net earnings required by subdivision (a) may be paid in cash, credits, written notices of allocation, or capital stock issued by the worker cooperative.

> *Ca. Corp. Code § 12201.5*
Added by Stats 2015 ch 192 (AB 816),s 4, eff. 1/1/2016.

Section 12202 - Applicability of provisions

(a) The provisions of this part apply to corporations existing pursuant to Part 2 (commencing with Section 12200) of Division 3 of Title 1 in effect immediately prior to January 1, 1984.

(b) The existence of corporations formed or existing on the date of enactment of this part shall not be affected by the enactment or reenactment of this part or by any change in the requirements for the formation of corporations or by the amendment or repeal of the laws under which they were formed or created.

(c) Neither the repeal of Part 2 (commencing with Section 12200) of Division 3 of Title 1 as in effect immediately prior to January 1, 1984, nor the reenactment or amendment of this part shall impair or take away any existing liability or cause of action against any corporation, its members, shareholders, directors, or officers incurred prior to the enactment of this part.

> *Ca. Corp. Code § 12202*
Repealed and added by Stats. 1982, Ch. 1625, Sec. 3. Operative January 1, 1984.

Section 12203 - Construction

Unless the provisions or the context otherwise requires, the definitions set forth in this part govern the construction of this part.

> *Ca. Corp. Code § 12203*
Repealed and added by Stats. 1982, Ch. 1625, Sec. 3. Operative January 1, 1984.

Article 2 - GENERAL PROVISIONS AND DEFINITIONS

Section 12210 - Suing corporation

A corporation may be sued as provided in the Code of Civil Procedure.

> *Ca. Corp. Code § 12210*
Added by Stats. 1982, Ch. 1625, Sec. 3. Operative January 1, 1984.

Section 12211 - Attachment of corporate property

Any corporation shall, as a condition of its existence as a corporation, be subject to the provisions of the Code of Civil Procedure authorizing the attachment of corporate property.

Ca. Corp. Code § 12211

Added by Stats. 1982, Ch. 1625, Sec. 3. Operative January 1, 1984.

Section 12212 - Fees for filing instruments

The fees of the Secretary of State for filing instruments by or on behalf of corporations are prescribed in Article 3 (commencing with Section 12180) of Chapter 3 of Part 2 of Division 3 of Title 2 of the Government Code.

Ca. Corp. Code § 12212

Added by Stats. 1982, Ch. 1625, Sec. 3. Operative January 1, 1984.

Section 12213 - Certificate of correction

Any agreement, certificate, or other instrument filed pursuant to the provisions of this part, may be corrected with respect to any misstatement of fact contained therein, any defect in the execution thereof or any other error or defect contained therein, by filing a certificate of correction entitled "Certificate of Correction of _____ (insert here the title of the agreement, certificate or other instrument to be corrected and the name of the corporation or corporations)." However, no such certificate of correction shall alter the wording of any resolution which was in fact adopted by the board or the members or delegates or effect a corrected amendment of articles which amendment as so corrected would not in all respects have complied with the requirements of this part, at the time of filing of the agreement, certificate or other instrument being corrected. Such certificate of correction shall be signed and verified or acknowledged as provided in this part with respect to the agreement, certificate or other instrument being corrected. It shall set forth the following:

(a) The name or names of the corporation or corporations.

(b) The date the agreement, certificate or other instrument being corrected was filed.

(c) The provision in the agreement, certificate or other instrument as corrected and, if the execution was defective, wherein it was defective. The filing of the certificate of correction shall not alter the effective time of the agreement, certificate or other instrument being corrected, which shall remain as its original effective time, and such filing shall not affect any right or liability accrued or incurred before such filing, except that any right or liability accrued or incurred by reason of the error or defect being corrected shall be extinguished by such filing if the person having such right has not detrimentally relied on the original instrument.

Ca. Corp. Code § 12213

Amended by Stats. 1983, Ch. 792, Sec. 1.

Section 12214 - Filing instruments

(a) Upon receipt of any instrument by the Secretary of State for filing pursuant to this part, if it conforms to law, it shall be filed by, and in the office of the Secretary of State and the date of filing endorsed thereon. Except for instruments filed pursuant to Section 12570 the date of filing shall be the date the instrument is received by the Secretary of State unless the instrument provides that it is to be withheld from filing until a future date or unless in the judgment of the Secretary of State the filing is intended to be coordinated with the filing of some other corporate document which cannot be filed. The Secretary of State shall file a document as of any requested future date not more than 90 days after its receipt, including a Saturday, Sunday or legal holiday, if the document is received in the Secretary of State's office at least one business day prior to the requested date of filing. An instrument does not fail to conform to law because it is not accompanied by the full filing fee if the unpaid portion of such fee does not exceed the limits established by the policy of the Secretary of State for extending credit in such cases.

(b) If the Secretary of State determines that an instrument submitted for filing or otherwise submitted does not conform to law and returns it to the person submitting it, the instrument may be resubmitted accompanied by a written opinion of a member of the State Bar of California submitting the instrument, or representing the person submitting it, to the effect that the specific provision of the instrument objected to by the Secretary of State does conform to law and stating the points and authorities upon which the opinion is based. The Secretary of State shall rely, with respect to any disputed point of law (other than the application of Section 12302), upon such written opinion in determining whether the instrument conforms to law. The date of filing in such case shall be the date the instrument is received on resubmission.

(c) Any instrument filed with respect to a corporation (other than original articles) may provide that it is to become effective not more than 90 days subsequent to its filing date. In case such a delayed effective date is specified, the instrument may be prevented from becoming effective by a certificate stating that by appropriate corporate action it has been revoked and is null and void, executed in the same manner as the original instrument and filed before the specified effective date. In the case of a merger agreement, such certificate revoking the earlier filing need only be executed on behalf of one of the constituent corporations. If no such revocation certificate is filed, the instrument becomes effective on the date specified.

(d) Any instrument submitted to the Secretary of State for filing pursuant to this part by a domestic corporation or foreign corporation that is qualified to transact business in California under Section 2105 shall include the entity name and number as they exist on the Secretary of State's records.

Ca. Corp. Code § 12214

Amended by Stats 2020 ch 361 (SB 522),s 10, eff. 1/1/2021.
Amended by Stats 2012 ch 494 (SB 1532),s 27, eff. 1/1/2013.

Section 12214.5 - Cancellation of filing of articles

The Secretary of State may cancel the filing of articles if a check or other remittance accepted in payment of the filing fee or franchise tax is not paid upon presentation. Within 90 days of receiving written notification that the item presented for payment has not been honored for payment, the Secretary of State shall give written notice of the applicability of this section and the cancellation date which shall be not less than 20 days from the date of mailing the written notice as certified by the Secretary of State, to the agent for service of process or to the person submitting the instrument. Thereafter, if the amount has not been paid by cashier's check or equivalent before the date of cancellation as stated in the written notice of cancellation, the cancellation shall thereupon be effective.

Ca. Corp. Code § 12214.5
Amended by Stats 2022 ch 617 (SB 1202),s 73, eff. 1/1/2023.
Amended by Stats. 1988, Ch. 508, Sec. 3.

Section 12214.6 - Failure to file statement

(a) A corporation that (1) fails to file a statement pursuant to Section 12570 for an applicable filing period, (2) has not filed a statement pursuant to Section 12570 during the preceding 24 months, and (3) was certified for penalty pursuant to Section 12670 for the same filing period of the prior year, shall be subject to suspension pursuant to this section rather than to a penalty under Section 12670.
(b) When subdivision (a) is applicable, the Secretary of State shall mail a notice to the corporation informing the corporation that its corporate powers, rights, and privileges will be suspended 60 days from the date of the notice if the corporation does not file the statement required by Section 12570.
(c) If the 60-day period expires without the delinquent corporation filing the required statement, the Secretary of State shall notify the Franchise Tax Board of the suspension, and mail a notice of the suspension to the corporation. Following completion of these notification requirements, except for the purpose of amending the articles of incorporation to set forth a new name or filing an application for exempt status, the corporate powers, rights, and privileges of the corporation are suspended.
(d) A statement required by Section 12570 may be filed, notwithstanding suspension of the corporate powers, rights, and privileges under this section or under provisions of the Revenue and Taxation Code. Upon the filing of a statement under Section 12570, by a corporation that has been suspended pursuant to this section, the Secretary of State shall certify that fact to the Franchise Tax Board and the corporation may, in accordance with Section 23305a of the Revenue and Taxation Code, be relieved from suspension, unless the corporation is held in suspension by the Franchise Tax Board pursuant to Section 23301, 23301.5, or 23775 of the Revenue and Taxation Code.

Ca. Corp. Code § 12214.6
Added by Stats. 1996, Ch. 589, Sec. 45. Effective January 1, 1997.

Section 12215 - Reference to mailing

Except as otherwise permitted, any reference in this part to mailing means first-class mail, postage prepaid, unless registered or some other form of mail is specified or permitted. Registered mail includes certified mail.

Ca. Corp. Code § 12215
Amended by Stats. 1983, Ch. 792, Sec. 2.

Section 12216 - Majority or other proportion of votes entitled to be cast; disqualification voting

If the articles provide for more than one vote for any member on any matter, the references in Sections 12223 and 12224 to a majority or other proportion of members mean, as to such matters, a majority or other proportion of the votes entitled to be cast. Whenever members are disqualified from voting on any matter, they shall not be counted for the determination of a quorum at any meeting to act upon, or the required vote to approve action upon, that matter under any other provision of this part or the articles or bylaws.

Ca. Corp. Code § 12216
Added by Stats. 1982, Ch. 1625, Sec. 3. Operative January 1, 1984.

Section 12217 - References to financial statements

All references in this part to financial statements of a corporation mean statements prepared in conformity with generally accepted accounting principles or some other basis of accounting which reasonably sets forth the assets and liabilities and the income and expenses of the corporation and discloses the accounting basis used in their preparation.

Ca. Corp. Code § 12217
Added by Stats. 1982, Ch. 1625, Sec. 3. Operative January 1, 1984.

Section 12218 - "Independent accountant" defined

As used in this part, "independent accountant" means a certified public accountant or public accountant who is independent of the corporation as determined in accordance with generally accepted auditing standards and who is engaged to audit financial statements of the corporation or perform other accounting services.

Ca. Corp. Code § 12218
Added by Stats. 1982, Ch. 1625, Sec. 3. Operative January 1, 1984.

Section 12219 - Reference to time notice is given or sent

Any reference in this part to the time a notice is given or sent means, unless otherwise expressly provided, the time a written notice by mail is deposited in the United States mails, postage prepaid; or the time any other written notice is personally delivered to the recipient or is delivered to a common carrier for transmission, or actually transmitted by the person giving the notice by electronic means, to the recipient; or the time any oral notice is communicated, in person or by telephone or wireless, to the recipient or to a person at the office of the recipient who the person giving the notice has reason to believe will promptly communicate it to the recipient.

Ca. Corp. Code § 12219
Added by Stats. 1982, Ch. 1625, Sec. 3. Operative January 1, 1984.

Section 12220 - Notice or report mailed or delivered as part of newsletter, magazine, or other organ regularly sent to members

A notice or report mailed or delivered as part of a newsletter, magazine or other organ regularly sent to members shall constitute written notice or report pursuant to this part when addressed and mailed postage prepaid by first or second class mail or delivered to the member, or in the case of members who are residents of the same household and who have the same address on the books of the corporation, when addressed and mailed postage prepaid by first or second class mail or delivered to one of such members, at the address appearing on the books of the corporation.

Ca. Corp. Code § 12220
Added by Stats. 1982, Ch. 1625, Sec. 3. Operative January 1, 1984.

Section 12221 - "Acknowledged" defined; certificate of acknowledgment

"Acknowledged" means that an instrument is either:
(a) Formally acknowledged as provided in Article 3 (commencing with Section 1180) of Chapter 4 of Title 4 of Part 4 of Division 2 of the Civil Code; or
(b) Accompanied by a declaration in writing signed by the persons executing the same that they are such persons and that the instrument is the act and deed of the person or persons executing the same. Any certificate of acknowledgment taken without this state before a notary public or a judge or clerk of a court of record having an official seal need not be further authenticated.

Ca. Corp. Code § 12221
Added by Stats. 1982, Ch. 1625, Sec. 3. Operative January 1, 1984.

Section 12222 - "Approved by (or approval of) the board" defined

"Approved by (or approval of) the board" means approved or ratified by the vote of the board or by the vote of a committee authorized to exercise the powers of the board, except as to matters not within the competence of the committee under Section 12352.

Ca. Corp. Code § 12222
Added by Stats. 1982, Ch. 1625, Sec. 3. Operative January 1, 1984.

Section 12223 - "Approval by (or approval of) a majority of all members" defined

"Approval by (or approval of) a majority of all members" means approval by an affirmative vote (or written ballot in conformity with Section 12463) of a majority of the votes entitled to be cast. Such approval shall include the affirmative vote of a majority of the outstanding memberships of each class, unit, or grouping of members entitled, by any provision of the articles or bylaws of this part to vote as a class, unit, or grouping of members on the subject matter being voted upon and shall also include the affirmative vote of such greater proportion, including all of the votes of the memberships of any class, unit, or grouping of members if such greater proportion is required by the bylaws or by this part.

Ca. Corp. Code § 12223
Added by Stats. 1982, Ch. 1625, Sec. 3. Operative January 1, 1984.

Section 12224 - "Approval by (or approval of) the members" defined

"Approval by (or approval of) the members" means approved or ratified by the affirmative vote of a majority of the votes represented and voting at a duly held meeting at which a quorum is present (which affirmative votes also constitute a majority of the required quorum) or written ballot in conformity with Section 12463 or by the affirmative vote or written ballot of such greater proportion of the votes of the memberships of any class, unit, or grouping of members as may be provided in the bylaws or in this part for all or any specified member action.

Ca. Corp. Code § 12224
Added by Stats. 1982, Ch. 1625, Sec. 3. Operative January 1, 1984.

Section 12225 - "Articles" defined

"Articles" includes the articles of incorporation, amendments thereto, amended articles, restated articles, and certificates of incorporation.

Ca. Corp. Code § 12225
Added by Stats. 1982, Ch. 1625, Sec. 3. Operative January 1, 1984.

Section 12226 - "Bylaws" defined

"Bylaws" includes amendments thereto and amended bylaws.

Ca. Corp. Code § 12226
Added by Stats. 1982, Ch. 1625, Sec. 3. Operative January 1, 1984.

Section 12227 - "Board" defined

"Board" means the board of directors of the corporation.
Ca. Corp. Code § 12227
Added by Stats. 1982, Ch. 1625, Sec. 3. Operative January 1, 1984.

Section 12228 - "Business corporation" defined

"Business corporation" means a corporation as defined in Section 162 of the General Corporation Law.
Ca. Corp. Code § 12228
Added by Stats. 1982, Ch. 1625, Sec. 3. Operative January 1, 1984.

Section 12228.3 - "Capital account cooperative"

"Capital account cooperative" is a worker cooperative in which the entire net book value is reflected in member capital accounts, one for each member, and an unallocated capital account, if any.
Ca. Corp. Code § 12228.3
Added by Stats 2015 ch 192 (AB 816),s 5, eff. 1/1/2016.

Section 12228.5 - "Chair" defined; reference to "chairperson of the board"

For the purposes of this part, all references to "chairperson of the board," other than in Section 12353, shall be deemed to refer to all permissible titles for a chair of the board, as permitted by Section 12353.
Ca. Corp. Code § 12228.5
Amended by Stats 2022 ch 617 (SB 1202),s 74, eff. 1/1/2023.
Amended by Stats 2015 ch 98 (SB 351),s 14, eff. 1/1/2016.
Added by Stats 2009 ch 631 (AB 1233),s 37, eff. 1/1/2010.

Section 12229 - "Chapter" defined

"Chapter" refers to a chapter of this part unless otherwise expressly stated.
Ca. Corp. Code § 12229
Amended by Stats. 1983, Ch. 792, Sec. 3.

Section 12230 - "Class" defined

"Class" refers to those memberships which:
(a) are identified in the articles or bylaws as being a different type of membership; or
(b) have the same rights with respect to voting, dissolution, redemption, distributions and transfer. For the purpose of this section, rights shall be considered the same if they are determined by a formula applied uniformly.

Ca. Corp. Code § 12230
Added by Stats. 1982, Ch. 1625, Sec. 3. Operative January 1, 1984.

Section 12230.5 - "Collective board worker cooperative"

"Collective board worker cooperative" means a worker cooperative in which there is only one class of members consisting of worker-members, all of whom are members of the board.
Ca. Corp. Code § 12230.5
Added by Stats 2015 ch 192 (AB 816),s 6, eff. 1/1/2016.

Section 12231 - "Constituent corporation" defined

"Constituent corporation" means a corporation which is merged with one or more other corporations and includes the surviving corporation.
Ca. Corp. Code § 12231
Added by Stats. 1982, Ch. 1625, Sec. 3. Operative January 1, 1984.

Section 12232 - "Corporation" defined

"Corporation" as used in this part means a corporation which is organized under, or subject to this part, including a central organization.
Ca. Corp. Code § 12232
Amended by Stats. 1983, Ch. 792, Sec. 4.

Section 12233 - "Directors" defined

"Directors" means natural persons, designated in the articles or bylaws or elected by the incorporators, and their successors and natural persons designated, elected, or appointed by any other name or title to act as members of the governing body of the corporation. "Directors" also means alternate directors described in Section 12331. A person who does not have authority to act as a member of the governing body of the corporation, including through voting rights as a member of the governing body, is not a director as that term is used in this part regardless of title. However, if the articles or bylaws designate that a natural person is a director or a member of the governing body of the corporation by reason of occupying a specified position within or outside the corporation, that person shall be a director for all purposes and shall have the same rights and obligations, including voting rights, as the other directors.
Ca. Corp. Code § 12233
Amended by Stats 2009 ch 631 (AB 1233),s 38, eff. 1/1/2010.

Section 12234 - "Disappearing corporation" defined

"Disappearing corporation" means a constituent corporation which is not the surviving corporation.

Ca. Corp. Code § 12234

Added by Stats. 1982, Ch. 1625, Sec. 3. Operative January 1, 1984.

Section 12235 - "Distribution" defined

"Distribution" means the distribution of any gains, profits or dividends to any member as such, but does not include patronage distributions.

Ca. Corp. Code § 12235

Added by Stats. 1982, Ch. 1625, Sec. 3. Operative January 1, 1984.

Section 12236 - "Domestic corporation" defined

"Domestic corporation" means a corporation formed under the laws of this state.

Ca. Corp. Code § 12236

Added by Stats. 1982, Ch. 1625, Sec. 3. Operative January 1, 1984.

Section 12237 - "Foreign corporation" defined

"Foreign corporation" means a foreign corporation as defined in Section 171.

Ca. Corp. Code § 12237

Added by Stats. 1982, Ch. 1625, Sec. 3. Operative January 1, 1984.

Section 12238 - "Member" defined

(a) "Member" means any person who, pursuant to a specific provision of a corporation's articles or bylaws, has the right to vote for the election of a director or directors, or possesses proprietary interests in the corporation.

(b) The articles or bylaws may confer some or all of the rights of a member, set forth in this part, upon any person or persons who do not have any of the voting rights referred to in subdivision (a).

(c) Where a member of a corporation is not a natural person, such member may authorize in writing one or more natural persons to vote on its behalf on any or all matters which may require a vote of the members.

(d) A person is not a member by virtue of any of the following:

(1) Any rights such person has as a delegate.

(2) Any rights such person has to designate or select a director or directors.

(3) Any rights such person has as a director.

(e) "Worker-member" means a member of a worker cooperative who is a natural person and also a patron of a worker cooperative.

(f) "Community investor" means a person who is not a worker-member and who holds a share or other proprietary interest in a worker cooperative.

(g) "Worker" means a natural person contributing labor or services to a worker cooperative. "Candidate" means a worker who is being considered for membership in a worker cooperative, as defined in the corporation's articles or bylaws.

   Ca. Corp. Code § 12238

Amended by Stats 2015 ch 192 (AB 816),s 7, eff. 1/1/2016.

Section 12239 - "Membership" defined

A "membership" refers to the rights a member has pursuant to a corporation's articles, bylaws and this part.

   Ca. Corp. Code § 12239

Added by Stats. 1982, Ch. 1625, Sec. 3. Operative January 1, 1984.

Section 12240 - "Membership certificate" defined

"Membership certificate," as used in this part, means a document evidencing a proprietary interest in a corporation.

   Ca. Corp. Code § 12240

Added by Stats. 1982, Ch. 1625, Sec. 3. Operative January 1, 1984.

Section 12241 - "Officers' certificate" defined

"Officers' certificate" means a certificate signed and verified by the chair of the board, the president, or any vice president, and by the secretary, the chief financial officer, the treasurer, or any assistant secretary or assistant treasurer.

   Ca. Corp. Code § 12241

Amended by Stats 2009 ch 631 (AB 1233),s 39, eff. 1/1/2010.

Section 12242 - "On the certificate" defined

"On the certificate," as used in this part means that a statement appears on the face of a certificate or on the reverse thereof with a reference thereto on the face.

   Ca. Corp. Code § 12242

Added by Stats. 1982, Ch. 1625, Sec. 3. Operative January 1, 1984.

Section 12242.5 - "Other business entity" defined

"Other business entity" means a domestic or foreign limited liability company, limited partnership, general partnership, business trust, real estate investment trust, unincorporated association, or a domestic reciprocal insurer organized after 1974 to provide medical malpractice insurance as set forth in Article 16 (commencing with Section 1550) of Chapter 3 of Part 2 of Division 1 of the Insurance Code. As used herein, "general partnership" means a "partnership" as defined in subdivision (9) of

Section 16101; "business trust" means a business organization formed as a trust; "real estate investment trust" means a "real estate investment trust" as defined in subsection (a) of Section 856 of the Internal Revenue Code of 1986, as amended; and "unincorporated association" has the meaning set forth in Section 18035.

Ca. Corp. Code § 12242.5

Amended by Stats 2009 ch 631 (AB 1233),s 40, eff. 1/1/2010.

Amended by Stats 2004 ch 178 (SB 1746),s 6, eff. 1/1/2005

Added September 21, 1999 (Bill Number: AB 198) (Chapter 437).

Section 12242.6 - "Parent party" defined

"Parent party" means the corporation in control of any constituent domestic or foreign corporation or other business entity and whose equity securities are issued, transferred, or exchanged in a merger pursuant to Section 12540.1.

Ca. Corp. Code § 12242.6

Added 9/21/1999 (Bill Number: AB 198) (Chapter 437).

Section 12243 - "Patrons" and "patronage" defined

(a)

(1) If the corporation is organized to provide goods or services to its members, the corporation's "patrons" are those who purchase those types of goods from, or use those types of services of, the corporation. If the corporation is organized to market, process, or otherwise handle its members' products or services, the corporation's "patrons" are those persons whose products or services are so marketed, processed, or handled by the corporation.

(2) "Patronage" of a patron is measured by the volume or value, or both, of a patron's purchases of products from, and use of services furnished by, the corporation, and by products and services provided by the patron to the corporation for marketing.

(b)

(1) If the corporation is organized as a worker cooperative, the corporation's "patrons" are its worker-members.

(2) If the corporation is organized as a worker cooperative, "patronage" may be measured by work performed, including, but not limited to, wages earned, number of hours worked, number of jobs created, or some combination of these measures.

Ca. Corp. Code § 12243

Amended by Stats 2015 ch 192 (AB 816),s 8, eff. 1/1/2016.

Section 12244 - "Patronage distribution" defined

"Patronage distribution" means any transfer made to a patron of the corporation the amount of which is computed with reference to the patron's patronage of the corporation.

Ca. Corp. Code § 12244

Added by Stats. 1982, Ch. 1625, Sec. 3. Operative January 1, 1984.

Section 12245 - "Person" defined

"Person," unless otherwise expressly provided, includes any association, company, domestic or foreign corporation, corporation sole, estate, individual, joint stock company, joint venture, partnership, domestic or foreign limited liability company, government or political subdivision, agency or instrumentality of a government.

Ca. Corp. Code § 12245

Amended by Stats. 1994, Ch. 1010, Sec. 66. Effective January 1, 1995.

Section 12245.2 - "Preferred memberships" defined

"Preferred memberships" means memberships that have a preference over any other memberships with respect to distribution of assets on liquidation or with respect to payment of distributions.

Ca. Corp. Code § 12245.2

Added by Stats 2013 ch 538 (AB 1255),s 1, eff. 1/1/2014.

Section 12246 - "Proper county" defined

"Proper county" means the county where the corporation's principal office in this state is located or, if the corporation has no such office, the County of Sacramento.

Ca. Corp. Code § 12246

Added by Stats. 1982, Ch. 1625, Sec. 3. Operative January 1, 1984.

Section 12246.2 - "Series" of memberships defined

"Series" of memberships means memberships within a class of memberships that have the same rights, privileges, preferences, restrictions, and conditions, but that differ in one or more rights, privileges, preferences, restrictions, or conditions from other memberships within the class. Certificated securities and uncertificated securities do not constitute a different series if the only difference is certificated and uncertificated status.

Ca. Corp. Code § 12246.2

Added by Stats 2013 ch 538 (AB 1255),s 2, eff. 1/1/2014.

Section 12247 - "Shareholder" defined

"Shareholder" shall have the same meaning as "member" as defined in Section 12238.
Ca. Corp. Code § 12247
Added by Stats. 1982, Ch. 1625, Sec. 3. Operative January 1, 1984.

Section 12248 - "Share certificate" defined

"Share certificate" shall have the same meaning as "membership certificate" as defined in Section 12240.
Ca. Corp. Code § 12248
Added by Stats. 1982, Ch. 1625, Sec. 3. Operative January 1, 1984.

Section 12249 - "Surviving corporation" defined

"Surviving corporation" means a corporation into which one or more other corporations are merged.
Ca. Corp. Code § 12249
Added by Stats. 1982, Ch. 1625, Sec. 3. Operative January 1, 1984.

Section 12250 - "Vacancy" defined

"Vacancy" when used with respect to the board means any authorized position of director which is not then filled, whether the vacancy is caused by death, resignation, removal, change in the number of directors authorized in the articles or bylaws (by the board or the members), or otherwise.
Ca. Corp. Code § 12250
Added by Stats. 1982, Ch. 1625, Sec. 3. Operative January 1, 1984.

Section 12251 - "Verified" defined

"Verified" means that the statements contained in a certificate or other document are declared to be true of the own knowledge of the persons executing the same in either:
(a) An affidavit signed by them under oath before an officer authorized by the laws of this state or of the place where it is executed to administer oaths; or
(b) A declaration in writing executed by them under penalty of perjury and stating the date and place (whether within or without this state) of execution. Any affidavit sworn to without this state before a notary public or a judge or clerk of a court of record having an official seal need not be further authenticated.
Ca. Corp. Code § 12251
Added by Stats. 1982, Ch. 1625, Sec. 3. Operative January 1, 1984.

Section 12252 - "Vote" defined

"Vote" includes, but is not limited to, authorization by written consent pursuant to subdivision (b) of Section 12351 and authorization by written ballot pursuant to

Section 12463.

Ca. Corp. Code § 12252

Added by Stats. 1982, Ch. 1625, Sec. 3. Operative January 1, 1984.

Section 12253 - "Voting power" defined

(a) "Voting power" means the power to vote for the election of directors at the time any determination of voting power is made and does not include the right to vote upon the happening of some condition or event that has not yet occurred.

(b) If different classes of memberships are entitled to vote as separate classes for different members of the board, the determination of percentage of voting power shall be made on the basis of the percentage of the total number of authorized directors that the memberships in question (whether of one or more classes) have the power to elect in an election at which all memberships then entitled to vote for the election of any directors are voted.

(c) Community investor voting power in a worker cooperative shall be provided in the articles or bylaws, and is limited to approval rights only over a merger, sale of major assets, reorganization, or dissolution. Approval rights shall not include the right to propose any action.

Ca. Corp. Code § 12253

Amended by Stats 2015 ch 192 (AB 816),s 9, eff. 1/1/2016.

Section 12253.5 - "Worker cooperative" or "employment cooperative"

"Worker cooperative" or "employment cooperative" means a corporation formed under this part that includes a class of worker-members who are natural persons whose patronage consists of labor contributed to or other work performed for the corporation. Election to be organized as a worker cooperative or an employment cooperative does not create a presumption that workers are employees of the corporation for any purposes. At least 51 percent of the workers shall be worker-members or candidates.

Ca. Corp. Code § 12253.5

Added by Stats 2015 ch 192 (AB 816),s 10, eff. 1/1/2016.

Section 12254 - "Written" or "in writing" defined

"Written" or "in writing" includes facsimile, telegraphic, and other electronic communication as authorized by this code.

Ca. Corp. Code § 12254

Amended by Stats 2004 ch 254 (SB 1306),s 35, eff. 1/1/2005

Section 12255 - "Written ballot" defined

"Written ballot" does not include a ballot distributed at a special or regular meeting of members.

Ca. Corp. Code § 12255

Added by Stats. 1982, Ch. 1625, Sec. 3. Operative January 1, 1984.

Section 12256 - Central organization

A central organization is a corporation whose membership is composed, in whole or in part, of other corporations organized under this part.

Ca. Corp. Code § 12256

Added by Stats. 1983, Ch. 792, Sec. 7.

Article 3 - FORMATION

Section 12300 - Formation

(a) One or more persons may form a corporation under this part by executing and filing articles of incorporation.

(b) Where initial directors are named in the articles, each director named in the articles shall sign and acknowledge the articles. Where initial directors are not named in the articles, the articles shall be signed by a person or persons described in subdivision (a) who thereupon are the incorporators of the corporation.

(c) The corporate existence begins upon the filing of the articles and continues perpetually, unless otherwise expressly provided by law or in the articles.

Ca. Corp. Code § 12300

Amended by Stats. 1983, Ch. 792, Sec. 8.

Section 12301 - Change of status to corporation

(a) In the case of an existing unincorporated association, the association may change its status to that of a corporation upon a proper authorization for such by the association in accordance with its rules and procedures.

(b) In addition to the matters required to be set forth in the articles pursuant to Section 12310, the articles in the case of an incorporation authorized by subdivision (a) shall set forth that an existing unincorporated association, stating its name, is being incorporated by the filing of the articles.

(c) The articles filed pursuant to this section shall be accompanied by a verified statement of any two officers or governing board members of the association stating that the incorporation of the association by means of the articles to which the verified statement is attached has been approved by the association in accordance with its rules and procedures.

(d) Upon the change of status of an unincorporated association to a corporation pursuant to subdivision (a), the property of the association becomes the property of the corporation and the members of the association who have any voting rights of the type referred to in Section 12238 become members of the corporation.

(e) The filing for record in the office of the county recorder of any county in this state in which any of the real property of the association is located, of a copy of the articles of incorporation filed pursuant to this section, certified by the Secretary of State, shall evidence record ownership in the corporation of all interests of the association in and to the real property located in that county.

(f) All rights of creditors and all liens upon the property of the association shall be preserved unimpaired. Any action or proceeding pending by or against the unincorporated association may be prosecuted to judgment, which shall bind the corporation, or the corporation may be proceeded against or substituted in its place.

(g) If a corporation is organized by a person who is or was an officer, director or member of an unincorporated association and such corporation is not organized pursuant to subdivision (a), the unincorporated association may continue to use its name and the corporation may not use a name which is the same as or similar to the name of the unincorporated association.

Ca. Corp. Code § 12301

Added by Stats. 1982, Ch. 1625, Sec. 3. Operative January 1, 1984.

Section 12302 - Names

(a) The Secretary of State shall not file articles setting forth a name in which "bank," "trust," "trustee," or related words appear, unless the certificate of approval of the Commissioner of Financial Protection and Innovation is attached thereto.

(b) The name of a corporation shall not be a name that the Secretary of State determines is likely to mislead the public and shall be distinguishable in the records of the Secretary of State from all of the following:

(1)The name of any corporation.

(2)The name of any foreign corporation authorized to transact intrastate business in this state.

(3)Each name that is under reservation pursuant to this title.

(4)The name of a foreign corporation that has registered its name pursuant to Section 2101.

(5)An alternate name of a foreign corporation under subdivision (b) of Section 2106.

(6)A name that will become the record name of a domestic or foreign corporation upon a corporate instrument when there is a delayed effective or file date.

(c) The use by a corporation of a name in violation of this section may be enjoined notwithstanding the filing of its articles by the Secretary of State.

(d) Any applicant may, upon payment of the fee prescribed therefor in the

Government Code, obtain from the Secretary of State a certificate of reservation of any name not prohibited by subdivision (b), and upon the issuance of the certificate the name stated therein shall be reserved for a period of 60 days. The Secretary of State shall not, however, issue certificates reserving the same name for two or more consecutive 60-day periods to the same applicant or for the use or benefit of the same person; nor shall consecutive reservations be made by or for the use or benefit of the same person of names so similar as to fall within the prohibitions of subdivision (b).

Ca. Corp. Code § 12302

Amended by Stats 2022 ch 617 (SB 1202),s 75, eff. 1/1/2023.
Amended by Stats 2022 ch 452 (SB 1498),s 58, eff. 1/1/2023.
Amended by Stats 2020 ch 361 (SB 522),s 11, eff. 1/1/2021.
Amended by Stats 2014 ch 401 (AB 2763),s 23, eff. 1/1/2015.

Section 12302.1 - Name prohibited by Financial Code

The Secretary of State shall not file articles for a corporation the name of which would fall within the prohibitions of Section 18104 of the Financial Code. This section shall not apply to articles filed for a corporation organized in accordance with Section 18100 of the Financial Code.

Ca. Corp. Code § 12302.1

Added 9/21/1999 (Bill Number: AB 1687) (Chapter 453).

Article 4 - ARTICLES OF INCORPORATION

Section 12310 - Articles of incorporation

The articles of incorporation of a corporation formed under this part shall set forth:
(a) The name of the corporation.
(b) The following statement: "This corporation is a cooperative corporation organized under the Cooperative Corporation Law. The purpose of this corporation is to engage in any lawful act or activity for which a corporation may be organized under the law." [The articles may include a further description of the corporation's purpose.]
(c) The name and street address in this state of the corporation's initial agent for service of process in accordance with subdivision (b) of Section 12570.
(d) The initial street address of the corporation.
(e) The initial mailing address of the corporation, if different from the initial street address.
(f) Whether the voting power or the proprietary interests of the members are equal or unequal. If the voting power or proprietary interests of the members are unequal, the articles shall state either (i) the general rule or rules by which the voting power and proprietary interests of the members shall be determined or (ii) that such rule or rules shall be prescribed in the corporation's bylaws. Equal voting power means voting power apportioned on the basis of one vote for each member. Equal proprietary rights means property rights apportioned on the basis of one proprietary unit for each

member.

(g) Pursuant to Section 12310.5, the articles of incorporation may state whether the cooperative has elected to be governed as a worker cooperative.

 Ca. Corp. Code § 12310

Amended by Stats 2015 ch 192 (AB 816),s 11, eff. 1/1/2016.

Amended by Stats 2012 ch 494 (SB 1532),s 28, eff. 1/1/2013.

Section 12310.5 - Election to be governed as worker cooperative

(a) A corporation organized under this part may elect to be governed as a worker cooperative by making the following statement in its articles of incorporation or its amended articles of incorporation: "This corporation is a worker cooperative corporation organized under the Cooperative Corporation Law."

(b) A corporation that makes the election to be governed as a worker cooperative, unless expressly exempted, shall be governed by all the provisions of this part.

 Ca. Corp. Code § 12310.5

Added by Stats 2015 ch 192 (AB 816),s 12, eff. 1/1/2016.

Section 12311 - Use of word "cooperative"

(a) The names of all corporations formed under this part shall include "cooperative." No corporation shall be formed under this part unless there is affixed or prefixed to its name some word or abbreviation which will indicate that it is a corporation, as distinguished from a natural person, a firm, or an unincorporated association.

(b) No person shall adopt or use the word "cooperative" or any abbreviation or derivation thereof, or any word similar thereto, as part of the name or designation under which it does business in this state, unless incorporated as provided in this part or unless incorporated as a nonprofit cooperative association under Chapter 1 (commencing with Section 54001) of Division 20 of the Food and Agricultural Code, as a stock cooperative, as defined in Section 11003.2 of the Business and Professions Code, as a limited-equity housing cooperative, as defined in Section 817 of the Civil Code, as a credit union or organization owned for the mutual benefit of credit unions, or under some other law of this state enabling it to do so. However, the foregoing prohibition shall be inapplicable to any credit union or organization owned for the mutual benefit of credit unions, any housing cooperative, the financing of which is insured, guaranteed, or provided, in whole or in part, by a public or statutorily chartered entity pursuant to a program created for housing cooperatives, a nonprofit corporation, a majority of whose membership is composed of cooperative corporations, or an academic institution that serves cooperative corporations.

(c) A domestic or foreign corporation or association which did business in this state under a name or designation including the word "cooperative" prior to September 19, 1939, and which conducts business on a cooperative basis substantially as set forth in this part, may continue to do business under that name or designation.

(d) Any person, firm, individual, partnership, trust, domestic corporation, foreign corporation, or association which did business in this state under a name or designation including the word "cooperative" prior to September 19, 1939, but which does not conduct business on a cooperative basis as contemplated by Section 12201 of this part, may continue to do business under that name or designation if the words "not organized under the law relating to cooperative corporations" are always placed immediately after the name or designation wherever it is used.

(e) Any foreign corporation, organized under and complying with the cooperative law of the state or other jurisdiction of its creation, may use the term "cooperative" in this state if it has complied with the laws of this state applicable to foreign corporations, insofar as those laws are applicable to it, and if it is doing business on a cooperative basis as contemplated by Section 12201.

Ca. Corp. Code § 12311
Amended by Stats 2011 ch 442 (AB 1211),s 28, eff. 1/1/2012.

Section 12312 - Statement limiting purposes or powers of corporation

The articles of incorporation may set forth a further statement limiting the purposes or powers of the corporation.

Ca. Corp. Code § 12312
Added by Stats. 1982, Ch. 1625, Sec. 3. Operative January 1, 1984.

Section 12313 - Additional provisions

(a) The articles of incorporation may set forth any or all of the following provisions, which shall not be effective unless expressly provided in the articles:

(1) A provision limiting the duration of the corporation's existence to a specified date.

(2) A provision providing for the distribution of the remaining assets of the corporation, after payment or adequate provision for all of its debts and liabilities, to a charitable trust.

(b) Nothing contained in subdivision (a) shall affect the enforceability, as between the parties thereto, of any lawful agreement not otherwise contrary to public policy.

(c) The articles of incorporation may set forth any or all of the following provisions:

(1) The names and addresses of the persons appointed to act as initial directors.

(2) Provisions concerning the transfer of memberships, in accordance with Section 12410.

(3) The classes of members, if any, and if there are two or more classes, the rights, privileges, preferences, restrictions, and conditions attaching to each class.

(4) Any other provision, not in conflict with law, for the management of the activities and for the conduct of the affairs of the corporation, including any provision which is required or permitted by this part to be stated in the bylaws.

(5) A provision conferring upon members the right to determine the consideration for which memberships shall be issued.

(6) A provision authorizing the board of directors, within any limits or restrictions stated, to fix the rights, privileges, preferences, restrictions, and conditions attaching to any wholly unissued class of memberships authorized in the bylaws or the articles.

(7) If the bylaws or articles authorize a class of memberships to be divisible into series, a provision authorizing the board of directors, within any limits or restrictions stated, to fix the rights, privileges, preferences, restrictions, and conditions attaching to any wholly unissued series of a membership class authorized to be divisible into series, and to fix the number of memberships in the series and the designation of the series. As to any series, the number of which is authorized to be fixed by the board, the articles may also authorize the board to increase or decrease, but not below the number of memberships then outstanding, the number of memberships of any such series subsequent to the issuance of that series. Unless the articles or bylaws provide otherwise, in case the number of memberships of any series is decreased, the memberships constituting this decrease shall resume the status which they had prior to the adoption of the board resolution originally fixing the number of memberships of the series.

Ca. Corp. Code § 12313
Amended by Stats 2013 ch 538 (AB 1255),s 3, eff. 1/1/2014.

Section 12314 - Unequal voting power of members provided in articles of incorporation of central organization

The articles of incorporation of a central organization, as defined in Section 12256, organized under or subject to this part may provide for unequal voting power of its members based upon the number of its members' members, the patronage of its members, or both. In no event shall any member have less than one vote.

Ca. Corp. Code § 12314
Amended by Stats. 1983, Ch. 792, Sec. 10.

Section 12315 - Certified copy of articles

For all purposes other than an action in the nature of quo warranto, a copy of the articles of a corporation duly certified by the Secretary of State is conclusive evidence of the formation of the corporation and prima facie evidence of its corporate existence.

Ca. Corp. Code § 12315
Added by Stats. 1982, Ch. 1625, Sec. 3. Operative January 1, 1984.

Section 12316 - Perfection of organization of corporation by incorporators

If initial directors have not been named in the articles of incorporation, the incorporators may do whatever is necessary and proper to perfect the organization of the corporation, including the adoption and amendment of bylaws of the corporation and the election of directors and officers, until the directors are elected.

Ca. Corp. Code § 12316
Added by Stats. 1983, Ch. 792, Sec. 11.

Section 12317 - Establishment as capital account cooperative

(a) A worker cooperative may, in its articles or bylaws, establish itself as a capital account cooperative.

(b) The articles or bylaws of a capital account cooperative may authorize assignment of a portion of retained net earnings and net losses to an unallocated capital account. The unallocated capital account in a capital account cooperative shall reflect any paid-in capital and retained net earnings not allocated to individual members. Earnings assigned to the unallocated capital account may be used for any and all corporate purposes, as determined by the board of directors.

(c) The system of member and unallocated capital accounts may be used to determine the redemption price of member shares, capital stock, and written notices of allocation. The articles or bylaws may provide for the capital account cooperative worker cooperative to pay or credit interest on the balance in each member's capital account.

(d) The articles or bylaws of a capital account cooperative may permit the periodic redemption of written notices of allocation and capital stock and shall provide for recall and redemption of membership shares upon termination of membership in the cooperative. However, no redemption may occur that would result in the liability of any director or officer pursuant to Article 3 (commencing with Section 12370) of Chapter 2.

(e) As used in this section, "written notice of allocation" has the same meaning as defined in Section 1388 (b) of the Internal Revenue Code.

Ca. Corp. Code § 12317
Amended by Stats 2018 ch 92 (SB 1289),s 48, eff. 1/1/2019.
Added by Stats 2015 ch 192 (AB 816),s 13, eff. 1/1/2016.

Article 5 - POWERS

Section 12320 - Powers

Subject to any limitations contained in the articles or bylaws and to compliance with other provisions of this part and any other applicable laws, a corporation, in carrying out its activities, shall have all of the powers of a natural person, including, without limitation, the power to:

(a) Adopt, use, and at will alter a corporate seal, but failure to affix a seal does not affect the validity of any instrument.

(b) Adopt, amend, and repeal bylaws.

(c) Qualify to conduct its activities in any other state, territory, dependency, or foreign country.

(d) Issue, purchase, redeem, receive, take or otherwise acquire, own, sell, lend, exchange, transfer or otherwise dispose of, pledge, use, and otherwise deal in and with its own memberships, bonds, debentures, notes, and debt securities.

(e) Pay pensions, and establish and carry out pension, deferred compensation, saving, thrift, and other retirement, incentive, and benefit plans, trusts, and provisions for any or all of its directors, officers, employees, and persons providing services to it or any of its subsidiary or related or associated corporations, and to indemnify and purchase and maintain insurance on behalf of any fiduciary of such plans, trusts, or provisions.

(f) Issue certificates evidencing membership in accordance with the provisions of Section 12401 and issue identity cards to identify those persons eligible to use the corporation's facilities.

(g) Levy dues, assessments, and membership and transfer fees.

(h) Make donations for the public welfare or for community funds, hospital, charitable, educational, scientific, civic, religious, or similar purposes.

(i) Assume obligations, enter into contracts, including contracts of guarantee or suretyship, incur liabilities, borrow or lend money or otherwise use its credit, and secure any of its obligations, contracts, or liabilities by mortgage, pledge, or other encumbrance of all or any part of its property and income.

(j) Participate with others in any partnership, joint venture, or other association, transaction, or arrangement of any kind whether or not such participation involves sharing or delegation of control with or to others.

(k) Act as trustee under any trust incidental to the principal objects of the corporation, and receive, hold, administer, exchange, and expend funds and property subject to such trust.

(l) Carry on a business at a profit and apply any profit that results from the business activity to any activity in which it may lawfully engage.

(m)

(1) In anticipation of or during an emergency, take either or both of the following actions necessary to conduct the corporation's business operations and affairs, unless emergency bylaws provide otherwise pursuant to subdivision (h) of Section 12331:

(A) Modify lines of succession to accommodate the incapacity of any director, officer, employee, or agent resulting from the emergency.

(B) Relocate the principal office, designate alternative principal offices or regional offices, or authorize the officers to do so.

(2) During an emergency, take either or both of the following actions necessary to conduct the corporation's business operations and affairs, unless emergency bylaws provide otherwise pursuant to subdivision (h) of Section 12331:

(A) Give notice to a director or directors in any practicable manner under the circumstances, including, but not limited to, by publication and radio, when notice of a meeting of the board cannot be given to that director or directors in the manner prescribed by the bylaws or Section 12351.

(B) Deem that one or more officers of the corporation present at a board meeting is a director, in order of rank and within the same rank in order of seniority, as necessary to achieve a quorum for that meeting.

(3) In anticipation of or during an emergency, the board may take any action that it determines to be necessary or appropriate to respond to the emergency, mitigate the effects of the emergency, or comply with lawful federal and state government orders, but shall not take any action that requires the vote of the members, unless the required vote of the members was obtained prior to the emergency.

(4) Any actions taken in good faith in anticipation of or during an emergency under this subdivision bind the corporation and shall not be used to impose liability on a corporate director, officer, employee, or agent.

(5) For purposes of this subdivision, "emergency" means any of the following events or circumstances as a result of which, and only so long as, a quorum of the corporation's board of directors cannot be readily convened for action:

(A) A natural catastrophe, including, but not limited to, a hurricane, tornado, storm, high water, wind-driven water, tidal wave, tsunami, earthquake, volcanic eruption, landslide, mudslide, snowstorm, drought, epidemic, pandemic, or disease outbreak, or, regardless of cause, any fire, flood, or explosion.

(B) An attack on or within this state or on the public security of its residents by an enemy of this state or on the nation by an enemy of the United States of America, or upon receipt by this state of a warning from the federal government indicating that any such enemy attack is probable or imminent.

(C) An act of terrorism or other manmade disaster that results in extraordinary levels of casualties or damage or disruption severely affecting the infrastructure, environment, economy, government functions, or population, including, but not limited to, mass evacuations.

(D) A state of emergency proclaimed by the Governor of this state, including any person serving as Governor in accordance with Section 10 of Article V of the California Constitution and Section 12058 of the Government Code, or by the President of the United States of America.

Ca. Corp. Code § 12320
Amended by Stats 2021 ch 523 (AB 663),s 19, eff. 1/1/2022.
Amended by Stats 2015 ch 98 (SB 351),s 15, eff. 1/1/2016.

Section 12321 - No assertion of limitation of powers; binding contracts or conveyances

(a) No limitation upon the activities, purposes, or powers of the corporation or upon the powers of the members, officers, or directors, or the manner of exercise of such powers, contained in or implied by the articles or by Chapters 15 (commencing with Section 12620), 16 (commencing with Section 12630) and 17 (commencing with Section 12650) shall be asserted as between the corporation or member, officer or director and any third person, except in a proceeding:

(1) by a member or the state to enjoin the doing or continuation of unauthorized activities by the corporation or its officers, or both, in cases where third parties have not acquired rights thereby,

(2) to dissolve the corporation, or

(3) by the corporation or by a member suing in any representative suit against the officers or directors of the corporation for violation of their authority.
(b) Any contract or conveyance made in the name of a corporation which is authorized or ratified by the board, or is done within the scope of authority, actual or apparent, conferred by the board or within the agency power of the officer executing it, except as the board's authority is limited by law other than this part, binds the corporation, and the corporation acquires rights thereunder whether the contract is executed or wholly or in part executory.

Ca. Corp. Code § 12321
Added by Stats. 1982, Ch. 1625, Sec. 3. Operative January 1, 1984.

Article 6 - BYLAWS

Section 12330 - Adoption, amendment, or repeal of bylaws

(a) Except as provided in subdivision (c) and Sections 12331, 12360, 12364, 12462, and 12484, bylaws may be adopted, amended, or repealed by the board unless the action would do any of the following:

(1) Materially and adversely affect the rights or obligations of members as to voting, dissolution, redemption, transfer, distributions, patronage distributions, patronage, property rights, or rights to repayment of contributed capital.

(2) Increase or decrease the number or members authorized in total or for any class.

(3) Effect an exchange, reclassification or cancellation of all or part of the memberships.

(4) Authorize a new class of membership.
(b) Bylaws may be adopted, amended or repealed by approval of the members (Section 12224); provided, however, that adoption, amendment, or repeal also requires approval by the members of a class or series if that action would do any of the following:

(1) Materially and adversely affect the rights or obligations of that class or series as to voting, dissolution, redemption, transfer, distributions, patronage distributions, patronage, property rights, or rights to repayment of contributed capital, in a manner different than such action affects another class or another series within the same class.

(2) Materially and adversely affect such class or series as to voting, dissolution, redemption, transfer, distributions, patronage distributions, patronage, property rights, or rights to repayment of contributed capital, by changing the rights, privileges, preferences, restrictions or conditions of another class or another series within the same class.

(3) Increase or decrease the number of memberships authorized for the class.

(4) Increase the number of memberships authorized for another class.

(5) Effect an exchange, reclassification or cancellation of all or part of the memberships of the class or series.

(6) Authorize a new class of memberships.
(c) The articles or bylaws may restrict or eliminate the power of the board to adopt, amend or repeal any or all bylaws, subject to subdivision (e) of Section 12331.
(d) Bylaws may also provide that repeal or amendment of those bylaws, or the repeal or amendment of specified portions of those bylaws, may occur only with the approval in writing of a specified person or persons other than the board or members. However, this approval requirement, unless the articles or the bylaws specify otherwise, shall not apply if any of the following circumstances exist:

(1) The specified person or persons have died or ceased to exist.

(2) If the right of the specified person or persons to approve is in the capacity of an officer, trustee, or other status and the office, trust, or status has ceased to exist.

(3) If the corporation has a specific proposal for amendment or repeal, and the corporation has provided written notice of that proposal, including a copy of the proposal, to the specified person or persons at the most recent address for each of them, based on the corporation's records, and the corporation has not received written approval or nonapproval within the period specified in the notice, which shall not be less than 10 nor more than 30 days commencing at least 20 days after the notice has been provided.

Ca. Corp. Code § 12330
Amended by Stats 2013 ch 538 (AB 1255),s 4, eff. 1/1/2014.
Amended by Stats 2009 ch 631 (AB 1233),s 41, eff. 1/1/2010.

Section 12331 - Number of directors

(a) The bylaws shall set forth (unless such provision is contained in the articles, in which case it may only be changed by an amendment of the articles) the number of directors of the corporation, or the method of determining the number of directors of the corporation, or that the number of directors shall be not less than a stated minimum or more than a stated maximum with the exact number of directors to be fixed, within the limits specified, by approval of the board or the members (Sections 12222 and 12224), in the manner provided in the bylaws, subject to subdivision (e). The number or minimum number of directors shall not be less than three. Alternate directors may be permitted, in which event, the bylaws shall specify the manner and times of their election and the conditions to their service in place of a director.
(b) Once members have been admitted, a bylaw specifying or changing a fixed number of directors or the maximum or minimum number or changing from a fixed to a variable board or vice versa may only be adopted by approval of the members.
(c) The bylaws may contain any provision, not in conflict with law or the articles, for the management of the activities and for the conduct of the affairs of the corporation, including, but not limited to:

(1) Any provision referred to in subdivision (c) of Section 12313.

(2) The time, place, and manner of calling, conducting, and giving notice of members', directors', and committee meetings, or of conducting mail ballots.

(3) The qualifications, duties, and compensation of directors; the time of their election; and the requirements of a quorum for directors' and committee meetings.

(4) The appointment of committees, composed of directors or nondirectors or both, by the board or any officer and the authority of these committees.

(5) The appointment, duties, compensation, and tenure of officers.

(6) The mode of determination of members of record.

(7) The making of reports and financial statements to members.

(8) Setting, imposing, and collecting dues, assessments, and membership and transfer fees.

(9) The time and manner of patronage distributions consistent with this part.
(d) The bylaws may provide for eligibility, the manner of admission, withdrawal, suspension, and expulsion of members, and the suspension or termination of memberships consistent with the requirements of Section 12431.
(e) The bylaws may require, for any or all corporate actions, the vote of a larger proportion of, or all of, the members or the members of any class, unit, or grouping of members or the vote of a larger proportion of, or all of, the directors, than is otherwise required by this part. A provision in the bylaws requiring a greater vote shall not be altered, amended, or repealed except by the greater vote, unless otherwise provided in the bylaws.
(f) The bylaws may contain a provision limiting the number of members, in total or of any class or series, which the corporation is authorized to admit.
(g) The bylaws may provide for the establishment by the corporation of a program for the education of its members, officers, employees, and the general public in the principles and techniques of cooperation.
(h)

(1) The bylaws may contain any provision, not in conflict with the articles, to manage and conduct the business affairs of the corporation effective only in an emergency as defined in Section 12320, including, but not limited to, procedures for calling a board meeting, quorum requirements for a board meeting, and designation of additional or substitute directors.

(2) During an emergency, the board may take any action that it determines to be necessary or appropriate to respond to the emergency, mitigate the effects of the emergency, or comply with lawful federal and state government orders, but shall not take any action that requires the vote of the members, unless the required vote of the members was obtained prior to the emergency.

(3) All provisions of the regular bylaws consistent with the emergency bylaws shall remain effective during the emergency, and the emergency bylaws shall not be effective after the emergency ends.

(4) Corporate action taken in good faith in accordance with the emergency bylaws binds the corporation, and shall not be used to impose liability on a corporate director, officer, employee, or agent.

Ca. Corp. Code § 12331

Amended by Stats 2021 ch 523 (AB 663),s 20, eff. 1/1/2022.

Amended by Stats 2015 ch 98 (SB 351),s 16, eff. 1/1/2016.

Amended by Stats 2013 ch 538 (AB 1255),s 5, eff. 1/1/2014.

Amended by Stats 2009 ch 631 (AB 1233),s 42, eff. 1/1/2010.

Section 12332 - Delegates

A corporation may provide in its bylaws for delegates having some or all of the authority of members. Where delegates are provided for, the bylaws shall set forth the delegates' terms of office, any reasonable method for delegates' selection and removal, and any reasonable method for calling, noticing, and holding meetings of delegates, may set forth the manner in which delegates may act by written ballot similar to Section 12463 for written ballot of members, and may set forth the manner in which delegates may participate in meetings of delegates similar to paragraph (6) of subdivision (a) of Section 12351. Unless delegates are directly elected by the membership, they shall be elected by a body or bodies directly elected by the membership. Each delegate shall have one vote on each matter presented for action. A delegate shall not vote by proxy. Delegates may be given a name other than "delegates."

Ca. Corp. Code § 12332

Amended by Stats 2021 ch 523 (AB 663),s 21, eff. 1/1/2022.

Amended by Stats. 1983, Ch. 792, Sec. 14.

Section 12333 - Voting by members or delegates

A corporation may provide in its bylaws for voting by its members or delegates on the basis of chapter or other organizational unit, or by region or other geographic grouping.

Ca. Corp. Code § 12333

Added by Stats. 1982, Ch. 1625, Sec. 3. Operative January 1, 1984.

Article 7 - LOCATION AND INSPECTION OF ARTICLES AND BYLAWS

Section 12340 - Location and inspection of articles and bylaws

Every corporation shall keep at its principal office in this state the original or a copy of its articles and bylaws as amended to date, which shall be open to inspection by the members at all reasonable times during office hours. If the corporation has no office in this state, it shall upon the written request of any member furnish to such member a copy of the articles or bylaws as amended to date.

Ca. Corp. Code § 12340
Added by Stats. 1982, Ch. 1625, Sec. 3. Operative January 1, 1984.

Chapter 2 - DIRECTORS AND MANAGEMENT

Article 1 - GENERAL PROVISIONS

Section 12350 - Board of directors

Each corporation shall have a board of directors. Subject to the provisions of this part and any limitations in the articles or bylaws relating to action required to be approved by the members (Section 12224), or by a majority of all members (Section 12223), the activities and affairs of a corporation shall be conducted and all corporate powers shall be exercised by or under the direction of the board. The board may delegate the management of the activities of the corporation to any person or persons, management company, or committee however composed, provided that the activities and affairs of the corporation shall be managed and all corporate powers shall be exercised under the ultimate direction of the board.

Ca. Corp. Code § 12350
Amended by Stats. 1996, Ch. 589, Sec. 47. Effective January 1, 1997.

Section 12351 - Meetings of board

(a) Unless otherwise provided in the articles or in the bylaws:

(1) Meetings of the board may be called by the chair of the board or the president or any vice president or the secretary or any two directors.

(2) Regular meetings of the board may be held without notice if the time and place of the meetings are fixed by the bylaws or the board. Special meetings of the board shall be held upon four days' notice by first-class mail or 48 hours' notice delivered personally or by telephone, including a voice messaging system or by electronic transmission by the corporation (Section 20). The articles or bylaws may not dispense with notice of a special meeting. A notice, or waiver of notice, need not specify the purpose of any regular or special meeting of the board.

(3) Notice of a meeting need not be given to any director who provides a waiver of notice or consent to holding the meeting or an approval of the minutes thereof in writing, whether before or after the meeting, or who attends the meeting without protesting, prior thereto or at its commencement, the lack of notice to that director. All waivers, consents, and approvals shall be filed with the corporate records or made a part of the minutes of the meetings.

(4) A majority of the directors present, whether or not a quorum is present, may adjourn any meeting to another time and place. If the meeting is adjourned for more than 24 hours, notice of any adjournment to another time or place shall be given prior to the time of the adjourned meeting to the directors who were not present at the time of the adjournment.

(5) Meetings of the directors may be held at any place within or without the state which has been designated in the notice of the meeting or, if not stated in the notice or if there is no notice, designated in the bylaws or by resolution of the board.

(6) Directors may participate in a meeting through use of conference telephone, electronic video screen communication, or electronic transmission by and to the corporation (Sections 20 and 21). Participation in a meeting through use of conference telephone or electronic video screen communication pursuant to this subdivision constitutes presence in person at that meeting as long as all directors participating in the meeting are able to hear one another. Participation in a meeting through use of electronic transmission by and to the corporation, other than conference telephone and electronic video screen communication pursuant to this subdivision constitutes presence in person at that meeting if both of the following apply:

(A) Each director participating in the meeting can communicate with all of the other directors concurrently.

(B) Each director is provided the means of participating in all matters before the board, including, without limitation, the capacity to propose, or to interpose an objection to, a specific action to be taken by the corporation.

(7) A majority of the number of directors authorized in or pursuant to the articles or bylaws constitutes a quorum of the board for the transaction of business. The articles or bylaws may require the presence of one or more specified directors to constitute a quorum of the board to transact business, as long as the death or nonexistence of a specified director or the death or nonexistence of the person or persons otherwise authorized to appoint or designate a director does not prevent the corporation from transacting business in the normal course of events. The articles or bylaws may not provide that a quorum shall be less than one-fifth the number of directors authorized in or pursuant to the articles or bylaws, or less than two, whichever is larger.

(8) Subject to the provisions of Sections 12352, 12373, 12374, and subdivision (e) of Section 12377, every act or decision done or made by a majority of the directors present at a meeting duly held at which a quorum is present is the act of the board. The articles or bylaws may not provide that a lesser vote than a majority of the directors present at a meeting is the act of the board. A meeting at which a quorum is initially present may continue to transact business notwithstanding the withdrawal of directors, if any action taken is approved by at least a majority of the required quorum for the meeting, or a greater number as is required by this division, the articles or bylaws.

(b) Any action required or permitted to be taken by the board may be taken without a meeting, if all directors shall individually or collectively consent in writing to that action. Such written consent or consents shall be filed with the minutes of the proceedings of the board. The action by written consent shall have the same force and effect as a unanimous vote of the directors.

(c) Each director shall have one vote on each matter presented to the board of directors for action. A director shall not vote by proxy.

Ca. Corp. Code § 12351

Amended by Stats 2020 ch 370 (SB 1371),s 40, eff. 1/1/2021.
Amended by Stats 2011 ch 442 (AB 1211),s 29, eff. 1/1/2012.
Amended by Stats 2009 ch 631 (AB 1233),s 43, eff. 1/1/2010.
Amended by Stats 2005 ch 102 (SB 119),s 6, eff. 1/1/2006
Amended by Stats 2004 ch 254 (SB 1306),s 36, eff. 1/1/2005

Section 12352 - Quorum; committees

(a) The board may, by resolution adopted by a majority of the number of directors then in office, provided that a quorum is present, create one or more committees, each consisting of two or more directors, to serve at the pleasure of the board. Appointments to such committees shall be by a majority vote of the directors then in office, unless the articles or bylaws require a majority vote of the number of directors authorized in or pursuant to the articles or bylaws. The bylaws may authorize one or more such committees, each consisting of two or more directors, and may provide that a specified officer or officers who are also directors of the corporation shall be a member or members of such committee or committees. The board may appoint one or more directors as alternate members of such committee, who may replace any absent member at any meeting of the committee. Such committee, to the extent provided in the resolution of the board or in the bylaws, shall have all the authority of the board, except with respect to:

(1) The approval of any action for which this part also requires approval of the members (Section 12224) or approval of a majority of all members (Section 12223) regardless of whether the corporation has members.

(2) The filling of vacancies on the board or in any committee which has the authority of the board.

(3) The fixing of compensation of the directors for serving on the board or on any committee.

(4) The amendment or repeal of bylaws or the adoption of new bylaws.

(5) The amendment or repeal of any resolution of the board which by its express terms is not so amendable or repealable.

(6) The appointment of committees of the board or the members thereof.

(7) The expenditure of corporate funds to support a nominee for director after there are more people nominated for director than can be elected.

(b) A committee exercising the authority of the board shall not include as members persons who are not directors. However, the board may create other committees that do not exercise the authority of the board and these other committees may include persons regardless of whether they are directors.

(c) Unless the bylaws otherwise provide, the board may delegate to any committee, appointed pursuant to paragraph (4) of subdivision (c) of Section 12331 or otherwise, powers as authorized by Section 12350, but may not delegate the powers set forth in paragraphs (1) through (7) of subdivision (a) of this section.

Ca. Corp. Code § 12352

Amended by Stats 2011 ch 442 (AB 1211),s 30, eff. 1/1/2012.

Amended by Stats 2009 ch 631 (AB 1233),s 44, eff. 1/1/2010.

Section 12353 - Officers

(a) A corporation shall have (1) a chair of the board, who may be given the title chair, chairperson, chair of the board, or chairperson of the board, or a president or both, (2) a secretary, (3) a treasurer or a chief financial officer or both, and (4) any other officers with any titles and duties as shall be stated in the bylaws or determined by the board and as may be necessary to enable it to sign instruments. The president, or if there is no president the chair of the board, is the chief executive officer of the corporation, unless otherwise provided in the articles or bylaws. Unless otherwise specified in the articles or the bylaws, if there is no chief financial officer, the treasurer is the chief financial officer of the corporation. Any number of offices may be held by the same person unless the articles or bylaws provide otherwise. Either the chair of the board or the president shall be elected from among those board members elected by the membership of the corporation.

(b) Except as otherwise provided by the articles or bylaws, officers shall be chosen by the board and serve at the pleasure of the board, subject to the rights, if any, of an officer under any contract of employment. Any officer may resign at any time upon written notice to the corporation without prejudice to the rights, if any, of the corporation under any contract to which the officer is a party.

Ca. Corp. Code § 12353

Amended by Stats 2022 ch 617 (SB 1202),s 76, eff. 1/1/2023.

Amended by Stats 2015 ch 98 (SB 351),s 17, eff. 1/1/2016.

Amended by Stats 2011 ch 442 (AB 1211),s 31, eff. 1/1/2012.

Amended by Stats 2009 ch 631 (AB 1233),s 45, eff. 1/1/2010.

Section 12354 - Authority of signing officers

Subject to the provisions of subdivision (a) of Section 12321, any note, mortgage, evidence of indebtedness, contract, conveyance or other instrument in writing, and any assignment or endorsement thereof, executed or entered into between any corporation and any other person, when signed by any one of the chairperson of the board, the president or any vice president and by any one of the secretary, any assistant secretary, the chief financial officer, or any assistant treasurer of such corporation, is not invalidated as to the corporation by any lack of authority of the signing officers in the absence of actual knowledge on the part of the other person that the signing officers had no authority to execute the same.

Ca. Corp. Code § 12354
Amended by Stats 2022 ch 617 (SB 1202),s 77, eff. 1/1/2023.
Amended by Stats. 1996, Ch. 589, Sec. 48. Effective January 1, 1997.

Section 12355 - Certified copy as prima facie evidence

The original or a copy in writing or in any other form capable of being converted into clearly legible tangible form of the bylaws or of the minutes of any incorporators', members', directors', committee or other meeting or of any resolution adopted by the board or a committee thereof, or members, certified to be a true copy by a person purporting to be the secretary or an assistant secretary of the corporation, is prima facie evidence of the adoption of such bylaws or resolution or of the due holding of such meeting and of the matters stated therein.

Ca. Corp. Code § 12355
Amended by Stats 2004 ch 254 (SB 1306),s 37, eff. 1/1/2005

Article 2 - SELECTION, REMOVAL AND RESIGNATION OF DIRECTORS

Section 12360 - Term of directors

(a) Except as provided in subdivision (d), directors shall be elected for terms of not longer than four years, as fixed in the articles or bylaws. In the absence of any provision in the articles or bylaws, the terms shall be one year. No amendment of the articles or bylaws may extend the term of a director beyond that for which the director was elected, nor may any bylaw provision increasing the terms of directors be adopted without approval of the members.
(b) Unless otherwise provided in the articles or bylaws, each director, including a director elected to fill a vacancy, shall hold office until the expiration of the term for which elected and until a successor has been elected and qualified, unless the director has been removed from office.
(c) The articles or bylaws may prescribe requirements for eligibility for election as a director.

(d) For the purposes of this subdivision, "designator" means one or more designators. Notwithstanding subdivisions (a) to (c), inclusive, all or any portion of the directors authorized in the articles or bylaws of a corporation may hold office by virtue of designation or selection by a specified designator as provided by the articles or bylaws rather than by election. Those directors shall continue in office for the term prescribed by the governing article or bylaw provision, or, if there is no term prescribed, until the governing article or bylaw provision is duly amended or repealed, except as provided in subdivision (f) of Section 12362. A bylaw provision authorized by this subdivision may be adopted, amended, or repealed only by approval of the members (Section 12224), except as provided in subdivision (d) of Section 12330. Unless otherwise provided in the articles or bylaws, the entitlement to designate or select a director or directors shall cease if any of the following circumstances exist:

(1) The specified designator of that director or directors has died or ceased to exist.

(2) If the entitlement of the specified designator of that director or directors to designate is in the capacity of an officer, trustee, or other status and the office, trust, or status has ceased to exist.

(e) If a corporation has not issued memberships and (1) all the directors resign, die, or become incompetent, or (2) a corporation's initial directors have not been named in the articles and all incorporators resign, die, or become incompetent before the election of the initial directors, the superior court of any county may appoint directors of the corporation upon application by any party in interest.

(f) If authorized in the articles or bylaws of a corporation, all or any portion of the directors may hold office ex officio by virtue of occupying a specified position within the corporation or outside the corporation. The term of office of an ex officio director shall coincide with that director's respective term of office in the specified position entitling him or her to serve on the board of directors. Upon an ex officio director's resignation or removal from that position, or resignation or removal from the board for any reason, the term of office as a director of the corporation shall immediately cease. At that time, the successor in office shall become an ex officio director of the corporation, occupying the place of the former director.

Ca. Corp. Code § 12360
Amended by Stats 2018 ch 322 (AB 2557),s 5, eff. 1/1/2019.
Amended by Stats 2009 ch 631 (AB 1233),s 46, eff. 1/1/2010.
Amended by Stats 2000 ch 485 (AB 1895), s 16, eff. 1/1/2001.

Section 12361 - Declaration of vacancy

The board may declare vacant the office of a director whose eligibility for election as a director has ceased, or who has been declared of unsound mind by a final order of court, or convicted of a felony, or, if at the time a director is elected, the bylaws provide that a director may be removed for missing a specified number of board meetings, fails to attend the specified number of meetings.

Ca. Corp. Code § 12361

Added by Stats. 1982, Ch. 1625, Sec. 3. Operative January 1, 1984.

Section 12362 - Removal

(a) Subject to subdivisions (b), (c) and (g), any or all directors may be removed without cause if one of the following applies:

(1) In a corporation with fewer than 50 members, the removal is approved by a majority of all members (Section 12223).

(2) In a corporation with 50 or more members, the removal is approved by the members (Section 12224).

(b) In a corporation in which the articles or bylaws authorize members to cumulate their votes pursuant to subdivision (a) of Section 12485, no director may be removed (unless the entire board is removed) when the votes cast against removal, or not consenting in writing to the removal, would be sufficient to elect the director if voted cumulatively at an election at which the same total number of votes were cast (or, if the action is taken by written ballot, all memberships entitled to vote were voted) and the entire number of directors authorized at the time of the director's most recent election were then being elected; and

(c) When by the provisions of the articles or bylaws the members of any class, voting as a class, are entitled to elect one or more directors, any director so elected may be removed only by the applicable vote of the members of that class.

(d) Any reduction of the authorized number of directors or any amendment reducing the number of class of directors does not remove any director prior to the expiration of the director's term of office, unless the reduction or amendment also provides for removal of one or more specified directors.

(e) Except as provided in this section and Sections 12361 and 12363, a director may not be removed prior to the expiration of the director's term of office.

(f) Where a director removed under this section or Section 12361 or 12363 was chosen by designation pursuant to subdivision (d) of Section 12360, then:

(1) Where a different person may be designated pursuant to the governing article or bylaw provision, the new designation shall be made; or

(2) Where the governing article or bylaw provision contains no provision under which a different person may be designated, the governing article or bylaw provision shall be deemed repealed.

(g) For the purposes of this subdivision, "designator" means one or more designators. If by the provisions of the articles or bylaws a designator is entitled to designate one or more directors, then:

(1) Unless as otherwise provided in the articles or bylaws at the time of designation, any director so designated may be removed without cause by the designator of that director.

(2) Any director so designated may only be removed under subdivision (a) with the written consent of the designator of that director.

(3) Unless as otherwise provided in the articles or bylaws, the right to remove shall not apply if any of the following circumstances exist:

(A) The designator entitled to that right has died or ceased to exist.

(B) If that right is in the capacity of an officer, trustee, or other status, and the office, trust, or status has ceased to exist.
Ca. Corp. Code § 12362
Amended by Stats 2009 ch 631 (AB 1233),s 47, eff. 1/1/2010.
Amended September 21, 1999 (Bill Number: AB 1687) (Chapter 453).

Section 12363 - Court order for removal

The superior court of the proper county may, at the suit of a director, or members possessing 5 percent of the voting power, remove from office any director in case of fraudulent or dishonest acts or gross abuse of authority or discretion with reference to the corporation and may bar from reelection any director so removed for a period prescribed by the court. The corporation shall be made a party to such action.
Ca. Corp. Code § 12363
Added by Stats. 1982, Ch. 1625, Sec. 3. Operative January 1, 1984.

Section 12364 - Filling vacancies

(a) Unless otherwise provided in the articles or bylaws and except for a vacancy created by the removal of a director, vacancies on the board may be filled by approval of the board (Section 12222) or, if the number of directors then in office is less than a quorum, by (1) the unanimous written consent of the directors then in office, (2) the affirmative vote of a majority of the directors then in office at a meeting held pursuant to notice or waivers of notice complying with Section 12351, or (3) a sole remaining director. Unless the articles or a bylaw approved by the members (Section 12224) provide that the board may fill vacancies occurring in the board by reason of the removal of directors, such vacancies may be filled only by approval of the members (Section 12224).

(b) The members may elect a director at any time to fill any vacancy not filled by the directors.

(c) Any director may resign effective upon giving written notice to the chairperson of the board, the president, the secretary, or the board of directors of the corporation, unless the notice specifies a later time for the effectiveness of such resignation. If the resignation is effective at a future time, a successor may be elected to take office when the resignation becomes effective.

Ca. Corp. Code § 12364
Amended by Stats 2022 ch 617 (SB 1202),s 78, eff. 1/1/2023.
Amended by Stats. 1985, Ch. 329, Sec. 5.

Article 3 - STANDARDS OF CONDUCT

Section 12370 - Duties and liabilities applicable regardless of compensation

Any duties and liabilities set forth in this article shall apply without regard to whether a director is compensated by the corporation.

Ca. Corp. Code § 12370
Added by Stats. 1982, Ch. 1625, Sec. 3. Operative January 1, 1984.

Section 12371 - Good faith; best interests of corporation

(a) A director shall perform the duties of a director, including duties as a member of any committee of the board upon which the director may serve, in good faith, in a manner such director believes to be in the best interests of the corporation and with such care, including reasonable inquiry, as an ordinarily prudent person in a like position would use under similar circumstances.

(b) In performing the duties of a director, a director shall be entitled to rely on information, opinions, reports or statements, including financial statements and other financial data, in each case prepared or presented by:

(1) One or more officers or employees of the corporation whom the director believes to be reliable and competent in the matters presented;

(2) Counsel, independent accountants or other persons as to matters which the director believes to be within such person's professional or expert competence; or

(3) A committee upon which the director does not serve that is composed exclusively of any or any combination of directors, persons described in paragraph (1), or persons described in paragraph (2), as to matters within the committee's designated authority, which committee the director believes to merit confidence, so long as, in any such case, the director acts in good faith, after reasonable inquiry when the need therefor is indicated by the circumstances and without knowledge that would cause such reliance to be unwarranted.

(c) A person who performs the duties of a director in accordance with subdivisions (a) and (b) shall have no liability based upon any alleged failure to discharge the persons's obligations as a director.

Ca. Corp. Code § 12371
Amended by Stats 2009 ch 631 (AB 1233),s 48, eff. 1/1/2010.

Section 12372 - Acts or omissions in connection with election, selection, or nomination of directors

(a) Section 12371 governs the duties of directors as to any acts or omissions in connection with the election, selection, or nomination of directors.
(b) This section shall not be construed to limit the generality of Section 12371.
  Ca. Corp. Code § 12372
Added by Stats. 1982, Ch. 1625, Sec. 3. Operative January 1, 1984.

Section 12373 - Interested or common director

(a) No contract or other transaction between a corporation and one or more of its directors, or between a corporation and any domestic or foreign corporation, firm or association in which one or more of its directors has a material financial interest, is either void or voidable because such director or directors or such other corporation, business corporation, firm or association are parties or because such director or directors are present at the meeting of the board or a committee thereof which authorizes, approves or ratifies the contract or transaction, if:

  (1) The material facts as to the transaction and as to such director's interest are fully disclosed or known to the members and such contract or transaction is approved by the members (Section 12224) in good faith, with any membership owned by any interested director not being entitled to vote thereon;

  (2) The material facts as to the transaction and as to such director's interest are fully disclosed or known to the board or committee, and the board or committee authorizes, approves or ratifies the contract or transaction in good faith by a vote sufficient without counting the vote of the interested director or directors and the contract or transaction is just and reasonable as to the corporation at the time it is authorized, approved or ratified; or

  (3) As to contracts or transactions not approved as provided in paragraph (1) or (2), the person asserting the validity of the contract or transaction sustains the burden of proving that the contract or transaction was just and reasonable as to the corporation at the time it was authorized, approved or ratified. Neither a mere common directorship nor a member-patron relationship on terms available to all members constitutes a material financial interest within the meaning of this subdivision. A director is not interested within the meaning of this subdivision in a resolution fixing the compensation of another director as a director, officer or employee of the corporation, notwithstanding the fact that the first director is also receiving compensation from the corporation.

(b) No contract or other transaction between a corporation and any corporation, business corporation or association of which one or more of its directors are directors is either void or voidable because such director or directors are present at the meeting of the board or a committee thereof which authorizes, approves or ratifies the contract or transaction, if:

(1) The material facts as to the transaction and as to such director's other directorship are fully disclosed or known to the board or committee, and the board or committee authorizes, approves or ratifies the contract or transaction in good faith by a vote sufficient without counting the vote of the common director or directors or the contract or transaction is approved by the members in good faith; or

(2) As to contracts or transactions not approved as provided in paragraph (1), the contract or transaction is just and reasonable as to the corporation at the time it is authorized, approved or ratified. This subdivision does not apply to contracts or transactions covered by subdivision (a).

Ca. Corp. Code § 12373
Added by Stats. 1982, Ch. 1625, Sec. 3. Operative January 1, 1984.

Section 12374 - Counting of interested or common directors

Interested or common directors may be counted in determining the presence of a quorum at a meeting of the board or a committee thereof which authorizes, approves or ratifies a contract or transaction as provided in Section 12373.

Ca. Corp. Code § 12374
Added by Stats. 1982, Ch. 1625, Sec. 3. Operative January 1, 1984.

Section 12375 - Loan to, or guarantee of obligation of, director or officer

(a) Unless prohibited by the articles or bylaws, a corporation may loan money or property to, or guarantee the obligation of, any director or officer of the corporation or of its parent, affiliate or subsidiary, provided:

(1) The board determines the loan or guaranty may reasonably be expected to benefit the corporation.

(2) Prior to consummating the transaction or any part thereof, the loan or guaranty is either:

(A) Approved by the members (Section 12224), without counting the vote of the director or officer, if a member.

(B) Approved by the vote of a majority of the directors then in office, without counting the vote of the director who is to receive the loan or the benefit of the guaranty.

(b) Notwithstanding subdivision (a), a corporation may advance money to a director or officer of the corporation or of its parent, affiliate or subsidiary, for any expenses reasonably anticipated to be incurred in the performance of the duties of the director or officer of the corporation or of its parent, affiliate or subsidiary, for any expenses reasonably anticipated to be incurred in the performance of the duties of the director or officer, provided that in the absence of such an advance the director or officer would be entitled to be reimbursed for these expenses by the corporation, its parent, affiliate, or subsidiary.

(c) The provisions of subdivisions (a) and (b) do not apply to credit unions, or to the payment of premiums in whole or in part by a corporation on a life insurance policy on the life of a director or officer so long as repayment to the corporation of the amount paid by it is secured by the proceeds of the policy and its cash surrender value, or to loans permitted under any statute regulating any special class of corporations.

Ca. Corp. Code § 12375

Repealed and added by Stats. 1983, Ch. 792, Sec. 17.

Section 12376 - Joint and several liability for approval of corporate actions

(a) Subject to the provisions of Section 12371, directors of a corporation who approve any of the following corporate actions are jointly and severally liable to the corporation for the benefit of all of the creditors entitled to institute an action under paragraph (1) or (2) of subdivision (c) or to the corporation in an action by members under paragraph (3) of subdivision (c):

(1) The making of any distribution or purchase or redemption of memberships contrary to Chapter 4 (commencing with Section 12450).

(2) The distribution of assets after institution of dissolution proceedings of the corporation, without paying or adequately providing for all known liabilities of the corporation, excluding any claims not filed by creditors within the time limit set by the court in a notice given to creditors under Chapters 15 (commencing with Section 12620), 16 (commencing with Section 12630), and 17 (commencing with Section 12650).

(3) The making of any loan or guarantee contrary to Section 12375.

(b) A director who is present at a meeting of the board, or any committee thereof, at which action specified in subdivision (a) is taken and who abstains from voting shall be considered to have approved the action.

(c) Suit may be brought in the name of the corporation to enforce the liability:

(1) Under paragraph (1) of subdivision (a) against any or all directors liable by the persons entitled to sue under subdivision (c) of Section 12455.

(2) Under paragraph (2) or (3) of subdivision (a) against any or all directors liable by any one or more creditors of the corporation whose debts or claims arose prior to the time of the corporate action who have not consented to the corporate action, whether or not they have reduced their claims to judgment.

(3) Under paragraph (3) of subdivision (a) against any or all directors liable by any one or more members at the time of any corporate action specified in paragraph (3) of subdivision (a) who have not consented to the corporate action, without regard to the provisions of Section 12490.

(d) The damages recoverable from a director under this section shall be the amount of the illegal distribution, or if the illegal distribution consists of property, the fair market value of that property at the time of the illegal distribution, plus interest thereon from the date of the distribution at the legal rate on judgments until paid, together with all reasonably incurred costs of appraisal or other valuation, if any, of that property, or the loss suffered by the corporation as a result of the illegal loan or guarantee, but not exceeding, in the case of an action for the benefit of creditors, the liabilities of the corporation owed to nonconsenting creditors at the time of the violation.

(e) Any director sued under this section may implead all other directors liable and may compel contribution, either in that action or in an independent action against directors not joined in that action.

(f) Directors liable under this section shall also be entitled to be subrogated to the rights of the corporation:

(1) With respect to paragraph (1) of subdivision (a), against the persons who received the distribution.

(2) With respect to paragraph (2) of subdivision (a), against the persons who received the distribution.

(3) With respect to paragraph (3) of subdivision (a), against the person who received the loan or guarantee. Any director sued under this section may file a cross-complaint against the person or persons who are liable to the director as a result of the subrogation provided for in this subdivision or may proceed against them in an independent action.

Ca. Corp. Code § 12376

Amended 9/21/1999 (Bill Number: AB 1687) (Chapter 453).

Section 12377 - Indemnification

(a) For the purposes of this section, "agent" means any person who is or was a director, officer, employee or other agent of the corporation, or is or was serving at the request of the corporation as a director, officer, employee or agent of another foreign or domestic corporation, partnership, joint venture, trust or other enterprise, or was a director, officer, employee or agent of a foreign or domestic corporation which was a predecessor corporation of the corporation or of another enterprise at the request of the predecessor corporation; "proceeding" means any threatened, pending or completed action or proceeding, whether civil, criminal, administrative or investigative; and "expenses" includes without limitation attorneys' fees and any expenses of establishing a right to indemnification under subdivision (d) or paragraph (3) of subdivision (e).

(b) A corporation shall have power to indemnify any person who was or is a party or is threatened to be made a party to any proceeding (other than an action by or in the right of the corporation to procure a judgment in its favor) by reason of the fact that the person is or was an agent of the corporation, against expenses, judgments, fines, settlements and other amounts actually and reasonably incurred in connection with the proceeding if the person acted in good faith and in a manner the person reasonably believed to be in the best interests of the corporation and, in the case of a criminal proceeding, had no reasonable cause to believe the conduct of the person was unlawful. The termination of any proceeding by judgment, order, settlement, conviction or upon a plea of nolo contendere or its equivalent shall not, of itself, create a presumption that the person did not act in good faith and in a manner that the person reasonably believed to be in the best interests of the corporation or that the person had reasonable cause to believe that the person's conduct was unlawful.

(c) A corporation shall have power to indemnify any person who was or is a party or is threatened to be made a party to any threatened, pending or completed action by or in the right of the corporation, to procure a judgment in its favor by reason of the fact that the person is or was an agent of the corporation, against expenses actually and reasonably incurred by the person in connection with the defense or settlement of the action if the person acted in good faith, in a manner the person believed to be in the best interests of the corporation and with that care, including reasonable inquiry, as an ordinarily prudent person in a like position would use under similar circumstances. No indemnification shall be made under this subdivision:

(1) In respect of any claim, issue or matter as to which the person shall have been adjudged to be liable to the corporation in the performance of the person's duty to the corporation, unless and only to the extent that the court in which the proceeding is or was pending shall determine upon application that, in view of all the circumstances of the case, the person is fairly and reasonably entitled to indemnity for the expenses which the court shall determine;

(2) Of amounts paid in settling or otherwise disposing of a threatened or pending action, with or without court approval; or

(3) Of expenses incurred in defending a threatened or pending action which is settled or otherwise disposed of without court approval.

(d) To the extent that an agent of a corporation has been successful on the merits in defense of any proceeding referred to in subdivision (b) or (c) or in defense of any claim, issue, or matter therein, the agent shall be indemnified against expenses actually and reasonably incurred by the agent in connection therewith.

(e) Except as provided in subdivision (d), any indemnification under this section shall be made by the corporation only if authorized in the specific case, upon a determination that indemnification of the agent is proper in the circumstances because the agent has met the applicable standard of conduct set forth in subdivision (b) or (c), by:

(1) A majority vote of a quorum consisting of directors who are not parties to the proceeding;

(2) Approval of the members (Section 12224), with the persons to be indemnified not being entitled to vote thereon; or

(3) The court in which the proceeding is or was pending upon application made by the corporation or the agent or the attorney or other person rendering services in connection with the defense, whether or not the application by the agent, attorney or other person is opposed by the corporation.

(f) Expenses incurred in defending any proceeding may be advanced by the corporation prior to the final disposition of the proceeding upon receipt of an undertaking by or on behalf of the agent to repay the amount unless it shall be determined ultimately that the agent is entitled to be indemnified as authorized in this section.

(g) No provision made by a corporation to indemnify its or its subsidiary's directors or officers for the defense of any proceeding, whether contained in the articles, bylaws, a resolution of members or directors, an agreement or otherwise, shall be valid unless consistent with this section. Nothing contained in this section shall affect any right to indemnification to which persons other than the directors and officers may be entitled by contract or otherwise.

(h) No indemnification or advance shall be made under this section, except as provided in subdivision (d) or paragraph (3) of subdivision (e), in any circumstance where it appears:

(1) That it would be inconsistent with a provision of the articles, bylaws, a resolution of the members or an agreement in effect at the time of the accrual of the alleged cause of action asserted in the proceeding in which the expenses were incurred or other amounts were paid, which prohibits or otherwise limits indemnification; or

(2) That it would be inconsistent with any condition expressly imposed by a court in approving a settlement.

(i) A corporation shall have power to purchase and maintain insurance on behalf of any agent of the corporation against any liability asserted against or incurred by the agent in that capacity or arising out of the agent's status as such whether or not the corporation would have the power to indemnify the agent against that liability under the provisions of this section.

(j) This section does not apply to any proceeding against any trustee, investment manager, or other fiduciary of a pension, deferred compensation, saving, thrift, or other retirement, incentive, or benefit plan, trust, or provision for any or all of the corporation's directors, officers, employees, and persons providing services to the corporation or any of its subsidiary or related or affiliated corporations, in the person's capacity as such, even though the person may also be an agent as defined in subdivision (a) of the employer corporation. A corporation shall have power to indemnify the trustee, investment manager or other fiduciary to the extent permitted by subdivision (e) of Section 12320.

   Ca. Corp. Code § 12377
Amended by Stats 2012 ch 61 (AB 2668),s 4, eff. 1/1/2013.

Chapter 3 - MEMBERS

Article 1 - ISSUANCE OF MEMBERSHIPS

Section 12400 - Consideration

Subject to the articles or bylaws, memberships may be issued by a corporation for no consideration or for such consideration as is determined by the board.

   Ca. Corp. Code § 12400
Repealed and added by Stats. 1982, Ch. 1625, Sec. 3. Operative January 1, 1984.

Section 12401 - Membership certificates; identity cards; disclosure document

(a) A corporation may issue, but is not required to issue, membership certificates. In the event that membership certificates are issued, the certificates shall state the information required to be contained in the disclosure document described in subdivision (b). Nothing in this section shall restrict a corporation from issuing identity cards or similar devices to members which serve to identify members qualifying to use facilities or services of the corporation.

(b) Except as provided in subdivision (e), prior to issuing a membership, the corporation shall provide the purchaser of a membership with a disclosure document. The disclosure document may be a prospectus, offering circular, brochure, or similar document, a specimen copy of the membership certificate, or a receipt which the corporation proposes to issue. The disclosure document shall contain the following information:

   (1) A statement that the corporation is a cooperative corporation.

(2) A statement that a copy of the corporation's articles and bylaws will be furnished without charge to a member or prospective member upon written request, and the address of the office of the corporation and the address to which such a written request is to be directed.

(3) If there are restrictions imposed by the corporation upon the transfer of membership, a statement to that effect and the restrictions imposed on transfer.

(4) If the corporation may levy dues, assessments, or membership or transfer fees, a statement to that effect and the conditions under which the corporation may make such a levy.

(5) If the member is required to contribute services to the corporation, a statement to that effect and the amount and nature of the services to be contributed to the corporation.

(6) Whether the membership is redeemable and the conditions under which the membership may be redeemed at the option of the corporation or the member.

(7) If the voting power or the proprietary interests of the members is unequal, a statement to that effect and the rule or rules by which the voting power and proprietary rights are to be determined.

(8) In lieu of specifying verbatim in the disclosure document the restrictions on the transfer of a membership, conditions of levy, amount and nature of services to be contributed, conditions under which memberships are redeemable, or the rules by which the voting power and proprietary rights of members are to be determined, the disclosure document may contain a statement that such information will be provided free of charge to a member or prospective member who requests it in writing. If the disclosure document contains such a statement it shall also set forth the address of the office of the corporation and the address to which such a request is to be directed.
(c) If the articles or bylaws are amended so that any statement required by subdivision (a) on outstanding membership certificates is no longer accurate, the board may cancel the outstanding certificates and issue in their place new certificates conforming to the articles or bylaws amendments.
(d) When new membership certificates are issued in accordance with subdivision (c), the board may order holders of outstanding certificates to surrender and exchange them for new certificates within a reasonable time fixed by the board. The board may further provide that the holder of the certificate to be surrendered shall not be entitled to exercise any of the rights of membership until the certificate is surrendered, but such rights shall be suspended only after notice of the order is given to the holder of the certificate and only until the certificate is surrendered. The requirement to surrender outstanding certificates may be enforced by civil action.
(e) A corporation shall issue a membership certificate, receipt, or written advice of

purchase to anyone purchasing a membership upon the member's first purchase of a membership of any class. No disclosure document need be provided to an existing member prior to the purchase of additional memberships if that member has previously been provided with a disclosure document which is accurate and correct as of the date of the purchase of the additional memberships.

(f) If a corporation does not issue new certificates as contemplated by subdivisions (c) and (d), and if a transferee of a membership certificate has not previously been provided with a disclosure statement which is accurate and correct as of the date of registration of the transfer, then the corporation shall provide a disclosure document to the transferee upon registration with the corporation of the transfer of the certificate.

   Ca. Corp. Code § 12401
Amended by Stats. 1983, Ch. 792, Sec. 19.

Section 12402 - New membership certificate in place of lost, stolen, or destroyed certificate

(a) A corporation may issue a new membership certificate in the place of any certificate theretofore issued by it, alleged to have been lost, stolen or destroyed, and the corporation may require the owner of the lost, stolen or destroyed certificate or the owner's legal representative to give the corporation a bond (or other adequate security) sufficient to indemnify it against any claim that may be made against it (including any expense or liability) on account of the alleged loss, theft or destruction of any such certificate or the issuance of such new certificate.

(b) If a corporation refuses to issue a new membership certificate or other certificate in place of one theretofore issued by it, or by any corporation of which it is the lawful successor, alleged to have been lost, stolen or destroyed, the owner of the lost, stolen or destroyed certificate or the owner's legal representative may bring an action in the superior court of the proper county for an order requiring the corporation to issue a new certificate in place of the one lost, stolen or destroyed.

   Ca. Corp. Code § 12402
Repealed and added by Stats. 1982, Ch. 1625, Sec. 3. Operative January 1, 1984.

Section 12403 - Admission to membership

(a) Except as provided in subdivision (b), or in its articles or bylaws, a corporation may admit any person to membership.

(b) A corporation may not admit its subsidiary to membership.

   Ca. Corp. Code § 12403
Repealed and added by Stats. 1982, Ch. 1625, Sec. 3. Operative January 1, 1984.

Section 12404 - Equal voting rights

Except as permitted in Sections 12314 and 12404.5, the voting power of members having voting rights shall be equal.

 Ca. Corp. Code § 12404
Amended by Stats 2015 ch 192 (AB 816),s 14, eff. 1/1/2016.

Section 12404.5 - Voting powers of worker-members of worker cooperative

(a) The worker-members of a worker cooperative shall have voting power as provided in subdivision (a) of Section 12253.

(b) Community investors have voting power only as provided in subdivision (c) of Section 12253.

 Ca. Corp. Code § 12404.5
Added by Stats 2015 ch 192 (AB 816),s 15, eff. 1/1/2016.

Section 12405 - No voting by proxy

There shall be no voting by proxy.

 Ca. Corp. Code § 12405
Amended by Stats. 1983, Ch. 792, Sec. 20.

Article 2 - TRANSFER OF MEMBERSHIPS

Section 12410 - Transfer of memberships

(a) Unless the articles or bylaws otherwise provide:

 (1) No member may transfer a membership or any right arising therefrom; and

 (2) Subject to the provisions of subdivision (b), Section 12422, and Section 12445, all rights as a member of the corporation cease upon the member's death or dissolution or the dissolution of a member which is a business entity.

(b) The articles or bylaws may provide for, or may authorize the board to provide for, the transfer of memberships, or of memberships within any class or classes, with or without restriction or limitation, including transfer upon the death, dissolution, merger, or reorganization of a member.

(c) Where transfer rights have been provided, no restriction of them shall be binding with respect to memberships issued prior to the adoption of the restriction, unless the holders of such memberships voted in favor of the restriction.

 Ca. Corp. Code § 12410
Amended by Stats. 1983, Ch. 792, Sec. 21.

Article 3 - TYPES OF MEMBERSHIPS

Section 12420 - Memberships having different rights privileges

preferences restrictions or conditions; additional classes of memberships

(a) Except as provided in subdivision (b), a corporation may issue memberships having different rights, privileges, preferences, restrictions, or conditions, as provided in its articles or bylaws. If the articles or bylaws authorize at least one class of voting memberships, a corporation may also authorize and issue additional classes of memberships, preferred or otherwise, that are divisible into a series or are nonvoting or both.

(b) All worker-members shall have the rights, privileges, preferences, restrictions, or conditions as provided in the articles or bylaws. This membership shall not be divided into partial memberships.

(c) A worker cooperative shall only make patronage distributions to the worker-member class.

   Ca. Corp. Code § 12420
Amended by Stats 2015 ch 192 (AB 816),s 16, eff. 1/1/2016.
Amended by Stats 2013 ch 538 (AB 1255),s 6, eff. 1/1/2014.

Section 12421 - Memberships having same rights, privileges, preferences, restrictions, and conditions

Except as provided in the articles or bylaws, all memberships shall have the same rights, privileges, preferences, restrictions and conditions.

   Ca. Corp. Code § 12421
Added by Stats. 1982, Ch. 1625, Sec. 3. Operative January 1, 1984.

Section 12422 - Redemption of memberships

(a) Unless the corporation's articles or bylaws so provide, memberships are not redeemable. A corporation may provide in its articles or bylaws for one or more classes or series of memberships which are redeemable, in whole or in part, for such consideration within such time or upon the happening of one or more specified events and upon the terms and conditions stated in the articles or bylaws. However, no membership shall actually be redeemed if prohibited by Chapter 4 (commencing with Section 12450).

(b) Nothing in this section shall prevent a corporation from creating a sinking fund or similar provision for, or entering into an agreement for, the redemption or purchase of its memberships to the extent permitted by Chapter 4 (commencing with Section 12450).

   Ca. Corp. Code § 12422
Amended by Stats 2013 ch 538 (AB 1255),s 7, eff. 1/1/2014.

Article 4 - TERMINATION OF MEMBERSHIPS

Section 12430 - Resignation

(a) A member may resign from membership at any time, although the articles or bylaws may require reasonable notice before the resignation is effective.
(b) This section shall not relieve the resigning member from any obligation for charges incurred, services or benefits actually rendered, dues, assessments or fees, or arising from contract, a condition to ownership of land, an obligation arising out of the ownership of land, or otherwise, and this section shall not diminish any right of the corporation to enforce any such obligation or obtain damages for its breach.
(c) A membership issued for a period of time shall expire when such period of time has elapsed unless the membership is renewed.

Ca. Corp. Code § 12430

Added by Stats. 1982, Ch. 1625, Sec. 3. Operative January 1, 1984.

Section 12431 - Expulsion, termination, or suspension

(a) No member may be expelled or suspended, and no membership or memberships may be terminated or suspended, except according to procedures satisfying the requirements of this section. An expulsion, termination, or suspension not in accord with this section shall be void and without effect.
(b) Any expulsion, suspension, or termination must be done in good faith and in a fair and reasonable manner. Any procedure that conforms to the requirements of subdivision (c) or (d) is fair and reasonable, but a court may also find other procedures to be fair and reasonable when the full circumstances of the suspension, termination, or expulsion are considered.
(c) A procedure is fair and reasonable if all of the following occur:

(1) The provisions of the procedure have been set forth in the articles or bylaws, or copies of such provisions are sent annually to all the members as required by the articles or bylaws.

(2) It provides the giving of 15 days' prior notice of the expulsion, suspension, or termination and the reasons therefor.

(3) It provides an opportunity for the member to be heard, orally or in writing, not less than five days before the effective date of the expulsion, suspension, or termination by a person or body authorized to decide that the proposed expulsion, termination, or suspension not take place.
(d) Any notice required under this section may be given by any method reasonably calculated to provide actual notice. Any notice given by mail must be given by first-class or registered mail sent to the last address of the members shown on the corporation's records.
(e) Any action challenging an expulsion, suspension, or termination of membership, including any claim alleging defective notice, must be commenced within one year after the date of the expulsion, suspension, or termination. In the event such an action

is successful the court may order any relief, including reinstatement, it finds equitable under the circumstances, but no vote of the members or of the board may be set aside solely because a person was at the time of the vote wrongfully excluded by virtue of the challenged expulsion, suspension, or termination, unless the court finds further that the wrongful expulsion, suspension, or termination was in bad faith and for the purpose, and with the effect, of wrongfully excluding the member from the vote or from the meeting at which the vote took place, so as to affect the outcome of the vote.

(f) This section governs only the procedures for expulsion, suspension, or termination and not the substantive grounds therefor. An expulsion, suspension, or termination based upon substantive grounds which violate contractual or other rights of the member or are otherwise unlawful is not made valid by compliance with this section.

(g) A member who is expelled or suspended or whose membership is terminated shall be liable for any charges incurred, services or benefits actually rendered, dues, assessments, or fees incurred before expulsion, suspension, or termination or arising from contract or otherwise.

   Ca. Corp. Code § 12431
Amended by Stats 2015 ch 192 (AB 816),s 17, eff. 1/1/2016.

Article 5 - RIGHTS AND OBLIGATIONS OF MEMBERS AND CREDITORS

Section 12440 - Liability

(a) A member of a corporation is not, as such, personally liable for the debts, liabilities, or obligations of the corporation.

(b) No person is liable for any obligation arising from membership unless the person was admitted to membership upon the person's application or with the person's consent.

(c) The ownership of an interest in real property, when a condition of its ownership is membership in a corporation, shall be considered consent to such membership for the purpose of this section.

   Ca. Corp. Code § 12440
Added by Stats. 1982, Ch. 1625, Sec. 3. Operative January 1, 1984.

Section 12441 - Dues, assessments, or fees

A corporation may levy dues, assessments, or fees upon its members pursuant to its articles or bylaws, but a member upon learning of them may avoid liability for them by promptly resigning from membership, except where the member is liable for them by contract, as a condition to ownership of an interest in real property, as an obligation arising out of the ownership of an interest in real property, or otherwise. Unless called to the attention of the member and agreed to in writing by the member, article or bylaw provisions authorizing such dues, assessments or fees do not, of themselves, create such liability. No action shall be brought by or on behalf of any creditor to levy or to require the levy of dues, assessments or fees upon the members of the corporation.

Ca. Corp. Code § 12441

Added by Stats. 1982, Ch. 1625, Sec. 3. Operative January 1, 1984.

Section 12442 - Liability of person holding membership as pledgee or membership in representative or fiduciary capacity

A person holding a membership as pledgee or a membership as executor, administrator, guardian, trustee, receiver or in any representative or fiduciary capacity is not personally liable for any unpaid balance of the purchase price of the membership, or for any amount owing to the corporation by the member, because the membership is so held, but the estate and funds in the hands of such fiduciary or representative are liable and the membership subject to sale therefor.

Ca. Corp. Code § 12442

Amended by Stats. 1983, Ch. 792, Sec. 22.

Section 12443 - Creditor's action

(a) No action shall be brought by or on behalf of any creditor to reach and apply the liability, if any, of a member to the corporation to pay the amount due on such member's membership or otherwise due to the corporation unless final judgment has been rendered in favor of the creditor against the corporation and execution has been returned unsatisfied in whole or in part or unless such proceedings would be useless.
(b) All creditors of the corporation, with or without reducing their claims to judgment, may intervene in any such creditor's action to reach and apply unpaid amounts due the corporation and any or all members who owe amounts to the corporation may be joined in such action. Several judgments may be rendered for and against the parties to the action or in favor of a receiver for the benefit of the respective parties thereto.
(c) All amounts paid by any member in any such action shall be credited on the unpaid balance due the corporation by such member.

Ca. Corp. Code § 12443

Added by Stats. 1982, Ch. 1625, Sec. 3. Operative January 1, 1984.

Section 12444 - No derogation of rights or remedies of creditor or member against promoter, member, director, officer, or corporation because of fraud or illegality

Nothing in this part shall be construed as in derogation of any rights or remedies which any creditor or member may have against any promoter, member, director, officer or the corporation because of participation in any fraud or illegality practiced upon such creditor or member by any such person or by the corporation or in derogation of any rights which the corporation may have by rescission, cancellation or otherwise because of any fraud or illegality practiced on it by any such person.

Ca. Corp. Code § 12444
Added by Stats. 1982, Ch. 1625, Sec. 3. Operative January 1, 1984.

Section 12445 - Manner of determining member's share of contributed capital or value of member's interest

The articles or bylaws shall prescribe:
(a) The manner of determining each member's share of the capital of the corporation contributed by the members and, if repayable, the time and manner for its repayment; and
(b) The manner of determining the value, if any, of the member's interest in the corporation apart from contributed capital and the time and manner of the corporation's purchase, if required, of such interest from a terminated member.

Ca. Corp. Code § 12445
Added by Stats. 1982, Ch. 1625, Sec. 3. Operative January 1, 1984.

Section 12446 - Proprietary interest in consumer cooperative corporation

(a) Subject to subdivision (b), Chapter 7 (commencing with Section 1500) of Title 10 of Part 3 of the Code of Civil Procedure shall not apply to any proprietary interest in a consumer cooperative corporation. Any proprietary interest that would otherwise escheat to the state pursuant to Chapter 7 (commencing with Section 1500) of Title 10 of Part 3 of the Code of Civil Procedure shall instead become the property of the corporation.
(b) Notwithstanding subdivision (a), no proprietary interest shall become the property of the corporation under this section unless the following requirements are satisfied:

   (1) The articles or bylaws shall specifically provide for the transfer of ownership of the otherwise escheated proprietary interests to the corporation.

   (2) At least 60 days prior notice of the proposed transfer of the proprietary interest to the corporation is given to the affected member by first-class or second-class mail to the last address of the member shown on the corporation's records, and by publication in a newspaper of general circulation in the county in which the corporation has its principal office. Notice given in the foregoing manner shall be deemed actual notice.

   (3) No proprietary interest shall become the property of the corporation under this section if written notice objecting thereto is received by the corporation from the affected member prior to the date of the proposed transfer.
(c) For purposes of this section, a "proprietary interest" shall mean and include any membership, membership certificate, membership share, or share certificate of any class or series representing a proprietary interest in, and issued by, the corporation

together with all accrued and unpaid dividends and patronage distributions relating thereto.

Ca. Corp. Code § 12446

Amended by Stats 2013 ch 538 (AB 1255),s 8, eff. 1/1/2014.

Chapter 4 - DISTRIBUTIONS

Article 1 - LIMITATIONS

Section 12450 - Applicability of chapter

This chapter does not apply to any proceeding for winding up and dissolution of corporations under Chapters 15 (commencing with Section 12620), 16 (commencing with Section 12630), and 17 (commencing with Section 12650).

Ca. Corp. Code § 12450

Repealed and added by Stats. 1982, Ch. 1625, Sec. 3. Operative January 1, 1984.

Section 12451 - Cap on distribution in any fiscal year

Distributions (Section 12235) in any fiscal year shall not exceed 15 percent, multiplied by contributions (whether by membership fees, capital credits, or otherwise) to capital.

Ca. Corp. Code § 12451

Amended by Stats. 1983, Ch. 792, Sec. 23.

Section 12452 - Purchase or redemption of memberships

A corporation may, subject to meeting the requirements of Section 12453 and any additional restrictions authorized by Section 12454, purchase or redeem memberships.

Ca. Corp. Code § 12452

Amended by Stats. 1985, Ch. 378, Sec. 7.

Section 12453 - No purchase or redemption of memberships, patronage distribution, or distribution if unable to meet liabilities

Neither a corporation nor any of its subsidiaries shall purchase or redeem memberships, or make a patronage distribution to members out of earnings of the corporation on nonmember patronage, or make a distribution, if the corporation or the subsidiary purchasing or redeeming memberships or making the distribution is, or as a result thereof would be, likely to be unable to meet its liabilities (except those whose payment is otherwise adequately provided for) as they mature.

Ca. Corp. Code § 12453

Repealed and added by Stats. 1982, Ch. 1625, Sec. 3. Operative January 1, 1984.

Section 12454 - Additional restrictions

Nothing in this chapter prohibits additional restrictions upon the purchase or redemption of a membership, upon distributions, or upon patronage distributions, by provision in a corporation's articles or bylaws or agreement entered into by the corporation.

Ca. Corp. Code § 12454

Added by Stats. 1982, Ch. 1625, Sec. 3. Operative January 1, 1984.

Section 12454.5 - Indivisible reserves account

(a) A worker cooperative may create an indivisible reserves account that shall not be distributed to members.

(b) Funds in the indivisible reserves account shall only derive from non-patronage-sourced income, in a manner provided in the articles or bylaws, or by the board, and shall be used as capital for the cooperative.

Ca. Corp. Code § 12454.5

Added by Stats 2015 ch 192 (AB 816),s 18, eff. 1/1/2016.

Article 2 - LIABILITY OF MEMBERS

Section 12455 - Liability for distribution

(a) Any person who with knowledge of facts indicating the impropriety thereof receives any distribution, including a payment in redemption of a membership, prohibited by this chapter is liable to the corporation for the amount so received by the person with interest thereon at the legal rate on judgments until paid.

(b) Any person who with knowledge of facts indicating the impropriety thereof receives any distribution, including a payment in redemption of a membership, prohibited by this chapter is liable to the corporation for the benefit of all of the creditors entitled to institute an action under subdivision (c) for the amount so received by the person with interest thereon at the legal rate on judgments until paid, but not exceeding the liabilities of the corporation owed to nonconsenting creditors at the time of the violation.

(c) Suit may be brought in the name of the corporation to enforce the liability to creditors arising under subdivision (b) for a violation of Section 12452 or 12453 against any or all persons liable by any one or more creditors of the corporation whose debts or claims arose prior to the time of the distribution and who have not consented thereto, whether or not they have reduced their claims to judgment.

(d) Any person sued under subdivision (b) may implead all other persons liable under subdivision (b) and may in the absence of fraud by the moving party compel contribution, either in that action or in an independent action against persons not joined in that action.

Ca. Corp. Code § 12455
Amended by Stats. 1984, Ch. 812, Sec. 17.

Chapter 5 - MEETINGS AND VOTING

Article 1 - GENERAL PROVISIONS

Section 12460 - Meetings of members

(a) Meetings of members may be held at a place within or without this state that is stated in or fixed in accordance with the bylaws. If no other place is so stated or fixed, meetings of members shall be held at the principal office of the corporation. Subject to any limitations in the articles or bylaws of the corporation, if authorized by the board of directors in its sole discretion, and subject to those guidelines and procedures as the board of directors may adopt, members not physically present in person at a meeting of members may, by electronic transmission by and to the corporation (Sections 20 and 21), electronic video screen communication, conference telephone, or other means of remote communication, participate in a meeting of members, be deemed present in person, and vote at a meeting of members, subject to subdivision (f).

(b) Except as provided in Section 12460.5, a regular meeting of members shall be held annually. In any year in which directors are elected, the election shall be held at the regular meeting unless the directors are chosen in some other manner authorized by law. Any other proper business may be transacted at the meeting.

(c) If a corporation fails to hold the regular meeting for a period of 60 days after the date designated therefor or, if no date has been designated, for a period of 15 months after the formation of the corporation or after its last regular meeting, or if the corporation fails to hold a written ballot for a period of 60 days after the date designated therefor, then the superior court of the proper county may summarily order the meeting to be held or the ballot to be conducted upon the application of a member, after notice to the corporation giving it an opportunity to be heard.

(d) The votes represented at a meeting called or by written ballot ordered pursuant to subdivision (c) and entitled to be cast on the business to be transacted shall constitute a quorum, notwithstanding any provision of the articles or bylaws or provision in this part to the contrary. The court may issue such orders as may be appropriate including, without limitation, orders designating the time and place of the meeting, the record date for determination of members entitled to vote, and the form of notice of the meeting.

(e) Special meetings of members for any lawful purpose may be called by the board, the chairperson of the board, the president, or other persons, if any, as are specified in the bylaws. In addition, special meetings of members for any lawful purpose may be called by 5 percent or more of the members, however, in a worker cooperative with more than four worker-members, a special meeting may only be called by the greater of three worker-members or 5 percent of the worker-members. In a worker cooperative with fewer than four worker-members, special meetings may be called by one worker-member.

(f) A meeting of the members may be conducted, in whole or in part, by electronic transmission by and to the corporation, by electronic video screen communication, conference telephone, or other means of remote communication if the corporation implements reasonable measures:

(1) to provide members a reasonable opportunity to participate in the meeting and to vote on matters submitted to the members, including an opportunity to read or hear the proceedings of the meeting concurrently with those proceedings,

(2) if any member votes or takes other action at the meeting by means of electronic transmission to the corporation, electronic video screen communication, conference telephone, or other means of remote communication, to maintain a record of that vote or action in its books and records, and

(3) to verify that each person participating remotely is a member. A corporation shall not conduct a meeting of members solely by electronic transmission by and to the corporation, electronic video screen communication, conference telephone, or other means of remote communication unless one or more of the following conditions apply:

(A) all of the members consent; or

(B) the board determines it is necessary or appropriate because of an emergency, as defined in paragraph (5) of subdivision (m) of Section 12320; or

(C) the meeting is conducted on or before June 30, 2022.
Ca. Corp. Code § 12460
Amended by Stats 2022 ch 617 (SB 1202),s 79, eff. 1/1/2023.
Amended by Stats 2022 ch 12 (AB 769),s 5, eff. 3/25/2022.
Amended by Stats 2021 ch 523 (AB 663),s 22, eff. 1/1/2022.
Amended by Stats 2015 ch 192 (AB 816),s 19, eff. 1/1/2016.
Amended by Stats 2004 ch 254 (SB 1306),s 38, eff. 1/1/2005

Section 12460.5 - Annual meeting of members not required

Notwithstanding Section 12460, a collective board worker cooperative shall not be required to hold an annual meeting of members.
Ca. Corp. Code § 12460.5
Added by Stats 2015 ch 192 (AB 816),s 20, eff. 1/1/2016.

Section 12461 - Notice of members' meeting or report

(a) Whenever members are required or permitted to take any action at a meeting, a written notice of the meeting shall be given not less than 10 nor more than 90 days before the date of the meeting to each member who, on the record date for notice of the meeting, is entitled to vote thereat; provided, however, that if notice is given by mail, and the notice is not mailed by first-class, registered, or certified mail, that notice shall be given not less than 20 days before the meeting. A worker cooperative shall provide notice of the meeting not less than 48 hours before the meeting if the meeting is a meeting of only worker-members, provided that the notice is delivered personally to every worker-member. Subject to subdivision (f), and subdivision (b) of Section 12462, that notice shall state the place, date, and time of the meeting, the means of electronic transmission by and to the corporation (Sections 20 and 21), electronic video screen communication, conference telephone, or other means of remote communication, if any, by which members may participate in that meeting, and (1) in the case of a special meeting, the general nature of the business to be transacted, and no other business may be transacted, or (2) in the case of the regular meeting, those matters which the board, at the time the notice is given, intends to present for action by the members, but, except as provided in subdivision (b) of Section 12462, any proper matter may be presented at the meeting for such action. The notice of any meeting at which directors are to be elected shall include the names of all those who are nominees at the time the notice is given to members.

(b)

(1) Notice of a members' meeting or any report shall be given personally, by electronic transmission by the corporation, or by mail or other means of written communication, addressed to a member at the address of such member appearing on the books of the corporation or given by the member to the corporation for purpose of notice, or if no such address appears or is given, at the place where the principal office of the corporation is located or by publication at least once in a newspaper of general circulation in the county in which the principal office is located. Notwithstanding the foregoing, the notice of a members' meeting or any report may be sent by electronic communication or other means of remote communication if the board determines it is necessary or appropriate because of an emergency, as defined in paragraph (5) of subdivision (m) of Section 12320. An affidavit of giving of any notice or report as permitted because of an emergency or otherwise in accordance with the provisions of this part, executed by the secretary, assistant secretary, or any transfer agent, shall be prima facie evidence of the giving of the notice or report.

(2) If any notice or report addressed to the member at the address of such member appearing on the books of the corporation is returned to the corporation by the United States Postal Service marked to indicate the United States Postal Service is unable to deliver the notice or report to the member at such address, all future notices or reports shall be deemed to have been duly given without further mailing if the same shall be available for the member upon written demand of the member at the principal office of the corporation for a period of one year from the date of the giving of the notice or report to all other members.

(3)

(A)Notice given by electronic transmission by the corporation under this subdivision shall be valid only if it complies with Section 20. Notwithstanding the foregoing, notice shall not be given by electronic transmission by the corporation under this subdivision after either of the following:

(i)The corporation is unable to deliver two consecutive notices to the member by that means.

(ii)The inability to so deliver the notices to the member becomes known to the secretary, any assistant secretary, the transfer agent, or other person responsible for the giving of the notice.

(B)This paragraph shall not apply if notices are provided by electronic communication or other means of remote communication as permitted because of an emergency.

(c)Upon request in writing to the corporation addressed to the attention of the chairperson of the board, president, vice president, or secretary by any person (other than the board) entitled to call a special meeting of members, the officer forthwith shall cause notice to be given to the members entitled to vote that a meeting will be held at a time fixed by the board not less than 35 nor more than 90 days after the receipt of the request. If the notice is not given within 20 days after receipt of the request, the persons entitled to call the meeting may give the notice or the superior court of the proper county shall summarily order the giving of the notice, after notice to the corporation giving it an opportunity to be heard. The court may issue such orders as may be appropriate, including, without limitation, orders designating the time and place of the meeting, the record date for determination of members entitled to vote, and the form of notice.

(d)When a members' meeting is adjourned to another time or place, unless the bylaws otherwise require and except as provided in this subdivision, notice need not be given of the adjourned meeting if the time and place thereof (or the means of electronic transmission by and to the corporation or electronic video screen communication, conference telephone, or other means of remote communication, if any, by which members may participate) are announced at the meeting at which the adjournment is taken. At the adjourned meeting the corporation may transact any business which might have been transacted at the original meeting. If the adjournment is for more than 45 days or if after the adjournment a new record date is fixed for the adjourned meeting, a notice of the adjourned meeting shall be given to each member of record entitled to vote at the meeting.

(e) The transactions of any meeting of members however called and noticed, and wherever held, are as valid as though had at a meeting duly held after regular call and notice, if a quorum is present, and if, either before or after the meeting, each of the persons entitled to vote, not present in person, provides a waiver of notice or consent to the holding of the meeting or an approval of the minutes thereof in writing. All such waivers, consents, and approvals shall be filed with the corporate records or made a part of the minutes of the meeting. Attendance of a person at a meeting shall constitute a waiver of notice of and presence at such meeting, except when the person objects, at the beginning of the meeting, to the transaction of any business because the meeting is not lawfully called or convened and except that attendance at a meeting is not a waiver of any right to object to the consideration of matters required by this part to be included in the notice but not so included, if such objection is expressly made at the meeting. Neither the business to be transacted at nor the purpose of any regular or special meeting of members need be specified in any written waiver of notice, consent to the holding of the meeting, or approval of the minutes thereof, unless otherwise provided in the articles or bylaws, except as provided in subdivision (f).

(f) Any approval of the members required under Section 12362, 12364, 12373, 12502, or 12658 other than unanimous approval by those entitled to vote, shall be valid only if the general nature of the proposal so approved was stated in the notice of meeting or in any written waiver of notice.

(g)A court may find that notice not given in conformity with this section is still valid, if it was given in a fair and reasonable manner.

(h) Subject to the provisions of subdivision (i), and unless prohibited by the articles or bylaws, before any regular or special meeting of members, the board may authorize distribution of a written ballot to every member entitled to vote at the meeting. Such ballot shall set forth the action proposed to be taken at the meeting, shall provide an opportunity to specify approval or disapproval of the proposed action, and shall state that unless revoked by the member voting in person at the meeting, the ballot will be counted if received by the corporation on or before the time of the meeting with respect to which it was sent. If ballots are so distributed with respect to a meeting, the number of members voting at the meeting by unrevoked written ballots shall be deemed present at the meeting for purposes of determining the existence of a quorum pursuant to subdivision (a) of Section 12462 but only with respect to the proposed action referred to in the ballots. These ballots shall be distributed in a manner consistent with the requirements of subdivision (b) and Section 12464.

(i) Unless prohibited by the articles or bylaws, written ballots may be distributed in a manner contemplated by subdivision (h) with respect to the election of directors, except that no ballots may be so distributed with respect to the election of directors if cumulative voting is permitted pursuant to Section 12484.

Ca. Corp. Code § 12461

Amended by Stats 2022 ch 617 (SB 1202),s 80, eff. 1/1/2023.
Amended by Stats 2021 ch 523 (AB 663),s 23, eff. 1/1/2022.

Amended by Stats 2015 ch 192 (AB 816),s 21, eff. 1/1/2016.
Amended by Stats 2004 ch 254 (SB 1306),s 39, eff. 1/1/2005

Section 12462 - Quorum

(a) The lesser of 250 members or members representing 5 percent of the voting power, shall constitute a quorum at a meeting of members, but, subject to subdivisions (b) and (c), a bylaw may set a different quorum. Any bylaw amendment to increase the quorum may be adopted only by approval of the members (Section 12224). If a quorum is present, the affirmative vote of the majority of the voting power represented at the meeting, entitled to vote, and voting on any matter shall be the act of the members unless the vote of a greater number or voting by classes is required by this part or the articles or bylaws.

(b) Where a corporation is authorized to conduct a meeting with a quorum of less than one-third of the voting power, then the only matters that may be voted upon at any regular meeting actually attended by less than one-third of the voting power are matters notice of the general nature of which was given, pursuant to the first sentence of subdivision (a) of Section 12461.

(c) Subject to subdivision (b), the members present at a duly called or held meeting at which a quorum is present may continue to transact business until adjournment notwithstanding the withdrawal of enough members to leave less than a quorum, if any action taken (other than adjournment) is approved by at least a majority of the members required to constitute a quorum or, if required by this division or the articles or the bylaws, the vote of the greater number or voting by classes.

(d) In the absence of a quorum, any meeting of members may be adjourned from time to time by the vote of a majority of the votes represented in person, but no other business may be transacted, except as provided in subdivision (c).

Ca. Corp. Code § 12462
Amended by Stats 2000 ch 485 (AB 1895), s 17, eff. 1/1/2001.

Section 12463 - Approval by written ballot

(a) Subject to subdivision (e), and unless prohibited in the articles or bylaws any action which may be taken at any regular or special meeting of members may be taken without a meeting if the corporation distributes a written ballot to every member entitled to vote on the matter. Unless otherwise provided by the articles or bylaws and if approved by the board of directors, that ballot and any related material may be sent by electronic transmission by the corporation (Section 20) and responses may be returned to the corporation by electronic transmission to the corporation (Section 21). That ballot shall set forth the proposed action, provide an opportunity to specify approval or disapproval of any proposal, and provide a reasonable time within which to return the ballot to the corporation.

(b) Approval by written ballot pursuant to this section shall be valid only when the number of votes cast by ballot within the time period specified equals or exceeds the quorum required to be present at a meeting authorizing the action, and the number of approvals equals or exceeds the number of votes that would be required to approve at a meeting at which the total number of votes cast was the same as the number of votes cast by ballot.

(c) Ballots shall be solicited in a manner consistent with the requirements of subdivision (b) of Section 12461 and Section 12464. All such solicitations shall indicate the number of responses needed to meet the quorum requirement and, with respect to ballots other than for the election of directors, shall state the percentage of approvals necessary to pass the measure submitted. The solicitation must specify the time by which the ballot must be received in order to be counted.

(d) Unless otherwise provided in the articles or bylaws, a written ballot may not be revoked.

(e) Directors may be elected by written ballot under this section, where authorized by the articles or bylaws, except that election by written ballot may not be authorized where the directors are elected by cumulative voting pursuant to Section 12484. When directors are to be elected by written ballot and the articles or bylaws prescribe a nomination procedure, the procedure may provide for a date for the close of nominations prior to printing and distributing of the written ballots.

(f) The secretary shall cause a vote to be taken by written ballot upon any action or recommendation proposed in writing by 20 percent of the members of the corporation.

Ca. Corp. Code § 12463
Amended by Stats 2004 ch 254 (SB 1306),s 40, eff. 1/1/2005

Section 12464 - Form of written ballot

(a) Any form of written ballot distributed to 10 or more members of a corporation with 100 or more members shall afford an opportunity on the form of written ballot to specify a choice between approval and disapproval of each matter or group of related matters intended, at the time the written ballot is distributed, to be acted upon by such written ballot, and shall provide, subject to reasonable specified conditions, that where the person solicited specifies a choice with respect to any such matter the vote shall be cast in accordance therewith.

(b) In any election of directors, any form of written ballot in which the directors to be voted upon are named therein as candidates and which is marked by a member "withhold" or otherwise marked in a manner indicating that the authority to vote for the election of directors is withheld shall not be voted for the election of a director.

(c) Failure to comply with this section shall not invalidate any corporate action taken, but may be the basis for challenging any written ballot and the superior court may compel compliance therewith at the suit of any member.

Ca. Corp. Code § 12464
Added by Stats. 1982, Ch. 1625, Sec. 3. Operative January 1, 1984.

Section 12465 - Court order that meeting be called or that written ballot

be authorized

(a) If for any reason it is impractical or unduly difficult for any corporation to call or conduct a meeting of its members, delegates or directors, or otherwise obtain their consent, in the manner prescribed by its articles or bylaws, or this part, then the superior court of the proper county, upon petition of a director, officer, delegate or member, may order that such a meeting be called or that a written ballot or other form of obtaining the vote of members, delegates or directors be authorized, in such a manner as the court finds fair and equitable under the circumstances.

(b) The court shall, in an order issued pursuant to this section, provide for a method of notice reasonably designed to give actual notice to all parties who would be entitled to notice of a meeting held pursuant to the articles, bylaws and this part, whether or not the method results in actual notice to every such person, or conforms to the notice requirements that would otherwise apply. In a proceeding under this section the court may determine who the members or directors are.

(c) The order issued pursuant to this section may dispense with any requirement relating to the holding of and voting at meetings or obtaining of votes, including any requirement as to quorums or as to the number or percentage of votes needed for approval, that would otherwise be imposed by the articles, bylaws, or this part.

(d) Wherever practical any order issued pursuant to this section shall limit the subject matter of the meetings or other forms of consent authorized to items, including amendments to the articles or bylaws, the resolution of which will or may enable the corporation to continue managing its affairs without further resort to this section. However, an order under this section may also authorize the obtaining of whatever votes and approvals are necessary for the dissolution, merger, sale of assets or reorganization of the corporation.

(e) Any meeting or other method of obtaining the vote of members, delegates or directors conducted pursuant to an order issued under this section, and which complies with all the provisions of such order, is for all purposes a valid meeting or vote, as the case may be, and shall have the same force and effect as if it complied with every requirement imposed by the articles, bylaws, and this part.

Ca. Corp. Code § 12465
Amended by Stats. 1986, Ch. 766, Sec. 34.

Section 12466 - Name signed on ballot, consent, or waiver

(a) If the name signed on a ballot, consent or waiver corresponds to the name of a member, the corporation if acting in good faith is entitled to accept the ballot, consent, or waiver and give it effect as the act of the member.

(b) If the name signed on a ballot, consent, or waiver does not correspond to the record name of a member, the corporation if acting in good faith is nevertheless entitled to accept the vote, consent, or waiver and give it effect as the act of the member if any of the following occur:

(1) The member is an entity and the name signed purports to be that of an officer or agent of the entity.

(2) The name signed purports to be that of an attorney-in-fact of the member and if the corporation requests, evidence acceptable to the corporation of the signatory's authority to sign for the member has been presented with respect to the vote, consent or waiver.

(3) Two or more persons hold the membership as cotenants or fiduciaries and the name signed purports to be the name of at least one of the coholders and the person signing appears to be acting on behalf of all the coholders.

(c) The corporation is entitled to reject a ballot, consent, waiver, or proxy appointment if the secretary or other officer or agent authorized to tabulate votes, acting in good faith, has a reasonable basis for doubt concerning the validity of the signature or the signatory's authority to sign for the member.

(d) The corporation and any officer or agent thereof who accepts or rejects a ballot, consent, waiver, or proxy appointment in good faith and in accordance with the standards of this section shall not be liable in damages to the member for the consequences of the acceptance or rejection.

(e) Corporate action based on the acceptance or rejection of a ballot, consent, waiver, or proxy appointment under this section is valid unless a court of competent jurisdiction determines otherwise.

Ca. Corp. Code § 12466

Added by Stats. 1996, Ch. 589, Sec. 51. Effective January 1, 1997.

Article 2 - ADDITIONAL PROVISIONS RELATING TO ELECTION OF DIRECTORS

Section 12470 - Reasonable nomination and election procedures

As to directors elected by members, there shall be available to the members reasonable nomination and election procedures given the nature, size and operations of the corporation.

Ca. Corp. Code § 12470

Amended by Stats. 1996, Ch. 589, Sec. 52. Effective January 1, 1997.

Section 12473 - Equal amount of space in material soliciting vote in corporate publication

Where a corporation distributes any material soliciting a vote for any nominee for director in any publication owned or controlled by the corporation, it shall make available to each other nominee, in the same material, an equal amount of space, with equal prominence, to be used by the nominee for a purpose reasonably related to the election.

Ca. Corp. Code § 12473
Added by Stats. 1982, Ch. 1625, Sec. 3. Operative January 1, 1984.

Section 12474 - Mailing to members

Upon written request by any nominee for election to the board and the payment of the reasonable costs of mailing (including postage), a corporation shall within 10 business days after such request (provided payment has been made) mail to all members, or such portion of them as the nominee may reasonably specify, any material, which the nominee may furnish and which is reasonably related to the election, unless the corporation within five business days after the request allows the nominee, at the corporation's option, the rights set forth in either paragraph (1) or (2) of subdivision (a) of Section 12600.

Ca. Corp. Code § 12474
Added by Stats. 1982, Ch. 1625, Sec. 3. Operative January 1, 1984.

Section 12475 - Declining to publish or mail material; liability

(a) Except as provided in subdivision (c), no corporation may decline to publish or mail material, otherwise required to be published or mailed on behalf of any nominee under this article, on the basis of the content of such material.

(b) Neither the corporation, nor its agents, officers, directors, or employees, may be held criminally liable, liable for any negligence (active or passive) or otherwise liable for damages to any person on account of any material which is supplied by a nominee for director and which it mails or publishes pursuant to Section 12473 or 12474 but the nominee on whose behalf such material was published or mailed shall be liable and shall indemnify and hold the corporation, its agents, officers, directors, and employees and each of them harmless from all demands, costs, including reasonable legal fees and expenses, claims, damages and causes of action arising out of such material or any such mailing or publication.

(c) Nothing in this section shall prevent a corporation or any of its agents, officers, directors, or employees from seeking a court order relieving the corporation from its obligation under Section 12473 or 12474 on the ground the material will expose the moving party to liability.

Ca. Corp. Code § 12475
Added by Stats. 1982, Ch. 1625, Sec. 3. Operative January 1, 1984.

Section 12476 - Expenditure of corporation funds prohibited

Without authorization of the board, no corporation funds may be expended to support a nominee for director after there are more people nominated for director than can be elected.

Ca. Corp. Code § 12476
Added by Stats. 1982, Ch. 1625, Sec. 3. Operative January 1, 1984.

Section 12477 - Action challenging validity of election, appointment, or removal of director

An action challenging the validity of any election, appointment or removal of a director or directors must be commenced within nine months after the election, appointment or removal. If no such action is commenced, in the absence of fraud, any election, appointment or removal of a director is conclusively presumed valid nine months thereafter if the only defect in the election, appointment or removal is the failure to give notice as provided in this part or in the corporation's articles or bylaws.

Ca. Corp. Code § 12477
Added by Stats. 1982, Ch. 1625, Sec. 3. Operative January 1, 1984.

Chapter 6 - VOTING OF MEMBERSHIPS

Section 12480 - One vote

Except as provided in Sections 12314 and 12484, each member entitled to vote shall be entitled to one vote on each matter submitted to a vote of the members. Single memberships in which two or more persons have an indivisible interest shall be voted as provided in Section 12482.

Ca. Corp. Code § 12480
Added by Stats. 1982, Ch. 1625, Sec. 3. Operative January 1, 1984.

Section 12481 - Record date

(a) The bylaws may provide or, in the absence of such provision, the board may fix, in advance, a date as the record date for the purpose of determining the members entitled to notice of any meeting of members. Such record date shall not be more than 60 nor less than 10 days before the date of the meeting. If no record date is fixed, members at the close of business on the business day preceding the day on which notice is given or, if notice is waived, at the close of business on the business day preceding the day on which the meeting is held are entitled to notice of a meeting of members. A determination of members entitled to notice of a meeting of members shall apply to any adjournment of the meeting unless the board fixes a new record date for the adjourned meeting.

(b) The bylaws may provide or, in the absence of such provision, the board may fix, in advance, a date as the record date for the purpose of determining the members entitled to vote at a meeting of members. Such record date shall not be more than 60 days before the date of the meeting. Such record date shall also apply in the case of an ajournment of the meeting unless the board fixes a new record date for the adjourned meeting. If no record date is fixed, members on the day of the meeting who are otherwise eligible to vote are entitled to vote at the meeting of members or, in the case of an adjourned meeting, members on the day of the adjourned meeting who are otherwise eligible to vote are entitled to vote at the adjourned meeting of members.

(c) The bylaws may provide or, in the absence of such provision, the board may fix, in advance, a date as the record date for the purpose of determining the members entitled to cast written ballots (Section 12463). Such record date shall not be more than 60 days before the day on which the first written ballot is mailed or solicited. If no record date is fixed, members on the day the first written ballot is mailed or solicited who are otherwise eligible to vote are entitled to cast written ballots.

(d) The bylaws may provide or, in the absence of such provision, the board may fix, in advance, a date as the record date for the purpose of determining the members entitled to exercise any rights in respect of any other lawful action. Such record date shall not be more than 60 days prior to such other action. If no record date is fixed, members at the close of business on the day on which the board adopts the resolution relating thereto, or the 60th day prior to the date of such other action, whichever is later, are entitled to exercise such rights.

Ca. Corp. Code § 12481

Added by Stats. 1982, Ch. 1625, Sec. 3. Operative January 1, 1984.

Section 12482 - Memberships in names of two or more members

Unless otherwise provided in the articles or bylaws, if a membership stands of record in the names of two or more persons, whether fiduciaries, members of a partnership, joint tenants, tenants in common, spouses as community property, tenants by the entirety, persons entitled to vote under a voting agreement or otherwise, or if two or more persons have the same fiduciary relationship respecting the same membership, unless the secretary of the corporation is given written notice to the contrary and is furnished with a copy of the instrument or order appointing them or creating the relationship wherein it is so provided, their acts with respect to voting shall have the following effect:

(a) If only one vote, such act binds all; or

(b) If more than one vote, the act of the majority so voting binds all.

Ca. Corp. Code § 12482

Amended by Stats 2016 ch 50 (SB 1005),s 24, eff. 1/1/2017.

Section 12483 - Inspectors of election

(a) In advance of any meeting of members the board may appoint inspectors of election to act at the meeting and any adjournment thereof. If inspectors of election are not so appointed, or if any persons so appointed fail to appear or refuse to act, the chairperson of any meeting of members may, and on the request of any member shall, appoint inspectors of election (or persons to replace those who so fail or refuse) at the meeting. The number of inspectors shall be either one or three. If appointed at a meeting on the request of one or more members, the majority of members represented in person shall determine whether one or three inspectors are to be appointed.

(b) The inspectors of election shall determine the number of memberships outstanding and the voting power of each, the number represented at the meeting, the existence of a quorum, receive votes, ballots or consents, hear and determine all challenges and questions in any way arising in connection with the right to vote, count and tabulate all votes or consents, determine when the polls shall close, determine the result and do such acts as may be proper to conduct the election or vote with fairness to all members.

(c) The inspectors of election shall perform their duties impartially, in good faith, to the best of their ability and as expeditiously as is practical. If there are three inspectors of election, the decision, act or certificate of a majority is effective in all respects as the decision, act or certificate of all. Any report or certificate made by the inspectors of election is prima facie evidence of the facts stated therein.

Ca. Corp. Code § 12483

Amended by Stats 2022 ch 617 (SB 1202),s 81, eff. 1/1/2023.
Added by Stats. 1982, Ch. 1625, Sec. 3. Operative January 1, 1984.

Section 12484 - Cumulative voting

(a) Except in the case of a central organization, cumulative voting shall not be permitted. In the case of a central organization, if the articles or bylaws authorize cumulative voting, but not otherwise, every member entitled to vote at any election of directors may cumulate such member's votes and give one candidate a number of votes equal to the number of directors to be elected multiplied by the number of votes to which the member is entitled, or distribute the member's votes on the same principle among as many candidates as the member thinks fit. An article or bylaw provision authorizing cumulative voting may be repealed or amended only by approval of the members (Section 12224), except that the governing article or bylaw provision may require the vote of a greater proportion of the members, or of the members of any class, for its repeal.

(b) No member shall be entitled to cumulate votes for a candidate or candidates unless such candidate's name or candidates' names have been placed in nomination prior to the voting and the member has given notice at the meeting prior to the voting of the member's intention to cumulate votes. If any one member has given such notice, all members may cumulate their votes for candidates in nomination.

(c) In any election of directors of a central organization by cumulative voting, the candidates receiving the highest number of votes are elected, subject to any lawful provision specifying election by classes. In any other election of directors, unless otherwise provided in the articles or bylaws, the candidates receiving the highest number of votes are elected.

(d) Elections for directors need not be by ballot unless a member demands election by ballot at the meeting and before the voting begins or unless the bylaws so require.

Ca. Corp. Code § 12484

Amended by Stats. 1984, Ch. 812, Sec. 17.5.

Section 12485 - Action to determine validity of election or appointment of director

(a) Upon the filing of an action therefor by any director or member or by any person who had the right to vote in the election at issue, the superior court of the proper county shall determine the validity of any election or appointment of any director of any corporation.

(b) Upon the filing of the complaint, and before any further proceedings are had, the court shall enter an order fixing a date for the hearing, which shall be within five days unless for good cause shown a later date is fixed, and requiring notice of the date for the hearing and a copy of the complaint to be served upon the corporation and upon the person whose purported election or appointment is questioned and upon any person (other than the plaintiff) whom the plaintiff alleges to have been elected or appointed, in the manner in which a summons is required to be served, or, if the court so directs, by registered mail; and the court may make such further requirements as to notice as appear to be proper under the circumstances.

(c) The court, consistent with the provisions of this part and in conformity with the articles and bylaws to the extent feasible, may determine the person entitled to the office of director or may order a new election to be held or appointment to be made, may determine the validity, effectiveness and construction of voting agreements and voting trusts, the validity of the issuance of memberships and the right of persons to vote and may direct such other relief as may be just and proper.

Ca. Corp. Code § 12485
Added by Stats. 1982, Ch. 1625, Sec. 3. Operative January 1, 1984.

Chapter 7 - MEMBERS' DERIVATIVE ACTIONS

Section 12490 - Members' derivative actions

(a) Subdivisions (c) through (f) notwithstanding, no motion to require security shall be granted in an action brought by the lesser of 100 members or 5 percent of the members.

(b) No action may be instituted or maintained in the right of any corporation by any member of such corporation unless both of the following conditions exist:

(1) The plaintiff alleges in the complaint that plaintiff was a member at the time of the transaction or any part thereof of which plaintiff complains, or that plaintiff's membership thereafter devolved upon plaintiff by operation of law from a holder who was a holder at the time of transaction or any part thereof complained of; and

(2) The plaintiff alleges in the complaint with particularity plaintiff's efforts to secure from the board such action as plaintiff desires, or the reasons for not making such effort, and alleges further that plaintiff has either informed the corporation or

the board in writing of the ultimate facts of each cause of action against each defendant or delivered to the corporation or the board a true copy of the complaint which plaintiff proposes to file.

(c) Subject to subdivision (a), in any action referred to in subdivision (b), at any time within 30 days after service of summons upon the corporation or upon any defendant who is an officer or director of the corporation, or held such office at the time of the acts complained of, the corporation or such defendant may move the court for an order, upon notice and hearing, requiring the plaintiff to furnish security as hereinafter provided. The motion shall be based upon one or both of the following grounds:

(1) That there is no reasonable possibility that the prosecution of the cause of action alleged in the complaint against the moving party will benefit the corporation or its members economically or otherwise.

(2) That the moving party, if other than the corporation, did not participate in the transaction complained of in any capacity. The court on application of the corporation or any defendant may, for good cause shown, extend the 30-day period for an additional period or periods not exceeding 60 days.

(d) At the hearing upon any motion pursuant to subdivision (c), the court shall consider such evidence, written or oral, by witnesses or affidavit, as may be material (1) to the ground or grounds upon which the motion is based, or (2) to a determination of the probable reasonable expenses, including attorneys' fees, of the corporation and the moving party which will be incurred in the defense of the action. If the court determines, after hearing the evidence adduced by the parties, that the moving party has established a probability in support of any of the grounds upon which the motion is based, the court shall fix the nature and amount of security, not to exceed fifty thousand dollars ($50,000), to be furnished by the plaintiff for reasonable expenses, including attorneys' fees, which may be incurred by the moving party and the corporation in connection with the action, including expenses for which the corporation may become liable pursuant to Section 12377. A ruling by the court on the motion shall not be a determination of any issue in the action or of the merits thereof. The amount of the security may thereafter be increased or decreased in the discretion of the court upon a showing that the security provided has or may become inadequate or is excessive, but the court may not in any event increase the total amount of the security beyond fifty thousand dollars ($50,000) in the aggregate for all defendants. If the court, upon any such motion, makes a determination that security shall be furnished by the plaintiff as to any one or more defendants, the action shall be dismissed as to such defendant or defendants, unless the security required by the court shall have been furnished within such reasonable time as may be fixed by the court. The corporation and the moving party shall have recourse to the security in such amount as the court shall determine upon the termination of the action.

(e) If the plaintiff shall, either before or after a motion is made pursuant to subdivision (c), or any order or determination pursuant to such motion, post good and sufficient bond or bonds in the aggregate amount of fifty thousand dollars ($50,000) to secure the reasonable expenses of the parties entitled to make the motion, the plaintiff has complied with the requirements of this section and with any order for security theretofore made pursuant hereto, and any such motion then pending shall be dismissed and no further or additional bond or other security shall be required.

(f) If a motion is filed pursuant to subdivision (c), no pleadings need be filed by the corporation or any other defendant and the prosecution of the action shall be stayed until 10 days after the motion has been disposed of.

Ca. Corp. Code § 12490

Added by Stats. 1982, Ch. 1625, Sec. 3. Operative January 1, 1984.

Chapter 8 - AMENDMENT OF ARTICLES

Section 12500 - Amendment of articles

(a) By complying with the provisions of this chapter, a corporation may amend its articles from time to time, in any and as many respects as may be desired, so long as its articles as amended contain only such provisions as it would be lawful to insert in original articles filed at the time of the filing of the amendment or as authorized by Section 12504 and, if a change in the rights of members or an exchange, reclassification or cancellation of memberships is to be made, such provisions as may be necessary to effect such change, exchange, reclassification or cancellation. It is the intent of the Legislature in adopting this section to exercise to the fullest extent the reserve power of the state over corporations and to authorize any amendment of the articles covered by the preceding sentence regardless of whether any provision contained in the amendment was permissible at the time of the original incorporation of the corporation.

(b) A corporation shall not amend its articles to add any statement or to alter any statement which may appear in the original articles of the initial street address and initial mailing address of the corporation, the names and addresses of the first directors, or the name and address of the initial agent, except to correct an error in the statement or to delete the information after the corporation has filed a statement under Section 12570.

Ca. Corp. Code § 12500

Amended by Stats 2012 ch 494 (SB 1532),s 29, eff. 1/1/2013.

Section 12501 - Adoption by writing signed by majority of incorporators

Any amendment of the articles may be adopted by a writing signed by a majority of the incorporators so long as:

(a) No directors were named in the original articles;

(b) No directors have been elected; and

(c) The corporation has no members.

Ca. Corp. Code § 12501

Added by Stats. 1982, Ch. 1625, Sec. 3. Operative January 1, 1984.

Section 12502 - Approval of board

(a) Except as provided in this section or Section 12503, amendments may be adopted if approved by the board and approved by the members before or after the approval by the board.

(b) Notwithstanding subdivision (a), the following amendments may be adopted by approval of the board alone:

(1) An amendment extending the corporate existence or making the corporate existence perpetual, if the corporation was organized prior to August 14, 1929.

(2) An amendment deleting the initial street address and initial mailing address of the corporation, the names and addresses of the first directors, or the name and address of the initial agent.

(3) Any amendment, at a time the corporation has no members.

(4) Any amendment authorized in the articles pursuant to subdivision (c) of Section 12313 fixing the rights, privileges, preferences, restrictions, and conditions attaching to any wholly unissued class of memberships.

(5) Any amendment authorized in the articles pursuant to subdivision (c) of Section 12313 fixing the designation, number of memberships and the rights, privileges, preferences, restrictions, and conditions attaching to any wholly unissued series of memberships, or an increase or decrease in the number of memberships of any series.

(c) Whenever the articles require for corporate action the approval of a particular class of members or of a larger proportion of, or all of, the votes of any class, or of a larger proportion of, or all of, the directors, than is otherwise required by this part, the provision in the articles requiring a greater vote shall not be altered, amended or repealed except by the class or the greater vote, unless otherwise provided in the articles.

Ca. Corp. Code § 12502

Amended by Stats 2013 ch 538 (AB 1255),s 9, eff. 1/1/2014.

Amended by Stats 2012 ch 494 (SB 1532),s 30, eff. 1/1/2013.

Section 12503 - Approval by members

(a) An amendment shall also be approved by the members (Section 12224) of a class, whether or not the class is entitled to vote thereon by the provisions of the articles, if the amendment would do any of the following:

(1) Materially and adversely affect the rights, privileges, preferences, restrictions or conditions of that class as to voting, dissolution, redemption or transfer, or the obligations of that class, in a manner different than such action affects another class.

(2) Materially and adversely affect such class as to voting, dissolution, redemption or transfer by changing the rights, privileges, preferences, restrictions or conditions of another class.

(3) Increase the number of memberships authorized for the class.

(4) Increase the number of memberships authorized for another class.

(5) Effect an exchange, reclassification or cancellation of all or part of the memberships of the class.

(6) Authorize a new class of memberships.
(b) An amendment shall also be approved by the members of a series whether or not the series is entitled to vote thereon by the articles or bylaws if the series is adversely affected by the amendment in a different manner than other shares of the same class.
   Ca. Corp. Code § 12503
Amended by Stats 2013 ch 538 (AB 1255),s 10, eff. 1/1/2014.

Section 12504 - Change of status

(a)A corporation may amend its articles to change its status to that of a nonprofit public benefit corporation, a nonprofit mutual benefit corporation, a nonprofit religious corporation, a business corporation, or a social purpose corporation by complying with this section and the other sections of this chapter.
(b) Except as authorized by Section 12501 or unless the corporation has no members, an amendment to change its status to a nonprofit public benefit corporation or a nonprofit religious corporation shall:

(1) be approved by the members (Section 12224), and the fairness of the amendment to the members shall be approved by the Commissioner of Financial Protection and Innovation pursuant to Section 25142; or

(2) be approved by the members (Section 12224) in an election conducted by written ballot pursuant to Section 12463 in which no negative votes are cast; or

(3) be approved by 100 percent of the voting power.
(c) Amended articles authorized by this section shall include the provisions which would have been required (other than the initial street address and initial mailing

address of the corporation and the name of the initial agent for service of process if a statement has been filed pursuant to Section 12570), and may in addition only include those provisions which would have been permitted, in original articles filed by the type of corporation (nonprofit public benefit, nonprofit mutual benefit, nonprofit religious, business, or social purpose) into which the corporation is changing its status.

(d)At the time of filing a certificate of amendment to change status to a nonprofit public benefit corporation, the Secretary of State shall make available the filed certificate to the Attorney General.

Ca. Corp. Code § 12504

Amended by Stats 2022 ch 617 (SB 1202),s 82, eff. 1/1/2023.
Amended by Stats 2022 ch 452 (SB 1498),s 59, eff. 1/1/2023.
Amended by Stats 2019 ch 143 (SB 251),s 31, eff. 1/1/2020.
Amended by Stats 2014 ch 694 (SB 1301),s 71, eff. 1/1/2015.
Amended by Stats 2012 ch 494 (SB 1532),s 31, eff. 1/1/2013.

Section 12505 - Certificate of amendment

(a) Upon adoption of an amendment, the corporation shall file a certificate of amendment, which shall consist of an officers' certificate stating:

(1) The wording of the amendment or amended articles is in accordance with Section 12507;

(2) That the amendment has been approved by the board;

(3) If the amendment is one for which the approval of the members (Section 12224) or the approval of 100 percent of the voting power is required, that the amendment was approved by the required vote of members; and

(4) If the amendment is one which may be adopted with approval by the board alone, a statement of the facts entitling the board alone to adopt the amendment.

(b) In the event of an amendment of the articles pursuant to a merger, the filing of the officers' certificate and agreement pursuant to Section 12535 shall be in lieu of any filing required under this chapter.

Ca. Corp. Code § 12505

Added by Stats. 1982, Ch. 1625, Sec. 3. Operative January 1, 1984.

Section 12506 - Certificate of amendment signed by incorporators

In the case of amendments adopted by the incorporators under Section 12501, the corporation shall file a certificate of amendment signed and verified by a majority of the incorporators which shall state that the signers thereof constitute at least a majority of the incorporators, that directors were not named in the original articles and have not been elected, that the corporation has no members and that they adopt the amendment or amendments therein set forth.

Ca. Corp. Code § 12506

Added by Stats. 1982, Ch. 1625, Sec. 3. Operative January 1, 1984.

Section 12507 - Wording of amendment or amended articles

The certificate of amendment shall establish the wording of the amendment or amended articles by one or more of the following means:

(a) By stating that the articles shall be amended to read as therein set forth in full.

(b) By stating that any provision of the articles, which shall be identified by the numerical or other designation given it in the articles or by stating the wording thereof, shall be striken from the articles or shall be amended to read as set forth in the certificate.

(c) By stating that the provisions set forth therein shall be added to the articles. If the purpose of the amendment is to reclassify, cancel, exchange, or otherwise change outstanding memberships the amended articles shall state the effect thereof on outstanding memberships.

Ca. Corp. Code § 12507

Added by Stats. 1982, Ch. 1625, Sec. 3. Operative January 1, 1984.

Section 12508 - Filing of certificate of amendment; certified copy of certificate

Upon the filing of the certificate of amendment, the articles shall be amended in accordance with the certificate and any change, reclassification or cancellation of memberships shall be effected, and a copy of the certificate, certified by the Secretary of State, is prima facie evidence of the performance of the conditions necessary to the adoption of the amendment.

Ca. Corp. Code § 12508

Added by Stats. 1982, Ch. 1625, Sec. 3. Operative January 1, 1984.

Section 12509 - Extension of term of existence

A corporation formed for a limited period may at any time subject to the expiration of the term of its corporate existence, extend the term of its existence by an amendment to its articles removing any provision limiting the term of its existence and providing for perpetual existence. If the filing of the certificate of amendment providing for perpetual existence would be prohibited if it were original articles by the provisions of Section 12302, the Secretary of State shall not file such certificate unless, by the same or a concurrently filed certificate of amendment, the articles of such corporation are amended to adopt a new available name. For the purpose of the adoption of any such amendment, persons who have been functioning as directors of such corporation shall be considered to have been validly elected even though their election may have occurred after the expiration of the original term of the corporate existence.

Ca. Corp. Code § 12509

Added by Stats. 1982, Ch. 1625, Sec. 3. Operative January 1, 1984.

Section 12510 - Restated articles of incorporation

(a) A corporation may restate in a single certificate the entire text of its articles as amended by filing an officers' certificate entitled "Restated Articles of Incorporation of (insert name of corporation)" which shall set forth the articles as amended to the date of filing of the certificate, except that the signatures and acknowledgments of the incorporators and any statements regarding the effect of any prior amendment upon memberships and any provisions of agreements of merger (other than amendments to the articles of the surviving corporation) and the names, addresses, signatures and acknowledgments of the first directors and the initial street address and initial mailing address of the corporation and of the initial agent for service of process shall be omitted (except that the initial street address and initial mailing address of the corporation and the names and addresses of the initial agent for service of process and the first directors shall not be omitted prior to the time that the corporation has filed a statement under Section 12570). Such omissions are not alterations or amendments of the articles. The certificate may also itself alter or amend the articles in any respect, in which case the certificate must comply with Sections 12505 and 12506, as the case may be, and Section 12507.

(b) If the certificate does not itself alter or amend the articles in any respect, it shall be approved by the board and shall be subject to the provisions of this chapter relating to an amendment of the articles not requiring approval of the members (Section 12224). If the certificate does itself alter or amend the articles, it shall be subject to the provisions of this chapter relating to the amendment or amendments so made.

(c) Restated articles of incorporation filed pursuant to this section shall supersede for all purposes the original articles and all amendments filed prior thereto.

Ca. Corp. Code § 12510

Amended by Stats 2012 ch 494 (SB 1532),s 32, eff. 1/1/2013.

Chapter 9 - SALES OF ASSETS

Section 12520 - Mortgage, deed of trust, pledge or other hypothecation of corporation's property

Any mortgage, deed of trust, pledge or other hypothecation of all or any part of the corporation's property, real or personal, for the purpose of securing the payment or performance of any contract or obligation may be approved by the board. Unless the articles or bylaws otherwise provide, no approval of the members (Section 12224) shall be necessary for such action.

Ca. Corp. Code § 12520
Added by Stats. 1982, Ch. 1625, Sec. 3. Operative January 1, 1984.

Section 12521 - Sale or other disposal of assets

(a) A corporation may sell, lease, convey, exchange, transfer or otherwise dispose of all or substantially all of its assets when the principal terms are:

  (1) Approved by the board; and

  (2) Unless the transaction is in the usual and regular course of its activities approved by the members (Section 12224) either before or after approval by the board and before or after the transaction.

(b) Notwithstanding approval by the members (Section 12224), the board may abandon the proposed transaction without further action by the members, subject to the contractual rights, if any, of third parties.

(c) Such sale, lease, conveyance, exchange, transfer or other disposition may be made upon such terms and conditions and for such consideration as the board may deem in the best interests of the corporation.

Ca. Corp. Code § 12521
Added by Stats. 1982, Ch. 1625, Sec. 3. Operative January 1, 1984.

Section 12522 - Certificate annexed to deed or instrument conveying or transferring assets

Any deed or instrument conveying or otherwise transferring any assets of a corporation may have annexed to it the certificate of the secretary or an assistant secretary of the corporation, setting forth that the transaction has been validly approved by the board and (a) stating that the property described in such deed or instrument is less than substantially all of the assets of the corporation or that the transfer is in the usual and regular course of the business of the corporation, if such be the case, or (b) if such property constitutes all or substantially all of the assets of the corporation and the transfer is not in the usual and regular course of the business of the corporation, stating the fact of approval thereof by the members (Section 12224) or all the members pursuant to this chapter. Such certificate is prima facie evidence of the existence of the facts authorizing such conveyance or other transfer of the assets and conclusive evidence in favor of any purchaser or encumbrancer for value who, without notice of any trust restriction applicable to the property or any failure to comply therewith, in good faith parted with value.

Ca. Corp. Code § 12522
Added by Stats. 1982, Ch. 1625, Sec. 3. Operative January 1, 1984.

Chapter 10 - MERGERS

Article 1 - MERGER

Section 12530 - Merger

Except as provided in Section 12530.5, any corporation may merge with another domestic corporation, foreign corporation, or other business entity. However, a merger with a nonprofit public benefit corporation or a nonprofit religious corporation must have the prior written consent of the Attorney General.

 Ca. Corp. Code § 12530
Amended by Stats 2015 ch 192 (AB 816),s 22, eff. 1/1/2016.
Amended September 21, 1999 (Bill Number: AB 198) (Chapter 437).

Section 12530.5 - Consolidation or merger of worker cooperative

Notwithstanding Section 12530, a worker cooperative that has not revoked its election to be governed as a worker cooperative under Section 12310.5 shall not consolidate or merge with another corporation other than another worker cooperative. Two or more worker cooperatives may merge or consolidate in a manner consistent with this chapter.

 Ca. Corp. Code § 12530.5
Added by Stats 2015 ch 192 (AB 816),s 23, eff. 1/1/2016.

Section 12531 - Agreement of merger

The board of each corporation that desires to merge shall approve an agreement of merger. The constituent corporations shall be parties to the agreement of merger and other persons may be parties to the agreement of merger. The agreement shall state all of the following:

(a) The terms and conditions of the merger.

(b) The amendments, subject to Sections 12500 and 12505 to the articles of the surviving corporation to be effected by the merger, if any; if any amendment changes the name of the surviving corporation, the new name may be the same as or similar to the name of a disappearing corporation, subject to subdivision (c) of Section 12302.

(c) The amendments to the bylaws of the surviving corporation to be effected by the merger, if any.

(d) The name and place of incorporation of each constituent corporation and which of the constituent corporations is the surviving corporation.

(e) The manner, if any, of converting memberships or securities of the constituent corporations into memberships or securities of the surviving corporation and, if any memberships or securities of any of the constituent corporations are not to be converted solely into memberships or securities of the surviving corporation, the cash, property, rights or securities of any corporation that the holders of those memberships or securities are to receive in exchange for the memberships or securities, which cash, property, rights or securities of any corporation may be in addition to or in lieu of memberships or securities of the surviving corporation or that the memberships are to be canceled without consideration.

(f) Other details or provisions as are desired, if any, including, without limitation, if not prohibited by this chapter, a provision for the payment of cash in lieu of fractional memberships or for any other arrangement with respect thereto.

   Ca. Corp. Code § 12531

Amended 9/21/1999 (Bill Number: AB 1687) (Chapter 453).

Section 12532 - Equal treatment of membership of same class

Each membership of the same class of any constituent corporation (other than the cancellation of memberships held by a surviving corporation or its parent or a wholly owned subsidiary of either in a constituent corporation) shall be treated equally with respect to any distribution of cash, property, rights, or securities unless:

(a) all members of the class consent or

(b) the Commissioner of Financial Protection and Innovation has approved the terms and conditions of the transaction and the fairness of such terms pursuant to Section 25142.

   Ca. Corp. Code § 12532

Amended by Stats 2022 ch 452 (SB 1498),s 60, eff. 1/1/2023.

Amended by Stats 2019 ch 143 (SB 251),s 32, eff. 1/1/2020.

Section 12533 - Approval by members

(a) The principal terms of the merger shall be approved by the members (Section 12224) of each class of each corporation which desires to merge. The approval by the members may be given before or after the approval by the board.

(b) Any member of any constituent corporation who voted against the merger may, without prior notice, but within 30 days following the effective date of the merger, resign from membership and, in the event of resignation, shall be:

   (1) Thereafter excused from all contractual obligations to the corporation which have not accrued prior to resignation; and

   (2) Shall be entitled to the same rights as would have existed if there had been no merger and the membership had been terminated.

   Ca. Corp. Code § 12533

Added by Stats. 1982, Ch. 1625, Sec. 3. Operative January 1, 1984.

Section 12534 - Signing agreement

Each constituent corporation shall sign the agreement by the chairperson of its board, president or a vice president and secretary or an assistant secretary acting on behalf of their respective corporations.

    Ca. Corp. Code § 12534

Amended by Stats 2022 ch 617 (SB 1202),s 83, eff. 1/1/2023.

Added by Stats. 1982, Ch. 1625, Sec. 3. Operative January 1, 1984.

Section 12535 - Filing agreement of merger

After approval of a merger by the board and any approval by the members under Section 12533, the surviving corporation shall file a copy of the agreement of merger with an officers' certificate of each constituent corporation attached stating the total number of memberships of each class entitled to vote on the merger, and that the principal terms of the agreement in the form attached were duly approved by the required vote of the members. The merger and any amendment of the articles of the surviving corporation contained in the merger agreement shall thereupon be effective (subject to subdivision (c) of Section 12214 and subject to the provisions of Section 12539) and the several parties thereto shall be one corporation. The Secretary of State may certify a copy of the merger agreement separate from the officers' certificates attached thereto.

    Ca. Corp. Code § 12535

Amended by Stats 2006 ch 773 (AB 2341),s 29, eff. 9/29/2006.

Section 12536 - Amendment to agreement

(a) Any amendment to the agreement may be adopted and the agreement so amended may be approved by the board and, if it changes any of the principal terms of the agreement, by the members, as required by Section 12533 of any constituent corporation in the same manner as the original agreement.

(b) If the agreement so amended is approved as provided in subdivision (a), the agreement so amended shall then constitute the agreement of merger.

    Ca. Corp. Code § 12536

Added by Stats. 1982, Ch. 1625, Sec. 3. Operative January 1, 1984.

Section 12537 - Abandoning merger

The board may, in its discretion, abandon a merger, subject to the contractual rights, if any, of third parties, including other constituent corporations, without further approval by the members at any time before the merger is effective.

    Ca. Corp. Code § 12537

Added by Stats. 1982, Ch. 1625, Sec. 3. Operative January 1, 1984.

Section 12538 - Copy of certified agreement of merger as conclusive evidence

A copy of an agreement of merger certified on or after the effective date by an official having custody thereof has the same force in evidence as the original and, except as against the state, is conclusive evidence of the performance of all conditions precedent to the merger, the existence on the effective date of the surviving corporation, and the performance of the conditions necessary to the adoption of any amendment to the articles contained in the agreement of merger.

Ca. Corp. Code § 12538
Added by Stats. 1982, Ch. 1625, Sec. 3. Operative January 1, 1984.

Section 12539 - Merger of corporations with foreign corporations, foreign business corporations, or domestic corporations

(a) Subject to the provisions of Section 12530, the merger of any number of corporations with any number of foreign corporations, foreign business corporations, or domestic corporations may be effected if the foreign corporations are authorized by the laws under which they are formed to effect the merger. The surviving corporation may be any one of the constituent corporations and shall continue to exist under the laws of the state or place of its incorporation.

(b) If the surviving corporation is a cooperative corporation, the merger proceedings with respect to that corporation and any domestic disappearing corporation shall conform to the provisions of this chapter and other applicable laws of this state, but if the surviving corporation is a foreign corporation, then, subject to the requirements of subdivision (d) and Section 12533, the merger proceedings may be in accordance with the laws of the state or place of incorporation of the surviving corporation.

(c) If the surviving corporation is a cooperative corporation, the agreement and the officers' certificate of each constituent corporation shall be filed as provided in Section 12535 and thereupon, subject to subdivision (c) of Section 12214, the merger shall be effective as to each corporation; and each foreign disappearing corporation that is qualified for the transaction of intrastate business shall, by virtue of the filing, automatically surrender its right to transact intrastate business.

(d) If the surviving corporation is a foreign corporation, the merger shall become effective in accordance with the law of the jurisdiction in which it is organized, but shall be effective as to any disappearing corporation as of the time of effectiveness in the foreign jurisdiction upon the filing in this state as required by this subdivision. There shall be filed as to the domestic disappearing corporation or corporations the documents described in any one of the following paragraphs:

(1) A copy of the agreement, certificate, or other document filed by the surviving corporation in the state or place of its incorporation for the purpose of effecting the merger, which copy shall be certified by the public officer having official custody of the original.

(2) An executed counterpart of the agreement, certificate, or other document filed by the surviving corporation in the state or place of its incorporation for the purpose of effecting the merger.

(3) A copy of the agreement of merger with an officers' certificate of the surviving foreign corporation and of each constituent domestic corporation attached.

(e) If the date of the filing in this state pursuant to subdivision (d) is more than six months after the time of the effectiveness in the foreign jurisdiction, or if the powers of the domestic corporation are suspended at the time of effectiveness in the foreign jurisdiction, the merger shall be effective as to the domestic disappearing corporation or corporations as of the date of filing in this state. Each foreign disappearing corporation that is qualified for the transaction of intrastate business shall automatically by the filing pursuant to subdivision (d) surrender its right to transact intrastate business as of the date of the filing in this state regardless of the time of effectiveness as to a domestic disappearing corporation.

Ca. Corp. Code § 12539

Amended by Stats 2006 ch 773 (AB 2341),s 30, eff. 9/29/2006.
Amended September 21, 1999 (Bill Number: AB 1687) (Chapter 453).

Section 12540 - Agreement of merger between cooperative corporation and one or more business or nonprofit corporations

If an agreement of merger is entered into between a cooperative corporation and one or more business or nonprofit corporations, Sections 12531, 12532, 12533, 12535, and 12536 shall apply to any constituent cooperative corporation. Sections 8011, 8011.5, 8012, and 8015 shall apply to any constituent mutual benefit corporation. Sections 6011, 6012, 6014, and 6015 shall apply to any constituent public benefit corporation. Sections 6014 and 6015 and subdivisions (c) and (d) of Section 9640 shall apply to any constituent religious corporation and Sections 1101, 1101.1, 1103, and 1104 shall apply to any constituent business corporation.

Ca. Corp. Code § 12540

Added by Stats. 1982, Ch. 1625, Sec. 3. Operative January 1, 1984.

Section 12540.1 - Merger between corporations and other business entities

(a) Any one or more corporations may merge with one or more other business entities (Section 12242.5). Subject to the provisions of Section 12530, one or more other domestic corporations or foreign corporations (Section 12237) may be parties to the merger. Notwithstanding the provisions of this section, such a merger may be effected only if:

(1) In a merger in which a domestic corporation or domestic other business entity is a party, it is authorized by the laws under which it is organized to effect the merger.

(2) In a merger in which a foreign corporation is a party, it is authorized by the laws under which it is organized to effect the merger.

(3) In a merger in which a foreign other business entity is a party, it is authorized by the laws under which it is organized to effect the merger.

(b) Each corporation, other domestic corporation, foreign corporation, and other business entity which desires to merge shall approve an agreement of merger. The board and the members of each corporation which desires to merge shall approve (Sections 12222 and 12224) the agreement of merger. The agreement of merger shall be approved on behalf of each other constituent party by those persons authorized or required to approve the merger by the laws under which it is organized. The parties desiring to merge shall be parties to the agreement of merger and other persons, including a parent party (Section 12242.6), may be parties to the agreement of merger. The agreement of merger shall state all of the following:

(1) The terms and conditions of the merger.

(2) The name and place of incorporation or organization of each party and the identity of the surviving party.

(3) The amendments, if any, subject to Sections 12500 and 12507, to the articles of the surviving corporation, if applicable, to be effected by the merger. The name of the surviving corporation may be, subject to subdivisions (b) and (c) of Section 12302, the same as, or similar to, the name of a disappearing party to the merger.

(4) The manner, if any, of converting the memberships or securities of each of the constituent corporations into shares, memberships, interests, or other securities of the surviving party and, if any memberships or securities of any of the constituent corporations are not to be converted solely into shares, memberships, interests, or other securities of the surviving party, the cash, rights, securities, or other property which the holders of those memberships or securities are to receive in exchange for the memberships or securities, which cash, rights, securities, or other property may be in addition to or in lieu of shares, memberships, interests, or other securities of the surviving party.

(5) Any other details or provisions required by the laws under which any party to the merger is organized, including, if a domestic limited partnership is a party to the merger, subdivision (a) of Section 15911.12, or, if a domestic general partnership is a party to the merger, subdivision (a) of Section 16911, or, if a domestic limited liability company is a party to the merger, subdivision (a) of Section 17710.12.

(6) Any other details or provisions as are desired.

(c) Each membership of the same class of any constituent corporation (other than the cancellation of memberships held by a party to the merger or its parent or a wholly owned subsidiary of either in another constituent corporation) shall be treated equally with respect to any distribution of cash, property, rights, or securities unless (i) all members of the class consent or (ii) the commissioner has approved the terms and conditions of the transaction and the fairness of those terms pursuant to Section 25142.

(d) Notwithstanding its prior approval, an agreement of merger may be amended prior to the filing of the agreement of merger if the amendment is approved by each constituent corporation in the same manner as the original agreement of merger. If the agreement of merger as so amended and approved is also approved by each of the other parties to the agreement of merger, as so amended it shall then constitute the agreement of merger.

(e) The board of a constituent corporation may, in its discretion, abandon a merger, subject to the contractual rights, if any, of third parties, including other parties to the agreement of merger, without further approval by the members (Section 12224), at any time before the merger is effective.

(f) Each constituent corporation shall sign the agreement of merger by its chairperson of the board, president, or a vice president and also by its secretary or an assistant secretary acting on behalf of their respective corporations.

(g) After required approvals of the merger by each constituent corporation and each other party to the merger, the surviving party shall file a copy of the agreement of merger with an officers' certificate of each constituent domestic and foreign corporation attached stating the total number of outstanding shares or membership interests of each class entitled to vote on the merger (and identifying any other person or persons whose approval is required), that the agreement of merger in the form attached or its principal terms, as required, were approved by that corporation by a vote of a number of shares or membership interests of each class which equaled or exceeded the vote required, specifying each class entitled to vote and the percentage vote required of each class, and, if applicable, by that other person or persons whose approval is required. If equity securities of a parent party (Section 12242.6) are to be issued in the merger, the officers' certificate or certificate of merger of the controlled party shall state either that no vote of the shareholders of the parent party was required or that the required vote was obtained. The merger and any amendment of the articles of the surviving corporation, if applicable, contained in the agreement of merger shall be effective upon the filing of the agreement of merger, subject to the provisions of subdivision (i). If a domestic reciprocal insurer organized after 1974 to provide medical malpractice insurance is a party to the merger, the agreement of merger or certificate of merger shall not be filed until there has been filed the certificate issued by the Insurance Commissioner approving the merger pursuant to Section 1555 of the Insurance Code.

In lieu of an officers' certificate, a certificate of merger, on a form prescribed by the Secretary of State, shall be filed for each constituent other business entity. The certificate of merger shall be executed and acknowledged by each domestic constituent limited liability company by all of the managers of the limited liability company (unless a lesser number is specified in its articles of organization or operating agreement) and by each domestic constituent limited partnership by all general partners (unless a lesser number is provided in its certificate of limited partnership or partnership agreement) and by each domestic constituent general partnership by two partners (unless a lesser number is provided in its partnership agreement) and by each foreign constituent general partnership or foreign constituent limited liability company by one or more managers and by each foreign constituent limited partnership by one or more general partners, and by each constituent reciprocal insurer by the chairperson of the board, president, or vice president, and by the secretary or assistant secretary, or, if a constituent reciprocal insurer has not appointed such officers, by the chairperson of the board, president, or vice president, and by the secretary or assistant secretary of the constituent reciprocal insurer's attorney-in-fact, and by each other party to the merger by those persons required or authorized to execute the certificate of merger by the laws under which that party is organized, specifying for such party the provision of law or other basis for the authority of the signing persons.

The certificate of merger shall set forth, if a vote of the shareholders, members, partners, or other holders of interests of the constituent other business entity was required, a statement setting forth the total number of outstanding interests of each class entitled to vote on the merger and that the agreement of merger or its principal terms, as required, were approved by a vote of the number of interests of each class which equaled or exceeded the vote required, specifying each class entitled to vote and the percentage vote required of each class, and any other information required to be set forth under the laws under which the constituent other business entity is organized, including, if a domestic limited partnership is a party to the merger, subdivision (a) of Section 15911.14, if a domestic general partnership is a party to the merger, subdivision (b) of Section 16915, and, if a domestic limited liability company is a party to the merger, subdivision (a) of Section 17710.14. The certificate of merger for each constituent foreign other business entity, if any, shall also set forth the statutory or other basis under which that foreign other business entity is authorized by the laws under which it is organized to effect the merger.

The Secretary of State may certify a copy of the agreement of merger separate from the officers' certificates and certificates of merger attached thereto.

(h) A copy of an agreement of merger certified on or after the effective date by an official having custody thereof has the same force in evidence as the original and, except as against the state, is conclusive evidence of the performance of all conditions precedent to the merger, the existence on the effective date of the surviving party to the merger, the performance of the conditions necessary to the adoption of any amendment to the articles, if applicable, contained in the agreement of merger, and of the merger of the constituent corporations, either by themselves or together with other constituent parties, into the surviving party to the merger.

(i)

    (1) The merger of domestic corporations with foreign corporations or foreign other business entities in a merger in which one or more other business entities is a party shall comply with subdivisions (a) and (g) and this subdivision.

(2) Subject to subdivision (c) of Section 12214 and paragraph (3), the merger shall be effective as to each domestic constituent corporation and domestic constituent other business entity upon filing of the agreement of merger with attachments as provided in subdivision (g).

(3) If the surviving party is a foreign corporation or foreign other business entity, except as provided in paragraph (4), the merger shall be effective as to any domestic disappearing corporation as of the time of effectiveness in the foreign jurisdiction upon the filing in this state of a copy of the agreement of merger with an officers' certificate of the surviving foreign corporation and of each constituent foreign and domestic corporation and a certificate of merger of each constituent other business entity attached, which officers' certificates and certificates of merger shall conform to the requirements of subdivision (g). If one or more domestic other business entities is a disappearing party in a merger pursuant to this subdivision in which a foreign other business entity is the surviving entity, a certificate of merger required by the laws under which each domestic other business entity is organized, including subdivision (a) of Section 15911.14, subdivision (b) of Section 16915 or subdivision (a) of Section 17710.14, if applicable, shall also be filed at the same time as the filing of the agreement of merger.

(4) If the date of the filing in this state pursuant to this subdivision is more than six months after the time of the effectiveness in the foreign jurisdiction, or if the powers of a domestic disappearing corporation are suspended at the time of effectiveness in the foreign jurisdiction, the merger shall be effective as to the domestic disappearing corporation as of the date of filing in this state.

(5) Each foreign disappearing corporation that is qualified for the transaction of intrastate business shall automatically by the filing pursuant to subdivision (g) surrender its right to transact intrastate business as of the date of filing in this state or, if later, the effective date of the merger. With respect to each foreign disappearing other business entity previously registered for the transaction of intrastate business in this state, the filing of the agreement of merger pursuant to subdivision (g) automatically has the effect of a cancellation of registration for that foreign other business entity without the necessity of the filing of a certificate of cancellation.

Ca. Corp. Code § 12540.1
Amended by Stats 2012 ch 419 (SB 323),s 13, eff. 1/1/2013, op. 1/1/2014.
Amended by Stats 2006 ch 773 (AB 2341),s 31.5, eff. 1/1/2007.
Amended by Stats 2006 ch 773 (AB 2341),s 31, eff. 9/29/2006.
Amended by Stats 2006 ch 495 (AB 339),s 15, eff. 1/1/2007.
Added September 21, 1999 (Bill Number: AB 198) (Chapter 437).

Article 2 - EFFECT OF MERGER

Section 12550 - Effect of merger

(a) Upon merger pursuant to this chapter the separate existences of the disappearing parties to the merger cease and the surviving party to the merger shall succeed, without other transfer, to all the rights and property of each of the disappearing parties to the merger and shall be subject to all the debts and liabilities of each and trust obligations upon the property of a disappearing party in the same manner as if incurred by the surviving party to the merger.

(b) All rights of creditors and all liens and trusts upon or arising from the property of each of the constituent corporations and other parties to the merger shall be preserved unimpaired, provided that these liens and trust obligations upon property of a disappearing party shall be limited to the property affected thereby immediately prior to the time the merger is effective.

(c) Any action or proceeding pending by or against any disappearing corporation or other party to the merger may be prosecuted to judgment, which shall bind the surviving party to the merger, or the surviving party to the merger may be proceeded against or substituted in its place.

 Ca. Corp. Code § 12550
Amended 9/21/1999 (Bill Number: AB 198) (Chapter 437).

Section 12550.5 - Assumption of liability

(a) Upon merger pursuant to this chapter, a surviving domestic or foreign corporation or other business entity shall be deemed to have assumed the liability of each disappearing domestic or foreign corporation or other business entity that is taxed under Part 10 (commencing with Section 17001) of, or under Part 11 (commencing with Section 23001) of, Division 2 of the Revenue and Taxation Code for the following:

 (1) To prepare and file, or to cause to be prepared and filed, tax and information returns otherwise required of that disappearing entity as specified in Chapter 2 (commencing with Section 18501) of Part 10.2 of Division 2 of the Revenue and Taxation Code.

 (2) To pay any tax liability determined to be due.

(b) If the surviving entity is a domestic limited liability company, domestic corporation, or registered limited liability partnership or a foreign limited liability company, foreign limited liability partnership, or foreign corporation that is registered or qualified to do business in California, the Secretary of State shall notify the Franchise Tax Board of the merger.

 Ca. Corp. Code § 12550.5
Amended by Stats 2006 ch 495 (AB 339),s 16, eff. 1/1/2007.

Amended by Stats 2006 ch 773 (AB 2341),s 32, eff. 9/29/2006.

Added by Stats 2005 ch 286 (AB 241),s 4, eff. 1/1/2006.

Section 12551 - Real property

Whenever a domestic or foreign corporation or other business entity (Section 12242.5) having any real property in this state merges with another domestic or foreign corporation or other business entity pursuant to the laws of this state or of the state or place in which any constituent party to the merger was organized, and the laws of the state or place of organization (including this state) of any disappearing party to the merger provide substantially that the making and filing of the agreement of merger vests in the surviving party to the merger all the real property of any disappearing party to the merger, the filing for record in the office of the county recorder of any county in this state in which any of the real property of the disappearing party to the merger is located of either (a) a certificate prescribed by the Secretary of State, or (b) a copy of the agreement of merger or certificate of merger, certified by the Secretary of State or an authorized public official of the state or place pursuant to the laws of which the merger is effected, shall evidence record ownership in the surviving party to the merger of all interest of the disappearing party to the merger in and to the real property located in that county.

Ca. Corp. Code § 12551

Amended 9/21/1999 (Bill Number: AB 198) (Chapter 437).

Section 12552 - Bequest, devise, gift, grant, or promise contained in will or other instrument of donation, subscription, or conveyance

Any bequest, devise, gift, grant, or promise contained in a will or other instrument of donation, subscription, or conveyance, which is made to a constituent corporation and which takes effect or remains payable after the merger, inures to the surviving party to the merger.

Ca. Corp. Code § 12552

Amended 9/21/1999 (Bill Number: AB 198) (Chapter 437).

Chapter 11 - BANKRUPTCY REORGANIZATIONS AND ARRANGEMENTS

Section 12560 - Law governing reorganizations

Any proceeding, initiated with respect to a corporation, under any applicable statute of the United States, as now existing or hereafter enacted, relating to reorganizations of corporations, shall be governed by the provisions of Chapter 14 (commencing with Section 1400) of Division 1 of Title 1, and for this purpose the reference in Chapter 14 to "shareholders" shall be deemed to be a reference to members and the reference to "this division" shall be deemed to be a reference to this part.

Ca. Corp. Code § 12560
Amended by Stats 2009 ch 500 (AB 1059),s 25, eff. 1/1/2010.

Chapter 12 - REQUIRED FILINGS BY CORPORATION OR ITS AGENT

Section 12570 - Statement

(a) Every corporation shall, within 90 days after the filing of its original articles and annually thereafter during the applicable filing period in each year, file, on a form prescribed by the Secretary of State, a statement containing:

(1) the name of the corporation and the Secretary of State's file number;

(2) the names and complete business or residence addresses of its chief executive officer or general manager, secretary, and chief financial officer;

(3) the street address of its principal office in California, if any;

(4) the mailing address of the corporation, if different from the street address of its principal office in California; and

(5) if the corporation chooses to receive renewal notices and any other notifications from the Secretary of State by electronic mail instead of by United States mail, the corporation shall include a valid electronic mail address for the corporation or for the corporation's designee to receive those notices.

(b) The statement required by subdivision (a) shall also designate, as the agent of the corporation for the purpose of service of process, a natural person residing in this state or any domestic or foreign corporation that has complied with Section 1505 and whose capacity to act as an agent has not terminated. If a natural person is designated, the statement shall set forth the person's complete business or residence street address. If a corporate agent is designated, no address for it shall be set forth.

(c) For the purposes of this section, the applicable filing period for a corporation shall be the calendar month during which its original articles were filed and the immediately preceding five calendar months. The Secretary of State shall provide a notice to each corporation to comply with this section approximately three months before the close of the applicable filing period. The notice shall state the due date for compliance and shall be sent to the last address of the corporation according to the records of the Secretary of State or to the last electronic mail address according to the records of the Secretary of State if the corporation has elected to receive notices from the Secretary of State by electronic mail. Neither the failure of the Secretary of State to send the notice nor the failure of the corporation to receive it is an excuse for failure to comply with this section.

(d) Whenever any of the information required by subdivision (a) is changed, the corporation may file a current statement containing all the information required by subdivisions (a) and (b). In order to change its agent for service of process or the address of the agent, the corporation must file a current statement containing all the information required by subdivisions (a) and (b). Whenever any statement is filed pursuant to this section, it supersedes any previously filed statement and the statement in the articles as to the agent for service of process and the address of the agent.

(e)The Secretary of State may destroy or otherwise dispose of any statement filed pursuant to this section after it has been superseded by the filing of a new statement.

(f)This section does not place any person dealing with the corporation on notice of, or under any duty to inquire about, the existence or content of a statement filed pursuant to this section.

Ca. Corp. Code § 12570

Amended by Stats 2022 ch 617 (SB 1202),s 84, eff. 1/1/2023.

Amended by Stats 2012 ch 494 (SB 1532),s 33, eff. 1/1/2013.

Amended by Stats 2012 ch 162 (SB 1171),s 22, eff. 1/1/2013.

Amended by Stats 2011 ch 204 (AB 657),s 11, eff. 1/1/2012.

Section 12571 - Resignation by agent designated for service of process

(a) An agent designated for service of process pursuant to Section 12570 may deliver to the Secretary of State, on a form prescribed by the Secretary of State for filing, a signed and acknowledged written statement of resignation as an agent for service of process containing the name of the corporation, the Secretary of State's file number of the corporation, the name of the resigning agent for service of process, and a statement that the agent is resigning. Thereupon the authority of the agent to act in that capacity shall cease and the Secretary of State forthwith shall mail or otherwise provide written notice of the filing of the statement of resignation to the corporation at its principal office.

(b) The resignation of an agent may be effective if, on a form prescribed by the Secretary of State containing the name of the corporation, the Secretary of State's file number for the corporation, and the name of the resigning agent for service of process, the agent disclaims having been properly appointed as the agent. Similarly, a person named as an officer or director may indicate that the person was never properly appointed as the officer or director.

(c) The Secretary of State may destroy or otherwise dispose of any resignation filed pursuant to this section after a new form is filed pursuant to Section 12570 replacing the agent for service of process that has resigned.

Ca. Corp. Code § 12571

Amended by Stats 2014 ch 834 (SB 1041),s 18, eff. 1/1/2015.

Amended September 21, 1999 (Bill Number: AB 1687) (Chapter 453).

Section 12572 - Designation of new agent

If a natural person who has been designated agent for service of process pursuant to

Section 12570 dies or resigns or no longer resides in the state or if the corporate agent for such purpose resigns, dissolves, withdraws from the state, forfeits its right to transact intrastate business, has its corporate rights, powers and privileges suspended, or ceases to exist, the corporation shall forthwith file a designation of a new agent conforming to the requirements of Section 12570.

Ca. Corp. Code § 12572
Added by Stats. 1982, Ch. 1625, Sec. 3. Operative January 1, 1984.

Section 12574 - Availability of business records to assessor

Upon request of an assessor, a corporation owning, claiming, possessing or controlling property in this state subject to local assessment shall make available at the corporation's principal office in California or at a place mutually acceptable to the assessor and the corporation a true copy of business records relevant to the amount, cost and value of all property that it owns, claims, possesses or controls within the county.

Ca. Corp. Code § 12574
Added by Stats. 1982, Ch. 1625, Sec. 3. Operative January 1, 1984.

Section 12575 - Joint and several liability of officers, directors, employees, or agents

Any officers, directors, employees or agents of a corporation who do any of the following are liable jointly and severally for all the damages resulting therefrom to the corporation or any person injured thereby who relied thereupon or to both:

(a) Make, issue, deliver or publish any prospectus, report, circular, certificate, financial statement, balance sheet, public notice, or document respecting the corporation or its memberships, assets, liabilities, capital, dividends, distributions, patronage distributions, business, earnings, or accounts which is false in any material respect, knowing it to be false, or participate in the making, issuance, delivery, or publication thereof with knowledge that the same is false in a material respect.

(b) Make or cause to be made in the books, minutes, records, or accounts of a corporation any entry which is false in any material particular knowing such entry is false.

(c) Remove, erase, alter, or cancel any entry in any books or records of the corporation, with intent to deceive.

Ca. Corp. Code § 12575
Added by Stats. 1982, Ch. 1625, Sec. 3. Operative January 1, 1984.

Section 12576 - Action by attorney general

The Attorney General, upon complaint of a member, director, or officer, that a corporation is failing to comply with the provisions of this chapter, Chapter 5 (commencing with Section 12460), Chapter 6 (commencing with Section 12480) or

Chapter 13 (commencing with Section 12580) may, in the name of the people of the State of California, send to the principal office of such corporation, (or, if there is no such office, to the office or residence of the chief executive officer, general manager, or secretary, of the corporation, as set forth in the most recent statement filed pursuant to Section 12570) notice of the complaint. If the answer is not satisfactory, or if there is no answer within 30 days, the Attorney General may institute, maintain, or intervene in such suits, actions, or proceedings of any type in any court or tribunal of competent jurisdiction or before any administrative agency for such relief by way of injunction, the dissolution of entities, the appointment of receivers, or any other temporary, preliminary, provisional, or final remedies as may be appropriate to protect the rights of members or to undo the consequences of failure to comply with such requirements. In any such action, suit or proceeding there may be joined as parties all persons and entities responsible for or affected by such activity.

Ca. Corp. Code § 12576
Added by Stats. 1982, Ch. 1625, Sec. 3. Operative January 1, 1984.

Chapter 13 - RECORDS, REPORTS AND RIGHTS OF INSPECTION

Article 1 - GENERAL PROVISIONS

Section 12580 - Record available in written form

If any record subject to inspection pursuant to this chapter is not maintained in written form, a request for inspection is not complied with unless and until the corporation at its expense makes such record available in written form. For purposes of this chapter, "written" or "in writing" includes cathode ray tube and similar electronic communications methods.

Ca. Corp. Code § 12580
Amended by Stats. 1983, Ch. 792, Sec. 28.

Section 12581 - Right of inspection

Any inspection under this chapter may be made in person or by agent or attorney and the right of inspection includes the right to copy and make extracts.

Ca. Corp. Code § 12581
Added by Stats. 1982, Ch. 1625, Sec. 3. Operative January 1, 1984.

Section 12582 - Records of subsidiary

Any right of inspection created by this chapter extends to the records of each subsidiary of a corporation.

Ca. Corp. Code § 12582
Added by Stats. 1982, Ch. 1625, Sec. 3. Operative January 1, 1984.

Section 12583 - Limitation of rights of members prohibited

The rights of members provided in this chapter may not be limited by contract or the articles or bylaws.

Ca. Corp. Code § 12583
Added by Stats. 1982, Ch. 1625, Sec. 3. Operative January 1, 1984.

Article 2 - REQUIRED RECORDS, REPORTS TO DIRECTORS AND MEMBERS

Section 12590 - Keeping records

(a) Each corporation shall keep:

(1) Adequate and correct books and records of account;

(2) Minutes of the proceedings of its members, board, and committees of the board; and

(3) A record of its members giving their names and addresses and the class of membership and number of membership units held by each.
(b) Those minutes and other books and records shall be kept either in written form or in any other form capable of being converted into clearly legible tangible form or in any combination of the foregoing. When minutes and other books and records are kept in a form capable of being converted into clearly legible paper form, the clearly legible paper form into which those minutes and other books and records are converted shall be admissible in evidence, and accepted for all other purposes, to the same extent as an original paper record of the same information would have been, provided that the paper form accurately portrays the record.

Ca. Corp. Code § 12590
Amended by Stats 2004 ch 254 (SB 1306),s 41, eff. 1/1/2005

Section 12591 - Annual report

(a) A corporation shall notify each member yearly of the member's right to receive a financial report pursuant to this subdivision. Except as provided in subdivision (c), upon written request of a member, the board shall promptly cause the most recent annual report to be sent to the requesting member. An annual report shall be prepared not later than 120 days after the close of the corporation's fiscal year. Unless otherwise provided by the articles or bylaws and if approved by the board of directors, that report and any accompanying material sent pursuant to this section may be sent by electronic transmission by the corporation (Section 20). That report shall contain in appropriate detail the following:

(1) A balance sheet as of the end of that fiscal year and an income statement and a statement of cashflows for that fiscal year.

(2) A statement of the place where the names and addresses of the current members are located.

(3) Any information required by Section 12592.
(b) The report required by subdivision (a) shall be accompanied by any report thereon of independent accountants, or, if there is no report, the certificate of an authorized officer of the corporation that the statements were prepared without audit from the books and records of the corporation.
(c) This section does not apply to corporations that do not have more than 25 members at any time during the fiscal year.
Ca. Corp. Code § 12591
Amended by Stats 2006 ch 214 (AB 1959),s 7, eff. 1/1/2007.
Amended by Stats 2004 ch 254 (SB 1306),s 42, eff. 1/1/2005

Section 12592 - Statement of transaction or indemnification

(a) Any provision of the articles or bylaws notwithstanding, every corporation shall furnish annually to its members and directors a statement of any transaction or indemnification of a kind described in subdivision (d) or (e), if any such transaction or indemnification took place. If the corporation issues an annual report to all members, this subdivision shall be satisfied by including the required information in the annual report. A corporation which does not issue an annual report to all members, pursuant to subdivision (c) of Section 12591, shall satisfy this section by mailing or delivering to its members the required statement within 120 days after the close of the corporation's fiscal year. Unless otherwise provided by the articles or bylaws and if approved by the board of directors, that statement may be sent by electronic transmission by the corporation (Section 20).
(b) Except as provided in subdivision (c), a covered transaction under this section is a transaction in which the corporation, its parent, or its subsidiary was a party, and in which either of the following had a direct or indirect material financial interest:

(1) Any director or officer of the corporation, or its parent or subsidiary.

(2) Any holder of more than 10 percent of the voting power of the corporation, its parent or its subsidiary. For the purpose of subdivision (d), an "interested person" is any person described in paragraph (1) or (2).
(c) Transactions approved by the members of a corporation, under subdivision (a) of Section 12373, are not covered transactions. For the purpose of subdivision (b), neither a mere common directorship nor a member-patron relationship on terms available to all members constitutes a material financial interest.

(d) The statement required by subdivision (a) shall describe briefly:

(1) Any covered transaction (excluding compensation of officers and directors) during the previous fiscal year involving more than one thousand dollars ($1,000), or which was one of a number of covered transactions in which the same interested person had a direct or indirect material financial interest, and which transactions in the aggregate involved more than one thousand dollars ($1,000).

(2) The names of the interested persons involved in such transactions, stating such person's relationship to the corporation, the nature of such person's interest in the transaction and, where practicable, the amount of such interest; provided, that in the case of a transaction with a partnership of which such person is a partner, only the interest of the partnership need be stated.

(e) The statement required by subdivision (a) shall describe briefly the amount and circumstances of any loans, guaranties, indemnifications, or advances aggregating more than one thousand dollars ($1,000) paid or made during the fiscal year to any officer or director of the corporation pursuant to Section 12377; provided that no such report need be made in the case of a loan, guaranty, or indemnification approved by the members under paragraph (2) of subdivision (e) of Section 12377 or a loan or guaranty not subject to the provisions of subdivision (a) of Section 12375.

Ca. Corp. Code § 12592
Amended by Stats 2004 ch 254 (SB 1306),s 43, eff. 1/1/2005

Section 12593 - Enforcement

(a) The superior court of the proper county shall enforce the duty of making and mailing or delivering the information and financial statements required by this article and, for good cause shown, may extend the time therefor.

(b) In any action or proceeding under this section, if the court finds the failure of the corporation to comply with the requirements of this article to have been without justification, the court may award the member reasonable expenses, including attorneys' fees, in connection with such action or proceeding.

Ca. Corp. Code § 12593
Added by Stats. 1982, Ch. 1625, Sec. 3. Operative January 1, 1984.

Section 12594 - Report on vote

For a period of 60 days following the conclusion of an annual, regular, or special meeting of members, a corporation shall, upon written request from a member, forthwith inform the member of the result of any particular vote of members taken at the meeting, including the number of memberships voting for, the number of memberships voting against, and the number of memberships abstaining or withheld from voting. If the matter voted on was the election of directors, the corporation shall report the number of memberships, or votes if voted cumulatively, cast for each nominee for director. If more than one class or series of memberships voted, the report shall state the appropriate numbers by class and series of memberships.

Ca. Corp. Code § 12594

Added 9/21/1999 (Bill Number: AB 1687) (Chapter 453).

Article 3 - RIGHTS OF INSPECTION

Section 12600 - Inspection of record of members' names, addresses and voting rights or obtaining list of names, addresses, and voting rights of members

(a) Subject to Sections 12601 and 12602 and unless the corporation provides a reasonable alternative pursuant to subdivision (c), a member may do either or both of the following as permitted by subdivision (b):

(1) Inspect and copy the record of all the members' names, addresses, and voting rights, at reasonable times, upon five business days' prior written demand upon the corporation which demand shall state the purpose for which the inspection rights are requested; or

(2) Obtain from the secretary of the corporation, upon written demand and tender of a reasonable charge, a list of the names, addresses, and voting rights of those members entitled to vote for the election of directors, as of the most recent record date for which it has been compiled or as of a date specified by the member subsequent to the date of demand. The demand shall state the purpose for which the list is requested. The membership list shall be made available on or before the later of 10 business days after the demand is received or after the date specified therein as the date as of which the list is to be compiled.

(b) The rights set forth in subdivision (a) may be exercised by:

(1) A member or members possessing 5 percent or more of the voting power for a purpose reasonably related to the members' interest as members. Where the corporation reasonably believes that the information will be used for another purpose, or where it provides a reasonable alternative pursuant to subdivision (c), it may deny the member access to the list. In any subsequent action brought by the member under Section 12606 the court shall enforce the rights set forth in subdivision (a) unless the corporation proves that the member will allow use of the information for purposes unrelated to the person's interest as a member or that the alternative method offered reasonably achieves the proper purpose set forth in the demand.

(c) The corporation may, within 10 business days after receiving a demand under subdivision (a), deliver to the person or persons making the demand a written offer of an alternative method of achieving the purpose identified in the demand without providing access to or a copy of the membership list. An alternative method which reasonably and in a timely manner accomplishes the proper purpose set forth in a demand made under subdivision (a) shall be deemed a reasonable alternative, unless within a reasonable time after acceptance of the offer the corporation fails to do those things which it offered to do. Any rejection of the offer shall be in writing and shall indicate the reasons the alternative proposed by the corporation does not meet the proper purpose of the demand made pursuant to subdivision (a).

Ca. Corp. Code § 12600

Repealed and added by Stats. 1982, Ch. 1625, Sec. 3. Operative January 1, 1984.

Section 12601 - Order setting aside demand

(a) Where the corporation, in good faith, and with a substantial basis, believes that the membership list, demanded by a member or members under Section 12600, will be used for a purpose not reasonably related to the interests as members of the person or persons making the demand (hereinafter called the requesting parties) or provides a reasonable alternative pursuant to subdivision (c) of Section 12600 it may petition the superior court of the proper county for an order setting aside the demand.

(b) Except as provided in subdivision (c), a petition for an order to show cause why a protective order pursuant to subdivision (d) should not issue shall be filed within 10 business days after a demand by a member or members under Section 12600 or receipt of a written rejection by the member or members of an offer made pursuant to subdivision (c) of Section 12600 whichever is later. The petition shall be accompanied by an application for a hearing on the petition. Upon the filing of the petition, the court shall issue a protective order staying production of the list demanded until the hearing on the order to show cause. The court shall set the hearing on the order to show cause not more than 20 days from the date of the filing of the petition. The order to show cause shall be granted unless the court finds that there is no reasonable probability that the corporation will make the showing required under subdivision (f).

(c) A corporation may file a petition under this section more than 10 business days after the demand or rejection under Section 12600 but only upon a showing the delay was caused by excusable neglect. In no event, however, may any petition under this section be considered if filed more than 30 days after the requesting party's demand or rejection, whichever is later.

(d) Upon the return day of the order to show cause, the court may issue a protective order staying production of the list demanded until final adjudication of the petition filed pursuant to this section. No protective order shall issue under this subdivision unless the court finds that the rights of the requesting parties can reasonably be preserved and that the corporation is likely to make the showing required by subdivision (f) or the court is likely to issue a protective order pursuant to subdivision (g).

(e) If the corporation fails to file a petition within the time allowed by subdivision (b) or (c), whichever is applicable, or fails to obtain a protective order under subdivision (d), then the corporation shall comply with the demand, and no further action may be brought by the corporation under this section.

(f) The court shall issue the final order setting aside the demand only if the corporation proves:

(1) That there is a reasonable probability that the requesting parties will permit use of the membership list for a purpose unrelated to their interests as members; or

(2) That the method offered by the corporation is a reasonable alternative in that it reasonably achieves the proper purpose set forth in the requesting parties' demand and that the corporation intends and is able to effectuate the reasonable alternative.

(g) In the final order, the court may, in its discretion, order an alternate mechanism for achieving the proper purposes of the requesting parties, or impose just and proper conditions upon the use of the membership list which reasonably assures compliance with Section 12600 and Section 12608.

(h) The court shall award reasonable costs and expenses including reasonable attorneys' fees, to requesting parties who successfully oppose any petition or application filed pursuant to this section.

(i) Where the corporation has neither, within the time allowed, complied with a demand by a member or members under Section 12600, nor obtained a protective order staying production of the list, or a final order setting aside the demand, which is then in effect, the requesting parties may petition the superior court of the proper county for a writ of mandamus pursuant to Section 1085 of the Code of Civil Procedure compelling the corporation to comply with the demand. At the hearing, the court shall hear the parties summarily, by affidavit or otherwise, and shall issue a peremptory writ of mandamus unless it appears that the demand was not made by a member or members possessing sufficient voting power, that the demand has been complied with, that the corporation, pursuant to subdivision (c) of Section 12600, made an offer which was not rejected in writing within a reasonable time, or that a protective or final order properly issued under subdivision (d), (f) or (g) is then in effect. No inquiry may be made in such proceeding into the use for which the list is sought. The court shall award reasonable costs and expenses, including reasonable attorneys' fees, to persons granted an order under this subdivision.

(j) Nothing in this section shall be construed to limit the right of the corporation to obtain damages for any misuse of a membership list obtained under Section 12600, or otherwise, or to obtain injunctive relief necessary to restrain misuse of a member list. A corporation shall be entitled to recover reasonable costs and expenses, including reasonable attorneys' fees, incurred in successfully bringing any such action.

Ca. Corp. Code § 12601

Repealed and added by Stats. 1982, Ch. 1625, Sec. 3. Operative January 1, 1984.

Section 12602 - Limitation or restriction of rights by court

(a) Upon petition of the corporation or any member, the superior court of the proper county may limit or restrict the rights set forth in Section 12600 where, and only where, such limitation or restriction is necessary to protect the rights of any member under the Constitution of the United States or the Constitution of the State of

California. An order issued pursuant to this subdivision shall provide, insofar as possible, for alternative mechanisms by which the persons seeking to exercise rights under Section 12600 may communicate with members for purposes reasonably related to their interests as members.

(b) Upon the filing of a petition under subdivision (a), the court may, if requested by the person making the petition, issue a temporary order suspending the running of any time limit specified in Section 12600 for compliance with that section. Such an order may be extended, after notice and hearing, until final adjudication of the petition, wherever it appears that the petitioner may prevail on the merits, and it is otherwise equitable to do so.

Ca. Corp. Code § 12602

Added by Stats. 1982, Ch. 1625, Sec. 3. Operative January 1, 1984.

Section 12603 - Accounting books and records and minutes

The accounting books and records and minutes of proceedings of the members and the board and committees of the board shall be open to inspection upon the written demand on the corporation of any member at any reasonable time, for a purpose reasonably related to such person's interests as a member.

Ca. Corp. Code § 12603

Added by Stats. 1982, Ch. 1625, Sec. 3. Operative January 1, 1984.

Section 12604 - Director's right of inspection

Every director shall have the absolute right at any reasonable time to inspect and copy all books, records and documents of every kind and to inspect the physical properties of the corporation of which such person is a director.

Ca. Corp. Code § 12604

Added by Stats. 1982, Ch. 1625, Sec. 3. Operative January 1, 1984.

Section 12605 - Frustration of proper purpose of person making demand

Where the proper purpose of the person or persons making a demand pursuant to Section 12600 is frustrated by (a) any delay by the corporation in complying with a demand under Section 12600 beyond the time limits specified therein, or (b) any delay caused by the filing of a petition under Section 12601 or Section 12602, or (c) any delay caused by the alternative proposed under subdivision (c) of Section 12600, the person or persons properly making the demand shall have, in the discretion of the court, a right to obtain from the superior court an order postponing any members' meeting previously noticed for a period equal to the period of such delay. The members may obtain such an order in a proceeding brought pursuant to Section 12601 upon the filing of a verified complaint in the proper county and after a hearing, notice of which shall be given to such persons and in such manner as the court may direct. Such right shall be in addition to any other legal or equitable remedies to which the member may be entitled.

Ca. Corp. Code § 12605

Added by Stats. 1982, Ch. 1625, Sec. 3. Operative January 1, 1984.

Section 12606 - Enforcement of demand for inspection or right of inspection

(a) Upon refusal of a lawful demand for inspection under this chapter, or a lawful demand pursuant to Section 12600 or Section 12603, the superior court of the proper county, or the county where the books or records in question are kept, may enforce the demand or right of inspection with just and proper conditions or may, for good cause shown, appoint one or more competent inspectors or independent accountants to audit the financial statements kept in this state and investigate the property, funds and affairs of any corporation and of any subsidiary corporation thereof, domestic or foreign, keeping records in this state and to report thereon in such manner as the court may direct.

(b) All officers and agents of the corporation shall produce to the inspectors or accountants so appointed all books and documents in their custody or power, under penalty of punishment for contempt of court.

(c) All expenses of the investigation or audit shall be defrayed by the applicant unless the court orders them to be paid or shared by the corporation.

Ca. Corp. Code § 12606

Added by Stats. 1982, Ch. 1625, Sec. 3. Operative January 1, 1984.

Section 12607 - Award of reasonable costs and expenses to member

In any action or proceeding under this article, and except as required by Section 12601, if the court finds the failure of the corporation to comply with a proper demand thereunder was without justification, the court may award the member reasonable costs and expenses, including reasonable attorneys' fees, in connection with such action or proceeding.

Ca. Corp. Code § 12607

Added by Stats. 1982, Ch. 1625, Sec. 3. Operative January 1, 1984.

Section 12608 - Membership list

(a) A membership list is a corporate asset. Without consent of the board a membership list or any part thereof may not be obtained or used by any person for any purpose not reasonably related to a member's interest as a member. Without limiting the generality of the foregoing, without the consent of the board a membership list or any part thereof may not be:

(1) Used to solicit money or property unless such money or property will be used solely to solicit the vote of the members in an election to be held by their corporation;

or

(2) Used for any purpose which the user does not reasonably and in good faith believe will benefit the corporation; or

(3) Used for any commercial purpose or purpose in competition with the corporation; or

(4) Sold to or purchased by any person.

(b) Any person who violates the provisions of subdivision (a) shall be liable for any damage such violation causes the corporation and shall account for and pay to the corporation any profit derived as a result of said violation. In addition, a court in its discretion may award exemplary damages for a fraudulent or malicious violation of subdivision (a).

(c) Nothing in this article shall be construed to limit the right of a corporation to obtain injunctive relief necessary to restrain misuse of a membership list or any part thereof.

(d) In any action or proceeding under this section, a court may award the corporation reasonable costs and expenses, including reasonable attorneys' fees in connection with such action or proceeding.

(e) As used in this section, the term "membership list" means the record of all the members' names and addresses.

Ca. Corp. Code § 12608

Amended by Stats. 1996, Ch. 589, Sec. 53. Effective January 1, 1997.

Chapter 14 - SERVICE OF PROCESS

Section 12610 - Law governing service of process upon corporation

Service of process upon a corporation shall be governed by Chapter 17 (commencing with Section 1700) of Division 1 of Title 1.

Ca. Corp. Code § 12610

Added by Stats. 1982, Ch. 1625, Sec. 3. Operative January 1, 1984.

Chapter 15 - INVOLUNTARY DISSOLUTION

Section 12620 - Involuntary dissolution

(a) A complaint for involuntary dissolution of a corporation on any one or more of the grounds specified in subdivision (b) may be filed in the superior court of the proper county by any of the following persons:

(1) One-half or more of the directors in office.

(2) A person or persons holding or authorized in writing by persons holding not less than 33^1/$_3$ percent of the voting power exclusive of memberships held by persons who have personally participated in any of the transactions enumerated in paragraph (5) of subdivision (b).

(3) Any member if the ground for dissolution is that the period for which the corporation was formed has terminated without extension thereof.

(4) Any other person expressly authorized to do so in the articles.
(b) The grounds for involuntary dissolution are that:

(1) The corporation has abandoned its activity for more than one year.

(2) The corporation has an even number of directors who are equally divided and cannot agree as to the management of its affairs, so that its activities can no longer be conducted to advantage or so that there is danger that its property will be impaired or lost or its activities impaired, and the members are so divided into factions that they cannot elect a board consisting of an uneven number.

(3) There is internal dissension and two or more factions of members in the corporation are so deadlocked that its activities can no longer be conducted with advantage.

(4) When during any four-year period or when all voting power has been exercised at two consecutive meetings or in two written ballots for the election of directors, whichever period is shorter, the members have failed to elect successors to directors whose terms have expired or would have expired upon election of their successors.

(5) Those in control of the corporation have been guilty of or have knowingly countenanced persistent and pervasive fraud, mismanagement or abuse of authority or persistent unfairness toward any member or the corporation's property is being misapplied or wasted by its directors or officers.

(6) The period for which the corporation was formed has terminated without extension of such period.
(c) At any time prior to the trial of the action any member or creditor may intervene therein.
(d) This section does not apply to any corporation subject to:

(1) The Public Utilities Act (Part 1 (commencing with Section 201) of Division 1 of the Public Utilities Code) unless an order is obtained from the Public Utilities Commission authorizing the corporation either (a) to dispose of its assets as provided in Section 851 of the Public Utilities Code or (b) to dissolve.

(2) The provisions of Article 14 (commencing with Section 1010) of Chapter 1 of Part 2 of Division 1 of the Insurance Code when the application authorized by Section 1011 of the Insurance Code has been filed by the Insurance Commissioner unless the consent of the Insurance Commissioner has been obtained.

Ca. Corp. Code § 12620

Added by Stats. 1982, Ch. 1625, Sec. 3. Operative January 1, 1984.

Section 12621 - Action by attorney general

(a) The Attorney General may bring an action against any corporation or purported corporation in the name of the people of this state, upon the Attorney General's own information or upon complaint of a private party, to procure a judgment dissolving the corporation and annulling, vacating or forfeiting its corporate existence upon any of the following grounds:

(1) The corporation has seriously offended against any provision of the statutes regulating corporations.

(2) The corporation has fraudulently abused or usurped corporate privileges or powers.

(3) The corporation has violated any provision of law by any act or default which under the law is a ground for forfeiture of corporate existence.

(4) The corporation has failed to pay to the Franchise Tax Board for a period of five years any tax imposed upon it by the Bank and Corporation Tax Law.

(b) If the ground of the action is a matter or act which the corporation has done or omitted to do that can be corrected by amendment of its articles or by other corporate action, such suit shall not be maintained unless (1) the Attorney General, at least 30 days prior to the institution of suit, has given the corporation written notice of the matter or act done or omitted to be done; and (2) the corporation has failed to institute proceedings to correct it within the 30-day period or thereafter fails to duly and properly make such amendment or take the corrective corporate action.

(c) In any such action the court may order dissolution or such other or partial relief as it deems just and expedient. The court also may appoint a receiver for winding up the affairs of the corporation or may order that the corporation be wound up by its board subject to the supervision of the court.

(d) Service of process on the corporation may be made pursuant to Chapter 17 (commencing with Section 1700) of Division 1 or by written notice to the president or secretary of the corporation at the address indicated in the corporation's last tax return filed pursuant to the Bank and Corporation Tax Law. The Attorney General shall also publish one time in a newspaper of general circulation in the proper county a notice to the members of the corporation.

Ca. Corp. Code § 12621
Added by Stats. 1982, Ch. 1625, Sec. 3. Operative January 1, 1984.

Section 12622 - Provisional director

If the ground for the complaint for involuntary dissolution of the corporation is a deadlock in the board as set forth in paragraph (2) of subdivision (b) of Section 12620 the court may appoint a provisional director. The provisions of subdivision (d) of Section 12365 apply to any such provisional director so appointed.
Ca. Corp. Code § 12622
Added by Stats. 1982, Ch. 1625, Sec. 3. Operative January 1, 1984.

Section 12623 - Receiver

If, at the time of the filing of a complaint for involuntary dissolution or at any time thereafter, the court has reasonable grounds to believe that unless a receiver of the corporation is appointed the interests of the corporation or its members will suffer pending the hearing and determination of the complaint, upon the application of the plaintiff, and after a hearing upon such notice to the corporation as the court may direct and upon the giving of security pursuant to Sections 566 and 567 of the Code of Civil Procedure (except that the Attorney General shall not be required to give security), the court may appoint a receiver to take over and manage the affairs of the corporation and to preserve its property pending the hearing and determination of the complaint for dissolution.
Ca. Corp. Code § 12623
Added by Stats. 1982, Ch. 1625, Sec. 3. Operative January 1, 1984.

Section 12624 - Orders and decrees

After hearing the court may decree a winding up and dissolution of the corporation if cause therefor is shown or, with or without winding up and dissolution, may make such orders and decrees and issue such injunctions in the case as justice and equity require.
Ca. Corp. Code § 12624
Added by Stats. 1982, Ch. 1625, Sec. 3. Operative January 1, 1984.

Section 12625 - Involuntary proceedings for winding up

(a) Involuntary proceedings for winding up a corporation commence when the order for winding up is entered under Section 12624.
(b) When an involuntary proceeding for winding up has commenced, the board shall conduct the winding up of the affairs of the corporation, subject to the supervision of the court, unless other persons are appointed by the court, on good cause shown, to conduct the winding up. The directors or such other persons may, subject to any

restrictions imposed by the court, exercise all their powers through the executive officers without any order of court.

(c) When an involuntary proceeding for winding up has commenced, the corporation shall cease to conduct its activities except to the extent necessary for the beneficial winding up thereof and except during such period as the board may deem necessary to preserve the corporation's goodwill or going-concern value, pending a sale or other disposition of its assets, or both, in whole or in part. The directors shall cause written notice of the commencement of the proceeding for involuntary winding up to be given by mail to all members and to all known creditors and claimants whose addresses appear on the records of the corporation, unless the order for winding up has been stayed by appeal therefrom or otherwise or the proceeding or the execution of the order has been enjoined.

Ca. Corp. Code § 12625

Added by Stats. 1982, Ch. 1625, Sec. 3. Operative January 1, 1984.

Section 12626 - Jurisdiction of court

When an involuntary proceeding for winding up has been commenced, the jurisdiction of the court includes:

(a) The requirement of the proof of all claims and demands against the corporation, whether due or not yet due, contingent, unliquidated, or sounding only in damages, and the barring from participation of creditors and claimants failing to make and present claims and proof as required by any order.

(b) The determination or compromise of all claims of every nature against the corporation or any of its property, and the determination of the amount of money or assets required to be retained to pay or provide for the payment of claims.

(c) The determination of the rights of members and of all classes of members in and to the assets of the corporation.

(d) The presentation and filing of intermediate and final accounts of the directors or other persons appointed to conduct the winding up and hearing thereon, the allowance, disallowance, or settlement thereof, and the discharge of the directors or such other persons from their duties and liabilities.

(e) The appointment of a commissioner to hear and determine any or all matters, with such power or authority as the court may deem proper.

(f) The filing of any vacancies on the board which the directors or the members are unable to fill.

(g) The removal of any director if it appears that the director has been guilty of dishonesty, misconduct, neglect, or breach of trust in conducting the winding up or if the director is unable to act. The court may order an election to fill the vacancy so caused, and may enjoin, for such time as it considers proper, the reelection of the director so removed; or the court, in lieu of ordering an election, may appoint a director to fill the vacancy caused by such removal. Any director so appointed by the court shall serve until the next regular meeting of members or until a successor is elected or appointed.

(h) The staying of the prosecution of any suit, proceeding, or action against the corporation and requiring the parties to present and prove their claims in the manner required of other creditors.

(i) The determination of whether adequate provision has been made for payment or satisfaction of all debts and liabilities not actually paid.

(j) The making of orders for the withdrawal or termination of proceedings, to wind up and dissolve, subject to conditions for the protection of members and creditors.

(k) The making of an order, upon the allowance or settlement of the final accounts of the directors or such other persons, that the corporation has been duly wound up and is dissolved. Upon the making of such order, the corporate existence shall cease except for purposes of further winding up if needed.

(l) The making of orders for the bringing in of new parties as the court deems proper for the determination of all questions and matters.

(m) The disposition of assets held in charitable trust.

Ca. Corp. Code § 12626

Added by Stats. 1982, Ch. 1625, Sec. 3. Operative January 1, 1984.

Section 12627 - Creditors and claimants

(a) All creditors and claimants may be barred from participation in any distribution of the general assets if they fail to make and present claims and proofs within such time as the court may direct, which shall not be less than four nor more than six months after the first publication of notice to creditors unless it appears by affidavit that there are no claims, in which case the time limit may be three months. If it is shown that a claimant did not receive notice because of absence from the state or other cause, the court may allow a claim to be filed or presented at any time before distribution is completed.

(b) Such notice to creditors shall be published not less than once a week for three consecutive weeks in a newspaper of general circulation published in the county in which the proceeding is pending or, if there is no such newspaper published in that county, in such newspaper as may be designated by the court, directing creditors and claimants to make and present claims and proofs to the person, at the place and within the time specified in the notice. A copy of the notice shall be mailed to each person shown as a creditor or claimant on the books of the corporation, at such person's last known address.

(c) Holders of secured claims may prove for the whole debt in order to realize any deficiency. If such creditors fail to present their claims they shall be barred only as to any right to claim against the general assets for any deficiency in the amount realized on their security.

(d) Before any distribution is made the amount of any unmatured, contingent or disputed claim against the corporation which has been presented and has not been disallowed, or such part of any such claim as the holder would be entitled to if the claim were due, established, or absolute, shall be paid into court and there remain to be paid over to the party when the party becomes entitled thereto or, if the party fails to establish a claim, to be paid over or distributed with the other assets of the corporation to those entitled thereto; or such other provision for the full payment of such claim, if and when established, shall be made as the court may deem adequate. A creditor whose claim has been allowed but is not yet due shall be entitled to its present value upon distribution.

(e) Suits against the corporation on claims which have been rejected shall be commenced within 30 days after written notice of rejection thereof is given to the claimant.

Ca. Corp. Code § 12627

Added by Stats. 1982, Ch. 1625, Sec. 3. Operative January 1, 1984.

Section 12628 - Order declaring corporation duly wound up and dissolved

(a) Upon the final settlement of the accounts of the directors or other persons appointed pursuant to Section 12625 and the determination that the corporation's affairs are in condition for it to be dissolved, the court may make an order declaring the corporation duly wound up and dissolved. The order shall declare:

(1) That the corporation has been duly wound up, that a final franchise tax return, as described by Section 23332 of the Revenue and Taxation Code, has been filed with the Franchise Tax Board, as required under Part 10.2 (commencing with Section 18401) of Division 2 of the Revenue and Taxation Code and that its known debts and liabilities have been paid or adequately provided for, or that those debts and liabilities have been paid as far as its assets permitted, as the case may be. If there are known debts or liabilities for payment of which adequate provision has been made, the order shall state what provision has been made, setting forth the name and address of the corporation, person, or governmental agency that has assumed or guaranteed the payment, or the name and address of the depositary with which deposit has been made or such other information as may be necessary to enable the creditor or other person to whom payment is to be made to appear and claim payment of the debt or liability.

(2) That its known assets have been distributed to the persons entitled thereto or that it acquired no known assets, as the case may be.

(3) That the accounts of directors or such other persons have been settled and that they are discharged from their duties and liabilities to creditors and members.

(4) That the corporation is dissolved.

(b) The court may make such additional orders and grant such further relief as it deems proper upon the evidence submitted.

(c) Upon the making of the order declaring the corporation dissolved, corporate existence shall cease except for the purposes of further winding up if needed; and the directors or such other persons shall be discharged from their duties and liabilities, except in respect to completion of the winding up.

Ca. Corp. Code § 12628

Amended by Stats 2006 ch 773 (AB 2341),s 33, eff. 9/29/2006.

Section 12629 - Filing of order, decree, or judgment; notification of Franchise Tax Board

Whenever a corporation is dissolved or its existence forfeited by order, decree, or judgment of a court, a copy of the order, decree or judgment, certified by the clerk of court, shall forthwith be filed. The Secretary of State shall notify the Franchise Tax Board of the dissolution.

Ca. Corp. Code § 12629

Amended by Stats 2006 ch 773 (AB 2341),s 34, eff. 9/29/2006.

Chapter 16 - VOLUNTARY DISSOLUTION

Section 12630 - Voluntary election to wind up and dissolve

(a) Any corporation may elect voluntarily to wind up and dissolve (1) by approval of a majority of all members (Section 12223) or (2) by approval of the board and approval of the members (Section 12224).

(b) Any corporation which comes within one of the following descriptions may elect by approval of the board to wind up and dissolve:

(1) A corporation which has been the subject of an order for relief in bankruptcy.

(2) A corporation which has disposed of all of its assets and has not conducted any activity for a period of five years immediately preceding the adoption of the resolution electing to dissolve the corporation.

(3) A corporation which has no members.

(c) If a corporation comes within one of the descriptions in subdivision (b) and if the number of directors then in office is less than a quorum, it may elect to voluntarily wind up and dissolve by any of the following:

(1) The unanimous consent of the directors then in office.

(2) The affirmative vote of a majority of the directors then in office at a meeting held pursuant to waiver of notice by those directors complying with subdivision (a) of Section 12351.

(3) The vote of a sole remaining director.

(d) If a corporation elects to voluntarily wind up and dissolve pursuant to subdivision (c), references to the board in this chapter and Chapter 17 (commencing with Section

12650) shall be deemed to be to a board consisting solely of those directors or that sole director and action by the board shall require at least the same consent or vote as would be required under subdivision (c) for an election to wind up and dissolve.

Ca. Corp. Code § 12630
Amended by Stats 2009 ch 631 (AB 1233),s 49, eff. 1/1/2010.
Amended by Stats 2009 ch 500 (AB 1059),s 26, eff. 1/1/2010.

Section 12631 - Certificate evidencing election

(a) Whenever a corporation has elected to wind up and dissolve a certificate evidencing that election shall forthwith be filed.

(b) The certificate shall be an officers' certificate or shall be signed and verified by at least a majority of the directors then in office or by one or more members authorized to do so by approval of a majority of all members (Section 12223) and shall set forth:

(1) That the corporation has elected to wind up and dissolve.

(2) If the election was made by the vote of members alone, the number of votes for the election and that the election was made by persons holding at least a majority of the voting power.

(3) If the certificate is executed by a member or members, that the subscribing person or persons were authorized to execute the certificate by persons representing at least a majority of the voting power.

(4) If the election was made by the board pursuant to subdivision (b) of Section 12630, the certificate shall also set forth the circumstances showing the corporation to be within one of the categories described in that subdivision.

(c) If an election to dissolve made pursuant to subdivision (a) of Section 12630 is made by the vote of all the members of a corporation with members or by a vote of all members of the board of a corporation without members pursuant to subdivision (b) of Section 12630 and a statement to that effect is added to the certificate of dissolution pursuant to Section 12635, the separate filing of the certificate of election pursuant to this section is not required.

Ca. Corp. Code § 12631
Amended by Stats 2014 ch 834 (SB 1041),s 19, eff. 1/1/2015.
Amended September 21, 1999 (Bill Number: AB 1687) (Chapter 453).

Section 12632 - Revocation

(a) A voluntary election to wind up and dissolve may be revoked prior to distribution of any assets:

(1) if the election was made pursuant to paragraph (1) of subdivision (a) of Section

12630, by the approval of a majority of all members;

(2) if the election was made pursuant to paragraph (2) of subdivision (a) of Section 12630, by approval of the board and approval of the members; or

(3) if the election was by the board pursuant to subdivision (b) of Section 12630, by approval of the board. Thereupon a certificate evidencing the revocation shall be signed, verified and filed in the manner prescribed by Section 12631.
(b) The certificate shall set forth:

(1) That the corporation has revoked its election to wind up and dissolve.

(2) That no assets have been distributed pursuant to the election.

(3) If the revocation was made by the vote of members alone, the number of votes for the revocation and that the revocation was made by persons representing at least a majority of the voting power.

(4) If the revocation was made by the approval of the board and the approval of the members, the certificate shall so state.

(5) If the revocation was made by the board alone, the certificate shall so state.
Ca. Corp. Code § 12632
Added by Stats. 1982, Ch. 1625, Sec. 3. Operative January 1, 1984.

Section 12633 - Commencement of voluntary proceedings for winding up

(a) Voluntary proceedings for winding up the corporation commence upon the adoption of the resolution required by Section 12630 by the members or by the board, electing to wind up and dissolve.
(b) When a voluntary proceeding for winding up has commenced, the board shall continue to act as a board and shall have full powers to wind up and settle its affairs, both before and after the filing of the certificate of dissolution.
(c) When a voluntary proceeding for winding up has commenced, the corporation shall cease to conduct its activities except to the extent necessary for the beneficial winding up thereof, to the extent necessary to carry out its purposes, and except during such period as the board may deem necessary to preserve the corporation's goodwill or going-concern value pending a sale or other disposition of its assets, or both, in whole or in part. The board shall cause written notice of the commencement of the proceeding for voluntary winding up to be given by mail to all its members (except no notice need be given to the members who voted in favor of winding up and dissolving the corporation), to all known creditors, and claimants whose addresses appear on the records of the corporation.

Ca. Corp. Code § 12633
Added by Stats. 1982, Ch. 1625, Sec. 3. Operative January 1, 1984.

Section 12634 - Superior court taking jurisdiction over voluntary winding up proceeding

If a corporation is in the process of voluntary winding up, the superior court of the proper county, upon the petition of (a) the corporation, or (b) a member or members possessing 5 percent or more of the voting power, or (c) three or more creditors, and upon such notice to the corporation and to other persons interested in the corporation as members and creditors as the court may order, may take jurisdiction over such voluntary winding up proceeding if that appears necessary for the protection of any parties in interest. The court, if it assumes jurisdiction, may make such orders as to any and all matters concerning the winding up of the affairs of the corporation and the protection of its members and creditors as justice and equity may require. The provisions of Chapter 15 (commencing with Section 12620) (except Sections 12620 and 12621) shall apply to such court proceedings.

Ca. Corp. Code § 12634
Added by Stats. 1982, Ch. 1625, Sec. 3. Operative January 1, 1984.

Section 12635 - Certificate of dissolution

(a) When a corporation has been completely wound up without court proceedings therefor, a majority of the directors then in office shall sign and verify a certificate of dissolution stating:

(1) That the corporation has been completely wound up.

(2) That its known debts and liabilities have been actually paid, or adequately provided for, or paid or adequately provided for as far as its assets permitted, or that it has incurred no known debts or liabilities, as the case may be. If there are known debts or liabilities for payment of which adequate provision has been made, the certificate shall state what provision has been made, setting forth the name and address of the corporation, person or governmental agency that has assumed or guaranteed the payment, or the name and address of the depositary with which deposit has been made or such other information as may be necessary to enable the creditor or other person to whom payment is to be made to appear and claim payment of the debt or liability.

(3) That its known assets have been distributed to the persons entitled thereto or that it acquired no known assets, as the case may be.

(4) That the corporation is dissolved.

(5) That a final franchise tax return, as described by Section 23332 of the Revenue and Taxation Code, has been or will be filed with the Franchise Tax Board, as required under Part 10.2 (commencing with Section 18401) of Division 2 of the Revenue and Taxation Code.

(b) The certificate of dissolution shall be filed and thereupon the corporate existence shall cease, except for the purpose of further winding up if needed. The Secretary of State shall notify the Franchise Tax Board of the dissolution.

Ca. Corp. Code § 12635

Amended by Stats 2006 ch 773 (AB 2341),s 35, eff. 9/29/2006.

Section 12636 - Expiration of term of existence

Except as otherwise provided by law, if the term of existence for which any corporation was organized expires without renewal or extension thereof, the board shall terminate its activities and wind up its affairs; and when the affairs of the corporation have been wound up a majority of the directors shall execute and file a certificate conforming to the requirements of Section 12635.

Ca. Corp. Code § 12636

Added by Stats. 1982, Ch. 1625, Sec. 3. Operative January 1, 1984.

Section 12637 - Petition for order declaring corporation duly wound up and dissolved

(a) The board, in lieu of filing the certificate of dissolution, may petition the superior court of the proper county for an order declaring the corporation duly wound up and dissolved. Such petition shall be filed in the name of the corporation.

(b) Upon the filing of the petition, the court shall make an order requiring all interested persons to show cause why an order shall not be made declaring the corporation duly wound up and dissolved and shall direct that the order be served by notice to all creditors, claimants, and members in the same manner as the notice given under subdivision (b) of Section 12627.

(c) Any person claiming to be interested as member, creditor, or otherwise may appear in the proceeding at any time before the expiration of 30 days from the completion of publication of the order to show cause and contest the petition, and upon failure to appear such person's claim shall be barred.

(d) Thereafter an order shall be entered and filed and have the effect as prescribed in Sections 12628 and 12629.

Ca. Corp. Code § 12637

Added by Stats. 1982, Ch. 1625, Sec. 3. Operative January 1, 1984.

The Legislature enacted two versions of § 12637. The text of each version has been set out with the same section number pending reconciliation by the legislature. .

Section 12638 - Disposal of known claims

(a) A corporation in the process of winding up may dispose of the known claims against it by following the procedure described in this section.

(b) The written notice to known creditors and claimants required by subdivision (c) of Section 12633 shall comply with all of the following requirements:

   (1) Describe any information that must be included in a claim.

   (2) Provide a mailing address where a claim may be sent.

   (3) State the deadline, which shall not be fewer than 120 days from the effective date of the written notice, by which the corporation must receive the claim.

   (4) State that the claim will be barred if not received by the deadline.

(c) A claim against the corporation is barred if any of the following occur:

   (1) A claimant who has been given the written notice under subdivision (b) does not deliver the claim to the corporation by the deadline.

   (2) A claimant whose claim was rejected by the corporation does not commence a proceeding to enforce the claim within 90 days from the effective date of the rejection notice.

(d) For purposes of this section, "claim" does not include a contingent liability or a claim based on an event occurring after the effective date of dissolution.

   Ca. Corp. Code § 12638

Renumbered from Ca. Corp. Code § 12637 and amended by Stats 2015 ch 303 (AB 731),s 46, eff. 1/1/2016.

The Legislature enacted two versions of § 12637. The text of each version has been set out with the same section number pending reconciliation by the legislature. .

Chapter 17 - GENERAL PROVISIONS RELATING TO DISSOLUTION

Section 12650 - Powers and duties of directors and officers

The powers and duties of the directors (or other persons appointed by the court pursuant to Section 12625) and officers after commencement of a dissolution proceeding include, but are not limited to, the following acts in the name and on behalf of the corporation:

(a) To elect officers and to employ agents and attorneys to liquidate or wind up its affairs.

(b) To continue the conduct of the affairs of the corporation insofar as necessary for the disposal or winding up thereof.

(c) To carry out contracts and collect, pay, compromise, and settle debts and claims for or against the corporation.

(d) To defend suits brought against the corporation.

(e) To sue, in the name of the corporation, for all sums due or owing to the corporation or to recover any of its property.

(f) To collect any amounts remaining unpaid on memberships or to recover unlawful distributions.

(g) To sell at public or private sale, exchange, convey, or otherwise dispose of all or any part of the assets of the corporation for an amount deemed reasonable by the board without compliance with the provisions of Section 12521, and to execute bills of sale and deeds of conveyance in the name of the corporation.

(h) In general, to make contracts and to do any and all things in the name of the corporation which may be proper or convenient for the purposes of winding up, settling, and liquidating the affairs of the corporation.

   Ca. Corp. Code § 12650

Added by Stats. 1982, Ch. 1625, Sec. 3. Operative January 1, 1984.

Section 12651 - Filling vacancy on board

A vacancy on the board may be filled during a winding up proceeding in the manner provided in Section 12364.

   Ca. Corp. Code § 12651

Added by Stats. 1982, Ch. 1625, Sec. 3. Operative January 1, 1984.

Section 12652 - Determination of identity of directors or appointment of directors

When the identity of the directors or their right to hold office is in doubt, or if they are dead or unable to act, or they fail or refuse to act or their whereabouts cannot be ascertained, any interested person may petition the superior court of the proper county to determine the identity of the directors or, if there are no directors, to appoint directors to wind up the affairs of the corporation, after hearing upon such notice to such persons as the court may direct.

   Ca. Corp. Code § 12652

Added by Stats. 1982, Ch. 1625, Sec. 3. Operative January 1, 1984.

Section 12653 - Distribution of remaining assets

(a) After determining that all the known debts and liabilities of a corporation in the process of winding up have been paid or adequately provided for, the board shall distribute all the remaining corporate assets in the manner provided in Sections 12655, 12656, and 12656.5.

(b) If the winding up is by court proceeding or subject to court supervision, the distribution shall not be made until after the expiration of any period for the presentation of claims that has been prescribed by order of the court.

(c) Anything to the contrary notwithstanding, assets, if any, that are not subject to attachment, execution, or sale for the corporation's debts and liabilities may be distributed pursuant to Sections 12655, 12656, and 12656.5 even though all debts and liabilities have not been paid or adequately provided for.

Ca. Corp. Code § 12653

Amended by Stats 2015 ch 192 (AB 816),s 24, eff. 1/1/2016.

Section 12654 - Payment of debt or liability

The payment of a debt or liability, whether the whereabouts of the creditor is known or unknown, has been adequately provided for if the payment has been provided for by either of the following means:

(a) Payment thereof has been assumed or guaranteed in good faith by one or more financially responsible persons or by the United States government or any agency thereof, and the provision (including the financial responsibility of such persons) was determined in good faith and with reasonable care by the board to be adequate at the time of any distribution of the assets by the board pursuant to this chapter.

(b) The amount of the debt or liability has been deposited as provided in Section 12659. This section does not prescribe the exclusive means of making adequate provision for debts and liabilities.

Ca. Corp. Code § 12654

Added by Stats. 1982, Ch. 1625, Sec. 3. Operative January 1, 1984.

Section 12655 - Assets held by corporation upon condition requiring return, transfer, or conveyance

After complying with the provisions of Section 12653 assets held by a corporation upon a valid condition requiring return, transfer, or conveyance, which condition has occurred or will occur, shall be returned, transferred, or conveyed in accordance with the condition.

Ca. Corp. Code § 12655

Added by Stats. 1982, Ch. 1625, Sec. 3. Operative January 1, 1984.

Section 12656 - Disposal of assets

After complying with the provisions of Section 12653 and except as otherwise provided in Section 12655, assets held by a corporation shall be disposed of on dissolution as follows:

(a) If the articles or bylaws provide the manner of disposition, the assets shall be disposed of in that manner.

(b) If the articles or bylaws do not provide the manner of disposition, the assets shall be distributed among the members in accordance with their respective rights therein.

Ca. Corp. Code § 12656

Added by Stats. 1982, Ch. 1625, Sec. 3. Operative January 1, 1984.

Section 12656.5 - Dissolution of worker cooperative; distribution of unallocated capital account

(a) After complying with the provisions of Section 12653, and except as otherwise provided in Section 12655, upon dissolution of a worker cooperative the majority of the unallocated capital account shall be distributed to members on the basis of any of the following, as specified in the articles of incorporation or bylaws of the cooperative:

   (1) Patronage.

   (2) Capital contributions.

   (3) A combination of patronage and capital contributions.

(b) A worker cooperative is authorized to include patronage provided by past and current members in its distribution of the unallocated capital account.

(c) Subdivision (a) shall not apply to any amounts in the indivisible reserve account. Any amount in the indivisible reserve account shall, upon dissolution, be allocated to a cooperative development organization designated in the articles of incorporation or the bylaws.

   Ca. Corp. Code § 12656.5

Added by Stats 2015 ch 192 (AB 816),s 25, eff. 1/1/2016.

Section 12657 - Distribution

Distribution may be made either in money or in property or securities and either in installments from time to time or as a whole, if this can be done fairly and ratably and in conformity with the provisions of the articles and bylaws and shall be made as soon as reasonably consistent with the beneficial liquidation of the corporation assets.

   Ca. Corp. Code § 12657

Added by Stats. 1982, Ch. 1625, Sec. 3. Operative January 1, 1984.

Section 12658 - Plan of distribution

(a) If a corporation in process of winding up has more than one class of memberships outstanding, a plan of distribution of the memberships, obligations, or securities of any other corporation, domestic or foreign, or assets other than money which is not in accordance with the liquidation rights of any class or classes as specified in the articles or bylaws may nevertheless be adopted if approved by (1) the board and (2) by approval by the members (Section 12224) of each class. The plan may provide that such distribution is in complete or partial satisfaction of the rights of any of such members upon distribution and liquidation of the assets.

(b) A plan of distribution so approved shall be binding upon all the members. The board shall cause notice of the adoption of the plan to be given by mail within 20 days after its adoption to all holders of memberships having a liquidation preference.

   Ca. Corp. Code § 12658
Added by Stats. 1982, Ch. 1625, Sec. 3. Operative January 1, 1984.

Section 12659 - Deposit with controller in trust

(a) If any members, creditors, or other persons are unknown or fail or refuse to accept their payment or distribution in cash or property or their whereabouts cannot be ascertained after diligent inquiry, or the existence or amount of a claim of a creditor, member, or other person is contingent, contested, or not determined, or if the ownership of any memberships is in dispute, the corporation may deposit any such payment, distribution, or the maximum amount of the claim with the Controller in trust for the benefit of those lawfully entitled to the payment, distribution, or the amount of the claim. The payment or distribution shall be paid over by the depositary to the lawful owners, their representatives or assigns, upon satisfactory proof of title.
(b) For the purpose of providing for the transmittal, receipt, accounting for, claiming, management, and investment of all money or other property deposited with the Controller under subdivision (a), the money or other property shall be deemed to be paid or delivered for deposit with the Controller under Chapter 7 (commencing with Section 1500) of Title 10 of Part 3 of the Code of Civil Procedure, and may be recovered in the manner prescribed in that chapter.

   Ca. Corp. Code § 12659
Amended by Stats. 1996, Ch. 860, Sec. 4. Effective January 1, 1997.

Section 12660 - Recovery of improper distribution

(a) Whenever in the process of winding up a corporation any distribution of assets has been made, otherwise than under an order of court, without prior payment or adequate provision for payment of any of the debts and liabilities of the corporation, any amount so improperly distributed to any person may be recovered by the corporation. Any of such persons may be joined as defendants in the same action or be brought in on the motion of any other defendant.
(b) Suit may be brought in the name of the corporation to enforce the liability under subdivision (a) against any or all persons receiving the distribution by any one or more creditors of the corporation, whether or not they have reduced their claims to judgment.
(c) Members who satisfy any liability under this section shall have the right of ratable contribution from other distributees similarly liable. Any member who has been compelled to return to the corporation more than the member's ratable share of the amount needed to pay the debts and liabilities of the corporation may require that the corporation recover from any or all of the other distributees such proportion of the amounts received by them upon the improper distribution as to give contribution to those held liable under this section and make the distribution of the assets fair and ratable, according to the respective rights and preferences of the memberships, after

payment or adequate provision for payment of all the debts and liabilities of the corporation.

(d) As used in this section, "process of winding up" includes proceedings under Chapters 15 (commencing with Section 12630) and 16 (commencing with Section 12630) and also any other distribution of assets to persons made in contemplation of termination or abandonment of the corporate business.

  Ca. Corp. Code § 12660

Added by Stats. 1982, Ch. 1625, Sec. 3. Operative January 1, 1984.

Section 12661 - Continued existence

(a) A corporation which is dissolved nevertheless continues to exist for the purpose of winding up its affairs, prosecuting and defending actions by or against it, and enabling it to collect and discharge obligations, dispose of and convey its property and collect, and divide its assets, but not for the purpose of continuing its activities except so far as necessary for the winding up thereof.

(b) No action or proceeding to which a corporation is a party abates by the dissolution of the corporation or by reason of proceedings for winding up and dissolution thereof.

(c) Any assets inadvertently or otherwise omitted from the winding up continue in the dissolved corporation for the benefit of the persons entitled thereto upon dissolution of the corporation and on realization shall be distributed accordingly.

  Ca. Corp. Code § 12661

Added by Stats. 1982, Ch. 1625, Sec. 3. Operative January 1, 1984.

Section 12662 - Enforcement of causes of action

(a)

  (1) Causes of action against a dissolved corporation, whether arising before or after the dissolution of the corporation, may be enforced against any of the following:

    (A) Against the dissolved corporation, to the extent of its undistributed assets; including, without limitation, any insurance assets held by the corporation that may be available to satisfy claims.

    (B) If any of the assets of the dissolved corporation have been distributed to other persons, against those persons to the extent of their pro rata share of the claim or to the extent of the corporate assets distributed to them upon dissolution of the corporation, whichever is less. The total liability of a person under this section may not exceed the total amount of assets of the dissolved corporation distributed to that person upon dissolution of the corporation.

(2) Except as set forth in subdivision (c), all causes of action against a person to whom assets were distributed arising under this section are extinguished unless the claimant commences a proceeding to enforce the cause of action against that person prior to the earlier of the following:

(A) The expiration of the statute of limitations applicable to the cause of action.

(B) Four years after the effective date of the dissolution of the corporation.

(3) As a matter of procedure only, and not for purposes of determining liability, persons to whom assets of a dissolved corporation are distributed may be sued in the name of the corporation upon any cause of action against the corporation. This section does not affect the rights of the corporation or its creditors under Section 2009, or the rights, if any, of creditors under the Uniform Voidable Transactions Act, which may arise against persons to whom those assets are distributed. This subdivision applies to corporations dissolved on or after January 1, 2000. Corporations dissolved prior to that date are subject to the law in effect prior to that date.

(b) Summons or other process against a dissolved corporation may be served by delivering a copy thereof to an officer, director, or person having charge of its assets or, if that person cannot be found, to any agent upon whom process might be served at the time of dissolution. If none of these persons can be found with due diligence and it is so shown by affidavit to the satisfaction of the court, then the court may make an order that summons or other process be served upon the dissolved corporation by personally delivering a copy thereof, together with a copy of the order, to the Secretary of State or an assistant or deputy secretary of state.

(c) Every dissolved corporation shall survive and continue to exist indefinitely for the purpose of being sued in any quiet title action. Any judgment rendered in any quiet title action shall bind each and all of its members or other persons having any equity or other interest in that corporation, to the extent of their interest therein, and that action shall have the same force and effect as an action brought under the provisions of Sections 410.50 and 410.60 of the Code of Civil Procedure. Service of summons or other process in any quiet title action may be made as provided in Chapter 4 (commencing with Section 413.10) of Title 5 of Part 2 of the Code of Civil Procedure or as provided in subdivision (b).

(d) Upon receipt of that process and the fee therefor, the Secretary of State forthwith shall give notice to the corporation as provided in Section 1702.

Ca. Corp. Code § 12662

Amended by Stats 2019 ch 143 (SB 251),s 33, eff. 1/1/2020.

Amended 9/21/1999 (Bill Number: AB 1687) (Chapter 453).

Section 12663 - Obligations of owners' association

Without the approval of 100 percent of the members, any contrary provision in this part or the articles or bylaws notwithstanding, so long as there is any lot, parcel, area, apartment or unit for which an owners' association, created in connection with any of the forms of development referred to in Section 11004.5 of the Business and Professions Code, is obligated to provide management, maintenance, preservation, or control, the following shall apply:

(a) The owners' association or any person acting on its behalf shall not do either of the following:

(1) Transfer all or substantially all of its assets.

(2) File a certificate of dissolution.

(b) No court shall enter an order declaring the owners' association duly wound up and dissolved.

    Ca. Corp. Code § 12663

Amended by Stats 2006 ch 538 (SB 1852),s 81, eff. 1/1/2007.

Chapter 18 - CRIMES AND PENALTIES

Section 12670 - Failure of corporation to file statement

(a) Upon the failure of a corporation to file the statement required by Section 12570, the Secretary of State shall provide a notice of that delinquency to the corporation. The notice shall also contain information concerning the application of this section, and shall advise the corporation of the penalty imposed by Section 19141 of the Revenue and Taxation Code for failure to timely file the required statement after notice of delinquency has been provided by the Secretary of State. If, within 60 days after providing notice of the delinquency, a statement pursuant to Section 12570 has not been filed by the corporation, the Secretary of State shall certify the name of the corporation to the Franchise Tax Board.

(b) Upon certification pursuant to subdivision (a), the Franchise Tax Board shall assess against the corporation a penalty of fifty dollars ($50) pursuant to Section 19141 of the Revenue and Taxation Code.

(c) The penalty herein provided shall not apply to a corporation which on or prior to the date of certification pursuant to subdivision (a) has dissolved, has been converted to another type of business entity, or has been merged into another corporation or other business entity.

(d) The penalty herein provided shall not apply and the Secretary of State need not provide a notice of the delinquency to a corporation the corporate powers, rights, and privileges of which have been suspended by the Franchise Tax Board pursuant to Section 23301, 23301.5, or 23775 of the Revenue and Taxation Code on or prior to, and remain suspended on, the last day of the filing period pursuant to Section 12570. The Secretary of State need not provide notice of the filing requirement pursuant to Section 12570, to a corporation the corporate powers, rights, and privileges of which have been so suspended by the Franchise Tax Board on or prior to, and remain suspended on, the day the Secretary of State prepares the notice for sending.

(e) If, after certification pursuant to subdivision (a) the Secretary of State finds the required statement was filed before the expiration of the 60-day period after providing notice of the delinquency, the Secretary of State shall promptly decertify the name of the corporation to the Franchise Tax Board. The Franchise Tax Board shall then promptly abate any penalty assessed against the corporation pursuant to Section 19141 of the Revenue and Taxation Code.

(f) If the Secretary of State determines that the failure of a corporation to file a statement required by Section 12570 is excusable because of reasonable cause or unusual circumstances which justify the failure, the Secretary of State may waive the penalty imposed by this section and by Section 19141 of the Revenue and Taxation Code, in which case the Secretary of State shall not certify the name of the corporation to the Franchise Tax Board, or if already certified, the Secretary of State shall promptly decertify the name of the corporation.

  Ca. Corp. Code § 12670

Amended by Stats 2014 ch 834 (SB 1041),s 20, eff. 1/1/2015.

Amended by Stats 2011 ch 204 (AB 657),s 12, eff. 1/1/2012.

Section 12671 - Issuance of memberships or membership certificates with intent to defraud

Any promoter, director, or officer of a corporation who knowingly and willfully issues or consents to the issuance of memberships or membership certificates with intent to defraud present or future members or creditors is guilty of a misdemeanor punishable by a fine of not more than one thousand dollars ($1,000) or by imprisonment in county jail for not more than one year or by both such fine and imprisonment.

  Ca. Corp. Code § 12671

Added by Stats. 1982, Ch. 1625, Sec. 3. Operative January 1, 1984.

Section 12672 - Unlawful distribution of assets

Any director of any corporation who concurs in any vote or act of the directors of the corporation or any of them, knowingly and with dishonest or fraudulent purpose, to make any distribution of assets, except in the case and in the manner allowed by this part, either with the design of defrauding creditors or members or of giving a false appearance to the value of the membership and thereby defrauding purchasers is guilty of a crime. Each such crime is punishable by imprisonment pursuant to subdivision (h) of Section 1170 of the Penal Code, or by a fine of not more than one thousand dollars ($1,000), or imprisonment in a county jail for not more than one year, or by both that fine and imprisonment.

  Ca. Corp. Code § 12672

Amended by Stats 2011 ch 39 (AB 117),s 68, eff. 6/30/2011.

Amended by Stats 2011 ch 15 (AB 109),s 44, eff. 4/4/2011, but operative no earlier than October 1, 2011, and only upon creation of a community corrections grant program to assist in implementing this act and upon an appropriation to fund the grant program.

Section 12673 - Unlawful making or publishing false report or statement; unlawful refusal to make book entry or post notice

(a) Every director or officer of any corporation is guilty of a crime if such director or officer knowingly concurs in making or publishing, either generally or privately, to members or other persons (1) any materially false report or statement as to the financial condition of the corporation, or (2) any willfully or fraudulently exaggerated report, prospectus, account, or statement of operations, financial condition, or prospects, or (3) any other paper intended to give, and having a tendency to give, a membership in such corporation a greater or lesser value than it really possesses.
(b) Every director or officer of any corporation is guilty of a crime who refuses to make or direct to be made any book entry or the posting of any notice required by law in the manner required by law.
(c) A violation of subdivision (a) or (b) of this section shall be punishable by imprisonment in state prison or by a fine of not more than one thousand dollars ($1,000) or imprisonment in the county jail for not more than one year or both such fine and imprisonment.
  Ca. Corp. Code § 12673
Added by Stats. 1982, Ch. 1625, Sec. 3. Operative January 1, 1984.

Section 12674 - Unlawful receipt of property; unlawful destruction or falsification of records

(a) Every director, officer or agent of any corporation, who knowingly receives or acquires possession of any property of the corporation, otherwise than in payment of a just demand, and, with intent to defraud, omits to make, or to cause or direct to be made, a full and true entry thereof in the books or accounts of the corporation is guilty of a crime.
(b) Every director, officer, agent or member of any corporation who, with intent to defraud, destroys, alters, mutilates or falsifies any of the books, papers, writings, or securities belonging to the corporation or makes or concurs in omitting to make any material entry in any book of accounts or other record or document kept by the corporation is guilty of a crime.
(c) Each crime specified in this section is punishable by imprisonment in state prison, or by imprisonment in a county jail for not exceeding one year, or a fine not exceeding one thousand dollars ($1,000), or both such fine and imprisonment.
  Ca. Corp. Code § 12674
Added by Stats. 1982, Ch. 1625, Sec. 3. Operative January 1, 1984.

Section 12675 - Unlawful exhibition of false or altered instrument of evidence to public officer or board

Every director, officer or agent of any corporation, or any person proposing to organize such a corporation who knowingly exhibits any false, forged, or altered book, paper, voucher, security, or other instrument of evidence to any public officer or board authorized by law to examine the organization of such corporation or to investigate its affairs, with intent to deceive such officer or board in respect thereto, is punishable by imprisonment pursuant to subdivision (h) of Section 1170 of the Penal Code, or by imprisonment in a county jail for not exceeding one year.

   Ca. Corp. Code § 12675
Amended by Stats 2011 ch 39 (AB 117),s 68, eff. 6/30/2011.
Amended by Stats 2011 ch 15 (AB 109),s 45, eff. 4/4/2011, but operative no earlier than October 1, 2011, and only upon creation of a community corrections grant program to assist in implementing this act and upon an appropriation to fund the grant program.

Section 12676 - Unlawful subscribing of another's name in prospectus, advertisement or announcement

Every person who, without being authorized so to do, subscribes the name of another to or inserts the name of another in any prospectus, circular or other advertisement or announcement of any corporation, whether existing or intended to be formed, with intent to permit the document to be published and thereby to lead persons to believe that the person whose name is so subscribed is an officer, agent or promoter of such corporation, when in fact no such relationship exists to the knowledge of such person, is guilty of a misdemeanor.

   Ca. Corp. Code § 12676
Added by Stats. 1982, Ch. 1625, Sec. 3. Operative January 1, 1984.

Section 12677 - No limitation on state's power to punish

Nothing in this chapter limits the power of the state to punish any person for any conduct which constitutes a crime under any other statute.

   Ca. Corp. Code § 12677
Added by Stats. 1982, Ch. 1625, Sec. 3. Operative January 1, 1984.

Section 12678 - Injunctive relief

Any person may be enjoined from violating the provisions of Section 12311. Any corporation may be enjoined from carrying on business outside of the purpose for which it was formed.

   Ca. Corp. Code § 12678
Added by Stats. 1982, Ch. 1625, Sec. 3. Operative January 1, 1984.

Section 12679 - Violation of Section 12311 or carrying on business outside purposes for which corporation was formed

Any person violating Section 12311, and any corporation carrying on business outside the purpose for which it was formed, is guilty of a misdemeanor punishable by a fine of five hundred dollars ($500), or by imprisonment for not more than one year, or by both such fine and imprisonment.

Ca. Corp. Code § 12679
Added by Stats. 1982, Ch. 1625, Sec. 3. Operative January 1, 1984.

Chapter 19 - FOREIGN CORPORATIONS

Section 12680 - Laws applicable to foreign corporations transacting intrastate business

Foreign corporations transacting intrastate business shall comply with Chapter 21 (commencing with Section 2100) of Division 1, except as to matters specifically otherwise provided for in this part and except that Section 2115 shall not be applicable.

Ca. Corp. Code § 12680
Amended by Stats. 1997, Ch. 187, Sec. 10. Effective January 1, 1998.

Chapter 20 - TRANSITION PROVISIONS

Section 12690 - Definitions

As used in Sections 12690 to 12704, inclusive, of this part:
(a) "New law" means Part 2 (commencing with Section 12200) of Division 3 of Title 1 of the Corporations Code enacted by the California Legislature during the 1981-82 Regular Session and operative January 1, 1984.
(b) "Prior law" means Part 2 (commencing with Section 12220) of Division 3 of Title 1 of the Corporations Code in effect on December 31, 1983.
(c) "Subject corporation" means any corporation described in subdivision (a) of Section 12202 and subject to the prior law.

Ca. Corp. Code § 12690
Added by Stats. 1982, Ch. 1625, Sec. 3. Operative January 1, 1984.

Section 12691 - Applicability of new law

(a) The new law shall apply to all corporations which are incorporated on or after January 1, 1984, under Part 2 (commencing with Section 12200) of this division or which are expressly governed by Part 2 pursuant to a particular provision of this division or other specific statutory provision.

(b) Except as otherwise expressly provided in this chapter, the new law shall apply to all subject corporations and to all actions taken by the directors, officers, or members of such corporations, on or after January 1, 1984.

(c) Except as otherwise expressly provided in this chapter, all of the sections of the new law governing acts, contracts, or other transactions by a subject corporation or its directors, officers, or members, shall apply only to the acts, contracts, or transactions occurring on or after January 1, 1984, and the prior law shall govern acts, contracts, or transactions occurring before January 1, 1984.

(d) Except as otherwise expressly provided in this chapter, any vote or consent by the directors or members of a subject corporation prior to January 1, 1984, in accordance with the prior law, shall be effective in accordance with that law. If any certificate or document is required to be filed in any public office of this state relating to such vote or consent, it may be filed on or after January 1, 1984, in accordance with the prior law.

Ca. Corp. Code § 12691

Added by Stats. 1982, Ch. 1625, Sec. 3. Operative January 1, 1984.

Section 12692 - Applicability of new law relating to contents of articles of incorporation

(a) The provisions of Sections 12310 and 12313 of the new law relating to the contents of articles of incorporation do not apply to subject corporations unless and until an amendment of the articles is filed stating that the corporation elects to be governed by all of the provisions of the new law not otherwise applicable to it under this chapter.

(b) The amendment described in subdivision (a) may be adopted by the board alone, except that if such amendment makes any change in the articles other than conforming the statement of purposes of the subject corporation to Section 12310, deleting any references to the location of its principal office, deleting any statement of par value or any statement regarding the number of directors, or conforming any such statement to Section 12331 (subject to Section 12694), the amendment shall also be approved by the members (Section 12224) if such approval is otherwise required for the changes made.

(c) The amendment shall not name the corporation's initial agent for service of process if a report required by Section 12570 has been filed.

Ca. Corp. Code § 12692

Added by Stats. 1982, Ch. 1625, Sec. 3. Operative January 1, 1984.

Section 12693 - Applicability of Section 12320

Section 12320 of the new law shall apply to subject corporations, but any statement in the articles of these corporations prior to an amendment thereof pursuant to Section 12692, relating to the powers of the corporation, shall not be construed as a limitation unless it is expressly stated as such.

Ca. Corp. Code § 12693
Added by Stats. 1982, Ch. 1625, Sec. 3. Operative January 1, 1984.

Section 12694 - Applicability of subdivision (a) of Section 12353

Subdivision (a) of Section 12353 of the new law shall apply to subject corporations, but the treasurer of these corporations shall be deemed to be the chief financial officer unless otherwise provided in the articles or bylaws.

Ca. Corp. Code § 12694
Amended by Stats 2009 ch 631 (AB 1233),s 50, eff. 1/1/2010.

Section 12695 - Applicability of new law governing indemnification

Section 12377 governs any proposed indemnification by a subject corporation after January 1, 1984, whether the events upon which the indemnification is based occurred before or after January 1, 1984. Any statement relating to indemnification contained in the articles or bylaws of a subject corporation shall not be construed as limiting the indemnification permitted by Section 12377, unless it is expressly stated as so intended.

Ca. Corp. Code § 12695
Added by Stats. 1982, Ch. 1625, Sec. 3. Operative January 1, 1984.

Section 12696 - Applicability of new law governing members' meetings

(a) The provisions of Chapter 5 (commencing with Section 12460) and Chapter 6 (commencing with Section 12480) of the new law shall apply to any meeting of members of a subject corporation, held on or after January 1, 1984, and to any action by such members pursuant to a written ballot, which becomes effective on or after January 1, 1984, and to any vote cast at such a meeting or ballot, given for such action, whether or not a ballot was executed by the member prior to January 1, 1984.
(b) Notwithstanding subdivision (a), the prior law shall apply to any meeting of members and to any vote cast at such a meeting if the meeting was initially called for a date prior to January 1, 1984, and notice thereof was given to members entitled to vote at the meeting.

Ca. Corp. Code § 12696
Added by Stats. 1982, Ch. 1625, Sec. 3. Operative January 1, 1984.

Section 12697 - Applicability of new law governing actions

Section 12490 of the new law shall apply to actions commenced on or after January 1, 1984, with respect to a subject corporation. The prior law shall govern actions which are commenced prior to January 1, 1984, but are still pending on January 1, 1984.

Ca. Corp. Code § 12697
Added by Stats. 1982, Ch. 1625, Sec. 3. Operative January 1, 1984.

Section 12698 - Applicability of new law governing transactions

Chapter 9 (commencing with Section 12520) and Chapter 10 (commencing with Section 12530) of the new law shall apply to transactions consummated by a subject corporation on or after January 1, 1984, unless the approval required by the prior law has been given prior to January 1, 1984, or has been given on or after January 1, 1984, at a meeting of members initially called for a date prior to January 1, 1984, in which case the transaction shall be governed by the prior law.

Ca. Corp. Code § 12698
Added by Stats. 1982, Ch. 1625, Sec. 3. Operative January 1, 1984.

Section 12699 - Applicability of new law governing involuntary dissolution

Chapter 15 (commencing with Section 12620) and Chapter 17 (commencing with Section 12650) of the new law shall apply to acts for involuntary dissolution of a subject corporation commenced on or after January 1, 1984. The prior law shall govern any of these actions which are commenced prior to January 1, 1984, but are still pending on January 1, 1984.

Ca. Corp. Code § 12699
Added by Stats. 1982, Ch. 1625, Sec. 3. Operative January 1, 1984.

Section 12700 - Applicability of new governing voluntary dissolution

Chapter 16 (commencing with Section 12630) and Chapter 17 (commencing with Section 12650) of the new law shall apply to any voluntary dissolution proceeding initiated with respect to a subject corporation by the filing on or after January 1, 1984, of an election to wind up and dissolve. The prior law shall govern any of these proceedings so initiated prior to January 1, 1984.

Ca. Corp. Code § 12700
Repealed and added by Stats. 1982, Ch. 1625, Sec. 3. Operative January 1, 1984.

Section 12701 - Service of process on designated agent

When any corporate agent has been designated for service of process prior to January 1, 1984, and such designation of an agent included a name of a city, town, or village where the corporate agent maintained an office, service on such an agent may be effected at any office of the agent set forth in the certificate of the corporate agent filed pursuant to Section 1505, 6213, 8213, or 12573, or filed pursuant to Section 3301.5, 3301.6, 6403.5, or 6403.6 as in effect prior to January 1, 1977.

Ca. Corp. Code § 12701
Repealed and added by Stats. 1982, Ch. 1625, Sec. 3. Operative January 1, 1984.

Section 12702 - Election to continue existence

Any subject corporation that existed on the first day of January 1873, was formed under the laws of this state, and which has not already elected to continue its existence under the prior law, may at any time elect to continue its existence under the provisions of this code applicable thereto, (a) by the unanimous vote of all its directors, (b) by the vote of the members representing a majority of the voting power of the corporation at an election held at any annual meeting of the members or at any meeting called by the directors for the express purpose of considering this subject, or (c) by action of the directors upon the written consent of the members representing a majority of the voting power of the corporation.

A certificate of the action of the directors, signed by the directors and the secretary, shall be filed in the office of the Secretary of State when the election is made by the unanimous vote of the directors or upon the written consent of the members. A certificate of the proceedings of the meeting of the members when the election is made at any such meeting, signed by the chairperson and secretary of the meeting and a majority of the directors, shall be filed in the office of the Secretary of State. Thereafter, the corporation shall continue its existence under the provisions of this code which are applicable thereto, and shall possess all the rights and powers, and shall be subject to all the obligations, restrictions, and limitations, prescribed thereby.

Ca. Corp. Code § 12702
Amended by Stats 2022 ch 617 (SB 1202),s 85, eff. 1/1/2023.
Repealed and added by Stats. 1982, Ch. 1625, Sec. 3. Operative January 1, 1984.

Section 12704 - Suspension of corporate rights, privileges, and powers

If the corporate rights, privileges, and powers of a subject corporation have been suspended and are still suspended immediately prior to January 1, 1984 pursuant to the prior law, as a result of its incorporation of the General Nonprofit Corporation Law (commencing with Section 9000) in effect on December 31, 1979, and the incorporation by the General Nonprofit Corporation Law of Sections 5700 through 5908 of the prior law (Section 2300), such sections and provisions continue to apply to such corporation until restoration by the controller pursuant to such sections.

Ca. Corp. Code § 12704
Repealed and added by Stats. 1982, Ch. 1625, Sec. 3. Operative January 1, 1984.

Made in the USA
Las Vegas, NV
04 January 2024

83853058R00431